W9-DJI-246

American Democracy

C O U 8 2 5

Robert K. Carr

AMERICAN COUNCIL ON EDUCATION

Marver H. Bernstein

PRINCETON UNIVERSITY

Walter F. Murphy

PRINCETON UNIVERSITY

Michael N. Danielson

PRINCETON UNIVERSITY

American Democracy

Sixth Edition

HOLT, RINEHART AND WINSTON, INC.

New York   Chicago   San Francisco   Atlanta   Dallas   Montreal   Toronto   London

Copyright © 1963, 1968, and 1971 by Holt, Rinehart and Winston, Inc.
Copyright, 1951 by R. K. Carr, D. H. Morrison, M. H. Bernstein, and R. C. Snyder.
Copyright © 1955 by Robert K. Carr, Marver H. Bernstein,
Donald H. Morrison, Richard C. Snyder, and Joseph E. McLean.
Copyright © 1959 by Robert K. Carr, Marver H. Bernstein,
Elizabeth Gibson Morrison, and Joseph E. McLean.

All rights reserved
Library of Congress Catalog Card Number: 75-137863
SBN: 03-084320-0
Printed in the United States of America
1 2 3 4 5   19   9 8 7 6 5 4 3 2 1

Design, illustrations, and cover by Incentra/McDade

Preface

In earlier editions of this book, we expressed many specific criticisms about the functioning of the American political system, and we supported many changes in that system. But we also thought that the general course of political development in domestic affairs since World War II was bringing the country closer to an approximation of a just society and doing so at a reasonable rate of progress. We saw the great problems of American politics as lying in the field of international relations, of trying to attain peace and security in an insecure and heavily armed world.

We still see those problems as serious. Indeed, they are more grave today than they have been since the days of the Korean War. But even if the United States reaches an effective agreement with the Soviet Union on arms control, finds an expeditious way out of IndoChina, helps negotiate a lasting peace in the Middle East, and adopts an acceptable stance somewhere between imperialism and isolation—as unlikely as these happenings appear in the fall of 1970—the country would still face a set of momentous problems in domestic politics. Events of the last few years have shown that racism, poverty, and violence are more deep-rooted than we had earlier believed. Urban blight, environmental pollution, and overpopulation now seem not merely worse but, despite brave words, to be escalating in seriousness.

To underline the importance of these problems and the way in which American government has coped and can cope with them, we have to some extent revised every chapter in this book. We have also written six new chapters—five of which appear in the Essentials Edition—on American political culture, the judicial process, the Supreme Court, the functioning of criminal justice, the new black politics, and the haphazard operations of welfare programs. In addition, we have heavily revised our treatment of federalism in general and urban problems in particular, both directly in Chapters 4 and 5 and indirectly in those portions of the book dealing with the legislative, executive and judicial processes as well as in those concerned more specifically with policy problems. We have also attempted to show in the chapter on foreign and military policy and at several other places, both the costs of maintaining the defense establishment and the risks of allowing it to atrophy.

We are not disillusioned by or alienated from the American political system. We do not preach revolution. But neither do we celebrate our system and pretend that all is well and that our problems will vanish like Fourth of July oratory behind a skyrocket, even if that rocket is heading for the moon. While we are more critical of what has been going on—and what has not been going on—in American politics than we have been in the past, we do not think that the system is inherently corrupt or is doomed by internal contradictions or foreign pressures. Yet we do believe that unless Americans quickly and successfully attack the root causes of their domestic political problems, their governmental system will survive only at a terrible price. And much of that price will be paid in the diminution or even loss of values and processes that the system has supposedly cherished, values like privacy and freedom of speech and association, processes like fair and public trials. We are not living in one of those happy times when problems can be solved by temporizing. In context of the 1970s, neglect can only be malignant; it cannot be benign.

It may be comforting to some to think that the United States is suffering from the defects of its virtues: that poverty is so ugly in America because most people in the country—and more each year—are prosperous; that racism is so vile because American ideals demand equal justice; that crime is so repugnant because opportunities for lawful advancement are so plentiful; that pollution is so reprehensible because the environment has been so generous both in material and aesthetic terms. But such consolation does nothing to fill the empty bellies of white children in Appalachia, of red children on the reservations, or of black children in Harlem or Chicago's South Side.

In the chapters that follow, we try to explain—we hope with more skill and clarity than we have in the past—the structure, processes, and products of American politics. We think that we best serve the cause of progress in this country by acting like political scientists, not like advocates, by telling it as we see it, which is as close as we can come to telling it like it is. We believe that the American political system needs revitalizing and is worth the great efforts that revitalizing requires. We hope to contribute to that process by helping to understand the system, both in its failures and in its successes.

Again our list of debts is long. Our greatest obligations are to the faculty and students who have used—and criticized—this book, and to our wives, who have for different reasons been even more sharply critical. We would also like to thank Mrs. Shirley Gilbert of the Office of Survey Research and Statistical Studies of Princeton University for computer programming, Professor Jameson Doig of Princeton University for reading and commenting on parts of the manuscript, and Dr. Herbert E. Alexander, Director of the Citizens' Research Foundation, for unpublished data on campaign spending. We, of course, assume full responsibility for all errors of commission and omission.

ROBERT K. CARR
MARVER H. BERNSTEIN
WALTER F. MURPHY
MICHAEL N. DANIELSON

November, 1970
Washington, D.C.
Princeton, N.J.

Contents

Introduction

The stuff of politics is power—who governs and how, the reciprocal relationships of authority and obligation between the governors and the governed as well as between different sets of governors and among the governed themselves. The product of political interaction is more than a series of particular policies like foreign aid or civil rights; it is a way of life.

Harold Lasswell[1] profanely but quite accurately defined politics as involving three questions: "Who gets what, when, and how?" More formally, we can say that politics is concerned with the authoritative processes which determine society's goals, mobilize its resources to achieve those goals, and distribute within society rights, duties, costs, benefits, rewards, and punishments. By authoritative processes, we mean those whose decisions the vast majority of the population, at least of those who are aware of what is going on, accept as binding. They may do so for a variety of reasons, including habit, tradition, respect for certain procedures, or loyalty to particular persons or institutions. In Western democracies citizens may tend to view most governmental decisions as authoritative, but in other systems people may not see public officials as legitimate rulers. In addition, under many circumstances, large segments of a population may look on other organizations or individuals as legitimate leaders, at least for some purposes. A bishop or a guerrilla chief, for instance, may make decisions which a sizable minority or even a majority of citizens consider binding.

Authoritative political decisions may promote order or provoke civil war, inflate the economy, maintain prosperity, exacerbate poverty, or bring on a depression. One's right to life and liberty are largely dependent on politics. The men who speak with the authority of the community usually also command a preponderance of the instruments of force. This means that they can imprison people for real or alleged crimes, conscript young men and women for regular armies or guerrilla cadres, exterminate groups of people as Hitler did with the Jews or Stalin did with his opponents, or keep slave laborers

1

without rights or dignity as Americans did with blacks until the Civil War. Alternatively, political action can remove conditions of terror and slavery, end famine and pestilence, discourage drug abuse, wipe out gangland rule, and restore civil rights. On the international scale, politics can trigger a war between individual countries and even incite a global conflict, but political action can also bring peace, orderly development, and a measure of prosperity.

We speak of the process by which political decisions are made in the United States as democratic but, unfortunately, the word *democracy* is among the most vague and value-laden terms in the vocabulary of any Western language. Democracy can refer to a town-meeting style of government in which all citizens are present and possess equal voting power; it can mean government by an Athenian assembly whose members are selected by lot or serve by rotation; it can refer to a representative form of government in which delegates are chosen through any of a variety of electoral forms. Democracy can also mean a limited or a totalitarian government. Totalitarian democracy is no contradiction in terms. "Democratic despotism" has a long history; the Greek city states were more totalitarian than many present day "people's republics."

When we speak of American democracy, then, we are talking about a concept of popular government operating in a particular cultural context and through a particular set of institutions and informal processes. It is a peculiar concept, one that is closely related to constitutional democracy in other Western countries and less closely to democracy as it is developing in other parts of the world. Democratic government implies a specific cluster of arrangements, not a universal idea.

American democracy means representative government. The people "rule" in the sense of having a right to speak their minds on public issues, to organize other citizens, and, at stated intervals, to vote for or against candidates who wish to govern them. The people also "rule" in the sense that public officials who are subject to periodic re-election are typically anxious to anticipate the moods and preferences of the voters—although how they anticipate or even discover those moods and preferences involves a process that is often more mystic than scientific. As V. O. Key[2] once quipped, "To speak with precision about public opinion is a task not unlike coming to grips with the Holy Ghost." Yet at election time public opinion can become as real to government officials as the Holy Ghost is to traditional Christian theologians.

American democracy also means limited government. Its practice includes the concept of minority rights as well as majority rule. Although that practice has by no means always respected the rights of all minorities, it is still true that the general culture, the formal institutions, and the informal processes of politics in the United States impose a network of moral and physical barriers against the exertion of governmental power.

The framers of the American Constitution, of course, did not try to construct a popular government by requiring all major officials to be directly elected by universal manhood suffrage. Because they shared the ancient fear of tyranny of the majority, the framers provided instead for only limited public participation. More important for the long run, they fragmented power for the explicit purpose of preventing a majority or a small combination of minorities from imposing their political will in a tyrannical fashion. The framers built well. Over time, their legal institutions have become latticed with informal arrangements that reinforce the proclivity of formal structures to divide and subdivide authority.

American democracy is also permeated with the concept of equality, a notion only slightly less varied in meaning than that of democracy itself. Juridical equality, equality before the law, is a constitutional command which orders at least "one man, one vote" in the political sphere, even-handed justice from the courts, and at the same time forbids government imposed restrictions on social mobility or economic opportunity because of race, religion, or ancestry. Living up even to these minimums has posed immense practical problems that the American system has not yet overcome.

Given the empirical fact that men are not equal in talent and ambition and do not share the same interests and moral code, political equality is a difficult state to maintain. If left alone, some individuals will inevitably want, seek, and obtain a disproportionately large share of many goods and services, including political power. It is obvious that all Americans are not equal in power. The candidates who compete for public office are rarely just plain folks, although they frequently pretend to be. They are members of an elite, usually a professional elite, typically better educated, wealthier, and far more astute in the arts of manipulation than the average citizen. They are often surrounded by other elites, bankers, financiers, union officials, lawyers, interest group leaders, or newspapermen, whose political resources also set them apart from the average man. Professional politicians compete with each other for power; one of the arenas of competition is the marketplace of popular votes. It is principally because of this competition in this particular market—and because of the anticipation of how that market will react—that one can speak of the United States as having a democratic government. And because in that marketplace all votes are supposed to count the same, one can speak of some measure of political equality.

The problem of equality has other troublesome dimensions. Even where practice diverges from ideals, there is a contagion among ideas. In the United States, the notion of political equality has been coupled with an ideal of social equality, an ideal that goes far beyond equal treatment by government officials or "one man, one vote." It means an absence of informal, social barriers as well. But because social practice, like political practice, has not always lived up to its ideals, governmental action is necessary to strike down and keep down unofficially imposed religious, economic, and, most important in the American context, racial barriers against social mobility. But the concept of limited government, made operational through fragmentation of power, hampers governmental action, just as does the concept of popular government made operational through the actual check and anticipated check of the ballot box. Ideals to the contrary notwithstanding, a majority of Americans have been quite willing to allow informal social barriers to exist. Indeed, they have spent a good deal of their ingenuity in constructing these barriers.

The problem of equality, particularly racial equality, is at the heart of the current crisis in American domestic politics, and it is closely linked to problems of poverty and crime. Surrounding this trio is a band of other serious problems like inflation, full employment, clogged transportation lines, urban growth, environmental pollution, and sickness, especially of the very young, the very old, and the very poor. International problems of foreign aid, war, peace, and survival create additional dimensions of concern. None of these has a simple solution, and many of them compete with each other for scarce resources like time, energy, and money. Building an anti-ballistic missile system may mean ending a school lunch program; a new network of highways may both increase air pollution and further upset black housing problems. At the same time, both may reduce unemployment and by putting more money into circulation increase government's tax revenues, thereby replenishing public capital resources.

Reconciling conflicting demands for government action and government economy, for freedom and equality, for governmental aid, regulation, and abstinence is inevitably complex. But as we said in the opening sentence, these power relationships form the stuff of politics.

This is a book about politics in the United States, about how those demands are met if not reconciled, about the benefits and the costs that accrue from problems solved and unsolved. Most of all, this is a book about how the processes of politics shape American life.

Footnotes

[1] Harold D. Lasswell, *Politics: Who Gets What, When, and How?* (New York: McGraw-Hill Book Company, 1936).

[2] V. O. Key, Jr., *Public Opinion and American Democracy* (New York: Alfred A. Knopf, 1961), p. 8.

Part I The Framework of American Politics

Involvement of Middle Class in the Narcotics Problem Arouses Demands for Action

By MARTIN TOLCHIN

When does a problem become a problem for politicians? When it afflicts the white middle class.

That is the answer of top officials in the Lindsay administration in explaining why there has been only limited government action—Federal, state and local—against narcotics, although these drugs have been the scourge of the black slums for several decades.

"As long as drugs were primarily a problem of the lower classes, there was a minimum amount of pressures from society to do any more than research the problem," says a chief Lindsay aide who asked not to be named.

Lawrence W. Pierce, chairman of the State Narcotics Addiction Control Commission, agrees with this assessment. "They simply haven't had the clout where it mattered," he says of slum dwellers who have pleaded vainly for years for government protection against drug abuse. "The facts speak for themselves."

Prof. Richard Cloward of the Columbia School of Social Work suggests another, more sinister reason for government inaction in the years when narcotics traffic was confined to the slums.

He believes that long-standing social outrages, such as the narcotics traffic, are tolerated by government when they aid the status quo. As long as slum dwellers remain on drugs, Professor Cloward theorizes, they cannot mobilize against landlords, or fight to dump political leaders.

"Cloward's theory is probably true," says Larry A. Bear, Commissioner of the city's Addiction Services Agency. "Drug addiction has prevented forceful social action from taking place."

Black Muslims and Black Panthers prohibit the use of drugs for just this reason.

They argue, much like the Chinese in the Opium War with Britain in the 19th century, that drugs would render their culture impotent. Commissioner Bear sees no political conspiracy to perpetuate narcotics traffic in the slums, but rather a tolerant attitude, buttressed by the feeling that "It doesn't make any difference if it's not bothering me."

All that has changed within the last six months. With increased use of heroin evident in high schools and junior high schools in more affluent neighborhoods—the Midwood section of Brooklyn, Riverdale in the Bronx, Scarsdale in Westchester and Great Neck on Long Island—and the deaths of heroin users who have barely approached puberty have aroused a politically potent middle class that vigorously insists on more action by government.

"The city is now dominated by the issue, in very much the same way as education dominated the city during the early part of last year," says Richard R. Aurelio, Deputy Mayor and Mr. Lindsay's chief of staff.

There is an awareness among public officials, moreover, that the public expects more than the punitive answers given by government in the past. Among these was Governor Rockefeller's program of compulsory confinement of narcotics users—a campaign promise made during the 1966 gubernatorial campaign when drug users were considered "them," not "us."

The difficulty of piecing together a narcotics program, these officials say, is uncertainty over the causes of drug addiction and abuse ("Is it a statement on our mental health as a nation?" asks one Lindsay official) and profound differences over possible solutions.

"You could pour millions and millions into this area and still not get a result if you weren't approaching it right," Mayor Lindsay said recently at a City Hall news conference. "What makes it even worse is that so much of what we have to do is experimental."

The drug subculture in the United States began 100 years ago. By an accident of history, the United States was the first nation to use morphine on a widespread basis. It was during the Civil War. The resulting addiction of 45,000 soldiers was called the "Army Disease." Europe learned from the American experience, and avoided using the drug.

After the war, the importation of Orientals—many of whom smoked opium—to work on the transcontinental railroad added another chapter in the nation's narcotics traffic. So did the widespread use of paregoric, an opium derivative—in the South.

In 1911, the narcotics problem became so acute that Congress passed the Narcotics Control Act, but marijuana was specifically exempted from the list of dangerous drugs that could not be sold without a physician's prescription. Marijuana was added in 1940 in a move that many regarded as repressive. In that decade, narcotics traffic proliferated in the slums.

Politicians offer various reasons for the breakout today into middle-class neighborhoods. Mayor Lindsay relates it to the hopelessness—over the Vietnam War, middle-class morality and an inability to find fulfillment in the adult world.

"The kids that are into drugs, whether from the ghetto or the Gold Coast, are looking for the right thing—some connection and human value," says Dr. Mitchell S. Rosenthal, deputy commissioner of the Addiction Services Agency. "They're just looking the wrong place, and they find out it doesn't work, but sometimes it's too late."

Some experts relate the drug scene to our high-speed, pill-popping culture and the teenage sub-culture that developed in the nineteen-sixties, when drugs in the music world became celebrated by the Beatles with songs like "Lucy in the Sky with Diamonds," a hymn to LSD.

"You try to teach your children against that kind of power, you have a very slim chance," says one Lindsay aide. "The most encouraging thing I know about the war against drugs is that the Beatles are off them—it's far more important than any plan that the Governor or Mayor will come up with."

© 1970 by The New York Times Company. Reprinted by permission.

Chapter 1 American Political Culture

THE PHYSICAL SETTING

Since politics is concerned with power relationships among human beings and the rewards and burdens those relationships carry, the political system of a nation is affected—although by no means determined—by its location, its natural resources, and its customs and ideals. At least in the first two respects, the United States could hardly have been more blessed. When it was a small, underpopulated, and weak nation, it was also remote, both in terms of interest and distance, from the great powers of the world. To the north Canada was a sparsely settled outpost of the British Empire, to the south Mexico wanted only peaceful coexistence once it gained independence. To the east was an ocean, and to the west an almost uninhabited subcontinent that invited exploitation.

Physical isolation was enhanced by a natural voluptuousness. On both sides of the Appalachians the climate was generally temperate and the soil fertile. A series of rivers provided a network of inland trade routes, and the coast was indented with sheltered harbors. Scattered about the country was an abundance of resources—wild animals for food, hides, and furs, grassy plains for cattle, timber for houses, gold and silver for adventure and quick wealth, and for the industry that would later come, oil, coal, natural gas, iron, copper, lead, and bauxite.

In 1840 Alexis de Tocqueville could speak of the "magnificent dwelling place" and the "immense booty" that fortune had left to Americans. That abundance has played a critical psychological as well as physical role in the American experience. The Protestant ethic of hard work could and did pay tremendous dividends in this environment. Great prosperity, and the illusion of even greater prosperity, brought wave after wave of immigrants, many of them already educated and trained, and sent them as well as older inhabitants searching out and developing the natural wealth of the country. These people may often have been the downtrodden, but they came to better themselves, not to accept poverty. In the relatively nontechnological age of the eighteenth, nineteenth, and early twentieth century, even their raw muscle power was much in demand. The myth of rags to riches may have seldom materialized, but social and economic advancement were possible and became the great American dream, creating a surge of energy and hope.

Immigration and social mobility, David M. Potter[1] points out, combined to help Americans maintain a myth of equality. It was not that all people were equal—they certainly were not in terms of wealth, education, talent, or political power. Rather it was the pull of expanding economy and the push of the next sweep of immigrants, who represented both producers and consumers, that would give most of the white-skinned poor more and more material benefits. It was not so much that their proportionate share of the good things of life increased, but that the number of good things available at a low price multiplied.

Industrialization and Urbanization

Until 1900, the frontier played a major role in American development. So did industrialization, but until 1860 its impact was more gradual. There had been some small-scale manufacturing during the colonial period and, shielded by a protective tariff, it had continued to grow slowly but steadily. The Civil War, however, created massive demands and started American—primarily northern—industry off on a spiraling curve that, despite frequent recessions and occasional depressions, has continued for more than a century. Technological advances in manufacturing were making a significant impact in the States at the same time as the great technological advances in transportation, the steamship and more important the railroad, had opened vast markets and made raw materials easily accessible.

European demands during World War I sent American industry burgeoning ahead again, so that by 1918 the United States had become not only the creditor of much of the world but also the biggest of the industrial giants. The Great Depression reduced all giants to pygmy size, but the Second World War catapulted the American economy off once more with a momentum it has not yet lost. Although the Soviet Union, West Germany, and Japan have taken long strides in production since 1945, further technological advances have widened the gap between American industry and that of most other nations. The ability to offer higher salaries, more research money, more sophisticated laboratory facilities, and in many instances a wider measure of freedom has created a "brain drain" of scientists from other countries to the United States, a phenomenon which is setting the stage for continued absolute and relative gains.

Industrialization has changed the character of the American population. The growth of factories and their demands for labor stopped new immigrants at the cities and also sparked a steady exodus from the farms to metropolitan areas. In 1800, only 6 percent of Americans were living in towns with populations over 2,500; by 1870 the proportion had risen to one quarter. By 1900 it was up to 40 percent, and by 1970 more than three out of four people in the United States were living in urban regions. Some 50 million of those people were in cities with populations of over 250,000. But even these figures understate urbanization. The arms of the megalopolis have been spreading out like hungry octopus tenacles, scooping up surrounding land for industrial parks, research laboratories, shopping centers, and suburban housing developments. "Strip Cities," like those reaching from north of Boston to south of Richmond, Virginia, or all around the southern arc of Lake Michigan, or from the California-Mexican border along the coast to the north of Santa Barbara, are turning huge stretches of country into solid concrete corridors and making old geographical and political boundaries impractical for control of social problems.

American Society

This collage of wealth, work, isolation, immigration, industrialization, and urbanization has produced a peculiar pluralism of several American societies. The dominant one, that of upper middle class whites, is easier to caricature than to describe. Its members have been driven by frenetic energy to earn their prosperity. It stands out as an example of the splendid affluence that a nation can produce and distribute widely, yet it does not quite succeed in painting over ugly scars of poverty. Its internal contrasts are as extreme: romantic love and high divorce rates, Hollywood sex symbols and Disneyland, urban blight alongside magnificent monuments, marvelous medical research and a mania for cigarette smoking, anger at the young for dulling their minds with marijuana but approval of cocktails before lunch and dinner, eminent symphony orchestras and blaring rock bands, resounding professions about human dignity and equality together with insidious racial discrimination.

These people have succeeded in maintaining fantastic rates of production that enable them and their employees to have the shortest work week of any industrial nation, to provide most citizens with comfortable housing, good food, and excellent medical and dental care. These people spend millions of dollars annually for recreation—books, color television sets, boats, second homes, second cars, golf, whiskey, and European or Caribbean vacations. Yet even play means hard work for Americans; they tend to consume rather than enjoy their leisure. Symbolic of the whole process of frantic leisure is the ubiquitous, noisy, and tense cocktail party that almost everyone who gives or attends claims to despise. At times it seems that the Protestant ethic of hard work has gone mad in American middle class society and has created a gruesome, mass rat race of people working compulsively harder and harder to get new jobs, higher salaries, more responsibility, and less enjoyment. The only two luxury items that seem to provide relaxation are the martini and the television, and they function more as soporifics.

Americans receive more formal education than any other citizen body. The median number of years of schooling for all adults in the United States is twelve years. A college education for their children has become the normal expectation of almost all middle class adults and probably of a majority of working class families as well. The marked correlation between income and formal education evidences the demands and the rewards that a highly technological society makes and bestows for advanced training. In 1970 over 7 million students were actually attending colleges and universities in the United States and the number is expected to approach 9 million by 1975.

Despite the great emphasis on education—even beyond the college level to graduate school—and despite the great respect Americans accord to academics, especially to those in the physical sciences, there is a noticeable current of anti-intellectualism in

"As I look back, I realize that everything I have I owe to the Protestant work ethic, and a few timely tips on the market."

Drawing by Donald Reilly. © 1969 by **The New Yorker** Magazine, Inc.

American thought.[2] Perhaps the challenge of survival on the frontier and later of competition in the dog-eat-dog laissez-faire economy of the last century encouraged pragmatic, even materialistic judgments and discouraged philosophical speculation. Does it work? does it make a profit? and does it allow me to get ahead? were—and are—the typical questions Americans have asked, not: How does it fit into a broad interpretation of the cosmos? Indeed, if Americans can be said to have developed any national philosophy, it is that of pragmatism, which, although hardly anti-intellectual, pushes aside abstract speculation and dogmatic propositions for more practical questions about actual effects.

The permissive nature of society in the United States is notorious. With Dr. Benjamin Spock's books on child raising the Bible of the last generation of parents, family life has become very democratic. In recent decades, many school teachers have urged children to express themselves, to give their own opinions rather than to regurgitate the rote recitations that used to characterize—and still characterize elsewhere—much of what we call education. The point is not that there is no discipline or authoritarianism in the family or school, but that there is considerably less than in the American past or in the present of most other nations.

The informality of American business life, where the president or owner of a firm often insists on being addressed by his first name or initials, may be partly a means of softening some of the savagery of competition. However, the usual practice of the more successful corporations has been to encourage employee initiative, at the blue collar level as well as among top officials. Even the military is becoming less authoritarian. As Morris Janowitz[3] has pointed out, the traditional model of the general as the "heroic soldier" who earned his reputation for blood and guts and demanded instant and unswerving obedience is being superseded by a managerial model, in which the general persuades and leads more like a civilian corporation executive.

THE CONCEPT OF POLITICAL CULTURE

Like a nation's physical setting and resources, its social customs and ideals can influence the character and operation of its governmental system. To take account of this shaping force, political scientists have developed the concept of political culture. Writers differ among themselves in precisely how they define this term, but in its most general—and useful—sense, it refers to politically relevant ideas and social practices.[4] Of course, not all social arrangements and not all prevalent ideas are politically important, but many are. Even a social artifact as basic as language may play a significant political role. One noted political philosopher has speculated that the existence of the word "leader" has increased the chances for the success of democratic government in English-speaking countries over countries such as Germany and Italy where the closest words are more equivalent to "commander" or "director."[5]

One would expect a society in which fathers usually exercised completely authoritarian control over family life and employers ordered workers around like drill sergeants to foster very different sorts of political relationships than a society in which there was considerable give and take in family decision-making and in which discussion, debate, and dissent were normal parts of business life. One would also expect people who had grown up under a rigid class structure, who cherished inherited status over individual accomplishment, and who thought that some races were inherently superior to others, to behave differently politically from people who had been reared in a classless society, who saw personal achievement as an overriding value, and who accepted racial equality as a fact of life.

Although few societies provide such neat contrasts, there is evidence to indicate that the expected relations between society and politics do take place to a large extent.

People who have been accustomed to participate in decision-making in the family, at school, or at work tend to participate more in political life and to feel more competent to influence governmental decisions. The connections, however, between social background and political behavior are neither simple nor universal. Among the factors also playing important roles is personality. For instance, people who feel least competent politically are usually not those who were denied opportunities to participate in other social situations, but those who had those opportunities and did not take advantage of them.[6]

Moreover, traffic between politics and other social relations is not along a one-way street. To say that to be stable a governmental system must be congruent with the broader social system does not imply a static relationship. The old saying "stateways cannot change folkways" is utter nonsense. New governmental policies frequently interact with old social customs to precipitate fundamental changes not only in the way people behave publicly but also in relationships within supposedly more basic groups like the family or the church.

Some of the most glaring examples are from the communist world. Karl Marx wrote that economic relations determined the shape and content of politics; economics was the substructure of society, politics the superstructure, a mere reflection of the economic base. Joseph Stalin was more ruthless as well as more realistic than his prophet. He practiced the theory that politics could reshape more fundamental economic relations. The radically altered character of society in Russia and in China provides vivid testimonial to his ability and that of his imitators to use political power to revolutionize society, albeit with much more pain and suffering than many utopians had imagined. Vietnam supplies another example. The pattern in the North has been more along the Soviet or Chinese models; in the South, the massive American military presence has apparently also made some radical changes in the social system, although mostly in an unplanned and almost haphazard manner.

Less dramatically but not necessarily less significantly in the long run, democratic governments can also bring about important and peaceful social changes. "Our government," Justice Louis D. Brandeis[7] once noted, "is the potent, the omnipresent teacher. For good or for ill, it teaches the whole people by its example." It is a plausible hypothesis that much of the permissiveness of current American life is also a byproduct of political democracy. There are considerable problems of logic and role adaptation involved in extolling the virtues of debate and participation in governmental affairs, but forbidding discussion in the family, classroom, or office. One of the objectives of the current "revolt" of college students has been to bring political democracy to the whole government of the college, not just to student-run organizations.

One can see similar influences at work outside the United States. Certainly the change in Ireland from a rural, agricultural society with rather strict patterns of discipline in the family, the school, and the church, to the beginnings of an urban, industrialized society with considerable easing of discipline is closely linked to the success of a liberal democratic government and its public policies. In Japan, too, a switch from an authoritarian to a democratic government has brought important changes in social structure and behavior. Even theologically oriented societies have felt the impact of political democracy. A great deal of the current ferment within the Catholic Church has been generated by a perceived incompatibility between the processes followed in secular and ecclesiastical government. In essence most of the modern church reformers are campaigning for wider participation in ecclesiastical affairs, more consultation between the rulers and the ruled, and a greater play for individual freedom—much the same fight waged by liberals all over the Western world.

Politics does not always predominate over other kinds of social relations, but there is interaction. The flow of influence is likely to be both continuing and reciprocating. Under certain conditions, folkways may be primary; under others stateways may principally shape societal development, but in no situation is either likely to be insignificant. What neither political scientists nor sociologists now know with any precision are the exact conditions which cause the relative importance of political or cultural factors to vary.

Belief Systems

There are a number of basic ideas about human nature, about authority, about religion, and about the purposes of life that have broad political relevance. The framers of the American Constitution, for instance, were deeply imbued with the idea of sin. Products of a Protestant religious culture, though many of them were Deists, they were influenced by the theological doctrine of original sin—human nature is fundamentally weak, wanting to do good but inclined toward evil and selfishness. Thus they found attractive a governmental scheme for checking ambition against ambition. "But what is government itself," Madison[8] asked in *The Federalist,* "but the greatest of all reflections on human nature? If men were angels, no government would be necessary."

Ideas about fundamental philosophic principles as well as beliefs directly linked to politics are more likely to be normative than descriptive. That is, they are more likely to consist of the notions that people have about what is right and proper—what they expect to happen or want to happen in particular kinds of situations—than descriptions of what actually transpires. These ideas thus form a kind of moral and intellectual screen through which people filter information, and perceive, misperceive, and pass judgments on political reality.

One can speak in gross terms of a belief system in American political culture in two senses. First, there is evidence that at least nine out of ten Americans endorse a whole set of political principles. These propositions include a belief that democracy is the best form of government, that public officials should be elected by a majority vote, that every citizen should have an equal opportunity to participate in politics, and that members of the minority have a right to criticize the majority's choices and to try to win a majority over to their own views.[9] The concept of the basic equality of human dignity would probably receive an equally thumping endorsement.

Second, in many important respects, the political outlooks of Americans differ from those of citizens of other countries. Compared to the British, Germans, Italians, and Mexicans, for example, Americans tend to be more trusting of their fellow man, to see more altruism in other people, to look more on political participation as a duty of the average citizen, to be prouder of their governmental institutions, to think of themselves as more influential in their national government, and, except for the British, more likely to expect fair and equal treatment from public officials.[10]

But the political system is not the passive recipient of values and beliefs any more than it is of social customs. Indeed, like customs, politically relevant ideas frequently change in the modern world; government officials have been teachers here, too. American concepts of equality owe much to Jefferson and Lincoln, nationalism to George Washington and Chief Justice John Marshall. Certainly Presidents Franklin D. Roosevelt, John F. Kennedy, and Lyndon B. Johnson were primarily responsible for converting minority views about the desirability of the welfare state into an accepted part of American life. Chief Justice Earl Warren's pronouncement for the Supreme Court in the School Segregation Cases of 1954[11] changed a great deal of thinking about human dignity in general and race relations in particular, not least markedly among clergymen, who, after the Supreme Court's decision, seem to have had revealed to them that God Almighty had always forbidden segregation.

CULTURAL DIVERSITY

One must talk of many political cultures when analyzing the United States or most modern nations. Predominance of a particular kind of pattern by no means implies its universality even within a single society. Patterns of child raising, educational and religious training, and economic relations vary greatly across social groups in America. An immigrant child raised in a strict Irish-Catholic family and educated by authoritarian nuns is apt to have been exposed to a very different set of influences from a black child who came to maturity in an urban ghetto or on a Mississippi cotton farm, or from a white Protestant youngster who grew up in an affluent suburb.

In similar fashion, we should not expect anything approaching unanimity on all politically relevant beliefs. What we know about public opinion in this country indicates that consensus on general principles rarely includes agreement on specific policies. To a middle class white, for example, equality of the black man may refer to his right to live in decent housing in the central city, not next door in a suburb, to compete for a blue collar job, not a managerial position. To a black militant, equality may mean preferential treatment to compensate for centuries of injustice. To an arch conservative, the right of a minority to try to persuade the majority of the error of its ways may not include the right of a socialist to speak in a public hall or at a street meeting. To a student radical, free speech may mean the right to shout down spokesmen for the "establishment."

The following table, summarizing the responses of samples of adults in Ann Arbor, Michigan, and Tallahassee, Florida, who had averaged over 95 percent agreement on the democratic principles we listed in the previous section, indicates just how quickly broad consensus disappears when it is confronted with practical problems of application. Of the seven statements listed, on only three, the rights of blacks to run for office and of socialists to speak and a desire to restrict voting on city tax measures to taxpayers, were about eight out of ten respondents in agreement. In no instance did the answers approach the consensus reached in reply to the questions about abstract principles.

The Silent Majority

We can speak of the dominant political culture as that of the white upper middle class. Its general beliefs are those of popular participation and election, of majority rule and minority rights, and of equality before the law. But, as we saw for the population as a whole, these beliefs are usually abstract rather than particular. They may or may not have much application to concrete problems of policy. Perhaps as a byproduct of pragmatism, there is deep affection for the political system; after all, it has generally worked very well for the white middle class. The Constitution is more than a charter for government, it has become a symbol of political virtue.

As a reflection of their individualism, Americans tend to be wary of governmental power. "I am not a friend to a very energetic government," Thomas Jefferson[12] wrote in 1787. Even today a majority of Americans are apt to respond suspiciously if not negatively to general questions about governmental power. On the other hand, on specific matters that affect them directly, they are perfectly willing, often eager, to accept governmental help and regulation. The paradox here is not only unresolved but generally unrecognized; it is clear that even well educated people can tolerate a high level of dissonance.

Political action to the middle class American means voting and perhaps writing to his senator or congressman or calling a local official about a problem. On the whole, to the average citizen "politics is a sideshow in the great circus of life."[13] Even in 1968, after thirty-five continuous years of extensive government regulation of the economy, only 1 percent of American adults believed that the outcome of the presidential election

RESPONSES TO QUESTIONS ABOUT CIVIL RIGHTS

Statement	Percent Agreeing
Antireligious speeches should be allowed	63
Socialist speeches should be allowed	79
Communist speeches should be allowed	44

Statement	Percent *Disagreeing*
Only informed people should have the right to vote on a city referendum	49
Only taxpayers should have the right to vote on city tax measures	21
Negroes should not be allowed to hold public office	81
Communists should not be allowed to hold public office	46

SOURCE: *James W. Prothro and Charles M. Grigg, "Fundamental Principles of Democracy: Bases of Agreement and Disagreement,"* Journal of Politics, 22 *(May 1960), p. 285.*

would affect them in a very important financial way, and two out of three said that the election would make no financial difference to them at all. As one would expect from these responses, the political knowledge of the middle class citizen is generally low; even during election campaigns he is unlikely to have detailed information about the specific issues that candidates, interest group leaders, journalists, and political scientists think are critical. He seldom engages in much political discussion, and when he does it is likely to be with people who agree with him.

There is a cluster of private citizens, mostly but not exclusively from the upper and upper middle class, who are highly informed and deeply concerned about politics. Their opinions about specific problems tend to be consistent and coherent pieces of a more general political ideology. As one would expect, they are typically well educated and sometimes have amateur experience in practical politics. But they are a small minority, all together they account for no more than 10 percent of the adult population.[14]

The Professional Politician

Even the very interested and articulate private citizen often differs from the professional politician in the way he looks at politics. The professional's world is shaped by the fact that he has far more political resources at his command. As a generalist, he may know less about some particular problems than many highly educated private citizens, but he knows where to find expertise if he needs it, and more important, he usually has a more instrumental understanding of the system as a whole. He devotes his working time to politics, not just his leisure. Acquiring technical knowledge and manipulative skills is his life's work; and this knowledge and skill can open up other resources. If he is an incumbent, he has at his disposal the authority of his office; if he is not in office, he may still have considerable influence with those who head governmental agencies.

Private citizens may tacitly or openly accept general principles of democratic government, but they seldom have a sophisticated understanding of how to make those general principles operative, how to translate those abstract propositions into workable rules to control the political game. To the professional, on the other hand, "the rules of the game"[15] are likely to be tangible guidelines. He may, unless he is especially reflective and articulate, have trouble spelling out just what those rules are, but he tends to internalize them in a meaningful way.

If he is a legislator, for example, the most basic rule will be acceptance of an election as the means of determining who should govern. Other rules include listening to all constituent complaints, permitting groups likely to be affected a chance to be heard before he takes action, allowing, even when in the majority, opposing legislators a reasonable opportunity to speak, keeping his word to officials from the opposing party as well as his own, not looking closely into the campaign financing or tactics of colleagues unless scandalous abuses come to light, and respecting the constitutional prerogatives of other governmental agencies, even while sharply disagreeing with their decisions. This list is illustrative rather than exhaustive; one could easily add other prescriptions such as restraints on campaign accusations. Certainly none of these, especially the last, is universally kept, but, on the whole, most professional politicians generally observe these and similar precepts. Because they are professionals, because they know that they have to work year after year with other professionals, that they will have to run for reelection at frequent intervals, and that in their careers they may hold a variety of offices in several branches of government, they have a long-range, vested interest in these rules.

Even the amateur activist who gets deeply involved in politics is apt to see a different world than does the professional. The amateur typically enters the political arena with a single, immediate policy goal in mind. The professional, on the other hand, is used to dealing with many issues so steadily and constantly "that few of them have the ultimate soul-saving importance for him that they do for the amateurs. . . . Politics for them [amateurs] is a means to an end, and what counts is to gain that end. To the professional, in contrast, what counts is to endure."[16]

The Poor

Cutting across other lines is another cultural dimension, a range of patterns of behavior, belief, and expectation held by those people who are more or less affluent and those who live in dire poverty. Many Americans tend to forget that prosperity has not been a universal happening in their society, that along with abundance there exists pitiful want, with perhaps as many as 25 million people in this country existing below the poverty level, and another 25 million just at that level or barely above it. Some of the people in the poorest categories are near starvation, but all of the poor are hungry, both for hope and for food. These new poor are not like the latest group of immigrants who lack material goods but who are propelled ahead by high aspirations. The new poor are the rejects from an urban, industrialized society, "those driven from the land and bewildered by the city."[17] While a majority of the poor are white, more than a third of blacks live below the poverty line.[18] Whether black or white or Indian, these people are disproportionately very old and very young. If old they tend to be sick, unemployed, and unemployable; if young, they often come from broken homes, to be receiving an education inadequate to equip them for competition in American society, and so to be doomed to live in the empty shadows of poverty, vulnerable to guilt and hate as they catch an occasional glimpse of the world of prosperity.

Michael Harrington,[19] whose book *The Other America* played a major role in awakening national interest in the problems of the poor, sees poverty as "a culture, an institution, a way of life." The poor have a different family structure, different sexual mores, and different political outlooks from those of middle class citizens. "To be impoverished is to be an internal alien, to grow up in a culture that is radically different from the one that dominates society."[20]

Poverty also has tremendous implications—although still largely potential implications—for the political system. Until the late 1960s, the poor were politically mute and unimportant, despite their huge numbers. More recently, poor people, especially blacks, Chicanos, Puerto Ricans, and Appalachian whites, have become "politically visible." But even with some encouragement from the federal government, the vast majority of the poor remain ineffective in the political arena. Only about three out of five adults with an annual income of under $4,000 even claims to vote, and the actual proportion is probably somewhat smaller. In comparison, about nine out of ten people with incomes over $15,000 go to the polls. A politically more significant difference is that the poor usually do not belong to unions, clubs, or any organizations that can dramatize their plight and represent their interests as poor people. They have been too resigned to their misery, too unaware that another life was possible, too ignorant, too young and unsophisticated, or too old and tired to achieve anything like their political potential.

The Blacks

The Kerner Commission on Civil Disorders stated in 1968 that the United States was "moving toward two societies, one black, one white—separate and unequal."[21] The striking eloquence of this sentence obscures the fact that it is fundamentally wrong.[22] The United States has always comprised many societies and the most obvious and enduring line of division has been race. Since the first slaves were taken ashore in Virginia in 1619, America has had a black society that has been separate from and unequal to white society. The black man, W. E. B. Du Bois[23] wrote at the beginning of this century, "ever feels his twoness—an American, a Negro; two souls, two thoughts, two unreconciled strivings; two warring ideals in one dark body."

No more accurately, of course, than with Caucasians can one speak of "a" black society. There are many social, economic, educational, and political differences among blacks. There are some rich blacks, although not very many; there is a black bourgeoisie, seemingly attached to white middle class values. There are black Uncle Toms, just as there are whites who would find masochistic joy in being slaves, and there are the masses of the black poor, people from the small rural farms or the large city ghettos. The poor of both races bear many of the same burdens, but the color of their skin has usually generated enough prejudice and distrust to have kept them from acting as close allies to promote similar goals; instead they merely share common suffering. In that respect they have been following a well-worn pattern. True assimilation of blacks into white American life at any social or economic level has been a rare phenomenon.

As a result of imposed separatism, a set of black subcultures has grown up, with some practices and speech patterns dating back to Africa via the slave cabins. Not only do customs and habits of dress frequently differ, but poorer rural and ghetto blacks often speak what is in many respects a different language from white middle class English.[24] The words are pronounced differently and have different meanings. The cadence is slower, more lilting, even the syntax is different. Gestures connote different kinds of emphases. Less formally, music plays a different role in the two subcultures. The Blues expresses much of the bitter lonesomeness of the black man's lot, and the concept "soul" signifies the greater seriousness and less inhibited pleasure that the black experiences.

The average black has grown up in a much more hostile environment than the typical Caucasian. If he is poor or near-poor, he witnesses violence almost every day of his life. The black trusts his fellow man less than does the white, and with good reason. He is four times more likely to be robbed than a white man, and a black woman is four times more likely to be raped than a Caucasian woman. Blacks are also much more likely than whites to be stopped by police and subjected to humiliating searches or to be hauled off to a police station for questioning.

A black can expect to live, on the average, seven years less than a white person of the same sex, to enjoy a little more than half the income—even if he has more education than his white brothers—and to suffer about twice the unemployment rate. Thus most blacks neither have nor can reasonably expect to gain in the near future the material goods that the average white earns. Discrimination, unemployment, and welfare are likely to be integral parts of the black man's life.

Under these circumstances, it is hardly surprising that a black is apt to carry his own political subculture. He, too, may endorse the basic principles of democracy, but majority rule may mean white domination and minority rights a black dream. Historically, a smaller proportion of blacks than of whites has voted and to a lesser extent this rule still holds, even where discrimination and retaliation are gone or were never practiced. When they do vote, blacks tend to be much more strongly Democratic than whites. Not unnaturally, they are more concerned about problems of discrimination; they perceive much more of it in American society than do whites and have personally experienced a great deal more of it.

The black man's expectations also tend to be different. College or even a high school diploma is often beyond his reach; formal education, after all, has often been totally irrelevant to survival in the rural South or in the northern ghetto and, at times, has been dysfunctional, even dangerous. Since they generally have less education, blacks typically have less political know-how than whites. Younger militant leaders, however, have taken over where older organizations like the National Association for the Advancement of Colored People leave off, and blacks are becoming more politically aware and more adept at using direct action like sit-ins or demonstrations to supplement or substitute for voting power.

When they express their political views, blacks, compared to whites, assert greater general trust in the federal government and are much more strongly in favor of specific federal programs to carry out school desegregation, to enforce fair employment practices, and to provide jobs and a minimum standard of living for all citizens. On the other hand, blacks register far less satisfaction with local government. They are much more critical

WHITE/BLACK OPINIONS ABOUT THE FEDERAL GOVERNMENT		
Statement	Percent Agreeing	
	Negroes	Whites
The federal government has gotten too powerful	15	59
The federal government should make sure everyone has a job and a good standard of living	81	30
The federal government should make sure Negroes get fair job treatment	89	38
The federal government should make sure Negro and white children can go to the same schools	89	37

SOURCE: *Survey Research Center, University of Michigan, 1968 Election Survey.*

of such public services as garbage collection, recreational facilities, schools, and most of all police protection.[25]

James Baldwin has described the police as "an army of occupation" in the ghetto, imposing an alien law to keep black people in their place. The riots in Watts, Newark, and a half-dozen other communities were sparked by rather minor incidents between blacks and police. To a middle class white, a policeman may be an annoying authority figure when it comes to a traffic ticket, but otherwise he is a welcome symbol of law and order. To the black, however, the policeman is "the Man"—the Man who stops and searches people without, it often seems to the suspect and witnesses, good reason, the Man who chases kids off street corners, shuts off fire hydrants on hot summer afternoons, worries people with questions, and takes them off to jail, sometimes with what seems to be unnecessary force and verbal abuse. He is also the Man who is seldom around when a black is robbed or threatened. To the policeman, on the other hand, work in the ghetto is both hard and dangerous; the rate of crime is fantastically high and cooperation with and respect for legal processes very low. He believes that to enforce the law he must act quickly and decisively. He may be far less sympathetic to the plight of the blacks than are social workers or educators, but there is some evidence that he is more sympathetic than whites are generally.[26]

Survey data indicate that blacks are only slightly less favorably disposed toward the police than whites and expect much the same kind of fair treatment as whites do. Deeper probing, however, as the following table indicates, often reveals bitter resentment and hostility, attitudes that have been reflected in action. Still ghetto residents need and want more police protection. This ambivalence explains demands of black power advocates for local, that is, neighborhood, control of police and schools.

One of the more important political differences between blacks and whites is not merely the way in which they judge events but also the way each group tends to see—or not see—the same event. For instance, almost eight out of ten whites interviewed during the 1968 presidential campaign said they thought that most black protests had been

WHITE/BLACK OPINIONS ABOUT THE POLICE		
Statement	Percent Agreeing	
	Negroes	Whites
Police do not answer calls fast enough	51	27
Police show disrespect and use insulting language	38	16
Police search people without good reason	36	11
Police rough up people unnecessarily when arresting or questioning them	35	10

SOURCE: *Angus Campbell and Howard Schuman, "Racial Attitudes in Fifteen American Cities," in* Supplemental Studies for the National Advisory Commission on Civil Disorders (*Washington, D.C.: Government Printing Office, 1968*), *pp. 42–43.*

violent, while fewer than three out of ten blacks so perceived the demonstrations. The
race riots of the 1960s underline these perceptual differences. As the following tables show,
blacks tend to find the causes primarily in social deprivation, the results of a discriminatory system. Whites, on the other hand, are far more likely to blame looters or "agitators."
Moreover, blacks look for a cure in social reform, while close to a majority of whites
sees a solution in stiffer police measures.

We shall have to return at frequent intervals to black-white differences, for the
race problem is at the core of the most grave issues of American domestic politics.
Furthermore, it is growing more and more serious as a political problem. As the condition of the black man improves, his awareness of his deprivation and of the possibility
of doing something about it increases. As he becomes more politicized, he wants more
rapid and more complete solutions, more rapid and more complete, perhaps, than the
white majority is ready to accept. The real revolution precipitated by the Supreme Court's
School Segregation Cases in 1954 may lie in its having created a new black awareness.
As Eldridge Cleaver,[27] Minister of Information for the Black Panthers, has written:

> Prior to 1954, we lived in an atmosphere of novocain. Negroes found it necessary, in
> order to maintain whatever sanity they could, to remain somewhat aloof and detached
> from "the problem." We accepted indignities and the mechanics of the apparatus of
> oppression without reacting by sitting-in or holding mass demonstrations. Nurtured
> by the fires of the controversy over segregation, I was soon aflame with indignation
> over my newly discovered social status, and inwardly I turned away from America
> with horror, disgust and outrage.

WHITE/BLACK OPINION ABOUT CAUSES OF URBAN RIOTS
"What do you think was the main cause of these disturbances?"

Most frequent types of spontaneous response[a]	Negroes	Whites
	(In percent)	
Discrimination, unfair treatment	47	25
Unemployment	23	13
Inferior jobs	12	5
Poor education	10	7
Poverty	9	10
Police brutality	7	2
Black Power or other 'radicals'	5	24
Looters and other undesirables	11	34
Communists	0	7

[a] *Since some people mentioned more than one cause, the percentages do not add up to a hundred.*
SOURCE: *Angus Campbell and Howard Schuman, "Racial Attitudes in Fifteen American Cities," in*
Supplemental Studies for the National Advisory Commission on Civil Disorders (*Washington,*
D.C.: Government Printing Office, 1968), *p. 48.*

WHITE/BLACK OPINION ABOUT SOLUTIONS TO URBAN DISORDERS

"What do you think is the most important thing the city government in _____ could do to keep a disturbance like the one in Detroit from breaking out here?"

First type of response mentioned	Negroes	Whites
	(In percent)	
Better employment	25	10
End discrimination	14	2
Better housing	8	4
Other social and economic improvements	6	4
Better police treatment	4	1
Improve communications between Negroes and whites; show Negroes whites care	12	11
More black control of institutions	0	0
More police control	9	46
Can't do anything; have already tried everything	4	8
Don't know	18	14
	100	100

SOURCE: *Angus Campbell and Howard Schuman, "Racial Attitudes in Fifteen American Cities,"* in Supplemental Studies for the National Advisory Commission on Civil Disorders (*Washington, D.C.: Government Printing Office, 1968*), p. 48.

VIOLENCE AS A CULTURAL TRAIT

A politically important strain running through American culture has been an exaltation of the rule of law and an emphasis on the necessity of public order, together with a condemnation of violence except in extreme cases of self-defense. Alongside this hallowed tradition, however, has been a clearly discernible thread of thought justifying, possibly even subconsciously glorifying, the use of violence. This latter strain may be a remnant from a frontier society that depended heavily on self-help for survival. In any event, historically there has been a strong theme of violence in the legends of Daniel Boone, Andrew Jackson, Davy Crockett, James Bowie, Wild Bill Hitchcock, and Buffalo Bill Cody. Moreover, much of what passes for literature today is often a chorale to assorted mixtures of sex and sadism. In the currently popular novels about Mike Hammer, Matt Helm, and Travis McGee, and in the television or comic page stories of the adventures of those upstanding peace officers Wyatt Earp, Matt Dillon, and Dick Tracy, and of those masked vigilantes, Bat Man and Robin, the heroes customarily, almost automatically, settle their disputes with guns, knives, lasers, knees, or, in moments of relative reason, fists. As one of Matt Dillon's victims observed from the perspective of the barroom floor, "That Marshal is awful sudden."

The Robin Hood theme of the generous criminal crusading against injustice has also been popular both in the movies and on television. The Hollywood productions of the lives of Frank and Jesse James made them out to be misunderstood lads whose murders and robberies were just boyish forms of social protest against overly acquisitive railroad officials. More recently, films such as "Bonnie and Clyde" and "Butch Cassidy and the Sun-dance Kid" were almost panegyrics to wild mayhem, making light of the slaughter of dozens of persons.

Even serious American writers like James Fenimore Cooper, Edgar Allan Poe, Stephen Crane, Jack London, Ernest Hemingway, John Dos Passos, and Norman Mailer have been fascinated by violence. At one level, they have seemed to deplore its use, but again and again they returned to it in their work, exploring in fine detail death struggles on the frontier, on the battlefield, or in the bullring. These writers have been indulging literary realism; all through American history there have been frequent resorts to illegal or "extra legal" violence.

Indeed, the country was conceived in a revolution against tax collectors and came to its maturity in a gruesome civil war. The Boston Tea Party, slave revolts, farmer rebellions, "Bloody Kansas," John Brown's raid, riots against the draft in New York during the Civil War, against Catholics in Philadelphia, against blacks in the Midwest, and against orientals in the Far West, night riders of the Ku Klux Klan, bounty hunters, Indian fighters, mountaineer feuds like that of the Hatfields and the McCoys, the Molly Maguires of the mines, Pinkertons and union men beating and bombing each other, the gang warfare of prohibition, illicit police assaults against the poor and the black, the assassination of four Presidents from 1865 to 1963 and serious attempts on the lives of three others, twenty-one bombings of Negro churches in Birmingham, and murders of a number of civil rights workers in the South—all form a gory chronicle that fits the current ghetto and campus riots into one niche of a much larger and even sadder picture.

When H. Rap Brown, the black militant leader, said that violence was as American as apple pie, he was offering a reasonably accurate description of a part, although only one part, of American culture. Despite the generally low importance of politics to most Americans, almost every group at one time or other has felt justified in using violence to achieve its goals. The thread of legal, peaceful change may be the stronger one; still the recurrence of violence indicates a persistent failure of the political system to achieve its avowed goals of ensuring both justice and domestic tranquility. But this failure is hardly unique among nations. In a generalization about European history that could easily be applied to Asia, Africa, or Latin America, Charles Tilly[28] has said that "collective violence has flowed regularly out of the central political processes. . . . The oppressed have struck in the name of justice, the privileged in the name of order, the in-between in the name of fear."

In defense of the American system, one can note, as has a British journalist,[29] that a nation has been carved out of a wilderness, and since 1820 the system has absorbed more than 44 million immigrants from varied and conflicting backgrounds. Under those circumstances, the significant points may be that there has been so little rather than so much violence, and that such a small proportion of what has occurred has been directed at the system itself. Furthermore, there is a difficult moral dilemma here that has confounded centuries of political philosophers. Under many circumstances, violence may be the only alternative to submission to tyranny and oppression. On the other hand, resort to violence to right fancied or minor grievances or even to correct major injustices when peaceful means are available can threaten the existence of society. No one has yet constructed a set of calipers to provide objective measurements in such matters.

POLITICAL SOCIALIZATION

Sociologists have called the process by which one generation passes on its civilization to the next socialization. Education is an older and perhaps more descriptive term, but political scientists have adopted their colleagues' jargon and speak of political socialization. It can be both a means of maintaining or changing a system by indoctrinating a new generation as well as a means by which members of the new generation learn to become mature political actors in society and perhaps to follow a different set of values.[30]

Experiences in early childhood, even though not directly political, begin the educational process. In his relations with his parents and perhaps his grandparents, aunts, and uncles, with his siblings, and with other playmates, the child discovers something about the nature of authority, the requirements of obedience, the existence of sanctions, and the opportunities, benefits, and costs of freedom. Indoctrination by the family or church of moral values helps the child construct ideas about justice, fair play, and the permissible limits of behavior.

Later, children can transfer these more universal notions to the political world and, at least in the United States, they begin to do so very early in life. Even before school, American children are very much aware—and proud—of their national identity. By second grade, if not before, many of them think of themselves as Democrats or Republicans, although the content of this partisan identity is almost totally emotional. Orientation toward authority is usually favorable. Perhaps as a carryover from a permissive family environment, most young American children look on the police, the mayor, and the President as "good men" who do "good things" for people. By their early teens, children are reasonably well informed—compared to their parents—about politics, and by their mid-teens their views are usually sufficiently formed to allow them to fit specific policy preferences into a more general political orientation.

It is probable that this learning process continues through much of life. As a young person builds up more experience with party workers and government officials like policemen, military officers, bureaucrats, or more occasionally legislators and judges, his initial uncritically favorable attitudes toward authority will probably moderate and become more sophisticated. But psychologists still believe that it is the early experiences that make the most lasting impact on a man's outlook on life; and it may well be that the strong emotional attachments to country and government that children form keep people loyal in later years to their political systems, despite the frequent failures of all such systems to fulfill their promises.

Political socialization operates in a number of formal and informal ways. As we have already mentioned, the patterns of trust, obedience, and freedom of pre-school years have important political spill-overs. In addition, the child may hear discussions of political affairs, and his parents or other family members may "explain" some current event to him. These "explanations" are likely to be very simplistic and highly moralistic, couched in such terms as the good guys (us) against the bad guys (them). In school, the authority roles of the teacher and the principal are added to those of the family, and freedom takes on a new dimension as do relations with other children. The child is probably taught, though he does not necessarily fully believe until he himself becomes a parent, such principles as "good boys and girls obey their teachers" or "good boys and girls settle their differences without hitting each other."

More formally, saluting the flag, reciting the pledge of allegiance, singing the national anthem, reciting legends of heroes like George Washington and Abraham Lincoln—whose truthfulness and honesty, in an interesting induction of general socialization from political culture, are often stressed more than their political accomplishments—reinforce national identity. Reading and teaching in history, geography, and civics provides a pool of specific information about national ideals and traditions.

Even religious instruction may play a role here. In inculcating ideas about the Deity, churchmen are indirectly teaching something about the nature of authority and the necessity of obedience. Furthermore, many religious groups, especially those associated with more recent immigrants, frequently go out of their way to praise the political system and to stress the smooth compatibility between fidelity to their theology and loyalty to America.

Not all groups in society go through the same socialization processes, either formal or informal, and, of course, not all persons react to the same influences in the same manner. Uniformity of socialization would be impossible in a culturally diverse country, especially one where wealth is so unequally divided. For even among young children, differences in social class, religion, and race are accompanied by difference in political orientation.

Adult immigrants go through the most obviously different form of political learning. They have, first of all, the difficult task of uprooting old national identifications and loyalties and building new ones, and perhaps also of creating new standards of civic conduct. Many older blacks are experiencing some of the same problems of re-education as immigrants. A number of younger militant black leaders complain of being frustrated by the effectiveness with which the older generation was habituated into a subservient political role. One of the reasons for low participation in politics has been acceptance of the norm that "politics is white folks' business," with consequent disinterest in governmental affairs and disbelief that public officials can or will do anything to change fundamentally the black man's life.

The immigrant's socialization is usually more formal and direct than that of the natural born citizen. Since he often has to learn as an adult, the immigrant is apt to get much more of his education from reading, from lectures, and from direct experiences with public officials, rather than from the slow process of gradually being exposed to more and more complex authority relations. The federal government suggests that all aliens interested in becoming citizens read several volumes[31] designed to provide quick socialization by listing the ideals of American government.

Historically, socialization of waves of immigrants often reversed the usual generational process. It was the children who passed on American culture to their parents. They learned the new ways in the neighborhood and more importantly in public schools and brought the new customs and beliefs home to their parents both verbally and by means of behavior that would not have been tolerated in the old country.

Government plays a direct role in the socialization process. As we have already seen, the example of public officials can stir respect or contempt for prevailing customs, processes, and values; and the speeches, opinions, and writings of presidents, governors, legislators, and judges can help shape political beliefs. The way in which the professional politician campaigns, runs his office, and trains other professionals makes him a carrier both of the general political culture and of the more particular rules that allow the system to function.

Socialization, of course, does not mean merely preserving the cultural status quo, although it often has that effect. It can also be an instrument for change. The Russians, the Chinese, the Japanese after World War II, and the Germans both under Hitler and since World War II have carefully and deliberately tried to educate children away from politically dominant norms and patterns of conduct. In the United States, the battle over school desegregation is in large part a struggle for control of one of the more important links in the socialization process. No educational system can ever be politically neutral. By its practices as much as by its precepts it inevitably encourages some kinds of political conduct and discourages others, just as the political system inevitably influences the content of beliefs transmitted.

Moreover, socialization may be so effective as to promote unintended change. It may imbue some people with such high political ideals that when they reach the age of adulthood, they cannot accommodate those ideals to a world inhabited by fallible men. Under those circumstances they may react against the system and become either bitter revolutionaries or cynical apoliticals. In neither case are they likely to see much use in working within the political system.

SELECTED BIBLIOGRAPHY

Almond, Gabriel A., and Sidney Verba, *The Civic Culture: Political Attitudes and Democracy in Five Nations* (Princeton, N.J.: Princeton University Press, 1963). A pathbreaking study of political culture in five democracies.

Brown, Claude, *Manchild in the Promised Land* (New York: The New American Library, Inc., 1965). A shocking but fascinating autobiographical account of life in the Harlem ghetto.

Commager, Henry Steele, *The American Mind: An Interpretation of American Thought and Character Since the 1880's* (New Haven, Conn.: Yale University Press, 1950). An incisive and readable intellectual history of Modern America.

Dahl, Robert A., *A Preface to Democratic Theory* (Chicago, Ill.: University of Chicago Press, 1956). An analysis of the underpinnings of American democracy that rejects much accepted lore.

Dawson, Richard E., and Kenneth Prewitt, *Political Socialization* (Boston, Mass.: Little, Brown and Company, 1969). The best introduction to the study of political socialization.

Frazier, E. Franklin, *Black Bourgeoisie* (New York: The Free Press of Glencoe, 1957). A jaundiced view of the black middle class, the group from which older black leadership was almost exclusively drawn until the mid-1950's.

Handlin, Oscar, *The Uprooted* (New York: Grosset & Dunlap, 1951). A first rate history of immigration to the United States and its impact on American life.

Harrington, Michael, *The Other America: Poverty in the United States* (Baltimore, Md.: Penguin Books, 1962). A social reformer's angry account of the disgraceful number and condition of the American poor.

Lerner, Max, *America as a Civilization: Life and Thought in the United States Today* (New York: Simon and Schuster, 1957). A lengthy interpretation—always interesting and always controversial—of American political, social, and intellectual life by a thoughtful social scientist-turned-journalist.

Lipset, Seymour Martin, *Political Man* (New York: Doubleday & Company, Inc., 1960). A series of essays by a political sociologist evaluating the conditions that make for democratic stability.

Lowi, Theodore J., *The End of Liberalism: Ideology, Policy, and the Crisis of Public Authority* (New York: W. W. Norton & Company, 1969). An analysis of the problems of American politics that lays the blame squarely on acceptance of what the author calls "interest-group liberalism."

Mason, Alpheus T., ed., *Free Government in the Making*, 3d ed. (New York: Oxford University Press, 1965). An extraordinarily useful collection of essays and documents illustrating the development of American thinking about politics.

Potter, David M., *People of Plenty: Economic Abundance and the American Character* (Chicago, Ill.: University of Chicago Press, 1954). A leading historian's view of the linkages between physical richness and the development of American life and "national character."

Tocqueville, Alexis de, *Democracy in America,* Phillips Bradley, ed.; (New York: Alfred A. Knopf, 1945). After more than 130 years still one of the most perceptive analyses of American democracy, a classic in the study of American politics.

Footnotes

[1] David M. Potter, *People of Plenty: Economic Abundance and the American Character* (Chicago, Ill.: University of Chicago Press, 1954), especially chap. 4.

[2] Richard Hofstadter, *Anti-Intellectualism in American Life* (New York: Alfred A. Knopf, Inc., 1963).

[3] Morris Janowitz, *The Professional Soldier: A Social and Political Portrait* (New York: The Free Press of Glencoe, 1960).

[4] Most of the literature on political culture has developed in the context of comparative politics. Among the more useful works are: Lucian W. Pye and Sidney Verba, eds., *Political Culture and Political Development* (Princeton, N.J.: Princeton University Press, 1965), especially the chapter on "Comparative Political Culture" by Verba; Harry Eckstein, "A Theory of Stable Democracy," reprinted as an appendix to his *Division and Cohesion in Democracy: A Study of Norway* (Princeton, N.J.: Princeton University Press, 1966); Gabriel A. Almond and Sidney Verba, *The Civic Culture: Political Attitudes and Democracy in Five Nations* (Princeton, N.J.: Princeton University Press, 1963); Eric A. Nordlinger, *The Working Class Tories* (Berkeley: University of California Press, 1967); and Lucian W. Pye, *Politics, Personality, and Nation Building* (New Haven, Conn.: Yale University Press, 1962). For a rather critical view of the way political scientists have used the concept of political culture, see Young C. Kim, "The Concept of Political Culture in Comparative Politics," *Journal of Politics,* 26 (May 1964), p. 313.

[5] Giovanni Sartori, *Democratic Theory* (New York: Frederick A. Praeger, 1965), p. 97.

[6] G. A. Almond and S. Verba, *The Civic Culture,* Chap. 12. For a useful overview—and an annotated bibliography—of the role of personality and politics, see Fred I. Greenstein, *Personality and Politics: Problems of Evidence, Inference, and Conceptualization* (Chicago, Ill.: Markham Publishing Company, 1969).

[7] *Olmstead v. United States,* 277 U.S. 438, 485, dissenting opinion (1928).

[8] *The Federalist,* No. 51 (New York: Random House, 1937), Modern Library Edition, p. 337.

[9] James W. Prothro and Charles M. Grigg, "Fundamental Principles of Democracy: Bases of Agreement and Disagreement," *Journal of Politics,* 22 (May 1960), p. 276.

[10] G. A. Almond and S. Verba, Parts II and III.

[11] *Brown v. Board of Education,* 347 U.S. 483 (1954).

[12] Jefferson to James Madison, December 20, 1787; quoted in Alpheus T. Mason, ed., *Free Government in the Making,* 3rd ed. (New York: Oxford University Press, 1965), p. 320.

[13] Robert A. Dahl, *Who Governs? Democracy and Power in an American City* (New Haven, Conn.: Yale University Press, 1961), p. 305.

[14] For a discussion of the scarcity of politically knowledgeable and sophisticated citizens, see Philip E. Converse, "The Nature of Belief Systems in Mass Publics," in David E. Apter, ed., *Ideology and Discontent* (New York: The Free Press of Glencoe, 1964), p. 206.

[15] The best discussion of the concept of the "rules of the game" can be found in David B. Truman, *The Governmental Process* (New York: Alfred A. Knopf, 1955), Chaps. 12, 14, and 16.

[16] Charles Frankel, *High on Foggy Bottom: An Outsider's Inside View of Government* (New York: Harper and Row, 1968), p. 108.

[17] Michael Harrington, *The Other America: Poverty in the United States* (Baltimore, Md.: Penguin Books, 1962), p. 17.

[18] The poverty line is defined by the U.S. Department of Commerce and the Bureau of the Census in terms of the amount of money it takes a family in a particular area to pay for minimally adequate food, shelter, and medical care. In 1970 the poverty line for a nonfarm family of four was approximately $3,700.

[19] Harrington, p. 22.

[20] Harrington, pp. 23–24.

[21] *Report of the National Advisory Commission on Civil Disorders* (Washington, D.C.: Government Printing Office, 1968), p. 1.

[22] See the data amassed to support this proposition by Angus Campbell and Howard Schuman, "Racial Attitudes in Fifteen American Cities," in *Supplemental Studies for the National Advisory Commission on Civil Disorders* (Washington, D.C.: Government Printing Office, 1968).

[23] W. E. B. Du Bois, *The Souls of Black Folk* (Chicago, Ill.: A. C. McClung & Co., 1903), p. 3.

[24] See William W. Ellis, *White Ethics and Black Power: The Emergence of the West Side Organization* (Chicago, Ill.: Aldine Publishing Co., 1969).

[25] See the data collected in Campbell and Schuman, especially in chapter 4.

[26] See David H. Bayley and Harold Mendelsohn, *Minorities and the Police* (New York: The Free Press of Glencoe, 1969), especially chapter 6.

[27] Eldridge Cleaver, *Soul on Ice* (New York: McGraw-Hill Book Company, 1968), pp. 3–4.

[28] Charles Tilly, "Collective Violence in European Perspective," in Hugh Davis Graham and Ted Robert Gurr, eds., *Violence in America: Historical and Comparative Perspectives,* A Staff Report to the National Commission on the Causes and Prevention of Violence (Washington, D.C.: Government Printing Office, 1969), I, 5.

[29] Henry Fairlie, "The Distemper of America," *Interplay,* 4 (November 1969), p. 6.

[30] There is a rapidly growing literature on political socialization. Among the more useful works are: Richard E. Dawson and Kenneth Prewitt, *Political Socialization* (Boston: Little, Brown and Company, 1969); David Easton and Jack Dennis, *Children in the Political System* (New York: McGraw-Hill Book Company, 1969); Fred I. Greenstein, *Children and Politics* (New Haven, Conn.: Yale University Press, 1965); and Robert D. Hess and Judith V. Torney, *The Development of Political Attitudes in Children* (Chicago, Ill.: Aldine Publishing Company, 1967).

[31] See the Becoming a Citizen Series prepared by the Immigration and Naturalization Service: Book 1: *Our American Way of Life;* Book 2: *Our United States;* Book 3: *Our Government* (Rev. ed.; Washington, D.C.: Government Printing Office, 1969).

Chapter 2 The Formation of a More Perfect Union

THE UNITED STATES: THE FIRST "EMERGING NATION"

The United States was in a very real sense the first "emerging nation" of modern times—the first "underdeveloped area" to throw off its colonial status and become an independent country. It is not surprising, then, that the Constitutional Convention of 1787 has always been of great interest to students of political institutions. This has never been truer than since World War II—years in which some 68 nations have achieved independence and, always the more difficult task, have tried to become countries in the sense of establishing a stable and effective self-government. Thus there has been a steady flow of books[1] dealing with the Philadelphia Convention. Their very titles—*The Great Rehearsal, 1787: The Grand Convention, Miracle at Philadelphia*—underscore the relevance of Jefferson's[2] words concerning America's "example of changing a constitution by assembling the wise men of the state, instead of assembling armies."

The Constitution Viewed as the Final Achievement of the American Revolution

The Constitutional Convention of 1787 was the penultimate event of a revolutionary period that began in 1763. The last event of the revolutionary period occurred in 1791 when the first ten amendments to the Constitution, known as the Bill of Rights, became effective. The opening of the period was marked by an ending—the ending of a series of armed conflicts in Europe and in America, variously known as the Seven Years' War, the Great War for the Empire, and the French and Indian War. By 1763, Britain, with the help of its thirteen American colonies, had driven the French out of Canada and out of the great wilderness west of the Appalachian mountains. It had, for the moment, obtained Florida from Spain, although that country still held the vast and vague territory known as Louisiana. Contrary to what might have been expected, this great victory of the English-speaking peoples did not usher in an era of harmony and further growth for the British Empire. Instead, peace and prosperity brought the British and the Americans to a series of quarrels over some basic issues—the control of trade, the levying of taxes, and the representation of local people and interests in the central councils of the government.

Students of the revolutionary period[3] have tried to do two things in recent years. First, looking beyond the much-told story of the great events of the period, they have concerned themselves with making a "quantitative analysis of massive amounts of hard social, economic and political data on such topics as economic development, social structure, voting behavior and religious divisions."[4] Second, they have sought a better understanding of "the total content" of the American Revolution, including "the implicit and underlying attitudes, values and beliefs . . . and [of] their broadest social and psychological meaning."

Viewing the American Revolution as a continuously evolving phenomenon, there were three fundamental and interrelated questions to be answered by the American people, either by force of arms or other means during the years from 1763 to 1791.

1.   Could the colonies reconcile their differences with the government in London and stay within the British Empire as an effective federation in which the local units were allowed reasonable measures of influence centrally and self-government locally? This question received a negative answer during the 1763–1776 period.

2.   Having declared their independence on July 4, 1776, could the colonies win their War of Independence? By 1783, they had answered this question in the affirmative.

3.   Could thirteen independent states effect a union through a constitutional settlement resulting in a durable nation organized as a republic? This was the major question with which men were concerned between 1783 and 1791.

The Meaning of Constitutional Government

From the time of the Mayflower Compact on, people in the New World gave much attention to the concept of a written charter of fundamental law that would determine the purpose, the precise character, and the limits of government. Until 1776, the colonies were typically governed under a written *charter* granted by the king. Between 1776 and 1787, the people of the thirteen states devoted much time and effort to the formulation of written *constitutions* fixing the political arrangements under which they would be governed at the state level. The Stamp Act Congress of 1765, the First Continental Congress of 1775, and the Second Continental Congress of 1776–1781, all efforts toward the formation of essential mechanisms of national government, took shape in the absence of any written constitution. It was expected that the Second Continental Congress would quickly write a constitution so that the War for Independence could be fought under the direction of a national government which had received formal authority and been told what its assignment was. The states, however, were slow to ratify this agreement. Therefore, between 1776 and 1781 the national government remained provisional. In 1781, the Articles of Confederation became effective as the nation's first written constitution. When the Founding Fathers met at Philadelphia in 1787 they operated within a political culture that accepted the concept of constitutional government. Their assignment was to set down on paper a series of written rules which would provide the country with "a more perfect union" than it had enjoyed up to then.

Constitutional government is an arrangement by which the people of a nation organize for collective action through government, while reserving to themselves an area of freedom upon which government is forbidden to encroach. The most important single factor in the meaning of constitutionalism is this concept of *limited government*. A constitution is the means whereby authority and liberty are balanced in a state. It is always a difficult undertaking to find a balance between liberty and authority that will work. In particular, it is difficult to set down in writing in a single document the terms of a constitutional settlement. If the document is too long or precise it may force the settlement into such a rigid mold that it will rapidly prove unsatisfactory in a changing world. If it is too short and vague it may fail to limit the power of the government sufficiently. In the history of government few actual constitutions have ever been very successful or lasted very long.

The Pattern of Revolutions

Students have been intrigued by indications that there is a common pattern in the great revolutions that have occurred in the Western World during the last two centuries. The pattern appears to run something like this: A revolutionary era opens with the growing decadence of the old order, its leaders stubbornly resisting changes that might enable it to survive. Important or influential intellectuals declare their dissatisfaction with the old order. A substantial number of political activists are impressed with the intellectuals' case against the old order and are also made aware of their own unsatisfactory role in society through direct personal experience. A crisis stage is reached, dissension progresses from polemics to coercion and violence. As this transition takes shape, the most radical of the revolutionaries seize leadership. Civil War or even a reign of terror ensues. The old order is supplanted, but after awhile the radicals begin to show signs of exhaustion or are unable to satisfy an equally exhausted populace with a stable new order. New leaders emerge and a more conservative, albeit still revolutionary period is ushered in. These new leaders manage to consolidate the principal gains of the revolution and a viable new social and political order is established.

Like all models, this one fails to explain in detail any specific instance such as the French Revolution, the Russian Revolution, or certainly the American Revolution. But it has its uses, one of which is to invite examination of the leadership of a revolution, which in turn is very likely to reveal that, while the leaders of a revolution necessarily have much in common, they can and do disagree sharply, both in their ideologies and on the practical matter of what to do at crucial moments throughout the revolutionary era. One group of leaders is often labeled radical and another conservative, although such terms are always relative. A conservative revolutionary position that proves workable can result in a far more lasting social change and thus be more significant historically than a more radical one that proves unacceptable or unworkable.

The Nationalists and Republicans

Viewing the American Revolution as a period of change that lasted for nearly three decades, its leaders do seem to have divided themselves into two such contrasting groupings. One group has been called the Nationalists and the other the Republicans. (For the final phase of the Revolution (1783–1791), it is customary to refer to the former as Federalists and the latter as Antifederalists.) From our perspective, the Nationalists seem the more conservative of the two groups. Basically they wanted a stable society that could preserve "law and order" and encourage a prosperous economy. They thought these goals could be reached more effectively through a national government than it could through the states. The Republicans appear radical in that they were more concerned with the rights of the individual than they were in the interests of society and believed that these rights could best be fostered by government at the state and even the local level through legislative bodies in which every social class or group would have its own representation. "Republicanism" for them was virtually synonymous with representative or legislative government.

The Nationalists had the upper hand between 1763 and 1775 when it seemed possible that the colonies would settle their differences with the British, remain a part of the Empire, and go on accepting the British system of "mixed government" that included elements of monarchy, aristocracy, and democracy. The Republicans become dominant in the 1770s, as the principal advocates of the Declaration of Independence and of the war that followed to give the Declaration meaning. With the winning of the war and the floundering of the state governments thereafter, the Nationalists slowly regained the dominant position and provided the leadership that led to the drafting of the Constitution and its ratification by the states. But the Republicans regrouped their forces during the ratification struggle and won a final victory in forcing the addition of a bill of rights to the Constitution.

The Republicans—Thomas Jefferson, Patrick Henry, Richard Henry Lee, Samuel Adams, John Adams, and John Hancock—declared and won the revolution. Idealistic and philosophical in outlook, they believed that through reason men could build a better, a more perfect social order. For them, government at best was a necessary evil, it existed to secure and protect the natural rights of man.

The Nationalists—Benjamin Franklin, Alexander Hamilton, Robert Morris, James Wilson, John Marshall, and George Washington—were the conservatives who consolidated the gains of a revolution after it was won. Pragmatic in outlook, "their systems were based in history, not in logic."[5] In their view, order and stability were essential if the individual was to be able to take advantage of the practical opportunities offered by life, and only a strong government could provide that tranquility.

Clearly there is much in this classification system (and most similar ones) that is overly simplistic. All of these people were revolutionaries. The Nationalists differed among themselves in conservatism, just as the Republicans advocated varying degrees of radicalism. Perhaps the most striking anomaly in all was George Washington who is viewed as the greatest of the Nationalists. But he was not sufficiently intellectual in style to have been consciously aware that he was basing his "system" in either logic or history. He was as essential to the winning of the violent phase of the Revolution as he was to consolidating its gains during "the conservative reaction."

Almost all of the leaders of both factions or parties, in addition to being Patriots, were members of the elite of colonial society. They were merchants, bankers, lawyers, college professors, or plantation owners in their occupations; they were, for their times, exceptionally well educated; they lived in cities, or on plantations that were not lacking in culture and urbanity. They had all found "room at the top." They had held political office and gained much political experience before they made the crucial decisions that shaped a new nation. All along they had been the men who "could afford the expensive business of public service."[6] In the end, the Republicans came to believe with the Nationalists in "the capacity of a conspicuous few to speak for the whole society," which a recent scholar of the revolutionary period has written "was to become in time the distinguishing feature of American democratic politics."[7]

This emphasis on elitism is not to say that all of the great events in American history between 1763 and 1791 were manipulated or conducted by the members of a small class of leaders who somehow managed to disagree among themselves sufficiently to enable history to sort them out as Republicans or Nationalists. Strong democratic or populist tides were running in America in these decades and it took the conscious support and enthusiastic participation of large segments of "the people" to conduct and complete the revolution. For one thing, the social and economic extremes of society were closer together at the end of the eighteenth century than the preceding discussion might suggest. Life was lived easily and luxuriously by very few men; but, except among the slaves, neither was there much abject poverty. In the city, the masses found means of livelihood as artisans and tradesmen; urban slums and ghettos were virtually unknown. In the countryside, and particularly on the frontier, men did not live like Washington at Mt. Vernon or Jefferson at Monticello, for subsistence farming was the rule for many. However, most men owned their farms and made modest progress. Since the suffrage was usually based on property, the right to vote was remarkably broad for the age. And though the American armies were frequently ill-manned and ill-equipped, the Revolution could not have been fought to its successful outcome without active participation of a large number of people in the military effort. At the very end of the period, as will be seen, the elite leaders recognized that the people must be sounded out before the Constitution could be viewed as properly ratified or put into operation. The concept "of the people" played a far more important part in determining the constitutional settlement that implemented the American victory won by force of arms than was true of the French revolution in the 1790s or the Russian revolution in the years after 1917.

National Government Under the Articles of Confederation

Article II of the Articles of Confederation provided, "Each state retains its sovereignty, freedom and independence, and every power, jurisdiction and right, which is not by this confederation expressly delegated to the United States, in Congress assembled." This meant that the "perpetual union" created by the Articles was that of "a firm league of friendship" of independent states rather than a federal union in which sovereignty rested in the nation. It also meant that the only constitutional agency of the central government was a unicameral Congress. The Articles established no executive branch. Congress was authorized to create national courts for the limited purposes of trying piracy and prize cases or settling disputes among the states. Congress itself was not so much a national legislative assembly as it was a conference of state ambassadors. Each state was authorized to send from two to seven delegates: but, as in the General Assembly of the United Nations, each state had but one vote in Congress regardless of its population. Important public laws required the approval of nine states rather than of a simple majority.

Congress under the Articles could coin money and borrow money, issue paper currency, establish a postal system, fix standards of weights and measures, regulate Indian affairs, and appropriate funds to meet governmental costs. In foreign affairs its powers were relatively extensive. It could negotiate treaties, send and receive ambassadors, raise and equip an army and a navy, appoint officers in these armed services, and declare war.

The Weaknesses of the Articles of Confederation

In several ways, the Articles proved seriously defective as an adequate constitutional basis for a system of government. First, the Articles ignored an executive branch. Therefore, the new government could legislate, that is, prescribe policy, but could not carry it out. In 1781, Congress did establish four executive departments. This administrative machinery, however, was largely ineffectual because the Articles did not provide for a chief executive to effect central unity and guidance. Second, it is an exaggeration to say that Congress could "legislate"; the laws it passed were merely directives to the states and did not bear directly on the people. Congress could "resolve and recommend but could not command and coerce."[8] Third, the powers actually granted to Congress were inadequate for the needs of a truly national government. Having no taxing power, Congress had to depend upon state contributions to the national treasury for its revenues. With no congressional power to regulate commerce among the states, each state was free to establish barriers against the trade of neighboring states. This made the establishment of a uniform national commercial policy almost a practical impossibility. Fourth, the Articles authorized Congress to supervise the settlement of disputes between states, but there was no way to settle conflicts between the national government and the states. Finally, the Articles were extremely difficult to amend; the legislatures in all thirteen states had to ratify changes proposed to them by Congress.

As soon as the Revolutionary War was won, the inadequacies of the Articles began to be felt in practice. In 1786, for example, the entire income of the national government would have paid less than one third of the interest on the national debt. Congress found it impossible to negotiate commercial agreements with foreign nations since it was clear that it could not carry out its promises. At home the commercial trade wars between the states were threatening to bring domestic commerce to a complete halt. These difficulties over trade led five states to send delegates to a meeting in Annapolis in 1786. The meeting did little to settle economic problems, but before it adjourned it issued a call for a second meeting to be held in Philadelphia the following year. In addition, it proposed that at this second meeting something more than the commercial difficulties be considered. It recommended that this new convention "take into consideration the situation of the United States, to devise such further provisions as shall appear to them necessary to render the constitution of the federal government adequate to the exigencies of the Union, and to report such an Act for that purpose to the United States in Congress assembled, as when 'agreed to by them and afterwards confirmed by the legislatures of every state' will effectually provide for the same."

Most delegates to Congress were reluctant to issue a call for a convention that might recommend sweeping political changes, but the fears created by Shays' Rebellion in Massachusetts late in 1786 and the fact that seven states had already appointed delegates led Congress to vote its approval in February of 1787.

THE ISSUES FACED BY THE PHILADELPHIA CONVENTION

This brief description of government under the Article of Confederation serves to underscore the basic questions that the Philadelphia convention had to try to answer. They were:

1.   Assuming that the national legislature must be given power to pass laws that would be binding on the people, not just the states, how should Congress be organized and, in particular, should the states be represented equally or on some weighted basis?

2.   Should provision be made in the Constitution for executive and judicial agencies at the national level and should this be done in such a way as to implement the principle of distribution of powers?

3.   The national government would presumably be empowered to provide for the common defense and to control foreign affairs so that the threat posed to the new nation by England, Spain, and France could be effectively dealt with at the same time that trade with these nations and their colonies was encouraged. But what other express powers should the national government be granted, particularly with respect to taxation, money, the public debt, and trade within the country?

4.   What should be done about the development of the vast western wilderness to which the new nation and the individual states laid claim?

5.   What provision should a constitution make for maintaining a division of power between a more powerful national government and the thirteen state governments?

6.   What provision should a constitution make for keeping straight the distinction between powers granted to governments and rights reserved to the people?

THE WORK OF THE CONVENTION

There were many reasons why the Philadelphia convention might have failed. The thirteen states shared a common language and, as the former colonies of a single nation, also shared "common legal and political institutions, common culture, common enemies, and common memories of a successful drive toward independence,"[9] but they had, in a century and a half, developed diverse social and economic interests and were as ready to quarrel among themselves as independent political states always have been. They were contiguous geographically, but the distance in miles from Massachusetts to Georgia was great. The eighteenth-century means of communication and transportation were poor and the way of thinking about goals in terms of *national* purpose and *national* opportunity was vague.

Yet the Founding Fathers managed to draft a Constitution that has since been regarded as a brilliant achievement in statecraft. They sensed the needs of a particular emerging nation and they correctly estimated the fact that the people would go along with a bold step toward a single country with a strong national government operated on republican principles, in order to achieve fundamental purposes and goals.

Organization and Procedures of the Convention

In seeking an explanation of the highly successful outcome of the American constitutional assembly, the procedures of the convention should be noted, for many a similar assembly has failed to accomplish its mission because of faulty organization and ways of going about its business.

The convention was in session from the end of May to the middle of September in 1787. In all, fifty-five delegates attended. Many of these were late in arriving, only forty-two stayed until the end, and only thirty-nine signed the finished Constitution. Twelve states were represented; Rhode Island refused to send any representatives. The states sent varying numbers of delegates, but, although the large states favored a weighted system of voting based on population, a decision was made early in the convention that each state would cast one vote. Thus there was a maximum of twelve votes on any question. A simple majority was sufficient to carry any proposal. Debate was not limited in any fashion; discussions were frequently lengthy and vigorous. The way was open for establishment of rapport among the delegates and for essentially simple, informal ways of doing business.

There is no official or formal record of the proceedings of the convention. The meeting appointed William Jackson to serve as its secretary, but he kept very sparse minutes of the sessions. Fortunately, other delegates also kept notes and recorded them in personal papers, diaries, and memoranda. The most valuable source of information is a diary kept by James Madison, in which he reported the story of the convention, including lengthy résumés of the speeches made by the delegates on the floor of the assembly.

Meeting as they did nearly two centuries ago, the delegates were able to make a decision that undoubtedly helped the convention to succeed but that almost certainly could not be done today. This was the adoption of a secrecy rule by which "nothing spoken in the house [was] to be printed, or otherwise published or communicated without leave." This rule was consistently adhered to throughout the sessions. It is clear that in those troubled times the work of the Philadelphia convention was greatly simplified because it took place behind closed doors. Madison himself wrote that "no Constitution would ever have been adopted by the Convention if the debates had been public."

The work of the convention over its four-month span was further facilitated by a

Docr. Franklin. It is too soon to pledge ourselves before Congress and our Constituents shall have approved the plan.

Mr. Ingersol did not consider the signing, either as a mere attestation of the fact, or as pledging the signers to support the Constitution at all events; but as a recommendation, of what, all things considered, was the most eligible.

On the motion of Docr. Franklin
N.H. ay. Mas. ay. Ct. ay. N.J. ay. Pa. ay. Del. ay. Md. ay. Va. ay. N.C. ay. S.C. divd. Geo. ay. [*] Genl. Pinkney & Mr. Butler disliked the equivocal form of the signing, and on that account voted in the negative.

Mr. King suggested that the Journals of the Convention should be either destroyed, or deposited in the custody of the President. He thought if suffered to be made public, a bad use would be made of them by those who would wish to prevent the adoption of the Constitution.

Mr. Wilson preferred the second expedient, he had at first liked the first best.; but as false suggestions may be propagated it should not be made impossible to contradict them.

A question was then put on depositing the Journals and other papers of the Convention in the hands of the President, on which,
N.H. ay. Mas. ay. Ct. ay. N.J. ay. Pena. ay. Del. ay. Md. no. Va. ay. N.C. ay. S.C. ay. Geo-

The negative of Maryland was occasioned by the language of the instructions to the Deputies of that State, which required them to report to the State, the proceedings of the Convention.

The President having asked what the Convention meant should be done with the Journals &c. whether copies were to be allowed to the members if applied for. Resolved nem: con: "that he retain the Journal and other papers, subject to be transferred hither & thither...

James Madison appointed himself unofficial secretary to the Constitutional Convention and kept a record of its activities. His lengthy résumés of remarks and speeches are recorded in his diary, Notes on the Federal Convention. *On this page of the journal, Madison discusses several proposals regarding the safekeeping of the papers of the Convention—whether they should be thrown out or deposited with the President.* (Library of Congress) plan of proceeding that was largely free from the complicated parliamentary devices that are used in most assemblies today. No use was made of standing committees.[10]

Early on, several members proposed a detailed substantive proposal for a new constitution which was laid before the convention by certain of its members. About two weeks later another group submitted a quite different proposal. Sitting as a "committee of the whole," the convention considered these and voted, six states to four in favor of one of these plans, which it then debated in detail for a month. The convention adjourned twice, once for ten days and once for two days, to permit two special committees to take stock of the convention's progress and, in the light of its decisions, to prepare new drafts of a constitution for its further consideration. The convention went over the report of the first of these agencies, known as the committee of detail, with great care for five weeks, debating the committee's proposed constitution section by section and attempting to make final decisions on each point. The second committee was appointed early in September "to revise the style of and arrange the articles which had been agreed to by the house." The convention then spent three days scrutinizing the committee's draft, a few last-minute changes were made, and the Constitution was ready to be signed.

At another point, midway in the convention, when the disputed issue of representation of the states in the two houses of a proposed Congress threatened to wreck the convention, a special committee, consisting of one delegate from each state, was appointed. This committee was able to make a recommendation for equal representation in one house and representation by population in the other that the delegates could accept.

Personnel

The fifty-five delegates who went to Philadelphia in 1787 were a remarkable group of men. Without doubt, they profoundly influenced the precise character of the Constitution. Twenty-six of them had college educations; two college presidents and three professors were present. More than thirty delegates had training in law. The delegates also had much practical experience in politics—forty-two of the delegates had been members of Congress; twenty had served in state constitutional conventions; seven had been state governors; thirty were serving in state legislatures at the time the Philadelphia convention met.

The Founding Fathers provide an example of men of widely differing ages working together to solve a common problem. The oldest, the most experienced, and the wisest in the ways of men, Benjamin Franklin, was a venerable eighty-one. The youngest delegate, Jonathan Dayton of New Jersey, was only twenty-six. Four delegates were in their twenties, fifteen in their thirties, twenty-two in their forties, seven, including Washington, in their fifties, and seven were sixty or older. The average age was just over forty-three.

Thomas Jefferson, from his diplomatic post in Paris, wrote John Adams in London that the convention was "an assembly of demigods." Many of the most famous men of the revolutionary period were there, including George Washington, Benjamin Franklin, Alexander Hamilton, James Madison, James Wilson, Gouverneur Morris, Roger Sherman, George Mason, Oliver Ellsworth, and Edmund Randolph.[11] It is an equally striking fact that others among the men who had played important roles during the Revolutionary years were missing. John Adams and Thomas Jefferson were abroad serving their country as diplomats. Samuel Adams was at home in Massachusetts, too old to come. John Hancock also stayed in Massachusetts, where he was governor of the state. Patrick Henry declined to serve; his laconic explanation was, "I smelt a rat!" Thomas Paine was in Europe. Among others who, for one reason or another, were missing were George Clinton and John Jay of New York and John Marshall of Virginia. Only eight of the fifty-six men who had signed the Declaration of Independence eleven years earlier were among the fifty-five delegates to the Philadelphia convention.

Although the fact of those present and those absent tends to support the notion that the Philadelphia convention was "the conservative reaction" phase of the American revolution, or the moment at which the Nationalists seized control away from the Republicans, agreement was far from easily achieved on all matters. As the business of the convention took shape it quickly became apparent that the states and delegates were almost evenly balanced between two contrasting positions. More than once along the way the convention almost broke up because of the failure of a dominant majority to emerge.

The Motives of the Framers

No aspect of the Constitutional Convention has received more attention as the years have gone by than has the issue of the character and motives of the fifty-five men who framed the Constitution. Throughout most of the nineteenth century a great tradition grew up to the effect that the framers were staunch patriots and wise statesmen who created the most remarkable constitutional system that history had yet seen and that they did this as men of vast erudition and experience, who rose above personal considerations in their common desire to serve the good of all the people. From today's vantage point with our more sophisticated knowledge that men's motives at best are likely to be mixed, this earlier viewpoint has an aura of lost innocence.

Thus, twentieth-century social scientists, utilizing their new viewpoints and research techniques, have turned anew to the record of the convention in a search for more complex and satisfactory explanations of what happened and why. This process began in 1913 when Charles A. Beard[12] published one of the most influential, albeit controversial books ever to be written by an American social scientist. His basic point was that the framers were much more influenced by personal considerations than had previously been recognized and that what they did was frequently consciously intended to protect and advance their own interests. As Beard saw it, those delegates who owned public securities were concerned about the inability or unwillingness of both state and national governments to meet payments on the interest and principal of the public debt. The western landowners wanted roads and protection against Indians. Creditors were worried about the increasing tendency of debtors to seek legislation from their state governments which freed them from part or all of their obligations. Merchants and manufacturers were handicapped by the lack of a uniform national currency and were suffering because of the disruption of America's foreign trade and the growing stagnation in interstate trade. These men all had strong personal reasons for desiring a strong, central government that would protect and promote their own economic interests.

For half a century after its appearance, Beard's book set the pattern for a widely accepted view of the framers and their work. Now during the last few decades, scholars have taken a further look at the motives of the framers, utilizing more careful research methods and a much larger body of data than were available to Beard. Beard's findings have been particularly challenged by Robert E. Brown and Forrest McDonald.[13] The conduct of most of the delegates, McDonald contends, rather than reflecting their own personal economic interests, "was to a much greater extent a reflection of the interests and outlooks of the states they represented."

Beard's thesis that the framers had personal economic motives has not been rejected outright. The framers did have good personal reasons to be concerned about such practical matters as what was to be done about the public debt, how trade on a national and international basis could be encouraged, and what steps might be taken to realize the potential of the western wilderness. Early scholars of the convention may not have known the exact pecuniary interest that each delegate had in such matters, but it was always known that many delegates were men with propertied and commercial interests. It has certainly always been known that the states they represented had strong and varied economic interests in such areas as trade, taxation, the public debt, and slavery. Since Beard's time, scholars have dug out a vast body of facts about all these matters. In the end the facts seem to show that men's motives in the convention were mixed. They were simultaneously concerned about the public good and their private interests. The senior Arthur Schlesinger[14] has written that analysis of the motives of the "Fathers of the Constitution" "forms an illuminating commentary on the fact that intelligent self-interest, whether conscious or instinctive, is one of the motive forces of human progress."

This recent research has also underscored another point that was more or less obvious all along. Many of the delegates, and the states and the people they represented, were frequently pulled in opposite directions on a specific issue because, from the point of view of their own selfish interests, there was something to be said for going in either direction. To take but one example, holders of western lands had to decide whether to support a stronger national government because it could provide protection against the Indians and somehow manage to expel the British from posts they continued to hold in violation of the Treaty of 1783, or to be apprehensive lest a strong Congress, beholden to states and people with other interests, might by law or treaty negotiate away the right of the Americans who would ultimately be living in the West to enjoy free use of the Mississippi River trade route to the high seas.[15]

For today's student of political institutions this problem of the motives of the framers is a rewarding one to explore, as he searches for useful models that will help explain why men behave politically as they do. The problem suggests a number of seemingly relevant questions: What importance should be attributed to consciously determined, more or less rational factors in the political ideas and actions of men? To what extent are events shaped by chance and confusion, or by rational interests or arguments that are so evenly balanced that men can come down on either side of a great issue with almost equal ease? How conscious were the subsistence farmers living in the frontier areas that their interests might be benefited or injured through the policies that a stronger national government might pursue? Did they actually know what their interests were and had they established a priority among these interests? Was it their debtor status that would suffer if the cheap money policies of the preceding decade were reversed? Do the data show that they were debtors? If so, what kind of debts did they owe and to whom?

How great was their concern about the danger from Indians? Or is it possible that the subsistence farmers and western settlers were simply too remote from the centers of information to know what was going on?

To put the question another way, were the people who lived in the cities and towns in the tidewater areas more aware than rural people that the social systems that were growing in the thirteen states were becoming so complex that men needed stronger and more effective governmental mechanisms through which to engage in the problem-solving required in such a complex society?

In spite of the difficulty of bringing to light all of the relevant data about the constitutional period, one can be certain that scholars will continue to search for additional evidence and to strive for a better understanding of the period as the data accumulate. Perhaps more importantly, this concern with the political happenings of nearly two centuries ago and of the roles that men played in them is indicative of the increasing interest of today's students in the contemporary behavior of men and his determination that the search for all relevant data concerning actual political behavior be broadened and intensified.

THE VIRGINIA AND NEW JERSEY PLANS

The two contrasting proposals for a new constitution that were introduced early in the convention were the Virginia Plan and the New Jersey Plan. The Virginia Plan proposed a bicameral congress in both of whose houses the states would have representation based on population. This congress would have all the powers of its predecessor under the Articles of Confederation, and in addition, the authority "to legislate in all cases in which the separate states are incompetent, or in which the harmony of the United States may be interrupted by the exercise of individual legislation." It could also veto all state laws that in its opinion violated the Constitution and thus would have power to draw the line between national and state authority and to determine the limits of is own powers. Congress was to choose a "national executive" and provision was made for a "national judiciary." The executive and judiciary would constitute a "council of revision" with a veto power over the congress; the vetoes, however, could be overridden by a subsequent vote of both houses.

The convention proceeded to consider this radical and far-reaching plan for some two weeks in a committee of the whole. At the end of that period, those delegates who advocated a more modest increase in the powers of the central government presented the New Jersey Plan, which retained a unicameral congress in which the states would have equal representation. To the existing powers of this congress would be added authority to tax and to regulate interstate commerce. Congress would also be given power to elect a "federal executive," and provision would be made for a "federal judiciary." Perhaps the most striking proposal in the New Jersey Plan was that federal laws and treaties were to be "the supreme law of the respective states" and that state courts were bound to enforce these federal enactments. This "was in reality the key to the solution of federalism, but at the time it escaped notice, for momentarily the Convention was altogether preoccupied with the legislature."[16]

As we have seen, by a vote of six to four, the committee chose the Virginia Plan as a basis for its further deliberations. The closeness of the vote indicated that there would have to be a good deal of negotiation and compromise if anything approaching consensus was to be reached by the end of the convention.

COMPROMISE IN THE CONVENTION

The framers found it quite easy to agree on many of the basic issues of the day. There was general accord on such propositions as (1) the need for a stronger government to cope with the nation's economic and social problems, (2) the wisdom of providing such increased power in the central government rather than in the states, and (3) the desirability of establishing in the national government some kind of executive and judicial agencies as well as a legislature and of arranging for checks and balances to prevent abuse of the increased powers the three agencies of the national government would possess. However, the differences that had to be reconciled were serious. The states, widely separated geographically and with many conflicting social and economic interests, had to be persuaded that a stronger national government, which most of them thought was desirable, would represent their separate interests fairly and substantially. Here, in the Philadelphia convention, an issue appeared that has troubled the nation throughout its entire history. How can each of the many states joined together in one great federal union be assured that its own economic and social interests will receive satisfactory consideration from the central government?

Compromise Between the Large and the Small States

It has been traditional to speak of the need to bridge a fundamental difference of positions in the convention between the "large" and the "small" states. The "large" states favored a stronger national government which they expected to dominate through a representational Congress based on population, and the "small" states favored a national government which was only modestly stronger than it was under the Articles of Confederation in which their interests would be secure because all states would enjoy equal representation in the congress. More careful consideration of relevant data has suggested that the patterns of state voting in the convention were more complex than this explanation suggests.

The data show that the strong central government position was initially supported by four states south of the Potomac River, only one of which, Virginia, was "large." It was supported by two of the eight states north of the Potomac, Massachusetts and Pennsylvania, both "large" states. The six other states, all north of the Potomac, were New Hampshire, Connecticut, New York, New Jersey, Delaware, and Maryland.[17] There seemed to be an essential six-to-six deadlock that would ultimately have to be broken by some means.

Further analysis shows that there were factors other than population that played a part in determining the two groupings. The "large" state group consisted of states that were torn internally by economic and social strife of kinds that they had reason to believe might be alleviated through the more aggressive policies of a stronger national government. The "small" states were more stable and prosperous internally and thus did not feel quite the same compulsion to change the existing political arrangements.

The political future of the West raised another decisive issue. The "large" states, having extensive access or title to western lands, favored a congress in which the states would have representation based on population so that a more systematic policy concerning the development of the West, which everyone agreed was desirable, would recognize the interests of these states in their lands. The "small" states, with few exceptions, had no direct claims to the West and thus favored a congress based on equal representation which might be expected to shape a western lands program in which all states and all persons could share alike in the economic and social advantages that would become available.

As discussion in the convention went on, it became apparent that the delegates were divided not so much on the issue of how much stronger the new national government ought to be as they were by the issue of equal vs. proportional voting power. John Dickinson,[18] a small state delegate, made this clear when he told Madison:

> Some of the members from the small States wish for two branches in the General Legislature, *and are friends to a good National Government;* but we would sooner submit to a foreign power, than submit to be deprived of an equality of suffrage, in both branches of the legislature, and thereby be thrown under the domination of the large States.

Finally, after prolonged discussions of the issue marked by much obtuseness and stubbornness, a solution was found in "the Connecticut Compromise." The compromise itself was an obvious one and had been suggested early in the convention: the states would be given varying representation based on population in the lower house of the congress and equal representation in the upper house. The details were apparently worked out by Oliver Ellsworth of Connecticut and John Rutledge of South Carolina in private negotiations, in which a complex series of small state concerns figured. Its final details took shape over a period of time, but it is said to have been based on Connecticut's wish to have access to enough land to enable the people of this overcrowded state to continue their system of farming and land speculation and on South Carolina's wish to protect its interests in the slave trade and the export business.[19] In one way or another the finished Constitution did take these interests into account.

Compromise over the Election of the President

Another perplexing problem concerned the election of the President. At least six methods for choosing the President were proposed. These included election by the people, by the state governors, by Congress, and by an electoral college. The convention twice gave its approval to election by Congress. Each time, those who favored a strong executive vigorously opposed this decision, arguing that legislative election would make the President ineffectual and subservient. Finally, toward the close of the convention, the electoral college system was approved.

The plan for the election of the President also involved a further compromise between the large and the small states. In the electoral college the large states would benefit, since the electoral vote of each state was to be equal to its representation in both houses of Congress. But if no candidate received a majority of the electoral vote, the House of Representatives, *voting by states,* was to elect a President from among the five highest candidates. In this event, the small states would benefit, because each state would have one vote. Moreover, since the electoral college would never sit together but rather each group of electors would meet in the state capital and cast their ballots it was probable that the presidential vote would frequently be widely distributed among several candidates, and election of a President by the House a fairly common occurrence.

Compromise on New States

Many delegates were apprehensive about the new states that might be carved out of the western wilderness. They felt that these states might reflect the radical interests of the debtor and small-farmer classes that they had learned to distrust during the Confederation period. Accordingly, they favored language in the Constitution restricting the admission of new states and providing for their membership in the Union on an inferior basis. As it turned out, there were enough delegates favoring free development of the West to insist upon compromise. It proved impossible to put into the Constitution a clause guaranteeing the right of new states to come into the Union "on the same terms with the original States," but neither was any express language adopted condemning new states to an inferior position. Instead, the power to finally decide the terms upon which new states might be accepted was delegated to Congress, which ultimately accepted fully the doctrine of complete equality.

Compromise and the Issue of Slavery

A geographical conflict separated the northern and southern states. The northern states had important interests in commerce and shipping and were ready for first steps toward a manufacturing economy that the next half century would bring. In the South, a large-scale plantation system of agriculture based on slavery was emerging. That section was producing increasingly large agricultural surpluses and was eager to exchange them in outside markets for the finished goods that were unavailable. Since the southern states were in a minority, they were apprehensive lest the increased power of the new central government be used to advance the economic interests of the North at their expense. To deal with this apprehension the delegates agreed that there should be an absolute prohibition upon export taxes. In this way the fear of the South that Congress might try to tax both the flow of the agricultural surplus out of and the flow of finished goods into its territory was quieted. A second compromise between North and South concerned the ratification of treaties. The South was concerned that the new government would enter into commercial agreements with foreign nations detrimental to its interests. The requirement of a two-thirds majority in the Senate for the approval of treaties assured the South of a veto power over agreements with foreign nations.

Slavery itself also was a source of disagreement between North and South. Some southerners wanted state representation in the lower house to be based upon total populations, including all slaves. Northern opponents of slavery, on the other hand, argued that none of the slaves be counted. The compromise spirit prevailing, it was agreed that three-fifths of the slaves would be counted in determining a state's quota of seats in the House of Representatives, as well as in calculating its quota whenever a direct tax was levied by the central government. Delegates from the deep South also were anxious to see the importation of slaves from Africa continue without restraint. The middle states, particularly Virginia, which bred their own slaves and had a surplus for sale, were willing to see the importation of slaves brought to an end, as were some of the northern delegates for moral reasons. A compromise decision finally allowed the slave trade to continue until 1808, when Congress might forbid further importation—which it promptly did when that year arrived. In the meantime, imported slaves were not to be taxed by the national government at a figure in excess of ten dollars a head.

None of these compromises, of course, improved the lot of those Americans whose color condemned them to slavery. Certainly the most fateful decision *not* taken at Philadelphia in 1787 was to deal with the institution of slavery itself, if not in the sense of abolishing it immediately, then at least in making provision in the Constitution for its ultimate abolition by peaceful means.[20] The institution of slavery and its impact upon the formation of "a more perfect union" should have been very much in the minds of the Founding Fathers since slavery was widely viewed as inconsistent with the ideas and principles of free government, at least half of the states having already made slavery unlawful.[21]

It took one of the bloodiest wars in history to abolish the institution of slavery. The United States is still striving to establish full racial justice and equality. One wonders whether the Founding Fathers might not have managed in their new Constitution to deal with this problem. This is, of course, one of the great "if onlys" of American history. The best judgment of scholars is that the basic issue of slavery itself could not have been dealt with by compromise—and certainly not by a frontal attack—at Philadelphia in 1787. All of the arguments against slavery were known and could have been voiced systematically on the floor of the convention. The issue could easily have been made the subject of a resolution that, in a showdown, would probably have been approved by a majority of the states. But it is even clearer that such a step would have been utterly unacceptable in 1787 to the five states south of Delaware. John Rutledge was undoubtedly correct when he told the convention that the question of what to do about slavery was in effect the question of "whether the southern states shall or shall not be parties to the Union."

RATIFICATION OF THE CONSTITUTION

The Extralegal Character of Ratification

The ingenuity of the delegates and the spirit of compromise that pervaded the convention's sessions had made possible the fashioning of a document that thirty-nine of the forty-two delegates who were present at the end were able to sign.[22] There was good reason to fear, however, that the Constitution might not be ratified by the states. By the terms of the Articles' amending clause, revision of the fundamental law could take place only by a vote of Congress and the approval of the *legislatures* in all *thirteen* states. Approval by the old

Congress was highly uncertain, and it was improbable that all thirteen state legislatures, including that of Rhode Island, which had refused to send delegates to the Philadelphia convention, would ratify. Accordingly, in wording the section of the Constitution that prescribed the manner in which it was to be ratified, the Fathers did not hesitate to depart from the stipulations of the Articles in three specific ways. They proposed to Congress that it send the Constitution to the several states without stopping to give the document its own consideration or approval; second, they recommended that consideration in the states be made by special conventions; and third, they provided that approval by nine states should be sufficient to put the new Constitution into operation in those states.

Antifederalist Opposition to Ratification

The men who supported the Constitution had to do more than discover a method of ratification that gave the document a chance of winning approval in the states. They had to mount and manage a campaign for such approval, to be conducted state by state and utilizing strong arguments and effective political maneuvering. For now at the end of 1787 and in the early months of 1788, the opponents to the kind of strong national government that was proposed in the new Constitution, bestirred themselves, making aggressive attempts at strong argument and effective political maneuvering. These opponents of the Constitution have come to be known as the Antifederalists. Looking back to earlier years, they had much in common with the Republicans of the revolutionary period. Looking ahead they would provide a link with the Republican-Democratic party that elected Jefferson to the Presidency in 1800 and controlled the national government almost continuously thereafter until 1840.

At first things went well for the Federalist supporters of the Constitution. Congress, at the end of September, 1787, voted to send the Constitution to the states without recommendation, pro or con, even though eighteen of the thirty-three congressmen present had served in the Philadelphia convention and might have chosen to do battle for a positive endorsement.[23] By January 9, 1788, five state conventions had ratified, three by unanimous votes and the other two by substantial majorities. These states, in order of action, were Delaware, Pennsylvania, New Jersey, Georgia, and Connecticut, which suggests that by now some if not all the "small" states had become enthusiastic supporters of the Constitution.

Thereafter, the battle raged for many months. New Hampshire was the ninth state to ratify in late June, 1788, but it took another month to add Virginia and New York to the list of favorable states. In this battle the Federalists had certain significant advantages. They were better organized, they proved to be more flexible in reacting to the needs of the changing situation as the scene shifted from one state convention to another. They had one other great advantage that their opponents were never able to match—that powerful series of letters explaining and extolling the Constitution written by Hamilton, Madison, and Jay, first published in newspapers of several states and, by the time the New York convention voted, available in pamphlet form. It is a mark of the strong roles that both principle and pragmatism have played in American politics that *The Federalist*, which has always been regarded as America's greatest contribution to the literature of political thought, was called forth by the practical necessity of winning votes for the proposed Constitution.

In part the Antifederalists were less effective than their opponents because the bulk of their support came from the less articulate groups in society, from the small farmers, rather than from the plantation owners or gentleman farmers, from debtors rather than from merchants and bankers, from local politicos rather than from nationally known figures. The Antifederalists had a few eloquent spokesmen like Robert Yates and Richard Henry Lee, and their writings are still being reprinted.[24] But, on the whole, those who talked and wrote against the new constitution lacked the skill, experience, and prestige of Federalist leaders like Madison, Hamilton, Jay, and Washington. There was no *The Antifederalist* that carried the kind of weight in crucial states like New York and Virginia that *The Federalist* did. As a loose coalition, the Antifederalists were slow to organize, often clumsy in their techniques, and lacked energy and leadership. Even Thomas Jefferson, who in the 1790s was to suture the remnants of the Antifederalists into an effective political party, was in favor of ratification, although he also urged adoption of a bill of rights. The Federalist victory, one recent scholar[25] concludes, "was actually more of an Antifederalist default." They simply "were not, as one Federalist put it, 'good politicians.'"

Antifederalist sentiments were widespread, however, and feelings went deep. As a rural member of the Massachusetts convention protested:[26]

> These lawyers, and men of learning, and moneyed men, that talk so finely, and gloss over matters so smoothly, to make us poor illiterate people swallow down the pill, expect to get into Congress themselves; they expect to be the managers of this Constitution, and get all the power and all the money into their own hands, and then they will swallow up all us little folks, like the great Leviathan, Mr. President; yes just as the whale swallowed up Jonah.

The Antifederalists, even though they failed in their ostensible purpose, did develop a case against the Constitution which was far from being totally ineffectual at the time and which has received a good deal of attention and respect in recent years. The strength of the Antifederalists was clearly demonstrated by the exceedingly close votes in three crucial states. The Massachusetts convention ratified by a vote of 187 to 168, the Virginia convention by a vote of 89 to 79, and the New York convention by a vote of 30 to 27. The diffuseness of the Antifederalist campaign against the Constitution makes it difficult to characterize the arguments or position of the Antifederalists concisely or accurately. Generally, however, they attacked the proposed Constitution for providing "a consolidated system" of government that would destroy individual freedom and republican principles. By republicanism, as we have seen, they meant a system of representative government or democracy in which every interest in society would have its own voice. "The only safeguard against the abuse of power was to keep it ever immediately visible before the eyes of the people."[27] This could not be done through a Congress operating at a location remote from most of the people and in which the representation in the two houses of Congress fell far short of permitting a separate voice for each interest in every state and local community. There would instead either be a dangerous intermingling of interests in this national legislature, or the wealthy interests would seize control and "the middling" class would lose out. The Antifederalists could hardly oppose the basic idea of a compromising of interests if any public policy was ever to take shape in any community large or small. But in the "consolidated government" of the proposed Constitution "laws in the interest of dominant groups would necessarily be imposed upon minority groups against their will and to their grave disadvantage."[28] Separation of legislative, executive, and judicial powers, the Antifederalists said, might have lessened the dangers from the proposed government, but the new Constitution contained a volatile blending of powers. Thus the Senate, instead of being exclusively a legislative body, shared judicial power with the courts in the matter of the trial of public officers on impeachment charges and the courts were to enjoy a "stupendous magnitude of power that was both legislative and judicial in nature."

Scholars have waged a battle through the years over the issue of the size of the electorate in 1787 and 1788, the nature of the voter turnout in the elections in which the delegates to the state conventions were chosen, and over the ultimate issue of what part of the electorate or "the people" actually favored the Constitution. Forty years ago, Charles and Mary Beard[29] went so far as to argue that these supporters did not exceed 100 thousand in a population of 4 million. But this estimate has been challenged by historians who believe that the idea of a severely restricted suffrage in the 1780s is an exaggerated one.[30] In any event, it is difficult, if not impossible, to speak with any accuracy of a popular vote "for" and "against" the Constitution, since in many districts the delegates to the state ratifying conventions were elected on an "uninstructed" basis, that is, they were elected without being told how to vote.

The Argument over the Bill of Rights

The Bill of Rights, which was proposed by Congress in 1789 as a series of amendments to the Constitution, and ratified by the required number of states in 1791, was the one great triumph of the Antifederalists during the struggle over ratification. The Antifederalists were not able to condition ratification of the Constitution in any of the states on an absolute requirement that a bill of rights would be adopted under the new government, and they certainly failed in their more extreme effort to force the calling of a second national convention to draft such a bill of rights and perhaps reopen the whole question of the nature of the constitutional settlement. Instead, they had to settle for ratification "in full confidence" that the new Congress would set things in motion for the adoption of a bill of rights. Nonetheless, they won this argument intellectually and politically, and they thereby provided the momentum that led to the very significant adjustment in the American constitutional balance between public authority and individual freedom that the first ten amendments provided. Still it has to be noted that it was that staunch and able Federalist, James Madison, who, as a member of the first House of Representatives, was the floor manager in what proved to be a surprisingly difficult task of securing approval by the House of the series of proposed amendments out of which the final Bill of Rights emerged two years later. Moreover, he found more support among the Federalist members of the House than he did the Antifederalists, for some of the latter, stubborn to the last, opposed the amendments, hoping that a second constitutional convention could still be forced on the country.

Perhaps the most important conclusion to be derived from the story of the adoption of the Constitution is that, everything considered, "the factors that united the Federalists and Antifederalists were stronger than those that divided them."[31] Something approaching consensus had to be, and was, achieved concerning many basic social and economic issues and concerning the need for a stronger national government. Otherwise, the thirteen states, with their shared victory against Britain in the Revolutionary War receding further and further into the past, might well have drifted into disaster as their economic rivalries and political quarrels grew ever more serious in the absence of any adequate national means of coping with them.

The final word can be given to the Federalists, for whom "the move for the new central government became the ultimate act of the entire revolutionary era; it was both a progressive attempt to salvage the Revolution in the face of its imminent failure and a reactionary effort to restrain its excesses."[32]

SELECTED BIBLIOGRAPHY

Bailyn, Bernard, *Ideological Origins of the American Revolution* (Cambridge, Mass.: Harvard University Press, 1967). Analyzes the relationship between political thought in America during the Revolutionary period and European traditions, particularly libertarian ones.

Beard, Charles A., *An Economic Interpretation of the Constitution* (New York: Crowell-Collier and Macmillan Company, Inc., 1913). Highly influential for half a century, this famous book argued the case that the Founding Fathers were strongly motivated by their own economic interests in the drafting of the Constitution. Its thesis of "economic determinism" has been much criticized by scholars in the last dozen years as overly simplistic and based on inadequate data.

Elliot, Jonathan, *The Debates in the Several State Conventions on the Adoption of the Federal Constitution* (Philadelphia: J. B. Lippincott Company, 1888). The standard source for the debates in state conventions that ratified the federal Constitution.

Farrand, Max, *The Framing of the Constitution* (New Haven, Conn.: Yale University Press, 1926). An authoritative account of the work of the Philadelphia convention, designed for the general reader.

———, *The Records of the Federal Convention of 1787* (4 vols.; New Haven, Conn.: Yale University Press, 1911). A compilation of documentary sources bearing on the work of the Philadelphia convention.

The Federalist, the title given to the collection of letters written by Hamilton, Madison, and Jay in support of the proposed constitution during the ratification period. See editions by R. H. Gabriel (New York: Liberal Arts Press, 1954); H. S. Commager, *Selections from the Federalist,* (New York: Appleton-Century-Crofts, 1949) : and Max Beloff (New York: Crowell-Collier and Macmillan Company, Inc., 1950).

Jensen, Merrill, *The Articles of Confederation* (Madison, Wis.: University of Wisconsin Press, 1940). An analysis of the drafting of the Articles and the system thereby established.

Kelly, Alfred H., and Winfred A. Harbison, *The American Constitution: Its Origins and Development,* 3d ed. (New York: W. W. Norton Company, Inc., 1963). One of a number of excellent histories of constitutional development from colonial beginnings to the present.

Lynd, Staughton, *Class Conflict, Slavery, and the United States Constitution* (Indianapolis: Bobbs-Merrill Co., Inc., 1968). A provocative "radical" view of social and economic factors that shaped decisions during the revolutionary and constitutional periods.

McDonald, Forrest, *We the People: The Economic Origins of the Constitution* (Chicago: University of Chicago Press, 1958). One of the leading critiques of Beard's thesis concerning the economic motivations of the framers of the Constitution.

Palmer, R. R., *The Age of the Democratic Revolution: A Political History of Europe and America 1760–1800* (Princeton: Princeton University Press, 1964). Includes a challenging examination of the political and constitutional significance of the American Revolution.

Rossiter, Clinton L., *Seedtime of the Republic* (New York: Harcourt, Brace & World, Inc., 1953). An excellent analysis of the intellectual ferment and political ideas current during the Colonial and Revolutionary periods.

Footnotes

[1] Carl Van Doren, *The Great Rehearsal* (New York: The Viking Press, Inc., 1948); Clinton Rossiter, *1787: The Grand Convention* (New York: The Macmillan Company, Inc., 1966); Catherine Drinker Bowen, *Miracle at Philadelphia* (Boston, Mass.: Little, Brown and Company, 1966).

[2] Letter to David Humphreys, March 18, 1789. *The Papers of Jefferson,* Julian P. Boyd, ed. (Princeton, N.J.: Princeton University Press, 1950), 14:678.

[3] Examples are Forrest McDonald, *E Pluribus Unum* (Boston, Mass.: Houghton Mifflin Company, 1965); Bernard Bailyn, *Ideological Origins of the American Revolution* (Cambridge, Mass., Harvard University Press, 1967); and Gordon S. Wood, *The Creation of the American Republic* (Chapel Hill: University of North Carolina Press, 1969).

[4] The quoted passages are from a review of Gordon Wood's book by Jack P. Greene in the *New York Times Book Review,* Oct. 26, 1969.

[5] McDonald, p. 5.

[6] McDonald, p. 6.

[7] Wood, p. 491.

[8] Rossiter, p. 52.

[9] Rossiter, p. 38.

[10] Instead the delegates basically relied on the "committee of the whole," a parliamentary device that has long been used by all kinds of assemblies that are attempting to do business under formal rules of procedure. As a "committee" made up of all the members of an assembly, it temporarily escapes from the rules and is able to consider business informally, taking votes and arriving at decisions that are tentative only. As a committee, it always reports back to the assembly itself as the official body. The assembly then usually ratifies the decision reached in the committee of the whole, although it need not do so if "second sober thought" suggests the wisdom of another outcome.

[11] Almost all accounts of the Convention, while stopping short of Jefferson's concept of "demigods," stress the high quality of the delegates. However, McDonald in *E Pluribus Unum* is highly critical of many of the delegates. He asserts, for example, that Benjamin Franklin was approaching senility and that Washington's knowledge of what to do in a convention "barely extended beyond rules of order."

[12] Charles A. Beard, *An Economic Interpretation of the Constitution of the United States* (New York: Crowell-Collier and The Macmillan Company, Inc., 1913).

[13] Robert E. Brown, *Charles Beard and the Constitution: A Critical Analysis of "An Economic Interpretation of the Constitution"* (Princeton, N.J.: Princeton University Press, 1956); Forrest McDonald, *We the People: The Economic Origins of the Constitution* (Chicago, Ill.: University of Chicago Press, 1958), p. 416.

[14] Arthur Schlesinger, *New Viewpoints in American History* (New York: The Macmillan Company, Inc., 1925), p. 189.

[15] This matter of the complex, contradictory nature of the framers' motives is examined in the long introduction to Cecelia Kenyon's *The Antifederalists* (Indianapolis: The Bobbs-Merrill Company, Inc., 1966). Professor Kenyon concludes that it "seems inevitable that diverse causes were at work in determining men's opinions of and votes on the Constitution. And this means that we shall probably never know with absolute certainty what factors were the crucial ones." (p. xxxvii.) Gor-

don Wood in *Creation of the American Republic* observes, "it is difficult, as historians have recently demonstrated, to equate the supporters or opponents of the Constitution with particular economic groupings." However, with particular reference to the ratification period, Wood then asserts that the struggle over the Constitution "can best be understood as a social one" and that the quarrel was one fundamentally between aristocracy and democracy." P. 484. It is possible that Wood is thereby merely substituting one simplistic interpretation of a great historical event for another one.

[16] A. H. Kelly and W. A. Harbison, *The American Constitution,* 3rd ed. (New York: W. W. Norton & Company, Inc., 1963), pp. 127–128.

[17] McDonald argues that the alleged difference between the states in these two groups in terms of population was not as great as the terms "large" and "small" might suggest. He finds that the average population of the "large" states was about 307,000 and that of the "small" about 278,000.

[18] James Madison, *The Debates in the Federal Convention of 1787 Which Framed the Constitution of the United States of America,* G. Hunt and J. B. Scott, eds. (New York: Oxford University Press, 1920), p. 102. (Italics added.)

[19] Substantial use has been made in this section of McDonald's provocative vo'ume, *E Pluribus Unum.*

[20] See Rossiter, p. 266.

[21] For a polemical, but provocative argument that the slavery problem in the United States could be solved only by war, see Arthur Schlesinger, Jr.'s article, "The Causes of the Civil War: A Note on Historical Sentimentalism," *Partisan Review,* October, 1949; reprinted in the Bobbs-Merrill Reprint Series in History, No. H-187.

[22] The three who refused to sign were Edmund Randolph and George Mason of Virginia and Elbridge Gerry of Massachusetts. However, Randolph later changed his mind and supported the Constitution in the Virginia ratifying convention.

[23] McDonald, Chap. 8, is a source of much of the data in this section.

[24] Two recent collections of these Antifederalist writings, with excellent introductions are found in Cecelia Kenyon's *The Antifederalists* and John D. Lewis's *Antifederalists vs. Federalists* (San Francisco: Chandler Publishing Company, 1967).

[25] Gordon S. Wood, p. 486.

[26] Jonathan Elliot, *The Debates in the Several State Conventions on the Adoption of the Federal Constitution* (Philadelphia: J. B. Lippincott Company, 1888), 2:102.

[27] Lewis, p. 23.

[28] Lewis, p. 13.

[29] Charles and Mary Beard, *The Rise of American Civilization* enlarged ed. (New York: Crowell-Collier and Macmillan Company, Inc., 1947), 1:332.

[30] Robert E. Brown, for example, has estimated that property qualifications in the original states in most cases excluded as little as 5–10 percent of the voters and in no case more than 25 percent. Brown attributes the low vote in the election of delegates to the state ratifying conventions to "indifference" and not to "disfranchisement."—Robert E. Brown, pp. 197–199. See also Chilton Williamson, *American Suffrage from Property to Democracy* (Princeton, N.J.: Princeton University Press, 1960); Martin Diamond, "Democracy and the Federalist: A Reconsideration of the Framers' Intent," *The American Political Science Review,* 53 (March 1959), p. 52.

[31] Kenyon, p. xcvii.

[32] Wood, p. 475.

Chapter 3   A Constitution Intended to Endure for Ages to Come

THE SUCCESS OF THE AMERICAN CONSTITUTION

The American Constitution has survived for nearly two centuries. This simple statement is as good a starting point as any of an examination of the American political system, because a reasonable measure of stability and continuity are always essential to a satisfactory society and a productive economy. To be sure, a stable and "successful" political arrangement has, upon occasion, lasted too long; it has ceased to serve the interests of the people governed under it. But far more often in history, political arrangements have been marked by instability; constitutional experiments have not lasted long enough to begin to serve the purposes that constitution-makers had in mind. Notice need only be taken of the instability that during the last two centuries has plagued the political systems of France, Italy, Germany, Russia, and almost all of the nations of Latin America, as well as most of the new nations that have emerged in Africa and Asia.

Why has the American constitutional system been so durable up to now? There are many ways of trying to answer this question. The framers of the Constitution understood and successfully implemented the fundamental value system favored by the majority of the people who were to be governed under the Constitution; they were aware that the needs of the culture and the economy of the country had to be kept in mind in creating a compatible, workable political framework; they grasped the basic concept that there were many competing interests in a democratic society and a capitalist economy and that these called for a political arrangement in which pluralistic forces could contend for advantages and support through governmental agencies that would check and balance each other as they exercised their "separated" or "distributed powers."

The American constitutional experiment has also been conducted in the presence of certain "propitious circumstances," particularly during its first century, that contributed greatly to the successful outcome: The American people during the formative years enjoyed a protective isolation from the rest of the world. There was a vast western wilderness and an unbelievably rich storehouse of natural resources to exploit. Most free Americans came

Law: Is It Dead or 'Breathing Hard?'

by CRAIG R. WHITNEY

Against a background of illegal strikes by postal workers, student disorders at major universities, draft resistance, rising crime rates and disruptions in courtrooms, Whitney North Seymour asked yesterday: "Is law dead?"

The question was considered, but not answered, yesterday by a convocation of professors, lawyers, judges and interested laymen at the Assocation of the Bar of the City of New York, under the chairmanship of Mr. Seymour, who ventured his own opinion that law was "breathing hard."

Six speakers rarely dropped out of the "philosophical stratosphere," in the words of one student in the audience, and six more will try again today.

Specifically, yesterday's discussions centered on the problem of civil disobedience in a society governed by the consent of the governed.

Spirit of Law

Hannah Arendt, the philosopher and author, said that civil disobedience had become a worldwide phenomenon, but that "the American Republic is the only Government which has at least a chance to cope with it, not perhaps in accordance with the statutes but in accordance with the spirit of its laws."

But Ronald Dworkin, a former master of Trumbull College at Yale, where thousands are planning a massive "convocation" this weekend over the upcoming murder trial of a Black Panther leader, questioned whether the spirit governs.

"The Government's present policy is to ignore the distinction between those who break the law on plausible claims of right and those who break it out of contempt for all rights," he said.

Another Yale professor, Eugene V. Rostow, argued that such distinctions may be meaningless, because "the use of illegal means to achieve political ends cannot be justified."

And a third professor, Robert P. Wolff of Columbia University, argued that it did not matter whether the law was dead or alive, because "no one, not even a citizen of a true democracy, has an obligation to obey the law."

Pointless Destruction

He went on to say that he regretted that his anarchism was a concept that had come to be associated with "pointless destructiveness of sick young people in this and other societies."

Mr. Rostow, noting that a "demonstration of mass hysteria" was perhaps under way at Yale this weekend, said: "Perhaps we are too fevered, too involved, to take an analytical look at individual liberty."

"Under circumstances of legal and social permissiveness," Professor Arendt said, "people will engage in the most outrageous criminal behavior and even if the police catch up with them, "it would mean the collapse of the already disastrously overburdened courts."

Law, she concluded, has lost much of its power.

A layman at the gathering in the neoclassical meeting room of the association's building at 42 West 44th Street, rose at one point to say, "The law may not be dead, but it's pretty dormant."

For a man presiding over what almost amounted to a coroner's inquest, Mr. Seymour seemed cheerful.

Waiting for one questioner to finish a five-minute inquiry, Mr. Seymour asked gently: "Would you creep up on your question mark, please?"

The conference had the serene atmosphere that used to prevail, and occasionally still does, on college campuses, and the professors who participated occasionally registered a note of defensiveness.

Harris Wofford, president-designate of Bryn Mawr College, took Vice President Agnew to task for his recent attacks on Yale's president, Kingman Brewster Jr., and on the press.

"He is deliberately using the power of the Vice Presidency of the United States to purge the president of a university and attack not only the press but the academy itself," he said.

Dangerous Polarizing

"The Vice President is wrong," he added, "in lumping together civil and uncivil disobedience. He is dangerously polarizing our politics."

For, Mr. Wofford said, true civil disobedience assumes that the law will be enforced. As another Yale professor, Peter Gay, said, " 'Law and order' is used as a code word concealing, or rather all too plainly revealing, its opposite: illegality and chaos."

Today's sessions beginning at 9:30 A.M., will examine "the capacity of the American social order to meet the changing demands for social justice through the methods of law."

© 1970 by The New York Times Company. Reprinted by permission.

from Western Europe and were bound by common ancestral habits or customs. (The great contrasting Afro-American stream of ancestral habits and customs was obscured, and in many ways suppressed, by the slave status of America's black people.) What in other societies proved to be "disturbing elements" among the people prospered under the calming influence of successful agricultural pursuits and the attractions of the western frontier so that, as one English observer[1] of the American scene has put it, "they paved the way for industry and became the pioneers of civilization" and formed "a society of expectant capitalists." Small wonder that "Constitution worship"[2] quickly became a persistent and significant element in the American political culture.

For all of this, the American constitutional system always has been and still is an experiment. Moreover, there are signs that Americans may be losing their habit of Constitution worship. The argument is beginning to be heard that the American Constitution has lasted too long, that up to now it has merely *endured* in spite of serious faults in original design and unsatisfactory results along the way during its long life. For all of the awareness that the framers of the Constitution had of practical social and economic problems and for all of their conscious effort to solve these problems through political means, we know that today culture and politics must be far more closely and effectively intertwined for successful results than the Fathers understood to be necessary. No one can ignore the present strains upon American institutions signaled by the violence that has flared up in scores of communities, large and small, since 1966. Nor can one ignore the social tensions that have been at the root of this violence—social tensions that are producing problems that may be beyond the ability of the present political mechanisms and processes, established by the Constitution, to deal with effectively. As far back as 1830, a Scots Tory, Thomas Hamilton,[3] having visited this country, conceded that America did indeed enjoy "propitious circumstances," but looked to the time "when the masses would be congregated in large cities plagued by economic strife." Then, he predicted, social pressures would be intensified and class antagonisms sharpened. Would the constitutional system be equal to these new circumstances and occasions?

The fact remains that the American Constitution has been successful, in the sense that it has worked and that it has endured. Whatever may lie ahead or whatever thoughts may be entertained about the need for drastic constitutional reform, or even political revolution, the starting point for the student who hopes to understand the American political system with all its contemporary weaknesses and needs must be the study of the formal structure of public authority. In politics as in medicine, the study of anatomy precedes the study of physiology and of psychology. In taking a broad overview of the constitutional structure, the anatomy of public authority, we are preparing for the study of the physiology and the psychology of American politics, the way the system functions as a whole and why.

The Dual Nature of the Constitution

American politics are conducted under a constitutional government. The term "constitution" has many connotations.[4] We use it here in what is a limited and perhaps a parochial sense, as a synonym for a charter of government that spells out both the extent of and the restraints on public power. A constitution in this sense is, both an instrument of power and a symbol of restraint.[5]

Certainly the American Constitution plays each of those functions. The framers in 1787 saw a need for action on a national scale to cope with the country's economic problems, and they tried to equip the new government with the necessary powers to meet those crises—to regulate commerce, to coin money, to make uniform regulations regarding bankruptcy, to levy taxes, to raise armies, and to enforce the laws through its own administrative and judicial officers. At the same time, the framers were concerned about governmental power. Most of them had just fought a long war against a government that they had judged to be tyrannical, and they were anxious not to convert their victories on the battlefield into a mere change of masters. The final document that emerged from the Philadelphia Convention—and even more so with the adoption of the Bill of Rights—was studded with prohibitions against certain kinds of governmental action.

Even before the Convention met, James Madison[6] set out the basic problem the framers, like all constitution-makers, had to face. The important aspect was to construct a governmental organization that would be able "to controul one part of society from invading the rights of another, and at the same time sufficiently controuled itself, from setting up an interest adverse to that of the whole society." Neither Madison nor his colleagues at Philadelphia were so naive as to believe that "the parchment barriers" of elegant constitutional phrases would of themselves prevent tyranny. But the framers realized, first, that, if these restrictions became part of what we would call the political culture and were absorbed as part of the moral luggage that each citizen and public official carried, such phrases could exert considerable restraining force. Second, without adopting democratic ideals as we know them, they realized that an electorate could help keep public officials acting within certain limits by requiring them to justify their actions periodically. The framers, therefore, made the members of the House of Representatives directly responsible to a broad popular electorate, and the members of the Senate and the President directly responsible to a rather small group of officials but indirectly to a much larger and more popular base.

Third, the framers realized that, as an organization of governmental officers, a constitution could protect against tyranny by fragmenting power. They did their best to splinter power by dividing it between state and national levels, then further subdividing national power among separate institutions with overlapping grants of authority. They were deliberately weaving a web in which power was checked by power, a web which supported and encouraged institutional rivalries and jealousies, giving office holders vested interests in restricting the authority of other institutions. As Madison[7] explained, "ambition must be made to counteract ambition. The interest of the man must be connected with the constitutional rights of the place. . . . A dependence on the people is, no doubt, the primary control on the government; but experience has taught mankind the necessity of auxilliary precautions."

CONSTITUTIONAL POWER SEPARATED, SHARED, AND PROHIBITED

Many lawyers, judges, and textbook writers speak of a separation of power in the Constitution, and it has proved useful to talk in such terms. In fact, it is more precise to accept the antifederalist charge and to say that as much as separating power, the Constitution provides for a sharing of different kinds of authority among public officials. The Constitution also expressly prohibits all state and federal officials from exercising certain powers. This combination of separating, sharing, and prohibiting powers can most fruitfully be analyzed under the headings of federalism, distribution of powers within the national government, and limited government.

Federalism: Nation and States

We may define federalism as a political system that divides power between a central government, having authority over the entire country, and a series of local governments, collectively covering the entire territory. In a true federal system, each of these two levels of government must be more or less independent of the other.

Federalism may be contrasted with unitary or centralized government, such as that found in Britain. In that country there are local units of government in addition to the central government in London, but these local divisions are created by and subject to the control of the central government. They can be changed or abolished at the will of Parliament. Federalism may also be contrasted with the political arrangement in a confederation, which is a league of independent states. Under the Articles of Confederation, for instance, the American national government did not govern the people directly, but operated only through state governments, each of which thought of itself as possessing the ultimate power to govern.

The Constitution of 1787 established a federal system in the United States in which the central government had authority to govern the people directly in regard to many matters of domestic as well as foreign policy. This authority was derived from "the people" of the United States, not from the several states as separate political entities. On the other hand, the states, while losing the sovereignty they possessed under the Articles of Confederation, did not become mere subdivisions of the central government.

Three sections of the Constitution have established the legal framework within which American federalism has developed. The most important of these is paragraph 2 of Article VI, which makes explicit the doctrine of national supremacy:

> This Constitution, and the laws of the United States which shall be made in pursuance thereof; and all treaties made, or which shall be made, under the authority of the United States, shall be the supreme law of the land; and the judges in every State shall be bound thereby, any thing in the Constitution or laws of any State to the contrary notwithstanding.

Clearly, this clause renders illegal any effort by a state to contravene the Constitution or any federal statute or treaty that lies within the authority of the national government to enact. Furthermore, it provides that in any area of public policy where both the national and state governments may legitimately be active—control of commerce, for example— the national enactment shall enjoy supremacy or take precedence over an inconsistent state enactment. In addition, state authority may have to give way completely before national authority, in certain vital areas such as national security, where Congress may claim a "dominant interest" and has enacted a pervasive scheme of public policy for the nation, even where the conflict between contradictory national and state enactments is potential rather than actual.[8]

A second constitutional provision for federalism is the doctrine of "reserved powers," or "states' rights," in the Tenth Amendment:

> The powers not delegated to the United States by the Constitution, nor prohibited by it to the States, are reserved to the States respectively, or to the people.

A hasty reading of this amendment might lead to the view that there are two watertight compartments of authority: the legitimate powers of the federal government as enumerated in the Constitution and a vast residue of state power. Unhappily for those who like simple political solutions, no such clear-cut division of power exists. The Tenth Amendment does serve as a constitutional reassurance of the viability of the states, but it does not restrict national authority to those functions specifically listed in the Constitution. The amendment does not say that the powers not *expressly* delegated are reserved to the states, only those "not delegated." Several times during the debate in Congress on this amendment, proponents of states' rights tried to insert the word "expressly," but each time they were voted down.

These matters are closely related to the provision of Article I, section 8, the so-called necessary and proper, or sweeping, clause, with its doctrine of implied national power:

> The Congress shall have power . . . to make all laws which shall be necessary and proper for carrying into execution the foregoing powers, and all other powers vested by this Constitution in the government of the United States, or in any department or officer thereof.

By the terms of this clause, Congress has authority that goes far beyond any listing of specific powers, for it is herewith granted whatever powers are "necessary and proper" to carry out its general and particular responsibilities.

In 1819, in *McCulloch v. Maryland,*[9] the Supreme Court spelled out the implications of the doctrine of implied powers. In question was the constitutionality of the Bank of the United States, a quasigovernmental institution that Congress had established. No clause of the Constitution mentioned congressional authority to charter banks or other corporations. But, speaking for a unanimous Court, Chief Justice John Marshall held that, when coupled with the sweeping clause, the expressly delegated powers of Congress to borrow and coin money, to collect taxes, to regulate commerce, to raise armies, and to wage war implied that Congress had authority to create institutions that would enable it to carry out its work. Marshall carefully rejected placing close limits on congressional power to choose means that legislators thought most convenient:

> we think the sound construction of the constitution must allow to the national legislature that discretion, with respect to the means by which the powers it confers are to be carried into execution, which will enable that body to perform the high duties assigned to it, in the manner most beneficial to the people. Let the end be legitimate, let it be within the scope of the constitution, and all means which are appropriate, which are plainly adapted to that end, which are not prohibited, but consist with the letter and spirit of the constitution, are constitutional.

The concept of implied powers in the federal government is not easy to reconcile with a doctrine of reserved state powers. Once it is conceded that the national government has implied as well as expressed powers, the exact limits of national authority become difficult to fix. How far can implied power be stretched? What laws can Congress pass on this basis without invading the realm of reserved state powers? Such questions have no clear-cut answers. Some answers have been given by federal judges appointed for all practical purposes for life, some by locally elected congressmen, and some by nationally elected or appointed administrators, including the President who must often work through state and city officials even though he is responsible to a national constituency.

Executive, Legislative, and Judicial Power

Federalism provides for a geographic distribution of power among national and state officials. The Constitution also provides for a distribution of powers among national agencies and officers of government on the basis of function. In so providing the framers of the Constitution were influenced by the French political theorist Montesquieu. To an independent Congress, they gave primary authority to legislate, to make the laws. "All legislative power herein granted," Article I reads, "shall be vested in a Congress of the United States. . . ." To an independent President they gave basic authority to administer, to carry out, and to enforce the commands of the laws. "The executive power," Article II says, "shall be vested in a President of the United States of America." To an independent judiciary the framers gave fundamental authority to adjudicate, to apply laws and executive orders to specific legal proceedings. "The judicial power of the United States," Article III provides, "shall be vested in one Supreme Court and in such inferior courts as the Congress shall from time to time ordain and establish."

The framers, however, provided then that these distinct and legally equal departments should share many powers. The President can participate in the legislative process through his authority to call special sessions of Congress, to negotiate treaties which, when approved by the Senate, enunciate aspects of our foreign policy, to propose domestic laws to Congress, to veto bills passed by Congress to which he objects, and to try to influence or bring pressure on Congress in informal but often effective ways concerning the making of specific laws. Legislators can participate in the administrative process through their authority to create federal executive agencies, to fix the basic rules under which these agencies operate, and to appropriate—or not appropriate—the funds without which they could not carry out their functions. Senators can further influence administrative action through their authority to advise and consent to the appointment of important executive officers. Federal judges participate in the legislative and administrative processes by deciding exactly what the words of a federal statute or executive order really mean. The President can participate in the judicial process through his authority to nominate judges and to pardon all persons convicted in federal courts. In case of impeachment, the Senate sits as a trial court; there is no appeal from its decision.

In providing for a system of shared powers among three branches of government, the Constitution in essence requires a consensus among public officials if a particular policy is to become effective. Thus the power of any single official or group of officials is restricted. In addition, the Constitution provides each of these three agencies with direct checks on the power of the other two. For example, judges can declare acts of Congress or the President unconstitutional, but the President can refuse to enforce judicial decisions, and the House can impeach and the Senate convict and remove a federal judge or any other federal official, including the President. Furthermore, Congress, by the express terms of Article III, has wide discretion in determining the kinds of cases that federal courts can hear and decide. The President, if balked in Congress, can appeal over the heads of legislators to the voters and ask them to send new men to Washington. Similarly, members of Congress can campaign against a President or refuse to appropriate money to carry out his programs, as was being threatened in May 1970, as a means of terminating American involvement in the war in Indo China. A mere one third plus one of the Senate can reject a treaty negotiated by the President.

Just as there are many uncertainties about the application of implied powers, national supremacy, and federalism, so too there are many serious problems concerning the distribution of power among federal officials. How far may Congress properly go in altering the jurisdiction of federal courts or in increasing the size of the Supreme Court? How far may the President properly go in trying to persuade congressmen to vote for particular proposals? How readily may judges substitute their judgment for the judgment of Congress as to whether a statute is constitutional? Or their judgment for that of Congress or a law enforcement officer as to what a statute means? The process of checking, like the process of implying, has no precise limits. Both leave much room for flexibility in the joints of the political system.

Limited Government

Like the other concepts we have been discussing, the concept of "limited government" permeates the Constitution in both explicit and implicit fashion. First, sections of the original Constitution and, of course, of the Bill of Rights expressly forbid government officials to perform certain kinds of acts. Second, whatever the effect of the doctrine of implied powers, the fact that the national government is based upon delegated power has become a part of American political culture and may often act as a significant psychological check on public officials. Reinforcing this limitation is the statement of the Tenth Amendment that some powers are reserved "to the people" and the explicit reminder of the Ninth Amendment that "enumeration in the Constitution, of certain rights, shall not be construed to deny or disparage others retained by the people." Also of great importance is the establishment of popular elections, which Madison called the primary check against the arrogance of officials, and which enable the people to remove at least some potential oppressors from public office and to keep others out of office.

This limiting concept is offset at many points. The doctrine of implied powers competes as much with the notion of limited government as it does with state autonomy in a federal system. Furthermore, many Supreme Court decisions have held that most of the Constitution's prohibitions against governmental action are relative. The First Amendment, for instance, explicitly says that Congress "shall make no law" abridging freedom of speech or press; but in times of national emergency, Congress has enacted, the President has signed, and the Supreme Court has approved the constitutionality of statutes restricting what American citizens may speak or write. In sustaining convictions under a 1917 sedition law, Justice Oliver Wendell Holmes[10] said for a unanimous Court:

> We admit that in many places and in ordinary times the defendants in saying all that was said in the circular [opposing the draft during World War I] would have been

within their constitutional rights. But the character of every act depends on the circumstances in which it was done. . . . The question in every case is whether the words used are used in such circumstances and are of such a nature as to create a clear and present danger that they will bring about the substantive evils that Congress has a right to prevent.

Later justices, most notably Hugo L. Black, have challenged the soundness of this relativistic attitude. To date, however, these justices, while winning specific cases, have not yet been able to persuade a majority of their colleagues to hold that as a matter of constitutional law, First Amendment rights are absolute.

CONSTITUTIONAL FLEXIBILITY AND CHANGE

The framers wished to give their new government sufficient authority to cope with national problems while minimizing the chances that officials would abuse that authority. In addition, the framers were aware of their own limitations; they realized that they could envision only a small portion of the problems that a new nation would encounter. Thus they deliberately refused to draw a detailed blueprint outlining specific political actions and instead tried to sketch a flexible governmental system that could cope with unforeseen crises. As Edmund Randolph,[11] an influential member of the convention's committee on detail, wrote:

> In the draught of a fundamental constitution, two things deserve attention:
> 1. To insert essential principles only lest the operations of government should be clogged by rendering those provisions permanent and unalterable, which ought to be accommodated to times and events; and
> 2. To use simple and precise language, and general propositions, according to the examples of the several constitutions of the several states; for the construction of a constitution necessarily differs from that of law.

Three decades later, in the great case of *McCulloch v. Maryland,*[12] Chief Justice John Marshall expressed much the same thought when he said: "we must never forget that it is a constitution we are expounding." To make clear what he meant by a "constitution," the chief justice stated:

> A constitution, to contain an accurate detail of all the subdivisions of which its great powers will admit, and of all the means by which they may be carried into execution, would partake of the prolixity of a legal code, and could scarcely be embraced by the human mind. It would probably never be understood by the public. Its nature, therefore, requires that only its great outlines should be marked, its important objects designated, and the minor ingredients which compose those objects be deduced from the nature of the objects themselves.

Then Marshall spoke of the American Constitution in particular, as

> a constitution intended to endure for ages to come, and consequently, to be adapted to the various crises of human affairs. To have prescribed the means by which government should, in all future time, execute its powers, would have been to change, entirely, the character of the instrument, and give it the properties of a legal code. It

has, in all but one instance, that involving the Twenty-first Amendment repealing pro-hibition, required state legislatures to make the choice.

There are many technical questions concerning the amending procedure that the Constitution does not answer. May the President veto a proposed amendment? How long a time may be allowed to secure ratification by three-fourths of the states? May a state, having ratified or rejected an amendment, change its mind? The Supreme Court has answered some of these questions, although in its latest decision the Court has indicated that Congress is the proper agency to give the final answer to such questions.[14] Actually, all these questions have been answered by one means or another. The President does not pass upon an amendment, having authority neither to approve nor to veto it. Congress may fix a time limit within which the necessary number of states must ratify an amend-ment if it is to go into effect. If Congress fails to do so, the Supreme Court has said that Congress itself must determine whether an amendment ratified over a long period of years should be put into effect. A state that has approved an amendment may not re-consider its action, but a rejection is not regarded as final action and may be reversed.

If the Bill of Rights, or the first ten amendments, is regarded as part of the original Constitution, the Constitution has been formally amended only fifteen times between 1791 and 1971. Moreover, two of the fifteen amendments cancel each other. The Eighteenth Amendment gave Congress the power to prohibit the sale of liquor and the Twenty-first Amendment withdrew that power.

Of the other thirteen amendments, three make relatively minor changes in the mechanics of government: The Twelfth corrected the manner in which members of the electoral college cast votes for a President and a Vice President; the Twentieth changed the calendar of the government so as to eliminate lame-duck sessions of Congress and provide for inauguration of the President in January rather than in March; and the Twenty-third gave residents of the District of Columbia the right to vote in presidential elections. One amendment, the Eleventh, withdrew part of the jurisdiction originally granted the federal courts in Article III by forbidding them to hear cases in which a state is sued by a citizen of another state. Three amendments, the Thirteenth, Fourteenth, and Fifteenth, defined United States citizenship and forbade the states to encroach upon cer-tain civil rights; and the Fifteenth outlawed all governmental efforts to interfere with the right to vote, if they were based upon race, color, or previous condition of servitude. The Sixteenth Amendment granted Congress authority to levy income taxes without apportioning them among the states on the basis of population. The Seventeenth Amend-ment provided for popular election of United States senators. Under the original provision, they were chosen by the state legislatures and only members of the House had to be directly elected. The Nineteenth Amendment conferred suffrage on women. The Twenty-second Amendment prohibited Presidents from serving for three or more full terms. The Twenty-fourth Amendment forbade both the United States and the states to deny the right to vote in federal elections because of failure to pay any poll tax or other tax. The Twenty-fifth Amendment makes detailed provisions for what is to happen if a President becomes disabled.

A number of these amendments have been far reaching in their consequences; yet it is very clear that the amendments added since 1791 hardly even begin to reveal the tremendous changes that have taken place in the American system of government in the eighteen decades that have gone by. The record of these changes has been made outside the language of the original Constitution or the amendments that have been added to it through a continuous process of interpreting and reinterpreting the language of the Constitution, through court decisions, through new statutes, through fresh administrative action, and through patterns of political behavior and usage transcending all formal written statements of structure or policy.

STRUGGLES FOR POLITICAL SUPREMACY

By establishing a government based upon shared powers, the framers achieved what Alpheus T. Mason has called "institutionalized tension,"[15] that is, Presidents, congressmen, and even Supreme Court justices compete to attain a dominant political position. Shortly before his death, Alexander Hamilton wrote that the resulting "vibrations of power are the genius of our government."[16] Tensions and vibrations connote a dynamic rather than a static system, precisely the kinds of terms one would expect to be descriptive of a flexible constitutional arrangement.

At times, in the nineteenth century, there seemed to be a real likelihood that power would be so concentrated in Congress that the United States would come close to having a parliamentary system of government. At the beginning of that century two developments threatened to make the President a mere servant of the legislature. One was the congressional caucus, by which congressmen selected nominees for the Presidency. The other was the power of the House of Representatives to elect a President in case of a tie vote or in the absence of a majority vote in the electoral college. This power was exercised in 1800 and again in 1824.

By the age of Jackson, however, the congressional caucus had given way to the national nominating convention in which congressmen had to share power with other party leaders, and 1824 proved to be the last election in which the House made the final selection of a President. Moreover, Andrew Jackson soon gave new vigor to the office of the President, leaving a series of precedents for his successors to utilize if and when they wished to exercise national leadership. On the other hand, the impeachment and near conviction of President Andrew Johnson in 1868 once again threatened to subordinate the executive to the legislature. Had Johnson been convicted, Congress might thereafter have used the threat of impeachment to curb initiative and independence in both the executive and judicial branches of government.

At other times in American history, there have been indications that power and prestige were being centered in the Presidency. In the last century, Jefferson, Jackson, and Lincoln all challenged Congress on various issues and, in winning their way, asserted the superiority of executive over legislature. In the present century, Wilson and the two Roosevelts brought the Presidency to a new high level. In fact, the movement toward executive supremacy, if not domination, seems to have become the more persistent tendency. The growing number and complexity of the problems, both domestic and foreign, that all nations face and the speed with which many of these problems must be met have tended to compel legislatures to confine lawmaking to broad declarations of policy and to confer wide discretionary power on executive officers.

The Supreme Court has at many points in history enjoyed great prestige and has wielded much influence in the conduct of public affairs in America.[17] As early as 1803, the justices asserted authority to invalidate acts of Congress, and during the Marshall period the Court rendered decisions that were profoundly important in shaping the fundamental character of American government as well as in laying down specific public policies. In particular, Marshall and his Court helped to establish for all time the principle that the national government possesses broad and flexible authority under the Constitution, authority sufficient to enable it to safeguard and promote the interests and needs of a developing nation in a changing world.

On the eve of the Civil War, when the executive and legislative branches were trying to solve the slavery problem, the Court attempted, in the ill-fated *Dred Scott* decision,[18] to prescribe its own solution. Again, at the end of the last century, the Court in a long series of decisions challenged the policies of the executive and legislative branches. In the present century, the Court's frontal attack upon New Deal policies in the mid-1930s provided a notable example of the justices' power to protect at least temporarily the status quo in the face of executive and legislative efforts at reform. In the 1950s and 1960s the Court displayed its power to bring about social change by reading into the Constitution: (1) prohibitions against all forms of state action establishing distinctions or discrimination based on race; (2) requirements that the U.S. House of Representatives and both houses of every state legislature be elected in substantial accordance with the principle of "one man, one vote"; and (3) extensions of the restrictions of the Bill of Rights to the states as well as the national government. Perhaps more than ever before in its history, the Supreme Court in recent years has been making fundamental public policy. Cases concerning segregation in the schools, rulings about "one man, one vote," and sharp limitations of police efforts to obtain confessions from suspected criminals have produced bitter criticism of the Court, some of it taking the form of efforts to amend the Constitution so as to undo the Court's work. The fact that most of these efforts have so far failed only emphasizes the extent to which the Court has shaped public policy in these areas.

CONTRACTING AND EXPANDING GOVERNMENTAL ACTIVITY

Vibrations of power within the political system have also had significant effects on the general scope of governmental activity. At times the restraining or limiting function of the Constitution has been stressed as a means of safeguarding "the free enterprise system" or of civil liberties. At other times the balance has been tilted in favor of the power aspect of the Constitution so that government might promote "the general welfare." A good example of this "vibration" in the American constitutional system is found in the protracted conflict that persisted for nearly half a century beginning about 1890 between the positive concept of governmental "police power" and the restraining concept of "due process of law." The words police power are nowhere found in the Constitution. More-over, this aspect of the authoritative side of the constitutional system is badly named. It might better be called the general welfare power, for it enables government to foster and protect the health, safety, morals, and well-being of all the people, or of groups such as children or the poor that are deemed to require special protection under law. "Strict" interpretation of our Constitution has tended to view police power as reserved to the states under the Tenth Amendment, for there is no expressed grant of police power to Congress in Article One of the Constitution.[19] But Congress has frequently used, with subsequent approval of the Supreme Court, such expressed powers as the commerce and taxing powers to enact federal statutes intended to serve police-power ends.

There are two due process of law restraints in the Constitution, one in the Fifth Amendment affecting the national government, and one in the Fourteenth Amendment affecting the states. These two constitutional provisions forbid all government officials—national, state, and local alike—to deprive any person of his life, liberty, or property "without due process of law." However the term due process is itself general and vague and it has taken on meaning only through application to specific circumstances.

In the face of social problems created by rapid urbanization and industrialization in the decades following the Civil War, state governments began passing numerous police-power measures, establishing safety and health standards, providing special protection to women and children, fixing minimum-wage and maximum-hour standards for labor, and generally extending government regulation of private enterprise as a means of promoting the public welfare. At about the turn of the century, the national government also undertook a somewhat similar but less extensive program of social legislation, which, inevitably, curbed the freedom of certain persons and business organizations at the same time that it promoted the interests of others. Accordingly, the contention was soon heard from those restricted that these federal and state interferences amounted to deprivations of liberty and property without due process of law and were thus contrary to the Constitution. The Supreme Court at first rejected this argument, but in the 1890s it began using the due process clauses to invalidate both federal and state statutes. For forty years conservative judges interpreted the Constitution so as to curb much police-power activity by government.[20] In 1936, in one of the last decisions of this type, the Court, by a five to four vote, invalidated a statute of the state of New York prescribing minimum wages for women and children.[21] In the very next year, however, in a decision upholding a minimum-wage law of the state of Washington, the Supreme Court not only reversed its decision of the year before but also generally repudiated the whole idea that the courts could properly use the due process clauses of the Constitution as a basis for finding certain social welfare laws invalid.[22]

The Supreme Court uses the due process clauses to invalidate a wide variety of laws, particularly at the state and local level, on the ground that they interfere with the civil rights of individual citizens. These laws are based on the police power or other federal or state powers, but unlike social welfare laws they are often motivated by a legislative wish to protect the social or political status quo. A number of these cases will be examined in the chapters of this book dealing with civil rights, but an example may be noted here of the group of cases in which laws providing for the censorship of speech, books, and motion pictures have been found to deny liberty without due process of law.

PROTECTING THE CONSTITUTION

The Constitution, in one of its great silences, fails to say who has primary responsibility to protect it. Often private citizens, elected and appointed officials, and judges themselves think of the judiciary as its chief guardian. To the extent that legislative and executive officers are content to dodge constitutional issues and pass them on to judges, this opinion is accurate; but judges have no legitimate monopoly at that task. All public officials, legislative, executive, and judicial, take an oath to support and defend the Constitution, and many presidential and congressional acts, especially those concerned with foreign affairs, can never be challenged in the courts. The President and members of Congress must frequently interpret their own powers and duties under the Constitution as Jefferson did when he agreed to the Louisiana Purchase, as Lincoln did when he determined to use force to save the Union, and as Franklin Roosevelt, Harry Truman, and Lyndon Johnson did when they decided to use American military power without a formal declaration of war.

SELECTED BIBLIOGRAPHY

Corwin, Edward S., *The Constitution and What It Means Today,* 12th rev. ed. (New York: Atheneum Publishers, 1964). A useful and authoritative analysis of the Constitution section by section and clause by clause, done briefly and concisely. (Paperback)

Elazar, Daniel, *American Federalism: A View from the States* (New York: Thomas Y. Crowell, 1966). A brief but comprehensive analysis of the American federal system which stresses the continuing vitality and integrity of the states.

Friedrich, Carl J., *Constitutional Government and Democracy* (Boston: Ginn & Company, 1946). A systematic analysis of present-day democratic constitutional institutions.

Grodzins, Morton, *The American System* (Daniel J. Elazar, ed.) (Chicago: Rand McNally and Company, 1966). A sympathetic examination of the operation of the American federal system in terms of the *what* and *how,* the *what* and *why,* and *with what result?*

Holcombe, Arthur N., *Our More Perfect Union* (Cambridge, Mass.: Harvard University Press, 1950). A systematic account and defense of the constitutional system created by the Founding Fathers.

Hyneman, Charles S. and Gilbert, Charles E., *Popular Government in America: Foundations and Principles* (New York: Atherton Press, 1968). Reexamines American democratic theory and practice in the light of contemporary problems involving political influence, participation, pluralism, compromise, etc.

Mitchell, William C., *The American Polity* (New York: The Free Press, 1962). An effort to analyze American politics as an integral part of a social system.

Small, Norman J., ed., *The Constitution of the United States of America: Analysis and*

Interpretation, revised and annotated (Washington, D. C.: United States Congress, Sen. Doc. No. 39, 88th Congress, 1st sess., 1964). The most complete and authoritative treatment of the interpretation of the federal Constitution; the 1964 edition relies heavily on an earlier edition by Edward S. Corwin.

Wildavsky, Aaron, *American Federalism in Perspective* (Boston: Little, Brown and Company, 1967). A collection of readings on varied aspects of federalism by contemporary political scientists.

Footnotes

[1] Henry Fairlie, "The Distemper of America," *Interplay,* November, 1969, p. 6.

[2] Max Lerner, *Ideas for the Ice-Age* (New York: The Viking Press, Inc., 1941) p. 238.

[3] Thomas Hamilton, *Men and Manners in America* (Philadelphia: Carey, Lea, & Blanchard, 1833).

[4] See Carl J. Friedrich, "Constitutions and Constitutionalism," *International Encyclopedia of the Social Sciences* (New York: Macmillan and the Free Press, 1968) III, 318–326.

[5] Edward S. Corwin, "The Constitution as Instrument and as Symbol," *American Political Science Review,* 30 (December 1936), p. 1071.

[6] James Madison, *Vices of the Political System in the United States* (1787); reprinted in Alpheus T. Mason, *Free Government in the Making,* 3d ed. (New York: Oxford University Press, 1965), p. 172.

[7] James Madison, *The Federalist* (New York: Random House, Inc., 1937), Modern Library Edition, No. 51, p. 337.

[8] See, for example, *Pennsylvania v. Nelson,* 350 U.S. 497 (1956).

[9] 4 Wheaton 316, 421 (1819).

[10] *Schenck v. United States,* 249 U.S. 47, 52 (1919).

[11] Max Farrand, ed., *The Records of the Federal Constitution of 1787,* 4 vols. (New Haven, Conn.: Yale University Press, 1911, 1937), 2:137.

[12] 4 Wheaton 316, 407, 415 (1819).

[13] *Marbury v. Madison,* 1 Cranch 137 (1803).

[14] See *Hawke v. Smith,* 253 U.S. 221 (1920); *Dillon v. Gloss,* 256 U.S. 368 (1921); and, in particular, *Coleman v. Miller,* 307 U.S. 433 (1939).

[15] Alpheus T. Mason, *The Supreme Court: Palladium of Freedom* (Ann Arbor, Mich.: University of Michigan Press, 1962), p. 8.

[16] Quoted in Mason, *The Supreme Court.* p. 8.

[17] See, for example, Charles G. Haines, *The American Doctrine of Judicial Supremacy,* 2d ed. (Berkeley, Calif.: University Press, 1932); and Robert G. McCloskey, *The American Supreme Court* (Chicago: University of Chicago Press, 1960).

[18] *Dred Scott v. Sandford,* 19 Howard 393 (1857).

[19] As a member of the Committee On Style in the Constitutional Convention of 1787, Gouverneur Morris tried to replace a comma with a semicolon in Article I, section 8 of the Constitution. The semicolon would have followed the words, "To lay and collect taxes, duties, imposts and excises" and would have made a separate and complete power of the words that follow, "to pay the debts, and provide for the common defence and general welfare of the United States." But Roger Sherman objected to the change in punctuation, so the comma remained. This supported the interpretation later favored by the Supreme Court that the tax power is granted to Congress in order to provide funds to support the common defence and general welfare.

[20] See, for example, *Chicago, Milwaukee and St. Paul Ry. v. Minnesota,* 134 U.S. 418 (1890); *Lochner v. New York,* 198 U.S. 45 (1905); *Adair v. United States,* 208 U.S. 161 (1908); *Adkins v. Children's Hospital,* 261 U.S. 525 (1923); *Tyson v. Banton,* 273 U.S. 418 (1927); and *Railroad Retirement Board v. Alton R. Co.,* 295 U.S. 330 (1936). Most of these due process cases involved state legislation. The Supreme Court was more inclined to find federal police power statutes invalid on the ground that Congress had exceeded the limits of the commerce or tax powers than it was to declare that they violated the due process clause of the Fifth Amendment.

[21] *Morehead v. Tipaldo,* 298 U.S. 587 (1936).

[22] *West Coast Hotel v. Parrish,* 300 U.S. 379 (1937).

Part II   Federalism in an Urban Society

President Nixon and the Cities

By ALICE M. RIVLIN

There is no doubt that our big cities are in desperate financial condition. Costs of providing city services mount steeply. Revenues rise slowly. The middle class is still moving out. The poor are still moving in. Traffic congestion, housing conditions, crime, and air pollution get a little worse every day, and no one knows how to combat them without spending a lot more money.

So far, the Nixon administration has not found a way to relieve the budgetary crisis of the cities. Its two boldest domestic proposals—welfare reform and revenue sharing—have been greeted with faint praise in the big cities. The urban spokesmen do not seem to be against the Nixon program in principle. Rather, the reaction is: "It sounds like a good idea, but what's in it for us?"

The big cities are almost all in states with welfare payment levels well above the new federal floor. These states would get considerable fiscal relief from the new planned 100 per cent federal contribution to the minimum payment level. But these gains would be partially offset by the loss of federal matching funds on payments above the minimum. As pressure continues—inevitably—for higher benefit levels under welfare programs, the urban states would be forced to respond to these demands without federal help.

The Administration's revenue sharing proposal has met with somewhat more enthusiasm in the capitals of urban states and for good reasons. The plan has two basic purposes: The first is to strengthen state and local governments by giving them access to a "better" tax source than they have now. With all its faults the federal income tax, is a far more equitable tax than the property and sales taxes on which states and localities rely so heavily. Moreover, as the economy grows, federal income tax receipts rise much faster than sales and property tax receipts. The second purpose is to help equalize the burdens of government by channelling resources where the needs for governmental services are greatest. In the Nixon plan, population is used as an index of need at the state level, and the populous industrial states of the North and West are not likely to quarrel with this index.

But the fact remains that the Nixon plan, if enacted, would not help the big cities significantly. In the first place, the administration has apparently not found a satisfactory way of "passing through" money from the states to the big cities. The problem is hard because states differ widely in the way in which they share functions between state and local governments. In New Jersey, the localities bear the main burden of government and the state has few functions. In North Carolina, the state runs the school system. Requiring states to pass through, say 50 per cent to local governments would be too much in some states and not enough in others.

The Nixon revenue-sharing plan also has a "pass-through" formula. It would require a state to pass along to all its local governments a fraction of the funds proportional to the revenue raised by the local unit itself. There are two problems with this. First, the money would go to too many units of government. There are about 40,000 general purpose local governments in the country, and there is nothing in the Nixon plan which would tend to reduce that excessive number. Second, there is apparently no recognition in the formula of the special needs of big cities. Since local governments would get funds in proportion to the revenue they raise, the rich suburbs would do well, and the inner city would do badly.

The "pass-through" formula can be adjusted. The real problem is that the sums contemplated are not large enough to make a major contribution to state and local budgets no matter how they are distributed within states. Together, state and local governments now spend well over $100 billion a year. State and local tax receipts have been rising at a rate of $10 billion a year. The Nixon plan would start by turning over federal revenues of half a billion dollars, rising to $5 billion a year by 1975. Sums of this magnitude are not going to revolutionize state and local finance. Half a billion could get lost in "petty cash.". . .

One possibility is to use Federal money to share the capital cost of making our big cities habitable again—urban mass transit, renovation and replacement of housing, hospitals and schools. The funds that could be absorbed in this way are staggering, but the relief to the city budget would not be immediate. Cities are in trouble now, and clamoring for help with their operating budgets.

The other possibility is to use federal funds to support urban services, especially urban education which everyone agrees is both costly and ineffective. One hope for the cities is a massive federally financed urban education program which would revitalize urban schools (perhaps stemming the outflow of middle-class parents), and lighten the big city budget load at the same time. It is not difficult to devise a formula which targets funds on areas of greatest need. In fact, Title I of the Elementary and Secondary Education Act already has a formula which funnels money directly to school districts with concentrations of low-income children.

But this approach has problems, too. First, no one knows what an effective urban education program would be like. Disenchantment with big city school systems makes even ardent educationists reluctant to pour more funds into the same old channels. The experience with the Elementary and Secondary Education Act has not provided a basis for faith that simply applying an extra billion or two to the education of low income children will make much difference. Making city schools attractive, effective places (if it can be done) will take radically new methods, new attitudes, and new kinds of people coming into the teaching profession.

The dilemmas of the administration are real, but one thing is clear: help for the big cities will take many billions more than are now budgeted.

© 1969 by The Washington Post. Reprinted by permission.

Chapter 4   The Nation and the States

Every functioning federal system is a compromise between concentration of power at the center and preservation of autonomy at the periphery. To endure, a federal system must be dynamic since the context in which the distribution of power was originally arranged never remains constant. In the United States, the bargain between nation and state was struck in an isolated, small, agrarian society. It has survived Civil War, territorial expansion across the continent and beyond, a fiftyfold increase in population, the development of an industrial economy and urban society, foreign wars, and a tremendous growth in the power and responsibilities of government. In the process, American federalism has been transformed from a relatively simple set of constitutionally prescribed relationships between nation and state into an increasingly complex mosaic of interactions among public agencies at the national, regional, state, metropolitan, county, municipal, and neighborhood levels.

FEDERALISM AND THE CONSTITUTION

Much of the time of the Founding Fathers was devoted to working out the general principles and details of a viable federal partnership. To ensure a strong central government, the Constitution assigned major powers to the national government. It also denied the states a role in foreign affairs, the taxation of foreign and interstate commerce, the issuance of legal tender, and certain other powers reserved exclusively to the national government. In addition, the Constitution made a sweeping grant of implied power to the federal government in the "necessary and proper" clause and established in Article VI the doctrine of national supremacy. All powers not delegated to the national government were reserved to the states and the people. The President and Congress were to be elected from state constituencies; the states were guaranteed equal representation in the Senate and given the power to accept or reject constitutional amendments.

Guarantees to the States

The Constitution also obligates the federal government to guarantee the states a republican form of government, to protect the states against invasion, and, upon application of the legislature or executive of a state, against domestic violence, and to refrain from changing the boundaries of a state without its consent.

The guarantee of a republican form of government has had little impact on federal–state relations since the Supreme Court has taken the position that enforcement of the guarantee is the function of the "political" branches of the national government.[1] Presidents and congressmen have been extremely reluctant to define the line between a state government that is republican and one that is not.

More controversial has been the obligation to protect a state against domestic violence. In general, the President has waited for a request from state authorities before he has acted. But on occasion, he has gone ahead without such a request and has defended his action by asserting that the enforcement of federal laws required the presence of federal troops within a state. For example, against the wishes of Governor John P. Altgeld of Illinois, President Grover Cleveland sent an army regiment to Chicago in 1894 during a railroad strike, claiming that this action was necessary to keep the mails moving and to protect interstate commerce.[2]

The practical effect of the federal guarantee of territorial integrity has been to freeze the boundaries of the states. Without the consent of state government, there is no way to implement the periodic restructuring proposals which seek to make the geographic jurisdictions of the states coterminous with contemporary patterns of social and economic development, or to satisfy those who would separate northern and southern California or have New York City secede from New York State. Not since 1820 when Maine was detached from Massachusetts as part of the Missouri Compromise has a state legislature actually consented to a revision of its boundaries. Nor are the circumstances which permitted West Virginia to secede from Virginia and join the Union likely to arise again. This event occurred during the Civil War and resulted from the unwillingness of the loyal western counties of Virginia to follow that state into the Confederacy. A pretense of obeying the requirement of the Constitution was made by obtaining from an allegedly Unionist or "restored" government of Virginia permission for a change in the state's boundaries. But in fact Virginia quite clearly did not give its consent.

Admitting New States

The Founding Fathers were aware of the country's vast potential for further growth, and they did not want to cut off the possibility of physical expansion. Thus, in Article IV of the Constitution they granted Congress virtually unrestricted power to admit new states to the Union. Vermont and Kentucky were admitted as the fourteenth and fifteenth states in 1791 and 1792. Alaska and Hawaii became the forty-ninth and fiftieth states in 1958 and 1959. Of the thirty-seven states admitted to the Union, two (Vermont and Texas) made the transition from the status of independent nation, one (California) was acquired from Mexico at the end of the Mexican War and passed directly to statehood, three (Kentucky, Maine, and West Virginia) were separated from existing states, and the remaining thirty-one first served periods of apprenticeship as territories.

Congress is under no legal obligation to admit a new state in any given situation. It can be arbitrary in refusing statehood to a territory, or it can make the process as easy as it wishes. Nonetheless, congressional practice over the years has set minimum requirements for statehood. These were explained in 1953 in a report of the Senate Interior and Insular Affairs Committee in these terms:

> 1. The inhabitants of the proposed new state are imbued with and are sympathetic toward the principles of democracy as exemplified in the American form of government.
> 2. A majority of the electorate wish statehood.
> 3. The proposed new state has sufficient population and resources to support state government and . . . carry its share of the cost of Federal Government.

Few territories, however, ever acquired statehood merely by meeting these conditions. This is illustrated by the case of the last two states to enter the Union. Long after Alaska and Hawaii had met the traditional requirements for statehood, their admission was blocked in Congress. Since both territories were noncontiguous to the existing states, many Congressmen felt a dangerous precedent would be established in granting them statehood, thereby breaking the geographical solidarity of the country. Opposition also came from southerners who believed that the congressmen from Alaska and Hawaii would support civil rights legislation. Partisan considerations also played a role, since Republicans feared that Alaska would send Democratic members to Congress, and Democrats objected to Hawaii for the opposite reason. Not until 1958 did the supporters of Alaskan statehood prevail in Congress. With Alaska's admission, it proved easy to enact a Hawaiian statehood bill one year later.

In 1796, in admitting Tennessee to the Union, Congress set a precedent by declaring the new state to be "one of the United States of America," "on an equal footing with the original states in all respects whatsoever." Did this mean that once in the Union a new state could throw off special conditions imposed upon it by Congress at the time of admission? New states have generally assumed they had such power, and special conditions have frequently been repudiated. In 1911, in the case of *Coyle v. Smith,* the Supreme Court ruled that Oklahoma, which had entered the Union in 1907, might change its capital from Guthrie to Oklahoma City, in spite of the fact that the congressional enabling act specifically forbade such a move before 1913. The Court held:[3]

> The power of Congress is to admit "new states into *this* Union." "This Union" was and is a union of states, equal in power, dignity, and authority, each competent to exert that residuum of sovereignty, not delegated to the United States by the Constitution itself.

For three quarters of a century following the adoption of the Constitution there was much argument as to whether states might withdraw from the Union. This issue was settled on the battlefields of the Civil War, and in 1869 the Supreme Court gave legal approval to what had been already determined by force of arms when it declared that the "Constitution, in all of its provisions, looks to an indestructible union, composed of indestructible states."[4]

Interstate Obligations

In their relations with each other, the states are directed by the Constitution (1) to give full faith and credit to each other's official acts; (2) to extend the same privileges and immunities to citizens from other states that they extend to their own citizens; and (3) to deliver up fugitives from justice at the demand of the executive authority of the states in which the crimes occurred. The first of these has had many applications and has been much interpreted by the courts. For example, the clause is held to require each state to give effect to private contracts made under the laws of other states. Thus, a contract for the sale of land made in Ohio can be enforced in the courts of Texas. Similarly, marriages performed or granted under the laws of one state are valid in all other states; divorce, however, raises more complicated problems[5] that may make it possible for a state to refuse to recognize a divorce granted by another state.

The privileges and immunities guarantee means generally that a state must extend to citizens from other states the rights to acquire and hold property, to make contracts, to engage in business, and to sue and be sued, on the same basis as these rights are enjoyed by its own citizens. But a state need not follow the literal meaning of the guarantee in all respects. It may, for example, deny to citizens of other states the "privilege" granted its own citizens to attend its university or to enjoy many other services that it renders. On the other hand, a state cannot deny citizens of other states a privilege such as use of its highways. Custom and common sense have had a good deal to do with drawing the line between privileges that must be granted and those that can be denied altogther or granted on a restricted basis. The same thing is true of the surrender of criminals. Although the obligation is prescribed in the Constitution in binding language, in practice state officials have occasionally refused to surrender fugitives at the request of other states. Federal courts have consistently refused to order state authorities to meet this obligation imposed by the Constitution.

The Place of Local Government

The Constitution deals only with the relations between the national government and the states. It makes no specific reference to local units of government, such as counties, cities, school districts, and townships. From the constitutional point of view, these units are all subdivisions of the states, created by the states and responsible to them. As such, they are subject to all of the same restrictions and prohibitions that the Constitution places on the states. Their purposes, powers, and status, however, are determined by the states, except, of course, that a state cannot grant authority or functions to a subdivision that it does not itself possess.

What the Constitution establishes as a two-way relationship between the nation and the states has become a three-way federal partnership, in which national, state, and local units interact in exceedingly varied and complex patterns. Varying degrees of autonomy have been granted by the states to their subdivisions, especially in the home-rule provisions affecting municipalities. During the past quarter century, the cities have increasingly bypassed the state capitals in their quest for help from Washington. Despite these developments, the powers and resources of all local jurisdictions remain subject to substantial state control.

NATIONAL POWER AND STATES' RIGHTS

Perhaps the most important feature of the Constitution with respect to federalism has been its flexibility concerning the boundaries of power between the national government and state and local governments. The Constitution has permitted national power to expand in response to social, economic, technological, territorial, and political changes. It also has facilitated innovation, adjustment, and proliferation in intergovernmental relations, all of which has contributed significantly to the steady enlargement of the responsibilities of the states and localities. Because of the fundamental issues involved, the evolution of the federal partnership has generated persistent conflict throughout American history between those favoring a stronger national government and those dedicated to preserving states' rights. Often those waving the banner of states rights have not been public officials but private groups—frequently corporations—who wish to escape federal regulation.

The Growth of National Power

Underlying the enormous expansion in the activities of the national government has been the development of a modern industrial society with a national economy, nationwide transportation and communications networks, and an increasingly interdependent and mobile urbanized population. With these developments, more and more problems have become national in scope and impact, generating demands for national action. State and local governments can deal with most serious national economic and social problems only in piecemeal fashion. The national government has the authority—though not always the capacity—to treat problems comprehensively. For example, in a period of wide-spread unemployment, the federal government can analyze the causes and centers of unemployment without regard to the political boundaries of the states. It can plan national policies with a view toward maintaining a minimum standard of welfare necessary for decent living and can attempt to eliminate gross differences among the states with regard to health, welfare, income levels, and economic development. Again, it can insist that there are certain essential standards of individual freedom, civil rights, and racial equality that must be accepted and maintained on a uniform basis throughout the entire nation.

The development of national power has also produced business, labor, farm, civil rights, and other groups which naturally focus their political energies on the federal government. Concentrating on Washington involves a considerable economy of effort for organized interests, since there is only one Congress compared with fifty state legislatures and thousands of local councils. The fact that Congress has been more responsive to the demands of many groups than the states and localities has served to reinforce the national focus of many organized interests.

A major reason for the greater responsiveness of the national government is the superiority of its fiscal resources. Throughout much of the nineteenth century, the expansion of federal activities was underwritten by the proceeds from the sale of the public domain, as well as through the transfer of public lands to state and local units. During the past forty years, the growth of the national government has rested on its formidable powers to raise money through taxation and borrowing. Of particular importance has been the progressive income tax, which has been largely preempted by Washington. Compared with the sales and property taxes on which most state and local governments must rely, the income tax is less regressive and a source of considerably less political pain to elected officials, in part because it is much more responsive to general economic growth than the other major revenue sources. In addition, programs financed at the national level overcome the inhibitions caused by the reliance of the states and localities on tax resources located within their borders. Federal taxes and standards have the advantage of nationwide application, which means they place no unit at a competitive disadvantage as state and local measures frequently do.

Federal involvement also has been spurred by the inability or unwillingness of state and local governments to respond effectively to widespread demands for government action. The failure of the states to regulate the giant industrial combines and emerging corporate empires of the late nineteenth century led to the expansion of national controls over business during the progressive era (1885–1915). The devastating impact of the Great Depression of the 1930s on state and local fiscal capabilities created a governmental vacuum in a time of intense national need which was filled by the far-reaching innovations of the New Deal. Many of the newer federal programs have resulted from pressures from the cities which had been systematically short-changed by state legislatures, most of which greatly overrepresented rural areas prior to the Supreme Court's reapportionment decisions of the 1960s.[6] A final stimulus to national action has been the ineffectiveness and inefficiency of many state and local governments. More than one third of the states lack genuine merit systems for selecting governmental personnel and only a handful pay salaries large enough to attract competent professional employees. Given these financial, political, and administrative weaknesses, citizens and groups who want government to "do something" turn, more often than not, to the national government for action.

States' Rights and Political Interests

Throughout the nation's history, social, economic, and political considerations rather than principle for principle's sake have determined most people's attitude toward the growth of national power. In taking a position, the practicing politician usually has asked himself: For what purpose is national or state power being used? What interests are likely to benefit and which to lose if the balance shifts from state activity toward national activity? How will these shifts affect me and my constituents?

The stands taken by the political parties on the issue reflect practical considerations. In the first years of the new government, the lines were drawn between the

Federalists who favored a strong central government and the Antifederalists who worked for a system in which state power would be dominant. The triumph of the Antifederalists in the election of 1800 drove the Federalists from power permanently and enhanced the position and power of the states in the Union. But it by no means resulted in a drastic reduction in national power. Under such Presidents as Thomas Jefferson and Andrew Jackson, groups that had distrusted and opposed centralized government made vigorous use of the national government to further ends that they supported.

The arguments of the Federalists and Antifederalists were taken up by the Republican and Democratic parties that succeeded them. The Republican party, born to fight for the cause of the Union, usually favored enhancement of national power as a superior means of protecting property, stimulating commerce and business enterprise, and serving conservative interests generally. State power, was distrusted by some Republicans because of its appeal to local interests having "radical" aims. In contrast, the Democratic party tended to distrust national power because of the traditional use of this power by business interests. It viewed state power more favorably because Democrats, particularly in the South, represented interests with more influence at the state than at the national level.

Whatever its position in principle, each party has tended to deplore national power when its rival is in office, only to make extensive use of this power when in office itself. The Democratic party was in power nationally during the two great wars of this century. That experience itself was sufficient to compel the party to pursue more highly centralized programs of governmental activity than its rival had ever dreamed of undertaking. But the change of heart was not the result of international developments alone. Under Wilson, Roosevelt, Truman, Kennedy, and Johnson, the national Democratic party made vigorous use of federal power to effect sweeping domestic reforms. In one of the basic shifts in American politics, the states' rights party of the nineteenth century became the agency through which a national welfare state was established, despite the continued espousal of the doctrine of states' rights by many of its adherents in the South.

The Republican party did not view with equanimity these attempts to use national power. Federal legislation providing for social security, public works, full employment, collective bargaining, wage and hour control, reciprocal trade agreements, rural electrification, rehabilitation of tenant farmers, governmental utilization of atomic energy for peacetime purposes, urban rehabilitation, and ultimately aiming at the elimination of poverty itself was regarded by most Republican leaders as endangering the interests of property and business. Republicans denounced centralization of governmental activity in Washington and argued for a return of political power to state capitals "where it belongs." Under Dwight Eisenhower, the New Deal drive toward centralization was slowed down, but little was done to satisfy the demands of "Old Guard" Republicans for a sharp reduction in federal programs. In 1964, the Republicans nominated a presidential candidate who vigorously advocated a drastic curtailment of federal power and programs, a position which contributed to one of the most decisive electoral defeats in American history. Four years later, the victorious Republican candidate was less outspoken in his views on the role of the national government, but Richard Nixon assumed the Presidency committed to searching out "every feasible means of decentralizing government, of getting it close to the people."[7]

States' Rights and Decentralization

"Government close to the people" has long been the rallying cry of the defenders of states' rights and the advocates of a decentralized federal system. State and local officials are seen as closer to and more responsive to the electorate than federal officials, as those able to adapt governmental action more effectively to diverse local needs. From this perspective, the dispersion of political power among state and local governments is considered essential to democracy because it forecloses national control by one party or group, affords minorities the opportunity to control some of the system's many components, and expands the opportunities for meaningful participation in the process of self-government. It also can be argued that the tasks of the national government are made more manageable and political stability enhanced by resolving conflict throughout a decentralized system rather than only at the top. Conflict is moderated and experimentation encouraged because the existence of many relatively autonomous centers of power permits groups in some localities to avoid policies locally which do not command a national majority.

One may ask, however, whether state and local governments are, in fact, closer to the people than the federal government. A larger proportion of voters participate in national than in state or particularly local elections; news media devote more attention to national affairs than to state or local politics; and survey research indicates that the average citizen tends to be better informed on national issues than those contested at the state capitol or in city hall. Moreover, the decentralized administration of many of the expanding responsibilities of the national government means that many citizens have more frequent contact with federal officials in agencies such as the Post Office, Social Security Administration, Office of Economic Opportunity, Veterans Administration, Federal Housing Administration, Internal Revenue Service, Department of Agriculture, or Selective Service System than with state and local officials.

Equally questionable is the assumption that small size promotes responsiveness on the part of a unit of government, or the protection of minority rights, or democratic government. States and cities which are small have not been more responsive to their constituents' demands than the larger ones or than the federal government. Quite the contrary, the larger jurisdictions tend to be more responsive to the multiplying demands of an industrialized and urbanized population, while many of the smaller units have consistently lagged behind. By the same token, the denial of minority rights and the support of oligarchies have posed a greater threat to democracy in smaller states and communities than in either the larger states and cities or the federal government.

More often than not, the minorities whose interests have been enhanced by decentralization have used their influence to frustrate rather than to advance democracy and the general welfare. As William H. Riker[8] points out: "The main beneficiary [of federalism] throughout American history has been the Southern whites, who have been given the freedom to oppress Negroes, first as slaves and later as a depressed caste." The cause of states' rights has usually enlisted the staunchest defenders of the status quo, who have sought to minimize governmental activity by lodging responsibilities in state capitals where the prospects of inaction were usually high, in part because their influence was greater than that of national majorities.

To be sure, the federal system does provide opportunities for those units which can muster the resources and the political support to innovate and expand. Wisconsin pioneered in the development of unemployment compensation; California led the nation in evolving a superb and costly system of higher education in which some form of advanced training is available to every high school graduate; New York City extended effective protection to an extremely wide range of civil rights far in advance of most jurisdictions. But states and localities that are less enterprising, poorer, or less influenced by national majorities have lagged far behind their more enterprising neighbors. As a result, the maintenance of states' rights and government close to the people has fostered the dissection of the general welfare along state and local boundaries. Per pupil expenditures for education, the level of welfare payments, unemployment compensation rates, the effectiveness of public utility and insurance regulation, the provision of food stamps for the hungry, and the availability and quality of hundreds of other public activities are intimately affected by where an American happens to live.

The Zero-Sum Fallacy

A favorite image of the champions of states' rights pictures the states and localities as shriveling appendages of an all-powerful national government manned by bureaucrats who seek to dominate every phase of public life in the United States. In support of this contention, candidates on the stump, congressional budget cutters, outraged governors, and conservative political commentators point to the enormous growth in the activities and domestic expenditures of the federal government and conclude that Washington's gains have been at the expense of the states and their subdivisions. The trouble with this "zero-sum" approach to federalism, which conceives of a static system in which increased national power automatically means reduced state and local authority, is that it ignores the fact that governmental activity has been expanding at all levels.

Today, state and local governments are spending more money, employing more people, and engaging in more functions than ever before. In fact, state and local government is one of the fastest growing sectors of the American economy. Between 1950 and 1968, state and local expenditures increased 290 percent; during the same period, the gross national product rose only 202 percent. In 1968, the states and localities spent $99.1 billion, compared with a $76.5 billion outlay by the national government for domestic purposes. Approximately 9.4 million people worked for state and local governments in 1968, which was double the number in 1950. By contrast, the federal government employed only 3 million civilians in 1968, not all of whom were engaged in domestic programs. Equally important, the state and local governments play a primary role in most of the areas of governmental activity which have the greatest bearing on the quality of individual and community life. Two-thirds or more of the burden for educating the young, building and maintaining roads, providing public health and hospital care, and securing police and fire protection falls on the state and local governments.

Most state and local governments are being overwhelmed by their expanding responsibilities. With few exceptions, their principal problem is not the lack of something to do, but the lack of resources to satisfy the burgeoning demands of a rapidly growing urbanized population for the vital services provided by the states and localities in the decentralized American federal system.

Federal Grants

An increasingly important source of funds for hardpressed state and local governments are federal grants, which make the superior resources of the national government available for financing services administered by the states and localities. A grant-in-aid is a sum of money derived from a tax levied and collected by a higher level of government for expenditure and administration by a lower level of government in accordance with certain standards or requirements. Although the system of federal grants to states developed very largely in the present century, its beginnings go back to 1785 when Congress, under the Articles of Confederation, set aside a section of every township in the Northwest Territory for the maintenance of local schools. During the nineteenth century Congress aided the states in a variety of ways, including distributing surplus federal funds, allocating grants of land for schools and colleges, and developing agricultural experimental stations. Since 1900 federal grants to states have been used to help finance construction of highways, development of forests, vocational education and rehabilitation, public health, school lunch, and social security programs. More recently, federal grants have been made directly to local governments to construct airports and public housing, to plan and renew cities, to improve water and sewer facilities, to acquire open space in metropolitan areas, and to finance antipoverty programs.

Through grants, the federal government has been able to advance national priorities without assuming full responsibility for functions within the traditional sphere of state and local responsibility. In the process, Washington has provided the states and their subdivisions with a substantial portion of the resources needed to tackle some of their most pressing problems. Federal aid has stimulated new state and local activity in a wide range of program areas. Because of the requirement that recipients meet federal administrative and technical standards, grant programs have raised the level of competence and professional skill of a substantial number of state and local employees. Moreover, by facilitating the geographic redistribution of wealth from prosperous to less prosperous areas, federal grants permit high standards of governmental service and performance to be set and implemented for the nation as a whole. Finally, the development of the grant mechanism has moderated demands for more drastic forms of centralization that would clearly diminish the state and local role in the federal partnership.

For many, however, federal grants are a mixed blessing. Some critics maintain that the haphazard and uncoordinated development of federal grants covering a large number of services and functions has weakened the states financially. As the first Hoover Commission[9] reported: "In order to secure the necessary revenues, the national tax base is expanded, which makes it more difficult for State and local governments to secure their own revenues, and hence stimulates pressure from more and more groups for more and more grants." Even more popular is the arguments that the "strings" attached to federal assistance inevitably destroy the initiative and independence of state and local government by shifting control of state and local responsibilities to Washington and by skewing state and local budgets along lines desired by the federal government.

Clearly, the basic decisions on the allocation of the limited funds available for grants are made in Washington. Furthermore, no state or local government can secure federal grants without meeting certain conditions which have been set by Congress or federal administrators. Almost every grant program requires that a proportion of the federal money be matched by the recipient. Often, the matching requirement weights the allocation of state and local funds in the direction of federal-assisted activities. For example, some states have developed excellent highway programs with the help of federal funds, but have failed to develop equally important programs for which limited or no federal aid was available. In addition, the recipient agrees to spend the funds for the specified purpose and to comply with a variety of program, performance, materials, administrative, and personnel standards, which range from civil service status for those paid with federal funds to detailed technical specifications for the design of public housing to a requirement for the maximum feasible participation of the poor in community action programs.

Counterbalancing these requirements and standards is the fact that primary responsibility for the implementation of federally aided activities is lodged with state and local officials. In almost all grant programs, the federal role normally remains financial and supervisory. State highway engineers locate and build the roads, local school superintendents hire the teachers and establish the curriculum, state welfare officials set the levels of payment and eligibility criteria for most forms of public assistance, and city redevelopment aides negotiate the complex arrangements which are involved in urban renewal. Other state and local officials make thousands of policy choices which largely determine who benefits from federal aid, under what conditions, and at what costs to the various components of a particular constituency. In large part because of this system of decentralized implementation, the over-all impact of federal grants has been to enhance rather than undermine the capabilities of state and local governments.

THE DECENTRALIZED BASE OF AMERICAN POLITICS

Why is the implementation of most federal programs left to the states and localities? Why has the growth of national power also bolstered the role of state and local governments? The answers to these questions lie largely in the decentralized nature of the American political system. Despite the development of a national economy and the growth of a strong central government, the political power of most elected officials in Washington remains rooted in state and local constituencies. As a result, both Congress and the federal executive are highly responsive to the needs and demands of the states and localities. This responsiveness assures state and local governments of a major role in federal programs. The fact that the states and localities share in the control of federal resources contributes to the dispersal of prizes and rewards which has produced political decentralization in the United States.

At the heart of this decentralized system are political parties which serve to devolve rather than to centralize power. It is difficult to find more decentralized national institutions in a modern society than the Democratic and Republican parties. The basic rules of the party system are usually determined by state law. Most party funds are collected and distributed by state and local party organizations. Both national party organizations are federations of fifty state parties. The national committees exercise no significant control over party personnel in the states. Normally, the national party leadership plays no role in selecting candidates for Congress, governorships, the state legislature, or local offices.

Underlying the lack of centralized political parties is the decentralization of the prizes and rewards of political activity. For most participants in politics, the opportunities for elective office, patronage, government contracts, and other benefits are greater at the state and local than at the national level. Of the 500,000-odd elected offices in the United States, only 537 are federal positions, and all but two of these have state and local constituencies. Patronage opportunities are more numerous at the state and local levels since three out of every four civilian government employees are hired by states and their subdivisions where merit systems are neither as extensive nor as effective as federal civil service. Moreover, many federal patronage jobs such as postmasterships are distributed to the party faithful through state and local party leaders. Party decentralization is also enhanced by the broad scope of the activities of state and local governments which enable them to control a significant proportion of the rewards essential to the sustenance of political parties. The fact that state and local officials play a major role in determining how an estimated $25 billion in federal grants in 1970 will be spent also helps nourish the parties at the grass roots.

Of all the products of the decentralized party system, none is more important than the state and local constituency base of the Congress. Locally elected, locally responsible, and wary of centralizing party or governmental power in Washington, congressmen usually make sure that all levels of government share in the spending of federal money. The sensitivity of the average congressman to the needs of his constituency also provides a built-in defense of state and local interests in the administrative process. A state's objections to regulations proposed by the federal Welfare Administration, a suburb's efforts to persuade the Bureau of Public Roads to reject a state highway department's proposed alignment for an interstate route, or a neighborhood's difficulty in securing a grant from the Office of Economic Opportunity—all draw congressmen into the administrative aspects of intergovernmental relations. This involvement produces what Morton Grodzins[10] has called "the comprehensive, day-to-day, even hour-by-hour impact of local views on national programs. No point of substance or procedure is immune from congressional scrutiny."

Congressmen are able to advance state and local interests successfully within the federal bureaucracy because of Congress's autonomous constituency base, the lack of party discipline, and the power of congressional committees. Administrators constantly need appropriations to carry out their programs, and they frequently need new legislation to make their work more effective. To get money and new laws, they must have the active cooperation of congressmen. To obtain that cooperation, administrators frequently rely on the President, but when they cannot, they have to have a reservoir of good will with congressmen or with interest groups who in turn can influence congressmen. Directly or indirectly, the bureaucrat "must find support from legislators tied closely to state and local constituents and state and local governments. The political activity of the administrator, like the administrative activity of the legislator, must often be turned to representing state and local interests in national programs."[11]

A GOVERNMENT OF SHARED POWER

The net effect of decentralized politics is to produce a widespread sharing of power within the American federal system. The money that comes from Washington is disbursed at the state and local level. Federal controls are tempered by political realities, as well as by the bonds of professionalism, and the sharing of goals among the federal, state, and local officials who work together in a program area. As a result, there is no neat division of functions between the nation and the states and their subdivisions. Instead, the various components of the federal partnership cooperate in a multitude of ways to provide the ever-widening range of public services that are the shared responsibility of federal, state, and local government. To illustrate this pervasive sharing, Grodzins[12] provides a striking but not atypical example of the local health officer:

> [He] is appointed by the state under merit standards established by the federal government. His base salary comes jointly from state and federal funds, the county provides him with an office and office amenities and pays a portion of his expenses, and the largest city in the county also contributes to his salary and office by virtue of his appointment as a city plumbing inspector. It is impossible from moment to moment to tell under which government [he] operates. His work of inspecting the purity of food is carried out under federal standards; but he is enforcing state laws when inspecting commodities that have not been in interstate commerce; and somewhat perversely he also acts under state authority when inspecting milk coming into the county from across the state border. He is a federal officer when impounding impure drugs shipped from a neighboring state; a federal-state officer when distributing typhoid immunization serum; a state officer when enforcing standards of industrial hygiene; a state-local officer when inspecting a city's water supply; and (to complete the circle) a local officer when insisting that the city butchers adopt more hygienic methods of handling their garbage.

Federal-State-Local Cooperation

Intergovernmental cooperation extends far beyond those activities financed in part by federal grants. Informal cooperation is the most pervasive form of sharing since federal, state, and local agencies with common concerns find it mutually advantageous to keep each other informed about their activities and problems and to profit by one another's experience. All the levels of government cooperate in the collection and share in the distribution of information on everything from prices and incomes to births and deaths. Federal and state officials jointly inspect banks, utilities, and food processors; they investigate many crimes and accidents together; and they work side-by-side in preserving order and providing relief during disasters and riots. As in the case of the local health officer, the federal partners share the services of many public servants. They also lend personnel and equipment to one another, train personnel across intergovernmental lines, and provide each other with various goods and services.

Law enforcement, an area of paramount state and local responsibility, illustrates the variety and adaptability of the modes of federal-state-local cooperation. For years, the Federal Bureau of Investigation has helped to train state and local police officers. Its fingerprint files were developed with the aid of local police officials, and these files as well as other information and technical resources are readily available to police departments throughout the nation. During the late 1960s, federal cooperation in law enforcement intelligence, planning, and training activities took on a new dimension in the wake of the racial violence which shattered Los Angeles, Detroit, Newark, and scores of other cities. The gathering of information of use in riot prevention and control was intensified and computerized so that it could be made available on short notice to state and local officials in a particular city. The Department of Justice organized conferences and seminars to exchange information and coordinate planning with police departments and, most importantly, to promote and provide instruction in techniques for riot control which minimize the use of force. This cooperative intergovernmental activity fostered the speedy adoption by many of the major police forces of the policy of restraint recommended by the President's Advisory Commission on Civil Disorders in 1968.[13]

Decentralized Federal Activity

Both sharing and the dispersion of power are promoted by the fact that the bulk of federal activities is administered in local communities by local people. The great majority of the employees of the largest federal agencies, including the Department of Defense, the Veterans Administration, and the Departments of Agriculture, the Treasury, and the Interior are scattered throughout the country in every state. By custom, U.S. Attorneys and marshals, federal district judges and, where possible, heads of F.B.I. offices, are residents of the localities in which they serve. These employees staff veterans hospitals, maintain national dams and flood control projects, keep the voluminous records of the old-age insurance program, operate the federal court system, help track down persons suspected of committing federal crimes, and operate military installations. By the nature of their work—and of congressional appropriations—most have to cooperate closely with their state and local counterparts. And almost all bring to their jobs not the outlook of faraway government officials intent on imposing discipline on a supine citizenry but the same range of values and attitudes that characterize Americans in each state and community throughout the country.

The success of the Tennessee Valley Authority illustrates another way in which the national government can exercise broad authority and responsibility without necessarily concentrating additional power in Washington. By creating a separate agency, the valley authority, with a broad grant of power to develop the natural and material resources of a region, to encourage economic development, and to provide for comprehensive utilization of water resources for flood control, hydroelectric power, irrigation, and recreational purposes, Congress was able to provide initiative and leadership at the top without undermining the capacity of state and local units for self-government.

Interstate Cooperation

Sharing within the federal system need not involve the national government. Through cooperative efforts, the states have met some of their needs for uniform or coordinated governmental activities without federal assistance. In 1933, the Council of State Governments was created to promote interstate cooperation through consultation and research. The council comprises nine affiliated organizations of state officials, including the National Governors' Conference. The council lobbies for the states' point of view in Washington and actively promotes improved state administrative organization and uniform state legislation.

The demand for uniform state laws arises from the need for identical treatment of certain issues by individual states. The plight of the trucker who carries freight from one state to another illustrates the obstacles that confront a businessman when different states apply different rules to a single business transaction. One state may allow a trucker to carry a load of ten tons, whereas a neighboring state to which the trucker is going allows only eight tons for the same type of truck. Similarly, a businessman may want to transfer property to a buyer from another state, or he may want to sign a contract to close a business deal. Unless he can be certain that all the states involved in the transaction will enforce the contract in their courts with reasonable uniformity, he will be discouraged from entering into the agreement. As of 1966, the National Conference of Commissioners on Uniform State Laws had prepared seventy-one bills that were recommended for adoption by all states on a uniform basis, eighteen acts recommended only as models because complete uniformity among the states was not deemed essential, and twenty-five acts that had not been widely adopted but that the Conference still chose to recommend for consideration by the states. Among the recommended acts that have been most widely enacted are a criminal extradition act, a gifts to minors act, a partnership act, a narcotics act, and a simultaneous death act. Since state courts are under no obligation to interpret identical laws in the same way, there is no guarantee that uniformity of administration will result from these enactments.

Another means of securing cooperation among states is the interstate compact, an agreement between two or more states that has been approved by Congress. Between 1789 and 1920, only thirty-five compacts were completed, all of which were used to settle boundary or jurisdictional disputes. Since 1921, over 100 compacts have been concluded, many of which established continuing interstate agencies to operate bridges, ports, parks, river basins, and educational programs. The earliest and perhaps best-known of the compact agencies is the Port of New York Authority, established in 1921 by joint action of New York and New Jersey to build and operate interstate transport and terminal facilities in the New York metropolitan area. One of the more interesting recent compacts created the Educational Commission of the States, whose task is to foster cooperation among the fifty states to safeguard their dominant policy-making role in education.

Interstate cooperation has not lived up to the expectations of those who have hoped that consultation, uniform state laws, and compacts would obviate the need for expansion of the national government. Nonetheless, these approaches have both provided useful answers to some important problems and broadened the opportunities for shared endeavor within the federal system.

A New Level of Government: Regional Councils

By JOHN HERBERS

Special to The New York Times

WASHINGTON, April 18—While the Federal system in the United States has been undergoing severe strain in recent years, an important new level of government has sprung up almost unnoticed by the public.

More than 140 councils of government—voluntary organizations of municipalities and counties—have been established across the country to attack areawide problem. Most have been established since 1966 under the incentive of Federal grants, and most are in metropolitan areas, which have scores and sometimes hundreds of separate governments, each with its own tax base, ordinance and services.

The only powers the councils have are those delegated by the member governments and increasing authority from Washington to review Federal grants flowing to the local governments and to decide whether the funded projects are regionally beneficial.

As a result, the councils or COG's as they are called, have been involved more in planning than action and have been reluctant to come to grips with the more controversial forces that are afflicting metropolitan areas.

But they have emerged as the chief regional instrument for preventing chaos and waste. Some of them are beginning to move into social action, and there is a vitality and enthusiasm among the membership that is rare on the current American scene.

Further, there is the possibility that as urban problems grow, the councils may assume power and authority approaching that of the areawide metropolitan government. In the Minneapolis-St. Paul area, for example, the Minnesota Legislature has given the Metro Council taxing authority and the power to plan and carry out anti-pollution measures, solid waste disposal, zoning and noise abatement in a seven-county area.

The typical metropolitan area consists of a central city and a proliferation of suburban municipalities and county governments. The central cities have encountered a declining tax base, due to the movement of wealth outward, and an inability to impose uniform standards for the police, utilities, transportation, pollution control and health and welfare services.

In the mid-Nineteen sixties, the enactment of Federal grant-in-aid programs ranging from sewage treatment plants to antipoverty programs, further increased the confusion.

In the Housing Act of 1965, Congress provided for direct Federal assistance to the councils. In the Model Cities Act of 1966, Congress required area-wide reviews of Federal grants to avoid conflicts, duplications and harmful effects. This task fell largely to the councils, which increased rapidly after Federal funds had been made available.

The Nixon Administration has further strengthened them by requiring more reviews. The Nixon policy of strengthening the role of the states in domestic affairs has helped the organizations in some instances. In Texas, the state government has joined with Washington in providing direct financial assistance, and the council there are flourishing.

But there is fear within some councils that cut across state lines that strengthening the state role in regional projects will harm the organizations.

For example, Walter A. Scheiber, director of the Metropolitan Washington Council, one of the oldest and most innovative of the councils, said that his group was increasingly concerned that Richmond and Annapolis, the Virginia and Maryland capitals, which have jurisdiction over the Washington suburbs would fail to give the council the support it needed.

The Metropolitan Area Planning Council in Boston, which represents 100 governments in Massachusetts, provides a case study in the problems and promises involved. Each government has one representative on the council. In addition, the Governor appoints 21 members from the area at large, and the chairman of state and local agencies are ex-officio members. Each of the 131 members has one vote.

"There were a lot of people who questioned us at first," said Richard M. Doherty, director of the council. "They thought of us as a monster who would eat up local boundary lines. But we don't have enough power to be controversial. We don't take property or spend their money."

In almost every city, there is a fear on the part of the small governments that the councils will become a government superstructure and fear among blacks that their strength will be diluted by the suburbs.

Robert Farley, deputy director of the Southwest Michigan Council, which represents 105 governments in the Detroit area, said that 18 governments had pulled out of the organization since it was formed in 1968 and 11 others had joined.

"Some of them don't want anything to do with inner city problems," he said, "and then some of the militant persons from the inner city see us as a plot to give control to the lilywhite suburbs."

One of the critics of the council is Mayor Orville Hubbard of all-white Dearborn who says, "We already have too many cooks in the kitchen, and one more would only further gum up the works. Cities need more home rule, not more regional control."

Nevertheless, the council has brought about a central water system in which Detroit leases water to 60 surrounding communities, is involved in a number of social programs to help the inner-city poor and is currently trying to persuade the state to enact uniform building codes to lower the cost of housing.

The councils cite a wide range of accomplishments. There are the elementary ones: The East-West Gateway Co-Ordinating Council in St. Louis stopped plans of two jurisdictions to build an airport runway and a highway in the same place.

And there are the more sophisticated examples: The Metropolitan Washington Council was responsible for the member governments adopting a uniform ordinance against air pollution rather than waiting for Federal directives.

© 1970 by The New York Times Company. Reprinted by permission.

FEDERALISM IN FLUX

Never were the dynamics of the American federal system more apparent than during the 1960s. New and expanded federal domestic programs were one of the keynotes of John F. Kennedy's New Frontier. The landslide election of Lyndon B. Johnson in 1964 provided an activist President with the congressional majorities needed to create a "Great Society" through the use of "creative federalism." From the unprecedented legislative activity of 1965–1966 came a tremendous increase in the scope and intensity of intergovernmental relations, as well as new problems and proposals for reform since growth was so rapid that the Great Society programs threatened to overwhelm the federal system.

New Patterns of Partnership

One of the most striking features of the contemporary federal system is the great variety in the forms of partnership. Not only is the federal government a partner of state governments and cities in carrying out national programs financed through grants, but it also has become a partner of nongovernmental groups, professional associations, and private businesses in administering important phases of public programs. In the war against poverty, for example, federal funds have become available to support programs administered by community action programs, which usually are established outside of regular governmental channels and administered by private boards of directors. In the medicare program, the federal government has in effect contracted with private insurance companies to handle claims of persons over sixty-five and with professional associations to determine the eligibility of hospitals and nursing homes for participation in medicare. Other federal partnership arrangements have developed in new programs in community development, urban transportation, air and water pollution, and manpower for state and local governments.

Stresses and Strains in the Partnership

Not everyone has welcomed the proliferation of recipients of federal assistance. Governors, who for years have argued against the enactment of federal programs which bypassed the state capitals, complain bitterly that the mushrooming of federal-local relationships pose a basic threat to the viability of state government. How, they ask, could the states oversee, coordinate, and allocate resources for their subdivisions when state officials were not even aware of, much less able to influence or control, many of the federal programs which made funds available directly to cities, counties, local public authorities, neighborhood councils, quasi-public agencies, and private contractors? Mayors who for three decades have urged Washington to ignore the states in making aid directly available to local governments now find the shoe is on the other foot; many of them echo the governors in protesting that the antipoverty and other federal programs which bypass city hall undermine the authority of popularly elected officials.

Complexity and confusion has resulted from the rapid and unplanned expansion of federal programs. By the end of the decade, state and local officials were confronted with a bewildering maze of over 400 federal grant programs, each a response to a particular set of problems and pressures, and each with its own funds, objectives, and requirements. Formidable obstacles have hindered the development of effective delivery systems for the new programs. At the state and local level, many agencies lack the political skills and organizational capabilities needed to master the increasingly esoteric art of "grantsmanship." At the federal level, programs frequently overlap, as in the case of water and sewer grants which are available from the Departments of Agriculture, Commerce, Interior, and Housing and Urban Development, as well as through the Appalachian Regional Development Commission. Coordination among agencies and programs often is weak, and interagency conflict common. Moreover, the administration of a number of programs has been overly centralized in Washington, producing inflexibility, long delays in processing applications, and failure to adapt federal standards and guidelines to local conditions.

Perhaps these administrative shortcomings would be more readily tolerated if the expanding federal grant programs had served to reduce significantly the fiscal pressures on state and local governments. This has not happened. What appears to be a spectacular increase in federal aid during the past decade, from $7 billion in 1960 to $25 billion in 1970, increased the federal share of all funds available to state and local governments from only 11.6 percent to 15.8 percent. The reason for the relatively mild impact of the rapidly expanding grant programs, is that state and local taxes were rising almost as fast as federal aid. As a result, increased federal assistance has not appreciably lessened the fiscal and political burdens of governors and mayors, most of whom eventually find themselves in a crossfire between inexorable pressures for more services and vociferous voter resistance to higher taxes. Some state and local leaders, particularly the big city mayors, have sought to alleviate these continuing fiscal pressures by intensifying their efforts to expand and enrich federal grant programs. But others, including many of the governors of the large urban states, have questioned whether more of the same from Washington can ever answer the mounting fiscal problems of state and local governments. They point to the bureaucratic morass of many of the grant programs, the imbalances in state and local budgets caused by variations in the availability of funds, and the uncertainty in planning and programming that results from the vagaries of the processes involved in obtaining approval for specific grants or congressional appropriations for general programs. At the same time, they emphasize the gap between the demands on state and local governments that will outrun their resources as long as the national government continues to monopolize the most effective revenue sources. And they conclude that more basic changes than additional grant money are needed in the federal system since, in the words of New York's Governor Nelson A. Rockefeller:[14] "We don't need Band-Aids on the problem, with little bitty Federal help. We need a blood transfusion."

Revenue Sharing and "Creative Federalism"

For most governors and a growing number of congressmen and other national leaders, some form of revenue sharing which would substitute federal for state and local taxes offers the most promising source of such a transfusion. The first revenue-sharing plan was developed in 1964 by Walter Heller, chairman of the Council of Economic Advisers, who was seeking a means of relieving the fiscal pressures on the states and localities, of increasing their fiscal independence, of supplementing programmatic grants with unconditional assistance, and of insuring that more of the annual increments of federal income taxes produced by the growth in GNP was spent for domestic public sector needs. Under the Heller Plan, one percent of federal income tax collections (about $2.5 billion in 1965) would be placed in a trust fund to be distributed to the states primarily on the basis of population for their unconditional use. Initially, President Johnson endorsed revenue sharing, but he backed off when premature disclosure of the plan stirred up a hornet's nest of opposition. Fear that the money would be misused led liberal, labor, and urban interests to object to unconditional grants to state governments and to insist that federal assistance continue to focus federal resources according to national priorities and national standards. Similar protests came from federal agencies administering grants and from groups that benefit from specific federal programs, both of whom preferred to see additional federal funds go into their particular programs.

With revenue sharing on the shelf, the Johnson Administration responded to the growing criticism of the Great Society programs by seeking to overhaul the grant system. Under the general guise of "creative federalism," efforts were made to reduce the number of grant programs, to loosen the strings on federal aid, and to encourage local solutions. A number of health programs were consolidated into a single comprehensive grant to the states, while block grants for law enforcement were made available in the Omnibus Crime Control and Safe Streets Act of 1968. Several new endeavors, such as the Model Cities program, placed heavy reliance on local initiative and innovation. Departmental reorganizations in the Department of Health, Education and Welfare (HEW) and the Department of Housing and Urban Development (HUD) were designed to facilitate program coordination and to improve the processing of grants. Steps were taken to delegate more power to regional offices of federal agencies, to improve interagency coordination in the field, and to insure consultation with governors and mayors on federal programs within their jurisdictions.

Despite the promise of many of these developments, creative federalism failed to satisfy the advocates of revenue sharing, whose ranks steadily grew during the late 1960s. The National Governors' Conference endorsed revenue sharing in 1965. Two years later, one fifth of the members of the Ninetieth Congress cosponsored revenue-sharing bills, while the Gallup Poll reported that 70 percent of the American public favored the concept. Both candidates backed revenue sharing during the 1968 presidential campaign. And in 1969, the Nixon Administration proposed to distribute $500 million in unconditional federal aid to the states, with the allotment for revenue sharing rising to $5 billion by 1976. Revenue sharing fitted in with President Nixon's desire to reduce Washington's direct involvement in domestic programs and to funnel federal assistance through the state capitals. The latter goal, however, roused the ire of the cities, who refused to support the proposal until the Administration agreed that a sizable proportion of the shared revenues would be earmarked for local governments.

Whatever the outcome of these most recent episodes in the continuing effort to adapt the American federal system to the needs of a dynamic society, certain trends seem clear. A national economy and an urban society combine with the superiority of the federal tax system to guarantee that more and more of the money needed to finance government will come from Washington. New packages will be developed, more activities will be covered by federal aid, and recipients will produce new patterns of cooperation and conflict within a partnership characterized by political decentralization and widespread sharing of power.

SELECTED BIBLIOGRAPHY

Anderson, William, *The Nation and the States: Rivals or Partners?* (Minneapolis, Minn.: University of Minnesota Press, 1955). One of the best general treatments of the American federal system.

Elazar, Daniel J., *American Federalism: A View from the States* (New York: Thomas Y. Crowell Company, 1966). A useful analysis of federal-state-local relations from the perspective of the state capital.

Goldwin, Robert A., ed., *A Nation of States: Essays on the American Federal System* (Chicago, Ill.: Rand McNally and Company, 1963). A series of provocative essays on federalism by a group of leading scholars.

Grodzins, Morton, *The American System: A New View of Government in the United States.* Daniel J. Elazar, ed. (Chicago, Ill.: Rand McNally and Company, 1966). The major writings of one of the most influential students of American federalism.

Macmahon, Arthur W., ed., *Federalism: Mature and Emergent* (New York: Doubleday & Company, Inc., 1955). A large collection of essays on various aspects of federalism in American politics.

Mason, Alpheus T., *The States Rights Debate: Antifederalism and the Constitution* (Englewood Cliffs, N.J.: Prentice-Hall, Inc., 1964). An analysis of the historical origins of the current and recurrent debate about national power and states rights.

Riker, William H., *Federalism: Origin, Operation, Significance* (Boston, Mass.: Little, Brown and Company, 1964). A systematic, original, and critical analysis of federalism.

Sanford, Terry, *Storm over the States* (New York: McGraw-Hill Book Company, 1967). An imaginative reappraisal of federal-state-metropolitan relations by a former governor of North Carolina.

Footnotes

[1] See, for example, *Luther v. Borden,* 7 Howard 1 (1849) and *Pacific Telephone Co. v Oregon,* 223 U.S. 118 (1912).

[2] See the decision of the Supreme Court in *In re Debs,* 158 U.S. 564 (1895), a case that grew out of this same episode.

[3] 222 U.S. 559 (1911).

[4] *Texas v. White,* 7 Wallace 700 (1869).

[5] See the two cases entitled *Williams v. North Carolina,* 317 U.S. 287 (1942) and 325 U.S. 226 (1945), which involved the obligation of North Carolina to recognize a Nevada divorce.

[6] See *Baker v. Carr,* 364 U.S. 339 (1960) and the following cases decided on June 16, 1964: *Reynolds v. Sims, WMCA v. Lomenzo, Maryland Committee v. Tawes, Davis v. Mann, Roman v. Sinock,* and *Lucas v. Colorado General Assembly.* These cases are discussed in detail in Chapter 8.

[7] Richard M. Nixon, radio address, June 27, 1968, quoted in the *New York Times,* June 28, 1968.

[8] William H. Riker, *Federalism: Origin, Operation, Significance* (Boston, Mass.: Little, Brown and Company, 1964), p. 152.

[9] Commission on Organization of the Executive Branch of the Government, *Overseas Ad-*

ministration, Federal-State Relations, Federal Research (Washington, D.C.: Government Printing Office, 1949), pp. 31–32.

[10] Morton Grodzins, *The American System; A New View of Government in the United States.* Daniel J. Elazar, ed. (Chicago, Ill.: Rand McNally and Company, 1966), p. 377.

[11] Morton Grodzins, "American Political Parties and the American system," *Western Political Quarterly,* 13 (December 1960), p. 991.

[12] "The Federal System," in the Report of the President's Commission on National Goals, *Goals for Americans* (Englewood Cliffs, N.J.: Prentice-Hall, Inc., 1960), pp. 265–266.

[13] See The National Advisory Commission on Civil Disorders, *Report* (Washington: U.S. Government Printing Office, 1968), pp. 267–292.

[14] Quoted in "Governor Plans Talk with Nixon on Aid to States," *New York Times,* February 8, 1969.

Chapter 5   The Nation and the Cities

The American political system—dynamic, decentralized, and challenged by the forces of change—reflects the rapidly growing, dispersed, and troubled urban society it serves. The sustained growth of the domestic activities of government at all levels is primarily a response to urbanization, which both draws people to the cities and moves them out to the suburbs. In the transition from a rural to an urban society, government has assumed functions once the responsibility of the family and the church, such as the care of the old and the poor and the jobless. The interdependence of life in densely settled urban communities necessitates increasingly sophisticated governmental involvement in health and housing conditions, police and fire protection, the supply of water and other public utilities, and the disposal of sewage and garbage. The complexity of urban life creates problems like traffic congestion which are almost unique to the city, as well as the need for public services which are rarely found outside metropolitan areas, such as rapid transit.

Urbanization produces mobility and dislocation: one-fifth of the population moves to a new address each year; residential densities increase; neighborhoods decay; and business firms leave the congested inner core of the city, depleting tax resources of the city center. Urbanization increases interdependence, while bringing diverse class, ethnic, and religious groups into close proximity. The urban process also breaks down the primary controls of the extended family, the church, and the small face-to-face community. Each of these aspects of urbanization generates conflicts. The demands of a heterogeneous urban society for a widening range of public services and goods compete for the limited public resources of a decentralized and fragmented governmental system.

In responding to the variegated needs and conflicts of an urban society, government has become increasingly complex. Existing units of government have added a bewildering array of new agencies, many of which enjoy considerable freedom from the normal processes of political and budgetary control. Over the past century, cities have developed police, fire, water, sewage, health, planning, and traffic departments, housing, airport, and parking authorities, and urban-renewal, antipoverty, and model-cities agencies. A similar process of institutional elaboration has occurred at the state and national levels, where the proliferation of agencies has complicated the tasks of coordination, integration, and control by chief executives and legislatures. In most metropolitan areas, suburbanization has spawned new general purpose governments. Because these new municipalities typically are too small to encompass all of the public consequences of urbanization, special districts abound in the suburbs to handle problems such as sewage, water supply, and flood control. While urban interdependence, overlapping jurisdictions, and the interdependence of governmental units necessitate coordination and cooperation, differences in resources and constituencies create conflict within and among the components of the political system which tries to govern an increasingly urban America.

EMERGENCE OF THE METROPOLIS

The problems of an urban society only recently have moved to the foreground of the American political scene, yet the history of the United States is one of continuous urban growth. Except for the period 1810–1820, urban population growth has outstripped the increase in rural areas in every decade since the first census in 1790. By 1920, more Americans were living in towns and cities of over 2500 than in the countryside. Thereafter, economic depression, the mechanization of farms, and wartime prosperity in industry and business speeded the flight of people from the countryside to the town and city. By 1960, seven out of every ten Americans were classified by the Census Bureau as urban dwellers. By 1980, perhaps 90 percent will be living in cities.

Even more important, the 1960 census[1] showed that nearly two-thirds of the nation's citizens—or 113 million people—were residing in 212 standard metropolitan statistical areas covering only 7 percent of the nation's land area. Since 1950, more than 85 percent of the nation's population growth has occurred in metropolitan areas, which account for 70 percent of all local government expenditures, more than 70 percent of the nation's taxable property, over two-thirds of the manufacturing establishments, and almost 80 percent of all bank deposits.

Metropolitan areas, in turn, have begun to merge into vast urban belts that form continuous urbanized areas, some hundreds of miles long. At present, the largest of these strip cities, or megalopolises, stretches along the Atlantic seaboard from Boston to Washington, D.C., south to Richmond. The potentially largest urban mass is incubating in California, sprawling from San Francisco Bay to Los Angeles, and eventually, may extend to San Diego. Half of all Americans now live within thirteen strip city areas. Moreover, these islands of dense population account for 60 percent of all factory workers, 62 percent of all manufacturing activity, and 55 percent of the country's retail trade. Population experts predict that by 1975 strip cities will contain 60 percent of the total U.S. population.

The growth of the city, metropolitan area, and the megalopolis is a consequence of what York Willbern[2] has called:

> two revolutions, one imposed upon the other, and the meaning of the second is partially obscured by the fact that the first, much older, revolution is continuing even as the second develops.

STANDARD METROPOLITAN STATISTICAL AREAS

Seattle-Everett

Spokane

Tacoma

Great Falls

Portland

Salem

Billings

Eugene

Fargo-Moorhead

Boise City

Reno

Ogden

Sioux Falls

Sacramento

Sioux C

Vallejo-Napa

Salt Lake City

San Francisco
Oakland

Stockton

Provo Orem

Denver

Lincoln

San Jose

Salinas
Monterey

Fresno

Colorado Springs

To

Santa Barbara

Las Vegas

Pueblo

Oxnard-Ventura

Wichita

Los Angeles-Long Beach

San Bernadino-Riverside-Ontario

Tulsa

Anaheim-Santa Ana-Garden Grove

Amarillo

Oklahoma City

San Diego

Albuquerque

Lawtor

Phoenix

Lubbock

Sherr
Deniso

Wichita Falls

Tucson

Dallas

Midland

Fort Worth

El Paso

Odessa

Abilene

Waco

San Angelo

Austin

San Antonio

Ho

Laredo

Corpus Ch

McAllen-Pharr-Edinburg

Honolulu

Brownsville-Harlingen-San Benito

Source: U.S. Bureau of the Census

The first of these revolutions, of course, is the rise of an urban way of life. The second is its diffusion and dispersal over the countryside.

Underlying the "first revolution" has been migration to the city, a process which has had three major elements. The first, and the oldest, is the flow of white families from farm to small town, from farm and small town to the city and, increasingly in recent years, from farm and small towns to suburbs. Second is the migration of immigrants, primarily from the rural areas of Europe to American cities. In 1910, at the height of European immigration, 72 percent of the foreign born lived in cities. The final element in American urban migration is the twentieth century movement of blacks, as well as Puerto Ricans, Mexican-Americans, and whites from depressed areas such as Appalachia, into the decaying neighborhoods of the older and larger cities.

The "second revolution," the rapid outward movement of urban populations, results from the tremendous acceleration of the natural tendency of cities to grow at their periphery. This development results from the mass production of the automobile and other technological, economic, and social changes which have facilitated the spread of a relatively low-density population engaged in urban economic pursuits. Since 1920, suburban areas have been growing increasingly faster than central cities. During the 1950s, the suburbs grew almost five times faster than the central cities. Suburban areas accounted for 75 percent of the total increase in metropolitan population during the decade. Between 1960 and 1965, the suburban share of metropolitan growth rose to 85 percent. By 1965, 68 million Americans lived in suburbs, seven million more than resided in central cities.

These data, however, understate the growth of the suburbs since 86 percent of the population increase in the central cities during the 1950s resulted from the annexation of suburban areas. If annexations are disregarded, suburban growth was more than forty times that of the central cities between 1950 and 1960; and suburban areas accounted

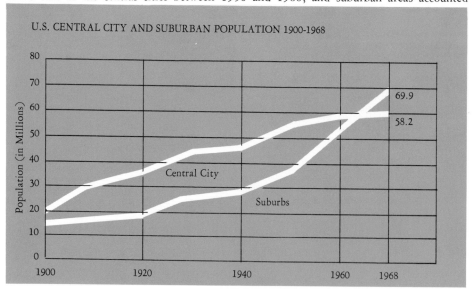

SOURCE: U. S. Bureau of the Census.

for 97 percent of the decade's total increase in metropolitan population.[3] Some of these new suburbanites are former rural dwellers who bypassed the city in the process of becoming urbanized; far more are the offspring of suburban parents. Over 80 percent of all the people who will be added to the population of the United States in the 1970s will be suburbanites, most of whom will be born in the suburbs. The most dramatic source of new suburbanites, of course, is the central cities. Approximately six million Americans, almost all of them white, abandoned central cities for the suburbs during the 1950s. The ten largest cities lost 3.5 million white residents. Between 1960 and 1966, the suburbs attracted close to 5 million more city dwellers.[4]

Because of these massive population shifts, most central cities have ceased to grow, and many have been losing population during the past two decades. In 1960, fourteen of the eighteen largest cities had fewer residents than in 1950; and two of the cities that grew did so only because of annexation. All twelve of the major cities in the heavily developed area east of the Mississippi River and north of the Ohio River registered losses totalling 850,000 during the decade. Three of these cities lost ten percent or more of their residents—Boston (13 percent), St. Louis (12.5 percent), and Pittsburgh (10.7 percent)—and another city, Detroit, declined by 9.7 percent. The nation's largest city, New York, dropped by 1.4 percent while its suburbs grew 38.9 percent, and the second largest city, Chicago, experienced a loss of 1.9 percent compared with a 64.9 percent increase in the metropolitan area outside the city.

In all of these cases, population losses would have been far greater had the strong outward movement of white families from the urban core not been offset by the growing migration of blacks, Puerto Ricans, and Mexican-Americans to the city. Between 1950 and 1966, central cities added 5.6 million black residents through migration and natural increase, which raised the proportion of black central-city residents 12–20 percent. By contrast, the number of blacks in suburbia rose only 780,000, and the black proportion of the suburban population dropped from 5 percent in 1950 to 4 percent in 1966. The black population has grown most rapidly in the larger urban centers, where it has become increasingly concentrated. In 1966, 26 percent of the population of central cities in metropolitan areas of one million or more was black, compared to only 12 percent in the core cities of metropolitan areas of 250,000 or less. One of every three blacks in the United States lives in one of the twelve largest cities, eight of which were 30 percent or more black in 1968.[5] As a consequence of these trends, cities are separated from the surrounding suburbs by sharpening racial, income, housing, and educational differences in most of the larger metropolitan areas, as well as in many smaller areas which have experienced similar population shifts.

Exceptions to these trends are found primarily in the South and West, where most cities are younger than those of the northeast and midwest. Developed in the automobile era at much lower densities than the older centers, cities in states such as Florida and Arizona are more suburbs than cities in the traditional sense. Many are growing rapidly: Albuquerque, El Paso, Jacksonville, Orlando, Phoenix, San Jose, Spokane, Tampa, and Tucson more than doubled their populations during the 1950s. As might be expected, central city-suburban differences are less sharp in these metropolitan areas. And in some of them, non-whites and low-income residents are more prevalent in the suburbs than in the city.

URBAN CHANGE AND THE CENTRAL CITY

The explosive growth of the metropolis has created serious problems for all the components of the American system, but it has exacted its heaviest toll from the older cities. Of the many factors which have contributed to the crisis of the American city, none is more basic than a half century of failure of most central cities to extend their boundaries at the periphery of the metropolis. As a result, most of the older cities have shared in relatively little of the tax revenues from new low-density residential, commercial, and industrial development. And while central cities have received few of the benefits of urban growth, they have had to bear most of the heavy social and financial burdens of urban change. Within the central city's boundaries are most of the blighted neighborhoods of the metropolis, the lion's share of its wornout housing, and a high proportion of its obsolescent factories and shopping districts, as well as most of the metropolitan area's less fortunate citizens.

The Decline of Annexation

Throughout the nineteenth century, urban growth was paralleled by the steady expansion of the city's territorial jurisdiction. Annexation often was a marriage of convenience, since the newly settled areas depended upon the city government for urban services and the financially hard-pressed cities normally were eager to increase their tax base. Through annexation, Chicago grew from a community of 10.5 to 190 square miles, Boston increased from 4.5 to 38.5 square miles, and Minneapolis from 8 to 53 square miles. The present area of Los Angeles is four and one half times greater than it was in 1910. The largest single annexation of territory by an American city took place in 1898, when Brooklyn, part of Queens County, and Staten Island, were added to New York City.

During the early years of the twentieth century, the pace of annexation slowed in many cities. In some cases, impediments to expansion were posed by topographic features, county and state boundaries, and the unwillingness of city taxpayers to finance costly capital improvements and unprofitable service extensions in the outlying areas. But the principal barrier in most instances was the opposition of the residents of the newly settled areas. Rather than be swallowed up by a large city with its distant city hall and its torrent of social problems, they preferred to live in a small and responsive political community which promised neighborhood control over municipal taxes and services, as well as insulation from the city's conflicts, immigrants, and corruption. In response to the suburban desire for separation and autonomy, many states prohibited their cities from annexing new territory without the consent of the residents of the target area. As a result of these developments, few of the major cities added significant new territory after 1920. And almost all of the large-scale annexations in recent years have been made by cities in the younger and rapidly growing metropolitan areas of the Southeast, Southwest, and the Upper Plains where city-suburban differences tend to be less pronounced than in the older metropolitan areas of the Northeast, Midwest, and Far West. Among the most successful of these cities were Houston, which grew from 160 to 447 square miles, and Oklahoma City, which became the most extensive city in the nation by annexing 533 square miles of new territory.

Help!

Herblock in the Washington Post.

The most important consequences of the failure of most cities to grow is the metropolitan area. Before the decline of annexation, the city and the metropolis were largely coincident, with a single political jurisdiction encompassing the socio-economic diversity of the urban community. Once the city stopped expanding, its boundary became the line between city and suburb. In the absence of natural boundaries, this line often is invisible as the middle-class neighborhoods on the periphery of the city blend into those of the inner suburbs. On one side of the line, there is a single city government, on the other, a multitude of small political fiefdoms. People on the city-side of this political boundary are older, more often unmarried, not as well educated, and less likely to own an automobile or home than those on the suburban side. City dwellers also are far more likely to be black, to live in substandard housing, to be unemployed or on welfare, and to commit or be victimized by crime than residents of the suburbs. In a particular metropolitan area, the extent of these socio-economic differences between city and suburb depends in part on when the city reached its territorial limits. Because Boston was encircled by independent suburban municipalities as early as 1873, even the middle-class development spurred by the extension of electric street-car lines fell largely outside the city limits. By contrast, the annexation of 177 square miles of farmland, primarily in the

San Fernando Valley, enabled Los Angeles to encompass a sizable number of the vast metropolitan area's single-family, low-density "suburban" neighborhoods. As a result, Los Angeles includes a much higher proportion of the area's middle-class population than does Boston.

The Exodus of the Affluent

City dwellers with the resources to buy or rent new residences have been moving out of the urban core for over a century. The oldest districts of New York and Philadelphia were losing population before the Civil War. As long as the city continued to annex the newly settled neighborhoods, the outward migration of upper- and middle-income families did not greatly affect the fortunes of the city, although it did add a significant spatial dimension to the conflict between the reformers, who drew their support primarily from the residential neighborhoods of the periphery, and the bosses, whose machines were rooted in the working class, ethnic wards of the inner city.

Once the city ceased to grow, the situation changed dramatically as the continued outflow progressively removed from the typical older city most of its upper-income residents, a significant proportion of its middle-class families, and, in the past two decades, a growing number of blue-collar workers and their families. City finances have been particularly hard hit by the movement of the higher salaried urban dwellers to the suburbs, since most of those who have left paid more local taxes and placed fewer demands on the city treasury than the urban newcomers who replaced them. In addition, many former city dwellers continue to work in the central business district where they benefit from city services to whose support they make little or no contribution, while others still use the parks, libraries, museums, and other public facilities supported by the city's taxpayers. The exodus also has deprived the city of the services of those who once were its civic leaders and most concerned citizens. Many of the upper-class notables on whom the city's charitable, cultural, and civic organizations depend for leadership and support have transferred their allegiances and energies to the suburbs, while most of the middle-class interest in "good government" and better schools is now focused on suburban councils and school boards.

The Influx of the Poor

One of the most important functions of the American city has been to turn impoverished newcomers into stable members of the urban community.

> For the American city during the past hundred and fifty years, the raw material was the stream of immigrants pouring in from Britain, Ireland, Germany, Norway, Russia, Italy, and a dozen other lands. The city needed these immigrants to build its streets and offices, to man its factories, service its houses and hotels and restaurants, and do all the dirty and menial jobs that older residents disdained. But the city did more than use its newcomers: it equipped them to take their place as fully participating members of U.S. society. Doing this—bringing people from society's back waters into the mainstream of American life—has always been the principal business, and the principal glory, of the American city.[6]

Report of The National Advisory Commission on Civil Disorders

Summary

The summer of 1967 again brought racial disorders to American cities, and with them shock, fear, and bewilderment to the Nation.

The worst came during a 2-week period in July, first in Newark and then in Detroit. Each set off a chain reaction in neighboring communities.

On July 28, 1967, the President of the United States established this Commission and directed us to answer three basic questions:

What happened?

Why did it happen?

What can be done to prevent it from happening again?

To respond to these questions, we have undertaken a broad range of studies and investigations. We have visited the riot cities; we have heard many witnesses; we have sought the counsel of experts across the country.

This is our basic conclusion: Our Nation is moving toward two societies, one black, one white—separate and unequal.

Reaction to last summer's disorders has quickened the movement and deepened the division. Discrimination and segregation have long permeated much of American life; they now threaten the future of every American.

This deepening racial division is not inevitable. The movement apart can be reversed. Choice is still possible. Our principal task is to define that choice and to press for a national resolution.

To pursue our present course will involve the continuing polarization of the American community and, ultimately, the destruction of basic democratic values.

The alternative is not blind repression or capitulation to lawlessness. It is the realization of common opportunities for all within a single society.

This alternative will require a commitment to national action—compassionate, massive, and sustained, backed by the resources of the most powerful and the richest nation on this earth. From every American it will require new attitudes, new understanding, and, above all, new will.

The vital needs of the Nation must be met; hard choices must be made, and, if necessary, new taxes enacted.

Violence cannot build a better society. Disruption and disorder nourish repression, not justice. They strike at the freedom of every citizen. The community cannot—it will not—tolerate coercion and mob rule.

Violence and destruction must be ended—in the streets of the ghetto and in the lives of people.

Segregation and poverty have created in the racial ghetto a destructive environment totally unknow to most white Americans.

What white Americans have never fully understood—but what the Negro can never forget—is that white society is deeply implicated in the ghetto. White institutions created it, white institutions maintain it, and white society condones it.

It is time now to turn with all the purpose at our command to the major unfinished business of this Nation. It is time to adopt strategies for action that will produce quick and visible progress. It is time to make good the promises of American democracy to all citizens—urban and rural, white and black, Spanish-surname, American Indian, and every minority group.

Our recommendations embrace three basic principles:

- To mount programs on a scale equal to the dimension of the problems;
- To aim these programs for high impact in the immediate future in order to close the gap between promise and performance;
- To undertake new initiatives and experiments that can change the system of failure and frustration that now dominates the ghetto and weakens our sociey.

These programs will require unprecedented levels of funding and performance, but they neither probe deeper nor demand more than the problems which called them forth. There can be no higher priority for national action and no higher claim on the Nation's conscience.

Today, however, instead of the city acculturating its newest citizens, the problems of the urban newcomers threaten to overwhelm the city. Most of the urban poor live in the central city because it has most of the metropolitan area's older and less expensive housing, and because suburban housing and land-use policies usually exclude the less affluent. The departure of the upper and middle class have increased the proportion of the poor in the city's population, while the political boundary between city and suburb has separated the suburbanites politically and financially from the problems of the disadvantaged. At the same time, the city offers the newcomer considerably less opportunity for employment than it did 50 or 100 years ago. Part of this decline in opportunity results from the growing gap between the skills required by an increasingly sophisticated economy and those possessed by the recent arrival in the city or the graduate of an ineffective slum school. It also reflects the decentralization of employment in the metropolis, which puts more and more jobs beyond the reach of the city dweller.

Intensifying all of these problems is the fact that most of those who have migrated to the older cities during the past quarter century are black. Racial prejudice has narrowed the urban black's opportunities for employment, education, and housing; and in so doing, excluded large numbers of blacks from the benefits of a booming urban economy and an exploding metropolis. Instead of liberating the black man from his crippling heritage of slavery, repression, and segregation, the move to the city, to the "promised land," usually has meant a lifetime spent

> in the teeming racial ghettos [where] segregation and poverty have intersected to destroy opportunity and hope and to enforce failure. The ghettos too often mean men and women without jobs, families without men, and schools where children are processed instead of educated, until they return to the street—to crime, to narcotics, to dependency on welfare, and to bitterness and resentment against society in general and white society in particular.[7]

From this bitterness and resentment has come a new militancy in the ghetto, demands for black power, the bifurcation of politics in many cities along racial lines, and riots and rebellions in the black ghettos of scores of American cities. The sharp increase in violence and racial conflict in the older cities has accelerated the escape of white families to the suburbs. As a result of these trends, there is a widening gap between two societies: one white, prosperous, and suburban; the other black, poor, and ghettoized.

Erosion of the Economic Base

Further complicating the central city's difficulties is the fact that jobs as well as people have been moving out to the suburbs. The popular myth that pictures urban decentralization as primarily a residential phenomenon with most suburbanites commuting to jobs in the central business district bears little relation to reality. Cultural centers are built in the suburbs; major league ballparks are found in Bloomington, Minnesota, and Anaheim, California; and the Mafia finds lucrative new opportunities in the spreading suburbs. Approximately half of all the jobs in the typical metropolitan area, particularly those in retail trade and services, are closely tied to residences. Industrial jobs also have been moving out of the urban core at a rapid rate. In suburbia, industrial managers can satisfy the space needs of modern manufacturing processes far more easily than in the crowded urban core with its lack of large parcels of land. Suburban locations also bring industry closer to skilled workers, who increasingly live in the suburbs. Many of the firms which have suburbanized are in the newer and rapidly growing industries, such as electronics and aerospace. Typical of this development are the sleek factories and laboratories which line suburban Route 128 as it loops around Boston. Even white collar jobs, which traditionally have been the most concentrated component of the urban economy, have been moving out of the city in order to escape the high taxes, expensive office space, labor shortages, and congestion imposed by locations in the central business district.

As a result of these trends, most of the older cities have stable or declining economies. Throughout the nation, downtown retail stores have declined in the face of competition from the burgeoning shopping centers which are far more convenient for the auto-oriented suburbanite than the crowded central business district with its inadequate parking. Central city newspapers have lost both readers and advertisers to suburban dailies and weeklies. And even where the central city economy is booming, almost all of the growth is centered in managerial and other skilled office jobs which afford few opportunities to the unskilled and poorly educated who form a growing proportion of the city's labor pool.

Intensified Pressures for City Services

The failure of the central city to grow has not been accompanied by a leveling off of municipal services and costs. Instead, the demand for increased expenditure is greater than ever. Higher salaries for teachers, policemen, garbage collectors, hospital workers, and other city employees have produced sharp increases in the costs of all municipal services. Social and economic decline in the city is reflected in rising crime and juvenile delinquency, which lead in turn to increased law-enforcement costs, as well as in soaring welfare outlays as dependency rates increase. Efforts to attract back the middle class, to resuscitate the city's flagging economy, and to improve housing and public services in the slums have added burdens to the city's treasury. Under these pressures, the costs of municipal government increase steadily; meeting them tries the political skill of the most resourceful city officials. At best, the tax resources of the central city are likely to be static; more often, they are declining as a consequence of the erosion of the city's economic base.

METROPOLITAN GROWTH AND THE SUBURBS

Suburbs come in a great variety of sizes and types; most are small, but some are larger than many central cities. Most are residential, but some are primarily commercial or industrial such as Chicago's steel-making suburb of Gary or Teterboro, New Jersey, where 40,000 work and only twenty-two live. Among the residential suburbs, especially in the larger metropolitan areas which have dozens or even hundreds of suburban jurisdictions, there are wide income, class, and status variations from suburb to suburb. At one extreme is the suburb with 3000 low-priced homes squeezed onto one square mile, each built from one of four plans, and with little or no provision for schools, water, sewage treatment, or other public services. At the other is the enclave of the well-to-do, where the most fortunate suburbanites enjoy expensive homes on large lots, protected by strict zoning regulations and provided with a high level of community services.

The Problems of Growth

Different kinds of suburbs face different problems. Many of the larger and older suburbs have begun to experience the same difficulties as the central cities as their neighborhoods decay, racial conflict grows, and commercial and industrial districts decline. School problems differ greatly in an industrial suburb with few residents, an older dormitory suburb with all its land developed, and a mushrooming development along the urban frontier. The most common problems in an era of accelerating decentralization, however, are those of growth. When the city dweller moves to a suburb, he is quick to demand the full range of public services to which he has been accustomed. Good schools are often his first interest, but he also makes known his desire for better roads, quicker snow removal in the winter, a more ample water supply for his lawn and swimming pool, regular garbage and trash collection, more efficient fire and police protection, not to mention a generous program of public utility services and parks and other recreational facilities. The effect of rapidly expanding services on the local tax rate can be catastrophic, especially since the tax base in many suburban communities is extremely narrow. Some communities are fortunate in having business and industrial enterprises within their boundaries, but the typical new residential suburb is often wholly dependent on the taxation of homes for its local revenues. Sooner or later, the dilemma of the typical residential suburb becomes clear: either services must be held to a modest level or property owners must be prepared to assume a heavy tax burden. Whichever alternative is elected in a particular community, life on the fringes of the metropolis can become something less than idyllic.

The Fragmentation of Suburban Government

In most metropolitan areas, the provision of public services in suburbia is complicated by the fragmentation of government. In 1968, there were 20,745 units of local government in metropolitan areas, for an average of forty-eight per metropolitan county. Since few of these units are large enough to provide economies of scale, costs to the taxpayer are increased by the proliferation of small suburban municipalities. Some units are even too small to afford anything but the most rudimentary public services; often they lack adequate fire protection or a public library or more than one or two poorly trained policemen. Facilities and services frequently are duplicated at high cost in adjacent suburbs because of the absence of the machinery for or an interest in joint ventures. More often than not, land is cleared, streets laid out, and public utilities installed with little or no coordination or joint planning with neighboring communities. Small size increases the problems of the limited tax base of most suburbs, while the crazy quilt of municipal boundaries almost always produces a mismatch between resources and needs. Suburbs with considerable industry and commerce often have few school children, sometimes by design,

It Turns My Stomach to See How We Pollute the Water—Draw the Drapes Please.

Fischetti in the Chicago Daily News. Courtesy Publishers-Hall Syndicate.

while suburbs with large numbers of school-age youngsters find it impossible to attract industrial and commercial tax ratables.

Fragmentation has its benefits as well as its costs. The existence of small suburban governments permits community control over the most important parameters of suburban life, including real estate taxes, land use (and therefore property values), and the local school system (which can account for as much as 80 percent of local taxes in a child-oriented suburbia). Far more than the resident of the city, the suburbanite can tailor the landscape, public services, and taxes to the needs and desires of his particular neighborhood or cluster of neighborhoods. In so doing, he has provided a wide range of choice among service and tax levels in individual communities for the potential suburban dweller, especially in the larger metropolitan areas. And in the process, the suburbanite can participate in a reasonable facsimile of the small-town democracy that is such a cherished aspect of American political mythology.

THE DIVIDED METROPOLIS

For most students of the metropolis, the costs of the fragmented metropolitan political system far outweigh the benefits of autonomy and smallness to suburbanites. The wide disparity between needs and resources produces significant variations in the level and quality of public services in different sections of the metropolis. The line between city and suburb concentrates the most serious urban problems in the older cities, while cutting them off from the tax resources generated by economic and population growth at the periphery of the metropolis. The separation of city and suburb also enhances the political significance of the socio-economic diversity of the metropolis. Unlike the nineteenth century city which fostered interdependence by encompassing all of the components of urban society with a single set of governmental institutions, the fragmented political system of the twentieth century metropolis reinforces social and economic differentiations between city and suburb and among suburbs. This differentiated system grapples with rising conflict and the problems of growth and change in a highly localized frame of reference. It lacks a regional political arena in which to resolve issues which have metropolitan implications, as well as popularly controlled central instrumentalities to deal with area-wide problems such as transportation, pollution, water supply, and open space.

Failure to Plan

Urban sprawl is not solely the result of population growth, human mobility, and technological change. It is also a consequence of the inability of the fragmented metropolis to plan adequately. The development of the nation's metropolitan centers has been almost wholly haphazard, at least so far as conscious human design is concerned. It seems clear that the metropolitan problem would be much less severe today if a few decades ago hardheaded men in the nation's communities had understood the need to "plan" a way out of the growing dilemma. Moreover, it is safe to assume that metropolitan areas will be in even worse shape tomorrow unless the planning of today is better than it was yesterday.

Water shortages in areas of the East that enjoy an abundant rainfall provides a graphic illustration of the price society pays for its failure to use planning to meet a predictable and measurable urban need. It is true that new forms of industrial production and domestic living have increased the demand for water, but the extent of current water needs was largely predictable, and some greater measure of foresight and action was possible. Many of the urban areas now experiencing severe water shortages would today have water to spare if in the past more rainfall had been captured and stored instead of being permitted to run out to sea. In many instances, some action to contain this water could have been taken as recently as the 1950s with relative ease and at reasonable cost. Today, the problem for many a community is frightening in its fiscal and engineering aspects. For example, as population and industry have expanded rapidly and spread into all areas of the country, the number of stream valleys providing low-cost reservoir sites has steadily been reduced. This need to take immediate and drastic remedial action, rather than the moderate, preventive action that might have sufficed in the past, characterizes the metropolitan problem. Solution by a single community is rarely feasible.

Metropolitan Government

Until recently, almost all urban specialists believed that the root of most urban deficiencies as well as the principal obstacle to their solution was the decentralized political system of the metropolis. The metropolis was seen as a socio-economic community whose common interests were not reflected in public policy because of the fragmentation of government. Thus, political decentralization was the cause rather than the result of urban differentiation and conflict. As has always been the case with the forces of reform in the United States, the metropolitan reformers were preoccupied with structural change and the values of economy and efficiency. For them, urban problems were the product of a lack of areal government rather than a consequence of the absence of shared interests or the result of conflict over values and goals. Concern with economy and efficiency led reformers to focus on the economies of scale produced by metropolitan government rather than on the local control and responsiveness associated with neighborhood government.

Despite the exhortations of planners, university professors, government groups, and downtown business interests, area-wide government has won little popular acceptance in most of urban America. In the larger metropolitan areas, size and complexity tend to rule out many of the advantages of area-wide government. New York City, a "metropolitan" government at the time of the creation of the greater city in 1898, is hardly an argument for economy and efficiency. Another obstacle is the tendency of each of the major urban governmental activities to have its own optimal service area. The ideal areas in which to provide water and drainage, secondary education, or police and fire protection rarely are identical and seldom similar. But the most important impediment to area-wide government is a lack of perceived common interests on the part of most residents of metropolitan areas and their concomitant concern with preserving the status quo. For the suburbanite, metropolitan government threatens the political independence and fiscal integrity of his local community. It implies "reunion . . . with the central city and its corrupt politics, its slums, immigrants, criminals, and the vicious elements from which [the suburbanite] only recently escaped;"[8] and raises the spectre of racial integration, public housing in the suburbs, and suburban school children being bussed to ghetto schools. In contrast, black leaders in the central city, see metropolitan government as a device for diluting the influence of blacks or foreclosing their capture of city hall through an enlargement of the urban constituency. Almost all local political organizations and government employees in the metropolis have opposed area-wide government as inimical to their interests.

Because of this formidable resistance, only a few of the many campaigns for metropolitan government have been successful. During the past twenty-five years, city and county governments have been consolidated into a single area-wide jurisdiction in Baton Rouge, Nashville, and Jacksonville, while county governments have assumed major metropolitan responsibilities in Miami and Indianapolis. In most of these instances, differences between the central city and the suburbs were not as great as in other metropolitan areas. In Miami-Dade County, for example, most residents had few emotional ties to the area, which resembled one big suburbia. The county commission commanded high respect and strong support, while the Miami city council was widely condemned. The city's businessmen were anxious to shift the financial burden of some of the city's area-wide functions (municipal hospital and port authority) to the county. Other favorable factors included the lack of a strong labor movement with vested interests in the central city, the relative absence of politically active racial or religious minorities, the rapidity of population growth with a high degree of turnover, and the absence of the traditional two-party system. All of these factors tended to minimize commitments to the status quo and to favor change. Finally, the Metro campaign was led very effectively and had strong support from newspapers, business groups, civic organizations, and state legislators.

The Adaptive Metropolis

If structural reform were the only means of coping with problems that transcend local jurisdictions, area-wide government would be the norm rather than the exception in the United States. Urban Americans, however, have proved to be remarkably inventive in developing piecemeal accommodations that have deflected the most intense pressures on suburban governments without undermining their political and fiscal autonomy or solving the basic problems.

One of the most popular forms of adaptation is the special district, which is a single or limited-purpose unit of government with a jurisdiction that can be as narrow as a subdivision within a municipality (as in the case of a local water district) or as broad as an entire metropolitan area (as with the Metropolitan Water District of Southern California). Among the most common responsibilities of special districts and public authorities are water supply, sewage disposal, parks, airports, toll roads, bridges and tunnels, ports, and parking lots. Objections to special districts are numerous. They add to the proliferation of overlapping governments in the metropolis; they rarely facilitate comprehensive planning; and they are usually insulated from the state or local political process and often undemocratic in organization and operation. Nonetheless, special districts and public authorities have the advantage of working. They permit expeditious action toward the solution of such a broad community need as development of a comprehensive water supply system, a need that simply cannot be met efficiently and economically by independent municipalities. One factor that helps to account for the increasing use of special districts to ease metropolitan problems is their acceptability to the plural interests in the local governmental system. They do not appear to threaten local community control. They do not raise taxes directly but tend to be financed by user fees. They can be tailored to fit the unique problems of a particular function in a particular area. They are usually free from the sort of restraints imposed by states on the tax and debt-incurring authority of local governments. And they appeal to citizens who tend to distrust politicians and normal processes of local government.

Interlocal cooperation is another common form of adaptation to the forces of urban growth and change. In many instances, central cities have rescued hard-pressed suburban towns by offering services such as water supply and public transportation on a pay-as-you-go basis. Similarly, the police and fire departments of separate municipalities frequently have understandings, formal and informal, by which they come to each other's assistance in time of need. Over 700 interlocal agreements have been negotiated by local governments in the Philadelphia metropolitan area. Counties also have helped local governments survive by assuming responsibility for a growing range of local services, including public health, administration of elections, library service, assessment and collection of taxes, fire and police protection, water supply, street maintenance, and recreation.

Suburbia is the prime beneficiary of these adaptive devices. Most have been developed to insure that suburbanites can enjoy the benefits of smallness and autonomy without having to pay all the costs which would otherwise be imposed by the fragmentation of government. Since all of these modes of accommodation are voluntary, they rarely encompass controversial issues or touch on the central problems of the older cities. Public authorities are not created to build low-income housing throughout a metropolitan area. Interlocal cooperation seldom extends to the large-scale transfer of students between suburban and city schools. Few suburbs are willing to assign control over local land-use to county government. Furthermore, most of these arrangements involve user charges, thereby foreclosing the transfer of resources from the wealthier municipalities to the poorer areas. As a result, they do little to ease the plight of the older cities or to lessen conflict between the city and the suburbs.

THE URBAN ROLE OF STATE AND NATIONAL GOVERNMENT

Throughout the twentieth century, urbanization has steadily increased the impact of urban voters and their problems on politics at the state and national level. At the same time, state and federal involvement in the problems of the metropolis have multiplied rapidly. These developments have usually reflected the diversity and political fragmentation of the metropolis rather than its interrelationships. Cities and suburbs rather than the metropolis as a whole press their claims in the state capitals and Washington. Few voters or their representatives in the state legislatures or Congress identify with the metropolis or metropolitan interests. By the same token, most state and federal programs have been directed at cities and suburbs rather than metropolitan areas as a whole.

Reinforcing Dominant Trends

In general, state and federal policies have tended to reinforce the dominant trends in urban America. They have facilitated the decentralization of urban development, particularly through massive state and federal highway programs which have greatly improved access to suburban areas and federal mortgage policies which have helped to bring home ownership within reach of large numbers of Americans. Despite state and federal investments in the cities, the over-all effect of state and federal activities has been to intensify rather than alleviate the problems of the older cities. Most states have taken more from the cities in taxes than they have returned in state aid, particularly in educational aid where suburban interests have regularly prevailed over those of the cities. Federal acceptance of municipal boundaries as the jurisdiction of local public housing and urban renewal agencies has helped to concentrate the poor and the black in the cities, because it has hindered construction of federally aided low-cost housing in the suburbs. In addition, the dedication of federal lending agencies to the ethnic integrity of neighborhoods has fostered racial segregation in the metropolis. The growing gap between city needs and state and especially federal help has darkened the prospects of most cities of checking, much less reversing, the downward spiral of physical deterioration, economic decline, and racial conflict.

The actions of the states and the national government have also contributed to the fragmentation of the metropolitan political system. Almost everywhere, the suburban quest for separation and political autonomy has received powerful assistance from the state capital. In some states, metropolitan districts were created which relieved suburbs from dependence on city services. In others, the state has used its power over local government to prohibit cities from denying their utility services as a means of forcing annexation. In response to suburban demands for protection from the imperialist designs of city hall, most state legislatures erected formidable barriers against annexation by the central cities. The common state-house alliance between suburban and rural Republicans has, however, produced or maintained state laws which erect few barriers against the incorporation of suburban municipalities and has facilitated defensive incorporation of areas threatened by annexation into the central city. Moreover, most state and federal aid programs have accepted the fragmented metropolis as given, thus reinforcing decentralization and the separation of city and suburb. By helping the suburbs to overcome some of the deficiencies of small size and limited resources, assistance from the state capitals and Washington has played an important role in permitting the decentralized system to flourish.

Finally, most of the massive state and federal investments in metropolitan areas have not been guided by any over-all strategies. Instead, highway plans, the construction of post offices, the location of military installations, and the development of airports have either followed the marketplace, the perspectives of a particular agency, or the desires of a powerful member of Congress. As a result, a tremendous opportunity has been lost to guide urban development through the planned and coordinated investment of state and federal resources in public facilities.

To a considerable degree, the pattern of state and federal policy in the metropolis reflects political realities. Functional interests and their clienteles usually prevail in the dispersed political systems found in Washington and most of the state capitals. Highway engineers traditionally have located new roads to serve traffic needs rather than to shape urban development along the lines desired by planners. Private real estate interests have had a great deal more to say about priorities in urban renewal than poor people who have the most pressing needs for shelter, but the least political sophistication. Furthermore, the steady movement to the suburbs has produced a substantial shift in the locus of political influence in a society where legislative power is rooted in geographic constituencies. The revolution in legislative apportionment during the 1960s has served to bolster the forces of suburbia in the state legislatures and Congress. Meanwhile, the beleaguered cities with their static or declining populations find their influence in these bodies declining at the same time that their problems are intensifying. The conflicts within the city between the poor, and the downtown business interests and between the blacks and the working-class whites further weaken the city in the political arenas of state and nation.

New Directions

Despite these strong political and policy trends, many of the newer state and federal programs and innovative proposals developed during the past several years offer promise of new directions in the metropolis. Several states have made it more difficult for suburbs to incorporate, while a large number have taken action to facilitate the creation of metropolitan planning agencies and regional councils of local officials. In 1969,

Michigan's governor proposed a uniform state-wide property tax for education, a move which if successful would remove city-suburban and other intermunicipal differentiations in per-pupil expenditures. A few years earlier, the New York legislature created a state Urban Development Corporation, empowered to supercede local land-use and building codes in the process of implementing broad scale development plans in urban areas. Across the Hudson River in New Jersey, state and local government have joined hands in an ambitious effort to develop cooperatively the Hackensack meadowlands, a vast underdeveloped area within fifteen minutes of the heart of the New York region.

Much of the recent emphasis in federal urban policy has been on improving planning, coordination, and local participation in the development and implementation of federally assisted programs in the metropolis. During the 1950s, federal funds became more readily available for urban renewal planning, local planning, and metropolitan planning. With the Highway Act of 1962 and the Urban Mass Transportation Act of 1964, Washington conditioned federal highway and transit assistance in metropolitan areas to the development of comprehensive area-wide transportation and land-use plans. Under the Demonstration Cities and Metropolitan Development Act of 1966 and subsequent administrative elaborations, all applications for federal aid for open spaces, hospitals, airports, libraries, water supply, sewage treatment, highways, mass transport, and similar programs must be reviewed for consistency with metropolitan plans and priorities by a regional agency on which the local governments of the area are represented. These new federal requirements have stimulated the establishment of a large number of metropolitan planning agencies and regional councils of local officials, as well as the preparation of metropolitan development plans and increased interaction among the officials of the many governments of the typical metropolitan area.

Another major new direction at both the state and federal levels has been the quest for greater coordination of local programs. A number of states have created agencies like New Jersey's Department of Community Affairs and enhanced the urban role and resources of state planning agencies. In Washington, the transformation in 1965 of the Housing and Home Finance Agency into the Department of Housing and Urban Development (HUD) with Cabinet rank symbolized the growth of the federal commitment to a coordinated attack on urban problems. Despite the creation of HUD, however, urban responsibilities remain scattered among a large number of agencies: health in the Department of Health Education and Welfare (HEW), urban transit and highways in the Department of Transportation, antipoverty programs in the Office of Economic Opportunity, and manpower training in the Department of Labor, to name only a few of the more important urban programs falling outside HUD's sphere of responsibilities. Moreover, as pointed out in the previous chapter, in the years since HUD's creation, the problems of coordinated federal urban efforts multiplied as a result of proliferation of new programs during the Great Society era. In an attempt to improve coordination, as well as to develop a national urban policy to guide federal efforts in the metropolis, President Nixon in 1970 created a Domestic Council as an internal counterpart to the National Security Council.

As the 1970s began, however, these new directions appeared to be inadequate to the task of rationalizing metropolitan growth, revitalizing the cities, and overhauling the cumbersome governmental structure of the metropolis. Rapid population growth centered in the suburbs continues to shape the future while local, state, and federal officials debate plans which often are outdated before they can be implemented. The new federal planning requirements have not come to grips with the underlying racial issues in the metropolis since they typically fail to deal with segregated education and housing. Because state legislators and congressmen reflect the desires of most of their constituents to maintain the governmental status quo in the metropolis, neither Washington nor the states have sought very energetically to foster the consolidation of local governments or the creation of general purpose metropolitan governments. By focusing on the problems of the poor and providing for participation by the local community, new federal programs in the city such as Model Cities have overcome some of the deficiencies of many past efforts. But they are yet to be financed at anything approaching the necessary scale by a society which continues to value space exploration and the development of a supersonic jetliner more highly than it values removing the corrosive consequences of poverty and racism in its urban centers.

SELECTED BIBLIOGRAPHY

Advisory Commission on Intergovernmental Relations, *Urban America and the Federal System* (Washington: U.S. Government Printing Office, 1969). A comprehensive review of urban and metropolitan problems based on a decade of research and recommendations by the Commission.

Banfield, Edward C., *The Unheavenly City* (Boston: Little, Brown and Company, 1970). An iconoclastic examination of urban problems and the role of government in their resolution.

Bollens, John C. and Henry J. Schmand, *The Metropolis: Its People, Politics, and Economic Life* (New York: Harper and Row, 1970). A detailed examination of the economic, social, and political systems of the metropolitan area.

Clark, Kenneth B., *Dark Ghetto: Dilemmas of Social Power* (New York: Harper and Row, 1965). A penetrating analysis by one of America's most distinguished social scientists.

Danielson, Michael N., *Federal-Metropolitan Politics and the Commuter Crisis* (New York: Columbia University Press, 1965). A study of transportation problems that emphasizes the interaction of the several governmental authorities acting within any metropolitan area.

Martin, Roscoe C., *The Cities and the Federal System* (New York: Atherton Press, 1965). A thorough analysis of direct federal-city relationships established to administer programs dealing with metropolitan problems.

National Advisory Commission on Civil Disorders, *Report* (Washington: U.S. Government Printing Office, 1968). The Kerner Commission report, which examines the urban riots of the 1960s and their causes.

Willbern, York, *The Withering Away of the City* (University, Ala.: University of Alabama Press, 1964). An excellent introduction to the problems of governance of the American metropolis.

Footnotes

[1] The Census Bureau defines a "standard metropolitan statistical area" as a county or two or more adjacent counties that contain at least one city of 50,000. Other counties than the one or ones in which such a city is located are included in such a standard metropolitan area if they are essentially metropolitan in character and socially and economically integrated with the central city. There were 233 SMSAs in 1968.

[2] *The Withering Away of the City* (University, Ala.: University of Alabama Press, 1964), pp. 9–10.

[3] Leo F. Schnore, *The Urban Scene* (New York: The Free Press, 1965), pp. 114–133.

[4] The National Commission on Civil Disorders, *Report* (Washington: U.S. Government Printing Office, 1968), pp. 118–120.

[5] See *ibid.*

[6] Charles E. Silberman, "The City and the 'Negro,'" *Fortune*, March 1962, pp. 88–89.

[7] The National Commission on Civil Disorders, *Report,* p. 91.

[8] Robert C. Wood, *Suburbia* (Boston: Houghton Mifflin, 1959), p. 83.

Part III The Processes of Politics

Politics of 70s to Skip Labels, Concentrate on Domestic Peace

By Richard Harwood

For more than 100 years, the American political system has been dominated by two amorphous institutions—the Republican and Democratic parties. The reason for this continuity has been that each new generation of Americans has inherited its politics as it has inherited its religion. Party loyalties have been passed on from fathers to sons.

Now and then there have been upheavals that have turned masses of Republicans into Democrats and vice versa. That happened in the Great Depression 40 years ago, and the Democrats have been the majority party ever since. The elections of 1968 did not change that fact.

It is thus both foolish and premature to write the obituary of the Democratic Party, no matter how disorganized and financially destitute it may appear at the top. Whether it survives in the 1970s as the majority party, however, is quite another matter.

The American electorate, former Census Director Richard Scammon keeps telling us, is "up for grabs." Party loyalties have been badly shaken in the last few years.

This volatility is especially pronounced among younger voters; in 1968 nearly two thirds of the voters under 30 split their tickets. It was the young who fueled the Wallace candidacy, with people under 30 giving him more support outside the South than any other age group. And it was the young, of course, who generated the splinter McCarthy movement in the primaries of 1968.

These younger voters will become increasingly important in the politics of the 1970s as the post-World War II baby crop comes of age; there are 43 million in the 20-to-34 age group today and there will be 58 million by 1980. They will be getting married, having children, buying houses and moving to the suburbs.

That is why Lawrence O'Brien, the new Democratic national chairman, is insisting that his party's future lies in suburbia and with the young. That is why the Republicans have identified the same targets for the 1970s.

They begin the competition of this new decade with no illusions on either side. The Democrats are well aware of the fragility of their "majority" status.

For their part, the Republicans are well aware, despite all the myths, that they are not going to become the majority party in the 1970s simply because people are moving to the suburbs. Democratic majorities in the suburbs of San Francisco, St. Louis, Buffalo, Pittsburgh, Boston and other cities are substantial and seem to be growing.

In dealing now with the political incoherency of the last few years, the parties are finding that the old formulas and cliches have lost their usefulness. The Democrats know that the "labor vote" has slipped out of their pockets; Hubert Humphrey got only about half of it in 1968. The Republicans know that the station wagon set that drove around with all those "I Like Ike" stickers in the 1950s, is driving around today in Volkswagens adorned with peace decals.

They believe, too, that what this faithless and turbulent electorate wants from government and from its politicians is not slogans but problem-solving and domestic tranquillity.

If that view is correct, the politics of the 1970s will be based less and less on party labels and party loyalties and more and more on strong personalities selling believable programs for the pacification of American life.

This is not a comfortable prospect for the political generation that came of age in the 1930s and 1940s—the elders of the ADA and Americans for Constitutional Action. But the unhappy truth is that their day is probably over and the parties will adjust to this fact or be replaced in the years ahead by more relevant political institutions.

© 1970 by The Washington Post. Reprinted by permission.

Chapter 6 The Party System

NATURE AND FUNCTION OF PARTY

A political party is an organization that attempts to acquire and maintain control of government. Political scientists distinguish a party from an interest group by the inclusiveness of the party's purposes and the basic means it uses to attain them. An interest group tries to influence a single policy or a set of public policies. To do so, it may or may not enter into electoral campaigns. In contrast, a party has as its goal not only influencing a wide range of public policies but also directing those policies through its own personnel. Thus, to democratically oriented parties, winning elections is vital in accomplishing these ends.

Ideally, political parties perform certain functions in a democracy. From the point of view of aspirants for public office, the party mobilizes electoral support, organizes a government if successful at the polls, and helps recruit new personnel to carry out these tasks. From the point of view of the citizen, the party supplies information about the nature of existing political problems, clarifies and simplifies alternatives, and offers a choice among solutions. In addition, the party serves as a continuing body on whom responsibility for achievements and failures may be placed and on whose future candidates rewards and punishments may be bestowed at the next election.

It takes only a passing acquaintance with the American scene to realize that political parties in the United States have not always performed each of these functions in a creditable manner. Nevertheless, as Lord Bryce[1] observed, "the spirit and force of party has in America been as essential to the action of the machinery of government as steam is to a locomotive engine." That spirit and force has, over the years, demonstrated three principal characteristics. First, America has a two-party system at the national level. Since the 1790s, there have almost always been two, and only two, serious contestants for control of the national government. Second, the parties appear to agree on many fundamentals of political philosophy and do not present radically different programs to the voters. Third, each of the two national parties is decentralized. Party policy is more apt to be the result of bargaining among leaders at many levels than of decisions made at the top of a formal hierarchy.

THE AMERICAN TWO-PARTY SYSTEM

The Attitude of the Framers toward Parties

The Constitution is entirely silent about political parties and about such all-important matters as presidential nominating conventions, direct primaries, caucuses, and other aspects of party machinery and procedure. Since political parties (though not in the fully modern sense) were known in 1787, these were probably deliberate omissions. There is no record of debate on party government in the Constitutional Convention, but George Washington apparently expressed the attitude of many of the Founding Fathers at the end of his Presidency when he warned against the "baneful effects of the spirit of party." It is possible that some members of the Philadelphia convention realized that the development of political parties in American government was inevitable. James Madison seemed to sense this in *The Federalist,* Number 10, originally published in November 1787. He wrote:

> A landed interest, a manufacturing interest, a mercantile interest, a monied interest, with many lesser interests, grow up of necessity in civilized nations, and divide them into different classes, actuated by different sentiments and views. The regulation of these various and interfering interests forms the principal task of modern legislation, and involves the spirit of party and faction in the necessary and ordinary operations of government.

Whatever the thoughts and wishes of the people at the Philadelphia convention, by the beginning of Washington's second administration there were already two political parties operating. Washington had gradually come under the influence of Alexander Hamilton and consistently sided with him against Thomas Jefferson in controversies over public policy. What may have remained a simple factional squabble within a ruling clique grew into the makings of a party battle when Thomas Jefferson and James Madison worked with members of Congress and local political leaders in southern and middle Atlantic states to create a coalition of small property owners and yeoman farmers to oppose Hamilton's policies. In 1793, Jefferson resigned from Washington's Cabinet, and in a few years the Republicans—or the Democracy or Mobocracy, as Hamilton's followers preferred to call the Jeffersonians—were a full-fledged political party, challenging the Administration's pro-British foreign policy and conservative domestic economic policy.

During this period, the followers of Washington and Hamilton preempted for themselves the name of Federalists, although the Jeffersonian ranks included many of those—including James Madison—who only a few years earlier had led what had then been the Federalist cause against the Antifederalists in the fight for adoption of the Constitution. The new Federalists, like the old, were predominantly an elite group, men of wealth and substance; but in contrast to their imaginative and energetic campaign of

1787 and 1788, they were curiously negligent about forming local party organizations that could mount an effective counter-appeal to the growing electorate. Out of touch with the newly enfranchised groups and lacking the machinery to mobilize the conservative vote, the Federalists were routed in the election of 1800 and by 1816 had ceased to exist as a party. The lesson of their disaster was not lost, however. Leaders of all succeeding parties have realized that to win office one must win votes; and to win votes one must have an effective organization at every electoral level.

After the demise of the Federalists the nation experienced a short period of one-party rule. Still, while the old Jeffersonian party tried to encompass all points of political view, it could not accommodate every political, economic, and social interest. By the mid-1820s there were two warring factions within the party, the Democratic Republicans and the National Republicans. The split grew until by 1840 the two factions, now called Democrats and Whigs, had become coalitions of economic and geographic interests and had taken on the character of national parties.

Through the mid-1850s the two parties fought on almost even terms, but with the death of old Whig leaders such as Henry Clay and Daniel Webster and the worsening of the crises over slavery, the Whig coalition between eastern capital and southern planters disintegrated. A number of third parties were agitating for national status, but many of the Whig rank and file as well as a large contingent of liberal Democrats found the new Republican party most attractive. In 1856, the Republicans rallied behind General John C. Fremont and made a respectable showing in the presidential campaign. In 1860, their candidate Abraham Lincoln carried only a minority of the popular vote but won a solid majority in the Electoral College. Not since that election has a third party even come close to capturing the White House; and only in 1912, when the progressive wing of the Republican party broke from the regulars to nominate Theodore Roosevelt as the Bull Moose candidate, has a third party polled as many votes as the loser of the major parties. Yet third parties have continued to have a voice in American politics. Henry Wallace in 1948 and George Wallace in 1968 offered the voters additional alternatives; and both before and after the 1968 election some militant black leaders spoke of establishing a black man's party at the national level.

Why Two Parties?

One of the questions that has most puzzled foreign observers of American politics is why the United States has a two-party rather than a multiparty system. After all, most modern democracies. France, Italy, Belgium, Holland, and Switzerland, for example, have a multiparty system, and even England and Canada have at times in this century had a three-party system. V. O. Key,[2] certainly one of the most astute students of American parties, concluded that there is no fully satisfactory answer. A number of forces have operated together to encourage a two-party system.

First, there have been historical factors. The colonists brought a two-party tradition with them. It is easy to exaggerate this influence, since England in the eighteenth century did not have a party system in the modern sense, yet the factional divisions between Whigs and Tories probably did have some effect on colonial ideas of party politics. After independence, there was the division between Federalists and Antifederalists over the adoption of the Constitution; then a few years later came the split between the Federalists in power and the Jeffersonians out of power. This latter division occurred at a time when the electorate was small and the social and economic structure of the country relatively uncomplex. The basic appeals to two different sets of social groups, by the Federalists to the mercantile class, men of means and substance, and by the Jeffersonians first to yeoman farmers and small property holders and later also to the small but rapidly growing working classes in the cities, set a pattern that, except for the period 1801–1824, has to a large extent been continued to the present day.

Institutional factors have also played a role. First was the Founding Fathers' choice of a presidential rather than a parliamentary form of democratic government. It is easier for a majority of multiparty representatives in a legislature to compromise their differences and pick a Prime Minister than it is for the masses of voters, owing allegiance to three or more parties, to select a President. Moreover, the specific language of the American Constitution requiring majority agreement, whether the President is chosen by the Electoral College or by the House of Representatives, has provided a further force limiting the number of presidential candidates and thus national political parties. The election of single chief executive at state and local levels of government has further served to encourage would-be factions to unite behind a single candidate and aim for that golden target, a majority vote.

Another institutional arrangement that has operated to foster a two-party system is the use of single-member districts for the election of members of Congress. In a single-member district only one party can win an election, and under such circumstances third parties are discouraged unless they can achieve a voting strength comparable to that of the established major parties. The Constitution does not require the election of members of the House of Representatives from single-member districts, but throughout most of American history Congress has required by law the use of the district system. Moreover, the election of senators is in effect a single-member district undertaking. Many state legislatures, however, utilize multimember districts, and there is no evidence that their use weakens the two-party system.[3]

Social factors probably have been more important than electoral arrangements in maintaining a two-party system. Where a society is beset by cleavages that follow geographic, socio-economic, ethnic, or religious lines, conditions are ripe for a multiparty system. Where there is relatively little class consciousness, and political divisions cut across religious, ethnic, geographical, and socio-economic lines, a two-party system has a far better chance of taking firm root. In such a situation, "the stakes of politics are smaller, and the kinds of tolerance, compromise, and concession necessary for a two-party system's majoritarian parties can prevail."[4]

In discussing class consciousness and other societal divisions, we are speaking only in relative terms. As we saw in Chapter 1, there is class consciousness in the United States, and there are societal divisions along economic, ethnic, geographic, religious, and, most important, racial lines. Each of the two major parties does tend to focus its appeals in considerable part on certain groups; and, as Chapter 10 will indicate, these groups often respond positively to these appeals. The point to be stressed, however, is that when compared to many countries, France and Italy, for example, class and other social divisions among whites in the United States are relatively indistinct and do not cut deeply into the vitals of the dominant society. As long as blacks and other racial minorities were more or less politically passive, caste differences imposed stresses on the governmental system that remained within limits that were tolerable to the system itself, although the pain to minorities was considerable. Whether the system can continue to bear these strains in the face of an ongoing black revolution depends in part on the government's ability to offer minority groups a real hope for a fair share of American abundance.

Because of their appreciation of the relative psychological homogeneity of the white electorate, leaders of both parties have tried to appeal to a wide spectrum of interests. Each party may gather its basic strength from particular ethnic, economic, or social groups, but each usually tries to gain support from all segments of society. It has been a rare platform that has not offered something to all parts of white society and even, although commonly on a smaller scale, to politically important parts of the black community as well. But the growing salience of racial cleavages and increasing black impatience at unfulfilled promises are complicating the tasks of building a biracial coalition. In fact in 1968 the Republican party followed a so-called southern strategy, which gave up any hope of winning over the black vote or any appreciable share of the liberal white votes of the northeast. Instead, the Republicans concentrated on capturing the South and picking up enough votes from traditional Republicans and worried whites in the border states, the Midwest, and California to obtain a majority in the Electoral College.[5]

Consequences of the Two-party System

Because there are only two major parties, it is probable that in a national election one or the other will win not only the Presidency but also a majority of both houses of Congress. The peculiarities of the American electoral system make it possible, of course, for one party to gain the White House while the other wins a majority of seats in both houses of Congress. This, however, has happened only twice since 1848—in 1956 and again in 1968. It is far more likely that the minority party will obtain control of both houses of Congress in an off-year election than in a presidential election, as has in fact occurred in ten of the twenty-two off-year elections since 1884. Nevertheless, during 106 of the 183 years from 1789 to 1972, the same party has controlled the Presidency and both houses of Congress.

In facilitating control of the government by one party, the two-party system places almost irresistible pressure on party leaders to achieve that goal. To do so they must win a majority or close to a majority of the popular vote. This means that a party cannot concentrate on one interest to the exclusion of all others, nor can it depend solely on one segment of the country for victory. Thus, the two-party system tantalizes party leaders into forming coalitions. Typically, the Republican party in this century has brought together the financial interests of the Northeast, the farmers and small-town residents of the Midwest, and white collar workers and many professional men throughout the nation. More recently, Republicans have also focused their attention on the prosperous states in the Rocky Mountain and Pacific Coast regions. The Democrats, on the other hand, have historically united—at least for purposes of electing a President—the South, blue collar workers in urban areas across the country, a portion of white collar workers, small farmers in the Midwest and Far West, northern liberals, and the blacks of the metropolitan ghettos.

Exceptions to the Two-party System

Although the United States has basically had a two-party system at the national level, a pair of reservations must be made. First, for long intervals many states have had one-party systems. The South for almost a century after the Civil War was the most obvious example of a regional one-party system. After analyzing electoral behavior in presidential, senatorial, and gubernatorial campaigns from 1914 to 1954, Austin Ranney and Will-moore Kendall[6] found that in only twenty-six of the then forty-eight states during this forty-year period did the minority party win 25 percent or more of these contests. On the basis of elections from 1946 to 1966, Duane Lockard[7] classifies twenty states as basically one party dominant and another ten as having only weak party competition.

Thus when we say the United States has a two-party system, we must be careful not to imply that the two parties compete effectively in each state. Indeed, as Chapter 8 will indicate, one-party domination of congressional districts, either because of deliberate rigging of district lines or because of the voting habits of the local population, is such that in less than half of the 435 districts can the election of congressmen be called serious two-party contests. Nevertheless, the trend in American politics has seemed to be away from one-party monopoly in national elections and, though less markedly, in state and local campaigns as well. As recent presidential elections have shown, it would be the height of folly for a Democratic candidate to assume that the South was solidly behind him or a Republican to act as though New England or the Midwest was in his camp.

The second reservation that must be made about the two-party system is that third parties have been a constant part of the American political scene. Freesoilers, Green-backers, Populists, Farmer-Laborites, Prohibitionists, Bull Moosers, Socialists, Dixiecrats, Progressives, and even Communists have been frequent contestants for state and national office. As we have already seen, however, no third party, with the possible exception of Theodore Roosevelt's Bull Moose group in 1912, has even come close to winning the Presidency since the Republicans did it in 1860. On the other hand, third parties, such as the Progressives in Wisconsin and the Non-Partisan League in the Dakotas, have often been influential in state politics and have sent representatives and occasionally senators to Washington.

Despite their short lifespans and the restriction of their tangible political power to single states or small geographic areas, third parties have often made important con-tributions to public policy. Many of them have won enough support among the voters to threaten the major parties with the possibility that they might gain a balance of power. This situation has sometimes forced the major parties to respond to pressures they would have preferred to ignore. Often the third party has taken a more decisive and more progressive stand on issues than has either of the major parties. But whenever it has appeared that any large number of voters were being attracted to such a party, sooner or later one (or both) of the major parties has been sufficiently impressed by its gains to take over at least a part of the third party's program, thus cutting the ground from beneath it. For example, the unexpectedly small vote polled by Henry A. Wallace's Progressive party in 1948 is in part explained by the extent to which the Democratic party under President Truman moved to the left on such issues as civil rights and labor-management relations to meet the threat offered by the new third party. So too in 1968,

Richard Nixon undercut some of George Wallace's support by implying that a Republican administration would slow down the push for black civil rights. Furthermore, once in the White House President Nixon continued to erode Wallace's power by means of lax enforcement of civil right laws and by nominating for the Supreme Court a pair of southern lawyers who had been staunch segregationists.

AMERICAN PARTIES AND IDEOLOGY

A second characteristic of the American party system is that the two major parties usually appear to differ slightly if at all in their basic ideology and in their general programs, when, indeed, a coherent program can be discerned in party platforms. American parties offer the voters a choice between politicians, but rarely do they present a clear-cut choice between specific political programs.

Two preliminary remarks must be made here. It is easy to exaggerate the ideological divisions among European parties, at least among those that have a chance of playing a major role in running the government. In England, for instance, the Labour party is something more than a vehicle for the labor unions and something less than a true Socialist party; the Conservative party is a good deal more than a party of business or of laissez-faire capitalism. Many contemporary issues provoke little or no disagreement between them. Second, the two parties in the United States do differ in their general policy orientations, though, of course, these differences cannot be compared to those between Fascists and Communists. The popular impression of the Democrats as the more liberal and the Republicans as the more conservative party is essentially accurate, although there are liberals and conservatives in each party. A study of the attitudes of delegates to the two national conventions—a group that includes senators, congressmen, governors, state and county chairmen, and petty party officials, as well as private citizens—showed that these leaders displayed marked differences in their respective attitudes toward a whole series of political problems in the fields of civil rights, governmental regulation of the economy, taxation, public ownership of natural resources, and foreign policy. As a group, the Democrats favored more governmental activity to protect the civil rights of minority groups, more governmental regulation of business, less regulation of labor, more public ownership of natural resources, higher taxes on business and upper income groups, and more of an internationalist orientation toward foreign policy than did Republican leaders.[8]

A 1968 survey of 200 administrative assistants of senators and congressmen produced similar results. As the following table shows, Democratic staff members were much more favorably disposed toward use of federal power in general and more specifically to increase medical care for the aged, improve education, control the economy, and desegregate public schools. In addition, Democrats were far more likely to find nothing wrong with racial intermarriage and to approve both recent Supreme Court decisions and the over-all way the Justices have been performing their governmental functions. As a whole, even southern Democrats tended to be more liberal than Republicans on most of these issues, although because of the small size of the groups involved only the differences between Republicans and southern Democrats on the broad issue of federal power and the specific policy of increased medicare are statistically significant.

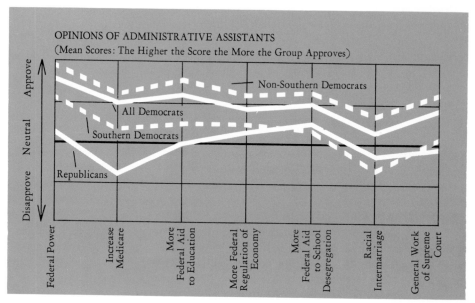

Source: Walter F. Murphy and Joseph Tanenhaus, *Public Opinion and the American Supreme Court* (forthcoming).
(Differences between All Democrats and Republicans are significant at the .005 level.)

The difference in approach between the two parties in America can also be gauged by comparing the concepts of the office of the Presidency held by Democratic Presidents Wilson, Franklin Roosevelt, Truman, Kennedy, and Johnson, with those of nearly all the Republican incumbents of this century. The Republican exception, Theodore Roosevelt, took a grand view of his office, as did each of the Democrats. For these men, the Presidency was a position of dynamic power, a post to control the executive bureaucracy, to push social and economic legislation through Congress, and to mold public opinion to accept, even to demand, such governmental action. For Taft, Harding, Coolidge, Hoover, Eisenhower, and even to some extent Nixon in domestic affairs, the Presidency was more a place for repose than for energetic action.

Another indication that there is a meaningful difference between the two parties is in their voting records in Congress. Party affiliation, Key[9] concluded, "appears to be the strongest and most persistent factor associated with the actions of Senators and Representatives." Roll call votes indicate that party unanimity in Congress is rare, but that party cohesion is not, as the following table indicates.

When these observations are made, it is apparent that the image that the two major parties present to the voters is more apt to differ in matters of style and policy detail than on fundamental issues of political philosophy. As already noted, both parties are likely to appeal to citizens of all social classes and geographical areas. Both accept the basic, though vague, principles of democratic government as embodied in the American Constitution. Both reject socialism and endorse a free enterprise system, though one modified by a degree of governmental regulation.

PARTY UNITY[a] SCOREBOARD

	Total roll calls	Party unity roll calls	Percent of total
1969			
Both chambers	422	144	34
Senate	245	89	36
House	177	55	31
1968			
Both chambers	514	172	33
Senate	281	90	32
House	233	82	35
1967			
Both chambers	560	198	35
Senate	315	109	35
House	245	89	36
1966			
Both chambers	428	198	46
Senate	235	118	50
House	193	80	41
1965			
Both chambers	459	213	46
Senate	258	108	42
House	201	105	52
1964			
Both chambers	418	171	41
Senate	305	109	36
House	113	62	55
1963			
Both chambers	348	166	48
Senate	229	108	47
House	119	58	49
1962			
Both chambers	348	149	43
Senate	224	92	41
House	124	57	46

[a] *"Party Unity" role calls are those on which a majority of voting Democrats oppose a majority of voting Republicans. It should be noted that this is only one of many possible indexes of party cohesiveness in Congress.*
SOURCE: Congressional Quarterly Weekly Report, *April 3, 1964, p. 650; October 25, 1968, p. 2934; and January 16, 1970, p. 172.*

Why Few Ideological Differences?

Part of the explanation of the lack of fundamental differences between the major parties can be traced to America's having a revered written Constitution that broadly defines the goals and so restricts the legitimate means that political parties may advocate. From time to time there have been extremist groups of abolitionists or segregationists, of radicals from the right or from the left who have attacked the Constitution, but these groups have been well outside the mainstream of American politics.[10]

Moreover, the United States has lacked a class consciousness of the sort that has divided many European nations. Without such class antagonism, development of ideological parties becomes very difficult. An appeal in this country pitched only to blue collar workers might well fall on uncomprehending if not deaf ears, as members of the Students for a Democratic Society discovered when they moved off the campuses and tried to "radicalize" factory workers. Whether this relative lack of a class struggle can be traced to the absence of a feudal tradition in American history, the comparative prosperity of the American economy, the existence of a frontier to absorb dissident elements, ideals of egalitarianism, the political castration of blacks, or to some combination of these and other factors, the dominant political standards of American society have been those of the white middle class. No nationally oriented party can wander very far from these standards without risking disastrous defeat. Even a national black party would have to face up to the fact that while blacks form a majority of many rural southern counties and northern central cities, in the country as a whole they are a small minority.

Furthermore, the two-party system encourages formation of coalitions. As we have seen, to control the national government party leaders must make a broad appeal. Given the diversity of background, outlooks, aspirations, and loyalties of the American people, it has been difficult, even in times of severe crisis, to organize a majority coalition behind a lucid, specific, and all-encompassing party program. An easier alternative for national party leaders is a vaguely worded statement of ultimate goals–glowing allusions to "The Great Society," for example, or to "binding up the nation's wounds"–with much hedging on specific proposals to achieve these noble purposes. Even the New Deal, which was the closest thing to a comprehensive governmental program the United States has ever had, was a combination of uncoordinated and at times conflicting individual policies, geared as much to satisfying each of the diverse groups in Roosevelt's grand coalition as to overcoming the depression through coherent, systematic governmental action.

An additional factor militating against ideological and programmatic parties is the indifference of many Americans to politics. In 1953, when debate in Congress and in the press over Senator John Bricker's proposed constitutional amendment to limit the President's treaty-making power was at its height, the Gallup poll reported that 81 percent of the persons interviewed disclaimed knowing anything about the proposal. In addition, public opinion may be so inchoate as to defy prediction of how it will respond to a given policy. Just before the 1968 election, after several years of intense debate on American policy in Vienam, the Survey Research Center of the University of Michigan found the following distribution of opinion about what the United States should do:

Pull out of Vietnam entirely	19.5%
Keep our soldiers in Vietnam but try to end the fighting	36.7

Take a stronger stand even if it means invading North Vietnam	33.5
Other	3.3
Don't know, no answer	7.0
Total number = 1557	100.0%

Finally, opinion where it does exist may be internally contradictory. The same people who disapprove of big government in Washington and want to cut federal spending may favor an antiballistic missile system, extended federal loyalty-security programs, increased aid to veterans, and an expanded network of jet ports.

Since available evidence, though not conclusive, indicates that the bulk of American voters tend to cluster just to the right or left of the political center, the magic goal of winning 50.1 percent of the electorate has pulled party leaders into aiming in large part for the same voters and then into making similar appeals. Barry Goldwater's debacle in 1964 stands as a warning to candidates for national office of the electoral consequences of even appearing to desert the middle of the road.

DECENTRALIZATION OF AMERICAN POLITICAL PARTIES

The third salient characteristic of the American party system is the decentralized organization of both major parties. Schattschneider[11] goes so far as to label decentralization as "the most important single characteristic" of the party system in the United States. Conventional wisdom often pictures the parties as having a pyramidal structure, with the membership at the base and the President or opposition leader at the apex and a chain of command running from top to bottom. This analogy, as we saw in Chapter 4, is picturesque but very misleading. First, it is difficult to speak of membership in either American political party. Membership does not involve paying dues or subscribing to any particular set of doctrines. In fact party membership is frequently only a state of mind—really about party identification —since many people who call themselves Democrats or Republicans never bother to vote, though voting in a primary is the usual way of asserting membership. In most states a citizen who votes in the primary of one party is barred from voting in the primary of another for a period of several months or years; but nothing can prevent that citizen from voting for the other party's candidates at the general election. In another group of states the primaries are "open." A citizen is legally free to change party allegiance and to vote in either primary. In fact, in the state of Washington it is possible for citizens to vote in both party primaries. And while both parties constantly solicit money from likely donors, neither even remotely hints that noncontributors are not welcome in the bosom of the party, at least on election day.

Second, party organization is complex and disorderly, with agencies of overlapping and conflicting jurisdiction. In addition, formal organization is frequently supplemented by an informal organization that wields the actual power within that segment of the party. For example, presidential candidates have typically put together personal staffs that usurp many of the campaigning functions of their respective national committees. As we have already seen, federalism, in providing independent bases of political power, also plays an important role in decentralizing American parties.

Party Machinery for Winning Elections

Generally speaking, party machinery, formal and informal, can be divided according to the two functions of winning elections and running the government. The basic unit in the American party corresponds to the basic unit of electoral administration, the precinct. Here the party organization may consist of one man, called a precinct captain or executive, or he may have a small staff of assistants, usually part-time volunteers. Historically, it was at this level that most of the personal contact between party officials and party constituencies occurred, though this is far less true today. Above the precinct in urban areas is the ward organization, again perhaps consisting of only a few people. In small towns and rural areas the unit above the precinct is the county committee. Its committeemen are usually the precinct captains, and its chairman, as Key[12] says, "may be a local political potentate of considerable significance." The 3000 or more county chairmen wield real power within each party organization.

One step above the county committee, at least on paper, is the state committee. Depending on local laws and customs, its members may be elected or hold their offices by virtue of their position in county organizations. The functions that state committees are supposed to perform vary widely from state to state, but they frequently include coordinating the campaign work of county committees, calling state party conventions to nominate candidates for office, and arranging the administrative details for primaries.

Much of the organization and operation of party machinery at the local and state level is prescribed by state law, while at the national level party machinery is strictly a matter of custom. The two parties, however, have established very similar patterns of organization. There are four main agencies—or agents—heading the national parties: the national convention, the national committee, the national chairman, and the national committee secretariat.

The national convention consists of some 1300 to 3000 delegates[13] from the fifty states and the federal territories who meet every four years to select the party's candidates for President and Vice President and to determine party policy through a platform in which a stand, forthright or evasive, is taken on the issues of the day. Apart from these functions, the national convention has little authority. It has nothing whatever to do with the nomination of the party's candidates for Congress, nor can it compel congressional candidates to pledge support to the party's platform.

National conventions have no authority of a continuous nature. During the four-year period between conventions a party is supposedly run by the national chairman and the national committee. The latter consists, in the case of the Democratic party, of 110 members—one man and one woman from each state, territory, and the District of Columbia. The Republican party has two men and one woman from each state plus one man and one woman from the District of Columbia, Guam, Puerto Rico, and the Virgin Islands, for a total of 158. Ordinarily, a national committee meets only on call by the chairman, and such calls are infrequent. Apart from offering advice and help during the campaign and meeting early in presidential years to determine the date and place of the national convention, a national committee more often than not exercises no further authority. The committee never actually runs the party, and it seldom determines party policy except in the sense of ratifying proposals laid before it by the chairman or party members holding public office. Individual members, known as national committeemen, however, frequently wield considerable power in their own states and within the federal government.

The national chairman is chosen by the national committee every four years following the nomination of the presidential and vice-presidential candidates. In practice the chairman is the personal choice of the presidential nominee and the committee merely ratifies the name suggested. The first and most important task confronting the new chairman is to organize and conduct the party's campaign for the Presidency. He is also active in the biennial congressional campaigns, but here he and the national committee share power and responsibility with the Senate and House campaign committees organized by the party groups in Congress. The national chairman's day-to-day duties are of a varying character, but are almost never concerned with the actual operation of the government itself unless he also holds a government post. He keeps in close touch with state and local party organizations, makes many speeches, and is engaged in an almost continuous effort to raise party funds. Seldom, if ever, does a national chairman become a "boss" in the sense that state and local chairmen sometimes do.

The vitality and effectiveness of the national party organization is in large measure affected by the caliber of the salaried secretariat that serves the national committee and the national chairman. In the main, this secretariat attracts little attention and its organization varies from time to time and party to party. Its functions are to write speeches for important party members, to supply research assistance, to help raise money, to keep track of political trends, to prepare publicity releases, to handle correspondence with state and local party agencies, and to engage in a great many housekeeping tasks whose successful performance affects party unity and strength in the next campaign.

Party Machinery for Running the Government

Party machinery for winning elections has little to do formally with running the government. County chairmen and other party officials may offer advice, however, on the distribution of patronage and frequently convey to office-holders constituents' requests for favors that may affect the formation or administration of important public policies. More formally, party influence makes itself felt through party organizations that parallel governmental machinery. Thus, each party has units inside Congress, such as a caucus, a steering (or policy) committee, and a floor leader to try to shape federal policy-making. The national chairman and the national committee have very little to do with the activity of party members in Congress. Any attempt by these people to exert pressure on congressmen is apt to be vigorously resisted. These agencies are supposed to be in close touch with the executive branch if the party controls the Presidency. But, even here, the President's Cabinet, his White House secretariat, or his informal advisers are more often the instruments through which party control of the administrative aspects of government is exercised.

The President, of course, is the chief of his party and in staffing his administration has responsibility not only to run the government efficiently but also to keep the party organization together by rewarding friends and punishing enemies. Although, as we shall discuss later, the President's control over party machinery is not necessarily as tight as one might think, his immediate access to mass media, the enormous prestige of his office, and his power over patronage do secure for him a position of party leadership, if he cares to use it. Like it or not, other party leaders have to live with the fact that the public at large usually identifies the President with his party, and the party's fate at the next election is heavily dependent on the public image of the President.

On the other hand the opposition party has no powerful, national leader around whom to rally. The titular leader of the minority party is the defeated presidential nominee, but his actual power position is ambiguous. The fact that he was rejected by the voters to some extent counterbalances the fact that he was chosen by the party for the country's highest office. As Adlai Stevenson,[14] twice titular leader of his party, commented:

> The titular leader has no clear and defined authority within his party. He has no party office, no staff, no funds, nor is there any system of consultation whereby he may be advised of party policy and through which he may help to shape that policy. There are no devices such as the British have developed through which he can communicate directly and responsibly with the leaders of the party in power.

Adding to the difficulties of the titular leader are the facts that the party leaders of the minority party who opposed his nomination are rarely persuaded of the error of their ways by having the electorate confirm their views, and new presidential hopefuls seldom see any point in helping to increase the prestige and powers of a prominent rival for the next nomination.

It this were all there was to the story, then the titular leader's position would be unambiguously impotent. But, as Stevenson himself admitted, the titular leader is generally looked on by press and public as the spokesman of his party, whether or not he deserves the accolade. This is true in great measure because there is rarely any other person who has a legitimate claim to speak for the party, if the titular leader asserts himself. Senators, congressmen, and governors represent interests that are too parochial, and new candidates have not yet received the mantle of nomination from a national convention. "Despite its ambiguity, perhaps even because of it," three close students[15] of the American party system have concluded, "the titular leadership has become a post that offers many opportunities for initiative, at least for a first time incumbent."

Federalism and Party Decentralization

The most important point about the decentralization of the American party system is that power within each party is diffused. There is little in the way of a chain of command from the top to the bottom of the party hierarchy, only many avenues of persuasion, of requests, demands, threats, and bargaining. Each of these is a two-way street, and often the traffic in demands and threats is heavier going up than down.

Federalism in the formal governmental structure of the nation increases the decentralization of power within the party system. There are approximately 90,000 units of government in the United States that are empowered to levy taxes and more than a half million elective political offices. An independent source of revenue or an elective office means that an independent power base may exist from which a party satrap can operate. The President cannot fire a mayor who refuses to support an urban renewal program on which the President's prestige depends. Nor can he dismiss a senator or representative who consistently attacks the administration's foreign policy or votes against administration bills. Each of these officials is elected by a local constituency and is legally responsible for his tenure of office only to that constituency. If he is sure of electoral support, he can thumb his nose at his colleagues, at the nation at large, or at any other governmental official or set of officials.

Even within the federal government, the President does not sit as a commander-in-chief of a united civilian army. As we have seen, Congress has been wary of centralizing power in the White House and usually stipulates that state and local officials will share in administering supposedly national programs. The man who actually spends federal money is often a political hybrid like the health officer described in Chapter 4. In addition, almost every congressman takes up a considerable part of his time—and his staff spends even more—talking to administrators about problems his constituents are experiencing. A congressman can apply more formal pressure in questioning agency heads or bureau chiefs during annual appropriations hearings or at special investigations. A federal bureaucrat who, even at the order of the President, tries to use his authority to build up a national party to compete with a congressman's local group is apt to find himself in difficulty when dealing, as he must, with Congress.

The key is that the President cannot always control Congress. And since the President cannot always control Congress he cannot always control his administrative subordinates. If caught in the middle of a power struggle between the White House and Capitol Hill, an administrator has to appear to cooperate with both. But to secure his own goals—which may be shared by neither Congress nor the President—he typically needs larger appropriations; and since Congress controls the purse, the bureaucrat frequently bargains with congressmen by becoming the defender of their local constituencies more than the promoter of the President's national constituency.

Party Discipline: The Local Machine

Decentralization, like two-party competition, may stop at the state and local level. There discipline may sometimes be strict and real power centered in the hands of one man or a small group of men. The literature and folklore on colorful, and not always honest, city and county bosses is as enormous as it is fascinating. The fragmented power structure of the national parties actually assists these people in running their machines. Decentralization of government and party power means local control and, as Lockard[16] says, "plays into the hands of the boss . . . he has contact with all the elements of the party system, but he usually is beyond the authority of any higher echelon of the party. He has and uses the weapons of discipline to keep control over his organization, but he is usually free of effective control or discipline from above."

Many eulogies have been recited at the supposed graveside of the local boss and his machine, but both of them seem able to survive the funeral and to enjoy the obituaries. Yet it is also true that increased prosperity, the spread of civil service, and wider assumption by government agencies of the social welfare functions that party officials once exercised to keep the poor immigrants loyal have cut into the number and efficiency of bosses.

Political machines, however, are still with us—now generally headed by "leaders" rather than bosses—and may, as the Byrd organization in Virginia did for so many years, bring all agencies of a state government under its taut discipline.

REFORM OF THE PARTY SYSTEM

At the turn of the century the American party system was the principal target for political reformers. Their goal was to curb the power of the party politician. To accomplish this, they fought, in some localities, for nonpartisan elections in which the party affiliation of candidates would not be labeled on the ballot. In other areas they fought for primary elections to take the power of nominating candidates away from party leaders. The party system is still the target of political reformers, but ironically the goal is now to strengthen party leadership, to centralize power within the parties, and to shore up party discipline. The over-all objective of the newer critics is to make the parties more responsive to the popular will and more responsible for the behavior of their elected candidates.

Critics of the Present System

The decentralized, compromise character of the national parties has been much criticized on the ground that such parties fail to fulfill two of the primary functions of a democracy. First, they do not present the voters with a clear choice on the really important public issues. Indeed, they often do not even discuss the really important issues. There is, James M. Burns[17] charges, "a vast boredom" in America with party politics. "Because it has failed to engage itself with the problems that dog us during our working days and haunt our dreams at night, politics has not engaged the best of us, or at least the best in us."

The second criticism of the American party system is that its diffusion of power causes a diffusion of responsibility. Because no one man or one committee or one convention can set party policy, no man or committee or convention can be held responsible. Some of these critics argue that we now have a four-party rather than a two-party system, with the Democrats and Republicans each having a congressional party and a presidential party. The parties are not able to effect consistent governmental policies and the voters are unable to hold either party, as a party, responsible for the action or inaction of its members while in office.

This criticism was eloquently voiced more than twenty years ago by a Committee on Political Parties set up by the American Political Science Association. In its report, "Toward a More Responsible Two-Party System," the committee[18] stated its dissatisfaction with the present party system:

> Historical and other factors have caused the American two-party system to operate as two loose associations of state and local organizations, with very little national machinery and very little national cohesion. As a result, either major party, when in power, is ill-equipped to organize its members in the legislative and the executive branches into a government held together and guided by the party program. Party responsibility at the polls thus tends to vanish. This is a very serious matter, for it affects the very heartbeat of American democracy. It also poses grave problems of

domestic and foreign policy in an era when it is no longer safe for the nation to deal piecemeal with issues that can be disposed of only on the basis of coherent programs.

Defenders of the Present System

On the other hand, many political scientists have defended the existing party system. For example, Pendleton Herring has developed the thesis that a democratic society can survive only where there is a constant reconciliation of conflicting economic and social interests. Herring argues that politicians perform an essential social role by acting as mediators, and he also defends the political party because of the way in which it appeals to a wide variety of groups and wins their support by offering something to each." The accomplishment of party government," Herring[19] says, "lies in its demonstrated ability for reducing warring interests and conflicting classes to cooperative terms." This also means that when parties write their platforms, however inconsistent and evasive, they make it possible for people who have clashing interests to live together in peace. In other words, opposing groups that are contending for power must keep their quarrels within narrow limits. Once the lines of conflict are too clearly drawn, once the stakes in politics are set too high, there is danger that the defeated faction in an election will refuse to accept the result in a peaceful manner. It may conclude that too much has been lost and that it is better to oppose the result with force and violence than to permit the government to pursue policies antagonistic to its interests.

THE PATTERN OF THE PARTY SYSTEM

We deliberately chose the term "party system" for this chapter, because "to speak of a party *system* is to imply a patterned relationship among elements of a larger whole."[20] What we have described and analyzed here is a pattern of relationships, although that pattern is dynamic rather than static. The three main characteristics we have been discussing are all parts of a larger pattern. They are so interrelated that it is difficult to say which are causes and which are effects of the others, or how the consequences of each shape the consequences of the others.

A two-party system encourages efforts to form majorities and thereby coalitions. The relative absence of deep and antagonistic class cleavages discourages strong ideological or programmatic stands as does a deeply respected written Constitution. These factors can also encourage coalitions, which in turn facilitate a two-party rather than a multiparty system. A presidential form of government and a winner-take-all electoral arrangement for congressional seats also encourage two parties and coalitions and move parties to stress social unity rather than divisiveness. At the same time, such political arrangements are feasible only where class consciousness is low. A pluralistic society spread over half a continent makes federalism an attractive political arrangement. Federalism, in turn, creates independent bases of power for local politicians and works against disciplined national parties. Undisciplined national parties are not apt to be able to unite on specific matters of ideology and comprehensive programs. A federal arrangement, in the absence of a presidential system, might work in favor of regional parties; but the electoral institutions counterbalance any such tendency, and when combined with federalism again encourage coalitions rather than splinter parties. The dangling bait of a majority vote and the apparent middle-of-the-road and rather indifferent political attitude of large portions of the electorate move the parties to make similar appeals to similar groups of voters; at the same time the similarity of these appeals may tend to make large blocs of voters somewhat lukewarm in their attention to politics and, after being educated in an environment of political moderation, to adhere to the middle of the political road.

This is not to claim that the party system has never changed or can never change. Surely in some respects it has changed over the years, and inevitably will change in the future. The attempt in 1964 by elements within the Republican party to swing that party away from the center would have, if continued for any length of time, brought about sweeping changes in the nature of the party system. The stinging defeat of Senator Gold-water in the presidential election of that year apparently convinced Republican leaders to halt popular abandonment of their party by uniting behind Richard Nixon, a more moderate conservative. An increasingly likely long-run trend is the spread of genuine two-party competition to more and more states. This is certainly true in the sense that the Republican party has made significant inroads into the traditionally Democratic South.

Nor does the description of the patterns of party behavior as a system imply that positive steps should not be taken to reform that system. What the concept of a party system does indicate is that reform is a much more difficult process than merely changing the mechanics of party organization and also that successful reform of the party system may have widespread effects throughout the entire governmental and social system in the United States. If power within the parties is in fact centralized and they are converted into disciplined, programmatic bodies, we should, for example, expect equally fundamental changes in the relationship between the states and national government and possibly even in the degree of political agreement in the country. These may or may not be desirable side effects of party reform, but we should be fully aware that they are very likely to occur.

SELECTED BIBLIOGRAPHY

Agar, Herbert, *The Price of Union* (Boston, Mass.: Houghton Mifflin Company, 1945). Stresses the role that political parties have played in American history in furthering compromise and building consensus.

Binkley, Wilfred E., *American Political Parties,* 4th ed. (New York: Alfred A. Knopf, 1963). Provides historical background for the present-day party system.

Cotter, Cornelius P., *Politics Without Power* (New York: Atherton Press, 1964). An analysis of the national committees of the two major parties.

Duverger, Maurice, *Political Parties: Their Organization and Activity in the Modern State* (New York: John Wiley and Sons, Inc., 1954). Still a leading comparative study of party systems in several countries.

Greenstein, Fred I., *The American Party System and the American People,* 2d ed. (Englewood Cliffs, N.J.: Prentice-Hall, Inc., 1970). A short but insightful introduction to American parties.

Key, V. O., Jr., *Politics, Parties, and Pressure Groups,* 5th ed. (New York: Thomas Y.

Crowell Company, 1964). The most recent edition of the standard—and, in many ways, the classic—textbook on American political parties.

———, *Southern Politics in State and Nation* (New York: Alfred A. Knopf, 1949). A brilliant analysis of the politics of one section of the United States.

McKean, Dayton, *The Boss* (Boston, Mass.: Houghton Mifflin Company, 1940). A detailed study of the late Mayor Hague of Jersey City and his political machine.

Michels, Robert, *Political Parties* (New York: Dover Publications, Inc., 1959), A sociological study of the emergence of leadership, the psychology of power, and the oligarchic tendencies of organization, first published in English in 1915.

Schattschneider, E. E., *The Struggle for Party Government* (College Park, Md.: University of Maryland Press, 1948). In contrast to volumes by Agar, Herring, Brogan, and others, this pamphlet presents a plea for stronger and more highly disciplined parties.

Footnotes

[1] James Bryce, *The American Commonwealth*, rev. ed. (New York: Crowell-Collier and Macmillan Company, Inc., 1914), II, 3.

[2] V. O. Key, Jr., *Politics, Parties, and Pressure Groups*, 5th ed. (New York: Thomas Y. Crowell Company, 1964), p. 207.

[3] See the interesting article by Maurice Klain, "A New Look at the Constituencies: The Need for a Recount and a Reappraisal," *American Political Science Review*, 49 (December 1955), pp. 1105–1119, in which it is shown that multimember state legislative districts are far more common in the United States than has generally been recognized.

[4] Frank J. Sorauf, *Political Parties in the American System* (Boston: Little, Brown and Company, 1964), p. 30.

[5] This southern strategy, usually credited to Attorney General William Mitchell, is outlined by one of Mitchell's former assistants, Kevin P. Phillips, in *The Emerging Republican Majority* (New Rochelle, N.Y.: Arlington House, 1969). In his dedication, however, Phillips gives Richard M. Nixon equal credit as the "architect" of this plan.

[6] Austin Ranney and Willmore Kendall, *Democracy and the American Party System* (New York: Harcourt, Brace and World, Inc., 1956), pp. 161–164.

[7] Duane Lockard, *The Politics of State and Local Government*, 2d ed. (New York: Crowell-Collier, Macmillan, Inc., 1969), pp. 176–177.

[8] Herbert McClosky, Paul Hoffman, and Rosemary O'Hara, "Issue Conflict and Consensus among Party Leaders and Followers," *American Political Science Review*, 54 (June 1960), pp. 406–427.

[9] P. 678.

[10] See Chapters 1 and 3.

[11] E. E. Schattschneider, *Party Government* (New York: Holt, Rinehart and Winston, Inc., 1942), p. 129.

[12] V. O. Key, Jr., *Politics, Parties, and Pressure Groups*, p. 327.

[13] There is a difference between "delegates" and "votes" in a national convention. Some delegates may have only a half-vote.

[14] Adlai Stevenson, *What I Think* (New York: Harper and Row, 1956), pp. ix–x.

[15] Paul T. David, Ralph Goldman, and Richard Bain, *The Politics of National Party Conventions* (Washington, D.C.: The Brookings Institution, 1960), p. 84.

[16] P. 211.

[17] J. M. Burns, *The Deadlock of Democracy*, rev. ed. (Englewood Cliffs, N.J.: Prentice-Hall, Inc., 1963), p. 1.

[18] *American Political Science Review*, Supplement, 44 (September 1950), p. v. Also published separately under the same title (New York: Holt, Rinehart and Winston, Inc., 1950).

[19] Pendleton Herring, *The Politics of Democracy* (New York: Holt, Rinehart and Winston, Inc., 1940), p. 132.

[20] V. O. Key, Jr., *Politics, Parties, and Pressure Groups*, p. 206.

Chapter 7   Interest Groups

An interest group is a formal organization of people who share one or more common objectives or concerns and who try to influence the course of public policy to protect and promote these aims. Such organizations differ widely: they are large or small, permanent or temporary, rich or poor, powerful or weak. Their exact number is impossible to calculate. Members and allies prefer the term "interest groups" to describe their organizations; enemies prefer the pejorative implication of "pressure groups." Since they are typically organized to protect an interest by exerting political pressure, each term is rather accurate, and we shall use them both with no moral judgment implied.

One way to understand an interest group is to note how it differs from a political party, although a party and an interest group overlap in many ways. As elaborated in Chapter 6, the Democratic and Republican parties are large agencies that seek to win the active support of 40 million or more voters. Consequently their appeals are broad and their programs deal with many problems. An interest group is seldom actively supported by more than a tiny minority of people. Consequently, its appeal is narrow and its program limited. In general, a party is primarily interested in winning control of and operating the government; an interest group is primarily interested in shaping a particular public policy. But these distinctions are not completely clear. Having won control of the government, a party can hardly avoid the responsibility of shaping many public policies, whereas to influence public policy an interest group may find it necessary to elect its supporters to public office.

THE SPECTRUM OF PRESSURE POLITICS

The spectrum of pressure politics is very broad indeed. Business, labor, agriculture, the professions such as law, medicine, and education, regional, racial, religious, and nationality groups, war veterans—almost every type of group allegiance known to man seems to be represented in the list of well-known organizations. The range of interest groups is suggested by some of the names of the organizations that annually spend $50,000 or more for lobbying activities in Washington. Each year's list will usually include the American Medical Association, the AFL-CIO, the American Farm Bureau Federation, the U.S. Savings and Loan League, the International Brotherhood of Teamsters, and the National Education Association.

It is probably safe to say that every white, middle-class American is identified with and represented by one or more interest groups. But not every interest is so represented. A striking and continuing phenomenon of pressure politics in the United States has been the relative lack of organization by the poor and by consumer groups. While there have been some recent changes, the poor have tended to be much less interested in politics than the middle class. Ill health, lack of education, and physical and cultural isolation help account for their absence of interest. Apathy among consumers is more difficult to explain. Every person is a consumer and complaints about high prices and low-quality merchandise and service are perennial, yet consumers have rarely organized for effective political action. With a few exceptions, Americans have preferred to express their interest as *producers* rather than as *consumers,* although the latent power of the consumer interest is obvious. Ralph Nader's successful lobbying for automobile safety regulations has barely scratched the surface of consumer resentment.

15 TOP SPENDERS

The 15 top spenders of the 269 organizations filing lobby spending reports for 1969, with comparative figures for 1968.

Organization	1969	1968
National Association of Letter Carriers (AFL-CIO)	$295,970	$ 63,797
United Federation of Postal Clerks (AFL-CIO)	250,827	170,784
Realty Committee on Taxation	229,223	—
AFL-CIO (headquarters)	184,938	154,466
American Farm Bureau Federation	146,337	147,379
National Committee for the Recording Arts	139,726	25,949
National Association of Home Builders of the United States	138,472	70,095
United States Savings and Loan League	126,421	119,784
Record Industry Association of America Inc.	115,334	111,394
American Legion	114,609	141,134
Council for a Livable World	112,603	541,022
National Education Association Office of Government Relations and Citizenship	97,537	84,146
National Housing Conference Inc.	95,562	96,935
American Medical Association	91,355	56,374
Railway Labor Executives Association	86,286	—

SOURCE: Congressional Quarterly Weekly Report, *July 31, 1970, p. 1967.*

Economic Interest Groups

Historically, the most effective pressure groups have been those based on the simple economic interests in earning a living and in acquiring, holding, and profitably using property. The associations that have most influenced government in the United States over the years have been those representing the three basic occupational groupings: business, labor, and agriculture. The recent activity of racial organizations may seem to mark a new trend, but even there economic factors are closely tied to problems of social justice.

It is commonly but erroneously believed that interest groups in a particular area are solidly united and always stand shoulder to shoulder in fighting this government measure or supporting that one. In fact, there are often serious divisions within apparently closely collaborating groups. Just as black civil rights leaders sometimes denounce each other and their white liberal allies with a vehemence that racists escape, labor is often torn between the rival aims of craft and industrial unions and of skilled and unskilled workers. Dairy farmers of the Midwest are sometimes pitted against cotton farmers of the South over an issue such as oleomargarine taxation. Similarly the manufacturer and independent retail merchant find themselves locked in a bitter struggle with chainstore operators and discount houses. The former want the support of government through "fair trade" laws fixing minimum retail prices; the latter want economic freedom to sell products at whatever prices they choose to charge. Moreover, segments of organized labor identified with certain businesses tend to reflect the industry position on some political issues to the point where certain businessmen and workers may be more closely identified with each other than either is with supposedly similar groups.

Noneconomic Interest Groups

When we move away from the economic area, the organizational loyalties of the American people become so numerous that it is impossible to present an inclusive analysis of the resulting interest groups. Furthermore, some associations that appear to be primarily noneconomic in character often show a very strong interest in economic issues. Some idea of the nature and complexity of these groups can be gained by noting their number and activity under such headings as race, religion, the professions, and veterans.

Many strong organizations represent the interests of racial and religious groups on the national scene. For example, two, the National Association for the Advancement of Colored People (NAACP) and the National Urban League, keep a constant watch over government policy as it affects the interests of blacks. Perhaps even more powerful today are the Southern Christian Leadership Conference (SCLC) and the Congress of Racial Equality (CORE), though both depend on methods of mass protest rather than conventional lobbying to pressure public officials. Protestants frequently seek to influence government through the National Council of Churches, Catholics through the National Catholic Welfare Council, and Jews through the American Jewish Committee, the American Jewish Congress, and the Anti-Defamation League.

Most professions have strong organizations which are active from time to time in pressure politics. This is particularly true of doctors and lawyers. Through the American Medical Association, doctors have tried strenuously to block or curtail federal programs to help finance medical care for the elderly and the poor. In 1965 the AMA admitted spending over $1.1 million in a vain effort to stop the passage of Medicare, which it had branded as "socialized medicine." The Association could claim some success, however, in restricting the coverage of the act and in helping to delay passage for seventeen years. The American Bar Association's interests have been more widely ranging, covering almost every proposal concerned with court structure, procedure, and personnel, as well as many substantive issues of public policy. It has, for instance, favored changes in antitrust law and opposed ratification of a treaty against genocide. In general, professional interest groups take very conservative positions, and while claiming to be anxious about maintaining high professional standards or serving the public good, often seem mainly concerned with protecting the vested interests of their members or clients.

Organizations representing war veterans find an immediate and powerful incentive for political activity in such issues as pensions for veterans and their dependents and relief and rehabilitation for the disabled. But their interest has also encompassed such issues as national defense and foreign policy. By all odds the largest veterans' organization today is the American Legion. Smaller organizations are the Veterans of Foreign Wars and the American Veterans of World War II (AMVETS). Like the Daughters of the American Revolution (DAR), the American Legion is controlled and administered by a group of very conservative leaders. Both of these organizations illustrate the enormous power often wielded, in interest groups of all kinds, by the professional secretariats at group headquarters. It is doubtful whether the average member of the DAR or the American Legion shares the ultraconservative views of the paid workers who run these particular organizations. This is one reason why public officers do not pay more attention to lobbyists. They know that on many issues professional lobbyists simply do not speak for any large number of rank-and-file members.

TECHNIQUES OF INTEREST POLITICS

To achieve its goals, an interest group can use three basic techniques. First, it can try to place in public office those persons most favorably disposed toward the interests it seeks to promote. This technique may be labeled *electioneering*. Second, an interest group can try to persuade public officers, whether they are initially favorably disposed toward it or not, to adopt and enforce the policies that it thinks will prove most beneficial to its interests. This technique may be labeled *lobbying*. Third, it can try to influence general public opinion and thereby gain an indirect influence over government, since government in a democracy is ultimately—albeit not always quickly—affected by public opinion. This technique may be labeled *propagandizing*.

Electioneering

Although interest groups and political parties are distinct and separate agencies, they are sometimes closely associated in their activities. In particular, an interest group often seeks to work within a party, since it is through parties that government is organized and public policy is shaped. This means that an interest group must be active at election time. Now and then an organization, such as the League of Women Voters, does succeed in maintaining neutrality between parties and candidates, even though it may be intensely interested in influencing public policy decisions. But such organizational neutrality is the exception rather than the rule. Most interest groups that become involved in electioneering campaign actively for particular candidates and vigorously support a particular party.

A typical interest group first undertakes to influence the nomination of congressmen, by trying to win promises of support from candidates in both parties and then by backing those candidates giving such a promise. It may even send representatives to the national party conventions to argue for inclusion in party platforms of a plank calling for enactment of the desired law. The association will thereafter take stock of its gains and losses, noting with pleasure the nomination of friendly candidates, marking for defeat unfriendly candidates, and perhaps sizing up the over-all situation with an eye toward supporting either the Republican or the Democratic party as such if either appears to be more strongly committed to the proposed law.

Having made these assessments, association leaders will then undertake to raise money in support of approved candidates, supplying them with favorable publicity and getting out votes for them on election day. Of course, the organization must watch its step very closely at this stage. Discretion may suggest some appearance of neutrality or even financial support for both sides, particularly in those areas in which both candidates are committed to support a bill, or where both are equally undecided about the proposal. For the real struggle still lies ahead—securing the enactment of the law when the newly elected Congress meets—and it is almost as important not to antagonize doubtful congressmen as it is to secure the election of fully committed congressmen.

It may be asked why an interest group, particularly if it is a large and important one, does not run candidates of its own for public office and seek direct control of government, thereby becoming a political party. If its purpose is to bring about the enactment of laws favorable to its cause and to kill those that it views as unfavorable, how can it better achieve this purpose than by electing its own men to office? As a matter of fact, many interest groups are tempted to do just that. The Prohibition party, a one-issue party that sought the outlawing of intoxicating beverages in the years before the adoption of the Eighteenth Amendment, is a good example. But much more often the temptation is resisted. No interest group, least of all a specific organization, has the support of more than a minority of the voters. Consequently, a direct attempt to take control of the government could not ordinarily hope to enjoy more than a very limited success. On the other hand, if a well-organized minority sells its support as dearly as it can to one of the major parties in an election, or remains neutral and then brings its pressure to bear upon the victorious party, threatening opposition in the next election, it has an excellent chance of influencing the course of government.

Unions, representing a large and well-organized minority, have often been tempted to form third parties, and in foreign countries such as England, Ireland, and Australia, and in a few American states as well, have done so. These attempts have met with some success, for labor in a highly industrialized area is a sufficiently numerous group to have a chance of winning an election, but at best that chance is less than even, unless a labor party is able and willing to broaden its appeal to include farmers, consumers, professional men, tradepeople, or other groups. In fact, to become one of Britian's two major parties the Labour party has had to pursue just such a policy, and in so doing it has ceased to be a pure labor party. In the United States, the labor movement, following the lead set by Samuel Gompers, has steadfastly refused to organize a national party and has instead tried to follow a policy of "rewarding its friends and punishing its enemies" without regard to party affiliations, although in national elections there has been a strong and positive correlation between being a Democratic candidate and being a "friend of labor."

Lobbying

The legislative process is, of course, the target of vigorous and conflicting activity by interest groups which bring pressure to bear directly upon public officers in an effort to shape governmental decisions. While this is a vital arena of lobbying activity, the influence of government upon the individual interests depends upon a great deal more than the words of statutes. The final impact of a law also depends upon the vigor with which it is enforced and upon the interpretation it receives through administrative rulings and court decisions. Accordingly, interest groups cannot limit their lobbying activity to legislators when they know that important decisions affecting government policy remain to be made in the executive and judicial arenas. Lobbying methods vary greatly.[1] An approach that is effective with one congressman may put off another, and even approaches generally useful in the legislative branch may be inappropriate in dealing with a regulatory commission, an agency chief, or a judge.

In the Legislative Branch

Lobbyists—or Washington representatives, as they usually prefer to be called—have sometimes found congressmen susceptible to influence through "wining and dining." Every few years a scandal breaks about a lobbyist showering favors—money, free plane trips, and hotel rooms, vicuna coats, deep freezes, or other gifts—on several legislators, administrators, and perhaps even White House staff members. These scandals make interesting reading, but they rarely reveal the more pervasive kinds of lobbying activities on Capitol Hill or in the executive agencies "downtown." Most lobbyists are too subtle and most federal officials too sophisticated for such crass efforts to pay off in much more than amused contempt.

Lobbyists typically concentrate on those legislators who are either already disposed to vote their way—the object is to re-enforce loyalty and to convert tacit into active support—or on those who are uncommitted and thus open to persuasion. Seldom do lobbyists spend time, energy, and other scarce resources on those who are committed to the other side, except perhaps to assuage any personal animosities so the legislator can be approached for support on other issues. Threats are also rarely used. Senators and representatives, as a general rule, are simply too powerful and independent to look kindly on those who threaten them. And legislators have nasty weapons that can be turned against annoying lobbyists.

A lobbyist has three principal instruments of persuasion. First are campaign contributions from his clients and their friends. As we shall see in Chapter 9, the costs of winning a contested election for a major office are always high. Thus, even the most honest of elected officials, unless he is himself a multimillionaire, cannot help but feel or anticipate a financial pinch that tempts him to be more sympathetic than he might to the pleas of special interests who are noted for making heavy contributions at election time. These contributions, incidentally, need not be monetary. They might include helping with registration drives, actually engaging in the campaign debates, or getting out the vote on election day. In any event, most legislators who possess any real measure of prudence and character can avoid total dependence on any one group, but it is hard for many legislators to be totally deaf to those who offer help when it is badly needed.

The second instrument is friendship. Legislators are incredibly busy men and can see only a few of the people who want to talk to them. Knowing this, many organizations hire former senators, congressmen, or staff members to represent them, because as a matter of professional courtesy, if not because of old friendships, these people can gain immediate access to their former colleagues. Obtaining access is critical, but using it fruitfully is even more so. Operating in a selfish world of demands and counter-demands, a legislator usually finds that he can trust only a small portion of those who come to him for help. As a result he tends to listen more to those whose reliability and personal loyalty have been tested over time. And the mark of a truly successful lobbyist is that officials on Capitol Hill look on him as a trusted friend and ally, not as an agent of an interest group.

Help in campaigning can predispose a legislator to treat a lobbyist seriously, perhaps even to trust him; but, even where a lobbyist's clients have not made any contributions a lobbyist has a third instrument that can work effectively on its own and can also help build up friendship and trust. One of the overpowering facts of a public official's life is that he needs information, accurate information about the nature and extent of a problem, about the feasibility of proposed solutions, and, not least, about how his constituents feel about the matter. Because of the thousands of demands on his time, a legislator can be personally and intimately familiar with only a narrow range of problems. Even with the help of a large staff he cannot give many important matters anything like the attention they deserve. Not only is his substantive knowledge likely to be deficient but he is often apt to be unaware of—though very concerned about—his constituents' reactions to certain developments. Thus, a lobbyist who can warn a legislator about important problems that are likely to arise, especially ones that will concern his state or district, and give him concise information about the nature of the problems and outlines of practical solutions, is soon likely to become a friend. These problems, incidentally, need have nothing to do with the lobbyist's own interest; in fact he may build up more credit—on which he can later draw—if they do not.

Since the legislator may depend on this information to reply to his constituents, to make speeches, or even to decide how to vote, the lobbyist has to draw a careful line between mustering evidence that presents his case persuasively and using specious information or arguments. A senator who is made to look like a fool in floor debate for citing false facts is not apt to go out of his way to help the man who led him to public embarrassment.

One particularly persuasive kind of information concerns what a proposal will do for—or to—a legislator's constituents. That is often the really decisive issue. When their own interests are at stake, lobbyists often try to capitalize on this fact by resorting to indirect tactics—by trying to generate a "grass roots" movement by having members of their group send letters and telegrams to their senators and congressmen. Any politician who plans to run for re-election has to pay some attention to mail from his constituents, but an experienced legislator can usually sniff out a phony campaign from a genuine popular outcry. The planted letters may sound too much alike, the arguments may be too pat and follow the group's line too closely, or the tactics of the lobbyist may be too well known. As a variant, some lobbyists prefer to have a few friends of the legislator from his constituency call on him and speak privately about what a bill is likely to do and how "the people" are viewing it.

Hearings on a bill provide a ready but not always useful forum for lobbyists. In part, congressional hearings are ritual performances that allow all points of view to be aired. In that sense, they do allow the lobbyist, simply by showing up and testifying, to get his clients' position on the official record and often in the newspapers as well. The drawback is that the records of hearings are frequently too voluminous for legislators to read with any care, and the hearings themselves are usually attended only by one or a few members of the committee. Therefore, the effect of what is said there is likely to be quite small.

A critically important fact about lobbying is that it is not a one-way street. Legislators can and frequently do use lobbyists for their own purposes. There is a kind of bargaining process at work. The legislator can do things for the lobbyist—give him publicity, leak some inside information to him, speak for him to an uncommitted colleague, introduce him to a member of an important committee, invite him to social functions so he can enlarge his contacts, and, of course, speak and vote for his proposals. Negatively, the legislator can refuse to cooperate with the lobbyist or even publicly attack him for trying to "pressure" votes. Popular feelings about lobbyists and lobbying are still sufficiently ambivalent for this to be a serious sanction, and it goes far to explain why lobbyists seldom threaten legislators.

The lobbyist can help the legislator by doing research, writing speeches, running errands, lining up friendly witnesses for committee hearings, soliciting campaign contributions, conducting an opinion poll, supplying information from his sources—which may include legislators from the other party—and using influence with other lobbyists and legislators to support proposals that the legislator wants enacted. In short, both lobbyists and legislators need each other and they use each other.

In addition, lobbyists' efforts to build up friendships are often based on mutual as well as selfish interests. Lobbyists and legislators frequently are natural allies who are working for many of the very same aims. Planning and carrying out a coordinated campaign to secure or block passage of legislation comes easily to them under such circumstances. This close relationship is readily understandable when one recalls that the congressman himself is frequently a lobbyist in the sense that he has been sent to Washington by a particular constituency to represent the economic and social interests of that area. A senator from Kansas has little difficulty cooperating with the lobbyists of the farm organizations, a senator from Texas readily accepts the help of the petroleum industry in working out the details of an oil bill, and a representative from Akron or Pittsburgh is likely to be predisposed to support organized labor's position on a "full-employment" bill.

It is generally true in all areas of government that the lobbyist who seeks to persuade public officers to act *positively* by adopting or enforcing a particular policy has a

more difficult task before him than the lobbyist whose purpose is a negative one of persuading government not to act, or to leave the status quo undisturbed. The Madisonian
system of fragmented power creates a tremendous inertia of rest. The difficulties of positive action are especially pronounced in Congress, where enactment of a bill usually
requires successfully surmounting half a dozen major hurdles. The lobbyist who wants
positive action must win at each of these. The lobbyist whose task is to kill a bill can
effect his purpose at any one of these hurdles. He can lose out at five points, win at the
sixth, and carry the day.

In the Executive Branch

There is a great deal more lobbying in the executive branch of government than is commonly realized. It begins with the opportunity that interest groups have of influencing the
appointments of administrative personnel to important posts. It continues through legislative hearings—particularly appropriations hearings—on the policies of the administrative
agency. Working through friends in Congress, a skillful lobbyist may nudge an agency one
way or another by sharp questions, praise, encouragement, and budgetary changes. In
dealing with Congress, administrators are often lobbyists, too. They want new laws and
more money and find effective many of the same tactics that lobbyists use for private
groups. In addition, they sometimes find it expedient to cooperate with a lobbyist and so
to exploit his as well as their own influence. This is the cause of the historic "triangular
alliance" that characterizes much of American politics: an interest group, an administrative agency, and a friendly majority on a congressional committee. Among themselves
they may establish or destroy public policy while the White House looks on helplessly.

The relationships between lobbyists and administrators continue through close and
sometimes friendly working contacts on a day-to-day basis. It is not surprising that corporation lawyers are in constant touch with the Antitrust Division of the Department of
Justice, businessmen with the Department of Commerce, trade union officials with the
Department of Labor, and farm organizations with the Department of Agriculture. This kind
of interaction means a frequent exchange of information, ideas, and solutions that can
bring about reciprocal influence. Exchanges of this sort are necessary consequences of the
concept of fair play that provides an opportunity for expression of opinions *before* rather
than *after* official decisions are made. But there is another kind of exchange as well, a
parade of government officials into executive positions in the very industries they previously regulated. It is not at all unusual, for example, for a procurement officer in the
Pentagon to retire from government service and accept an important post with a defense
contractor, or a director of the Federal Aviation Administration to resign to become a
vice president of a major airline. More discreetly, a senior lawyer from the Antitrust
Division or from the Internal Revenue Service may go into private practice and within a
short time have as his clients many of the corporations he was recently investigating and
prosecuting.

These shifts of personnel go in both directions, from private industry and private
practice to government as well as vice versa. Despite the obvious integrity of many of the
people involved, crossing career patterns are a source of concern, doubly so since it has
often happened that a regulatory agency has become the captive of the very groups it was
established to control.

In the Judicial Branch

In the sense that the term is used in the legislative process, there is little if any room for "lobbying" in the courts. Indeed, such lobbying is usually unethical and frequently illegal. Yet, in a broader sense, interest groups do lobby in the judicial process. Such lobbying is also inevitable, since court decisions play a crucial role in molding public policy. The interest of the NAACP, for instance, in a favorable judicial interpretation of a civil rights statute is hardly less salient than its interest in getting the law passed in the first place.

"Judicial lobbying" takes several forms. First, interest group leaders can use their influence in the executive or legislative process to help select judges whose general philosophy of government may be favorable to the group's aims. Second, interest groups can carry on lawsuits themselves or can help others in court actions challenging or defending the legality of governmental or private action. This sort of aid is more important than it might at first appear. The American legal process is typically slow and costly. It often takes a large amount of money to pay for lawyers, research expenses, and court fees. The cost merely of printing the briefs and records for a case brought to the Supreme Court can easily run into thousands of dollars. Third, if it can meet certain technical requirements, an association can enter a legal dispute already in progress as *amicus curiae,* a friend of the court, and offer its views as to the proper decision.

These kinds of interest group activities come as a surprise to many people and there is some conflict with the naïve view that courts and judges are remote from struggles over public policy-making. But judges are often intimately involved in these struggles, and the U.S. Supreme Court has held that the First Amendment's protection of freedom of speech, association, and petition gives organizations a right to use the courts to further their policy aims.[2]

Lobbying with the Home Organization

A Washington representative has to devote much of his time to channeling information and advice back to his home organization. After years of dealing with various government agencies, a lobbyist often develops personal sources of information about public policies planned for the future as well as a keen sense of likely official reactions to suggestions for changes in existing policies. This sort of intelligence can be of great use to his organization in responding to proposed legislative or administrative action, and if it is a business group, in designing products intended to be sold to the government.

Curiously, a lobbyist is often more perplexed about his relations with his employers than with public officials. To facilitate his work, a Washington representative would prefer that he be considered as an ambassador from his organization to the federal government, not only transmitting specific information and performing set tasks but also advising and being consulted on broad policy issues. At least among business firms, however, the tendency has been for the home office to take a more limited view of the lobbyist's functions.[3]

Propagandizing

An interest group can seldom afford to limit its operations to lobbying alone. Occasionally in an area of policy which has only narrow appeal or is exceedingly technical, an organization may concentrate all its energies on a few government officials, but it is more typical of successful interest groups to try to persuade both officials and public opinion. Indeed, as we just saw, influencing public opinion is often the most effective means of winning over officials. Thus propaganda and its arch-manipulators, public relations experts, come into play. Although much has been written about propaganda, the term remains a vague and inexact one. Propaganda may contain true, false, or distorted information; it may restrict itself to rational argument or become an emotional screed. Propaganda may be aimed at the most narrow and selfish aims or it may seek the broadest national good, but it always has one fundamental purpose: to influence public opinion on certain issues. And to accomplish this objective, public relations experts generally rely on the same kind of techniques used by the large advertising firms to mass-merchandise soap, automobiles, or patent medicines. In fact, the more affluent interest groups, like candidates for many political offices, are apt to use as their PR men some of the better known Madison Avenue advertising agencies.

The long attack of the American Medical Association against Medicare is one of the more striking examples of a combination of lobbying and propaganda.[4] Pressure on Capitol Hill was only a small part of a gigantic "educational" campaign, directed for the AMA by the public relations firm of Whitaker and Baxter. Thousands of billboards, newspaper advertisements, radio commercials, and literally millions of leaflets decried "socialized medicine." Paintings of a physician at the bed of sick child were sent to individual doctors to be displayed in their waiting rooms over the caption:

KEEP POLITICS OUT OF THIS PICTURE

When the life—or health—of a loved one is at stake hope lies in the devoted service of your Doctor. Would you change this picture?

Compulsory health insurance is political medicine. . . .

Supplementing this approach, Whitaker and Baxter persuaded almost 10,000 smaller organizations to endorse the AMA's position, and even went so far as to distribute "canned" editorials to a number of newspapers so they could more easily denounce the evils of federal aid. In great part because of the effectiveness of this opposition, as we noted earlier, the elderly had to wait until 1965 for the United States to begin to develop a national health plan, and the poor are still dependent on a hodgepodge of schemes that vary widely in the degree of care available.

Protest

Half-way between propaganda and lobbying is an old technique that has been most recently used by civil rights groups—public protest. The immediate purpose of a minority protest is less to persuade those against whom it is seemingly directed than to dramatize grievances and by so doing arouse the opinion of outside groups to whom the apparent target is sensitive.[5] For instance, when in 1960 a group of black students in Greensboro, North Carolina, staged the first sit-in at a chain store, they did not impose any serious financial threat to the corporation. But what the chain store executives could not ignore were the moral and financial pressures ignited by liberal sympathizers all around the country. Demonstrations in Greensboro were a trivial problem, but pickets in major cities in the

"That's the kind of thinking you can expect from anyone over thirty! ...

GRIN & BEAR IT by Lichty. Courtesy Publishers-Hall Syndicate.

North and Midwest, all presented in living color on evening television programs, were a different matter. So too, the apparent self-destruction of the burnings in the black ghettos, insofar as they had any purpose, was a means of dramatizing the black man's plight, just as similar burnings in the Catholic ghettos of Ulster drew attention to the religious discrimination being practiced there.

REGULATION OF INTEREST GROUPS

Interest groups are inevitable products of a pluralistic society that chooses many of its officials by popular elections and recognizes freedom of speech, petition, assembly, and association as constitutionally protected rights. It may even be argued that interest groups do contribute to the democratic character of government by providing an institutional means through which segments of public opinion can be brought directly to bear on public officials between elections. Historical experience has shown, however, that, like the individuals who compose them, interest groups sometimes succumb to temptations to act selfishly and even greedily and that lobbying presents dangers both of deception and corruption. To combat these perils, more than three-quarters of the states[6] as well as the national government, have enacted laws to regulate lobbying. Many of these statutes make use of *registration* and *disclosure*. Organizations, as well as their agents, that seek to influence government policy and practices are compelled to register with a public agency and to disclose certain information about themselves. Behind such regulations is the hope that if voters know about the extent and character of lobbying, they can more intelligently evaluate the performance of their representatives and so provide officials with a powerful incentive to resist pressure. This hope, however, has been largely unfulfilled. First, there is no evidence that any significant number of voters take any continuing interest in the lobbying information available. An occasional juicy scandal sparks considerable public interest but of a kind that quickly flickers out. Second, because of technical defects in most lobbying legislation, many active groups can completely avoid registration and those who do register are usually not obliged to disclose some of the most important facts about their operations. A close look at the federal statute reveals many of the problems typical of such laws.

The Federal Regulation of Lobbying Act

In 1946, Congress undertook for the first time to control interest groups in the Regulation of Lobbying Act.[7] Actually, the law is poorly named, since it provides for little actual *regulation*. Any person or organization soliciting or receiving money to be used "principally to aid," or any person or organization whose "principal purpose" is to aid, the passage or defeat of legislation before Congress is required to register with the clerk of the House of Representatives and to file quarterly reports showing all money actually received and expended, including the names and addresses of all persons contributing $500 or more, or to whom $10 or more has been paid. Each lobbyist is required to disclose

> the name and address of the person by whom he is employed, and in whose interest he appears or works, the duration of such employment, how much he is paid and is to receive, by whom he is paid or is to be paid, how much he is to be paid for expenses, and what expenses are to be included.

The law further requires that the reported data shall be published at quarterly intervals in the *Congressional Record*. Severe penalties for those convicted under the act are prescribed, ranging up to a $10,000 fine and a five-year prison term, and including a three-year ban against further lobbying.

Like many state laws, the 1946 act is vague and confusing where it needs to be specific and sharp.[8] Muddy phrases like "principal purpose" allow some active organizations to refuse to register on the grounds that lobbying is only incidental to their objectives. Compounding the difficulties, Congress did not establish any special agency to enforce the statute. Nor does publication of the required data do much to improve the situation. The *Congressional Record* is hardly regular reading fare even for most well informed voters, and newspaper and television analysts have generally shown scant interest in the available information, perhaps because it is incomplete and at times misleading.

Like similar state statutes, the 1946 act suffers from the further difficulty of having to operate under tight constitutional restrictions. The First Amendment, which forbids Congress to make any law abridging the right of the people to assemble and to petition the government for a redress of grievances, protects the basic right of lobbying against any outright federal prohibition. The extension of the right petition through the due process of law clause of the Fourteenth Amendment similarly bars state or local governments from such action.

In spite of the fact that the Regulation of Lobbying Act of 1946 provides for only an extremely weak measure of control, some serious constitutional objections have been raised against it. For example, the three-year ban against further lobbying by anyone convicted under the law might in effect deprive such persons of their right of petition. Similarly, it has been argued that the act is so vague and indefinite that it fails to provide an ascertainable standard of guilt and thus violates an essential requirement of due process of law. In 1954, the Supreme Court upheld the validity of the act, stating that Congress was not "constitutionally forbidden to require the disclosure of lobbying activities. To do so would be to deny Congress in large measure the power of self-protection."[9] The Court, however, avoided some of the more difficult constitutional questions by giving the statute the narrowest possible interpretation. According to the majority opinion, the act applies only to lobbyists who enter into direct communication with members of Congress with respect to pending or proposed federal legislation and does not extend to lobbyists who seek to influence the legislative process indirectly by working through public opinion.

The dangers inherent in "regulation" of lobbying became evident when, after the Supreme Court's decisions in the *School Segregation* cases, a number of southern states attempted to curb or outlaw the activities of the NAACP within their borders. The unconstitutionality of these campaigns was made clear in 1958 when the Supreme Court temporarily checked efforts by the attorney general of Alabama to enjoin the NAACP from further activities and to oust it from the state. In particular, the Justices ruled that the state could not compel the association to disclose the names of is members. Speaking for a unanimous Court, Justice John Harlan[10] observed:

> It is beyond debate that freedom to engage in association for the advancement of beliefs and ideas is an inseparable aspect of the "liberty" assured by the Due Process Clause of the Fourteenth Amendment. . . . it is immaterial whether the beliefs sought to be advanced by association pertain to political, economic, religious or cultural matters, and state action which may have the effect of curtailing the freedom to associate is subject to the closest scrutiny.

SELECTED BIBLIOGRAPHY

Bentley, Arthur F., *The Process of Government* (Bloomington, Ind.: The Principia Press, 1949). A theory of the role of interest groups in politics.

Blaisdell, Donald C., *American Democracy under Pressure* (New York: The Ronald Press, 1957). A vigorous account of the operations of several interest groups, and a theoretical statement of their role and status.

Childs, Harwood L., *Public Opinion: Nature, Function, and Role* (Princeton, N.J.: Van Nostrand Company, Inc., 1965). A comprehensive text by one of the pioneers in the study of public opinion.

Herring, E. Pendleton, *Public Administration and the Public Interest* (New York: McGraw-Hill, Inc., 1936). A study of the impact of interest groups on day-to-day administration of federal regulatory programs.

Key, V. O., Jr., *Public Opinion and American Democracy* (New York: Alfred A. Knopf, 1961). A thoughtful attempt to place sociological knowledge about public opinion into a meaningful political context.

Milbrath, Lester W., *The Washington Lobbyists* (Chicago, Ill.: Rand McNally and Company, 1963). An interesting analysis of the strategy and tactics of lobbyists, based on a series of interviews with both lobbyists and legislators.

Odegard, Peter H., *Pressure Politics: The Story of the Anti-Saloon League* (New York: Columbia University Press, 1928). A classic account of the efforts of one group to control the legislative process.

Salisbury, Robert H., ed., *Interest Group Politics in America* (New York: Harper and Row, 1970). A useful collection of articles and selections from books dealing with pressure groups.

Truman, David, *The Governmental Process* (New York: Alfred A. Knopf, 1951). A comprehensive analysis of the operation of the American political system as seen through interest group activities.

Zeller, Belle, *Pressure Politics in New York* (Englewood Cliffs, N.J.: Prentice-Hall, Inc., 1937). An excellent study of regional pressure politics and interest groups.

Footnotes

[1] Among the best general descriptions of lobbying in the legislative process are: Donald R. Matthews, *U.S. Senators and Their World* (Chapel Hill, N.C.: University of North Carolina Press, 1960), Chapter 8; and Lester W. Milbrath, *The Washington Lobbyists* Chicago, Ill.: Rand McNally and Company, 1963).

[2] *National Association for the Advancement of Colored People v. Button,* 371 U.S. 415 (1963).

[3] For an interesting analysis of the problems of the Washington representative of the large business firm, see Paul W. Cherington and Ralph L. Gillen, *The Business Representative in Washington* (Washington, D.C.: The Brookings Institution, 1962).

[4] For an excellent analysis of the early stages of this campaign, see Stanley Kelley, Jr., *Professional Public Relations and Political Power* (Baltimore, Md.: The Johns Hopkins Press, 1956), Chap. 3.

[5] Michael Lipsky, "Protest as a Political Resource," *American Political Science Review*, 62 (December 1968), p. 1144.

[6] These state regulations are analyzed in Edgar Lane, *Lobbying and the Law: State Regulation of Lobbying* (Berkeley, Calif.: University of California Press, 1964).

[7] 60 *Stat.* 839. The act is a "Title" of the Legislative Reorganization Act.

[8] See Belle Zeller, "The Federal Regulation of Lobbying Act," *American Political Science Review,* 42 (April 1948), pp. 239, 245.

[9] *United States v. Harris,* 347 U.S. 612, 625 (1954).

[10] *National Association for the Advancement of Colored People v. Alabama,* 357 U.S. 449, 460–461 (1958). After this decision the Alabama supreme court refused to reverse its decision sustaining the injunction against the NAACP because, the judges claimed, the U.S. Supreme Court had misunderstood the case. A second U.S. Supreme Court decision, 360 U.S. 240 (1959), affirmed that Court's 1958 decision. The Alabama courts, however, refused to take any action until a third U.S. Supreme Court decision, 368 U.S. 16 (1961), ordered a federal district court to hear the case if state courts did not act promptly. It was not until December 1961, more than five years after the "temporary" injunction had gone into effect, that the NAACP had its first full hearing in an Alabama court. The trial court made the injunction permanent, and the state supreme court affirmed. In its fourth decision in the case, the U.S. Supreme Court again reversed the Alabama courts and sharply rebuked them for their violation of the NAACP's constitutional rights. The Court then said that if the Alabama supreme court did not quickly dissolve the injunction, the Justices in Washington would do that themselves. 377 U.S. 288 (1964). The Alabama judges complied several months later.

Chapter 8 Electing the Policy Makers

SUFFRAGE AND DEMOCRACY

Certainly a minimum requirement of any modern democracy is that the principal officers who make public policy should be elected by the people for limited terms. This general statement, however agreeable to current tastes, leaves open such specific questions as who are "the people?" who are the "principal officers?" from what constituencies shall different sets of officers be chosen? and what constitutes "limited terms" of office? In the American context, colonial history made it pretty much inevitable that legislators in any national government would be chosen from within the states, although as we saw in Chapter 2, the problems surrounding the executive branch were not so easily resolved. Once, however, the Convention had decided on a single executive chosen independently from Congress, a national constituency, though not necessarily a popular one, also became almost inevitable.

"Limited terms" posed an additional set of serious problems, and the Framers came up with a pragmatic, compromise solution of two years for representatives, six for senators, and four for the President. Like many compromises, this solution has not ended debate. The proposal has frequently been made to lengthen representatives' terms to four years, and the Twenty-Second Amendment limits a President to two four-year terms or, if he initially succeeds to the Presidency on the death or disability of the incumbent, to a maximum of ten years.

WHO ARE THE PEOPLE?

The Framers eloquently spoke of "We, the people," but they skillfully avoided offering a definition of who were "the people." Indeed, it is not likely that a majority in the Convention would have accepted an arrangement under which each mature and sane member

151

of society would have one vote, equal in weight and effect to the vote of every other mature and sane member. Alexander Hamilton's alleged reference to the people as a "great beast" probably did not accurately reflect the Framers' sentiments, but it is evident that many of them had deep fears of democracy. As part of their artful dodging, the Framers left the question of suffrage pretty much to the states. For example, senators were to be elected by the state legislatures, congressmen by voters who possessed "the qualifications requisite for electors of the most numerous branch of the state legislature," and members of the Electoral College, who formally choose the President, were to be selected in each state "in such manner as the legislature thereof may direct."

Nevertheless, the concept of "one man, one vote" has over the years become an ideal of American political culture, and the system has been moving—rapidly in the last decade—toward that goal. Formal constitutional amendments have played a part in the shift from narrower to broader suffrage and from state to national control. In forbidding states to deny persons equal protection of the laws, the Fourteenth Amendment prohibits discriminatory regulations of the right to vote. To make crystal clear the intended safeguard of Negroes' rights, the Fifteenth Amendment specifically outlaws state or federal abridgement of the right to vote "on account of race, color, or previous condition of servitude." The Nineteenth Amendment forbids discrimination because of sex. The Seventeenth Amendment provides for direct, popular election of U.S. senators by those persons qualified to vote for congressmen. The Twenty-third Amendment gives residents of the District of Columbia a voice in presidential elections by awarding the District three votes in the Electoral College, although the Amendment made no provision for representation in Congress, which acts as the District's municipal legislature.

Formal constitutional amendments tell only a part of the story, however. Broadening suffrage to white adult males was accomplished without amendment to the U.S. Constitution. One can view the Seventeenth Amendment as extending suffrage in an important area, and the Twenty-third and Twenty-fourth Amendments have had some marginal effects. The Fourteenth Amendment, as recently applied by the Supreme Court, has become the instrument used to strike down gerrymandering. But the great victories in the march toward white male suffrage came in the state political processes before the Civil War.

Where constitutional amendments have been quickly and more or less fully successful, they have been reflections of deep-rooted and long-ranged changes in political power. For example, before the Seventeenth Amendment was proposed most states had already informally provided for popular choice of senators. Similarly, the adoption of the Twenty-fourth Amendment occurred after the poll tax had become politically unpopular and had been about to die a natural death. Only five states still used such a levy in 1962, when Congress proposed the Amendment; and, two years after it was ratified, the Supreme Court declared the Amendment redundant by holding that a poll tax violated the Fourteenth Amendment.[1]

The story was much the same with the Nineteenth Amendment's extension of suffrage to women. Adoption in 1920 culminated nearly a century of agitation, marked toward the end by bitter recriminations, mass demonstrations, violence, and jailings. But the Amendment came at the end of that struggle, after fifteen states had granted full female suffrage and many others had conferred limited voting rights. In their platforms in

1916 both parties had advocated state—but not national—action to enfranchise women, and the suffragette movement, while dramatizing its objectives by picketing and hunger strikes, had solid backing around the country both among men and women who were politically prominent. Getting congressional approval of the amendment was not easy, but ratification in the states took less than fourteen months.

The history of the Fourteenth and Fifteenth Amendments has been radically different. The Civil War made it evident that the United States could not allow slavery to continue. Less certain was the status the newly freed blacks were to enjoy. These two amendments were not anchored in established customs, nor were they products of long debates on the specific point—black suffrage—supposedly settled. Moreover, in the states most immediately and dramatically affected, those of the old Confederacy, the amendments lacked legitimacy because not only did they go against the substantive wishes of the whites, but the Radical Republicans had also made ratification a prerequisite for southern states to regain their prewar status. Further complicating the situation was the general lack of even elementary political knowledge among the newly freed slaves and the consequent lack of black leadership. These amendments did not create the kind of opportunity for political power that has come more recently to blacks. They represented the hopes of a group of whites and blacks temporarily dominant in the federal government. But without a strong power base either in the North or South, the amendments signaled a beginning rather than an end to the struggle for full black participation in the political processes.

In Chapter 21 we discuss the long fight for black equality in American life. Here we would note only that after the end of Reconstruction there was some degree of surface acceptance of black voting, even in the South. There were, of course, more instances of racial violence and institutional racism during this period than the Constitution—or justice—permits, but the movement to disenfranchise blacks picked up its real momentum in the 1890's. "It is perfectly true," C. Vann Woodward[2] notes, "that Negroes were often coerced, defrauded, or intimidated, but they continued to vote in large numbers in most parts of the South for more than two decades after Reconstruction. In the judgment of the Abolitionist [Thomas Wentworth] Higginson, 'the Southern whites accept them precisely as Northern men in cities accept the ignorant Irish vote—not cheerfully but with acquiescence in the inevitable. . . .'" After the failure of the Populist Revolt of small farmers and poor city dwellers to capture political power in the South, many of the old Populists turned on the black man as a scapegoat, blaming their own failure on the Bourbons' ability to buy the black vote. While their earlier efforts at social justice in the economic sphere largely failed, the Populists' later efforts at apartheid succeeded. What Woodward[3] calls "permissions to hate" came from many sources:

> They came from the federal courts in numerous opinions, from Northern liberals eager to conciliate the South, from Southern conservatives who had abandoned their race policy of moderation in their struggle against the Populists, from the Populists in their mood of disillusionment with their former Negro allies, and from a national temper suddenly expressed by imperialistic adventures and aggressions against colored peoples in distant lands.

Historically, whites have used three different means of keeping blacks from the polls. The first, simple physical violence and threats of violence, has been patently illegal, although no less effective for this fact. The second means, economic reprisal, has also usually been illegal but more subtly so. Third, there has been a continuous search for a "legal" means of keeping blacks from voting: literacy tests carefully administered to allow discrimination against both blacks and poor whites, "understanding clauses" that required a voter to explain to a state official's satisfaction that he "understood" the state or federal constitution, "grandfather clauses" that permitted a citizen to vote without taking a literacy test if his grandfather had voted, "white primaries," which barred blacks from participation in what, until recently, were the only generally meaningful elections in the South, and poll taxes, often cumulative, which again discriminated against poor whites as well as blacks.

Since World War I, the Supreme Court has declared many of these games of legal charades unconstitutional,[4] but it often seemed that southern state officials could pass new laws as fast as judges could invalidate old statutes. The court victories made little immediate change in black political power in the South, but when combined with the *School Segregation* decisions of 1954, these rulings helped create a public and official mood that was receptive to campaigns for national legislative and administrative action to end discriminatory voting practices. After passing a pair of awkward and ineffective statutes in 1957[5] and 1960,[6] Congress, prodded anew by federal judges, by the U.S. Commission on Civil Rights, and by the growing political power of northern blacks, zeroed in on the principal evils of literacy tests and voter registration procedures.

In the South, White Citizens' Council leaders and state officials—in many instances state officials *were* White Citizens Council leaders—cooperated to administer reading tests to fail blacks. Council leaders and state officials also cooperated to purge already registered blacks from voting lists. Black men attempting to register for the first time were often confronted with a battery of evasive maneuvers. Some registrars held office hours at irregular times and were simply not available when blacks showed up. In other instances, registrars refused to accept from blacks such standard identification as drivers' licenses and required that a prospective black voter bring in two already registered voters (that is, whites) to identify him. There were also cases in which registrars rejected black applicants for such minor errors as underlining rather than circling "Mr." on an application form.

To counter these tactics, the Civil Rights Act of 1964[7] made a sixth-grade education a presumption of literacy and required that all literacy tests be administered in writing unless the Attorney General of the United States gives special permission. The statute also forbade unequal administration of registration requirements and made it illegal for state officials to refuse to allow a prospective voter the franchise because of immaterial errors or omissions on registration forms. The 1964 act also strengthened earlier statutes permitting the Attorney General to intervene in voting cases, and directed the Bureau of the Census to gather registration and voting statistics based on race, color, and national origin.

Although less awkward than its predecessors, this statute proved to be an ineffective answer to discrimination against voting rights, and Congress passed a new act in 1965,[8] one even more complex than any previous civil rights law, but complex in the sense of having interlocking rows of sharp teeth rather than layers of gummy verbiage. The heart of the statute is a series of specific, practical remedies. First, the U.S. Attorney General may suspend operation of any state, county, or parish voting test of literacy, education, or character that he believes has been used to discriminate in the last five years if less than

half the residents of voting age in that governmental unit were not registered to vote in
November 1964 or did not vote in the 1964 presidential election. Second, any new state or
local rules affecting voting rights may not go into effect until either the Attorney General
finds no objection against them or the state obtains a judgment from the U.S. District
Court for the District of Columbia—not from the local federal district judge—that the
new regulations not discriminate on racial grounds.

Third, the Attorney General may declare that federal supervision in an area is
necessary to ensure fair voting procedures. The U.S. Civil Service Commission must then
assign examiners to determine who are qualified voters, and state officials must register
anyone certified by a federal examiner as a qualified voter. If requested by the Attorney
General, the Commission must also assign federal officers as poll watchers to make certain
that qualified voters are allowed to cast their ballots.

Each of these provisions applies to all elections, general or primary, whether of
state, local, or federal government officials, political party officers, or popular determinations of public policy issues. Furthermore, where a voting case is brought before a federal
district court in the regular course of litigation, the judge may, in addition to his usual
authority, exercise powers substantially similar to those of the Attorney General. Attempts
to interfere with the administration of this statute or to intimidate anyone trying to vote
or trying to persuade others to vote are felonies, punishable by prison terms of up to
five years.

Initial enforcement[9] of the 1965 Voting Rights Act was hampered by a lack of
trained personnel who could investigate complaints or serve as examiners, but this show of
force by the federal government encouraged civil rights organizations—SNCC, CORE,
and the NAACP, in particular—to intensify their voter registration drives in the South and
in the North as well. Black registration figures climbed dramatically. Even in states in the
deep South black voters have become an important political force, and black elected officials are now serving in every state of the old Confederacy.

How effective a political voice blacks will have depends on several factors. Insofar
as black power in the South is concerned, the attitude of the U.S. Attorney General and
his staff will be important, since both the Civil Rights Acts of 1964 and 1965 rely
heavily on federal administrative action. The key to the "southern strategy" of the
Nixon Administration has been to win over southern whites to the Republican party by
slowing down federal action on school desegregation and black civil rights generally, and
the Administration's attempt, defeated in Congress by passage of a law extending the full
force of the 1965 Act until 1975, to weaken federal protection of black voting rights
hardly augurs well for vigorous enforcement. This effort to soften the effect of the 1965
statute, incidentally, runs against the logic of one of the publicists of the "southern
strategy," who argues that since blacks are apt to be Democrats, a Republican administration should do all it can to encourage blacks to vote, and, by increasing black influence
within the Democratic party, propel southern whites into Republican ranks.[10]

Second, black migration to metropolitan areas is reducing their vulnerability to discrimination, at least insofar as voting is concerned. The anonymity of big city life and the
existence of a black urban power base, although in many cases a small one, make such discrimination more difficult. Rural counties, especially one-crop areas where blacks tend to
be sharecroppers, are rife with opportunities to punish blacks for trying to vote. "Where

Negroes do not vote," the U.S. Commission on Civil Rights[11] has noted, "they are for the most part subservient to crop, land, and landlord. . . . It is easier to retaliate against someone for whom there is declining need, and more difficult to prove that the reprisal was in fact racially motivated."

Third, the future of black suffrage lies in the hands of blacks themselves. Militancy has not yet made significant inroads on political apathy in many jurisdictions, nor has it always encouraged blacks to use the ballot box to achieve their goals. There is no doubt that the opportunity now exists for further development of black power within the American political system. Whether, or how skillfully, blacks exploit that opportunity depends in part on the wisdom of their own actions. How the political system would respond to the strains of that new power is a different—and equally critical—question.

PRESENT-DAY VOTING REQUIREMENTS

Voters are required to meet five general conditions today: these concern citizenship, residence, age, and registration.

There is nothing in the Constitution that forces states to limit voting to citizens, and in the past many states did allow aliens to vote. Now, however, citizenship is an absolute requirement for voting in every state. Each state also has a residence provision, although the specific length of time varies from three months to two years. There have been several recent lawsuits challenging the reasonableness of lengthy residence requirements. None of these had been successful in federal courts through the end of 1970, but the increased mobility of large segments of the population has put pressure on state and national legislation to reduce residency requirements. And, in the Voting Rights Act of 1970,[12] Congress provided that thirty days residence is sufficient to qualify a citizen to vote in a presidential election.

This statute also made a long-awaited change in the minimum voting age. Twenty-one had been the traditional minimum in state law, and this figure was given negative recognition in the "penalty" clause of the Fourteenth Amendment.[13] Over the last few decades, several states reduced the minimum age to eighteen, others to nineteen and twenty years. And since 1954, when President Eisenhower urged Congress to propose a constitutional amendment setting a uniform minimum of eighteen years, there has been growing agitation for national action. In 1970, Congress opted for a quicker but more controversial course: it established by statute that anyone over eighteen was, if he met other legal requirements, eligible to vote for federal officials. A number of people believed that this portion of the Voting Rights Act was an invasion of state authority and promised an immediate court suit to test its constitutionality.

Qualifications for voting are administered almost everywhere through a registration system. Under state law, persons desiring to become voters must appear before election officials, indicate their ability to meet legal requirements, and have their names placed on the voting list. Most states maintain permanent registration lists; a few have periodic registration systems by which voters must register anew at regular intervals. Recurrent registration may limit the possibility of fraud by eliminating inactive names, but it also discourages voting because of the annoyance of new registration. In 1969, the American

Institute of Public Opinion found that one out of every four adults was not registered to vote. These people were disproportionately young (under 30) and two out of three expressed a preference for the Democratic party.

Before passage of the Voting Act of 1965, about a third of the states employed a literacy test of one kind or another as a prerequisite to voting. After passage of that statute, many states suspended such tests—or had them suspended by the federal government. That statute and the Voting Rights Act of 1970 have cast a pall over the legitimacy of all tests of literacy, moral character, and political understanding.

Disqualification by Gerrymandering

Unfair apportionment of population for election purposes, or gerrymandering, may be accomplished by positive legislative action in which lines of electoral districts are deliberately drawn so as to give one party or set of interest groups advantages over another. Gerrymandering may also be achieved by default, by legislative inaction in the face of major population shifts. The latter method has been widely "used" in this century and, with the mass exodus from farms to cities, has been effective in overweighting rural representation in state legislatures as well as in Congress. As late as 1964 it was not unusual to find urban and suburban congressional districts with populations three or four times the size of rural districts in the same state, and there was an even more pronounced pattern of imbalance in most state legislatures.

In a series of decisions over the years, the Supreme Court had refused to hear lawsuits asking judges to command reapportionment. The Justices were often divided in their reasoning, but most observers interpreted these refusals as based on the doctrine that reapportionment was not a justiciable but a political question; that is, it was a problem that the Constitution left to be resolved by legislators and administrators rather than by judges. In 1962, however, the Court in *Baker v. Carr*[14] ruled that gerrymandering by default was a violation of the Constitution that courts could remedy. The *Baker* case, however, involved only the lower house of a state legislature, and it was not until *Wesberry v. Sanders*[15] in 1964 that the Court ruled that such malapportionment of congressional districts was also an infringement of the right to vote that courts could order corrected.

Later in 1964 a majority of the Justices held in *Reynolds v. Sims* that even the seats in the upper house of a state legislature had to be apportioned on the basis of population. The Court rejected the analogy to the U.S. Senate in favor of a ruling that the democratic ideal of "one man, one vote" was a constitutional command subject only to the specific exceptions of the Senate and the Electoral College. "Legislators," Chief Justice Warren[16] said for the Court, "represent people, not trees or acres. Legislators are elected by voters, not farms or cities or economic interests. As long as ours is a representative form of government . . . the right to elect legislators in a free and unimpaired fashion is a bedrock of our political system."

These decisions and their later extension to municipal elections[17] have stirred what eventually may turn into major changes in the nature of American politics by strengthening the political power of the cities and even more so of the suburbs, since it was the most recently developed areas that suffered most from gerrymandering by default. Since 1962, every state legislature in the country has, voluntarily, as a result of a court order, or because of a threat of such an order, undergone some reapportionment. For similar reasons a great majority of states have redrawn the lines of their congressional districts and, if the Supreme Court insists, as it appears to be doing,[18] on almost perfect mathematical uniformity, only those states that elect their congressmen at large are apt to escape redistricting.

These political results were not easily achieved. In each state groups that were faced with loss of influence fought doggedly to retain as much of the status quo as possible, and in many instances succeeded in delaying reapportionment and in minimizing their losses through clever drawing of district lines. The reapportionment decisions, especially *Reynolds v. Sims,* also ran into heavy congressional opposition. Led by the late Senate Minority Leader Everett Dirksen, the foes of the "one man, one vote" doctrine mounted several counterattacks that came close to pushing through Congress a proposed constitutional amendment to modify the effect of the Court's decisions. Indeed, on two occasions Dirksen's proposal to allow states to apportion one house of the legislature on grounds other than population received 57 to 39 and 55 to 38 majorities in the Senate, falling just short of the two-thirds vote needed to propose a constitutional amendment.

The end of the reapportionment struggle is not yet in sight. New legislative and court battles will be waged as political parties and interest groups vie for advantage. Moreover, analyses of the 1970 census will undoubtedly reveal fresh discrepancies in district populations and touch off another round of maneuvering. It is probably not possible to draw electoral lines without conferring some partisan advantages and disadvantages. Positive gerrymandering of electoral districts of substantially equal population but of such geographical configurations as to benefit one party or set of interest groups remains a practical if not a legal possibility.

In 1961, a full year before *Baker v. Carr,* the Supreme Court held unconstitutional Alabama's gerrymandering of the town of Tuskegee,[19] but there were special circumstances. Alabama's redistricting had been a crass effort to disfranchise black citizens, and the Court specifically declared that this sort of positive action violated the Fifteenth Amendment's prohibition against racial discrimination in voting. Judges are quite aware of the possibilities of gerrymandering, but whether they will—or can—prevent such maneuvers where nonracial factors are dominant remains to be seen.[20]

Even if each state eventually makes all of its congressional districts almost exactly equal in population, the federal nature of American government will still cause some areas to be overrepresented in Washington. First, unequal representation in the Senate necessarily results from each state's electing two senators regardless of its population. In 1970, the number of people represented by two senators ranged from about 20 million in California to about 300,000 in Alaska. Any alteration of this arrangement would require a constitutional amendment that would have to be ratified by all fifty states, since the Constitution provides that no state shall be deprived of its equal representation in the Senate without its consent.

A second difficulty is found in the unequal representation in the House of Representatives. The apportionment following the 1960 census of 435 seats in the House among the fifty states provided a reasonably close approximation of representation based on population. Under the Constitution each state must be given one seat. This resulted in three states obtaining a seat even though their populations were less than the average-size district, then about 410,000. After that, the remaining 385 seats were assigned. In effect a state got an additional seat for each additional 410,000 people. But no fractional seats could be assigned, so some states got a final seat for less than 410,000 people, whereas others failed to get such a seat because the remainder after their populations had been divided by 410,000 was not large enough. For example, the 1960 apportionment gave Kentucky one less congressman than Maryland, even though Kentucky's population was only 62,000 less than Maryland's.

WHICH OFFICES SHOULD BE ELECTIVE?

In our earlier discussion of elections, we noted that one requirement of a democratic government is that the principal policy-making officials should be elected. We put aside, however, the question of who are the principal policy-making officials. This was a prudent move for there is no political litmus paper that provides a means of distinguishing clearly between major and minor policy-makers. Certainly legislators and the heads of executive departments make important policy choices, but to some extent so do most government officials. A policeman's decision not to give speeding tickets unless offenders exceed posted limits by more than five miles an hour in effect modifies a legislative policy, just as a bureau chief's heel dragging can reshape a presidential decision. So too, a judge in interpreting the general phrases of the Constitution or the sometimes ambiguous wording of a statute finds that he must make policy to decide the specific cases before him. The Framers of the Constitution provided for popular election only of members of the House, but the Seventeenth Amendment formally requires senators to go through a similar election process. Practice has also changed the original form of the Electoral College so that the popular vote typically—though not necessarily—determines the choice of a President. Federal judges, cabinet members, and all lower ranking administrators are, appointed, not elected.

Thus in national elections each voter helps choose not more than four or five federal officers—a President, a Vice President, a senator (in two of three sequential elections), a representative from the voter's district, and occasionally a representative from the state at large. Moreover, with one "X" the voter expresses his preference for both a presidential and vice-presidential candidate. There is a sharp contrast between this federal short ballot and the long or "jungle" ballot that is widely used by state and local governments in the United States. State and local ballots vary considerably, but the typical state or city elects not only its chief executive and the members of its legislature but also a variety of subordinate executive officers and a number of judges. Evidence indicates that voters seldom know anything about more than a few of these candidates, and, where party identification is not clear, choice has an element of randomness.

On the other hand, the federal ballot is not short compared with the ballot in a British national election. There the voter helps select just one officer directly, the member of the House of Commons from his home district. The Prime Minister is not directly elected by British voters. Instead, the party that wins a majority of the seats in the House of Commons chooses one of its leaders to serve as Prime Minister and he is appointed to that post by the Queen. This is the short ballot reduced to its absolute minimum.

TWO STAGES IN ELECTING PUBLIC OFFICERS

The election of public officers in the United States by the voters is usually a twofold process consisting of nomination and then election. These two stages are quite distinct from each other, and each has been institutionalized in elaborate, highly formalized procedures. The nomination of national officers is nowhere referred to in the federal Constitution. In a two-party system nomination of candidates for public offices by the parties is of great significance, for it limits the choice of the voters to just two possibilities—a very substantial restriction.

The development of a separate, formalized nomination stage in the electoral system of a democracy is not inevitable. In Britain nomination has remained relatively uncomplicated; any properly qualified person can declare his candidacy for a seat in the House of Commons by obtaining the signatures of ten voters and posting a deposit of £150 which he forfeits if he fails to poll one-eighth of the total vote in his district on election day. In fact, however, most candidates running for the House of Commons are chosen by the party organizations in a quite informal way.

A party nomination in the American political system is, more often than not, much sought after. And this pressure at the nomination stage has resulted in the development of complicated mechanisms to determine party candidates. V. O. Key[21] mentioned three other reasons why "nominating processes in the United States are much more elaborate than in any other democratic regime." One is the long list of elective offices in federal, state, and local government which gives the nominating process great significance. Second is the existence of numerous one-party areas in the United States in which the nomination is equivalent to election and is thus certain to be vigorously sought after. And third is the similarity of the two major parties which tends to blur voter's choices *between* parties and thereby accentuates the importance of choice *within* a party.

ELECTING CONGRESSMEN

Provisions of the Constitution

Every two years the entire membership of the House of Representatives and one-third of the members of the Senate are chosen by the voters of the states in a November election. The Constitution provides that representatives shall be apportioned among the states on the basis of population. Although it does not say so, the implication is that Congress shall make a new apportionment every ten years following the taking of the census. The Constitution does not fix the number of seats in the House, leaving that to be determined by Congress itself, and Congress has set the number at 435. The Constitution does fix terms and minimum qualifications of senators and representatives. Senators must be thirty years of age and citizens of the United States for nine years; they serve for six years. Representatives must be twenty-five years of age and citizens for seven years; they serve for two years. Both senators and representatives are required to be inhabitants of their states at the time of their election, but as shown by the election in 1964 of Robert Kennedy as senator from New York, the term "resident" may sometimes be liberally construed. Representatives are not required by law or the Constitution to be residents of the districts they serve; however, by practice this is almost invariably the case.

The most important provision in the federal Constitution concerning the conduct of congressional elections is the paragraph in Article I, section 4, which states: "The times, places and manner of holding elections for Senators and Representatives, shall be prescribed in each State by the legislature thereof; but the Congress may at any time by law make or alter such regulations. . . ." By and large Congress has left it to the states to regulate national elections, although it has utilized its authority to protect voters against violence, intimidation, and fraud, and to enact "corrupt practices" legislation which has placed easily evaded limitations on campaign spending. Congress might also invoke this clause to safeguard the voting rights of blacks, but the Fifteenth Amendment supplies a more specific justification. For a time there was a live question whether Article I, section 4 conferred authority on Congress to regulate primaries. After some confusing dicta, the Supreme Court finally ruled that congressional primaries fell within national power.[22]

Article I, section 5 states: "Each House shall be the judge of the elections, returns and qualifications of its own members." The provision seemed to confer full and exclusive authority on the two houses, and on several occasions Congress established qualifications for membership that went beyond those enumerated in the Constitution. In 1900, for instance, the House refused to seat a polygamist, and in 1919 it barred a Socialist who had been convicted under the sedition laws. In 1926 the Senate would not seat senators from Illinois and Pennsylvania because they had spent too much money in their election campaigns.

The broad language of Article I, section 5 and congressional practice seemed to settle the matter by barring the possibility of a court suit to test any adverse legislative decision. But Rev. Adam Clayton Powell, black congressman from Harlem, thought otherwise. In 1967 the Ninetieth Congress had refused to seat him after hearing evidence that he had "wrongfully and willfully" misspent government funds and had abused his privileges and immunities as a congressman by defying court judgments against him for libel. Rev. Powell, however, did not meekly accept this punishment for his sins. He stood for reelection to his vacant seat in the Ninetieth Congress and won over 86 percent of the vote without campaigning. But, instead of returning to Washington to claim his seat, he stayed in Bimini and filed a lawsuit demanding back pay from the day of his exclusion. While the case was pending, Powell was reelected to the Ninety-first Congress and seated without incident.

Lower federal courts thought the question of barring Powell from the Ninetieth Congress was a matter under the exclusive jurisdiction of the House, but in a 7–1 decision the Supreme Court[23] ruled that "in judging the qualifications of its members Congress is limited to the standing qualifications prescribed in the Constitution." Any effort, as in Powell's case, to impose additional qualifications for membership was invalid. Either house, the Justices conceded, could punish a member for offensive conduct or even expel him; but, as provided by section 5 of Article I, expulsion required a two-thirds rather than a majority vote.

The Nomination of Congressmen

Today the party primary is widely used to nominate both senators and representatives. In 1968, only Delaware used the convention system for the nomination of both. In Connecticut senators and representatives are nominated by party conventions, but any unsuccessful candidate who receives at least 20 percent of the convention vote may, if he can obtain 750 to 5000 signatures on a petition—the number varies with the office being sought—run against the convention's nominee in a primary election. Indiana nominates its senatorial candidates by convention and representatives by primaries. All other states use the primary system. There are, however, wide differences in types of state primaries.

In a majority of states congressional primaries are of the so-called closed type. Voting in such a primary is limited to party members. Voters must declare their party affiliation either at registration or at the primary election. Some provision is made for voters to change party allegiance from time to time. A few states use the open primary, which allows voters to make up their minds on the day of the primary election in which party primary they will participate. Actually the distinction between these two types is not always a sharp one; in some states the closed primary is so loosely organized or administered that it allows almost the same freedom of action possible in the open system.

Oklahoma and ten southern states use a runoff primary system. Here, if the leading candidate in the first primary fails to poll a majority of the vote, a second, or runoff, primary is held in which the choice is narrowed to the two highest candidates in the first primary. In one-party states this system has the advantage of guaranteeing that the person who wins the nomination—and thereby the election—has the support of something more than the small plurality that is often enough to win a race in which three or more strong candidates are seeking nomination. Few of these states, however, can count on being one-party any longer. It remains to be seen what effects this will have on primary systems.

A further variation is found in the timing of primary elections. Some states nominate their congressional candidates as early as April in election years, whereas others do not do so until September. This staggering of primaries has a pronounced decentralizing effect upon the selection of national legislators, making it extremely difficult to focus voters' attention upon the same issues. Because of this lack of focus and the independent power bases of local politicos, national party organizations and leaders are ordinarily unable to exert much influence upon the selection of congressional candidates.

The primary election is usually viewed as a means of nominating candidates for Congress, but in fact it serves very widely as the means by which congressmen are elected. A study[24] of elections to the House of Representatives showed that 53.5 percent of victorious candidates between 1896 and 1946 won by at least a 60 to 40 margin. This suggests that the outcome of the final election in these instances was never much in doubt and that the real decision was made by the voters in the primary election of the dominant party. Data from the congressional elections of 1956 through 1970 demonstrate an even clearer pattern. On the average, about 261 seats, 60 percent of the total, were won by a margin of 60–40 or higher. While "safe" districts in one election can become bitterly contested districts a few years later, the important point is that more often than not it has been the congressional primary that constituted the real elecion. This phenomenon is by no means confined to southern states.

Moreover, only a rather small number of seats change party hands. In 1956, Democrats won eleven seats from Republicans, and the latter won nine seats from Democrats. In 1960, Republicans captured twenty-eight Democratic seats and Democrats eight Republican districts. 1964 was a disastrous year for Republicans, yet they lost only forty-eight seats to Democrats and, in turn, won ten, for a net loss of only thirty-eight. 1968 saw the Republicans victorious in nine formerly Democratic districts, but they lost five of their own. These were all years of presidential elections, and while party shifts in off-year elections are generally greater, as the chart shows, these changes, except for 1938 and 1946, are still rather small.

ELECTING THE PRESIDENT

The Original Method

The method of present-day presidential elections has been seriously criticized for its undemocratic character; yet, when compared to the method the Framers established, current practice seems relatively democratic, though far from perfect. The Convention finally approved a plan for the selection of the President and Vice President by an Electoral

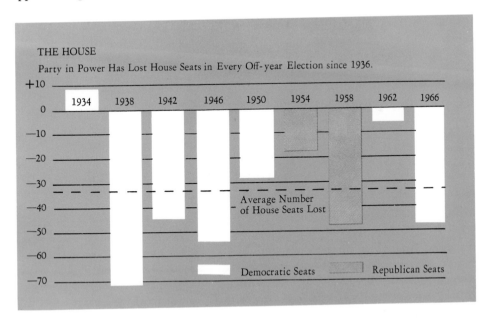

SOURCE: *The New York Times*, November 6, 1966 and *Congressional Quarterly Weekly Report,* November 11, 1966.

College—actually "colleges" would have been a more accurate title since these groups were to meet in the several states, never as a national body. Each state legislature was authorized to choose its members of the College in any manner it saw fit, and each state was to have as many electors as it had senators and representatives. The electors were to meet in their respective states at a time designated by Congress and to vote for two persons. The ballots were to be forwarded to Congress and opened and counted in the presence of both houses. The person having the largest number of votes, providing it was a majority of the total number of electors, was to be President, and the person with the second highest number Vice President. If no person had a majority, the House of Representatives was to select one of the five highest on the list to serve as President; each state was to have one vote in this process, and a majority of all the states was required for election.

The election of 1800 showed the need for a change in at least the mechanics of the operation. All the electors pledged to the Republican party cast their two votes for Thomas Jefferson and Aaron Burr, intending the first to be President and the latter Vice President. But, since both men had the same number of electoral votes, there was no legal way of carrying out the intention of the electors, and the House of Representatives had to break the tie. It was clear that the same result would prevail in subsequent elections if political parties continued to be active. Accordingly, the Twelfth Amendment was added to the Constitution in 1804, directing the electors to cast one of their votes specifically for President and one for Vice President.

Not a word appears in the Constitution about the nomination of presidential candidates. It was regarded as a foregone conclusion that George Washington would be the first President. But thereafter the Convention apparently expected that in each election the members of the Electoral College would have a free hand in canvassing a wide list of possible candidates and that there would be no "nominees" in any formal sense. Since the electors were never to meet in any one place as a single unit, this was almost certain to mean that the electoral vote would be widely distributed. It seems likely that many members of the Convention viewed the Electoral College as an agency that would *nominate* up to five candidates for the Presidency, and the House of Representatives as the agency that would frequently have to *elect* the President. The system, however, rapidly began to operate along quite different lines. During the first third of the nineteenth century it remained in a state of flux, but in the Jacksonian era the method of electing the President, as we know it today, more or less crystallized.

Nominating Presidential Candidates

Political parties have made an all-important contribution to the American electoral system, for it is not too much to say that the means by which the practical choice of the voters is narrowed to two or at most three candidates are almost completely controlled by the parties. Not only is the Constitution utterly silent concerning the nomination of presidential candidates, but there is little statutory control over this phase of the election system. A small body of state law deals with some of the details of convention organization and procedure, such as the method of selecting the delegates and the manner in which some of the state delegates cast their votes in the convention, but neither the states nor the federal government have attempted to regulate the larger aspects of the convention system—

the total number of delegates, the time and place of the meeting, or the vote required for nomination. Instead, the organization and the control of a national convention are largely the responsibility of the party and are determined for the most part by custom.

In recent decades the Democratic and the Republican national conventions have had from 1200 to 3000 delegates (many with only a one-half vote), with each state having a number of votes roughly equal to twice the size of its congressional delegation. Actually, both parties now use modified formulas by which states giving a party substantial election support enjoy increased voting power in that party's convention. In order to reduce the power of delegations from states with weak party organizations, the Republicans in 1924 adopted a system of granting bonus votes to delegations from states carried by Republican candidates for various national offices in recent elections. The bonus system was adopted by the Democrats in 1944 and has been expanded since. Democrats have tended more than Republicans to use fractional votes and oversized delegations. In the 1968 conventions, the Democrats had 2622 votes, and the Republicans 1333. Despite these changes, "the apportionment rules tend to over represent the small states and under represent the large. They also over represent the areas of low voter turnout and under represent those of higher voter turnout. In states where one party is much stronger than the other, the rules tend to over represent the weaker party and under represent the stronger."[25]

Both parties leave it to the individual states to determine how their delegates will be selected. Two methods are widely used—the convention system and the primary system. Throughout the nineteenth century delegates were chosen by state and local conventions or caucuses. Early in the present century a desire to make the presidential election system more democratic led to the presidential primary, in which the rank and file of party members in a state were not only allowed to choose the state's delegates to the national convention but were often given an opportunity to express their preferences for a presidential candidate. At first it appeared that the primary would soon entirely replace the state convention as a means of choosing delegates, but after 1916 a reaction set in. By 1968 only fourteen states and the District of Columbia held presidential primaries. Moreover, in many of the states the primary has become a formality. In the last few presidential election years the number of significant presidential primaries has not exceeded five or six. Still, a candidate who has not run well in these elections is usually in serious trouble at the national convention.

The regulations—usually state laws—surrounding presidential primaries often operate in favor of established political organizations by requiring long notice and many signatures before a name can be placed on the ballot. Thus, as supporters of Eugene McCarthy and George Wallace found in 1968, an insurgent candidate is often locked out not only of state conventions staffed by party regulars but also of more popularly oriented primaries.

Procedure in the Convention: Adopting a Platform

When a national convention meets there are two important items of business to be transacted: drafting and adopting the party platform and nominating the candidates for President and Vice President. The platform is drafted by a committee on resolutions consisting

of one man and one woman from each state and territory selected by their own delegations. This committee usually holds public hearings at which representatives of interest
groups are given a chance to present their views. Much of the platform, however, is often
prepared in advance by a small group of party leaders or, in the case of the party in
power, by the President and his advisers. The platform is submitted to the delegates on
the floor of the convention on the second or third day and is usually approved with a
minimum of debate or controversy. Occasionally, as when a public is badly divided on an
issue like Vietnam, an effort is made to amend the platform from the floor, and once in
a while such a move succeeds.

It is easy enough to ridicule the average platform, for as V. O. Key[26] says, it
"speaks with boldness and forthrightness on issues that are already well settled; it is likely
to be ambiguous on contentious questions." But such criticism frequently overlooks the
importance of compromise in politics. The evasive platform is one of the forces that
makes it possible for parties to hold together at least long enough to elect every four
years a President who has the backing of 40 million or more voters. This is an achievement whose importance should not be minimized. At the same time, the price paid for it
is sometimes a heavy one in terms of muddling issues that ought to be brought out
in the open and intelligently discussed.

Procedure in the Convention: Nominating Candidates

Both major party conventions now employ much the same method of nominating candidates. First, the roll of the states is called so that the candidates for the presidential nomination may be placed before the convention in formal nominating speeches. Then the
balloting begins, each state casting its votes orally as the roll is called from Alabama to
Wyoming. The District of Columbia and the territories and dependencies also cast a small
number of votes. A majority of all votes cast is necessary for nomination, and successive
ballots are taken until a majority is obtained by one of the candidates. The first ballot
frequently proves effective; in fact, from 1900 until 1968, fifteen Republican and twelve
Democratic candidates were chosen on the first ballot.

Following the presidential nomination, the convention quickly names a vice-
presidential candidate. The presidential nominee's advice is sought and usually accepted.
The vice-presidential candidate may be some one who could not have been nominated and
elected President, but whose qualities offset and complement those of the presidential
nominee. The heart attacks of Eisenhower and the assassination of Kennedy have increased
awareness of the possibility of the Vice President's becoming the Chief Executive and thus
focused attention on the abilities of vice-presidential candidates. It is probable that this
concern narrowed Nixon's margin of victory in 1968.

The Dynamics of the Presidential Nominating Process

Unless it is clear that a party is committed to the renomination of a President in office,
anywhere from two to a dozen candidates will be active in the preconvention campaign.
Most of these men will have long records in politics. Only rarely does a businessman or
military figure step directly into the role of a party's standard bearer with little or no

previous experience in politics, as did Wendell Willkie in 1940 or Dwight Eisenhower in 1952.

State politics has historically been a very important training ground for presidential candidates. Eleven of the twenty men nominated by the two major parties for the Presidency between 1900 and 1956 were state governors or former governors. With the increased importance of foreign policy, however, the Senate is becoming the spawning ground for leading presidential hopefuls. Each of the presidential candidates in 1960, 1964, and 1968, Barry Goldwater, Lyndon B. Johnson, John F. Kennedy, Hubert H. Humphrey, and Richard M. Nixon, had been senators, as had several of their major rivals for the nomination.

Despite such exceptions as Al Smith in 1928, John F. Kennedy in 1960, and Eugene McCarthy in 1968, most leading candidates for a major party nomination have been Protestant. Geography is also an important factor in determining the availability of presidential candidates. A candidate from a state with a large electoral vote that is also "doubtful" politically, such as California, New York, Ohio, Pennsylvania or Illinois, will seem much more attractive to the party than a man from a small state that is sure to be in one party column or the other. Beyond that, if an aspirant has a large and attractive family, a pleasing appearance and personality, and, above all, a knack for campaign oratory, he may be able to qualify as an available candidate. Whether lightning will finally strike him depends upon a further complex of forces and circumstances in which luck is by no means the least important factor.

The notion that a few party leaders get together in a smoke-filled room and agree upon a candidate, who is then meekly accepted by the delegates, does not fit the facts. Two forces operate in the present-day national convention to bring about the nomination of a candidate who has strong backing among the rank-and-file party members. One is the influence of the public opinion poll, which unquestionably carries great weight with both convention leaders and delegates. Indeed, since surveys have come to occupy such a prominent place on the American scene, both parties have almost always nominated the candidate who stood at the top of the polls. In 1964 the Republicans violated this practice and paid a high price at the ballot box.

Second, the presidential primary, for all of its shortcomings, continues to have some value as an indicator of public opinion. For example, in 1952 the first state primary, that in New Hampshire, substantially affected the chances of leading candidates in both parties. In the Republican primary Eisenhower won a decisive victory over Senator Robert Taft, giving great impetus to the Eisenhower movement at a time when the General was seemingly not sure whether he wanted to run for the Presidency. And Senator Estes Kefauver's victory over President Truman in the Democratic primary was apparently a major factor in the President's decision not to seek reelection in 1952. In 1960, Kennedy's strong showing in Wisconsin and West Virginia made him the frontrunner and ended Senator Hubert Humphrey's campaign. Similarly, in 1964 Barry Goldwater's victory in California made him the candidate whom no other Republican hopeful could reach. Primaries in 1968 did not play a critical role in determining the eventual nominee that they have in some other years. In part, this occurred because the candidate whose fortunes were most dependent on the primaries, Senator Robert F. Kennedy of New York, was assassinated and in part because the other major Democratic primary winner, Senator

Eugene McCarthy of Minnesota, was unacceptable to the dominant factions of the Democratic party.

The Final Election of a President

In presidential elections over 70 million voters go to the polls to select the members of the Electoral College. Before election day each of the parties selects a full slate of candidates for the seats to which a state is entitled in the Electoral College. The identity of these candidates and the manner of their selection are of little consequence, provided there is no question of a revolt on the part of a state's electors against their party's candidate for the Presidency. Indeed, in most states the names of the candidates for the Electoral College no longer appear upon the ballot. Instead, the ballots in these states carry only the names of the party candidates for President and Vice President, and a phrase for each party column indicating that the proper number of candidates for the Electoral College is pledged to vote for the party's nominees. This is known as the presidential short ballot.

In all the states the electors are chosen at large, which means that the entire slate of the party receiving the most votes in the state-wide election is elected and the electoral vote of the state is thereafter cast as a unit. There is nothing in the Constitution to prevent a state legislature from providing for choosing electors from single-member districts, an arrangement that would make possible a divided state electoral vote. No state has followed such a plan since 1891 (and few before that date) because the dominant party in each state naturally opposes giving the minority party a chance to win any electoral votes. Moreover, state legislators have reasoned that the possibility of a divided electoral vote would lessen their state's influence and prestige in national politics.

By midnight of election day it is usually possible to determine which party has the majority of the votes in the Electoral College and thus to know who will be the next President. But technically the voting for President and Vice President occurs in December when, on a day fixed by federal law, the victorious electors meet in their respective state capitals and formally cast their ballots. The outcome is not officially recognized until the new Congress assembles in January, counts the ballots of the electors in a joint House-Senate session, and proclaims the result. It is at this point that the House of Representatives would proceed to elect a President in case of a tie vote or in case no candidate had a clear majority of electoral votes, the Senate electing a Vice President under similar conditions. Since the Twentieth Amendment fixes January 20 as Inauguration Day, Congress would have to act promptly were the electoral vote to prove ineffective.

Defects of the Electoral College System

Although the Electoral College has functioned reasonably well through the years, the system has three serious weaknesses, each of which threatens the democratic character of presidential elections. In the first place, there is no provision in the federal Constitution or federal law to prevent an elector from voting for someone other than his party's candidates, and in 1948, 1960, and 1968 at least one elector voted for an "outside" candidate. Only a few states expressly compel electors to fulfill their pledges, although several others have laws that make an incidental recognition of this obligation.

The second weakness is the ever-present possibility that the popular vote and the

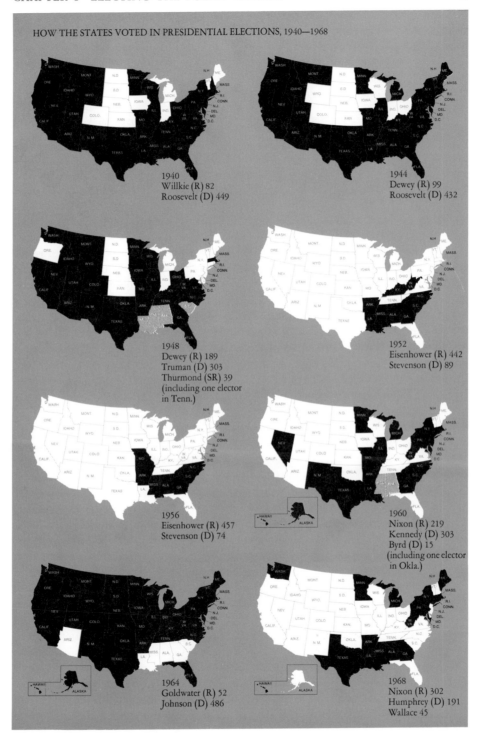

HOW THE STATES VOTED IN PRESIDENTIAL ELECTIONS, 1940–1968

1940
Willkie (R) 82
Roosevelt (D) 449

1944
Dewey (R) 99
Roosevelt (D) 432

1948
Dewey (R) 189
Truman (D) 303
Thurmond (SR) 39
(including one elector
in Tenn.)

1952
Eisenhower (R) 442
Stevenson (D) 89

1956
Eisenhower (R) 457
Stevenson (D) 74

1960
Nixon (R) 219
Kennedy (D) 303
Byrd (D) 15
(including one elector
in Okla.)

1964
Goldwater (R) 52
Johnson (D) 486

1968
Nixon (R) 302
Humphrey (D) 191
Wallace 45

SOURCE: Data from *The New York Times* and *Congressional Quarterly Weekly Report.*

electoral vote will get out of line and that the victor in the electoral vote will actually receive fewer popular votes than his opponent. This possibility results primarily from the fact that in each state the winning candidate receives the state's entire electoral vote regardless of the popular vote won by the losing candidate. This imbalance has occurred in two elections since the Civil War:

Year	Candidates	Popular Vote	Electoral Vote
1876	Hayes (Rep.)	4,033,768	185
	Tilden (Dem.)	4,285,992	184
1888	Harrison (Rep.)	5,439,853	233
	Cleveland (Dem.)	5,540,329	168

Moreover, the same result could have occurred in many other elections, including 1968, had small blocs of popular votes been cast the other way in certain states.

The third weakness is the possibility that the Electoral College may fail to give a majority to any candidate and the election will be thrown into the House of Representatives. This has happened only twice in American history and only once since the adoption of the Twelfth Amendment: in 1824, four presidential candidates divided the electoral vote in such a way that no one of them had a majority. But there have been other elections in which strong third-party candidates threatened to win enough electoral votes to throw the election into the House. The 1968 election provides a good example. The third party candidate, George Wallace, won in five states and received 46 electoral votes. Had Humphrey rather than Nixon carried Alaska, Delaware, Missouri, Nevada, and Tennessee (Nixon's combined margin of victory in these five states was less than 91,000), Nixon's electoral vote would have been 269 and Humphrey's 223. Both would have been short of a majority—270—and the House would have been called upon to choose among Humphrey, Nixon, and Wallace.

It may be asked why there should be any misfortune about having a presidential election thrown into the House of Representatives. Two difficulties should be mentioned. In the first place, the voting in the House for President is by states and not by members. It is entirely possible for the minority party in the House to have control of a majority of the state delegations and thereby to be in a position to elect its candidate to the Presidency even though he stood second in both popular and electoral votes. The constitutional requirement that the winning candidate receive the votes of a majority of all the states poses a second problem. It is possible for party control of state delegations to be so scrambled that the House would have great difficulty in selecting a President, if, indeed, it could do so at all. In the Ninety-first Congress, the one that would have been saddled with the task of unsnarling a Nixon-Humphrey-Wallace deadlock, the Republicans had a majority in only 19 state delegations. The Democrats had an apparent majority in 27 delegations, but these included the 11 states of the old Confederacy, five of whose voters had chosen electors pledged to Wallace. What would have happened in those delegations or in the four equally divided between Democrats and Republicans teases the imagination.

If the House were unable to choose a President by Inauguration Day, the Vice President, elected by the Senate from the two candidates with the highest electoral votes for that office, would serve until the House could reach a majority decision or, if that did not happen, until the end of a regular four-year term. If the Senate were unable to elect a Vice President—51 votes are needed and enough senators might abstain to keep either candidate from winning—the Speaker of the House of Representatives would serve as President, again until the House reached a decision or until the end of a four-year term. These defects have been obvious for many years, but many conservative congressmen and many of those from the smaller states have been reluctant to upset the status quo lest they increase the political power of the states with huge metropolitan areas. Finally, however, in the closing days of the 1970 session of the Ninety-first Congress, both houses proposed a constitutional amendment that provided for direct election of the President and Vice President by popular vote. The proposal stipulated that if no candidate received at least 40 percent of the total number of votes cast, there would have to be a run-off election between the two top ranking candidates for each office. As with all amendments, ratification by three quarters of the states is necessary to make the proposal a part of the Constitution.

SELECTED BIBLIOGRAPHY

David, Paul T., Ralph M. Goldman, and Richard C. Bain, *The Politics of National Party Conventions,* paperback edition, K. Sproul, ed. (Washington, D.C.: The Brookings Institution, 1960). Brings together a wealth of information on and interpretations of the operations of national party nominating conventions.

David, Paul T., Malcolm Moos, and Ralph M. Goldman, *Presidential Nominating Politics* (Baltimore, Md.: The Johns Hopkins Press, 1954), 5 vols. A monumental study of the Eisenhower and Stevenson nominations of 1952.

Dixon, Robert G., Jr., *Democratic Representation: Reapportionment in Law and Politics* (New York: Oxford University Press, 1968). A superb examination by a lawyer-political scientist of the problems, past and future, of legislative reapportionment.

Downs, Anthony, *An Economic Theory of Democracy* (New York: Harper & Row, Publishers, 1957). A challenging investigation of the rational bases of political behavior.

Lubell, Samuel, *The Future of American Politics* (New York: Harper and Row, 1952). Lubell's future has long come to pass, but this is still an interesting analysis of the American political system.

Polsby, Nelson W., and Aaron B. Wildavsky, *Presidential Elections: Strategies of American Electoral Politics* (New York: Charles Scribner's Sons, 1964). An excellent introduction to the American electoral process and the implications of some reform proposals.

U.S. Congress, House Committee on the Judiciary, *Report: Direct Popular Election of the President*, Ninety-first Congress, first session (1969). A thorough examination of the problems of the Electoral College and a reasoned justification for changing to a system of direct elections.

Footnotes

[1] *Harper v. Virginia*, 383 U.S. 663 (1966). In two earlier decisions, the Court had held poll taxes to be constitutional: *Breedlove v. Suttles*, 302 U.S. 277 (1937), and *Butler v. Thompson*, 341 U.S. 937 (1951).

[2] C. Vann Woodward, *The Strange Career of Jim Crow,* 2d rev. ed., (New York: Oxford University Press, 1966), pp. 53–54.

[3] *Ibid.,* p. 64.

[4] In 1890 the Court upheld the constitutionality of a Mississippi literacy test, *Williams v. Mississippi,* 170 U.S. 213 (1890), although the Justices conceded it was possible to administer the test unfairly. The Court took a similar view 60 years later: *Lassiter v. Northampton,* 360 U.S. 45 (1959). The Court's record, however, has generally been better. See the following decisions invalidating:

"Understanding clauses": *Schnell v. Davis,* 336 U.S. 933 (1949); and *Louisiana v. United States,* 380 U.S. 145 (1965);

"Grandfather clauses": *Guinn v. United States,* 238 U.S. 347 (1915); and *Lane v. Wilson,* 307 U.S. 268 (1939);

"White primaries": *Smith v. Allwright,* 321 U.S. 649 (1944); and *Terry v. Adams,* 345 U.S. 461 (1953); earlier the Court had vacillated, first striking down crude white primaries, *Nixon v. Herndon,* 273 U.S. 536 (1927), and *Nixon v. Condon,* 286 U.S. 73 (1932), then sustaining a more subtle plan in *Grovey v. Townsend,* 295 U.S. 45 (1935). *Allwright,* however, reversed *Grovey,* and lower federal courts continued to strike down even more esoteric efforts; see especially *Rice v Elmore,* 165 F.2d 387 (1947); and *Baskin v. Brown,* 174 F.2d 391 (1949).

[5] 71 *Stat.* 634.

[6] 74 *Stat.* 90.

[7] 78 *Stat.* 241.

[8] 79 *Stat.* 437.

[9] The Supreme Court has upheld the constitutionality of the 1965 Act in the first three challenges: *South Carolina v. Katzenbach,* 383 U.S. 301 (1966); *Allen v. Board of Elections,* 393 U.S. 544 (1969); and *Gaston County v. United States,* 395 U.S. 285 (1969).

[10] Kevin P. Phillips, *The Emerging Republican Majority* (New Rochelle, N.Y.: Arlington House, 1969), p. 464.

[11] *Report of the United States Commission on Civil Rights 1961* (Washington, D.C.: Government Printing Office, 1961), Book I, pp. 190–91.

[12] Public Law 91–285. This is the same statute that extended the life of the Voting Rights Act of 1965.

[13] This clause provides that when a state abridges, except as a punishment for criminal acts, the right of males over twenty-one to vote for national or state officials, that state's representation in the House of Representatives "shall be reduced in the proportion which the number of such male citizens shall bear to the whole number of male citizens twenty-one years of age in such State."

[14] 369 U.S. 186 (1962).

[15] 376 U.S. 1 (1964).

[16] 377 U.S. 533, 562 (1964).

[17] *Avery v. Midland County,* 390 U.S. 474 (1968); *Hadley v. Kansas City,* 397 U.S. 50 (1970).

[18] *Duddleston v. Grills,* 385 U.S. 455 (1967), *Kirkpatrick v. Preisler,* 394 U.S. 526 (1969); and *Wells v. Rockefeller,* 394 U.S. 542 (1969).

[19] *Gomillion v. Lightfoot,* 364 U.S. 339 (1961).

[20] See, for example, the Court's dodging of this issue in *Wright v. Rockefeller,* 376 U.S. 52 (1964).

[21] V. O. Key, Jr., *Politics, Parties, and Pressure Groups,* 3d ed. (New York: Thomas Y. Crowell Company, 1953), p. 399.

[22] *United States v. Classic,* 313 U.S. 299 (1941), settled the issue. *Newberry v. United States,* 256 U.S. 232 (1921), had caused much of the uncertainty.

[23] *Powell v. McCormack,* 395 U.S. 486 (1969). Three years earlier *Bond v. Floyd,* 385 U.S. 116 (1966), had given a warning that exclusion of a member of the House or Senate would be subject to judicial review. There the Court had held unconstitutional as a violation of the First and Fourteenth Amendments the refusal of the Georgia House of Representatives to seat Julian Bond, a black man, because of his sharp criticism of American po'icy in Vietnam and of the Selective Service Act.

[24] Cortez Ewing, "Primaries as Real Elections," *Southwestern Social Science Quarterly,* 29 (March 1949), pp. 293–298.

[25] Paul T. David, Ralph M. Goldman, and Richard C. Bain, *The Politics of National Party Conventions,* paperback edition, K. Sproul, ed. (Washington, D.C.: The Brookings Institution, 1960), p. 108.

[26] Pp. 462–463.

Chapter 9 Political Campaigning

THE CHARACTER OF A CAMPAIGN

The ideal functions of political parties in a democracy include informing the public about urgent problems, clarifying alternative courses, and offering choices among solutions as well as candidates to execute those solutions; and the political campaign should be a prime arena for the performance of these tasks. Certainly much frenzied talking, writing, arguing, and haranguing goes on in an American campaign. Housewives cannot go to the supermarket or city subway riders to work without shaking the hand of seemingly indefatigable candidates for local office. Candidates for state office seem to try to eat the favorite food of every nationality their voters represent, shake every hand, and kiss every baby in their districts.

For some eight weeks before a presidential election the country is treated to one of its most colorful and exhausting political spectacles. The candidates for the Presidency are involved in the most intensive and prolonged effort to win high office that takes place in any modern democracy. In contrast, a British national campaign is traditionally limited to a seventeen-day period between the dissolving of Parliament and Election Day.

Traveling in elaborately manned and equipped campaign trains and planes, American candidates follow each other across the country, making a series of carefully planned addresses in key cities, as well as scores of informal talks to the thousands who come to see them. Television and radio reach millions of listeners who, for a time, find presidential sweepstakes almost as exciting as the Super Bowl. Party machinery is oiled, tens of thousands of campaign workers toil endlessly to win votes, millions of pieces of campaign literature are distributed, debates are held, promises are made, names are called, the air is full of prophecies of peace, war, prosperity, and depression. Hundreds of millions of dollars are spent to influence the voter to go the polls and to vote wisely—that is, for whichever candidate is talking.

Yet when one looks beyond the hullaballo, he usually finds that real debate on major issues has been sparse. The candidates tend to talk past each other. More often both candidates come out strongly for virtue and the betterment of mankind. Each campaign seems to stress the candidate's charm and personality at the expense of a clear-cut delineation of the issues, a detailed explanation of alternatives, and an intellectually satisfying justification of policy solutions. Differences in approach to problems are frequently evident both from campaign speeches and from candidates' public records or party affiliations, but a campaign seldom forms the stage on which two or three presidential aspirants perform according to the script of democratic government, giving voters a choice between legible blueprints of and reasoned justifications for proposed policies.

The causes are not hard to find. At root are two factors. First is a necessity to appeal to a broad spectrum of voters to build a winning majority. To stitch together a national coalition large enough to put him in the White House, a candidate often finds it advantageous to speak in general terms, lest a specific commitment that would please one group alienate another. How general his speeches will be depends in large part on the pattern of the coalition he is attempting to weave. Aiming at an alliance of liberal whites and black urban voters, Hubert Humphrey in 1968 or Lyndon Johnson in 1964 could speak forcefully and candidly about the need not only for the federal government to increase protection of black civil rights, but also to take positive steps to foster black economic advancement. Because Richard Nixon wanted to gain the votes of whites, southern and non-southern, who were worried about black power as well as win to support from more liberally oriented people who were disenchanted with the Democrats on Vietnam, he had to speak in evasive terms about the dangers of creeping federal power and the federal government's "going too far" in threatening to cut off funds from school districts that refused to desegregate. In contrast, because of the nature of their alliance, Humphrey and Johnson had to speak vaguely about law and order, lest specific proposals offend blacks or white liberals; while here Nixon, like Barry Goldwater in 1964, could come down hard, attacking the Supreme Court for protecting defendants' rights, promising firm police action, and pledging to appoint tougher-minded judges to the bench.

The second and equally basic factor behind the evasive tendency of campaign oratory is that in peacetime politics is not a fundamental concern of most Americans. As we noted in Chapter 1 few people make a serious effort to achieve a detailed, sophisticated understanding of what is going on about them, unless their own self-interest is immediately involved; even then their commitments are apt to be more intense than informed. There is constant competition for the voters' attention. To compete successfully over a long period of time, most politicians believe, one cannot offer detailed discussions of intricate political problems. To rally supporters a candidate must first attract attention, and a pretty wife and children, an emotional charge of corruption in the opposition's ranks, and other sorts of Madison Avenue gimmickry can be more effective than a discussion of a brooding policy problem.

PRESIDENTIAL CAMPAIGNS

Do Campaigns Make a Difference?

Does all the frenzied activity in which candidates, their staffs, and supporters engage make a substantial difference on election day? There is no simple answer. A large body of survey research indicates that in presidential elections 60–75 percent of those who actually vote make up their minds by the time the national conventions have nominated their candidates.[1] But this statistic conceals as much as it reveals. It reveals that presidential campaigns, at most, have a real chance of shaping the choices of only a third of the voters. It also suggests what further research substantiates: a large share of the uncommitted are Independents, who, as a group, are generally less informed about and interested in politics than those who claim party fealty. This, of course, reinforces the temptation to substitute histrionics for intellectual debate.

This statistic also conceals one of the purposes of a campaign: to bring the committed to the polls. A preference expressed at a cocktail party may be nice to hear, but only when that preference is registered at the ballot box does it do a candidate much good. This statistic also obscures the fact that in many presidential elections—1948, 1960, and 1968, for example—a small switch in voting alignments can be decisive. Harry Truman's hard-hitting, whistle-stop tour in 1948 eroded just enough of Dewey's support to put Truman back in the White House. John F. Kennedy's effectiveness in the television debates of 1960 has been widely credited with providing his margin of victory. When a shift of one or only a few percentage points means the difference between winning and losing, campaigns become vitally important. They are waged "to make marginal changes in political alignments."[2]

Campaign Strategy

Candidates usually want to maximize the turnout of friendly voters and to persuade the largest possible numbers of uncommitted to come over.[3] At times sheer chance—as when Charles Evans Hughes in 1916 inadvertently left the impression of having snubbed Hiram Johnson[4]—or the dynamics of an existing political situation or an opponent's bad judgment may accomplish these goals. While every candidate prays for all of these happenings to be favorable to his cause, he must operate on the assumption that victory will come only as a result of hard work and shrewd campaign strategy. The first steps a candidate has to take are choosing—or sometimes allowing himself to be chosen by—a set of close advisers on whose loyalty and judgment he can rely and with whose help he can create a larger organization to carry out campaign strategy. Not least, as we shall shortly discuss, among staff competences is an ability to raise money, for political campaigning is a fantastically expensive business.

Most candidates select a campaign manager to organize and direct staffs and study groups, promote fund raising, negotiate for support, arrange travel schedules, and help with strategic decisions. The candidate cannot supervise the performance of all of these functions himself while traveling, shaking hands, making speeches, and, if he is an incumbent, doing a bit of store tending. In turn, a campaign manager has to build up his own staff, for he too would be quickly swamped. One of the less pleasant tasks of the campaign manager is to say no for the candidate in a way that the candidate himself cannot without digging deep wounds. Coordinating, directing, organizing, and deciding are all important jobs, but the campaign manager's critical function is to create in voters' minds an appealing image of his candidate.[5] Image building is the concern of the public relations expert, and many PR firms specialize in political campaigning, claiming, with some support from the election returns, that they can merchandise a President using much the same techniques as in selling lingerie or detergents.[6]

The candidate and his manager face a whole series of choices about campaign strategy. The following list suggests only a few of the problems that confront them.

ORGANIZATION Should primary dependence for organization effort be placed upon the party machine or should formation of "independent committees" be encouraged? Most seasoned politicians distrust the latter and are inclined to rely upon traditional party machinery. Yet the Independent Citizens for Eisenhower organization seemingly contributed substantially to the Republican victory in 1952, and various "nonpartisan" committees for Johnson helped swell his huge majority in 1964. One value of such independent organizations is the way in which they can appeal to dissatisfied members of the opposition party. A disgruntled Democrat who might find it hard to listen to the siren song of the Republican organization can much more readily be persuaded to become a member of an "independent citizens' committee."

APPROACH To what extent should the campaign rely on a "mass appeal" via television, radio, and huge rallies? To what extent should the candidate try to reach down to a personal, hand-shaking level? Meeting people individually is far more feasible in a congressional race, where the geographic scope of the campaign and the number of voters are limited, but presidential candidates often feel a need to talk directly to small groups of voters. Even in 1960, when the four televised debates gave John Kennedy and Richard Nixon a total audience of 120 million people,[7] both candidates thought it necessary to spend much of their time on tours, making brief talks and shaking countless thousands of hands. In 1964 and 1968, with no televised debates, each of the candidates spent most of his time traveling around the country.

APPEAL How can a winning coalition of voters be pieced together? To what extent should the candidate pitch his campaign at party regulars, to what extent at Independents, and to what extent to disaffected members of the other party? Since the New Deal, registration statistics have pretty well dictated each party's rational choice in this regard. Because Democrats have usually heavily outnumbered Republicans over the last three decades, the Republicans, as Nixon tried unsuccessfully in 1960 and successfully in 1968, must play down party labels and convince many wavering Democrats as well as a large proportion of Independents in order to win. The Democrats, on the other hand, can win by holding their party members together and swinging some Independents. The simplicity of Democratic strategy may be ending because white Southerners are becoming less and less willing to vote for a racially liberal candidate. But the percentage of voters who think of themselves as Democrats appears to have remained rather stable, though it may be declining among younger people.

Group and geographic appeals also present problems in coalition building. Each party has certain initial advantages, for instance, the Democrats with labor and Republicans with the upper-middle class. But both parties need broader support to win. How to keep these core groups enthusiastic and still bring in enough others to form a majority is a staggering task. A straight appeal to farmers may irritate urban and suburban housewives worried about food prices. Promises of public power may carry the Missouri Valley but generate a reaction in California against "creeping socialism." Similarly, the black vote is important in the urban centers in big states like Pennsylvania, New York, Illinois, Michigan, and California, but the combined Electoral College total of southern states is

PARTY IDENTIFICATION									
	1952	1954	1956	1958	1960	1962	1964	1966	1968
Democratic	47%	47%	44%	49%	45%	46%	51%	45%	45%
Independent	22	22	24	19	23	22	23	28	30
Republican	27	27	29	27	30	28	24	25	24
None or other	4	4	3	4	3	4	2	1	2
	100%	100%	100%	99%	101%	100%	100%	99%	101%

SOURCE: *Survey Research Center, University of Michigan. (Percentages may not equal 100 because of rounding.)*

an attractive prize. In 1960 John Kennedy came up with an interesting solution for racial and regional dilemmas. With Lyndon Johnson of Texas as his running mate, each man assumed primary responsibility for quieting fears in his own area. Richard Nixon in 1968 followed the so-called southern strategy formulated largely by his then Wall Street law partner and later Attorney General, John Mitchell: Forget about the black vote, forget about the liberal Northeast; instead, concentrate on the deep South, the border states, the rural Midwest, the Rocky Mountain states, and California. Appeal to the white middle class on issues like law and order; imply a go-slow attitude on black civil rights in the South, but say nothing directly that would alienate Republican liberals or Independents outside the old Confederacy.[8]

STYLE   Should the candidate take the offensive, as did Truman in 1948 and Nixon in 1968, or play it safe as Johnson did in 1964? If he takes the offensive, in what way should he do so? Should he stress particular policies or problems? Should he attack opposition personalities or exploit possible scandals? To what extent should he try to answer opposition charges? Or should he, like Roosevelt in 1936 and 1940, blithely ignore his opponent? To some extent a man's previous record shapes his answers. An Eisenhower who goes into a campaign a beloved father figure can avoid the risk of offending anyone by speaking in the vaguest and kindest of generalities. A John Kennedy or a Barry Goldwater, on the other hand, has little choice but to hammer away at issues.

TIMING   Finally, there are the all-important issues of travel and timing. Should the candidate try to visit as many states as possible or should he concentrate on those areas that are doubtful? Since the first alternative risks exhausting the candidate without building enough support to carry more than a few states and the second runs the danger of not turning-on partisans, most candidates opt for a mixed strategy, but the exact kind of mixture needed to win is difficult to concoct. Timing is critical both in scheduling visits to particular areas and in setting the over-all tempo of the campaign. Activity must be started neither too early nor too late and must be brought to a crescendo at just the right moment to sway the greatest number of voters. In 1960 Nixon peaked too early and faded at the close; In 1968 Humphrey got into high gear too late and needed more time to close the narrowing gap between him and Nixon.

TIME OF VOTING DECISION IN THE PRESIDENTIAL ELECTIONS
(voters only)

QUESTION: "How long before the election did you decide that you were going to vote the
way you did?"

	Percentage					
	1948	1952	1956	1960	1964	1968
Knew all along	37	30	44	24	13	20
Before the conventions, when knew candidates would run	a	4	14	6	17	14
At the time of the conventions	28	31	18	30	19	23
During the campaign	14	20	12	25	16	18
In the last two weeks	12	11	8	11	10	21
Don't remember, not ascertained	9	4	4	4	25	4
	100	100	100	100	100	100

a *Data not available.*
SOURCE: *Survey Research Center, University of Michigan.*

CONGRESSIONAL CAMPAIGNS

On a smaller scale the candidate for Congress has to face and make many of the same decisions that confront presidential candidates. But in other ways his problem is a different one.

If he is running for the House of Representatives from one of the 260 or more districts considered to be pretty safely in one party column or the other or for the Senate from a presumed "safe" state, his real campaigning must be done prior to the primary and be aimed at winning the nomination. His opponents will be members of his own party, which means that issues will probably play an even less important role than they ordinarily do in general elections. Candidates within the same party can and do disagree about issues, but the appeal to party voters is likely to be couched in terms of "I am an honest man who would greatly appreciate your personal support. I promise you that if I am nominated and elected I will serve the interests of this district to the best of my ability." There is no institutional arrangement that compels a candidate for Congress to seek the endorsement of a national party organization. If his local prestige is sufficient, he may even win the nomination in the face of active opposition by the national leaders of the party.

In presidential years congressional candidates usually try to ride on the coat tails of the presidential candidates. They tend to leave the discussion of issues to the national candidates and to concentrate upon winning friends among the voters and making certain that the local party machinery is in good running condition. In midterm elections the national parties are relatively inactive; there is no party platform; the 1966 and 1970 debates over Vietnam notwithstanding, issues generally recede into the background. The influence of the President is usually less strong than in a presidential year, voter interest wanes, and the size of the vote declines sharply. Under these circumstances campaigning is apt to be both decentralized and demoralized. Local interests, local personalities, and local party organizations influence the result even more than they do in presidential years. If the state or district is a "safe" one, the candidate of the dominant party can coast along, quite certain of election or reelection while his opponent goes through the forms of campaigning without creating even an illusion of victory. If the district is a marginal one, the candidate of the President's party will find himself at a disadvantage, for in every midterm congressional election since the Civil War, save that of 1934, the President's party has lost seats in Congress. Even in 1970, one of the most successful off-year elections for any administration, the Republicans lost 10 seats in the House while gaining 2 in the Senate. And yet these marginal districts are the ones most likely to be bitterly contested, for here campaigning can affect not only the immediate choice among candidates but also the structure of power in Congress. Curiously, these midterm losses of the party in the White House do not necessarily foreshadow defeat in the next presidential election.

Congressional campaigns and to a greater extent state and local contests are vulnerable to "dynamiting"—smearing a candidate by innuendo or even by direct, false, and defamatory charges. While presidential campaigns are not immune—as evidenced by the phony accusation in 1964 that Barry Goldwater had once suffered a mental breakdown or in 1960 that the election of John F. Kennedy would mean Papal control of America— they are relatively free of slander when compared to campaigns at other levels. There are a few public relations experts who are quite adept at the art of character assassination. Armed with an intimate knowledge of the loopholes in the law of libel, they can practically guarantee to enter a campaign at the last moment—so the opposition cannot have an opportunity to reply—and brand the other candidate as anything from a practicing homosexual to a card-carrying communist, and do so with complete legal impunity.[9]

The Supreme Court has made control of smears doubly difficult by ruling, first, that a state cannot require that campaign literature indicate who is responsible for its publication,[10] and, second, by holding that to win a libel suit a public official must show not only that an accusation against him was untrue, but also that it was "made with 'actual malice'—that is, with knowledge that it was false or with reckless disregard of whether it was false or not."[11] Lower courts have extended this principle to candidates as well as to office holders. The Justices were trying to foster free speech and to protect minority groups against oppression, but they have succeeded in discouraging political debate that clarifies rather than obfuscates policy issues.

MONEY AND POLITICS

Financing Campaigns

Political campaigning in the United States is an increasingly costly undertaking. In 1956, national-level committees of the two major parties spent $17.2 million; in 1960, $25 million; in 1964, almost $35 million; and in 1968, almost $60 million. The money spent

POLITICAL SPENDING AT THE NATIONAL LEVEL, 1964 AND 1968

	1964	1968
Republicans	$17,187,000	$28,851,000
Democrats	11,973,000	13,169,000
George Wallace	—	7,223,000
Labor	3,665,000	6,056,000
Miscellaneous	1,963,000	4,124,000
Total:	$34,788,000	$59,423,000

SOURCE: *Herbert E. Alexander*, Financing the 1964 Election (*Princeton, N.J.: Citizens' Research Foundation, 1966*), p. 8; and Herbert E. Alexander, "*Financing Parties and Campaigns in 1968*," *A Paper Presented to the 1969 Meetings of the American Political Science Association, p. 1.*

for nominating and electing all federal, state, and local officials probably totaled $140 million in 1952, $155 million in 1956, $175 million in 1960, about $200 million in 1964, and more than $300 million in 1968.[12] When one realizes that the cost of postage alone for sending a single postcard to each eligible voter would come to nearly $5 million, the wonder is that the total expenditures are not higher.

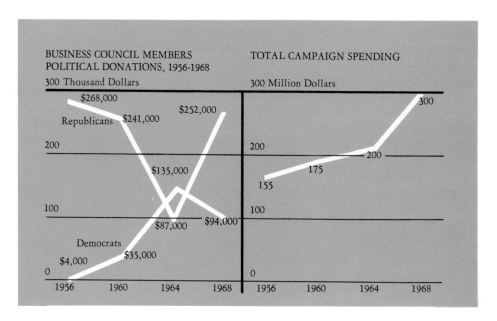

SOURCE: Data from *Herbert E. Alexander*, Director of the *Citizens' Research Foundation*, Princeton, N.J.

The threat that certain candidates will "buy" their way into public office, or that certain interests will "buy" public policies favorable to their cause, is always present. The result is one of the most difficult dilemmas of American politics: parties and candidates must be allowed to spend money in campaigns so that the voters may acquire necessary information; yet huge expenditures can corrupt the entire electoral process.

How Money Is Spent

While it is not possible to compile an exhaustive list of the ways in which campaign money is used, we can suggest six purposes that illustrate how a party organization can legitimately spend large sums of money during a campaign: (1) *general overhead*—for headquarters at national, state, and local levels, including salaries, office rent, postage, and telephones; (2) *field activities*—the speaking trips, often by leased jet aircraft, of

CAMPAIGN FINANCING: 1954, 1958, 1962, AND 1966
Reported campaign spending included in reports to the Clerk of the House for the mid-term campaigns since 1954. Numbers on the committee line indicate the number of groups reporting.

	Committee spending reported nationally			
	1954	1958	1962	1966[a]
Republican committees	27	14	11	21
Receipts	$ 5,380,994	$4,686,423	$ 4,674,570	$ 7,640,760
Expenditures	$ 5,509,649	$4,657,652	$ 4,637,586	$ 7,863,092
Percentage of total spending	53.5	53.7	39.4	41.5
Democratic committees	13	7	8	8
Receipts	$ 2,168,404	$1,733,626	$ 3,699,827	$ 4,055,410
Expenditures	$ 2,224,211	$1,702,605	$ 3,569,357	$ 4,282,007
Percentage of total spending	21.6	19.6	30.3	22.5
Labor committees	41	32	33	42
Receipts	$ 1,822,157	$1,854,635	$ 2,112,677	$ 4,262,077
Expenditures	$ 2,057,613	$1,828,778	$ 2,305,331	$ 4,289,055
Percentage of total spending	20.0	21.1	19.6	22.7
Miscellaneous committees	15	11	26	44
Receipts	$ 517,804	$ 492,710	$ 1,313,959	$ 2,123,868
Expenditures	$ 514,094	$ 486,430	$ 1,271,214	$ 2,545,080
Percentage of total spending	5.0	5.6	10.8	13.3
Totals				
Receipts	$ 9,949,359	$8,767,394	$11,801,033	$18,082,015
Expenditures	$10,305,567	$8,675,465	$11,783,488	$18,979,234

[a] *The 1966 expenditures are "less transfers," that is, lateral payments between national level committees have been deducted.*
SOURCE: Congressional Quarterly Weekly Report, *August 11, 1967.*

candidates, the costs of renting halls, stadiums, and auditoriums, and the other expenses involved in organizing mass meetings; (3) *publicity*—telecasts and radio broadcasts, spot commercials, newspaper advertisements, campaign literature, special buttons and souvenirs, and to these must be added the fees charged by the public relations firms that handle the campaign; (4) *grants to subsidiary committees*—tranfers of funds from national organizations to state and local organizations and to special committees and groups; (5) *election day expenses*—transportation of voters to the polls and payments to watchers at the polls and to party workers who try to bring out the vote; (6) *public opinion polling* to gauge the effects of various campaign strategies. The table below gives an idea of some of incidental costs incurred by the Republicans in 1968.

In presidential campaigns a high proportion of campaign funds is spent for national television speeches and programs. But even in state-wide elections up to a third or more of all funds may be spent for television. A half hour on a nation-wide television hook-up will cost almost $100,000—more than Abraham Lincoln spent on his entire campaign in 1860. Because of this high price both parties tend to rely more on spot announcements of from forty seconds to one minute than on long programs. In the 1960 presidential campaign the two parties at the national level spent approximately $4.7 million for television and radio time, and the networks donated $4 or $5 million in free time to the candidates. With no time donated by the networks in 1964 and 1968 for debates, the cost to both parties was substantially higher, totaling $11 million in 1964 and about $21 million in 1968.[13]

The Cost of Campaigning for the Senate

The cost of getting elected to the Senate, where a candidate has serious, organized opposition, ranges from about $100,000 into the millions. While a senator cannot personally spend more than $25,000 on his campaign, there is no limit to the number of committees that can be formed on his behalf by friends and supporters. In the largest states

INCIDENTAL COSTS, REPUBLICAN NATIONAL COMMITTEE 1968

Number	Item	Cost
20,500,000	Buttons	$ 300,000
9,000,000	Bumper strips	300,000
560,000	Balloons	70,000
400,000	Posters and placards	70,000
28,000	Straw skimmers	30,000
3,500,000	Copies of brochures, speeches, and position papers	500,000
12,000	Paper dresses	40,000
	Jewelry	50,000
	Total:	$1,360,000

SOURCE: *Herbert E. Alexander, "Financing Parties and Campaigns in 1968." A Paper Presented to the 1969 Meetings of the American Political Science Association, p. 55.*

perhaps 25,000 to 30,000 persons may contribute to the campaign fund of a senatorial candidate.

Where the Money Comes From

Apart from the size of the sums raised to meet campaign expenses, the most striking thing about party finances is how few people give money to a party or a candidate. Historically, political leaders have had to rely on large contributors for party funds. During the 1950s about 90 percent of all money came from less than 1 percent of the population. The Gallup poll reported in 1954 that only one family in eighteen contributed to that year's election campaigns. In 1968 the Survey Research Center of the University of Michigan found that this number had increased to one out of thirteen, hardly a broad base. As Sir Dennis W. Brogan,[14] a leading British interpreter of American politics, has commented:

> the American, normally so generous, normally so gullible, willing to subscribe to all funds, from community chests in very rich suburban communities to pensions for the widow of the unknown soldier, has proved curiously reluctant to contribute to his party. And the party has been forced to appeal to the hopes and fears of those with more to give than a few dollars.

The 1964 and 1968 elections present several interesting paradoxes. One would expect a strong and positive correlation between the number of campaign contributors and the size of popular vote. But Barry Goldwater received direct contributions from far more small donors—probably a total of 650,000—than did Lyndon Johnson, yet Johnson clobbered Goldwater at the polls. In 1968, the number of small contributors to Nixon's campaign dropped off by about 200,000 from the 1964 figure, while George Wallace received direct donations from 750,000 to 900,000 people, about as many as contributed directly to Humphrey and Nixon together; yet outside the South, Wallace received the smallest share of votes of the three. Despite these relatively large numbers of small gifts, each party in both elections had to depend heavily on large contributions to meet its expenses.[15]

In addition to small contributions from ordinary citizens, there are four principal sources of campaign funds. Most important are the political angels, known inelegantly as "fat cats," wealthy people who are willing to give large sums. In the past the Republican party has benefited far more than the Democrats from such donations. In 1956, for example, of the contributions of $500 or more by officers and directors of the 225 largest corporations in the United States, $1.82 million went to the Republicans and only $103,725 to the Democrats. In 1964, however, there was an abrupt turnabout, with the Democrats raising more than $4.8 million and the Republicans less than $3.5 million from contributions of $500 or over. 1968 saw a return to normalcy.

Unions, the second major source of funds, have increased their political contributions in recent years. The bulk of their gifts go to the Democratic party. Since 1936, when John L. Lewis gave $469,000 to aid the re-election of Franklin D. Roosevelt, labor organizations have donated less spectacularly but more steadily. In 1960, union organizations filed reports with the clerk of the House of Representatives stating that they had contributed $2.45 million to the campaign that year, a sum that is probably less than actual expenditures. Alexander estimates that labor groups in 1964 spent over $3.6 million, with the AFL–CIO Political Action Committee putting out over a million dollars in voter-registration drives. Labor organizations spent almost $6 million in the 1968 campaign, much of it in the preconvention stage, supporting first Lyndon Johnson and then Hubert Humphrey against Robert Kennedy and Eugene McCarthy.

Government employees represent a third source of funds. While federal law prohibits government workers from soliciting funds from their co-workers, no law forbids spontaneous giving by government employees. Many may be moved by conviction or expediency to make a contribution, and state officials who want to keep their jobs are quick to donate money. Indeed, many organizations have unofficially although effectively prescribed sliding scales of regular contributions to the party treasury. The amount "spontaneously" given varies with the salary of the job, and may for prestigious offices like judgeships involve an initial gift that approaches the equivalent of several months' or even a year's salary. Some, though not necessarily all, of this money is used for campaign expenses. A portion of it is usually siphoned off for more personal pleasures.

The underworld, from petty hoodlums to Cosa Nostra chieftains, constitutes a fourth source of funds. To run large scale number games, gambling establishments, prostitution rings, shakedowns, labor racketeering, and even to penetrate legitimate business enterprises, organized crime must have the insulation of governmental protection—police officials who look the other way or who warn about impending crackdowns, district attorneys who do not prosecute, judges who set minimum bail, dismiss charges or give light or suspended sentences, state and federal legislators who, along with executive officials from the mayor's staff on up, will pressure police, prosecutors, and judges. The return from the racket industry is immensely lucrative, totalling untold—and untaxed— billions each year; and campaign contributions to cooperative politicians or, perhaps without his knowing it, to an opponent of an uncooperative official, are cheap forms of insurance.

An underworld leader may make another kind of contribution to a campaign, for he, like the old time city boss, may have votes as well as money to throw onto the political scales. As Mario Puzo[16] describes it in his chillingly realistic novel about a Cosa Nostra family, the "Godfather" achieved much of his power by doing favors for little people, protecting them against the malice of their fellow men or correcting injustices that a complex governmental structure inadvertently perpetrated. "It was only natural then," Puzo writes, that when these poor people were puzzled about whom to vote for they should ask the advice of their Godfather.

In 1966 Congress created a potentially huge source of funds by authorizing each taxpayer to indicate on his income tax form if he desired one dollar of his taxes (two dollars for joint returns) to be placed in a fund to help finance the next presidential campaign. A rather complex formula would have controlled disbursement of the money, but in general the two major parties would have received equal shares, not in excess of the amount spent in the last campaign. If a minor party candidate had polled more than 5 million votes, for the next campaign his party would have been entitled to one dollar for each vote over 5 million.

If every taxpayer had contributed, the fund would have received over $100 million a year, enough to purchase a handsome set of campaign chests, even at current prices.

In 1967, however, many congressmen had second thoughts about how party officials might spend the huge sums to which they would be entitled and passed a new law suspending operations of the 1966 act until Congress set guidelines for distribution of the money. Four years later, at the close of the Ninety-first Congress, no such guidelines had been established and the statute remained in Limbo.

Even in years when there is no important election at stake, the parties require considerable amounts of money to finance their activities. In 1967, national level expenditures by the Democrats were over $2 million and Republicans spent $5.8 million.[17] Costs are continually rising, but, when compared to 1965 when the two parties spent $8.5 million at the national level, 1967 does not seem to be an unusually expensive year. Operating costs for a national political organization are always large. A staff must be maintained, debts from the last campaign paid off, research carried on, registration programs kept in operation, and capital accumulated for the next campaign. Obviously, fund raising has to be a continuous process.

FEDERAL CONTROL OF PARTY FINANCES

Certain Contribution Sources Are Prohibited

As early as 1907 Congress forbade corporations chartered under federal law, such as national banks, to make contributions to *any* political campaign, federal or local, and forbade all corporations to make contributions in *national* campaigns. Labor unions were subjected to a similar ban in 1943. In the 1944 campaign the CIO refrained from making any contributions to the Roosevelt campaign fund, but it spent over $1 million on direct aid to the Roosevelt ticket through its own Political Action Committee. Accordingly, the Taft-Hartley Act of 1947 renewed the ban on labor union contributions and also extended it to cover direct expenditures by unions themselves as well as by business corporations on behalf of candidates for federal office. There is doubt about the constitutionality of such a ban on direct expenditures by labor unions and business corporations.[18] Since 1883 Congress has tried to protect government employees from requests for contributions to campaign funds. As noted, this protection extends only to the solicitation of funds by one government employee from another and not to solicitation by private persons.

The Hatch Act of 1940 limits individual contributions to national party organizations to $5000 in a national campaign, and it also limits the total contributions that any one political committee may receive to $3 million.[19] The act also limits expenditures by a political committee to a maximum of $3 million in any one year. In 1925, Congress also placed limitations on the amounts that may be spent by candidates for Congress. These amounts were fixed at $10,000 for senatorial candidates and at $2500 for candidates for the House. However, recognizing that candidates in the populous states may legitimately incur greater expenses, Congress approved an alternative formula that allows a candidate to exceed these limits by spending three cents for every vote cast in the last general election, although in no event may the amount exceed $25,000 for senatorial candidates and $5000 for candidates for the House.

Since 1910 Congress has enacted laws requiring political committees and candidates for Congress to file statements at certain intervals with the clerk of the House of

CAMPAIGN COSTS PUT AT ZERO BY 7

Senators' Reports Point Up Loopholes in Legislation

By Congressional Quarterly

WASHINGTON, Dec. 10— Seven Senators have reported to the Senate that it cost them nothing to get elected last year. Five others said that last year's campaign cost them less than $5,000.

The reports by Senatorial candidates, whose actual campaign costs sometimes exceed $1-million, point up the broad loopholes in the Federal law requiring disclosure of campaign spending. The law permits Congressional candidates to declare only a small fraction—or none—of their expenditures.

Many House candidates also reported to Congress that their 1968 campaign costs were meager. In Michigan, 28 of 37 major party candidates for Congress stated that their campaigns cost less than $5,000.

In the Senate, those who reported spending nothing were Barry Goldwater, Republican of Arizona; J. W. Fulbright, Democrat of Arkansas; Alan Cranston, Democrat of California; Herman E. Talmadge, Democrat of Georgia; George S. McGovern, Democrat of South Dakota; George D. Aiken, Republican of Vermont; and Robert J. Dole, Republican of Kansas.

Those who reported spending less than $5,000 were Daniel K. Inouye, Democrat of Hawaii; Birch Bayh, Democrat of Indiana; Russell B. Long, Democrat of Louisiana; Stephen M. Young, Democrat of Ohio; and Norris Cotton, Republican of New Hampshire.

Federal-State Contrast

House candidates reported under Federal law spending a total of $5,768,393 last year, or $13,261 for each of the 435 Congressional districts. However, under state law, candidates in Florida's 12 Congressional districts alone reported combined 1968 campaign spending of $1,139,274.

Candidates running for the 34 Senate seats at stake in 1968 reported combined campaign spending of $2,714,464 to the Senate. But expenditures of $4,451,849 were reported to the State of California by Mr. Cranston, Max Rafferty, Republican candidate, and former Senator Thomas H. Kuchel, Republican, for the combined cost of their Senate campaigns alone.

The wide discrepancies between figures filed under state laws and those filed with Congress are largely a result of loopholes in the Federal law that requires disclosure of campaign spending. The Corrupt Practices Act of 1925 requires that Senate candidates file spending reports with the Secretary of the Senate and House candidates file with the Clerk of the House.

Under the act, a candidate must list only those expenses of which he has personal knowledge. As a result, some candidates report no campaign spending under the rationale that they did not have personal knowledge of the exact amounts involved.

"We are very careful to make sure that Senator McGovern never sees the campaign receipts; they go right to the committee," said George V. Cunningham, Mr. McGovern's executive assistant. Representative Brock Adams, Democrat of Washington, said the standard campaign practice was to "compartmentalize your operation so you don't handle money."

Primaries Not Covered

Many candidates take advantage of the provision in the Federal law that campaign committees are not required to report spending to Congress unless they operate in more than one state. In addition, primary election expenses are not covered by the Federal law.

Traditionally there has been almost no effort to enforce the Corrupt Practices Act against Congressional candidates. But last January the Clerk of the House, W. Pat Jennings, sent to the Justice Department the names of 107 House candidates who had not filed spending reports. A Justice Department spokesman told Congressional Quarterly last week that the matter was still "under investigation."

Many candidates take state laws on campaign spending far more seriously. "I filed my campaign costs with the State of Maine," said Representative William D. Hathaway, a Democrat. "If anyone wants to look it up, he can go to the Secretary of the State of Maine." Mr. Hathaway said he reported no campaign spending to the House, because "it is a nuisance to fill out more than one form."

In 1968, 43 states required Congressional candidates to report campaign spending. Of these, 31 states also demanded reports from campaign committees.

Although generally more effective than the Federal law state statutes provide few incentives for accurate reporting of campaign spending. Of the 43 states that require disclosure, only 16 require that the reports be inspected for accuracy.

The Corrupt Practices Act places a ceiling of $25,000 on the cost of any Congressional race, although there are many exempted expenses. Thirty states also limit campaign spending and in most of them the statutory maximum for a Congressional race is under $100,000.

© 1969 by The New York Times Company. Reprinted by permission.

Representatives concerning contributions received and expenditures made. Among the required data are the name and address of each person contributing more than $100 and the names of persons to whom more than $10 is paid. Such information is then available for public inspection, and a certain amount of it is usually reported by the press in rather sketchy fashion.

In the end, most of the corrupt-practices legislation now in existence fails to achieve the specific purposes for which it was enacted. The limitation of $3 million on the total expenditure of a political committee is also meaningless because it does not prevent two or more separate "committees" from spending up to $3 million each in support of the same party ticket. Certainly the Hatch Act has not brought about any reduction in the total amount of money spent by the major parties in presidential elections. About all it has done is to encourage a decentralization of expenditures, a change of doubtful value to the public good, since decentralized expenditures are much more difficult to keep track of.

The limitations on the expenditures of individual candidates are apt to be meaningless because of the impossibility of calculating the vast sums that may be and are spent directly by private persons on behalf of a candidate, without the candidate's receiving the money or even necessarily knowing that it is being used to aid him. Similarly, the $5000 limitation on the contributions of a single person is ineffectual because every member of a family, even infants, can give such an amount, and every member can donate $5000 to as many different committees as he can afford to subsidize. In 1968, for instance, Nelson Rockefeller's stepmother managed, quite legally, to give over $1.4 million to his unsuccessful campaign to win the Republican presidential nomination.[20]

The corrupt-practices laws do not make much of an attempt to regulate contributions and spending in congressional primaries or in preconvention campaigns of persons seeking the presidential nominations. For a while there was doubt whether Congress had power under the Constitution to establish such federal controls at the nomination stage of the national elections, but the Supreme Court finally ruled that such power does exist.[21] Congress took a tentative step toward the establishment of such controls in the Taft-Hartley Act of 1947 by providing that the ban on contributions and expenditures by business and labor should cover the nomination of candidates as well as the election of public officers.

These legislative efforts to curb the use of money in politics may not be completely without value. Such laws may serve to remind parties, candidates, and voters alike that the proper use of money in campaigns is to provide the public with necessary informtaion and not to "buy" public office. It is likely that these laws have restrained individuals and organizations from the bold and corrupt use of money that characterized certain earlier periods in American politics. Nonetheless, satisfactory control of money in American elections has not yet been achieved.

PROPOSALS TO IMPROVE CAMPAIGN FINANCING

To date, federal regulation of campaign financing has been negative in character, limiting the amount of money that may be given or expended. Even if these laws had no loopholes, serious problems would still exist. The costs of running a political campaign

are enormous; the money must come from somewhere—from borowing if not from contributions. As Herbert Alexander[22] has pointed out: "Political parties that are beholden
to a small number of large contributors constitute an unhealthy element in the body
politic. Debt-ridden parties that exist from hand-to-mouth at the mercy of a few large
creditors are in some respects even worse." The two parties were able to finance the 1960
campaign only by going heavily into debt. The Republican National Committee ended
up $993,000 in the red; the Democrats $3.82 million. The Republicans finished the 1964
campaign with a surplus of several hundred thousand dollars, but the Democrats ran into
debt again, although probably by only a little more than a million dollars. In 1968 the
Republicans pretty well broke even, but once more the Democrats had serious difficulties
and had to borrow more than $6 million to keep their campaign going.

In 1907, President Theodore Roosevelt proposed to Congress that the federal
government subsidize political campaigns, but it was not until 1961 that a President
initiated and supported an attempt to reform the American system (or lack of system) of
financing election campaigns. Within a year after taking office, President Kennedy appointed a distinguished bipartisan commission of political scientists and practicing politicians to recommend means of improving the collection and expenditure of money in
presidential elections.

In 1962, the commission filed a concise report outlining a program of positive federal action.[23] The commission recommended repealing meaningless ceilings on
expenditures and contributions, making campaign contributions up to $1,000 tax deduc-
tible, establishing a federal Registry of Elections to enforce statutes, and amending the
Federal Communications Act to allow broadcasters to provide free time to major party
candidates without having to do so for all minor parties as well. Further, the commission
suggested that if these measures did not bring marked improvement, the federal government should consider directly subsidizing the campaign costs of the major parties. Despite
urging by two Presidents, the only legislative action that had resulted by the end of the
Ninety-first Congress was the tax check-off plan, and that, as we just saw, has not yet been
put into operation.

SELECTED BIBLIOGRAPHY

Bullitt, Stimson, *To Be a Politician* (New York: Doubleday and Company, Inc., 1959).
    An interesting and thoughtful description of what it is like to run for office.
Heard, Alexander, *The Costs of Democracy* (Chapel Hill, N.C.: University of North
    Carolina Press, 1960). A remarkable study of money in politics, with data on who
    contributes, why, in what amounts, and for what purposes.
Jennings, M. Kent and L. Harmon Zeigler, eds., *The Electoral Process* (Englewood Cliffs,
    N.J.: Prentice-Hall, Inc., 1966). A useful collection of original essays on campaign
    strategy and finance.
Kelley, Stanley, Jr., *Political Campaigning: Problems in Creating an Informed Electorate*
    (Washington, D.C.: The Brookings Institution, 1960). The central concern here
    is how the discussion of policies and candidates in campaigns might make a greater
    contribution to electoral rationality.
————, *Professional Public Relations and Political Power* (Baltimore, Md.: The Johns

Hopkins Press, 1956). A highly interesting account of the use of high-pressure public relations techniques on behalf of issues and candidates for office.

Kessel, John H., *The Goldwater Coalition: Republican Strategies in 1964* (Indianapolis, Ind.: The Bobbs-Merrill Company, Inc., 1968). A scholarly but readable analysis of how the Republicans tried to capture the White House in 1964.

Lane, Robert E., *Political Life* (New York: The Free Press, 1959). A study of "why people get involved in politics."

Shadegg, Stephen C., *How To Win an Election* (New York: Taplinger Publishing Company, 1964). A controversial account of political campaigning by an aide of Senator Barry M. Goldwater.

Footnotes

[1] P. Lazarsfeld, B. Berelson, and H. Gaudet, *The People's Choice: How the Voter Makes Up His Mind in a Presidential Campaign* (New York: Duell, Sloan and Pearce, Inc., 1944); B. Berelson, P. Lazarsfeld, and W. McPhee, *Voting* (Chicago: University of Chicago Press, 1954); Angus Campbell, Philip E. Converse, Warren E. Miller, and Donald E. Stokes, *The American Voter* (New York: John Wiley and Sons, Inc., 1960), espec. Chap. 4; and data released by the University of Michigan's Survey Research Center after the 1960, 1964, and 1968 elections.

[2] Stanley Kelley, Jr., "The Presidential Campaign," in Paul T. David, ed., *The Presidential Election and Transition 1960–1961* (Washington, D.C.: The Brookings Institution, 1961), p. 57.

[3] William Riker, in his *The Theory of Political Coalitions* (New Haven: Yale University Press, 1962), argues that it is not rational for a leader to strive to build up a coalition greater than the 50.1 percent vote needed to win a particular election. Riker adds the qualification that because a candidate is usually uncertain about the number of votes he has nailed down, it is rational for him to go after more than a mere majority, but under conditions of perfect information this would not be true. Riker thus attacks Anthony Downs' contention, *An Economic Theory of Democracy* (New York: Harper and Row, 1957), that a political party should maximize its electoral support. We would dispute both Downs and Riker. There are "costs" in winning votes—time, energy, money, and perhaps policy promises; therefore, to go willy-nilly after every possible vote may be ruinous. On the other hand, there are advantages in winning big. If nothing else one may discourage future opposition. More immediately, in a political system with separately elected officials, the man who has won big has a psychological edge over the man who barely squeaked by. A President, for example, who ran behind a congressman in the congressman's district is hardly in a position to threaten to withdraw his support from that congressman at the next election. We think a marginal cost–marginal value approach is more rational. While the value of votes declines once a candidate—or a political leader in any institution that makes choices by means of voting—has the magic 50.1 figure, the value of additional votes is never zero. Thus the candidate has to weigh the marginal costs of the additional votes against the marginal value they would bring to him. See Walter F. Murphy, *Elements of Judicial Strategy* (Chicago: University of Chicago Press, 1964), Chap. 3.

[4] F. M. Davenport, "Did Hughes Snub Johnson?—An Inside Story," *American Political Science Review,* 43 (April 1949), p. 321; and Merlo J. Pusey, *Charles Evans Hughes* (New York: The Macmillan Company, 1952), I, 344–349.

[5] Stephen C. Shadegg, Barry Goldwater's campaign manager, has written an interesting account of a campaign manager's functions: *How to Win an Election* (New York: Taplinger Publishing Company, 1964).

[6] See Stanley Kelley, Jr., *Professional Public Relations and Political Power* (Baltimore: The Johns Hopkins University Press, 1956).

[7] Theodore H. White, *The Making of the President 1960* (New York: Atheneum Publishers, 1961), p. 296.

[8] Kevin P. Phillips, *The Emerging Republican Majority* (New Rochelle, N.Y.: Arlington House, 1969).

[9] See Frank Jonas, "The Art of Political Dynamiting," *Western Political Quarterly,* 10 (June 1957), p. 374.

[10] *Talley v. California,* 363 U.S. 60 (1960). See also *Golden v. Zwickler,* 394 U.S. 103 (1969).

[11] The basic case is *New York Times v. Sullivan,* 376 U.S. 254 (1964).

[12] Herbert E. Alexander, *Financing the 1964 Election* (Princeton, N.J.: Citizens' Research Foundation, 1966), p. 7, and Herbert E. Alexander, "Financing Parties and Campaigns in 1968: A Preliminary Report," A Paper Presented to the 1969 Meetings of the American Political Science Association. Throughout this section we rely heavily on Alexander's work.

[13] These figures include only the money spent in the general election campaigns for the Presidency. The total campaign costs for television in 1968 was $40.4 million.

[14] *Politics in America* (New York: Harper and Row, 1954), p. 259.

[15] Alexander, *Financing the 1964 Election* and "Financing Parties and Campaigns in 1968."

[16] Mario Puzo, *The Godfather* (New York: G. P. Putnam's Sons, 1969), p. 216.

[17] *Congressional Quarterly Weekly Report* (February 16, 1968), p. 298.

[18] See *United States v. Congress of Industrial Organizations,* 335 U.S. 106 (1948), in which five Justices held that the Taft-Hartley Act was not intended to prevent a labor organization from supporting a congressional candidate in a newspaper that it publishes. However, four Justices felt that the act was intended to ban such activity and that, so construed, it was unconstitutional. *I. A. M. v. Street,* 367 U.S. 740 (1961), continued the debate in a different context; but once again a majority of the Court decided the case on statutory rather than constitutional grounds.

[19] A "political committee" is defined by the Federal Corrupt Practices Act as "any committee, association, or organization which accepts contributions or makes expenditures for the purpose of influencing the election of candidates . . . in two or more states. . . ." 2 U.S.C. § 241.

[20] Herbert E. Alexander, "Financing Parties and Elections in 1968," p. 10.

[21] See *Newberry v. United States,* 256 U.S. 232 (1921), and *United States v. Classic,* 313 U.S. 299 (1941). The power of Congress to control the financing of congressional elections is clearly derived from the "times, places, and manner" clause of Article I of the Constitution. Its power to regulate the finances of presidential elections is less explicit but has been upheld by the Supreme Court on an implied-power basis. See *Burroughs v. United States,* 290 U.S. 534 (1934).

[22] Herbert E. Alexander, "Financing the Parties and Campaigns," in Paul T. David, ed., *The Presidential Election and Transition 1960–1961* (Washington, D.C.: The Brookings Institution, 1961), p. 148.

[23] *Financing Presidential Campaigns: Report of the President's Commission on Campaign Costs* (Washington, D.C.: Government Printing Office, 1962).

Chapter 10   Voting Behavior

VOTING STUDIES

It is far easier to describe in gross terms the behavior of American voters than to subject that behavior—or more properly those many kinds of behavior—to scientific analysis. There is little difficulty in obtaining complete and accurate statistics about the number and way in which votes were cast in an election. Furthermore, since these figures are usually available for subdivisions down to the precinct level, one can readily describe voting behavior along geographic lines. But official records have limited usefulness when trying to find out how different segments of the electorate, such as men or women, whites or blacks, Protestants or Catholics, have voted. Moreover, such records never reveal the "why" of election results.

Over a period of years students of political behavior have experimented with several techniques to minimize these difficulties. Commercial pollsters such as the Opinion Research Center have tended to rely on a "national sample." To obtain data about preferences and actions the polling agency interviews on a one-time basis a small number of people, usually about thirteen hundred to two thousand, selected at random from the nation as a whole. The questions are often drawn up to be answered "yes" or "no," or "approve," "approve strongly," "disapprove," "disapprove strongly," or "no opinion," although many agencies are now relying more heavily on "open-ended" questions—such as "What do you think are the major differences between the two parties?"—to which the respondent replies in his own words.

"The panel method" is a somewhat different approach. By this technique a group of people, again selected at random and often from one community, is interviewed not once but several times during a campaign to try to capture changes in individual reactions over time and correlate these changes with specific events. This method provides greater depth for opinion analysis, but there is no assurance that voters in one community will react like voters in another locality. The most promising—and expensive—kind of panel research is that in which the respondents are drawn from a national rather than a local sample. The Survey Research Center at the University of Michigan has been using this technique since 1948. Not only has SRC been interviewing voters during and after a presidential campaign but it has also tried to interview the same people in the succeeding off-year congressional election and during and after the next presidential campaign to see what kinds of changes develop over a period of years. The research techniques of the various studies[1] have been very different, and analysts have not always drawn the same conclusions from the same evidence. In fact, on longer reflection some of the researchers have changed their minds about the meaning of the information they had earlier collected. Nevertheless, their findings are similar though not identical. This indicates that reliable research methods are being developed, but the substance of the evidence is less heartening to those who hope to uncover evidence of an informed and interested citizenry. Indeed, a nearly universal finding of large-scale interview studies has been that a large majority of voting age adults lack anything like a detailed knowledge of politics, even during a campaign when all the news media are saturated with political information. A few weeks after the 1966 congressional election, for example, only about one out of every five respondents in an SRC sample could recall the name of one congressional candidate for whom he had just been eligible to vote and name a national problem—almost any answer would do except "don't know"—and name one policy issue on which the two parties differed—again, almost any answer other than "don't know" was scored as "correct." This is hardly a stiff test; one would hesitate to describe the fifth of the sample who passed it as necessarily being well-informed.

Responses to questions about specific policy preferences are also highly unstable over time. Questioning the same panel three times over a four-year period, SRC found that for a large segment of the population answers to identical questions varied almost randomly. The questions, incidentally, concerned such basic issues as the proper roles of the federal government and private enterprise in the fields of housing and public utilities.

These data hardly fit what we might call the classic democratic model of the voting decision: an aware, informed, and concerned body of citizens calmly weighing the costs and benefits of the policy alternatives proposed by candidates and then after discounting these alternatives by past party performance arriving at a decision. Before, however, concluding that this model is entirely inappropriate and before accepting any other, it would be well to examine some of the other findings of the voting studies.

Several preliminary caveats are in order. First, none of the analyses of voting behavior claims to explain the political choices of all individual voters. Each explanation is hedged by such words as "usually," "generally," "typically," or "tend to." Second, most of the intensive studies of electoral behavior concern presidential or off-year congressional campaigns. We can extrapolate most of the conclusions based on national elections to local contests, but only as hypotheses worth testing. Third, even at the national level, we have close investigations of only a handful of elections over a span of less than thirty years. We should be careful not to assume that we are dealing with a static phenomenon. We may have discovered invariant patterns of behavior, but that should be a conclusion based on research over a long time period, not an assumption built into analysis.

This third caveat requires some additional elaboration. Judging from the sweep of American history, presidential elections might be classified as (1) *maintaining,* in which prevailing patterns of party loyalties persist; (2) *deviating,* in which basic partisan loyalties remain intact, but for some reason enough voters support the minority party candidate to swing this particular election for him; (3) *reinstating,* in which the majority party regains control following a deviating election; and (4) *realigning,* in which old loyalties are disrupted to such an extent as to reshuffle majority and minority party statuses.[2] The elections of 1940, 1944, and 1948 were fundamentally all maintaining elections. Thus the close correlation between the 1940 and 1948 findings may mean that only in the same kind of election situations most people reacted in the same fashion.

The 1952 and 1956 presidential elections were deviating elections. Dwight D. Eisenhower won handily, but a large number of the voters who cast their ballots for him continued to think of themselves as Democrats and in 1954, 1956, and 1958 elected a Democratic majority to both houses of Congress. By a razor-thin margin the 1960 election would be classed as a reinstating election, and 1964 was another maintaining one. 1968 was a deviating election. Richard M. Nixon captured the Presidency but with only 43.4 percent of the popular vote, and, at the same time, the Democrats retained control of both houses of Congress. Thus we still lack a study in depth of an election that can be classified as realigning. This lack makes a full comparison impossible. Realigning elections are relatively rare, those of 1896 and 1932 being the most recent two. The panic of 1893 was apparently the catalyst that raised Republicans to majority-party status. For various reasons 1912 and 1916 have been classified as deviating elections. The depression of 1929 started another cycle that restored the Democrats to majority status in 1932.

When comparative information of the same kind is available on each type of presidential election some conclusions about political behavior may become apparent that are very different from those we have now. There have already been some modifications of early conclusions. The first studies, limited to maintaining elections, agreed that a person's party preference was the best single determinant of his final vote. In the deviating elections of 1952 and 1956, however, large numbers of voters who continued to call themselves Democrats voted Republican, clearly swayed by the attractiveness of General Eisenhower as a candidate. Even in the reinstating election of 1960, a considerable number of Democrats again voted Republican. In 1964, vast numbers of Republicans supported the Democratic candidate, and in 1968 a smaller number of Democrats cast their ballots for Nixon or Wallace. One cannot, therefore, think of parties as holding together "like a sticky ball of popcorn. Rather, no sooner has a popular majority been constructed than it begins to crumble."[3] Even a finding that the proportion of votes going to each party remains constant would not necessarily mean that the same people are always voting the same way. New voters come of age or decide to participate in politics; old ones die or lose interest in government. Other voters may become disenchanted with the administration and support the opposition; still others may be won over to administration policies and, for this election at least, vote for the incumbents.

GROUP INFLUENCES

Socialization

Even where a voter believes he is making a clear-cut choice between candidates based solely on policy considerations, innumerable factors in his background have helped form attitudes and outlooks that affect and perhaps even distort the image that candidates try to project. Psychologists have demonstrated time and again the phenomenon of "selective perception"—what people see in a particular situation is greatly influenced by their own values. And early political socialization may affect both perceptions and preferences.

An intensive study of Erie County, New York, in 1940 disclosed the cohesiveness of voting within the family, a striking fact that has been largely confirmed by subsequent investigations. Since husbands and wives tend to vote together, children are normally reared in a one-sided political atmosphere. It is not surprising, then, to find that when they come of age children are disposed to vote as their parents have. This, however, is only a general rule. Changes in social status, disagreements on important public policy questions, or an increasing age gap between the two generations may weaken "inherited" party allegiance. Still, probably three out of four voters who vote the first time in a presidential election vote for the same party their parents supported.

When the second generation marries, it is the wife who typically votes with her husband, assuming that the two partners come from different political backgrounds. The Erie County investigation showed that twenty-one out of twenty-two couples voted alike in 1940, and the Michigan Survey Center found a similar ratio of eleven out of twelve in the 1952 election. Looking over the evidence, an Elmira, New York,[4] study concluded in 1954: "In the end many American families vote *as a unit,* making joint decisions in voting as in spending parts of the common family incomes. Indeed, it would not be inappropriate to consider the family as the primarily unit of voting analysis. . . ."

Social Class

In most American communities there are no rigid class distinctions among whites comparable to those of European society. Nevertheless, there is a kind of stratification that is sufficiently recognizable to delineate in a rough way social classes. Although these classes have never existed as formal, organized groups and their lines of demarcation are frequently only dimly perceived by their respective members, social structure can affect individual motivation. Moreover, social structure does influence the availability of certain resources—money, leisure, and education, for example—needed to exploit fully the opportunities of the political process.

One of the chief difficulties in evaluating the effect of social class on any aspect of behavior lies in establishing criteria to differentiate one class from another. This is especially hard to do in America, and unfortunately no fine calibrators exist, but one can still speak in general terms with reasonable accuracy. If occupation, income, and education are used as three indexes of class (or socio-economic status, as some sociologists prefer), the results show that generally the higher his education and income and the more professional the nature of his work, the more likely a voter is to be a Republican. Conversely, the lower a voter's income and education and the more closely his occupation is related to manual, unskilled labor, the more likely he is to be a Democrat. There is, therefore, some evidence behind the old cliché that the rich tend to be Republicans and the poor to be Democrats, but the full truth is far more complex. Republican voting strength is largely based on middle-class white collar workers and semiprofessionals, and the Democrats have often drawn their leaders from the ranks of the wealthy. It should also be noted that there is a significant exception to the rule of the better educated being Republican. People who have had some college training do tend to vote Republican, but American intellectuals, particuarly social scientists, are overwhelmingly Democratic.

Despite trade union claims to the contrary, there is probably more political cohesiveness among businessmen than among workers. If this were not the case and the general lines of socio-economic division were followed in every election, the Republicans would be hard put to win any offices above the ward level, or they would be forced into becoming a more liberal party. Perhaps one of the basic reasons for absence of political solidarity among working-class people is that American culture has predominantly been white middle class.

Furthermore, as the authors of *The American Voter* have pointed out, the general relationship between social status and party loyalty is dynamic. At times the relationship has been marked, at other times almost trivial. Geographical influences also cut across class lines. In small cities outside the South, where the community is normally Republican, factory workers are less inclined to vote Democratic than are people who do the same work in large cities.

Religion

Religion, too, is often associated with partisan political loyalty. White Protestants in northern states tend to vote Republican. Since the 1920s the Jewish vote has been heavily Democratic by about a four to one margin. Historically, Catholics have been much more likely to vote Democratic, even those in upper income brackets. Despite this traditional orientation. Catholic voters in 1952 and 1956 shifted their votes to the Republican column. Only slightly more than half supported Stevenson in 1952, and slightly more than half voted for Eisenhower in 1956. With Kennedy the candidate in 1960, however, four out of five Catholics voted Democratic, and analyses of the 1964 and 1968 returns indicate that most Catholics have stayed in the Democratic fold.

Religion is a dangerous issue when it comes out openly in a campaign, and most politicians are careful to avoid the subject. In 1928, Al Smith's Catholicism was a major factor in his defeat. Again in 1960, it played a significant role, although this time its ultimate effect is more difficult to assess because the number of Catholic voters had heavily increased in the intervening thirty-two years. On balance, however, it would appear that John F. Kennedy's religion cost him more votes than it gained him. "Probably the best guess," V. O. Key, Jr.[5] wrote, "is that Kennedy won in spite of rather than because of the fact that he was a Catholic." If Kennedy's narrow victory in 1960 did not end the ban against a Catholic candidate, his brutal assassination did. Being a Catholic helped William Miller secure the 1964 Republican vice-presidential nomination, and in 1968 two of the front runners for the Democratic presidential nomination, Robert F. Kennedy and Eugene McCarthy, were Catholics. If he had not been assassinated, Robert Kennedy would probably have been chosen by the Democratic convention. All of this is not to say that religious bigotry is dead, but rather indicates a belief among practicing politicians, supported by survey data, that by and large, even in 1960 "Protestant Democrats were more likely to behave as Democrats than as Protestants, and Catholic Republicans were more likely to behave as Republicans than as Catholics."[6]

Race

Like religion, minority racial status can also be used as an indication of likely party choice. From Emancipation to the New Deal, blacks, at least those who voted, were strongly Republican; but Franklin D. Roosevelt won the black vote away from the party of Lincoln. Although the Republicans made a number of serious attempts to woo back black support and black leaders frequently urge their followers to vote more selectively, since 1932 blacks have remained solidly Democratic. It was in part Republican despair at cracking the black vote in northern metropolitan areas that made the southern strategy of 1968 attractive.

Migration to the Suburbs

Some writers have speculated about the political implications of the movement of people away from central cities to the burgeoning suburbs. There has been an expectation that because this normally involves moving from a lower-income bracket to a higher one, a change in political values and partisan preferences would follow. Although evidence seems to indicate that Republicans are more likely than Democrats to move out of the cities to the suburbs, the Michigan survey finds little evidence of a great Republican upsurge among former city dwellers.

The Rural Vote

Voting studies have confirmed the long-suspected fact that farmers react to politics in a very different style than city people. But one can speak of either a rural or an urban vote only in gross terms. Any remarks about voting behavior must be made with qualifications about income, race, religion, and a host of other factors, including geography. Northern farmers, for example, have a generally Republican tradition, southern farmers, at least until recently, a Democratic one. Outside the South, however, a considerable number of small farmers are quite likely to be Democrats; and even in the deep South, there have been rural Republican enclaves that trace their party loyalty back to the Civil War.

Historically, farmers have been a prolific source of radical third parties, parties that have received impressive local support in rural areas at one election only to vanish within an election or two. This tendency to support third parties may be dying out; but, according to the Michigan Survey Center, the two-party division among farmers outside the South still shows sharp fluctuations. Moreover, not only are farmers indisposed to carry over party loyalties from one election to another but they are also less likely than city dwellers to vote a straight party ticket in any one election. Finally, farmers' voting participation is erratic. They may turn out in mass for one election only to stay quietly at home for the next.[7]

Many explanations have been offered for the lack of a coherent pattern in rural political behavior. Economic vulnerability is undoubtedly a partial reason for farmers voting the way they do, or not voting. Another important aspect is the farmer's isolation— not only physical but to some extent cultural isolation from the rest of the nation. He tends to have less formal education. He is less exposed to the mass media. One could make similar observations about semiskilled factory workers, but there are differences. The farmer usually works pretty much alone. He is less likely to be approached by a party worker or to be reminded of his duty to vote "correctly" by a group official—despite lobbyists' claims, few farmers are active in farm organizations. The farmer is also less likely to have an opportunity to discuss politics. In short, many of the factors that operate in a city environment to stir up and maintain political interest and partisan loyalty operate far less efficiently or not at all in rural areas. Since he is unencumbered by party loyalty, the farmer is free of one of the principal emotional attachments that steady the vote of the urban worker. Without compunction the farmer can "vote the rascals out," whether

VOTING TRENDS AMONG SOCIAL CATEGORIES SINCE 1948
(Presidential Vote, 1948–1968)

Percent Democratic of two-party vote for President (three-party in 1968)

	1948	1952	1956	1960	1964	1968
Female	49	40	37	46	68	42
Negro	68[a]	76[a]	63[a]	66[a]	98	94
Under 35	57	45	41	52	71	40
35–44	57	45	41	50	67	44
45–54	44	42	39	54	68	36
55–64	40[a]	34	32	43	68	37
65 or over	46[a]	36	43	37	53	40
Metropolitan areas	56	42	44	57	71	46
Cities over 50,000	c	51	33	50	66	50
Towns, 2500–50,000	c	37	36[b]	40	60	40
Rural	61	39	42	47	67	29
Protestant	43	36	35	36	61	32
Catholic	62	51	45	82	79	54
Jewish	b	71[a]	77[a]	89[a]	89[a]	85[a]
Business and professional	19[a]	31	31	44	57	34
White collar	47[a]	35	39	48	63	38
Skilled and semiskilled	72	51	44	57	76	43
Unskilled	67	67	47	59	80	53
Farm operator	59[a]	37	46	33	63	34
Union member	76[a]	55	51	62	83	47
Grade school	63	48	41	54	78	48
High school	51	43	43	52	68	40
College	22[a]	26	31	35	53	33

[a] *Fewer than 100 cases: sampling error may be sizable.*
[b] *Too few cases to compute a stable proportion.*
[c] *Data not available.*
SOURCE: *Survey Research Center, University of Michigan.*

they be Republicans, Democrats, or members of some agrarian party. This political style, of course, is not altogether different from that of the independent voter in the city, but the urban independent voter is greatly outnumbered by his committed neighbors. On the other hand, the independent farmer is apparently in the majority within his occupational grouping.

Age

Age is a stabilizing factor in party preference. The Michigan Survey Research Center reports that about two-thirds of its respondents who can recall their first vote still identify with the same party, and a little more than half claim never to have crossed party lines in a presidential election. Typically, a young voter's loyalty to either party is not firm, but as he grows older this attachment apparently often hardens until it becomes very difficult for him to vote against his traditional party. Moreover, since the young voter's party loyalty is relatively weak, his party preference may shift, especially if his social status and income change. In fact, the young citizens who vote for the same party their parents have are quite apt to call themselves independents. Available statistics indicate that it is far more likely that young Democrats will switch to the Republican party in middle age than that young Republicans will ever become Democrats, a difference usually accounted for by the explanation that as one grows older one becomes more conservative and also that it has been more likely that a voter's income will increase as he grows older, at least until he approaches retirement.

Still, as the table on p. 197 shows, a significant minority of older and even elderly people vote Democratic, and in 1964 a majority of them did. In part, this shift was a reflection of the general trend away from Senator Goldwater, but it may have also been due to his critical comments about social security. Most of these people supported Richard Nixon in 1968, although more than two out of five voted for Humphrey.

Just as it would be a mistake to label all older people Republicans, it would be wrong to identify all or even most young voters with the radical left that has been so vocal on campuses. George Wallace drew heavy support from the young; indeed, outside the South, he received heavier support from those under 30 than from any other age group. Activists among college students may have seen themselves as battling a cynical and corrupt older generation, but "a more head on confrontation at the polls . . . was with their own age mates who had gone from high school off to the factory instead of college. . . . Outside of the election period, when verbal articulateness and leisure for political activitism count most heavily, it was the college share of the younger generation—or at least its politicized vanguard—that was most prominent as a political force. At the polls, however, the game shifts to 'one man, one vote,' and this vanguard is numerically swamped even within its own generation."[8]

Personality

One of the most fascinating aspects of political behavior is the effect of individual personality traits on the voting decision. Since political choice is influenced by nonrational forces, electoral behavior cannot be explained fully without some comprehension of the way in which individual mental attitudes shape political opinions and selectively tune out some messages and tune in others. Some highly provocative studies in psychology and politics have been written,[9] but to date this research, for all its fascination, has not lent itself to clear-cut conclusions about specific aspects of political choice.

The Independents

Since membership in American political parties is loose and informal, it is not easy to determine what proportion of the electorate can accurately be labeled as "independent." Many of the people who claim to be Independents actually support one party with considerable regularity. The best guesses place the number of real Independents at somewhere between one-quarter and one-third of the electorate.

There is a venerable body of middle-class opinion that asserts the moral and intellectual superiority of the independent voter. It is true that national surveys have found that a majority of the most sophisticated respondents call themselves Independents, but this group is small. On the lower and more crowded rungs of the ladder of political knowledge, Independents again outnumber those who identify with either party. The authors of *The American Voter* found that the typical Independent had less political interest, awareness, concern, and knowledge than the voter who asserted party allegiance.

Continued disaffection with the inability of either party to end the war in Vietnam and to cope with urban problems in domestic politics may swell, at least for a time, the ranks of those who call themselves Independents and change the composition of the group. The Gallup organization reported in 1969 that 52 percent of college students refused to identify with any party, as compared with 39 percent in 1966.

RATIONALITY AND ELECTORAL CHOICE

Certainly none of these findings changes the conclusion that the classic democratic model does not fit the behavior of the mass of American voters. Nor does a model of highly informed opinion leaders guiding policy choices of the less sophisticated provide an acceptable fit for the data we now have. While a certain amount of opinion leadership obviously exists, "it seems doubtful that it represents the dominant, effective phenomenon . . . that succeeds in lending shape to mass politics despite the absence of more detailed individual comprehension of the political context."[10]

Different segments of the electorate follow different patterns in making their voting choices. For a small portion, perhaps about 10 percent of the adult population but about 15 percent of those who actually vote, the classic democratic model is not too far wrong. These are the minority who are deeply interested in political affairs and possibly personally active as well. At the other extreme, about 20–25 percent of the population—representing a considerably smaller proportion of voters—react without much knowledge and less understanding about either past performance or future promise. Insofar as they are revealed by survey research, the choices of a third, inbetween group are based on somewhat hazy perceptions of problems and are mainly the result of party loyalty and gut reactions.

It is easy to conclude that most members of the first group are voting rationally. It is more difficult to justify drawing the opposite conclusion about the behavior of the other two, at least in presidential elections.[11] Most of our information comes from surveys of large samples in which individuals respond to about 60–90 minutes of set questions. While many of these queries allow respondents to couch replies in their own words, this kind of formal interviewing process requires a degree of articulation—in the word's double sense of verbal facility and organization—of which many people may not be capable on short notice. Less structured and more informal interviews in which many hours over a period of days or weeks are spent talking to respondents have produced a picture of somewhat more coherence—though not necessarily of more sophistication—to opinions that at first glance appear disparate, even mutually contradictory.[12] This latter type of interview, however, may itself help produce coherence and consistency by forcing respondents to think hard about political problems, something they might never do unless prodded by a persistent interviewer.

In addition, there is a distinction between acting on little information and acting irrationally. One simply cannot say that a gut reaction about politics is necessarily irrational or even unintelligent. Rationality depends on the man's gut and his reaction. For example, it makes excellent sense in terms of economic self-interest for blacks, poor whites, and working-class families in urban areas to vote for Democratic presidential candidates, just as it makes sense in the same terms for middle and upper-class white Protestants, especially businessmen and their families, to vote Republican. By and large Democratic Presidents of this century have tried to use federal power to help the economically less fortunate. Republican President have not necessarily been insensitive to demands for social justice, but since Theodore Roosevelt they have been more suspicious than Democrats of federal power, more afraid of moving too swiftly along the road to economic reform, and more concerned to protect the gains of middle and upper-class whites. Younger voters, more interested in change, may reasonably prefer the more liberal party, just as those who look to the past for guidance may prefer the more conservative. Catholics and Jews, underdogs in a predominantly Protestant society and strongly motivated by religious teachings about the positive obligations of the state, would be acting logically to pick the candidate who preached social justice.

Candidates and parties may provide weak or even confusing clues to their stands on specific problems, but the general policy orientation fo presidential candidates since 1932 has been rather clear. The substance of the findings of the voting studies is that in presidential elections, various groups tend to vote in a logical fashion, though the individuals cannot describe their personal ideologies with any precision.

Linkage among mass responses to policy questions, party stands on these issues, and party preferences of the respondents may be weak, but this weakness may be due in part to the interview problems we discussed previously. This weakness may also be partly due to the fact that parties take stands on many issues, and voters' perceptions of the relative importance of these issues may vary widely. There is a well-known psychological phenomenon that may be at work, the tendency of people to visualize more congruence among their views than actually exists. It would hardly be surprising to see a white laborer, worried about his job and afraid of having blacks as neighbors, vote for a Democratic presidential candidate who was pressing for civil rights, *if* the white worker also associated the Democrats with prosperity. Economic advancement might be more important to him than dislike of blacks. Besides, with more money he might be able to move into an all-white suburb. If this man used such social science jargon as "rank ordering of values" and "efficient allocation of resources," political scientists would be quick to proclaim the rationality of his decision, although they might deplore his goals. In short, we should be slow to equate lack of sophistication and knowledge with irrational behavior.

The real danger here is that the least informed voters—who also tend to be the least committed to either party—form the bulk of the swing vote in presidential elections and often supply the decisive margin of victory. The campaign or some outside event draws them into the electoral process to vote one way in a presidential election, leaves them cold and at home two years later at the off-year congressional election, and draws them out again at the subsequent presidential election, perhaps to vote for the other party's candidate. Campaign managers, as we saw in Chapter 9, aim much of their propaganda at the uncommitted and uninformed and often do so with gimmickry rather than with evidence and logic about policy problems. If political campaigns were waged with greater concern for projecting true images, the visceral reactions of the relatively uninformed voter would cause less concern. On the other hand, if more citizens would take the time to inform themselves about the political problems that so vitally affect their lives, political campaigns would probably be pitched more toward policy issues.

POLITICAL NONPARTICIPATION

So far we have been treating electoral behavior as if it involved only the basic question of which party or which candidate to support. In fact, there is a crucial question that must be answered first: whether to vote at all. As the most cursory glance at election and population statistics will show, nonvoting is a common phenomenon in American politics. Not since 1916 has more than two-thirds of the potential electorate turned out for a presidential election, and on two occasions (1920 and 1924) less than half actually voted. But in recent presidential elections, about three out of every four of those registered actually voted. This figure, roughly equivalent to the turnout in Canada, England, and France, suggests that getting people registered may be the crucial step in getting out the vote in presidential elections. Statistics for congressional elections, however, manifest less citizen interest and more serious problems. In a presidential year up to 4 million persons who vote for President do not bother to vote for a congressman, and in a congressional election following two years after a presidential election the size of the national electorate falls off anywhere from 5 to 20 million votes.

Even though registration and voting involve inconveniences, they are relatively easy forms of political action. Writing letters to government officials, contributing money to a party or a candidate, ringing doorbells to encourage voter registration or to acquaint neighbors with a candidate, or actually running for office, all require considerably more effort and reflect far greater interest. The percentage of the population engaging in such activities is small indeed. A 1946 Gallup poll reported that only 14 percent of American adults claim ever to have written their senator or congressman in Washington. And participation does not seem to have dramatically increased over the years, as the following table of responses for 1966 indicates.

HAVE YOU EVER DONE ANYTHING TO INFLUENCE A GOVERNMENTAL DECISION?	At Local level	At National level
Yes, worked through informal groups	8.2%	2.3%
Yes, worked through parties or other formal groups	1.6	1.0
Yes, as an individual	7.8	9.4
Yes, took part in demonstrations	0.1	0.1
Yes, other kinds of activity	5.8	1.8
No, never	76.3	85.4
Total	99.8%	100.0%
	N = 1277	N = 1279

SOURCE: *Survey Research Center, University of Michigan.*

Group Differences in Voting Turnout

On the basis of recent studies it is possible to state the basic facts about voting participation by various groups. More men than women vote, although the gap between the sexes has narrowed as women have gained more experience in voting since 1920. The proportion of people casting ballots varies directly with education; those with more education are more likely to vote than those with less. Similarly, people in upper income brackets are more likely to vote than those in lower income groups. Persons between the ages of thirty-five and fifty-five show greater interest in voting than do those in both younger and older age groups. Urban dwellers turn out in greater numbers than rural residents. Persons with strong attachments to a political party vote in relatively larger numbers than do political independents or those with weak party affiliations. Westerners have the highest rate of voting and southerners the lowest. Protestants are less likely to vote than Catholics and Jews.

As discussed in Chapter 8, legal and extralegal devices in southern communities discourage blacks from voting, but, as the Civil Rights Commission has said, so do lethargy, lack of education, and simple despair at the efficacy of the political process. In the North blacks are still less likely to vote than whites, but this statement conceals as much as it reveals. Blacks tend to come from the lower-income and lower-educated strata of society, in which nonvoting runs high among people of all races. Still, even where such economic and educational factors are held constant, blacks are less likely to be registered to vote than whites.

Why People Stay Home

Tabulating group differences in voting participation still does not explain *why* some people do not go to the polls. Certain pressures placed on a voter may cancel the effect of other pressures. Typical of the cross pressures that seem particularly onerous are having been reared in a home in which the mother and father were partisans of different parties or having recently changed one's socio-economic status or having moved from a community predominantly of one party to one predominantly of the other. Voting studies have shown that many people respond to such electoral cross pressures by staying home on election day.

Nonvoting may also be the result of a rational decision. Registration and voting consume time and energy, involving what economists call "opportunity costs." A study published in 1967[13] has shown that, as one would guess, registration regulations have a very significant impact on voting. Length of required residence, however, is apparently less important than is the length of time in which citizens are allowed to register. There are similar convenience costs attendant to obtaining information needed to arrive at an intelligent choice between offered alternatives. These costs also explain in part why so many people find the party label a handy guide to decision-making. In addition, the effect one hopes to obtain through his vote must be discounted by the number of other voters. In any election above the ward or precinct level one vote more or less is unlikely to have any effect on the final outcome. And when one man stays away from the polls he is not apt to create a chain effect unless he announces his intention not to vote and tries to persuade others of the correctness of his choice. It was probably on the basis of such an analysis that the late Judge Learned Hand remarked that voting was "one of the most unimportant acts of my life."

What is known of the typical nonvoter, however, does not fit the picture of the shrewdly calculating man (or woman) employing his available time, energy, and money with meticulous economy. On the contrary, the nonvoter is usually relatively uneducated and hardly disposed to tolerate coldly rational analysis or to indulge in it himself. Yet it is still possible that the nonvoter's decision to abstain is not altogether irrational. Registration takes time and effort, usually more so than does voting itself, and political participation may not have sufficient meaning for him to be worth the bother. Lacking the technical information and skills to utilize the other advantages of the political process, he has little reason to believe that casting a ballot will make much difference in his life.

Certainly nonvoters constitute a potentially volatile element in American politics. Pollsters assert that these people divide in party preference pretty much as do voters, although somewhat more in favor of the Democrats. But, since nonvoters generally have little loyalty to either party, an astute leader might rally them, along with those disaffected from both major parties, into a third party that could influence if not determine any national election. There is a more explosive possibility here. To the extent—which we simply now do not know—that nonvoting may be a reflection of alienation from the political system, these people form a group that might be welded into a revolutionary force to destroy that system.

WHY PEOPLE PARTICIPATE IN POLITICS

If there is a broad though vague consensus on political fundamentals, and if Americans are still basically oriented toward individual rather than governmental action to achieve their goals, it might well be asked why people participate in politics at all. First of all, that consensus, as we have seen, does not imply agreement even on rather fundamental practical questions. Anything approaching a public policy is bound to be controversial. Second, one would hope that most people realize that intelligent public participation in government is one of the principal ways through which the general consensus can be carried out in practice and the many disagreements on specifics compromised. While few reliable statistics are available,[14] this sense of civic duty, drummed into children during their school years and into adults during every political campaign, is undoubtedly one of the more important reasons why 60 percent or more of the electorate actually vote in presidential elections.

In addition, politics fills a number of rather basic human needs, some conscious, others subconscious. Robert Lane[15] has offered a grammar of these needs. His categories are hardly mutually exclusive, but they do form a useful frame of analysis. Through political activity, people may seek:

1. To advance their economic or material well-being, their income, their property, and their economic security;
2. To satisfy their needs for friendship, affection, and easy social relations;
3. To understand the world, and the causes of the events which affect them;
4. To relieve intrapsychic tensions, chiefly those arising from aggressive and sexual impulses;
5. To obtain power over others (to satisfy doubts about themselves);
6. To defend and improve their self-esteem.

Economic Gain

There can be little doubt that for many people, participation in politics is spurred by economic motives. Political activity may mean a government job or a contract; it may mean governmental policies of more generous tax exemptions, subsidies to business or farm groups, a closed or open shop for labor, protection for—or from— a Cosa Nostra family, or increased social security benefits and medical care for the aged. But economic gain is neither the sole nor the principal force behind political activity. Few Americans believe that a national election will personally affect them in a financial way, and thus they are unlikely to perceive a great economic stake in voting or working for either candidate. As we saw in Chapter 1, the lower-income groups, with the most to gain from governmental welfare programs, are usually the most apathetic politically. Upper-income groups, with their stake more immediately visible, are far more likely to be political activists.

Social Drives

The back-slapping, fast-talking politician is a caricature, but it does contain enough truth to suggest that politics is an important avenue to social acceptance. Political meetings and conferences, doorbell ringing, and other forms of campaigning are all means of meeting people and making friends. Many extroverts prefer a life in which they are socializing during most of their waking hours; and politics, whether it be merely discussing current affairs or actually running for office, provides many such opportunities. Politics, however, is neither the only nor the major, outlet for such social drives.

The Need to Understand

The need to understand the world in which we live is a motivation that can be readily grasped. Despite popular indifference, political decisions do vitally affect our everyday lives. Questions of war or peace, hydrogen-bomb testing or an atomic weapons moratorium, tariffs or free trade, school segregation or integration, government regulation of business or laissez faire, all are ultimately settled in the political process. It is normal that people want to know how such momentous decisions are made and perhaps even to have a voice in the final choice. Such people range from the "inside dopester" who merely wants to impress his friends with odd tidbits of information, to the serious student who tries to understand current happenings in terms of a broad philosophy, and to the practitioner who feels he must influence as well as comprehend his political environment.

Relief of Psychic Tensions

All human beings are beset by inner conflicts between opposing psychic drives or between drives and conscience. Some degree of aggression, frustration, guilt, and tension seems to be inevitable. Political participation is one of many means of letting off these pressures. The white man who actively supports school integration may be assuaging guilt feelings over personal or public unfairness toward blacks. Another white man, brought up to believe racial intermarriage is wrong, may become an avid supporter of white supremacy as he recoils in guilt over being attracted to a black woman. The housewife who is dissatisfied with her home life may find political activity a welcome outlet for her pent-up emotions. So, too, a man who wishes to escape from some personal problem may immerse himself in politics (or in business) as a form of diversion or escape. The classic example is the Germans in the early 1930s who, still rankling over the humiliation of the Treaty of Versailles and bankrupted by the runaway inflation of the 1920s, had a ready means of release for their frustrations in the superemotional rituals of Nazism and its accompanying glorification of the Reich.

Voting, as one psychiatrist[16] has said, "is more than a political act. It is an expression of affirmation or protest and is therefore an emotive as well as an instrumental act. The act of voting or of non-voting [as well as other forms of political activity] fulfills covert and unconscious as well as overt and conscious needs and wishes." Thus for many Americans membership in the Communist party during the 1930s was not just a manifestation of economic despair. It was also an extreme form of protest against what these people saw as the rank injustices of the existing political and social system. One could make similar observations about student participation in radical groups of the late 1960s and early 1970s.

There is no known correlation between neurosis and political activism. Although the evidence is inconclusive, it points the other way. What little research has been done indicates that the deeper an individual's inner conflict, the more apt he is to be politically apathetic. This does not mean that certain types of emotional problems are not more likely than others to move a man to political participation. Lane[17] reports that twenty case studies of political self-analysis have led him to believe that "persons who have a capacity for externalized aggression are more likely to become politically oriented than those for whom such external expression is inhibited."

The Quest for Power

Power motivation has always been recognized as a primary factor behind political activity. As Hobbes[18] noted over three centuries ago: "in the first place, I put for a general inclination of all mankind, a perpetual and restless desire of Power after power, that ceaseth only in death." Whether or how much this is an exaggeration, the pursuit of power remains a fact of life confirmed by daily experience. And politics is an excellent way (though, again, by no means an exclusive one) of expressing the power urge, even if political activity is restricted to casting a ballot for a winning candidate. On the other hand, in a democracy, a person who is not able to control, or at least to conceal, a burning power drive will usually exclude himself from positions of leadership by alienating his colleagues (who usually also have power ambitions) and followers.[19]

The Need for Self-esteem

The individual's need for personal status "is apparently insatiable. Whether we say that he longs for *prestige,* for *self-respect, autonomy,* or *self-regard,* a dynamic factor of this order is apparently the strongest of his drives."[20] Again, politics is one of many avenues to increased self-esteem. Seeing oneself or a member of one's family in the White House has historically been the apex of American ambition. Simply being informed about political affairs can be a source of prestige in a group. So, too, the act of voting, of participating in the choice of national leaders, is a status symbol.

Politicians are acutely aware of the local notoriety as well as self-esteem that comes to those who "know" a celebrity. This psychological knowledge explains in part the vast amount of handshaking in which candidates engage and the carefulness of most successful politicians to remember names and faces and to reward with some small personal attention all those who worked to elect them. No one who has watched the reaction of party workers who receive notes of thanks from the White House can doubt the effectiveness of appeals to self-esteem.

VOTING STUDIES AND DEMOCRATIC THEORY

The picture of the American citizen that the voting studies develop is not one that would overjoy naive apologists for democracy; it is also a disquieting picture for those theorists who argue that stable democratic government must rest on a well-informed, highly active citizen body. Clearly, political participation of any sort is not attractive to a large minority, and a majority of those who do vote do not base their choices on an informed judgment of public issues. One can, however, offer rational and intelligent explanations for the choices that most voters make in presidential elections, although possibly not in state and local contests. It is probable that many psychic drives and extrarational forces influence political actions, but this probability should come as no surprise to a society in which Freud is a household word. The important point is that no evidence has been offered that American voting choices in particular or political behavior in general are more influenced by nonrational factors than are other aspects of human life.

SELECTED BIBLIOGRAPHY

Campbell, Angus, Philip E. Converse, Warren E. Miller, and Donald E. Stokes, *The American Voter* (New York: John Wiley and Sons, Inc., 1960).

———, *Elections and the Political Order* (New York: John Wiley and Sons, Inc., 1966). The two most thorough and insightful analyses of voting behavior in national elections, based on polls conducted by the University of Michigan's Survey Research Center.

Eulau, Heinz, Samuel J. Eldersveld, and Morris Janowitz, eds., *Political Behavior* (New York: The Free Press, 1959). A collection of essays on the sociology of politics.

Fuchs, Lawrence P., *The Political Behavior of American Jews* (New York: The Free Press, 1956). An informative account of the political behavior of one group of Americans.

Lane, Robert E., *Political Ideology: Why the American Common Man Believes What He Does* (New York: The Free Press, 1962). An effort to describe the sources and consequences of the ideology latent in the mind of "the urban common man," based on long and intensive interviews with fifteen lower-middle-class workers.

———, *Political Thinking and Consciousness: The Private Life of the Political Mind* (Chicago, Ill.: Markham Publishing Company, 1969). A study, based on indepth interviews with 24 young men, of how motivation shapes thinking about politics.

Lazarsfeld, Paul F., Bernard Berelson, and Hazel Gaudet, *The People's Choice: How the Voter Makes Up His Mind in a Presidential Campaign* (New York: Duell, Sloan and Pearce—Meredith Press, 1944). The first of the modern voting studies, interesting both for its status as a piece of intellectual history and for its substantive findings.

Rogers, Lindsay, *The Pollsters* (New York: Alfred A. Knopf, 1949). An examination of the failure of the pollsters to predict the 1948 election that questions many of the fundamental assumptions and techniques of mass opinion surveys.

Scammon, Richard M., *America Votes* (Washington, D.C.: The Governmental Affairs Institute, 1956, 1958, 1960, 1962, 1964, 1966, and 1968), 7 vols. Extremely useful collections of voting statistics.

Thompson, Dennis F., *The Democratic Citizen: Social Science and Democratic Theory in the Twentieth Century* (Cambridge: Cambridge University Press, 1970). An interesting effort to reconcile the empirical findings of voting studies with attempts of normative political philosophers to construct a democratic political theory.

Tufte, Edward R., ed., *The Quantitative Analysis of Social Problems* (Reading, Mass.: Addison-Wesley Publishing Company, Inc., 1970). A good collection of quantitative studies, many of which deal with voting behavior.

Footnotes

[1] The most important of the voting studies are: Paul F. Lazarsfeld, Bernard B. Berelson, and Hazel Gaudet, *The People's Choice: How the Voter Makes Up His Mind in a Presidential Campaign* (New York: Duell, Sloan & Pearce-Meredith Press, 1944); Bernard B. Berelson, Paul F. Lazarsfeld, and William N. McPhee, *Voting: A Study of Opinion Formation in a Presidential Campaign* (Chicago: University of Chicago Press, 1954); Angus Campbell, Gerald Gurin, and Warren E. Miller, *The Voter Decides* (New York: Harper & Row, Publishers, 1954); Angus Campbell, Philip E. Converse, Warren E. Miller, and Donald E. Stokes, *The American Voter* (New York: John Wiley and Sons, Inc., 1960) and *Elections and the Political Order* (New York: John Wiley and Sons, Inc., 1966); and V. O. Key, Jr., *The Responsible Electorate* (Cambridge, Mass.: Harvard University Press, 1966).

[2] This classification has been developed and explained in V. O. Key, Jr., "A Theory of Critical Elections," *Journal of Politics*, 17 (February 1955), p. 3; and Campbell, Converse, Miller, and Stokes, *Elections and the Political Order,* Chaps. 2 and 3.

[3] Key, *The Responsible Electorate,* p. 30.

[4] Berelson, Lazarsfeld, and McPhee, pp. 92–93.

[5] V. O. Key, Jr., "Interpreting the Election Results," in Paul T. David, ed., *The Presidential Election and Transition 1960–1961* (Washington, D.C.: The Brookings Institution, 1961), p. 175.

[6] Campbell, Converse, Miller, and Stokes, *Elections and the Political Order,* p. 123.

[7] See the discussion in Campbell, Converse, Miller, and Stokes, *The American Voter,* Chap. 15.

[8] Philip E. Converse, Warren E. Miller, Jerrold G. Rusk, and Arthur G. Wolfe, "Continuity and Change in American Politics: Parties and Issues in the 1968 Election," *American Political Science Review,* 63 (December 1969), pp. 1104–1105.

[9] Among the more interesting studies are: Harold D. Lasswell, *Psychopathology and Politics* (Chicago, Ill.: University of Chicago Press, 1930); Herbert McClosky, "Conservatism and Personality," *American Political Science Review,* 52 (March 1958), p. 27; M. Brewster Smith, "Opinions, Personality and Political Behavior," *American Political Science Review,* 52 (March 1958), p. 1; E. Victor Wolfenstein, *The Revolutionary Personality: Lenin, Trotsky, Gandhi* (Princeton: Princeton University Press, 1967); Paul Roazen, *Freud: Political and Social Thought* (New York: Alfred A. Knopf, 1968); Fred I. Greenstein, *Personality and Politics: Problems of Evidence, Inference, and Conceptualization* (Chicago, Ill.: Markham Publishing Company, 1969); Robert E. Lane, *Political Thinking and Consciousness: The Private Life of the Political Mind* (Chicago, Ill.: Markham Publishing Company, 1969); and Leroy N. Rieselbach and George I. Balch, eds., *Psychology and Politics: An Introductory Reader* (New York: Holt, Rinehart and Winston, Inc., 1969).

[10] Philip E. Converse, "The Nature of Belief Systems in Mass Publics," in David E. Apter, ed., *Ideology and Discontent* (New York: Free Press of Glencoe, 1964), p. 233.

[11] V. O. Key, Jr., *The Responsible Electorate,* interprets much of the Gallup election data as indicating that genuine concern about political issues does influence a large portion of voters.

[12] See Robert E. Lane, *Political Ideology: Why the American Common Man Believes What He Does* (New York: Free Press of Glencoe, 1962).

[13] Stanley Kelly, Jr., Richard E. Ayres, and William G. Bowen, "Registration and Voting," *American Political Science Review,* 61 (June 1967), p. 359.

[14] For one attempt to gather such statistics see Campbell, Gurin, and Miller, pp. 194–199. See also Albert Somit, Joseph Tanenhaus, Walter H. Wilke, and Rita W. Cooley, "The Effect of the Introductory Political Science Course on Student Attitudes Toward Personal Political Participation," *American Political Science Review,* 52 (December 1958), p. 1129; these authors found no measurable change in student attitudes. See also the studies of political socialization cited in Chapter 1, p. 28.

[15] Robert Lane, *Political Life: Why People Get Involved in Politics* (New York: The Free Press, 1959), p. 102.

[16] C. W. Wahl, "The Relation between Primary and Secondary Identifications," in Eugene Burdick and Arthur J. Brodbeck, eds., *American Voting Behavior* (New York: Free Press of Glencoe, 1959), p. 280.

[17] *Political Life,* p. 119.

[18] Thomas Hobbes, *Leviathan,* Part I, Chap. 11.

[20] Harold D. Lasswell, "The Selective Effect of Personality on Political Participation," in R. Christie and M. Jahoda, eds., *Studies in the Scope and Method of "The Authoritarian Personality"* (New York: Free Press of Glencoe, 1954).

[20] Gordon Allport, The Psychology of Participation," *Psychological Review,* 52 (May 1945), p. 122.

Part IV The Congress

Confrontation in Capital

Disputes Between Nixon and Congress Reflect a Struggle for Reins of Power

By MAX FRANKEL
Special to The New York Times

WASHINGTON, Dec. 23— School's out at the Capitol for the last time in the sixties and the decade ends as it began, with a President and the legislators confronting each other like a stern principal and rebellious pupils. Congress passes one kind of tax bill one week, then, under the lash of Executive threat, settles for another. The President devises a plan to place more Negroes in construction jobs, and the legislators resolve to prevent it, except that in their eagerness to get away for a three-week holiday they decide they better let him have it. Mr. Nixon retires to compose a budget of social spending on health, education and welfare through June, 1971, while Congress retires without even formally appropriating the money spent in these areas since July, 1969.

Though it all looks bizarre from the outside, Washington has had its senses dulled to such confusion. Often, the confusion is even flattered as the essence of democracy, the highest expression of the constitutional checks and balances and the happy resolution of otherwise irreconcilable interests and pressures.

Thus weakened in this decade, the legislators have seemed to the Executive to have taken out their frustrations in delay, distortion, petulance and rebellion. They have distorted the proposed spending pattern. They have hamstrung the foreign aid program. They have even imposed total spending limits without bothering to make their own appropriations conform.

President Nixon, it is known, shares some of the same apprehensions. And he is plainly preparing, out of both frustration and ambition, to argue next year that the obstructing Democrats have impeded his fight against crime and inflation and that the national interest now requires the election of a "loyal" Republican legislature.

But the causes of the confusion and often debilitating stalemate here go far beyond partisan division. Mr. Kennedy always needed Republican support to prevail in a Democratic Congress. Mr. Nixon's most conspicuous setbacks found liberal Republicans voting with liberal Democrats or conservative Republicans with conservative Democrats.

Lyndon B. Johnson's landslide victory over Barry Goldwater gave him a tremendous mandate and majority on Capitol Hill, but they worked for him, legislatively, for only about 18 months and are not likely to be given to another President soon.

In fact, the issues of efficient and representative government here go far beyond the question of a President's year-end report card of measures passed and failed. It is only in the last 50 years that Congress has encouraged the President to be the legislator in chief, proposing while Congress only disposed, and keeping control of the nation's budget and therefore spending priorities. Before then, the members of Congress often resented the intervention of the President in their deliberations, and they went to the White House to give advice more often than to receive it.

Only in this century has Congress surrendered the essential power of the purse to the Executive while technology and modern weapons have simultaneously deprived it of significant participation in the making of foreign policy. With his command of the armies and of the budget-making process, the President has been cast in the role of not only leader but also disciplinarian: Do it my way because you don't have the means to offer real alternatives.

If you add the members of Congress who are determined, after Vietnam, to trim back the President's power to go to war without their consent to the members who are struggling to recapture control over the allocation of funds and the setting of domestic priorities, you can see the outline of a formidable army— perhaps half the Senate and between a third and half of the House.

But the irony is that those who wish to reassert the prerogatives of Congress have been unable to diminish the prerogatives of the Congressional elders, who rule by seniority, in largely safe and often Southern districts, with extraordinary powers in the committees that manage the money, monitor the military and hold enormous power over the political fortunes of the other members.

As John Gardner has pointed out, the Speaker of the House is 78. Thirteen Senate and House Committee chairmen are over 70, six of them over 75, two over 80.

The very weakness of the Congress has therefore produced rebellion without reform, leaving the President with enormous responsibility yet often a beggar of authority. The very strength of the Presidency has provoked leaderless resentments and challenges in Congress, without coherent alternatives.

These are not the checks and balances envisioned by the founding fathers. In fact, James Madison looked to the budget-making process as the essential counterweight to executive power.

"This power over the purse may, in fact, be regarded as the most complete and effectual weapon with which any constitution can arm the immediate representatives of the people," he wrote, "for obtaining a redress of every grievance and for carrying into effect every just and salutary measure."

Yet that power now resides in the White House and in a few closed circles of authority in Congress. The majority of the members are not equipped to assume it or even to police the budget work of others.

If they really wish to reform the American system of Government this will be the arena of struggle in the seventies, as some members have promised. If they truly intend to redirect the Executive, however, they must first find the means to reform themselves.

© 1969 by The New York Times Company. Reprinted by permission.

Chapter 11   The Legislative Process

The Congress of the United States was a product of the golden age of the legislature. The doctrine of legislative supremacy dominated the thinking of democratic theorists in the eighteenth century. The British parliament was emerging from the shadow of the crown, while power was lodged in the assembly in revolutionary France. On this side of the Atlantic, the revolt of the colonies was as much a protest against unbridled executive power as it was against England. Reflecting their commitment to representative democracy and the young nation's distrust of executive power, the Founding Fathers created a strong national legislature to determine public policy, spend public funds, and constrain the executive.

Today Congress functions in an era of legislative decline. The development of the modern social service state and its large bureaucracies, the enlargement of the stakes and instruments of diplomacy and warfare in the twentieth century, and the ability of mass communications to dramatize and personalize presidents and prime ministers, all have contributed to the eclipse of the legislature by the executive. Party discipline and the growth in the influence of the prime minister and his cabinet have severely limited the role of the individual member of the House of Commons. The contemporary national legislature in France is a pale shadow of the once-dominant assembly of the Third Republic, its power eroded by the steady growth of an increasingly autonomous bureaucracy and the creation of a plebiscitary presidency under the Fifth Republic of Charles De Gaulle and his successors.

Congress clearly has not been immune to these trends. In comparison with the executive branch, its *relative* importance in the national government inevitably has declined as a result of the phenomenal growth of governmental activity, international interests, and bureaucracy. In particular, Congress has lost much of the responsibility for initiating policy to the Presidency which more or less commands the services of three million federal employees and controls the information which directs the spending of $200 billion a year. But unlike most other national legislatures in the contemporary world, Congress has survived the growth of executive and bureaucratic power without losing either its vitality or its independence. If it is no longer the first branch of government neither has it become the captive of a centralized party system or a rubber stamp for the actions of the chief executive and his agents.

CONGRESS AND POLICY MAKING

Under the classical theory of representative democracy, the legislature has the primary responsibility for determining public policy through its power to make laws which are enforced by the executive and the judiciary. Article I of the Constitution provides that: "All legislative power herein granted shall be vested in a Congress . . ." Laws such as the Social Security Act, the Wages and Hours Act, the Elementary and Secondary Education Act, the Selective Service Act, and the various housing and highways acts passed by Congress over the past half century are some of the most important public policies currently being pursued in the United States. But a statute is only the most highly formalized of policy statements; policy in its broader and all-encompassing aspects takes many other forms, such as customs, court decisions, executive orders, and administrative rulings. In fact, most of the rules that govern human conduct are found in these, and a policy expressed in a statute can always be traced back to a *prestatutory* phase and is certain to have an important *poststatutory* development. Often a rule of society begins as a custom that men observe more or less voluntarily. Somewhat later this custom may find expression in judicial decisions or administrative orders. In the absence of a pertinent statute a judge may find it necessary to make his own law in deciding a dispute between opposing parties.[1] Similarly, an administrator may find it necessary to evolve rules of his own to cover certain problems where there is no statute to guide him.[2] Thus when the time arrives for the legislature to enact a statute in a particular field there is almost certain to have been a good deal of earlier policy formation in this same field. Indeed, in most law-making situations the legislature does not initiate completely new policy but, instead, selects from or ratifies certain rules that have already taken shape.

A good illustration is the development of the American program of aid to the allies in World War II. This program was eventually formalized by Congress in the Lend-Lease Act of 1941, which authorized the President to aid those foreign nations whose defense was deemed vital to American security. Actually, in September 1940, the President had already supplied England with fifty "over-age" destroyers and had accepted certain concessions in return, such as naval and air bases in Bermuda and Newfoundland. He took this step on the basis of his own constitutional power and certain vague congressional enactments authorizing him to dispose of governmental property. By this action he clearly gave shape to the main lines of the American policy that Congress later formally approved.

The process of policy formation by no means comes to an end when the legislature has acted. No matter what the character of a statute, a certain measure of policy refinement and extension is inevitable through the years as it is enforced. The complex problems of modern society compel legislatures to adopt statutes in more and more general terms. Many problems have become so technically complex and difficult that the legislature does not dare to attempt to deal with detail, but contents itself with indicating the broad lines of policy, leaving elaboration to other governmental agencies. This is an aspect of the governmental process that has always existed. Although the condition has become more striking in recent decades, the change is one of degree.

A good illustration is the parity-price aspect of the American farm program. In statutes Congress has set the ideal, that farmers ought to receive an income from the sale of their crops that will bring them into a position of parity with respect to the prices of the nonfarm goods that they must buy. But Congress has delegated to administrative officers a considerable measure of discretionary power to work out the details of this program. Thus the day-to-day meaning of the parity-price system is to be found very largely in administrative rulings.

Constitutionally, Congress retains the power at any time to veto or to alter such rulings by enacting new amending laws, but Congress does not legislate easily. The national legislative process is exceedingly difficult and complex. Occasionally sufficient public opinion takes shape and congressional majorities can be organized to put through an important piece of legislation. But often once a statute is passed its moment is gone— public attention is diverted elsewhere, legislative coalitions dissolve, and new ones take their place. As a general rule congressmen have been unable, or unwilling, to follow up initial policy decisions with precise, periodic revisions. Congressmen cannot follow on a regular and intimate basis the work of the innumerable courts and administrative agencies to which they entrust the interpretation and enforcement of a wide variety of statutes; nor can they ratify or repudiate the more or less continuous legislative rulings of these bodies.

Policy Making without Statutes

The days when governmental policy was evolved in the complete absence of statutes are by no means gone. At many points in the governmental process policy is still formulated by agencies other than the legislature. This is particularly true of foreign policy. The Constitution gives such a large measure of power to the President in this field that he is capable of acting independently of Congress in a great many ways. The Monroe Doctrine is a famous example. Usually, the President takes influential members of Congress into his confidence and tries to make the legislative branch a cooperative partner when he undertakes to shape or revise foreign policy. Occasionally, as in the case of the Gulf of Tonkin Resolution which Congress passed in 1964 during the initial stages of the escalation of the Vietnamese conflict, the President seeks direct congressional approval of actions he has already taken in the international sphere. In addition, Congress possesses an important check over presidential foreign policy-making through its control of the purse strings. The power of Congress to appropriate funds, however, is of limited usefulness in checking the executive in many of the most important areas of foreign policy. This is especially the case once the President commits the armed forces since, as congressional behavior during the War in Vietnam illustrates, few congressmen even among the critics of military involvement abroad are willing to leave themselves open to the charge that they failed to support "our boys" who are risking their lives.

The President also can make domestic policy without the benefit of statutes. A good example is provided by the loyalty program for employees of the federal government, originally announced by President Truman in 1947 by means of an executive order and continued in effect in revised form by Presidents Eisenhower, Kennedy, Johnson, and Nixon. This controversial program has subjected federal employees, actual and prospective, to intensive loyalty and security checks. Congress might well have made the original provision for such a program through the enactment of a statute. But it chose to operate only on the margins of this problem, leaving it largely to the President, as Chief Executive, to decide just how the loyalty of federal employees should be judged.

Sharing the Legislative Function

The role of Congress, then, is limited by the fact that policy-making in a complex government inevitably involves more than law-making. It is further circumscribed because Congress must share the legislative function with the President. From the Constitution the chief executive derives the power to veto legislation, call Congress into special session, report to the House and Senate on the State of the Union, and "recommend to their consideration such measures as he shall judge necessary and expedient." Only in the past half century, however, have the Presidents regularly employed and expanded their constitutional powers so as to occupy an increasingly important role in the legislative process. Today, the President is the chief source of legislative initiative and leadership in the Congress. The executive branch formulates most of the major bills considered by Congress. Through its preparation of the budget, the executive determines national priorities and, as a consequence, the legislative agenda, both of which are transmitted to Congress in the State of the Union message, the budget message, the economic report, and a series of special legislative messages on the various components of the President's legislative program. The White House also plays a key role in organizing political support for its program in Congress, employing its own legislative liaison forces and those of the departments and agencies, frequent meetings between the President and the congressional leadership, and presidential lobbying and pleas for public support.

Despite constant grumbling, frequent frustration, and an occasional revolt, Congress by and large accepts the President's initiative—although not necessarily his specific policies—because it has no alternative given the size and complexity of its contemporary legislative task. Because power is dispersed in Congress and its resources limited, the congressional leadership rarely is able to establish priorities or a legislative agenda. The President fills this gap with his legislative program and the leadership he provides for its enactment. In the process, as Richard E. Neustadt[3] points out:

> . . . Congress gains . . . a prestigeful "laundry-list, a starting order-of-priority to guide the work of each committee in both houses in every session. Since it comes from downtown, committee and house leaders—and all members—can respond to or react against it at *their* option. But coming from downtown it does for them what they, in their disunity, cannot do for themselves: it gives them an agenda to get on with, or depart from.

Congress usually "gets on" with a fair amount of the President's program, but never with all of it. Between 1964 and 1966, Lyndon Johnson dominated Congress as no President had since the early years of the New Deal. Yet the Eighty-ninth Congress rejected Johnson's proposal for home rule for the District of Columbia, blocked the Administration's plan for merging the National Guard and the Reserves, refused to appropriate funds for the newly enacted rent supplement program, forced the White House to accept limitations on the Secretary of Defense's right to close military bases, and killed the attempt of the President and organized labor to repeal the provision of the Taft-Hartley Act which permits states to enact "right to work" laws.

Under more normal circumstances, Congress plays an even larger part, despite the growing involvement of the executive branch in all aspects of the legislative process. Tax legislation continues to be written primarily by the House Ways and Means Committee rather than by the Department of the Treasury. In 1969, for example, leadership for an extensive tax reform program came from Wilbur Mills of Arkansas, the influential chairman of the Ways and Means Committee. Moreover, much of the legislative initiative in recent years in such areas as air and water pollution, mass transportation, consumer protection, overhaul of the Electoral College, and reform of the federal system has come from congressmen. Often, the congressman responsible for legislative innovation is the chairman of a key committee or subcommittee, as in the case of Representative John Blatnik of Minnesota who became Washington's prime mover in the field of water pollution control after assuming the chairmanship of the Subcommittee on Rivers and Harbors of the House Committee on Public Works in 1955. In other instances, constituency problems produce congressional innovation in the legislative process, as with Senator Harrison Williams of New Jersey who developed the initial federal mass transportation legislative proposals as a means of alleviating the desperate problems of rail commuters in the New York and Philadelphia metropolitan areas.

As long as there are concerned and ambitious members of Congress and Administrations are unable to respond adequately to the legislative desires of 535 representatives and senators, congressmen will continue to play an important role in developing legislative proposals. Foresight in the selection of an issue can catapult an obscure congressman into the national limelight as occurred with Senator Edmund Muskie of Maine, the prime architect of the Clean Air Act of 1963. Legislative initiative on the part of congressmen also affords an opportunity for the opposition party to force the Administration's hand on issues that it would prefer to duck, as was the case with Democratic bills dealing with the questions of electoral college reform and the 18-year-old vote in the early years of the Nixon Administration.

THE LEGISLATIVE STRUGGLE

The legislative process is often viewed as a continuous "struggle" on the part of opposing "groups" for power and control of public policy.[4] To bring about the enactment of a statute, groups form coalitions. It is usually much more difficult to forge a coalition majority for positive action than it is to organize a coalition strong enough to prevent action from being taken. As Stephen Bailey[5] concludes in his study of the adoption by Congress of the Employment Act of 1946.

> Put in its baldest form, the story of S.380 adds up to the fact that majority sentiment expressed in popular elections for a particular economic policy can be, and frequently

is, almost hopelessly splintered by the power struggles of competing political, administrative, and private interests, and is finally pieced together, if at all, only by the most laborious, complicated, and frequently covert coalition strategies.

Put in somewhat different terms, the legislative scene is frequently a confused one in which the individual legislators are subject to a wide variety of conflicting forces and influences. Many people regard the political party as dominating the action of congressmen. But pitted against the factor of party may be additional forces reflecting economic, sectional, and social considerations of much greater strength and importance.

Take, for example, the plight of a hypothetical congressman from an urban district in New England confronted with the necessity of making up his mind concerning a request by the President that the minimum-wage level be raised. If he belongs to the opposition party he will be inclined to oppose the measure; his own personal economic philosophy perhaps also tempts him to vote against it as a further instance of "government regulation"; the heavy labor vote in his urban district provides a tug on him to vote for the bill; and finally, the strong possibility that such a law may help New England stem the loss of its textile industry to the South also inclines him toward support. His decision will almost certainly be the product of a combination of influences rather than of one isolated force.

This situation illustrates the way in which pressures that are brought to bear upon the policy-making process often tend to offset one another. This conflict of interest has two sides. At times it brings about a balance or equilibrium in social forces which is highly desirable in a democratic, pluralistic society. It prevents any one group of forces from winning total power and compels all groups to accept bargaining and compromise as a price they must pay for partial victories. But the formulation of national policy on such a compromise basis also has it dangerous side. This is particularly true when fundamental human rights are compromised or in the case of foreign policy, where granting of concessions to particular groups may weaken policy and jeopardize national interests. Thus development of a sound program of economic and military aid to friendly nations may be weakened by the necessity of meeting the demands of shipping interests that a certain fixed percentage of goods sent to foreign nations be carried in American merchant vessels, or of farming interests that a fixed amount of the aid be farm produce, available in surplus supply in this country.

Moreover, under this "you scratch my back and I'll scratch yours" approach to policy-making, the conflicting forces present may offset one another to a point at which no action is possible. The various groups in a community may simply be unable to bridge the gaps between their interests. A striking example of such a failure occurred in the 1966 session of Congress when the Senate allowed the administration's civil rights bill to die. To begin with, there was a division over the bill's fundamental provisions, southern Democrats, of course, being bitterly opposed to any such proposal. Still, it seemed that there was a large majority for the bill, but soon its proponents began to splinter over the details of how far the federal government should go to guarantee open housing for people of all races. Complicating the situation were strident calls for black power from a new generation of black leaders and destructive riots in several metropolitan areas. These events cooled the ardor of some civil rights supporters and made less committed senators waver.

In the end the administration could not work out a compromise with potential Republican allies or muster enough votes to break a southern filibuster. It took two more years of pressure from the Johnson Administration—and the murder of Martin Luther King—before the bill became law.

Whatever the result of a particular legislative struggle, it should be stressed that the choices of an individual congressman are usually no more predetermined than those of Congress as a whole. In fact, except on one or two issues—say the race question for a Mississippi senator—a congressman typically enjoys considerable leeway. Rarely can he ignore the group struggle; neither can he always be deaf to pleas from party leaders or demands from his own constituents. But a shrewd legislator quickly becomes adept at playing interest groups off against one another, at bargaining with party leaders, and at taking advantage of public ignorance or apathy. He is seldom free to act completely as he pleases, but neither need he be a mere pawn who responds mechanically to external pressures.

Who Wants Action and Who Does Not

Since every group at some time desires positive legislative action and at other times opposes action, all groups must be experienced in the use of techniques both to facilitate and to frustrate the law-making process. Few groups are consistent over any long period of time in supporting or opposing "government regulation" or in defending or attacking legislative procedures that help or hinder positive action. The American farmer is often thought of as a conservative individual who is anxious to preserve his freedom to grow or not to grow crops, but he nonetheless comes to Congress again and again with demands for positive, remedial legislation. Similarly, conservative business groups frequently want action by the government. Manufacturers, for example, demand that state legislatures and Congress enact legislation permitting them to fix the retail prices at which their products may be sold and to compel retailers to observe these prices. On the other hand, labor, which is ordinarily thought of a "liberal" and thus desirous of much legislative action, is sometimes strongly opposed to the enactment of a particular law. In 1947, it vigorously opposed the Taft-Hartley bill, dealing with employee-employer relations, and was equally vehement in 1959 in trying to persuade Congress to shelve the Landrum-Griffin bill, which attempted to curb labor leaders' freedom to use union funds. Neither effort was successful.

Group attitudes toward particular legislative procedures are naturally also affected by the ways in which such procedures affect their interests. Among the legislative procedures that are frequently under attack by some group or other as "bad" are the Senate filibuster, the seniority rule for the selection of committee chairmen, and the power of the House Rules Committee to police the flow of bills to the floor of the House. A strong case can be made that each of these procedures is in some way undemocratic and that reform is necessary if the American legislative process is to be perfected. But there is almost no group that is unwilling to make use of these procedures if by so doing it can promote its own interests.

In 1964 and 1965, for instance, a number of liberal Senators who had repeatedly gone on record as favoring a change in Senate rules to curb filibustering used those very rules to "educate" their colleagues and the nation about the evils of efforts to thwart implementation of the Supreme Court decisions ordering legislative reapportionment. This educational process continued for a sufficient length of time to defeat all the objectionable bills and resolutions.

The observer who undertakes to predict whether a controversial bill will be passed or defeated in Congress must answer many questions. What groups are supporting the bill and what groups are opposing it? How strong numerically and how closely knit is each of these coalitions? Can the coalition that supports the bill muster the majority vote that is necessary at several crucial points along the way if the bill is to become law? On which side does time fight? Is there a deadline that one side or the other must meet if it is to control the result? Is public opinion moving noticeably toward support of one side, thereby compelling the other side to press for a quick decision if it is to win out? What is the procedural situation? What use may each coalition be expected to make of certain procedural opportunities and how effective is this use likely to be?

THE OTHER FUNCTIONS OF CONGRESS

Law-making usually is considered to be the paramount function of the legislature. But the work of Congress is not limited to enacting statutes. It also controls the budget, supervises administrative agencies, represents the interests of constituents, and influences public opinion. In performing these functions, Congress often has as much or more influence on policy-making than it does through its power to legislate.

The Power of the Purse

Controlling the purse strings is one of the oldest of legislative functions; for example, it had much to do with the emergence of Parliament as an important part of the British government. As one authority puts it:[6]

> In the thirteenth century the kings called together on various occasions not only the chief magnates of the realm, a traditional practice, but also knights from the shires and burgesses from the towns. The purpose in assembling these enlarged councils was not the consideration and enactment of legislation in the modern sense but the obtaining of consent to new tax levies, since even in the thirteenth century it was a constitutional principle, sometimes honored in the breach, that the King could impose no new burden without the approval of the Great Council.

In the American Colonial period the rallying cry of "no taxation without representation" indicated how important the notion of legislative control of tax policy had become. The related notion that funds could be appropriated from the public treasury only by legislative action was only a little slower to take root. By 1787, it had become such a firmly established concept of Anglo-American political practice that the framers of the Constitution without hesitation prescribed that "no money shall be drawn from the treasury, but in consequence of appropriations made by law."

Congress has informally delegated much of its power over the purse to the Appropriations Committee of the House of Representatives. Acting through subcommittees

"I've always prided myself as spokesman for the grassroot voters... Lately though, I'm worried about the image of the word 'grass'!..."

GRIN & BEAR IT by Lichty. Courtesy Publishers-Hall Syndicate.

constituents who call on their representative or senator for help on everything from information on how to vote to intercession in a federal criminal case. This "case work" usually preoccupies one or more of the members of the congressman's Washington staff, as well as the personnel in his district office. Representation of constituency interests, as pointed out in Chapter 4, also involves congressmen in a wide range of federal programs which affect his state and the local governments within his district, as well as in federal decisions which affect the major economic interests of his constituency.

In addition, the growing impact of federal spending on state and local economies has made congressmen increasingly active in the promotion of their localities as sites for federal facilities, and industries within their constituency as the recipients of federal contracts. Of particular importance because of their magnitudes are federal outlays for defense, aerospace, and science. Like former Secretary of Defense Robert McNamara,[8] congressmen are aware that "the award of new defense contracts and the establishment of new defense facilities in a particular area can make the difference between prosperity and depression." They also understand that federal research and development expenditures "have an extraordinarily powerful impact on the educational, industrial, and employment sectors of every region's vitality."[9] The size of these stakes has intensified congressional involvement in decisions involving the location of military installations and research facilities, the continued use of bases and weapons systems, and the selection of prime and subcontractors. The larger the prize, the greater legislative involvement, as indicated by the major roles of congressmen from Texas and Washington in the celebrated battle between General Dynamics (Fort Worth) and Boeing Aircraft (Seattle) for the $6.5 billion TFX fighter plane contract in the early 1960s. The prospects of a congressman delivering on campaign promises such as Senator Edward M. Kennedy's 1962 pledge to "do more for Massachusetts" depends largely on his ability to increase his constituency's share of defense and space contracts. Several state delegations in Congress have organized committees which work closely with state and local officials and industry lobbyists from their states in the quest for contracts and installations. One of the most active congressional delegations in this respect is California's, whose goal is to maintain and expand the state's dominant role in military and space spending. Midwestern congressmen, on the other hand, have sought to alter the present pattern since their region has fared poorly in the competition for federal military and science dollars in the years since World War II; and some of these efforts were rewarded in 1966 when the Atomic Energy Commission decided to locate the world's largest atom smasher, costing $400 million and involving 10,000 jobs, thirty-five miles from Chicago in Weston, Illinois.

Shaping Opinion

The final function, influencing public opinion, often is overlooked. In a democracy, government has a particular obligation to acquaint the people with the nature of social problems under consideration and with alternative courses of action that may be followed. Moreover, it is to the legislature as the chief agency *representing* the people and their interests that a considerable part of this educational responsibility falls. Much of the justification for legislative investigations is based on this function.

A speech on the floor of the House or the Senate by a well-known member of Congress may influence both public opinion and administrative action. In January 1945, Senator Arthur Vandenberg of Michigan made a speech in which he repudiated his earlier isolationist leanings and announced that he would henceforth support an American foreign policy looking toward closer cooperation with the wartime allies. This address was important not only because it indicated the probable future course that an influential senator would follow, but also because it undoubtedly impressed many Americans who had hitherto hoped that their country "might go it alone," but who had learned to trust Senator Vandenberg's integrity and judgment. It also encouraged the Roosevelt Administration to adopt a bolder course of action. Similarly, Senator William Fulbright's attacks on President Johnson's policies in Vietnam established an important rallying point for all groups who had doubts about the wisdom of American military participation in the Vietnamese war.

Such influential speeches are not made in Congress every day or even in every session. But from time to time the stage is set for an address that will profoundly affect the thinking of important segments of the American public. Such remarks need not even be spoken on the floors of Congress. So great is the attention paid by the press, radio, and television to certain congressmen that a few chance words uttered at a press conference or over the air may drastically alter the course of public thinking or of administrative policy. For instance, Senator Joseph McCarthy's speech in Wheeling, West Virginia, in 1950, in which he announced that he held in his hands the names of 205 persons "that were made known to the Secretary of State as being members of the Communist party and who nonetheless are still working and shaping policy in the State Department," marked the beginning of his strong influence on American public opinion. That he never succeeded in documenting his charge—and kept changing the number of alleged communists in the State Department from 205, to 57, to 81, to 10, to 116, to 121, and to 106—did not alter the effect of his speech. When a United States senator makes sensational charges, people listen and are impressed.

SELECTED BIBLIOGRAPHY

Bailey, Stephen K., *The New Congress* (New York: St. Martin's Press, 1966). An interpretative analysis which stresses the growing strength of centralizing forces in Congress in recent years.

Berman, Daniel M., *In Congress Assembled* (New York: Crowell-Collier & Macmillan, Inc., 1964). A fine introduction to the national legislative process.

Galloway, George B., *The Legislative Process in Congress* (New York: Thomas Y. Crowell Company, 1953). A standard general treatment.

Griffith, Ernest S., *Congress: Its Contemporary Role* (New York: New York University Press, 1951). A defense of congressional pluralism and an argument against the need for more party discipline in Congress, by a former director of legislative reference in the Library of Congress.

Gross, Bertram, *The Legislative Struggle: A Study in Social Combat* (New York: McGraw-Hill, Inc., 1953). A lively portrayal of the legislative process in terms of intergroup conflict.

Jewell, Malcolm E. and Samuel C. Patterson, *The Legislative Process in the United States* (New York: Random House, 1966). An extremely thorough comparative analysis of Congress and the state legislatures which synthesizes a great deal of contemporary research on legislative behavior.

Wilson, Woodrow, *Congressional Government: A Study in American Politics* (Boston: Houghton Mifflin Company, 1885). A classic study analyzing the way in which nineteenth-century Congresses predominated over the Presidency.

Young, Roland, *The American Congress* (New York: Harper and Row, 1958). An attempt to develop a systematic framework for the analysis of legislative processes. Contains a useful research guide, including bibliography.

Footnotes

[1] On the participation of judges in the lawmaking process see Chapters 18 and 19.

[2] For a further discussion of the relationship between policy-making and the administrative process see Chapters 14–17.

[3] "Politicians and Bureaucrats, The American Assembly," David B. Truman, ed., *The Congress and America's Future* (Englewood Cliffs, N.J.: Prentice-Hall, 1965), p. 111.

[4] Bertram Gross, *The Legislative Struggle* (New York: McGraw-Hill, Inc., 1953).

[5] *Congress Makes a Law* (New York: Columbia University Press, 1950), p. 237. Bertram Gross was a member of the professional staff of one of the legislative committees that considered this same law. Thus the Bailey and Gross volumes reflect in part the same data and the same experience.

[6] Hiram M. Stout, *British Government* (New York: Oxford University Press, 1953), pp. 89–90.

[7] Stephen K. Bailey, *The New Congress* (New York: St. Martin's Press, 1966), p. 84.

[8] Quoted in "Rivalry Is Keen for Defense Contracts," *New York Times,* June 9, 1963.

[9] U.S. Congress, House of Representatives, Select Committee on Government Research, *Federal Research and Development Programs: First Progress Report* (Washington, D.C.: U.S. Government Printing Office, 1964), p. 8.

Chapter 12 Congressmen and the Legislative System

Who are the 535 members of Congress? Are they honest and able? Would Congress or its record be much changed if these people were suddenly replaced by 535 others? Or, to put the question differently, to what extent is the work of Congress affected by the people who operate it, the constituencies they represent, the political parties they identify with, and the organization and procedures of Congress itself? Such questions are never easy to answer, because the behavior of any complex institution is always affected by many different factors. Most experts agree, for example, that Congress today is handicapped in its work by faulty organization and outworn procedures. Many also believe that the decentralizing forces in Congress—such as constituency pressure and the committee system—are too powerful, and the centralizing influence of the President and the political party are too weak to produce a responsible and responsive national legislature.

Students of American government have also been concerned about the caliber of congressional personnel. A variety of criticisms comes from every direction: the congressman is called an ignoramus, a self-seeker; critics charge that he loafs on the job, puts persons on the public payroll who "kickback" their salaries to him (and he occasionally goes to jail as a result), votes himself a pension or an increase in salary, goes "junketing" to the far corners of the earth at the taxpayers' expense, criticizes administrators for accepting "gifts" or failing to break their connections with private business while being guilty of the same offenses himself, holds blindly to outmoded, inefficient procedures, and has no interest in modernizing congressional organization. It is easy to illustrate the validity of each of these criticisms by pointing to particular members of Congress, because stupid, selfish, and dishonest men do get elected to Congress. However, such criticism is frequently overdone, for congressmen share the good and bad qualities of people everywhere.

The "Average" Congressman

In the Ninety-first Congress, the "average" congressman was a 53-year-old white male. Only eleven women and ten blacks (including one woman) were members of Congress in 1970. This "average" congressman had served for ten years, and had political experience before coming to Congress, most likely as a member of his state legislature. He had a college degree, was a lawyer by profession, and a veteran. He was born in a small town and spent most of his life prior to his election near his place of birth. Before coming to Congress, he was a well-known and popular member of the community, involved in a wide variety of civic activities. Although reasonably successful in law or business, the typical congressman had not been so successful that he sacrificed a huge income in giving up his private occupation. Nor did he necessarily reduce his involvement, since many congressmen continue to practice law or engage in other businesses on a part-time basis. He stepped into a job that in 1970 paid $42,500 a year and provided, in addition, about $30,000 a year for representatives and $65,000 for senators to employ an office staff (the exact amount of a senator's allowance depending on the population of his state). He was also given a travel allowance of twenty cents a mile for one round trip per session between Washington and his home, free office space in Washington and in his home state, free use of the mails, and substantial allowances for air mail and special delivery stamps, stationary, and long-distance calls and telegraph messages.

Congress is clearly not an accurate cross section of the American people, nor is it a community of intellectuals and technicians. Although a majority of congressmen are lawyers, one can usually find a fair number of senators and representatives who are former businessmen, bankers, journalists, farmers, and teachers, as well as some physicians, ministers, and labor leaders. This diversity is one of the strengths of Congress. Legislators should be able to grasp not only which of the alternative public policies are the most efficient or even the most just, but they must also perceive what the people will see, or can be persuaded to see, as best or most just. This kind of perception requires intelligence, hard work, and social sensitivity far more than it requires technical expertise.

The Congressional Setting

Congressional behavior is influenced by many factors, not the least of which is the fact that each of the 100 senators and 435 representatives is an individual. No two have identical personal philosophies, perceptions of their roles, or work habits. Some are conservatives, other liberals; many are pragmatists, a few ideologists. Most work hard, seek the respect of their colleagues, and conform to the internal mores of the two houses, but not all. Constituency concerns preoccupy numerous congressman, but many of the most senior and influential representatives and senators have safe seats and thus rarely feel constrained by the periodic necessity of facing the voters. A majority are party regulars who seldom deviate from the party line, but an influential minority are mavericks who pursue an independent course much of the time.

Despite these individual differences, every member of Congress is influenced by certain features of the congressional setting. Each has a constituency which makes the most important judgment about his political fate. All congressmen are members of one of the two political parties. And each senator and representative interacts in an institutional arena with certain structural characteristics such as bicameralism and the committee system, formal rules and procedures such as those that govern the role of the presiding officer, and informal practices such as seniority.

The dominant characteristic of Congress in the twentieth century has been the increasing dispersion of power. The number of competitive districts has been declining, which has increased tenure, enhanced the importance of seniority, lessened the influence of party leaders, and bolstered the autonomy of the individual congressman. In the House of Representatives party leadership is much weaker than it was during the half century following the Civil War. In both houses, committees and subcommittees have steadily enhanced their role in the legislative process, contributing further to the decentralization of influence in Congress.

CONGRESSMEN AND THEIR CONSTITUENCIES

Behavior in every legislative assembly is conditioned in part by the process by which its members are nominated and elected to office. In the case of Congress, these procedures are highly decentralized, reflecting the areal dispersion of influence in the American party system. Congressmen rely on state and district party leaders and supporters within their constituency rather than the national parties for nomination, campaign assistance, and reelection. Consequently, few congressmen feel indebted to the national party or to the President for their seat. Those that do—largely first-term legislators from marginal districts who owe their unexpected victory to presidential coattails—usually discover that the dictates of political survival in the next election demand that constituency interests prevail should they conflict with party policy or the President's program. Because seats in the House and in the Senate are rooted in state and local constituencies, party discipline and other countervailing national pressures tend to be weak in a showdown with strongly articulated constituency interests.

Not only are the congressman's primary sources of political support embedded in state and local politics, as is control over the electoral system that determines the composition of his constituency. State legislatures, not Congress itself or some other national agency, determine congressional district boundaries, a task they often perform with considerable imagination. Careers in the House of Representatives have been abruptly terminated by redistricting following a shift in party power in the state legislature. For example, after capturing control of the California legislature in 1960, the Democrats ensured the defeat two years later of Republican congressman John Rousselot, an avowed member of the John Birch Society, by tacking heavily Republican sections of the San Gabriel Valley on to an adjoining district. Other House members have been shielded from electoral risk by friendly state legislators. For years, both House Speaker Sam Rayburn and Rules Committee Chairman Howard Smith represented undersized rural districts that were zealously safeguarded from potentially hostile urban voters by the Texas and Virginia legislatures. Political futures in both the House and Senate also are affected by the state legislature's control over participation in party primaries, the scheduling of primary elections, and eligibility to vote in general elections. For almost a century, state restrictions on the voting of blacks in primaries and general elections in the South enhanced the electoral prospects of conservative congressmen and contributed to the development of safe one-party constituencies. The restrictions also helped southern Democrats in Congress acquire seniority and legislative influence far greater than warranted by their numbers alone.

The autonomy of congressional constituencies does not mean that congressmen are ciphers slavishly serving the interests of their districts. Such interests are not clearcut on most issues. Most districts have a multitude of interests and these often cancel out one another, providing the congressmen with considerable freedom of choice. On many questions, little or no concern is articulated by constituents. Most Americans never communicate with their congressmen; and in the average district a majority do not even know his name. As a result, other considerations, such as personal conviction, party loyalty, committee concerns, and commitments to other congressmen or lobbyists, often prove more persuasive than constituency interests. Nonetheless, constituency has a pervasive influence on the congressional setting, as H. Douglas Price[1] explains:

> An understanding of the risks of the electoral arena is important for an understanding of Congress, not because local pressures are always decisive on particular votes but because the local basis of election tends to promote a local orientation toward issues in general. Specific local pressures may only infrequently be decisive, but they constitute the pervasive milieu within which congressmen and senators operate.

A good example of this local orientation toward issues is provided by the growth of congressional opposition in the late 1960s to the deployment of an anti-ballistic missile weapons system. Relatively few congressmen initially opposed the $58-billion Sentinel ABM system proposed by the Johnson Administration as a means of protecting American cities from a nuclear missile attack. Once Congress approved the program, the Army began to acquire sites in a number of metropolitan areas. What happened next has been graphically described by John W. Finney:[2]

> In Boston, Chicago, Detroit, Seattle, San Francisco, Los Angeles and Honolulu, objections [were] raised by city councils, church groups, conservationists, union leaders, real estate developers, peace groups and scientists to the emplacement of nuclear-tipped missiles in their cities or suburbs. . . . What had been an abstract, highly technical issue suddenly acquired a direct political interest for many Senators and Representatives. When opposition began mounting in Hawaii, for example, Senator Daniel K. Inouye, a Democratic member of the Senate Armed Services Committee, came out firmly against Sentinel deployment on the ground that it would be 'a dangerous step backward' into a nuclear arms race. Senator Harry M. Jackson of Washington, who had championed the system on the Senate floor, found himself running into political flak back home when the Army proposed to put a Sentinel site at Fort Lawton in the heart of Seattle. At Senator Jackson's suggestion, the Army agreed to move the site to Bainbridge Island, across Puget Sound, but that only served to arouse Representative Thomas M. Pelly, who has a home on the island. . . . The Army [also proposed] to establish a Sentinel base at Cheli Air Force Base in the southeastern section of Los Angeles, only half a mile from [Representative Chet] Holifield's home in Montebello. This . . . brought protests from the Los Angeles County Board of Supervisors, which [wanted] to use the World War II base for industrial and housing development, and

suggestions from Mr. Holifield that the Army should not build its Sentinel bases in populated areas.

Similar constituency pressures influenced the views of many other congressmen, who combined with those opposed to the Sentinel for foreign policy, scientific, budgetary, and humanitarian reasons to threaten seriously the future of the ABM program. In 1969, the Nixon Administration was able to secure funds for the ABM by the margin of a single vote in the Senate, and only after the ABM concept was modified from the defense of cities to the defense of nuclear weapons bases, thus permitting the removal of ABM sites from metropolitan areas.

Most congressmen fit easily into the localistic milieu engendered by the decentralized constituency system. The average member of Congress is a "local" rather than a "cosmopolitan," to use Robert K. Merton's[3] terms. He has spent most of his life in his district, reads local newspapers, and employs many district residents on his staff. As a result, he tends to perceive most issues in a local rather than national frame of reference. In addition, his political experience before coming to Congress has been in local or state politics. It is a rare congressman who has been active on the national scene prior to his election to Congress. The most common stepping stone to Congress is the state legislature where the relationship between the legislator and his constituency is very similar in most states to that between the congressman and his district. The freshman in Congress who has served in the state legislature already has learned to rely on his own resources and supporters for nomination and election, and to assign constituency interests considerable weight in his evaluation of issues.

Job security is the object of much of the congressman's constituency-oriented activity. To a remarkable degree these efforts have been successful, especially in the House of Representatives. During the 1960s, approximately three-quarters of all the seats in the House were "safe," a proportion that has been rising steadily. In 1871, only 53 percent of the House had served one or more terms; by 1915 74 percent of the Representatives were in their second or subsequent term; and in 1969, only 8 percent were first termers. As a result, extended tenure has become much more common than in the past. Less than 10 percent of the House had served ten or more years in 1900, while in 1969, 52 percent had won five or more terms. These trends have increased the importance of seniority and made extended tenure a requirement for leadership, particularly in the House. Consequently, the leaders tend to be from the least competitive districts, while those who aspire to power in Congress are led to redouble their efforts to enhance the security of their seats.

Urbanization, reapportionment, and the enfranchisement of the southern blacks may reduce the number of safe seats in the House of Representatives in the future. Stephen K. Bailey[4] believes that:

> The long-range effect of the *Wesberry* case, and of the Civil Rights Act of 1965, which opened the gates for massive Negro registrations in the South, will be to make the constituencies of the overwhelming majority of congressional districts across the land socially and economically variegated. This increased pluralism will inevitably move House constituencies in the direction of becoming microcosms of senatorial and presidential constituencies: metropolitan rather than rural, complex rather than simple, changing rather than stable.

Bailey, however, is probably too optimistic. In the larger metropolitan areas, House districts tend to reflect the socio-economic differences between the poorer and more affluent neighborhoods of the city, and between the central city and the suburbs. Many safe seats—Democratic in the inner city districts and Republican in the suburbs—are in the New York, Chicago, Los Angeles, and Philadelphia metropolitan areas. Nor can we ignore the tremendous advantages conferred by incumbency, especially since they have been contributing to increased senatorial tenure despite the urbanization of most Senate "districts." Overstating his case only slightly, Representative Michael J. Kirwan,[5] longtime chairman of the Democratic Congressional Campaign Committee, argues:

> No Congressman who gets elected and who minds his business should ever be beaten. Everything is there for him to use if he'll only keep his nose to the grindstone and use what is offered.

THE ROLE OF POLITICAL PARTIES IN CONGRESS

The autonomy of constituencies is both a major product of the decentralization of the political parties and the principal factor underlying the inability of the parties to secure the steadfast support of their adherents in Congress. The weak national organs of the decentralized parties cannot even control the use of their party's label, which is borne by the winner of the primary in his state and district, although it may be the only thing he has in common with his party colleagues in the Senate or the House. Except in landslides of the dimensions of 1936 and 1964, incumbency in a safe seat insulates the vast majority of congressmen from the ebb and flow of national party fortunes. Decentralized constituencies also protect party mavericks from retribution by the President or the national party or the party's leadership in Congress. The rare presidential efforts to purge recalcitrant party members have almost always ended in failure, most notably in the case of President Roosevelt's unsuccessful forays in the primary elections of 1938 against conservative Democratic congressmen.

Despite these weaknesses, however, the two political parties are the most comprehensive groupings in Congress. Every member of the Ninety-first Congress was a Democrat or a Republican. A congressman's party is his primary identification both in Congress and on the ballot. Party affiliation determines which side of the aisle he will sit on, which legislative leaders he will follow, and whether he will be chairman or the ranking minority member of a committee or subcommittee once he has served long enough to rise to the top of the seniority list. His association with his party's label provides him with most of the support he receives on election day. Party is also the symbol of traditions and convictions the congressman shares with most of his fellow party members in Congress. It offers a source of support for his efforts to enact a favored bill, investigate the bureaucracy, or secure a prize for his constituency. It provides most of his associations with his colleagues. And it is something to be loyal to and to expect loyalty from, albeit not all of the time since every congressman has other ties—geographic, ideological, economic, and social—which also make demands on him.

Party is also the single most important influence on congressional voting behavior.

During the past half century, between two-thirds and three-quarters of the Democrats and Republicans in Congress have voted with a majority of their party colleagues on contested votes. Voting patterns in the House and Senate are more closely related to party affiliation than they are to constituency factors, including urban-rural and sectional differences. Party cohesiveness in Congress is primarily a product of strong party identification ties. Most Republicans tend to think and vote more like other Republicans than like Democrats—which is why they are Republicans—even though the instruments of party discipline are relatively weak. Moreover, as Jewell and Patterson point out:[6]

> on many issues the pressure for conformity to a party position is immediate and direct, whereas constituency pressures are often distant, vague, ill-informed, and contradictory.

Yet party cohesiveness is not sufficient in either house to guarantee victory to the majority party on most major issues. Except in periods such as 1935–1938 and 1965–1966 when congressional majorities were huge, bipartisan coalitions usually are needed to pass controversial legislation. One of the most durable bipartisan coalitions has been the alliance of conservative Republicans and Southern Democrats which has played an influential, if largely negative, role in Congress, particularly the House of Representatives for over thirty years.

Although party lines often break down when Congress turns its attention to legislation, they hold fast in the work of organization. The party groups in each house hold separate caucuses and agree upon their candidates for Speaker of the House and President *pro tempore* of the Senate. The party floor leaders, whips, and policy committees are also selected at these caucus meetings. All party members are expected to support the party position on these matters when the House and Senate vote.

The selection of committee personnel is also strictly a partisan affair. In both houses each party sets up its own committee on committees. These four committees, functioning independently, then proceed to dole out committee assignments. Before their work can begin, however, the majority party in each house must decide the ratio that is to prevail between Democrats and Republicans on each standing committee. There has long been a tradition accepted by both parties that the ratio must reflect fairly accurately the division between the two parties in the houses. The slates prepared by the party committees on committees are ratified by the party caucuses and the two houses, but this action is almost without exception a mere formality. Actually, in the House as well as in the Senate, the standing committees are reasonably continuous bodies; the party task every two years is merely one of filling vacancies. This usually involves allowing some of the senior congressmen to move up to the vacancies on the more important committees and filling the vacancies at the bottom with the freshman members of Congress. The Democrats in the Senate are currently following a policy of trying to give each newly elected Democratic senator one appointment to a major committee and one to a minor committee. Most newly elected Republican senators must still be content with appointment to two minor committees and await their turn for appointment to major committees.

Aside from its role in organizing Congress, the party caucus is an agency of declining importance. At the height of its power the caucus was a meeting of all members of a party in the House or the Senate called to determine party position on a controversial bill. Each congressman was expected to cast his vote on the floor of the house in accordance with a party decision made in the caucus. Today this binding character of the caucus decision has almost wholly disappeared, although party caucuses are still held from time to time during the session to discuss legislative strategy.

THE STRUCTURE OF CONGRESS

Two Houses

The most obvious structural fact about the American Congress is its bicameral organization. It was by no means inevitable that Congress should be bicameral. Its parent legislative body, the Congress under the Articles of Confederation, consisted of a single house, as did all of the *national* assemblies of the American Colonial and Revolutionary periods. On the other hand, practically all of the assemblies in the thirteen American colonies and the legislatures set up in the American states after 1776 consisted of two houses. The British Parliament, with which most Americans were familiar, was a bicameral body.

Faced as they were with definite precedents in either direction, why choose a bicameral Congress? Of course, the Connecticut Compromise necessitated a bicameral arrangement. It seems likely, however, that the convention would have preferred this structure anyway, for bicameralism was consistent with the principal of checks and balances, one of the strongest forces that motivated the work of the convention. The story is told that when Thomas Jefferson returned from France after the Philadelphia convention he objected to the bicameral feature and asked Washington why the convention had taken such a step. The conversation occurred at breakfast, and Washington is said to have asked Jefferson, "Why did you pour that coffee into your saucer?" "To cool it," was Jefferson's reply. "Even so," answered Washington, "we pour legislation into the senatorial saucer to cool it"[7]

This original expectation has long since ceased to be realized. The Senate does not function primarily as a "check" upon the House. Legislation, with very few exceptions, originates as readily in one house as in the other. The filibuster has proved to be a weapon that a conservative minority can use to prevent favorable action on a bill in the Senate. Pigeonholing a bill in committee or killing it in the Rules Committee by failing to give it the right of way on the floor are weapons that enable small groups of representatives to defeat bills in the House.

Bicameralism affects the nature of the congressional setting in a number of ways. The difference in their constituency bases affects the behavior of the two houses. Representatives are chosen from districts with an average population (in 1970) of approximately 475,000, while senators represent states which range in population from 250,000 in the case of Alaska to 19 million in the case of California. Despite the constitutional "malapportionment" of the Senate, the upper house has been the more liberal and responsive chamber during much of the twentieth century. The Senate, in the half century following the Civil War, had earned a reputation as the citadel of wealth and privilege. The democratization of the Senate came about through the adoption of the direct primary, the growth of party competition, the spread of urbanization and industrialization, and the

Seventeenth Amendment which substituted population election for the selection of senators by the state legislature. Regardless of their size, statewide constituencies tend to be more heterogeneous than House districts. As a result, senators are subject to a greater variety of pressures than the typical House member; there are fewer safe seats and less immunity to national political trends in the Senate than in the House of Representatives.

The Senate is a much smaller body than the House, consequently, the 100 senators function in a less formally structured environment than do the 435 members of the House. The pace in the Senate is more leisurely; there is more opportunity for debate and deliberation. The individual senator also has greater independence and visibility than his counterpart in the House. In addition, specialization is less intensive since in the smaller house each senator serves on two major committees. Finally, senators enjoy a six-year term, while House members must face the ordeal of re-election every two years, which in a competitive district involves almost perpetual campaigning. Because of the advantages of the Senate's size and term of office, as well as the greater prestige associated with being a U.S. Senator, many representatives—especially those unwilling to wait out the long climb up the seniority ladder to a place in the sun in the House—aspire to and eventually win a seat in the Senate.

A New Congress Every Two Years

Congress operates on a two-year cycle. The Congress that convened early in January, 1971, was the Ninety-second Congress, there having been ninety-one previous Congresses in one hundred and eighty-two years. The Constitution does not clearly prescribe this biennial cycle, but it was the logical result of an election system whereby all the seats in the House of Representatives and one third of the seats in the Senate become vacant every two years. Accordingly, the Congress that meets in January of an odd-numbered year is a new body, many of its members having just been elected to their offices two months before. The meeting in the odd-numbered year is thus the "first" session, and, assuming that no special session is called, the meeting in the following even-numbered year is the "second" and final session of a Congress. Very early in a first session the two houses proceed to organize, and the resulting arrangements prevail for the two-year period. Any bill introduced in the first session of a Congress may be taken up without backtracking during the second session. But when the final session in the two-year cycle comes to an end all unfinished business automatically dies.

The opening days of a new Congress are marked by activity and excitement as the business of organizing is carried out. The presiding officers and other officials must be elected, members must be assigned to standing committees, a chairman selected for each committee, and parliamentary rules of procedure agreed upon. These tasks of organization give the House of Representatives a good deal more concern than they do the Senate, since only one third of the senators must run for reelection every two years. Of course, since there are likely to be a few elections to fill the unexpired terms of senators who have died, retired, or resigned, slightly more than one third of the Senate may be new members; but unless party control of the Senate is changing in a new Congress, the process of organizing is apt to be a mere formality. Moreover, the Senate has always regarded itself as a continuing body, and therefore has never reaffirmed its rules.

THE LEADERSHIP

The primary centralizing force within Congress is the leadership, composed of the presiding officers and the party leaders who manage the flow of business through the House and the Senate. As one would expect, the leaders are among the most influential and respected men in Congress. With the lengthening of congressional service, most are career congressmen with long tenure who identify closely with the internal norms of their chamber. Nonetheless, the leaders have modest formal powers at best. They play a secondary role in determining the legislative agenda which is set—increasingly so—at the White House. The authority of the leaders over the chairmen of committees and subcommittees is limited. The leaders attempt to lead a diverse legislative party whose members are not sufficiently dependent on the leadership to follow it on every controversial issue.

Presiding Officers

The most important formal officers of Congress are those who preside over the two houses: in the House, the Speaker, chosen by the majority party caucus; in the Senate, the Vice President, who holds the post of presiding officer by constitutional direction. Each house has a second presiding officer. In the Senate he is the President *pro tempore,* who also is chosen on a party basis and presides in the absence of the Vice President. (In fact the Vice President or the President *pro tempore* rarely presides; this dull duty is usually passed around among the most junior senators.) In the House it is the chairman of the Committe of the Whole. Technically speaking, the latter is not a House but a committee officer. Nonetheless, he is the officer who presides while the House is transacting much of its important business. He is not a permanent officer but is appointed from time to time by the Speaker as the House rises and goes into the Committee of the Whole.

In part the authority and influence wielded by the presiding officers depends upon their formal powers. To a large extent, the leaders' importance is controlled by such intangible factors as their personalities, the respect they command from their colleagues, their political skill, their party standing, the over-all strength and cohesion of the party groups, and the state of relations between Congress and the President. The Speaker of the House is almost always one of the two or three most respected and influential members of the majority party. The position of the Vice President is more uncertain. He may have little influence, as was true in the case of Henry Wallace. Or he may be an influential ex-senator and popular among his former colleagues, as Lyndon Johnson and Hubert Humphrey were. Accordingly, even though the Speaker and the Vice President have many of the same formal powers, their prestige and power vary considerably. The Speaker is a party leader, chosen by his colleagues. In addition, he is a regular member of the House. He retains his right to vote and speak on any proposal, whereas the Vice President has no regular right to participate in debate and may vote only to break a tie. Upon occasion the Speaker does leave the chair to enter the debate, and when he does he is apt to exert great influence.

No member of the House or Senate may address his colleagues or offer any motion without first being recognized by the presiding officer. Occasionally in moving from one piece of business to another the course of the legislative process may be profoundly affected by the recognition of a certain member at a particular moment, and the Speaker and Vice President sometimes deliberately give the floor to members with such considerations in mind. But in the course of debate on a particular measure the power of recognition is usually exercised on an impartial basis.

The presiding officer also has the authority to interpret and apply the rules when any question of proper procedure is raised. The routine use of this authority is rather unspectacular and noncontroversial, for mere reference to precedent is often enough to indicate the proper interpretation.[8] Every textbook cites the famous exercise of this power made by Speaker Thomas B. Reed in 1890 when he changed the interpretation of the quorum rule so as to include in the quorum count those members present but not voting yea or nay on a bill and thereby frustrated the attempts of the Democratic minority to prevent the transaction of business by not voting either way. But the opportunity to make a new and significant interpretation of the rules is rare. In both houses any ruling of the presiding officer may be appealed to the floor and reversed by a majority of the members present, so that the power to determine the meaning of a rule ultimately rests with a simple majority of the members of the House or Senate.

In both houses the presiding officers refer the many bills introduced by the members to standing committees for consideration and action. The Legislative Reorganization Act of 1946 delineates committee jurisdictions in detail. Occasionally, however, a bill may be sent to any one of two or more committees, and the presiding officer may choose a friendly or unfriendly committee.

In addition, the presiding officers of the House and Senate are frequently called upon to name the members of special committees, such as special investigating committees and conference committees organized to work out the differences in the bills passed by the two houses into a mutually acceptable form. This action, however, is usually so controlled by tradition that it leaves very little freedom of choice. For example, it is the almost unvarying practice in both houses to name the members of conference committees in order of seniority from the standing committees that originally considered a bill; if there is any question, the presiding officer usually defers to the chairman of the appropriate standing committee.

Prior to 1910, the powers of the Speaker of the House were far greater. As chairman of the Rules Committee, the Speaker controlled the flow of legislation in the House. He had the ability to reward and punish, because he appointed the committee members and chairmen. And he also had absolute discretion in recognizing members on the floor. All of these powers were lost as a result of the revolt of 1910–1911 against the strong central leadership of Speaker Joe Cannon. Since then, as Richard F. Fenno, Jr.,[9] indicates:

> the Speaker's formal authority has been modest, and his centralizing influence has been more informal and interstitial than formal and comprehensive. Sam Rayburn's success as Speaker was a triumph of personal skill and only served to obscure the essential modesty of his formal powers.

Floor Leaders and Other Party Officers

Next to the Speaker, the most important officers in Congress are the majority and minority floor leaders in each house. These men are chosen by the party caucuses, and, as their titles indicate, their main duty is to watch over and control business on the floor of the House or Senate from a strictly party point of view. A floor leader keeps in touch with party members, tries to persuade them to vote in accordance with the wishes of party leaders, supervises debate, directs the activity of the party whips, and is in general the party's chief strategist. The majority floor leader in each house also undertakes to plan and control the order of business, usually doing so on a weekly basis. This, however, is a power that he must share with other party agencies, such as the steering or policy committees, and in the House with the Rules Committee and with the Speaker.

Each party in each house chooses a whip. His function is supposedly to secure the attendance of the party rank and file at votes and to inform party members of the wishes of the leadership. Aiding the whip is an organization of perhaps fifteen to twenty deputies and assistants. All whips are, of course, members of Congress. Although they do notify party members of votes and convey the wishes of the leadership (sometimes without visible effect on voting behavior), the whips also help inform the party leadership of the views of the rank and file.

The Legislative Reorganization Act of 1946 established in the Senate a Democratic and a Republican policy committee. Each of these groups has a small staff and an annual budget paid for out of federal funds. The Reorganization Act charges the two committees with "the formation of over-all legislative policy of the respective parties." Practice, however, has failed to conform to this mandate. While the two parties have used their committees in somewhat different fashions, some generalizations can be made. Hugh A Bone, the closest student of their work, has concluded that the committees have been helpful in accommodating factionalism within each party, in collecting, analyzing, and disseminating data about public issues, and even sometimes in clearing legislation for floor action. But, Bone[10] has said, the committees "have never been 'policy' bodies in the sense of considering and investigating alternatives of public policy, and they have never put forth an over-all congressional party program."

In the House both parties use steering committees, though since 1949 the Republicans have called theirs the House Republican Policy Committee. It has been facetiously observed that the steering committees seldom meet and never steer. This is an overstatement, but it is clear that the committees are not in fact powerful or even very important agencies of party government in the House. This failure of the steering committees to function more actively illustrates the weakness of centralized leadership. Within Congress the power to lead is diffused among a wide number of officers and agencies and at best is exercised on a collective basis. One of the few recent periods of aggressive and effective congressional leadership was from 1954 to 1960 when Lyndon B. Johnson was Senate majority leader; but, while Johnson's influence in the Senate was great, he had far less influence in the House, where he had to rely on his old friend from Texas, House Speaker Sam Rayburn.

THE COMMITTEE SYSTEM

Power is dispersed in the United States Congress because most of the work of the House and Senate is done in committees and subcommittees which enjoy considerable autonomy from the central leadership. The committee system facilitates a division of labor in dealing with the numerous and complex proposals that come before Congress. It also fosters specialization on the part of congressmen, most of whom develop detailed knowledge only in those areas of governmental activity which fall within the purview of their committee. Specialization is a key norm in Congress. Respect and influence among colleagues are won primarily by working hard in committee and developing expertise. In the words of one Representative:[11]

> The members who are most successful are those who pick a specialty or an area and become real experts in it. As a consequence, when they speak they are looked upon as authorities and are highly respected. Even though they may be an authority in only one field, their influence tends to spread into other areas.

Committee influence in the legislative process rests largely on the deference of congressmen to committee members in their area of specialization. The relationships are reciprocal: the congressman who relies on his colleagues' judgment on an issue within their special sphere of competence expects their deference on matters that come before his committee. However, as Fenno[12] points out:

> The conditions of committee influence vary. Members are likely to defer to a committee, for example, when the issues are technical and complicated, when large numbers do not feel personally involved, or when all committee members unite in support of the committee's proposal. . . . Conversely, members are less likely to defer to the judgment of a committee when the issue is of a broad ideological sort, where national controversy has been stirred, or where the committee is not unanimous. . . . Under such circumstances committee influence may be displaced by the influence of party, of constituency, or of a member's social philosophy.

Committees and Subcommittees

The House of Representatives has twenty, and the Senate sixteen, permanent committees, each of which watches over a particular segment of legislative business. While the number of committees in the two houses differs slightly, the division of legislative responsibility among committees is very similar in both houses. Both houses have committees on agriculture, appropriations, the armed services, banking and currency, civil service, the District of Columbia, government operations, public works, rules, labor, taxation, foreign relations, the judiciary, and interstate and foreign commerce. In general, each senator is assigned to two of these committees and each representative to one. Prior to the enactment of the Legislative Reorganization Act of 1946 there were more than 80 committees. Congressmen had twice as many committee assignments as they do now. The drastic reduction in the number of committees has served to enhance the influence of the remaining committees and their chairmen, broadening their sphere of operations and greatly reducing overlapping jurisdictions and the possibility of conflicting expertise.

The streamlining of the committee system in 1946 also fostered the proliferation of subcommittees. There are now more than 250 subcommittees, most of which are permanent and many of which are subject to little control by the parent committee. In many committees, the most important determinations are made in subcommittee since many members of the committee defer to the specialists on the subcommittees, thus further dispersing power in Congress.

Many state legislatures make use of joint committees in an attempt to bridge the gap between the two houses. In Congress the parallel committee structures of the House and Senate are conducive to joint committee hearings and deliberations, but such sessions are seldom held. Instead, the committees of each house jealously guard their separate prerogatives. Congress, however, does make some use of such committees. Most influential are the conference committees; but a conference committee stays in existence only until the particular bill it was created to facilitate has either been passed or rejected by Congress. The House and Senate have also established a few permanent joint committees. Among these are the joint committees on Printing, the Library of Congress, Atomic Energy, Internal Revenue Taxation, and the Economic Report. Except for the Joint Committee on Atomic Energy, which is the only joint committee authorized to report legislation and which is a major influence on atomic energy policies, these committees have not played important roles.

From time to time the House or Senate creates a special committee to conduct a temporary investigation. From 1938 to 1945 the House Un-American Activities Committee was such a committee. In 1945, however, the House voted to make it a standing committee. In recent years the number of special committees has declined, and investigations have been assigned instead to the relevant standing committees or subcommittees thereof.

All of the standing committees in both houses are bipartisan. Most Senate committees have fourteen to nineteen members, and House committees range from nine to fifty members. Because of its size and its bipartisan membership, a committee inevitably possesses a certain cross-sectional character, but it is a mistake to think of each committee as constituting a House or a Senate in miniature, at least so far as the interests and voting inclinations of the members are concerned. Committee and subcommittee assignments determine to a considerable degree the policy areas in which a congressman will specialize, the administrative agencies on which he will have the greatest influence, and the subjects on which he is likely to generate the most publicity. Constituency considerations are usually an important factor in the choice of a committee assignment. Many committees—especially Agriculture, Interior, Merchant Marine and Fisheries, Armed Services, Aeronautical and Space Sciences, and Banking and Currency—have a larger percentage of their membership with constituency interests in the committee's substantive work than does Congress as a whole.

The Role of Committee Chairmen

It is almost impossible to overestimate the importance of the role played by committee chairmen in the legislative process. To a chairman belongs the power to arrange the meetings of his committee; to select much of its professional staff; to appoint the personnel of its subcommittees; to determine the order in which it considers bills; to decide whether public hearings shall be held on a bill; to arrange to have a bill, which the committee has reported favorably, brought to the floor of the house; to manage the floor debate on the bill; to ward off unwanted amendments; and, should a conference on a particular bill be necessary, to serve as a member of this committee and sometimes to influence the choice of other conference members from his house. The manner in which a chairman exercises these powers is supposedly subject to review and even control by the committee as a whole, but it is a rare committee that ever undertakes to check or rebuke its chairman. The 1967 action of the House to remove the chairman of the Committee on Education and Labor, Adam Clayton Powell, is a notable as well as a highly unusual exception.

Chairmen exercise their powers largely independently of one another and in very large measure, independently of the presiding officers, floor leaders, and other congressional and party officials. This is a crucial factor explaining the absence of centralized leadership in Congress. As Woodrow Wilson[13] said more than seventy years ago: "The chairmen of the Standing Committees do not constitute a cooperative body like a ministry. They do not consult and concur in the adoption of homogeneous and mutually helpful measures; there is no thought of acting in concert." After a finely detailed study of the voting patterns in the Eighty-first Congress (1949–1950), David Truman[14] wrote that "no reason exists for revising Wilson's conclusion that the seniority leaders do not function as a collegial body. If they consult, they do not concur."

Committee Chairmen and the Seniority Rule

In each house the committee on committees of the majority party formally designates committee chairmen. In practice, however, each assignment goes automatically to that member of the majority party who has the longest unbroken service on a committee. Exceptions to this "seniority rule" are virtually unknown. No aspect of congressional organization is more controversial than this rigid system of selecting committee chairmen.

The case against the seniority rule is a strong one. Seniority ignores ability; it puts a premium upon mere continuous service; it discourages any attempt to achieve recognition and high office by hard work and demonstration of interest or skill; and it sentences junior congressmen to a long period of apprenticeship that deters able and mature men from seeking election to Congress. It is further argued that the seniority rule is undemocratic in that it tends to place in office as committee chairmen men from "safe" congressional districts that are often politically stagnant. Because of the certainty of their election to Congress these men may be insensitive to changing public opinion and represent a point of view current at the time of their original election to Congress. For example, the election of President Dwight D. Eisenhower in 1952 unquestionably represented a victory for the moderate faction of the Republican party, but it resulted in a large number of committee chairmanships going to conservative or "old guard" members of the President's party. Similarly, Democratic congressional victories in the 1960s automatically placed in positions of great power as committee chairmen a score of southern Democrats who were hostile toward most of the domestic programs recommended by Presidents Kennedy and Johnson.

The seniority rule also weakens the role of the parties in Congress. A committee chairman usually can blithely ignore the party leadership; for, as long as he has the support of a majority of voters in his state or district, his seat in Congress is safe, and under the seniority rule, so too is his chairmanship of a committee (provided his party is in power). The House of Representatives supplied a blatant case in point in 1967 when it selected William Colmer of Mississippi as Chairman of its powerful Rules committee. This selection came strictly on the basis of seniority. Colmer had twice, in 1948 and 1960, publicly supported third party candidates for the Presidency and had time and again

"Don't look back men. Some problem may be gaining on us."

Fischetti in the Chicago Daily News. Courtesy Publishers-Hall Syndicate.

spoken and voted against the liberal policy proposals of Presidents from his own party. Critics of the seniority rule argue that one of the most effective ways of providing for increased party discipline and regularity in Congress would be to assign committee chairmanships on the basis of service and loyalty to the party and to insist upon such continued service and loyalty as the price of retention of a chairmanship over a period of years.

The argument against abandoning the seniority system that carries the greatest weight with congressmen is a negative one. Any attempt to get away from a purely automatic method of selecting chairmen would result in a high degree of intraparty bickering and intrigue. It is contended that congressmen seeking good committee assignments and committee chairmanships would be forced to engage in all sorts of wirepulling and logrolling with their fellow party members. Admittedly, this is possible. Intrigue is particularly strong in a decentralized party, where vigorous leadership and discipline are absent. But opponents of the seniority rule argue that putting the selection of congressional officers on a merit basis would itself provide a real impetus for the development of a stronger party organization with sufficient power to enable it to control the assignment of its members to posts on a merit basis without undue bickering and intrigue. Moreover, the intraparty arguing that might accompany the making of these assignments could hardly be more demoralizing to party organization than is the seniority rule itself, under which party members know that party regularity has absolutely nothing to do with receiving the important posts that the party has to bestow upon its members.

Another argument that is seldom voiced publicly but that carries weight with the supporters of the seniority rule is that the rule strengthens the hand of the conservative elements in both parties and serves to minimize the influence of liberals. The senior members of Congress, having first been elected a generation or more ago and often having held their seats through the years without facing any real opposition, are apt to reflect political attitudes and pressures of the past rather than the present.

STAFFING CONGRESS

Over the years the volume of government business has forced congressmen to build up a bureaucracy of their own that employs more personnel than many federal agencies. These professional staff members, often with technical experience and expertise that exceeds that of the representatives and senators for whom they work, have come to play an important part in the legislative process.

Each member of Congress is given an allowance for the maintenance of a personal office staff. In the case of representatives, these funds enable him to employ an administrative assistant, a legislative assistant, a professional secretary, and several clerk-stenographers. A senator's allowance is more generous, and a senator from a populous state may have a dozen or more persons working for him in his office. It is difficult to generalize about the duties of these administrative assistants or of professional secretaries, for much depends upon the care with which they are selected and the work that is delegated to them. A competent assistant can act as executive director of a congressman's office, answer much of his mail, deal with visitors to his office, keep in touch with the executive agencies of the government, run many of the errands to these agencies for constituents, and offer the congressman advice and assistance in studying bills, researching, writing speeches, and running for reelection. In short, an able, shrewd, and loyal professional man can serve his employer as a sort of "assistant congressman."

The many committees of Congress, standing and special, employ over 1200 staff members. The Legislative Reorganization Act of 1946 authorized each committee to engage up to four professional experts and six clerks. While many appointments have been on the basis of merit, party affiliation remains an important factor in the selection of a sizable number of these employees.

A number of staff services are also available to the two houses of Congress at large. Chief among these are the Legislative Reference Service and the Office of Legislative Counsel. The former was established in 1914 but has been greatly expanded since the 1946 statute. It is a general research agency in the Library of Congress, which supplies various services and materials—pamphlets, digests of bills, data for use in speeches, abstracts of current literature, and studies of special legislative problems—requested by individual congressmen or by committees. In 1970, it had a professional and clerical staff of almost 300 and an annual budget of more than $3.3 million. The Office of Legislative Counsel was established in 1918 and has also grown rapidly since 1946. Its chief function is to draft bills at the request of congressmen or committees, making certain that their technical legal language accomplishes the purposes that their sponsors have in mind. A former official in the agency[15] has testified, "Our office has nothing to do with policy whatsoever. We try to find out what the committee wants to do and help them do it." This may be an accurate statement of the way in which the Legislative Reference Service and the Office of General Counsel operate; but the intricacies and complexities of public problems make such demands on the time and energy of most congressmen, that other staff members have considerable opportunity to exercise their own discretion and so to influence policy-making.

SELECTED BIBLIOGRAPHY

————, "The American Assembly," David B. Truman, ed., *The Congress and America's Future* (Englewood Cliffs, N.J.: Prentice-Hall, 1965). Perceptive essays by eight leading students of congressional behavior and national politics.

Bailey, Stephen K., *Congress Makes a Law* (New York: Columbia University Press, 1950). A lively study of the enactment of the Employment Act of 1946.

Clapp, Charles L., *The Congressman: His Work as He Sees It* (Washington, D.C.: The Brookings Institution, 1963). The House of Representatives from the perspective of the individual congressman.

De Grazia, Alfred, *Public and Republic: Political Representation in America* (New York: Alfred A. Knopf, Inc., 1951). A history of the practice of representation in legislatures.

Fenno, Richard F., Jr., *The Power of the Purse* (Boston: Little, Brown & Company, 1966). An exhaustive account of the political processes involved in congressional appropriations.

Kofmehl, Kenneth, *Professional Staffs of Congress* (West Lafayette, Ind.: Purdue University Studies, 1962). A useful analysis of the development since 1946 of professional staffs for congressional committees.

MacNeil, Neil, *The Forge of Democracy* (New York: David McKay Company, Inc., 1963). An informative study of the House of Representatives.

Matthews, Donald R., *U.S. Senators and Their World* (Chapel Hill, N.C.: University of North Carolina Press, 1960). A detailed and well-written analysis of the formal and informal ways of the Senate.

Steiner, Gilbert Y., *The Congressional Conference Committee* (Urbana, Ill.: University of Illinois Press, 1951). A case study of this committee's operations from the Seventieth to the Eightieth Congress.

Truman, David, *The Congressional Party* (New York: John Wiley & Sons, Inc., 1959). A case study of party leadership and cohesiveness in the 81st Congress.

Turner, Julius, *Party and Constituency: Pressures on Congress* (Baltimore, Md.: The Johns Hopkins Press, 1952). Seeks to measure the influence of party and constituency on congressmen over a twenty-five year period.

White, William S., *Citadel: The Story of the U.S. Senate* (New York: Harper & Row, 1958). An admiring account of the unique qualities of the Senate.

Footnotes

[1] "The Electoral Arena," in The American Assembly, David B. Truman, ed., *The Congress and America's Future* (Englewood Cliffs, N.J.: Prentice-Hall, 1965), p. 32.

[2] "Halt of Sentinel Is Traced to a 10-Month-Old Memo," *New York Times,* February 9, 1969.

[3] See "Patterns of Influence: A Study of Interpersonal Influence and Communications Behavior in a Local Community," Paul Lazarsfeld and Frank Stanton, eds., *Communications Research, 1948–1949* (New York: Harper, 1949), pp. 180–219.

[4] *The New Congress* (New York: St. Martin's Press, 1966), p. 3.

[5] *How to Succeed in Politics* (New York: Macfadden Books, 1964), p. 20.

[6] Malcolm E. Jewell and Samuel C. Patterson, *The Legislative Process in the United States* (New York: Random House, 1966), p. 417.

[7] Max Farrand, *The Framing of the Constitution* (New Haven, Conn.: Yale University Press, 1926), p. 74.

[8] See Asher C. Hinds, *Precedents of the House of Representatives* (Washington, D.C.: Government Printing Office, 1907), 8 vols.: Clarence Cannon, *Precedents of the House of Representatives* (Washington, D.C.: Government Printing Office, 1936–1941), 11 vols., (the first five of these volumes are a reprint of Hinds's *Precedents*); H. H. Gilfrey, *Precedents, Decisions on Points of Order with Phraseology, in the Senate* (Washington, D.C.: Government Printing Office, 1914); and C. L. Watkins and F. M. Riddick, *Senate Procedure: Precedents and Practices* (Washington, D.C.: Government Printing Office, 1958).

[9] "The Internal Distribution of Influence: The House, in The American Assembly," David B. Truman, ed., *The Congress and America's Future* (Englewood Cliffs, N.J.: Prentice-Hall, 1965), p. 63.

[10] *Party Committees and National Politics* (Seattle, Wash.: University of Washington Press, 1958), p. 186.

[11] Quoted in Charles L. Clapp, *The Congressman: His Work as He Sees It* (Washington: The Brookings Institution, 1963) p. 24.

[12] *Op. cit.,* p. 54.

[13] *Congressional Government* (Boston: Houghton Mifflin Company, 1885), p. 61.

[14] *The Congressional Party: A Case Study* (New York: John Wiley & Sons, 1959), pp. 134, 237–238.

[15] Quoted in George B. Galloway, *The Legislative Process in Congress* (New York: Thomas Y. Crowell Company, 1953), p. 409.

Chapter 13 Congress at Work

A DISAPPOINTING SCENE: CONGRESS IN SESSION

The visitor to the House or Senate galleries is often disillusioned. He has envisaged an impressive parliamentary panorama with traditional ceremony, dignified debate, and high drama with the clash of political personalities. Instead, more often than not he finds a dull and inactive scene. Of the 435 representatives, or 100 senators, perhaps 30 or 40 of the former or a dozen of the latter are present. A lone figure has the floor, and while he drones along in an unexciting monologue a few inattentive colleagues read newspapers, work at their desks, or sit talking in back rows.

Such a glimpse of the House or Senate in session is hardly a reliable guide to the nature and importance of the legislative process. "Like a vast picture thronged with figures of equal prominence and crowded with elaborate and obtrusive details," Woodrow Wilson[1] once said, "Congress is hard to see satisfactorily and appreciatively at a single view and from a single stand-point." While a visitor to the galleries today witnesses forms and procedures that are more than a century and a half old, changing times have placed a steadily greater burden upon government, and Congress has adapted those forms and procedures to new needs. Assuredly Congress is not perfectly equipped to perform its functions in late twentieth century. But Congress has changed, and it does go about its work today by means of a complex institutional system that has evolved slowly through the years, and only part of which can be understood by observing the House and Senate in formal session.

A CONGRESSMAN'S DAY

If a Congressman, then, does not put in a great deal of time on the floor of the House or Senate, how does he spend his day? Although it is obvious that there can be no "typical day, or "average" congressman, much can be learned about the complex responsibilities and functions of all congressmen by introducing Representative Malcomb Durbin, a hypothetical member of Congress from a mixed urban-suburban district, and following him through a day's work in Washington.

Office Activity

Congressman Durbin arrives at his office at nine o'clock, having already breakfasted with a lobbyist who works for one of the civil rights organizations. Durbin finds his desk piled high with business, old and new. His first attention goes to the newly arrived mail, for letters are one of his most valuable contacts with the people back home. If the session of Congress has reached a climactic point, his letters may number hundreds, or even thousands each day. Mail must be handled rapidly, yet given close attention. The long sessions of modern times that keep the congressman in Washington the better part of each year make it relatively difficult for him to keep in close personal touch with many of his constituents. Thus the wise congressman tries to make sure that a member of his staff acknowledges every letter that comes into his office from his home district.

By 9:20 A.M. Durbin is consulting with his office staff. A weekly newsletter for publication in the newspapers of his district must be ready for the noon mail, and a final draft awaits polishing. The congressman's secretary has some information about witnesses who are scheduled to appear later that morning before the Committee on Education and Labor, of which he is a member, to testify on a bill in which he is interested. Another staff member has been in touch with the offices of several other congressmen and has a report on the status of a bill that Durbin has introduced to provide increased federal financial aid to cities trying to maintain racially integrated schools.

Soon a steady stream of visitors begins to flow through the legislator's office. A few will be constituents from back home who must be courteously received. Some will have business to transact; some merely "want to say hello." Other congressmen will drop in to discuss legislative issues, to exchange views, and to seek advice. A newspaperman comes in to talk about a speech Durbin is to give before his home town Lions Club, for rumor has it that he intends to criticize sharply administration of the minority-business loan program.

Running Errands for Constituents

Between chats with visitors Congressman Durbin is on the telephone, and before the morning is over he has been in communication with a dozen administrative agencies of the government. Some of these calls provide the congressman with information needed in his work, but many of them are made to help him meet the inquiries and requests of constituents. He checks with the Department of Agriculture concerning the availability of agricultural agents to assist suburban home owners to keep their lawns green during the summer drought. Then he calls the Defense Department to arrange an interview for a businessman who is coming to Washington from his district. Next he puts in a request to the Legislative Reference Service for data to be used in the Lions Club speech. Finally, he gets in touch with the Civil Service Commission to inquire about the rating of a constituent on an examination recently taken. In the meantime several of his assistants have been making a series of similar telephone calls and talking with constituents before and after they see Durbin himself. In between times, they will have been working on drafts of his

Lions Club talk and preparing a more formal speech for him to give on the floor of Congress.

Meeting with Interest Groups

Throughout the day a considerable portion of Durbin's time is taken up by discussions with lobbyists or government officials about legislative matters. Much of this time may seem wasted; the requests of many persons seeking to influence legislation are unreasonable or cannot possibly be met; or the congressman finds it difficult to maintain his dignity and his honesty in resisting the pressures that are exerted upon him. Still, he cannot refuse to listen: legislative policies are about to be determined; it is the congressman's duty to give representation to his constituents, and so he must listen patiently to requests or demands that he support this bill or oppose that one. Moreover, Durbin has discovered by experience that lobbyists and administrative officials are often experts in the areas in which they operate. Even when he disagrees with them, they can help him learn about policy problems.

Attending Committee Meetings

At 10:30 A.M. Congressman Durbin leaves his office and walks down to the first floor of the office building to the room where the Committee on Education and Labor is scheduled to continue its sessions. Durbin has served on the Committee for nine years, and he is now the third member of his party in seniority. Long ago he became aware that the most important work of Congress is done in committee. He has come to give an increasing amount of time and energy to his committee responsibilities, and through hard work he has made himself something of an expert on educational policy. For two weeks the committee has been holding hearings on a bill to provide stronger federal support for higher education, and it will soon go into executive, that is, secret, session to determine the final language of the bill. During this period Durbin has found it necessary to devote much time to the careful study of the transcripts of hearings, the wording of proposed amendments, and data supplied by the committee's staff. This morning the chief witness is the head of a major organization of private colleges and universities. Durbin does not see eye to eye with this witness, and he intends to question him vigorously on a number of points. Indeed, he spent most of last evening studying several of the organization's reports in preparation for this questioning and Durbin's staff has turned up earlier statements of the witness contradicting his present stand.

Attending Sessions of Congress

Promptly at noon the committee adjourns. The session has been a lively one, and Durbin pressed the witness hard with a series of searching questions. Now he travels by an underground tunnel from his office building to the Capitol and comes on to the floor of the House, which convened at noon. The "morning hour" is in effect. Petitions, memorials, and messages from the President, heads of departments, and the other house are being presented, and bills and resolutions introduced. Durbin does not linger long and at 12:20 P.M. goes downstairs to the congressional dining room for lunch. During the afternoon he is on and off the House floor several times. Twice he is called off the floor to talk with visitors, one a constituent from his home town and the other an official of one of the large farm organizations, who talks with him at some length about a pending farm bill. Durbin is no expert on agricultural matters and the lobbyist knows it. What the lobbyist suggests —subtly and obliquely—is that if the congressman can persuade some of his friends to vote for the farm bill, he, the lobbyist, can swing his farm organization behind the congressman's education proposals. Durbin is not sure that this trade is entirely in his interest; but he needs all the votes he can get for his own bill, and he promises to talk to the lobbyist again in a few days.

At 3:30 P.M. Durbin gets word that there will probably be no voting until the next day, and he goes back to his office to resume his work there, knowing that he will be warned by a bell should a vote be reached and that he will have ample time to get back to the floor to answer his name when it is called. Next month, when the higher education bill is brought to the floor of the House, he plans to speak at some length. Although Durbin is a respected member of Congress, he is not known as an active participant in debate. Occasionally he asks another member a question or raises a point of order, but his formal speeches seldom exceed three or four a year, and he wants them to be good—concise, informative, and persuasive.

Homework

The House recesses for the day at 5:30 P.M., but Durbin remains in his office for almost an hour more, reading and signing outgoing letters. When he leaves for home he takes with him a bulky brief case. It contains the *Congressional Record* for the previous day's session, which he has not yet found time to examine, the morning newspapers, which have had only a quick glance, the rough draft of a committee report on the education bill that the committee staff has been working on, some notes for his Lions Club speech, a long letter from a trusted political adviser in his home town, which will have to be answered tomorrow with some care, and a thick file of education statistics and data recently supplied him by the Department of Health, Education and Welfare. After dinner and a visit with his children he will settle down to a long evening with these materials and his problems. As he drives his car away from the Capitol his mind runs ahead to next year and the election it will bring. His friend writes that he may face a strong rival in the party primary who is prepared to attack him on the ground that his "catering to blacks" has cut into the civil rights of whites. Furthermore, yesterday he read in his local paper that two black leaders had asserted that black power was the only answer to discrimination and that blacks should force Durbin's party to nominate a black candidate for Congress next year. Durbin asks himself for the thousandth time why he stays in politics.

THE MAKING OF A FEDERAL STATUTE

It is difficult to exaggerate the importance of an adequate system of rules to a modern legislative body, and these rules are bound to be the result of a slow, evolutionary development in which conflicting forces contribute to the final result. The business of legislating for a country like the United States is a tremendous responsibility, and technical procedures concerning order of business, length of debate, amending bills, methods of voting, and reconciliation of House and Senate differences must be carefully prescribed. Yet there is constant danger that procedure will become so detailed and circumscribed that business can be transacted only with difficulty. Both houses have in part solved this dilemma by creating two entirely different sets of rules: a formal set that recognizes each distinct problem of parliamentary procedure and provides an official mode of action to take care of it; and an informal and largely unwritten set that makes it possible for the legislative body to transact much of its business in disregard of prescribed procedures. It has been said[2] that the Senate "has operated so long as a gentlemen's club that two sets of rules have developed, one written and the other based on custom. Only after specific warning is it considered fair to enforce the written rules."

One manifestation of informal procedure in both houses is the extensive transaction of business by unanimous consent. Either house can violate its formal rules at any time so long as no member objects. Even though members of Congress have widely varying interests and points of view, they often recognize the necessity of preferring the informal to the formal rules in transacting much legislative business. Yet they know that the formal rules may be invoked when the issues at stake are vital or when the conflict of interests is not being compromised.

Perhaps the clearest way to illustrate the importance of legislative rules and to indicate something of their substance is to describe the process by which a bill becomes a statute. Leaving aside for the moment the approval or rejection of bills by the President, there are six major stages through which a major bill usually passes before it becomes law. These are (1) drafting and introduction of the bill; (2) consideration and approval by committee in the house in which the bill is introduced; (3) consideration and approval by that house itself; (4) consideration and approval by committee in the second house; (5) consideration and approval by the second house; and (6) ironing out differences between the two houses in conference.

Drafting and Introduction of Bills

With very few exceptions any member of either house may introduce a bill or resolution dealing with any subject over which Congress has power. The exceptions are quickly stated. The Constitution requires that revenue bills be introduced in the House of Representatives, and, by custom, appropriation bills are also considered there first. Resolutions proposing the impeachment of federal officers may also be introduced only in the House. Consent to treaties, confirmation of appointments, and trial of impeachment cases are all restricted by the Constitution to the Senate, and accordingly any motion or resolution bearing on these matters can be presented only by a senator.

Bills and resolutions are designated as follows: A bill carries the prefix "HR" in the House, "S" in the Senate, and a number that indicates the order of its introduction. Joint resolutions are labeled "HJ Res" or "SJ Res." Bills enacted into law are also numbered in sequence. The Voting Rights Act of 1965, for example, is Public Law (or P. L.) 89–110, and 110th public law adopted by the Eighty-ninth Congress. The title "public law" is used to differentiate statutes of general application from private laws, such as an act to admit a particular person to the United States as an exception to current immigration rules.

Concurrent resolutions are labeled "H Con Res" or "S Con Res," and resolutions, "H Res" or "S Res." While bills and joint resolutions, if enacted, have the force of law, neither concurrent resolutions nor resolutions have such authority. A resolution is a statement by one house and a concurrent resolution, a statement by both houses. For example, a change in the rules of either house is affected by a resolution; a special House-Senate investigating committee is established by a concurrent resolution.

A legislative idea in Congress may originate in many ways. Some bills have their origins primarily within Congress and may reflect the wishes and labors of the congressmen who introduced them. Or a bill may have its birth in the deliberations of a standing committee which has given much time and consideration to the need for new legislation in a particular field. Other bills have their origins primarily outside of Congress, some originate with interest groups. A majority of the more important proposals enacted into law are initially developed in one of the executive departments or agencies. The language of a major statute usually is determined by many persons. Few congressional committees report bills in exactly the same language that may originally have been suggested by an executive agency or interest group. On the other hand, almost no major legislation is written within Congress without any outside help or advice.

Committee Action on Bills

With very few exceptions all bills are referred to standing committees for consideration. The committee stage is the most crucial in the life of a bill. Here the great majority of bills introduced in Congress are pigeonholed and never heard of again. Here the bills that do emerge for later floor action are carefully scrutinized and their final language often determined. There is a great deal of variation in committee procedure. Important bills are often made the subject of public hearings, but such hearings are far from uniform. They may be impressive sessions at which committee members honestly seek the advice and assistance of informed persons interested in the proposed legislation. Or they may be carefully staged proceedings in which a committee chairman seeks to confirm and give publicity to his own prejudices. Because the two houses accept so many committee recommendations without change, interest groups are quite active at committee hearings.

Following these public hearings, a committee meets in executive session to determine a bill's fate. If it views the legislative proposal favorably, it usually proceeds to "mark up" (revise) the bill and to prepare a formal report on it. Often the committee is split, and both majority and minority reports are submitted to the House or Senate. These reports are printed and, together with copies of the final bill, are made available to all members of the House or Senate.

Floor Action on Bills

A bill that has been reported by a committee is placed on a calendar to await consideration by the House or Senate. Its position on the calendar, however, has little to do with the order in which it is actually considered. Instead, both houses have developed varying procedures for determining the order of business. Since the committees report their bills without regard for each other's actions, some system of priorities has to be established.

Under the Senate rules any senator is entitled to move that the Senate take up any bill that has been reported by committee. If the motion is adopted by a majority vote, the Senate turns to the bill in question. In practice such motions are usually offered by the majority floor leader, who acts after consultation with other party leaders, such as the majority policy committee and the committee chairmen who have bills awaiting consideration. A motion to call up a bill is debatable, which means that a minority of senators can try to prevent consideration of a bill by filibustering against this motion. Noncontroversial bills are taken up by the "call of the calendar." This call takes place at irregular intervals. Each senator is limited to five minutes of debate on bills called up in this way.

Because of the size of its membership, the House system of determining the order of business is much more complex. Very few bills can be called up by a simple motion from the floor, as in the Senate. A few committees may do so and are said to be "privileged" in this respect. The Ways and Means Committee can move to call up a tax bill whenever it wishes; the Appropriations Committee can do the same with appropriation bills; and the Rules Committee can move at any time to call up any rule that it has reported.

Important public bills are brought to the floor of the House by means of a special rule or order prepared by the Rules Committee and adopted by the House by majority vote. It is standard procedure for the chairman of the standing committee reporting a bill to go to the Rules Committee to ask for such a rule. Often the committee has refused a special rule to bills supported by standing committees and by the majority party leadership. If granted, the special rule usually fixes the time that consideration of a bill by the House shall begin, limits the period of general debate, and guarantees the bringing of the bill to a final vote. Most special rules are "open," but a few are "closed" or "gag" rules, which limit or forbid the offering of amendments to a bill from the floor. For example, the Ways and Means Committee usually elects to bring tax bills before the House by means of a closed rule, so that they will not be subject to amendment from the floor.

In the wake of their landslide victory in 1964, the liberal Democrats pushed through two major changes in House rules at the opening of the Eighty-ninth Congress to reduce the authority of the Rules Committee. The first change allowed the House, by a majority vote and without Rules Committee action, to send to a conference committee a bill passed by both houses in different form. The second change was more important, but short-lived. It allowed a member of a standing committee to bring before the House a bill favorably reported by his committee if that bill had been before the Rules Committee for twenty-one days. Two years later, a reinforced conservative Republican-southern Democratic coalition succeeded in repealing the twenty-one day rule.

A bill may also be brought to the floor of the House by discharging a standing committee from further consideration of it. Discharging a committee requires that a majority of all House members sign a petition and that the House then approve the motion to discharge by a majority vote of those present. Such action takes a bill away from committee and brings it to the floor of the House. If the Rules Committee refuses to report a special order for a bill, the same discharge petition method can be used to force a House vote on the special order. This procedure is rarely successful, in part because of the influence of senior members of committees, who are able to take revenge against those who sign a discharge petition by pigeonholing bills.

The House of Representatives transacts much of its most important business while sitting as the Committee of the Whole, on which all 435 members of the House serve. Traditionally, the Committee of the Whole was employed by a parliamentary body to permit preliminary and tentative action, with the possibility of changing its mind later when it gave final, official consideration to a matter. In practice, however, action taken by the House of Representatives while sitting as the Committee of the Whole tends to be decisive. Normally, no further debate or amendments are in order when the committee rises and reports its recommendations to the House for final action. The chief reason for the use of this arrangement is that it enables the House to escape from its own rules, some of which are prescribed by the Constitution, and to operate instead under a different set of rules designed to expedite business. For example, a quorum is fixed at 100 members in the Committee of the Whole, whereas the Constitution fixes the quorum for the House and Senate at a majority of all the members (51 in the Senate; 218 in the House).

The Limitation of Congressional Debate

In a democracy it is important that proposed public policies be carefully debated before they are adopted and that such proposals be brought finally to a vote so that they may be accepted or rejected by decision of the majority. Thus both houses of Congress have adopted rules that make it possible to bring debate to a close. Before turning to these rules we again should note that both houses transact most of their business in routine fashion with great dispatch. In the House and Senate bills debated over a period of several days number no more than a dozen or so a session. This indicates, first, that many legislative proposals are noncontroversial and, second, that controversial issues are often thrashed out elsewhere than on the floor of the House or the Senate—at the time a bill is being drafted or at the time of committee consideration.

Under the House rules each member is entitled to speak for one hour on the subject under consideration. But this right means little in practice. First, it is usually in order for the member who has the floor to move the previous question. This motion must be voted on immediately. If it is supported by a majority, debate ends at once, and the bill or proposal, whatever it may be, is brought to a final vote. Furthermore, the House debates virtually all important measures while sitting as the Committee of the Whole. Here debate is divided into two sections: a period of general debate on a bill and a period when the bill is read section by section for amendment. The length of the period of general debate is fixed in advance by the Rules Committee, and two members, one favoring and one opposing the bill, have control of the time. In the second period debate occurs under the so-called five-minute rule, by which five-minute speeches are in order for or against proposed amendments. Debate in the House is thus apt to be brief and lively. But a bill may nonetheless be before the House for a considerable period. In the case of important bills, it is not unusual to allow two or three days for the period of general debate. Further debate under the five-minute rule may on occasion lengthen House consideration of a bill to a period of a week or more.

Under Senate rules, it is never in order to move the previous question. Except when "the calendar" is being called, senators may speak as long as they please on the matter under consideration. It is this situation that makes possible the Senate practice of filibustering, which usually means prolonged debate by a minority in an attempt to prevent the majority from passing a bill. From the point of view of the majority right to rule, logic is against the filibuster, for it enables a very small minority to frustrate the will of the majority. But the defenders of the Senate's unlimited debate argue that it protects the right of the minority to present its views and to prevent hasty action. As the pressure of legislative business has mounted in modern times, however, and the enormity of the power wielded by a small group of filibustering senators has been realized, the Senate has been forced to utilize certain means of limiting debate.

1. THE TWO-SPEECH RULE No member may speak more than twice on a single subject on the same legislative day. By recessing, rather than adjourning, at the end of a day's session the Senate can prolong a "legislative day" indefinitely, and thereby limit the amount of speaking that can be done on a single item of business.

2. THE CLOTURE RULE The Senate adopted a specific cloture rule in 1917 prior to American entry into World War I, after a particularly unpopular filibuster against a proposal by President Wilson for arming American merchant ships. Under the original version of the rule, sixteen senators might petition the Senate to close debate upon a pending measure. If such a petition were approved by a two thirds vote of the members present, no senator could thereafter speak for more than one hour on the measure and amendments pending thereto. But in 1948, the cloture rule was weakened. In the course of a filibuster against an anti-poll tax bill, the President *pro tempore* of the Senate. Senator Arthur H. Vandenberg, ruled that cloture was not applicable to debate on a motion to call up a bill but could be invoked only during debate on a bill itself. This ruling meant that if a group of minority senators started a filibuster on a motion to call up a bill, the cloture rule could not be used against them. In 1949, the Senate amended its rule to make cloture applicable to debate on motions to call up measures as well as to debate on measures themselves. But the price of this reform was a further change requiring that two thirds of the entire membership must vote to support cloture.

Since 1957, at the beginning of each new Congress, liberal senators have waged hard campaigns to strengthen the cloture rule. Despite vague pledges in both platforms, up to 1971, the most the liberals had been able to accomplish was a return to the older rule allowing debate to be limited by a vote of two-thirds of the senators actually present. In practice, cloture has been extremely difficult to invoke. Only thirty-six cloture petitions were brought to a vote between 1917 and 1966, and the victory of the liberals during the debate on the 1965 Voting Rights Act was only the seventh time that the necessary two thirds vote has been attained to limit debate.

3. CURTAILMENT OF DEBATE BY UNANIMOUS CONSENT AGREEMENTS Debate on most major bills is now brought to a close in the Senate, surprisingly enough, by unanimous consent agreements that a final vote will be taken at a set hour. How is it possible to obtain such unanimous consent when the two third majority needed to invoke cloture can almost never be obtained? The explanation is that attempts are

made to invoke the cloture rule only in the face of an extensive filibuster against a highly controversial bill, whereas debate is closed by unanimous consent as a matter of convenience where there is no real opposition to letting a bill come to a vote, particularly if the majority has allowed a reasonable time for debate.

Methods of Voting

Both House and Senate employ several methods of voting. The simplest and most common form is a voice vote, in which the members in turn call out the yeas and nays and the presiding officer judges which side has prevailed. Any member who doubts the results can ask for a rising, or division, vote in which the two groups rise alternately and are counted. In the House only, one fifth of a quorum may request a teller vote, by which the two groups leave their seats, pass between tellers, and are counted. Finally, in both houses, one fifth of the members present may demand a record vote, in which the roll is called and members are recorded by name as voting yea or nay.

Conference Committee Action on Bills

Many important public bills pass the two houses in differing versions. These differences must be compromised if any further progress in the enactment of a law is to take place. One house may vote to give way and accept the version approved by the other. Where the differences are slight or time is an important factor or the bill is an unimportant one, this often occurs. But if each house stands fast on its version of a bill, it is then necessary to make use of the conference committee as a means of effecting a compromise. The members of the conference committees are formally chosen by the Speaker and the Vice President. However, the selection is usually made in bipartisan fashion from the standing committee in each house that originally considered the bill; if any question of selection arises, the standing committee chairman normally has the decisive word. Supposedly, a conference committee must produce a compromise version of a bill that falls somewhere between the House and Senate version. But conference committees sometimes find it necessary to introduce new ideas or provisions into bills, even though technically this is a violation of congressional rules. When the conference committee reports a compromise version, it must be accepted or rejected as it stands by both houses, and no amendments may be proposed on the floor of either house. Either house, however, may reject a conference report and send a bill back to conference a second time, making it clear that it desires a particular change before it will accept the bill.

CONGRESSIONAL REFORM

The cards are stacked against action by Congress. Bills can be sidetracked at any one of these stages in either house, while to be adopted they must be affirmed by both House and Senate at each step in the process. The fact that it is far easier to kill a bill than to secure its adoption has led critics of Congress to assert that the national legislative process is not only seriously defective in organizational and procedural efficiency but is undemocratic as well. These critics argue that it ought to be easier for majority public opinion to take

Those Powerful 'Conferees' of Congress

by Arlen J. Large

... In these rooms meet the mysterious and powerful "conferees," senior members of the House and Senate whose job is to put the final touches on almost every important bill passed. Here, more than at any other stage of the legislative process, is the quintessential Congress—a closed-door world of horse-trading, double-crosses and sordid sellouts. It has been going on for 181 years.

Conferees' decisions are responsible for strange items of law that over the years became taken for granted. The famous 27½% oil depletion allowance is an example. The Senate in 1926 voted to set the allowance at 30%; the House wanted 25%. The conferees argued and argued and, unable to think up anything more imaginative, exactly split the difference at 27½%. Last year the House voted a deep cut to 20%, the Senate a shallower reduction to 23%. The conference compromise of 22% was closer to the Senate's figure, but in return the House men wrung other tax concessions from their Senate counterparts.

This kind of swapping and bluffing and conniving—done in secret—can touch the lives of every citizen, and not always for the best. But in a bicameral legislature with houses of equal power, there's really no alternative. A major reason for having two houses is to get diversity. After one house passes a bill, the other will—in theory—improve upon it with amendments reflecting second thoughts and new facts. Then the whole thing must be brought back together again, and that's the responsibility of the 10 or 15 members of the "Committee of Conference."

... One exchange, as reported by somebody who was there, illustrates nicely the poker-table atmosphere in which the nation's laws are made.

Under discussion was the health warning on the cigaret pack. The House version of the bill attributed the warning of dangers from lung cancer and other diseases to the surgeon general; the Senate didn't attribute its warning to anybody. The House conferees were determined to hang the responsibility on the surgeon general, not on Congress. Rep. Haarley Staggers of West Virginia, chairman of the House Commerce Committee and a 21-year veteran in Congress, read out a proposed compromise text: "Warning: The Surgeon General Has Determined That Cigaret Smoking Is Dangerous to Your Health."

"Agreed?" said Mr. Staggers, all business and ready to get on to the next item.

"*Tentatively* agreed," said Sen. Norris Cotton of New Hampshire, laden with 15 years' seniority. "I want to see what we'll be getting in return." The Senate, in the end, got plenty.

There's no set rule on how many conferees there should be, but 15 is a common number. In case a disagreement must be settled by a vote, the question isn't put to the entire group. The eight Senators, for example, would vote among themselves on whether to accept a House provision, while the seven House conferees just watch. But veterans of many conferences say an impressive number of decisions are reached by a sort of rolling consensus, without

formal votes. Rep. Wilbur Mills of Arkansas, who often heads conferences on tax legislation, is renowned for guiding the discussion to an "everybody agreed?" conclusion.

How do you get to be a conferee? Generally, the seniority system will do it for you, if you keep getting elected. Conferees usually are selected from the most senior members of the House and Senate committees that originally considered the bills. This, in turn, means that key conference decisions often rest in the hands of conservative Southerners.

In theory, each chamber's conferees must fight to the bitter end to preserve their version of a bill, even if they personally disagree with it. In practice, conferees sometimes can't wait to sell their colleagues out.

Three years ago, the House approved a bill saying Congressional districts in a state would meet the Supreme Court's one-man, one-vote test if there were no more thaan 30% population difference between the biggest and smallest. The 30% rule would apply to the 1968 and 1970 elections. The Senate voted for a tougher 10% test promoted by Sens. Edward Kennedy of Massachusetts and Howard Baker of Tennessee.

But five of the six Senate conferees, picked from the conservative seniors on the Judiciary Committee, had voted against the Kennedy-Baker test on the floor, and quickly abandoned it in conference. The full conference group recommended no numerical test for the 1968 and 1970 elections. However, both houses of Congress must agree on a conference bill before it can be sent to the President, and the House asked the conferees to try again. But the Senate rejected the second bill, and the effort was permanently scuttled.

The system also can put conferences into the hands of liberals, and then the conservatives lose. Recently, members of the liberal-dominated Senate and House Labor committees—an unusually swollen conference of 12 Senators and 24 Representatives—were in charge of settling differences over a bill extending Federal school aid. The biggest problem was a Senate amendment requiring uniform enforcement of desegregation rules, North and South. Sponsored by John Stennis of Mississippi, the amendment had put the Senate through an unusual emotional wringer before passing, 56 to 36.

A decisive roll-call vote like that was, in theory, supposed to put iron in the will of the Senate conferees. It apparently did, for a while, though only four of the 12 Senators had voted with the majority. The House conferees, described as adamantly opposed to any Stennis-type amendment, opened with a demand for total deletion, but the Senators refused. When Rep. Albert Quie of Minnesota then proposed language changes thaat would have nullified the amendment, the Senators turned him down twice. There was more haggling, and then Rep. William Ford of Michigan proposed inserting other words that, according to Sen. Stennis, ruined the amendment. At that point the Senator conferees caved in, and ... they persuaded the Senate to accept defeat.

©1970 by The Wall Street Journal. Reprinted by permission.

shape in the United States and to find positive expression in the adoption of national legislation, particularly that proposed by the President since he is chosen by the nation as a whole.

Party Government

For most of the would-be congressional reformers of the past quarter century, the key to a more efficient and democratic Congress has been a strengthening of the role of the political parties in Congress so as to increase the centripetal forces within the House and Senate, decrease the centrifugal forces, and enhance the legislative prospects of both congressional majorities and the President. One of the more comprehensive statements of the "party government" position was prepared in 1950 by the American Political Science Association's Committee on Political Parties[3] which recommended that:

1. "Leadership Committees" should be created by each party in House and Senate. Powers now scattered through such agencies as the steering or policy committees, the committees on committees, and the House Rules Committee would be concentrated in these new agencies. They would draw up the slates of committee assignments, issue calls for party caucuses, and, in the case of the majority party leadership committees, control the legislative schedule in the House and Senate.
2. The party caucus should be revived and strengthened as a means of allowing democratic discussion of the party program by all of a party's members in each house, and of providing for a *binding* decision on important legislative proposals that would force all party members to vote in accordance with the party's established principles and platforms.
3. Assignment of committee posts and distribution of patronage should deliberately be used to encourage congressmen's loyalty to the established party platform.
4. The seniority rule should be modified to permit the party leadership to name as committee chairmen senior members who are loyal to the party program.
5. Control of the legislative schedule in the House of Representatives should be transferred from the Rules Committee to the leadership committee of the majority party.
6. The Senate rule on freedom of debate should be modified to permit debate to be closed by a simple majority vote.

Reform of Congress along these lines has failed to make much headway largely because of the opposition of those who have a vested interest in the existing committee and seniority system. It is also extremely difficult to centralize the parties in Congress as long as they remain decentralized in the congressional constituencies. As a result, most of the changes that have enhanced the centripetal forces tend to come from without rather than within Congress, primarily through the growth of the legislative role of the President and the executive departments.

Modernizing Congressional Procedures

To date, Congress has made little use of modern methods which are available to assist organizations in coping with the vast flow of information that characterizes complex modern societies. A growing chorus of reformers, both inside and outside of Congress, argue that the House and Senate with their nineteenth century procedures and techniques cannot hope to match an increasingly sophisticated executive branch with its banks of computers, program budget specialists, and the like. Reformers advocate widespread congressional use of computers and other electronic information storage and retrieval devices, as well as the employment by Congress of technicians trained in systems analysis, operations research, and related skills. For example, in 1966 the Joint Committee on the Organization of the Congress recommended that the appropriations committees use automatic data processing to handle budget information. Other frequently advanced proposals for accelerating the pace of congressional activity and improving its efficiency include electronic voting and joint hearings by House and Senate committees.

Congressional Ethics

Another concern of congressional reformers has been the individual behavior of members of Congress. Public attention to congressional ethics tends to be attracted by the occasional spectacular scandal, such as those involving Senator Thomas Dodd of Connecticut, Representative Adam Clayton Powell of New York, former Secretary to the Senate Majority Leader, Bobby Baker, and a staff assistant of Speaker of the House John McCormack. Such affairs may involve personal appropriation of money contributed for campaign expenses, diversions of public funds for private pleasures, or use of a congressman's name, office, and influence to further personal financial interests.

But more insidious than the occasional scandal is the pervasive practice of members of Congress not only engaging in private business while in public office, but also of sitting on committees considering new laws and overseeing administration of existing statutes regulating the very businesses in which they themselves are involved. Without a doubt, a member of the House Banking or Senate Finance Committee who maintains his position as a bank executive, a member of the Commerce Committee who owns an interest in a radio or television station, a member of the Judiciary Committee who retains a partnership in a law firm that regularly argues before federal judges, or the owner of a large farm who sits on the Agriculture Committee has an impossible job of serving the twin masters of the public good and his own financial interest. Even if he does succeed in this task, it is not likely that he can *appear* to succeed. At the very least, he makes not only himself but Congress vulnerable to a charge of corruption.

Despite the serious implications of the widespread congressional mixing of public and private responsibilities, Congress has been remarkably insensitive to the conflict of interest issue where its own members have been involved. Congressmen have been quick to attack administrators and judges for possible violation of ethical standards; but except in the most flagrant cases, Congress has been extremely reluctant to take action to clarify the ethical standards expected of members of the national legislature. In 1962, Congress passed a far-reaching conflict of interest statute governing the behavior of almost all employees of the federal government. But neither in 1962 nor in the intervening years have congressmen seen fit to include themselves under the terms of federal laws regulating conflict of interest.

CONGRESSIONAL INVESTIGATIONS

While the visitor to the House or Senate gallery is frequently disappointed by the routine activity he sees, the visitor to a hearing of a congressional investigating committee seldom voices a similar complaint. If the committee is well known, and if the subject of investigation is important and controversial, the most ample room in the office buildings of the House or Senate will prove none too large for its meeting. Hundreds of people and dozens of press, radio, and television representatives will watch and listen as a parade of witnesses testify on an issue of great public interest—the "truth" about Pearl Harbor, Cuba, Vietnam, or Laos, cost overruns in the Department of Defense, the safety of birth control pills, labor racketeering, allegations that a leading political official has used his public office for private gain, or charges that corporations have earned "windfall" profits in their contractual dealings with the government.

Types of Investigating Committees

A congressional investigation is to be contrasted with the normal, routine consideration of bills by the standing committees of Congress. An investigation is an inquiry into a *subject* or a *problem* rather than a specific legislative proposal. The most formal investigation occurs when Congress specifically authorizes an inquiry into a particular subject, designates a committee to make this study, votes an appropriation to cover the costs of the inquiry, and grants the committee power to subpoena witnesses. Most investigations are authorized by the House or Senate acting independently of one another, although on occasion the two houses take concurrent action and set up a joint investigating committee. Separate House and Senate investigations are today most often turned over to the relevant standing committees or subcommittees.

Purposes of Congressional Investigations

The motives that lead congressmen to authorize an investigation are varied. First is the obvious need to obtain detailed and accurate information if Congress is to take intelligent action. A good illustration is the Wall Street investigation in 1933, in which Congress sought and obtained data about banking and stock exchange practices that led to the enactment of statutes establishing the Securities and Exchange Commission. A second purpose, only slightly less important, is the use of investigations by Congress to supervise or check the work of administrative agencies charged with enforcement of laws. Each house has a committee on government operations which frequently conducts such inquiries. A third purpose of investigations is to influence public opinion by giving wide circulation to certain facts or ideas, as Senator William Fulbright tried to do through his committee's 1966 hearings on the war in Vietnam. As far back as 1885, Woodrow Wilson[4] called attention to "the instruction and guidance in political affairs which the people might receive from a body which kept all national concerns suffused in a broad daylight of discussion." And, he asserted, "The informing function of Congress should be preferred even to its legislative function."

These three purposes are often supplemented by others of a more personal and partisan character. Senator Joseph McCarthy was following a well-worn path in employing sensational investigatory techniques. More than one legislator has advanced his career—usually for a longer period than did McCarthy—through a reputation made as a hard-headed investigator. Hugo L. Black, who later became a Supreme Court justice, and Harry S. Truman, who spent some years in the White House, are cases in point. Accordingly, it is not surprising that hope for political advancement should strongly motivate congressmen to seek authorization for new investigations. Similarly, a political party often undertakes investigations to advance its own interests or to embarrass its adversary. In the 1920s and 1930s the Democratic party did its best to discredit the Republicans through investigations into the Harding Administration scandals and the misdeeds of bankers and businessmen. When the Republicans won control of Congress in the 1946 election, they facetiously announced that each day's session of the Eightieth Congress would "open with a prayer and close with a probe."

Committee and Witnesses: Constitutional Issues

Congressional investigating committees sometimes encounter witnesses who refuse to appear before a committee or to answer its questions. Out of such episodes have come congressional statutes and Supreme Court decisions concerning the relative status and rights of investigating committees and witnesses. In particular, answers have been sought to these questions:[5] What subjects may Congress properly investigate? On what grounds may a witness properly refuse to answer a committee's questions? To what extent may Congress provide for the punishment of uncooperative witnesses?

The Supreme Court[6] has held that the "power of the Congress to conduct investigations is inherent in the legislative process."

> That power is broad. It encompasses inquiries concerning the administration of existing laws as well as proposed or possibly needed statutes. It includes surveys of defects in our social, economic or political system for the purpose of enabling the Congress to remedy them. It comprehends probes into departments of the Federal Government to expose corruption, inefficiency or waste.

In this same opinion the Court also pointed out:

> It is unquestionably the duty of all citizens to cooperate with the Congress in its efforts to obtain the facts needed for intelligent legislative action. It is their unremitting obligation to respond to subpoenas, to respect the dignity of the Congress and its committees and to testify fully with respect to matters within the province of proper investigation.

As early as 1857, Congress enacted a statute[7] directing private persons to appear before investigating committees when subpoenaed and to answer pertinent questions or risk a criminal prosecution in the courts and imprisonment up to one year for failure to do so. The constitutionality of this statute has repeatedly been upheld by the Supreme Court.

According to the Supreme Court, there are three situations in which a witness may properly refuse to cooperate with an investigating committee of Congress:

1. If the subject under examination lies outside the authority of the investigating committee, a witness is under no legal obligation to answer its questions. In 1953, for instance, the Supreme Court[8] set aside the conviction of Edward Rumely, who had been prosecuted under the 1857 statute for refusing to answer questions about the financing of publications designed to influence public opinion. A majority of the justices found that the resolution of the House of Representatives establishing the committee had authorized it to investigate only lobbying activities which were intended to influence Congress directly, not indirectly, as had Rumely's activities.

2. If a committee asks a witness questions that are not pertinent to the subject under investigation, the law allows him to refuse to answer. Thus, in 1957, in the case of *Watkins v. United States,*[9] the Supreme Court set aside the conviction of a witness for contempt of Congress because the questions he had refused to answer had not been demonstrated to be pertinent to a proper line of inquiry.

3. If a witness's answers would provide evidence that might be used against him in a criminal proceeding, he can invoke the privilege of the Fifth Amendment against self-incrimination and refuse to reply to a committee's questions. The Court has made it clear that to invoke the privilege a witness need only believe that his answer *might tend* to incriminate him. Thus a silent witness is not necessarily guilty of the "offense" he refuses to discuss. Nonetheless, many of the witnesses who have lawfully invoked the privilege before congressional committees have been subjected to certain social sanctions.[10] Many such witnesses have been dismissed from their jobs, sometimes on the ground that they failed to meet a test of good citizenship by refusing to cooperate with a legislative committee, and sometimes on the ground that their silence created a presumption that they had been engaging in unlawful activity.

Improving Congressional Investigations

In a democratic state a citizen must be protected against arbitrary and unjust governmental procedures. Some of the practices of particular investigating committees have abused this right; and in so doing, have tended to bring Congress itself into disrepute.

Some observers argue that Congress should delegate the conducting of its investigations to administrative agencies and other bodies of experts who would report their findings and recommendations back to it. A precedent for this suggestion is the British Parliament's practice of having investigations made by so-called royal commissions, consisting of experts outside Parliament, usually in the administrative offices. When, however, investigations are undertaken by experts in the United States, it is sometimes difficult to obtain sufficient publicity for their findings or action upon their recommendations.

Perhaps the mixed commission, consisting of congressmen, administrators, and private citizens, provides a means of meeting both the objection that purely congressional committees are apt to be unfair or incompetent and the objection that purely administrative commissions have too little influence or publicity-getting power. The two Hoover Commissions on the Organization of the Executive Branch of the Government were good examples of a mixed commission. Both of these commissions conducted their inquiries in a generally careful and responsible way. Both received excellent publicity and their findings led to a number of important changes in federal administrative organization and practice.

A good deal of attention has been given in recent years to the development of a code of fair procedures for congressional investigating committees. Certain specific committees have voluntarily adopted some of the recommended procedures, and in 1956, the House of Representatives prescribed a rudimentary code for all of its committees to follow. But neither house has yet been willing to put into effect a comprehensive set of procedural regulations with teeth in it. One difficulty lies in securing agreement among the experts as to which procedures should be prescribed, for most students of the subject agree that Congress must be careful not to go so far that it hamstrings its committees. There is, however, fairly general agreement on including the following procedures: hearings should be held only when authorized by a majority of a committee's members and only in the presence of two or more committee members representing both political parties; no committee reports or statements to be issued without the approval of a majority of committee members; witnesses should enjoy the assistance of counsel; persons attacked by witnesses should enjoy a reasonable right of reply; no radio or television broadcasts should be permitted without the approval of witnesses.

Many critics of congressional investigations have demanded a stricter measure of supervision by the courts. In particular, in cases in which witnesses are prosecuted for contempt, it is argued that the courts should carefully scrutinize committee authority and procedures for full compliance with the Constitution and statutes. As early as 1881, the Supreme Court checked the authority of a congressional investigating committee, but the Court has always been reluctant to impose any drastic restraints upon the legislative power of inquiry. The late Justice Jackson[11] once said, "I think it would be an unwarranted act of judicial usurpation to strip Congress of its investigatory power, or to assume for the courts the function of supervising congressional committees, I should . . . leave the responsibility for the behavior of its committees squarely on the shoulders of Congress."

In 1957, in the *Watkins* case, the Supreme Court indicated that it was prepared to exercise a tighter control over congressional inquiries. After a coalition of conservative Republicans and southern Democrats waged a narrowly unsuccessful fight to rebuke the justices for protecting the rights of witnesses, however, the Court executed a tactical withdrawal.[12] The Court has continued to reverse contempt of Congress convictions but has restricted itself to the most technical kinds of issues.[13]

Congressmen themselves must be persuaded to make a more responsible use of their investigating power. This means that both House and Senate must give greater attention to the authorization of specific investigations and refuse to approve those inquiries that seem primarily motivated by personal ambitions or by hopes for sensational hearings. Congressmen must also see to it that difficult investigations into complex, controversial subjects are made by colleagues who are respected for their integrity, their sense of fair play, their understanding of national needs, and their respect for the rights of individuals. And no code of fair procedures, however carefully drawn or complete, can excuse the House and Senate from the need to keep a close watch over all committees of inquiry and to employ a restraining hand at the first sign of abuse of the investigating power.

SELECTED BIBLIOGRAPHY

Bolling, Richard W., *House Out of Order* (New York: Dutton, 1965). A critical analysis of the House of Representatives by an experienced congressman who favors far-reaching reforms.

Carr, Robert K., *The House Un-American Activities Committee* (Ithaca, N.Y.: Cornell University Press, 1952). A thorough account of the role and activities of one of the most publicized congressional committees in decades.

Clark, Joseph S., *Congress: The Sapless Branch*, rev. ed. (New York: Harper & Row, Publishers, 1965). A liberal senator's biting critique of Congress and his passionate plea for reform.

Congress and the Public Trust (New York: Atheneum, 1970), Report on the Association of the Bar of the City of New York Special Committee on Congressional Ethics, James C. Kirby, Executive Director. A study of conflicting interests and ethical standards in Congress with recommendations designed to increase public confidence in the legislative process.

DeGrazia, Alfred, ed., *Congress, The First Branch of Government* (Garden City, N.Y.: Anchor Books, 1967). Twelve studies of congressional organization based on the premise that Congress itself must be strengthened, not made more dependent on party or the presidency.

Froman, Lewis A., Jr., *The Congressional Process: Strategies, Rules, and Procedures* (Boston: Little, Brown and Company, 1967). An analysis of the effects of congressional organization and rules of procedure on public policy formulation.

Haynes, George H., *The Senate of the United States* (New York: Russell & Russell, 1960), 2 vols. A reissue of a classic work on the Senate, originally published in 1938.

Miller, Clem, *Member of the House* (New York: Charles Scribner's Sons, 1962), ed. by John Baker. A view of life in the House of Representatives as seen by a brilliant young congressman.

Tacheron, Donald G. and Morris K. Udall, *The Job of the Congressman* (Indianapolis and New York: The Bobbs-Merrill Company, 1966). A handbook for members of the House, full of useful insights into the congressional setting.

Taylor, Telford, *Grand Inquest* (New York: Simon and Schuster, Inc., 1955). Probably the best general account of congressional investigating committees, treated historically and critically.

Footnotes

[1] *Congressional Government* (Boston: Houghton Mifflin Company, 1885), p. 58.

[2] O. R. Altman, "Second and Third Sessions of the Seventy-Fifth Congress, 1937–38," *American Political Science Review*, 32 (December 1938), pp. 1099, 1116.

[3] "Toward a More Responsible Two-Party System," *American Political Science Review*, Supplement, 44 (September 1950), p. 57. Also published separately under the same title (New York: Holt, Rinehart and Winston, Inc., 1950).

[4] *Op. cit.*, pp. 297, 303.

[5] Among the most important decisions of the Supreme Court bearing on the congressional power of investigation are: *Anderson v. Dunn*, 6 Wheaton 204 (1821); *Kilbourn v. Thompson*, 103 U.S. 168 (1881); *McGrain v. Daugherty*, 273 U.S. 135 (1927); *Sinclair v. United States*, 279 U.S. 263 (1929); *United States v. Rumely*, 345 U.S. 41 (1953); *Quinn v. United States*, 349 U.S. 155

(1955); *Watkins v. United States*, 354 U.S. 178 (1957); and *Barenblatt v. United States*, 360 U.S. 109 (1959).

[6] *Watkins v. United States*, 354 U.S. 178, 187–188 (1957).

[7] 11 *Stat.* 155, 2 U.S.C. § 192.

[8] *United States v. Rumely*, 345 U.S. 41 (1953).

[9] 354 U.S. 178 (1957).

[10] See *Quinn v. United States*, 349 U.S. 155 (1955); and *Emspak v. United States*, 349 U.S. 190 (1955). See also *Slochower v. Board of Higher Education*, 350 U.S. 551 (1956); and *Beilan v. Board of Education of Philadelphia*, 357 U.S. 399, 409 (1958).

[11] Dissenting in *Eisler v. United States*, 338 U.S. 189, 196 (1949), Jackson's colleagues did not necessarily disagree with him on this point.

[12] For a full account of the congressional battle over the decisions of the Warren Court, see Walter F. Murphy, *Congress and the Court: A Case Study in the American Political Process* (Chicago: The University of Chicago Press, 1962).

[13] See, for example, *Deutch v. United States*, 367 U.S. 456 (1961); *Yellin v. United States*, 374 U.S. 109 (1964); and *Gojack v. United States*, 384 U.S. 702 (1966).

Part V The Presidency

PRESIDENTS LOOK AT THE PRESIDENCY

REPUBLICAN VIEWS Was it possible to lose the nation and yet preserve the Constitution? By general law, life and limb must be protected, yet often a limb must be amputated to save a life. . . . I felt that measures, otherwise unconstitutional, might become lawful by becoming indispensable to the preservation of the Constitution through the preservation of the nation.—*ABRAHAM LINCOLN, in a letter to A. G. Hodges, April 4, 1864.*

The most important factor in getting the right spirit in my Administration . . . was my insistence upon the theory that the executive power was limited only by specific restrictions and prohibitions appearing in the Constitution or imposed by Congress under its constitutional powers. . . . I decline to adopt the view that what was imperatively necessary for the nation could not be done by the President unless he could find some specific authorization to do it.—*THEODORE ROOSEVELT, in "An Autobiography," 1913.*

Any American who had a modicum of modesty would at times be overcome by the intensity and the importance of the problems that he would meet if he were called upon to serve in the chief official position of this country.—*DWIGHT D. EISENHOWER, in an address at Charlotte, N. C., May 18, 1964.*

DEMOCRATIC VIEWS He [the President] is expected by the nation to be the leader of his party as well as the Chief Executive officer of the Government, and the country will take no excuses from him.

. . . He must be prime minister, as much concerned with the guidance of legislation as with the just and orderly execution of law, and he is the spokesman of the nation in everything, even in the most momentous and most delicate dealings of the Government with foreign nations.—*WOODROW WILSON, in a letter to A. Mitchell Palmer, Feb. 5, 1913.*

The Presidency is not merely an administrative office. That is the least part of it. . . . It is preeminently a place of moral leadership. All our great Presidents were leaders of thought at times when certain historic ideas in the life of the nation had to be clarified. . . . Without leadership alert and sensitive to change, we are bogged up or lose our way.—*FRANKLIN D. ROOSEVELT, speech, Nov. 12, 1932.*

The President must know when to lead the Congress, when to consult it and when he should act alone . . . and he must be prepared to use all the resources of his office to ensure enactment of legislation—*JOHN F. KENNEDY, January 1960.*

I have watched it [the Presidency] since Mr. Hoover's day and I realize[d] the responsibilities it carried and the obligations of leadership that were there, and the decisions that had to be made, and the awesome responsibilities it carried. . . . But I must say that when I started to make those decisions . . . the Presidency looked a little different . . . than it did . . . in the Congress.—*LYNDON B. JOHNSON, March 14, 1964.*

Chapter 14 Presidential Leadership

NATURE OF THE PRESIDENCY

In societies all over the world the twentieth century has seen a turning of people toward strong central executive power to solve their most troublesome problems. In its rawest, most extreme form, the result has been absolute dictatorship. More moderately, most Western democracies have tried to srengthen the resources of executive leadership without abandoning the customary restraints that hold the executive within constitutional bounds.

The American Presidency has been deeply affected by these general trends. A summary view of presidential leadership shows a mixture of traditional duties and recently acquired responsibilities. Today a President of the United States is expected to symbolize the aspirations, grandeur, and unity of the American people; run the immense and complex machinery of the federal government; keep a firm hand on relations with foreign governments whose activities may affect the peace, prosperity, and the very existence of the United States; weld together America's allies in concerted action; command the armed forces of the United States; initiate and actively promote legislation to combat poverty and pollution of the environment; lead his political party so that it may continue in power; see that timely and sufficient measures are taken to avoid inflation and economic depression; and maintain order if state and local authorities are unable to do so.

A Product of Many Forces

Over the years the Presidency has been a constantly evolving institution. The more important forces affecting it include the ideas of the framers of the Constitution, changing social and economic conditions, and the personalities of the Presidents.

Discussions of the nature of the executive occupied the members throughout the Constitutional convention. The problem was two-sided: to create an executive whose authority would energize the government and to surround him with sufficient safeguards to make dictatorship unlikely. One group of delegates shared the view of Roger Sherman,[1] who preferred the executive to be only an institution for carrying out the will of the legislature and thought that the executive "ought to be appointed by and accountable to the Legislature only, which was the depository of the supreme will of society." For a time this group was attracted to the idea of a plural executive, possibly three men, on the grounds that it would be less dangerous to liberty and would permit representation of the South and West as well as the East.[2] Finally, however, a majortity of the convention came over to the view that the executive should be a single individual, with wide, though limited, authority.

"The executive power shall be vested in a President of the United States of America." This terse opening statement is characteristic of the sparse prose of Article II of the Constitution: "the President shall be Commander-in-Chief of the Army and Navy"; "he shall nominate, and, by and with the advice and consent of the Senate, shall appoint ambassadors, other public ministers and consuls, judges of the Supreme Court, and all other officers of the United States whose appointments are not herein otherwise provided for, and which shall be established by law"; "he may require the opinion, in writing, of the principal officer in each of the executive departments"; "he shall receive ambassadors and other public ministers"; and "he shall from time to time give to the Congress information of the state of the Union, and recommend to their consideration such measures as he shall judge necessary and expedient."

This enumeration of powers is brief and, if we look beyond the literal terms of the Constitution to the working Presidency, woefully incomplete. Yet Article II does provide the legal framework within which a President must operate. Each of the specific powers authorized by the article forms a nucleus around which cluster dozens of other powers brought into existence by legislation, judicial interpretation, custom, and, most of all, by varying presidential practices.

The demands created by changing social and economic conditions have also been a major shaping influence on the Presidency. To maintain the political support needed for survival, any government institution must to some extent be able to meet pressing demands, to satisfy existing needs, whether or not particular office holders wish to pay attention to such issues. Thus a President does not have a completely free hand in choosing what problems he wishes to devote his resources to solving—assuming, that is, that he wants to be re-elected or to see his party's candidates win in the next election. Indeed, the matter may go deeper, even to the question of survival of a particular kind of government or of the nation itself. If the federal government had not been able to cope with—not necessarily immediately end—the depression of the 1930s, popular despair might have brought about a drastic change in the American form of government. Failure in the 1970s to mount a successful attack against the causes of racial discrimination, crime, poverty, and environmental pollution could produce widespread demands for drastic restructuring of the constitutional system. The inability of any administration to deal effectively with foreign policy problems since the end of America's nuclear monopoly might lead to annihilation of the American people.

This is not to say that a President is a mere prisoner of his times. Some problems may be thrust on him, but he still has a choice in deciding which other problems to attack.

And he has wide leeway in selecting the means he deems most appropriate to deal with any problem. There are times, of course, especially in domestic politics, when doing nothing, that is, leaving a problem to be worked out by nongovernmental processes, may be an attractive and effective way of handling an issue.

In choosing how to attack a problem, a third shaping influence on the Presidency has been the personality of the Chief Executive. Historically, there has been such a close relationship between office and personality that it is difficult to discuss the real power of the Presidency except in terms of specific men. Presidential powers under Lincoln were very different from those under Buchanan, just as Andrew Jackson's Presidency was hardly the same office that John Quincy Adams had held. The subtlety of Franklin D. Roosevelt's leadership was far different from the bluntness of Harry Truman. Eisenhower's reluctance to immerse himself in politics stands in sharp contrast to the bubbling energy and curiosity of Presidents Kennedy and Johnson. In an interview in 1967, Richard Nixon said that "this country could run itself domestically without a President; all you need is a competent Cabinet to run the country at home. You need a President for foreign policy. . . ."[3] Once in the White House, however, Mr. Nixon found that he could not avoid domestic affairs, especially those relating to inflation and poverty, but he did devote himself overwhelmingly to foreign affairs, which tend to respond more directly to presidential actions. In a major campaign address in September 1968, Nixon indicated his conception of the Presidency:

> The President is the only official who represents every American—rich and poor, privileged and underprivileged. He represents . . . also the great, quiet forgotten majority—the nonshouters and the nondemonstrators, the millions who ask principally to go their own way in decency and dignity, and to have their own rights accorded the same respect they accord the rights of others. . . .

Strong and Weak Presidents

We might range all American Presidents along an action spectrum. At one extreme would be the "literalists."[4] Men like Rutherford Hayes, William Howard Taft, Warren Harding, and Calvin Coolidge viewed the Presidency as a place of repose. They saw the President's main function as carrying out policy decisions made within Congress. Any positive presidential action had to be justified by a clear constitutional command. As Taft[5] phrased his philosophy:

> The true view of the Executive functions is, as I conceive it, that the President can exercise no power which cannot be fairly and reasonably traced to some specific grant of power or justly implied and included within such express grant as proper and necessary to its exercise. Such specific grant must be either in the Federal Constitution or in an act of Congress passed in pursuance thereof. There is no undefined residuum of power which he can exercise because it seems to him to be in the public interest.

At the other end of the spectrum have been "strong" Presidents like Lincoln, both Roosevelts, Woodrow Wilson, and Lyndon Johnson. They have thought of the Presidency as the center of a tornado of activity, an ideal vantage point from which they could lead the nation. Theodore Roosevelt[6] summed up to the outlook of these men when he said:

> My view was that . . . every executive officer in high position was a steward of the people bound actively and affirmatively to do all he could for the people, and not to content himself with the negative merit of keeping his talents undamaged in a napkin. I declined to adopt the view that what was imperatively necessary for the Nation could not be done by the President unless he could find some specific authorization to do it. My belief was that it was not only his right but his duty to do anything that the needs of the Nation demanded unless such action was forbidden by the Constitution or by the laws. . . . I did not usurp power, but I did greatly broaden the use of executive power. In other words, I acted for the public welfare, I acted for the common well-being of all our people, whenever and in whatever manner was necessary, unless prevented by direct constitutional or legislative prohibition.

Most Presidents, like Richard Nixon, do not fall so neatly at one extreme or the other but are somewhere in between. During their office many behave at some times more like literalists, at others more like strong Presidents, but each incumbent has helped shape the office.

PRESIDENTIAL STYLES

Among recent Presidents, only Eisenhower might be described as an antipolitician. He achieved national support as a great war hero and father-figure, but he often was unable to utilize this support to achieve political or public objectives. In his attempt to place the Presidency "above politics," Eisenhower put heavy emphasis on tidy administrative arrangements and careful staff work, and relied on assistants for information, ideas, analyses, and insights. The staff system, as developed by Eisenhower, gave him the help he wanted and made the President's tasks, as he perceived them, more manageable. But in the process "he became typically the last man in his office to know tangible details and the last to come to grips with acts of choice."[7]

Most of the biographical evidence suggests that considerations of personal advantage played little, if any, role in Eisenhower's conduct. Given the irrelevancy of military experience for White House occupants, his insensitivity to political factors and forces is explainable. To paraphrase Neustadt, Eisenhower sought national unity, not personal power; he disliked the political process and partisan politics; he saw his role as reconciling differences among Americans and among nations. He preferred to moderate rather than to initiate proposals.

From the moment he assumed office President Kennedy gave every indication of loving his job. Reporters repeatedly described him as a constant source of fresh ideas and energy, as the focus of attention in American politics, and as a center of action. Kennedy maintained and even expanded an enormous command of information on a wide range of matters and issues. Impatient with large staff meetings and regularly scheduled Cabinet sessions, he preferred direct exposure to the free flow of argument. He resisted summaries and synopses of reports and memoranda and readily absorbed details.

The Kennedy White House staff reflected directly the habits, talents, and preferences of its chief. While Eisenhower functioned more like a chairman of the board, waiting for the staff and advisers to resolve policy controversies and bring to him for ratification decisions commanding wide agreement, Kennedy tackled problems personally, seeking out information, reading half a dozen newspapers thoroughly every day. Kennedy's assistants had no carefully staked out areas of concern or operation, although they may have tended to concentrate in one area rather than another. They obviously worked *with* the President and never *instead of* him in disposing of White House business.

As a result, Kennedy's White House office was not very tidy. As one Washington observer stated, coordination was a minor pastime, and failures of coordination may have had disastrous consequences, as the crushing defeat at the Bay of Pigs in 1961 illustrated. The President actively fought against the diffusion of leadership through layers of committees, and he often cut across normal administrative channels to keep informed about developments or to communicate ideas to others.

A leader by temperament, President Johnson had worked closely with Presidents, senators, and congressmen for twenty-five years before he assumed the Presidency on the death of President Kennedy on November 22, 1963. During the Eisenhower years Johnson had acquired a reputation for political genius in his astute management of the Democratic majority in the Senate. Probably none of the other seven Vice Presidents who succeeded to the Presidency upon the death of Presidents was as thoroughly prepared for the highest office. Starting as a country schoolteacher in the Texas hills, he had been known for cyclonic energy, a zest for crisis reminiscent of the Roosevelts, and an iron will in facing up to tough decisions. Whereas Kennedy tended to be dashing and even electric in style, Johnson was flamboyant and emotional, yet acutely sensitive to the "art of the possible" in domestic politics. Until he deeply committed himself to massive military involvement in Vietnam, he displayed a highly developed sense of the limitations of political power. He began office with a belief in a strong Presidency, an immense reserve of congressional good will, and a respected capacity for designing accommodations needed to reach majority agreement. A man of many moods, he was often described as a bundle of paradoxes, easy to caricature but impossible to paint. His decision not to seek re-election in 1968 was just one more unexpected piece in an incomplete jigsaw puzzle.

With the crucial exception of Vietnam, criticism was directed more at Johnson's style and operating methods than his policies. As one journalist[8] summarized the complaints heard in Washington:

> The President drives people too hard, is too high-handed and arrogant, doesn't really want argument and independent points of view . . . he is too preoccupied with his popular image, is too sensitive to criticism, spends too much of his time answering attacks he should ignore . . . he tends to whine over his troubles and blame others for his mistakes . . . when things go truly wrong, he frequently turns nasty.

Whatever validity there may have been in such criticism, it is clear that Johnson lacked the warmth of Eisenhower and the wit and grace of Kennedy. He was rather the clever, hard-driving, purposeful, and somewhat ornery Texan.

While President Johnson typically worked his staff very hard, he tended to rely heavily on department and agency heads. He permitted no one to interpose himself as an Assistant President between himself and his Cabinet secretaries. In working with his immediate staff he alone set the schedule and determined the priorities. As a top aide[9] concluded:

> By this avoidance of commitments, by the avoidance of fixed routines of government, a President is able better to keep on top of a job that, if he submits himself to routines, can quickly become so burdensome, so time consuming, that he himself can never apply any new initiatives to the job.

At the outset of his administration President Nixon counseled his key aides to lower their voices, speak calmly, and "bring us together." He may have been reacting to the contentiousness of his predecessor and his combative personality. At any rate Nixon's Presidency has become a relatively low key, low profile, methodical administration, whose chief earmark thus far has been the President's preference for introspection, solitary decision, and time to think in privacy. He has insisted that his staff bring to him not bland consensus but the conflicts, so that he would be making the important choices after hearing all sides of an issue. By all accounts he is a good listener and a perceptive questioner. He has consciously tried to resist Johnson's tendencies to become involved in every detail of government and to hold out far-reaching promises that could not be readily or easily fulfilled. Rather he keeps himself remote from day-to-day governmental concerns in order to concentrate as much as possible on one issue at a time. As one reporter of the Washington scene wrote:

> Johnson drew his strength from the people, whom he longed to touch and hear. Nixon tends to place his faith in the executive machinery of Government and his own carefully contrived decision-making process.[10]

Because of his penchant for privacy, he has tended to isolate himself from the press and the public. Yet he has obviously enjoyed the Presidency. He told reporters in mid-1969, "The Presidency has not yet become for me that awesome burden that some have described." The storm of protest against his decision to invade Cambodia in the spring of 1970 marked the end of the honeymoon period of his administration.

SOURCES OF PRESIDENTIAL POWER

The major work of the President, Harry Truman[11] liked to say, consists in "trying to persuade people to do the things they ought to have sense enough to do without my persuading them." There may be serious doubts whether the President's judgment is always correct, but Truman was certainly right in stressing that the power of the President, in both national and international politics, is based on persuasion rather than command. In domestic affairs both state and national legislators, as well as governors, mayors, and a host of other officials, have an independent electoral base, and federal judges have virtual life tenure. Thus there are few people outside the executive branch whom the President may command, and even there he may have problems. In dealing with foreign nations, the need to rely on persuasion is obvious. Even use or threats of force, such as Kennedy's in dealing with Soviet missiles in Cuba, are typically designed to compel an opponent to negotiate rather than to obliterate him. In Vietnam Johnson first used air strikes against the North and later American troops in the South in a vain effort to convince the North

Vietnamese and the Vietcong that it was too expensive to continue trying to conquer South Vietnam. His later decision to end the bombing and Nixon's step-by-step withdrawal of troops were open invitations to compromise.

The unique constitutional and political position of the President allows him to play many different roles, and in each role he may exercise different kinds of persuasion. But two facts must be kept in mind when looking at presidential roles. First, the President "plays every 'role,' wears every 'hat' at once. Whatever he may do in one role is by definition done in all. . . . He is one man, not many."[12] Second, neither in any particular role or combinations of roles is the President assured of exercising effective persuasion. Even as strong and able a leader as Lyndon Johnson may end his term in tragedy. Each facet of the Presidency presents the incumbent with an opportunity—and in another sense, a menace—not a guarantee.

Party Leader

First and foremost the President is the leader of his party. When a candidate for the presidential office receives the nomination, he becomes head of his party and continues to be head after election. He cannot be elected and cannot effectively perform his duties without his party's support. Since American parties are in reality loosely knit coalitions of state and local factions, they cannot be directed easily from the central point—by the President or by anyone else. If he is a strong vote-getter, state and local leaders may feel indebted to him for helping them to stay in power. As often as not, however, these leaders boast of their achievement in electing a President who, they claim, would have failed without their support. If he is to be at all successful, he must use charm, patience, patronage, and federal funds to weld these factions into some reasonable facsimile of a political organization.

Chief of State

To Americans and to the rest of the world the President symbolizes the government of the United States. Like the British monarch, he reigns; like the British prime minister and cabinet, he governs. As the representative of the entire nation, the President can, when he thinks it necessary, rise above partisan politics and claim authority to lead in the name of America, gathering to himself all the emotions aroused by appeals to patriotism. It is most difficult for any American to ignore a President who says that the national interest requires a certain policy. A member of Congress or a private citizen may not necessarily be convinced by the President's logic, but it is very likely that he will listen attentively and respectfully.

Chief Diplomat

The Constitution makes the President the principal officer in foreign affairs, though in some respects he shares authority with Congress. The President alone receives ambassadors and thus "recognizes" foreign governments. With "the advice and consent of the Senate" he appoints American ambassadors and top-level State Department officials. Only the

President or his agents can communicate officially with other governments in the name of the United States. Only the President or his agents can negotiate treaties or other international agreements, although to be binding a treaty must be approved by a two-thirds vote of the Senate. In addition, to become fully effective some treaties need to be supplemented by legislation, such as an appropriation, that must be passed by both houses of Congress.

Judicial interpretations of the Constitution have increased the importance of the President's position in foreign affairs. The authority of the federal government in international politics, the Supreme Court[13] has ruled, is not limited to those powers specifically listed or implied in the Constitution. "The powers to declare and wage war, to conclude peace, to make treaties, to maintain diplomatic relations with other sovereignties, if they had never been mentioned in the Constitution, would have vested in the Federal government as necessary concomitants of nationality." Moreover, the Court[14] has said that the power of the national government to deal with foreign affairs is also plenary in the sense that it is not limited by the powers reserved to the states. As Edward S. Corwin[15] once remarked, this power is inherent in the federal government in the sense that it "owes its existence to the fact that the American people are a sovereign entity at international law."

What the Constitution has allowed, political reality has demanded. The rapidity with which crises develop in foreign relations and the magnitude of their consequences require, if the nation is to survive, that federal authority not be shared with the states and that, at least for those issues demanding quick decisions, authority be centralized. Given the awesome potential of the American military establishment and the persistent recurrence of international crises, it is inevitable that the White House be a place from which a President can influence the course of world politics. His words and actions are taken seriously in Moscow, Peking, Hanoi, and Havana no less than in London, Paris, Bonn, or Ottawa.

Chief Legislator

As discussed in the preceding chapters, it is so difficult for effective leadership to develop within Congress that Presidents have taken over the role of chief legislator. While four or five Presidents of this century have dramatized their legislative role, it is hardly a recent innovation. Thomas Jefferson was one of the most effective Presidents in this respect. Over the years success in leading Congress has been one of the principal standards by which the caliber of a President's administration is gauged.

A President may not be able or may not choose to give Congress such leadership. The alternative of Congress' doing nothing is always open. Presidential leadership usually means positive action, and many congressmen prefer not to act and many prefer to act in ways other than those advocated by the White House. The problems can be exacerbated when a President, as did Eisenhower in six of his eight years and Nixon throughout his first term, faces a Congress controlled by the other party.

Commander-in-Chief

Article II of the Constitution confers on the President the title of commander-in-chief of the armed forces of the United States. Thus, while only Congress can declare war, the President is responsible for the way a war is fought. Indeed, he can act as Thomas Jefferson did against the pirates of Tripoli, as Abraham Lincoln in the opening months of the Civil War, Franklin Roosevelt in the early stages of World War II, Harry Truman in the Korean conflict, and Lyndon Johnson in the Vietnamese war, that is, commit American military and naval personnel to combat without a declaration of war. A President can gain —or lose—considerable influence in international politics by his astuteness as commander-in-chief.

The way a President plays this role can also have a significant impact on domestic politics. A decision to fight an undeclared war can materially change a President's popularity at home and impair or enhance his ability to get measures through Congress or to carry out programs already approved by the legislature. The saddest case in point is the way the war in Vietnam blasted Lyndon Johnson's plans to build the Great Society. Lesser decisions such as hiring and firing professional soldiers can affect a President's standing with Congress or the electorate, as Lincoln found out as he shuffled generals during the Civil War and Truman when he dismissed General Douglas MacArthur during the Korean conflict.

As commander-in-chief the President may make a very different kind of impact on domestic affairs. Section 4 of Article IV of the Constitution directs the national government to protect each state "on application of the legislature, or the executive (when the legislature cannot be convened), against domestic violence." Congress has authorized[16] the President to use federal forces, including the National Guard and the state militia, in discharging this obligation. It was this authority that Lyndon Johnson utilized in the summer of 1967 when, at the request of Governor George Romney, he sent troops into Detroit to help put down race riots. Congress[17] also has provided for the use of troops when the enforcement of laws of the United States by ordinary judicial proceedings is, in the President's judgment, impracticable. Congress lists as obstacles to judicial enforcement "unlawful obstructions, combinations, or assemblages of persons, or rebellion." It was this latter authorization that President Eisenhower used in 1957 to dispatch troops to Little Rock, Arkansas, and President Kennedy in 1962 to send troops into Mississippi to enforce federal court decisions ordering desegregation of educational facilities. Before he can employ the armed forces under either of these two provisions the President must issue a proclamation commanding the "insurgents to disperse and retire peaceably to their respective abodes."[18] The issuance of this proclamation does not establish martial law. The military does not replace civilian agencies but merely assists them to maintain their authority and normal operations.

The President's responsibility to "take care that the laws be faithfully executed" also carries with it authority to use federal troops when federal property or activities are endangered. In its most drastic form use of military power within the United States means establishment of martial law and replacement of civil law and civilian courts by military law enforced by military tribunals. In Chapter 19 we discuss the implications of martial law on civil liberties.

Head of the Executive Branch

The Constitution charges the President "to take care that the laws be faithfully executed." The burden of executing or administering laws is increased by the vague language of many statutes. Choosing a general rather than a specific phrase is often used by congressmen as a means of compromise. Unable to agree on how to settle some policy issues, legislators may opt for a broad but not very clear provision, leaving final resolution of the problem to administrators, to judges, or perhaps to a future legislative decision. Furthermore, because of the great complexity of many problems with which the federal government deals, congressmen frequently find it expedient to lay down only guiding principles and leave it to administrative agencies to formulate more precise regulations. During the 1930s a majority of the Supreme Court held that there were close limits to valid congressional delegation. Congress could not delegate legislative power; it had to prescribe standards to direct administrative discretion.[19] Since the 1930s the justices have taken a more liberal view of congressional power in this regard and have upheld as constitutional congressional instructions to agencies to formulate regulations that are "fair and equitable," "just and reasonable," or "in the public interest."[20]

The task of translating laws from statute books to real life requires a large administrative staff. Reacting against the evils of a spoils system whereby even low-level federal jobs changed hands with every major shift in party fortunes, Congress established a civil service system that attempts to put on a merit basis the recruitment, retention, and advancement of the overwhelming majority of government employees. A President, however, may still nominate, for whatever reason he considers sufficient, a large number of officials, mostly at the top ranks of executive agencies or at the level of ambassador or federal judge. President-elect Nixon found in late 1968 that he had available about 500 appointments subject to Senate confirmation ranging from Cabinet officers to ambassadors. Below this level he could fill some 2,000 positions of a "policy determining" or "confidential" nature; but like other Presidents before him, Nixon appointed senior civil servants to many of these positions.

The Constitution states that except where Congress provides otherwise—and it often has—presidential appointments are to be made "by and with the advice and consent of the Senate." While senators have usually given the President a relatively free hand in choosing such national officials as members of his Cabinet, ambassadors, and, to a lesser degree, Supreme Court justices, a different practice has grown up for more locally oriented appointments—postmasters and district judges, for example. Since George Washington, it has been customary for a President, before nominating an official to serve in a particular state, to consult with the senator from that state if he is a member of the President's party. In effect this "consultation" often means that the senator proposes a list of candidates from whom the President's advisers choose. If the President skips this consultation phase, the senator may ask his colleagues to vote against confirmation, and under the rule of "senatorial courtesy" they will reject the nomination. If there are two senators from that state from the President's party, his task is more complicated, but his power may be increased since he may be able to play one off against the other and in the end name his own man. If neither senator from a state belongs to the President's party, the President—or again, more commonly one of his staff—usually discusses candidates with state and local party leaders before making a nomination.

The framers of the Constitution expected that the Senate would use the confirmation power to scrutinize the qualifications of the President's nominees. After a searching inquiry into the practice of senatorial confirmation, however, Joseph P. Harris[21] concluded: The principal effect of senatorial confirmation of appointments has not been to subject the

President's nominees to careful scrutiny of their qualifications, but has served rather to perpetuate patronage appointments to many offices and positions which should be placed in the career service, and to afford the opposition party and insurgents within the ranks of the President's party an opportunity to attack his administration by contesting his nominations. Whatever its defects, the constitutional provision of senatorial confirmation is not likely to be changed.

OBSTACLES TO PRESIDENTIAL INFLUENCE

As noted earlier, the various roles the President may play provide him with opportunities to influence and persuade others. A President who wants to have his policies accepted and put into operation must persuade large segments of the voting public, a working majority of Congress, executive officials, and, often, many state officers. He must also consider judicial opinions, for in very different ways federal judges may also block attainment of presidential goals.

The President and Public Opinion

In dealing with other public officials a President's professional reputation for having both the ability and the desire to exploit his position is crucial. So too is the President's prestige —what other government officials think the general public thinks about the President. Voters can defeat the President or his party only at election time, but their opinions, at least what officials perceive to be their opinions, can ignite or extinguish enthusiasm in Washington or a state capital for a President's plans. Many legislators are as reluctant to support an unpopular President's program as they are to oppose the proposals of a popular Chief Executive. Administrative officers too are often sensitive to fluctuations in both congressional and popular opinion.

Antagonisms between the President and Congress

Congress presents a second major obstacle to achievement of a President's program. Many Presidents have started out to lead Congress but have found the way long and hard. Whether the President is a Democrat or a Republican, to all senators and representatives he is to some extent a dangerous rival. The complexity of modern problems has more and more required the President to undertake major initiatives in formulating legislative proposals and in establishing policy goals subject to enactment by Congress. In turn Congress and individual legislators, especially the ranking members and chairmen of subcommittees in both houses, have become increasingly adept in inventing ways of intervening in administrative operations. The traditional pattern of legislative-executive relations, in which Congress enacts broad policy and the President, with help from administrative agencies, formulates specific policies and is responsible for administration, has been at least partially reversed. The President has become the key actor in the drama of legislating, while Congress spends much of its time intervening in the activities of the executive branch.

The constant broadening of the scope of federal operations has made it more difficult for a congressman to understand, much less carefully control, more than a small portion of executive action. Increasing American involvement in world affairs, the growth of personal rather than institutional diplomacy, and the frequent necessity for quick decisions based on secret information have combined to weaken congressional power. As the power of Congress to influence the grand design of public policies has eroded, its propensity to delve deeply into the details of administrative activities has grown.

Legislators may be displeased by the accretion of executive authority, yet they often need the President's help in influencing other congressmen, in signing legislation, in making appointments, or in campaigning for re-election. So, too, the President may often be frustrated by congressional action—or, more often, inaction—yet his power is also limited, and he needs the assistance of members of Congress if he is to govern efficiently and legitimately. The relationship between Congress and the President is thus complex. There is inevitable friction and conflict, but there must also be agreement and cooperation if either is to accomplish policy goals. In such situations, of course, the most likely tactics are negotiation and compromise. At times a strong President may dominate Congress, the extreme cases being those of Franklin Roosevelt in 1933 and Lyndon Johnson in the early months of 1964. Such periods of domination, however, have been short. More often there is the give and take of bargaining, sometimes expressed, sometimes tacit. Lyndon Johnson[22] once remarked: "I've never seen a Congress that didn't eventually take the measure of the President it was dealing with." "Eventually," however, can be a long time, and, as Johnson's own record demonstrates, a President can accomplish a great deal before being checked.

The reasons for presidential-congressional friction are many. First, some conflict is built into a system of shared powers. The purpose of this constitutional arrangement, as designed by James Madison, is to check the power of one group of officials by the power of another group so that no one person or faction can obtain a monopoly of political authority.

Second, the President and the members of Congress are chosen by very different constituencies and this influences each in quite different directions. The President is chosen in a national election and must receive the support of 30–40 million or more voters to win his post. He naturally tends to think and act in terms of grand strategy of national policy. A senator or representative, on the other hand, is chosen by a single state or district and must necessarily be sensitive to the demands of more local constituencies. There is no institutional reason that compels him to have a national point of view. These contrasting influences are bound to result in argument and conflict.

Moreover, the President is often led to recommend a positive attack upon social problems, whereas congressmen frequently prefer to take a let-well-enough-alone attitude. The causes of this condition are varied. For example, a congressman's sensitivity to the diverse and conflicting interest groups of his district often leads him to try to preserve the status quo. Further, the President has superior access to information. He may be a conservative person, disinclined to approve vigorous or broad exercise of the power of government. But when his advisers and subordinates in the executive branch brief him concerning the facts of a social problem, the case for positive action by government often becomes compelling. Congressmen, on the other hand, usually do not have such direct access to data, and such information that reaches them secondhand may not seem so compelling.

The President and the Bureaucracy

Officials of administrative agencies may present a third set of obstacles to achievement of presidential goals. One might think that as Chief Executive the President would be able to command his subordinates in much the same way as a general commands an army. In practice, however, bureaucracy, "more nearly resembles the arena of international politics than a group of disciplined subordinates responsible to the control of common superiors."[23] Two points stand out: the size of the President's job and the pluralism of interests that may be reflected in the federal executive establishment.

The sheer magnitude of the President's job, the heavy burden of work, and the limited amount of time available to cope with any single problem combine to complicate his relations with the bureaucracy. Only on the most pressing matters does a Chief Executive have more than an occasional opportunity to check closely on what has actually happened since he issued an order. Of necessity he must rely heavily on his subordinates to carry out his wishes; and these officials in turn must rely on their own subordinates to complete the tasks. "Like our governmental structure as a whole," Neustadt has observed, "the executive establishment consists of separated institutions sharing power. The President heads one of these; Cabinet officers, agency administrators, and military commanders head others. Below the departmental level, virtually independent bureau chiefs head others."[24]

Furthermore, since a President can inform himself personally of only a few problems, he is dependent on others to provide the information he needs to make decisions. Even when there is no conscious effort at deception or deviousness, fully briefing a President is not easy. A fact omitted because a subordinate thought it unimportant, forgot about it, or was simply unaware of it can have a significant influence on the way a President views the alternatives open to him.

Adding to the President's burdens is the pluralism of interests that may exist within the bureaucracy. Career civil servants at the senior level have usually been working for many years in specialized fields and often feel that they, not their appointed or elected superiors who stay for only relatively short periods, really know what policies are best. Heel-dragging by these people can hamper execution of many policies. "Were the Presidents of the last fifty years to be polled on this question," Clinton Rossiter[25] claims, "all but one or two, I am sure, would agree that the 'natural obstinacy' of the average bureau chief or commissioner or colonel was second only to the 'ingrained suspicions' of the average congressman as a check on the President's ability to do either good or evil."

A similar situation may obtain where appointed officials are concerned. To gain nomination and win election a President may have had to promise certain appointments in exchange for support. These appointees may not necessarily agree with him or each other on policy matters, but as long as they retain their base of political support and conduct their feuds and opposition with circumspection a President may find it inexpedient to fire them. In addition, some appointees may feel that they owe their position not to the President but to some other powerful person, perhaps a governor, senator, or member of the party's national committee, and give their loyalty to one of these men.

The discussion in Chapter 6 on the party system notes that an administrator may find that the White House is unable to protect him in dealing with Congress. In order to carry out his policy aims—which may or may not be those of the President—he must enter into an alliance with some legislators and perhaps also with certain interest group leaders. "The conditions which a system of fragmented power sets for the success and survival of a Cabinet officer," Richard F. Fenno, Jr.,[26] has observed, "encourage him to consolidate his own nexus of power and compel him to operate with a degree of independence from the President." This point is no less true of high level officials below Cabinet rank.

Ambition may also enter the picture. Charles G. Dawes, Budget Director under President Hoover and Vice President under President Coolidge, used to say that Cabinet members were a President's natural enemies. Dawes may have been exaggerating, but it has not been unknown for a Cabinet officer, or even a lesser-ranking official, to harbor hopes of seeing himself one day in the White House or on Capitol Hill. Such a man is apt to look on the President as an instrument to be used or as a rival to be thwarted than as a revered commander-in-chief.

Judges and State Officials

The Constitution makes federal judges virtually independent of presidential control once they are nominated and confirmed, and many executive policies face major tests before the courts. Judges may be asked to pass on the constitutionality of legislation or executive orders or to interpret a statute to determine whether Congress in fact has authorized a particular course of action.

State officials may also check presidential policies. Given the federal nature of American political parties, state and local officials can help shape the reactions of senators, legislators, and even administrators to presidential proposals. Conversely, again in part because of the federal nature of the party structure, the success of many supposedly national programs depends on the cooperation of state and local officials.

INSTRUMENTS OF PERSUASION

Despite these interlocking checks, a President is still in a position of immense influence—provided he has the desire, energy, and ability to exploit his opportunities for persuasion. He has at his command a number of instruments, not the least of which are the availability of evidence to support his arguments and the use of reason in convincing others. In addition, he has the respect and prestige of his office, unequaled access to the mass media, and certain specific constitutional grants such as the appointing power. He also may possess personal charm and skill in human relations. None of these instruments is likely to be effective alone, but if several of them are combined expertly they may yield some measure of success.

To a certain extent a President may be hampered by the Twenty-second Amendment,[27] which stipulates that a President may not serve for more than two full terms. In his second term and especially in his last year, rival candidates for the nomination may attract considerable political support to themselves and away from the incumbent. But if he uses his instruments of persuasion to control his party's choice of a candidate, a President may still retain much of his power during this bowing-out period.

Molding Public Opinion

With mass media at his disposal, the President has an unequaled opportunity to mold public opinion. For important speeches he may preempt prime television and radio time, newspapers carry his remarks on their front pages, and magazines publish feature articles on him and his family. His press conferences allow him to engage in give-and-take discussions with news analysts from all over the country. By displaying confidence, knowledge, and mental agility, an adroit President may do much at these conferences to build up a highly favorable public image that will affect not only newspaper readers the next day but also the stories that reporters will write for months to come. President Kennedy made full use of his quick wit by having his press conferences televised; President Johnson preferred to operate in a less spontaneous environment; and President Nixon in his first year experimented with different formats for his rather infrequent press conferences.

Since a President finds it difficult to escape publicity, he must be wary of overexposure. Everything he or his family does is newsworthy; the trivial as well as the important events are faithfully reported. Whether he tries to take a long walk, golf, sail, swim, or vacation in an isolated Bahama cay, he is always front page news.

Influencing Congress: Formal Powers

To induce members of Congress to cooperate or at least compromise, a President has a number of instruments. First is his ability to recommend legislation and, in effect, to set the agenda of Congress. This power is most important because it gives the President the initiative in the legislative process. Article II of the Constitution instructs the President to "give the Congress information of the state of the Union" and to "recommend to their consideration such measures as he shall judge necessary and expedient." In addition the President can call Congress into special session to act on his recommendations. These clauses legitimize necessity. In a few areas, such as taxation, congressmen have been able to retain much of the initiative in drafting legislation, but in general the diffusion of power within Congress, the many demands on a legislator's time, and the complexity of most policy issues have interacted to shift the burden of preparing important bills to the executive branch and to require that the President play his roles as Chief of State, Chief Legislator, and Party Leader if the bills are to become law.

Presidential capture of legislative initiative has been gained only at a price. One element of that cost has been that the scope of congressional business makes it impossible for the Chief Executive to work constantly and directly with Congress. There are simply too many issues coming up on Capitol Hill and too many competing problems from domestic and international affairs. More and more, Presidents have had to depend heavily on legislative liaison staffs and other presidential assistants to coordinate the efforts of various executive departments to persuade Congress to adopt or reject legislation. We discuss the work of various presidential assistants in detail in Chapter 15.

In inducing Congress to take favorable action, a President may invoke party loyalty. While that loyalty may be a sometime thing for most senior legislators, it can tug at their self-interest more insistently than at their emotions. Even if their own re-election is certain, if their party does not win the Presidency again, the congressmen's ability to influence appointments may vanish. If their party does not retain control of Congress, their leadership positions and committee chairmanships will go to other men.

Still, the weak, decentralized structure of both major parties cannot be depended upon to bridge the gap between the executive and legislative branches. Far more often than not, only by means of bipartisan majorities is the President able to get measures through Congress. Piecing these majorities together is delicate work. On almost every issue the President is likely to be opposed by some members of his own party who are in genuine disagreement with him on substantive grounds and to whom considerations of party loyalty are not sufficiently strong to outweigh their distaste for the President's position. On the other hand, some members of the opposition party may agree with the President on substantive grounds, but will nonetheless vote against him because the opportunity to embarrass him politically is too strong to be resisted. And yet, if the President is to secure the legislation he wants, he must persuade some members of one or the other of these groups to abandon their inclination to vote against him. Often it is the opposition congressman, rather than the member of the President's own party, who decides to go along with the White House.

The President has another powerful weapon, the veto, that he can use both as roadblock against unwanted legislation and as a prod to move congressmen to pass the bills he wants in the form he wants them. The Constitution is specific in its provisions: Every bill, order, resolution, or vote to which the concurrence of the Senate and the House of Representatives may be necessary (except a question of adjournment) shall be presented to the President of the United States for his approval or disapproval. Although the language of the Constitution seems to permit only the exception just noted to the requirement, others have been added. Concurrent resolutions need not be submitted to the President, and the same is true of proposed constitutional amendments.[28]

The President has four choices when he receives a bill. The first and most obvious is to sign it, in which case the bill becomes law. The President may veto the bill, and return it without his signature to the house where it originated. If the bill is repassed by each house with a two-thirds majority, it becomes law without the President's approval; otherwise the bill dies. Or the President may let a bill remain on his desk ten days without either signing it or returning it to Congress; in this case it becomes law without his signature. Presidents have not often done this. The fourth possibility is a variation of the third: if during the ten-day period that the President holds a bill without signing it Congress ends its session and adjourns, the bill automatically dies instead of becoming law. This is the so-called pocket veto. It is effective from the President's point of view, since adjournment of Congress eliminates any possibility that his veto will be overridden. Because Congress, like many state legislatures, tends to pass a great many bills during the closing days of a session, a President is apt to have extensive opportunity to use the pocket veto.

The veto power has had a long, varied, and controversial history. Early Presidents made very sparing use of it, and until the time of the Civil War most vetoes were justified on the ground of a bill's doubtful constitutionality. It was even contended by some that this was the only reason for which a President should exercise the power. Since the Civil War, however, Presidents have based their objection to a bill far more often on its lack of wisdom. Eight Presidents vetoed no bills at all during their terms of office. Grover

Cleveland and Franklin Roosevelt each vetoed more than five hundred bills and together account for about half of all vetoes since George Washington.

Relatively few bills are ever repassed over the President's veto.[29] The Constitution makes reconsideration mandatory, but this requirement is fulfilled by mere reference of the bill back to the standing committee that reported it to the house in which it originated.

The President does not possess an item veto power, as do the governors of some American states. Accordingly, he must accept or reject a bill in its entirety. A sweeping grant of an item veto power would require a constitutional amendment, although it seems permissible for Congress to write into each appropriation bill a clause authorizing the President to suspend items from operation if he wishes. But Congress has shown little inclination to give the President any such discretionary power. Presidents, however, have occasionally exercised this kind of power simply by declining to spend appropriated funds on projects authorized by Congress.

The veto power is of far greater importance than the mechanics of its operation indicate. Its use by modern Presidents has led congressmen to have great respect for executive power. The mere threat of its exercise frequently influences congressional action during the stages when legislation is being formulated. In other words, the veto has come to have a positive as well as a negative significance. By reminding Congress of the possibility that he may use it, a President is frequently able to persuade Congress to shape the language of a bill to his liking. For example, the conference committee charged with revising the tax reform measure in December 1969 attempted to avoid a veto by taking account of some of President Nixon's known objections to the measure. To bring a wavering legislator into line, the President's legislative liaison team may intimate that the White House is considering vetoing a bill the congressman desperately wants or needs. Roosevelt's strategy in asking his staff to find bills for him to veto often provided him with both of these options.

Another constitutional grant allows the President a minor measure of control over the length of congressional sessions. Article II provides that the two houses must agree before either house can adjourn or recess for more than three days, and then adds the provision that, in case of the inability of the two houses to so agree, the President may order an adjournment of Congress "to such time as he shall think proper." There is not a single instance of the use of this power. It seems likely that the political repercussions that might follow will continue to dissuade Presidents from exercising it in any but a grave emergency.

Influencing Congress: Informal Means

To lead Congress a President must depend on informal methods of persuasion as well as formal powers. He must learn to be a consummate manipulator of men, alternately friendly and firm, now shrewd and calculating, now open and frank, by turns the suppliant and the bully, the flatterer and the threatener. He has a wide field on which to practice such talents. Because of the way power is divided in Congress, he must deal with majority and minority leaders and committee chairmen, as well as with influential members of the rank and file. He must weld them into an effective team when possible, play them off against each other when necessary, and somehow persuade at least a majority of them

Philadelphia Plan: How White House Engineered Major Victory

By ROBERT B. SEMPLE Jr.
Special to The New York Times

WASHINGTON, Dec. 25—It was near midnight last Monday, and the Senate, in a major reversal of sentiment, had just voted to give the Administration authority to compel labor unions to hire more Negroes. . . .

Accused by his critics of ambiguous leadership, the President had rallied his forces in a moment of legislative crisis and had won a major victory. . . .

As reconstructed from a dozen sources inside and outside the Administration, the campaign started in midsummer, when the Administration proposed the Philadelphia plan as but a forerunner of similar programs in other cities. The plan would require bidders on federally assisted projects costing more than $500,000 to work toward "specific goals" for improving minority employment in the craft unions, where only 8.4 per cent of 1.3 million union members are black.

A contractor would not have to meet all of these goals if he could prove "good faith" efforts to hire more Negroes during the life of the contract. Attorney General John N. Mitchell said last summer that this did not set racial employment quotas in violation of the Civil Rights Act of 1964.

Later, however, Controller General Elmer Staats ruled that the plan did violate the act. . . .

Late Wednesday night. Dec. 17, the Senate Appropriations Committee, dominated by Southerners, voted to attach a rider, or extraneous amendment, to a supplemental appropriations bill specifying that no funds could be spent on any program or contract that the Controller General thought to be in violation of Federal law. . . .

Yet even in disarray, the Nixon forces, quarterbacked by the President, managed to produce three important decisions Thursday: To concentrate their lobbying efforts in the House (nobody doubted that the Senate would approve the rider that evening); to emphasize the civil rights rather than the struggle, and to give the problem White House visibility.

The Senate met that evening and delivered two crushing blows. It accepted the rider by a 73-to-13 vote and rejected, 52-to-35, a Mitchell-written amendment designed to permit the Philadelphia Plan to continue while the constitutional struggle between the Executive and Mr. Staats was being resolved in the courts.

For the White House, there were two bright moments in an otherwise gloomy day.

First, John W. Gardner, head of the Urban Coalition, authorized the use of his and the coalition's prestige in the fight to save the plan. . . .

Second, before the evening was out, John Ehrlichman, the President's assistant for domestic affairs, called Mr. Garment, the President's special consultant on civil rights, and told him the civil rights community was missing from the forces striving to revive the plan. . . .

Early Friday morning, the White House staff met to parcel out lobbying responsibilities. Bryce N. Harlow, the President's counselor and legislative aide, was to approach his sources in the House; Mr. Rumsfeld, a former Representative, would telephone as many people as he knew; Mr. Garment would do what he could in the civil rights community.

At some point in the meeting, Mr. Ehrlichman suggested drafting a Presidential statement outlining the civil rights issues involved in the rider, the statement, released later that day, declared that "the civil rights policy to which this Administration is committed is one of demonstrable deeds—one of the things that counts most is earning power."

Mr. Harlow's most immediate worry was the Senate-House conference committee meeting scheduled for the next day. He felt that the committee was stacked against the Philadelphia Plan and sensed that it would quickly ratify the Senate's decision.

But he also knew that the House, which had never actually voted as a body on the Philadelphia Plan, would have to meet Monday to accept or reject the conference committee's decision. . . .

The conference committee, as anticipated, aproved the supplemental appropriations bill with the damaging rider. Yet the White House kept its sights trained on the House vote scheduled for Monday.

As the conference committee was voting, Mr. Shultz and his assistant secretary, Arthur Fletcher, a Negro, appeared on television. . . .

Some of those who worked in the President's behalf say now that they were skeptical of his motives. They did not doubt, they say, his commitment to minority employment, but they have privately suggested that he might have sensed political profit in pitting the civil rights movement against its natural allies in the labor movement.

The White House denies this, asserting that the President gave no thought to the politics involved and was moved largely by a genuine fear that repeal of the Philadelphia Plan would mean the destruction of the strategy for increased minority employment.

Whatever his motives, the President clearly wanted the plan preserved. On Sunday, after a White House church service, he called the Wednesday action by the Senate committee "dirty pool," and on Monday morning he presided over what participants described as one of the most extraordinary leadership meetings of this or any other Administration. . . .

The President opened with a few remarks, then Mr. Fletcher gave an off-the-cuff talk that participants later described as "brilliant."

He poured out statistics on minority employment in the craft unions, pointing out that of the 1.3 million workers employed in the $24-billion space program, fewer than 4 per cent were black.

After the meeting, events moved very swiftly.

In early evening, the House voted 208 to 156 to reject the controversial rider; the Senate followed suit four hours later by a margin of 39 to 29. . . .

© 1969 by The New York Times Company. Reprinted by permission.

that his program is good for the country, good for their constituents, and therefore good for themselves. A President must also carefully choose for his liaison with Congress people of utmost diplomatic skill. A busy man himself, a congressman is more apt to forgive a harassed chief executive than he would a thoughtless White House aide. Annoying a member of Congress can have serious consequences. Bryce N. Harlow of President Nixon's staff incensed Senator Margaret Chase Smith in 1970 by telling other senators that she was going to support the nomination of G. Harrold Carswell for the Supreme Court. Harlow's action insured that Senator Smith would vote against the administration and materially contributed to Carswell's rejection by the Senate. Franklin Roosevelt suffered an analogous difficulty when in 1937 his attempt to use one of his sons to negotiate with senators on his plan to increase the size of the Supreme Court succeeded only in solidifying the opposition.

Presidents go out of their way to woo congressmen through friendly gestures and sociability. Calvin Coolidge invited Republican congressmen to the White House for breakfast; Franklin Roosevelt entertained Democratic congressmen at clambakes on an island in Chesapeake Bay; Harry Truman now and then appeared suddenly at the Capitol and modestly asked to eat lunch with some of his old colleagues; Dwight Eisenhower offered lunch at the White House to Republicans and Democrats alike. John F. Kennedy often extended the hospitality of a formal White House dinner with vintage wine, French cuisine, and music from the Marine band. Lyndon Johnson used the telephone to keep in touch with members of Congress at all hours of the day—and night, and his entertaining was more folksy than that of his two immediate predecessors. Richard Nixon has regularly breakfasted with invited legislative leaders.

It is doubtful that these gestures have often paid off in bills passed or not passed by Congress. But no President can afford to ignore the friendly gesture as part of his program to lead Congress. There are so many occasions when he must play the role of the stern taskmaster that he must seize every opportunity to persuade congressmen that he is a decent human being, not a harsh tyrant.

The President may also use public opinion to influence congressmen. By utilizing his access to the mass media of communications, he can do more than increase his own popularity or his party's chances at the next election. More immediately—if he does not try this tactic too often or too crassly—he can cause constituents to put heavy pressure on members of Congress.

Sometimes the President can trade measures with members of Congress. A promise of support for a congressman's pet bill, or a threat of presidential opposition to it, may produce support for the President's own program. Frequently the President must bargain with congressmen about the details of his own measures. One of the chief purposes of the regular consultations between the President and congressional leaders is to determine whether the lines can be held fast for the President on one of his proposals or whether compromise, and if so, how much, is in order.

Perhaps the most famous of the President's informal powers for use in influencing Congress is distribution of patronage. Use of the appointing power by the President to win favor with members of Congress dates back to George Washington. This does not mean that Presidents have often indulged in a crude business of purchasing votes in Congress for legislation by offering to make appointments according to the wishes of congressmen. A President is likely to use the patronage power more subtly as a means of cultivating

friendly relations with members of Congress, thereby encouraging sympathetic consideration of executive proposals. This kind of approach was illustrated in the special session
of Congress in 1933 at which many of the most important of Roosevelt's New Deal
measures were passed. The administration let it be understood that patronage would not
be distributed until after the session. In this way congressmen eager to control certain
appointments were compelled to give favorable consideration to the President's legislative
requests.

In recent decades the development of the merit system has lessened the value of
patronage as a means of influencing Congress, just as long years of prosperity have eased
much constituent pressure on legislators for government jobs. The Eisenhower Administration has so little patronage to distribute in 1953 that it experienced difficulty in meeting
congressional requests for favors that were exceedingly modest by past standards. Still
there are certain highly sought-after federal offices—federal judgeships, for example—
that become vacant from time to time and are then filled in such a way as to curry favor
with congressmen in the states in which these officers serve.

Patronage, however, is a two-edged sword. For one thing, an appointment that
pleases one congressman may irritate other legislators as well as disappointed candidates.
Second, by trading patronage for congressional votes a President may be weakening his
control over administration, since the appointees may feel a stronger loyalty to members
of Congress than to the Chief Executive. President Taft summed up these problems in his
lament that every time he made an appointment he created nine enemies and one ingrate.

A promise of presidential support at the next election campaign can be an effective
instrument of persuasion. In extreme circumstances the President may threaten political
reprisals against uncooperative congressmen. But he must think twice before he actually
carries out this threat, for institutional arrangements are not entirely in his favor. He
cannot dissolve Congress or call a new election as can a prime minister. Even though a
regular election may be impending, if his quarrel is with members of his own party the
President cannot very well ask for the election of members of the opposite party. To
secure the defeat of his own party colleagues he must go into state primaries and conventions and try to persuade party voters to replace these men with new legislators who will
be more loyal to him.

Persuading Judges and State Officials

In dealing with state officials a President can use almost the same instruments and
tactics that he employs with Congress—reason, prestige, publicity, personal charm, promises of campaign support, patronage, and old-fashioned bargaining. In contrast, a President has as little chance of charming judges into agreement as he does of over-awing
them with his prestige or with promises of patronage. Of course, since federal judges are
not elected, campaign support is of no value to them, although a chance of promotion
might be enticing. Reasoned argument, usually presented by the solicitor general and members of his staff from the Department of Justice, is the instrument most often used in
dealing with judges. But a President's appointing power can also be important, both in
selecting men to run the solicitor general's office and initially choosing and later promoting
judges whose basic views tend to coincide with his own.

In addition, if courts hand down a decision or series of decisions that threaten his policy objectives, the President may deploy his instruments of persuasion against Congress to obtain some counteraction—perhaps a constitutional amendment, a more clearly worded statute, a change in the kind of cases the courts can hear, or an increase in the number of judges. As a last resort a President may refuse to enforce a court decision, as Lincoln declined to do during the Civil War when Chief Justice Roger B. Taney ordered a southern sympathizer released from a military prison.[30]

In influencing public opinion in general a President may also influence judges, not in the crude sense of courts following election returns but in the deeper sense of creating a climate of opinion in which all citizens must live. "The great tides and currents," Justice Cardozo[31] once wrote, "which engulf the rest of men do not turn aside in their course and pass the judges by."

ROLE OF THE VICE PRESIDENT

Historically, the Vice Presidency generally has not attracted able and vigorous men who could render substantial service as a member of the President's working team. Until recently a vice-presidential candidate was usually selected to reward an "elder statesman," to placate or weaken a party faction, or to sidetrack a rival candidate. Furthermore, the Constitution does not give the Vice President the position or powers of an Assistant President. Heads of departments and other top officials expect presidential decisions, not the advice and direction of the Vice President.

From time to time Presidents have attempted to utilize the services of Vice Presidents, but with uneven success. President Truman, by statutory authority, appointed Alben Barkley a member of the National Security Council. After President Eisenhower's illness in September 1955, Vice President Richard Nixon took over many ceremonial activities. He also presided over meetings of the Cabinet and the National Security Council, but he could not assume any important executive responsibility. The vacuum caused by the President's temporary inability was not filled by the Vice President but by the White House staff and key Cabinet officers.

In the days immediately following the election of 1964, President Johnson and the Vice President-elect, Hubert H. Humphrey, held numerous conferences to determine how Humphrey could become maximally useful to the President. But, while Johnson used Humphrey as a "trouble shooter" in a variety of fields, he did not permit his Vice President to develop a national political following of his own, a decision that made Humphrey's 1968 presidential campaign all the more difficult.

The considerations that led President Nixon to select Spiro T. Agnew as his running mate in 1968 may never be completely revealed. It seems likely that the qualities the President perceived in Agnew as a possible successor in the event of his own disability or death did not play as significant a role as in his choice of Henry Cabot Lodge as his running mate in 1960 or in Johnson's choice of Humphrey in 1964. While Vice Presidents have been generally unsuccessful in their search for something to do, Vice President Agnew within a year commanded attention and controversy by giving speeches that delighted conservatives and outraged liberals. To an unusual degree he appeared to carve out for himself an area of political independence mainly in support of the efforts of the Republican party to win more adherents, especially in the South. By statute, Agnew is chairman of five interagency councils, and supervisor of an office that oversees federal relations with the nation's governors and mayors; yet his involvement in policy matters remains modest.

PRESIDENTIAL INABILITY

An emergency arises in the Presidency when a President dies in office or is incapacitated by illness. Article II, section 1 of the Constitution states that the Vice President shall succeed to the Presidency upon the removal, death, resignation, or inability of the President to discharge his duties and authorizes Congress to provide by law for the succession in the event that the Vice President is unable to carry on the office. Two questions arise under these provisions: Who determines whether the President is unable to discharge his duties? Who succeeds the Vice President in the event that both the President and the Vice President die, resign, or are removed?

Two cases have arisen in which Presidents have been incapacitated for extended periods. President Garfield was unable to discharge the duties of his office for several weeks after he was shot, and President Wilson was seriously ill for several months following a cerebral hemorrhage in September 1919. On both these occasions there were extended discussions about the steps that should be taken. It was variously suggested that the Vice President decide whether the President was able to work, that it be decided jointly by the Vice President and Congress, and that it be decided by Congress alone. In each case, what happened was that the President's family and intimate associates determined he was able to carry on his duties, even though the evidence indicated that he was disabled.

The determination of when a President is in fact unable to serve remains a critical question today. Since 1958, Presidents and their Vice Presidents have made private agreements about the assumption of the President's duties by the Vice President should the President become incapacitated. They provided that the Vice President shall serve as acting President if the President asks him to do so or if it is otherwise clear that the President cannot function. The decision as to his ability is left to the President himself. Thus there was still no provision for action in a case where the President is not fit to serve but is unwilling to relinquish the powers and duties of his office.

The further possibility that a President and key officials might be obliterated in a sudden and devastating attack on Washington has not received the consideration it deserves, but the law at least is clear. The Speaker of the House of Representatives acts as President upon the death, removal, or resignation of both the President and the Vice President. Next in the line of succession are the President *pro tempore* of the Senate and the Cabinet members. A Cabinet member may serve only until a Speaker of the House or a President *pro tempore* of the Senate is available and qualified to supersede him.

Twenty-fifth Amendment

The Twenty-fifth Amendment, adopted in 1967, spells out a procedure that permits the Vice President to become acting President if the President is disabled and provides for filling a vacancy in the office of Vice President. The President informs the Speaker and the President *pro tempore* of the Senate that he is unable to perform the duties of the

Presidency; in that event the Vice President would serve as acting President until the President sends a written declaration to the contrary to the Speaker and the Senate leader.

The amendment also authorizes the Vice President to assume the office of acting President whenever he and a majority of the Cabinet—or a majority of another body to be prescribed by Congress—declare the President to be disabled. Under these circumstances the President could resume power upon declaring his disability ended, unless the Vice President and a majority of the Cabinet disagreed and informed Congress of their disagreement within four days. If this happened, Congress would decide the issue. If, within twenty-one days, Congress decided that the President was unable to resume his duties, the Vice President would continue as acting President. Otherwise the President would resume his office. The new amendment also provides that a vacancy in the office of Vice President may be filled by a person nominated by the President and confirmed by a majority vote of both houses of Congress.

PRESIDENTIAL TRANSITIONS

For the great body of American voters the inaugural ceremony at noon on January 20 every four years signifies the orderly transfer of constitutional authority from the outgoing President to the President-elect. In fact, the ritual of oath-taking on inauguration masks a complex and uncertain process through which the President and the President-elect have prepared for the transfer of political power.

This transfer involves two broad requirements. The first is the continuity of presidential leadership in national and international affairs and the stability of administrative performance by the machinery of government. Because of the enormous increase in the significance of the international position of the United States and the strategic role played by government decisions and actions in the economic life of the country, the instabilities of a presidential transition generate powerful pressures that threaten the continuity of responsible leadership and expert management. The second requirement concerns the responsiveness of the government to new political leadership. In addition to continuity in presidential leadership and administrative performance, it is equally important that the incoming President be given a fair chance to bring about changes in policies reflecting his objectives.

From 1933 to 1952 unbroken control of the White House by the Democrats reduced the problems of transferring presidential power. Since then, the old, improvised ways of ushering in a new administration, ready to govern, have been increasingly regarded as inadequate and impractical.

The first modern President to consult with his successor shortly after election day was Herbert Hoover. Generally, both Presidents Franklin Roosevelt and Harry Truman, while running for re-election, permitted their subordinates to maintain informal confidential communication with rival presidential candidates. The first organized attempt to achieve an orderly transfer of presidential power came in 1952 when President Truman arranged, during the election campaign, to keep the candidates informed about critical matters facing the nation. Truman should also be credited with establishing the precedent that the outgoing President must accept responsibility for facilitating the transfer of power to his successor, a precedent that both Presidents Eisenhower and Johnson followed. Eisenhower and Johnson also continued the practice of giving intelligence briefings to rival party candidates in 1956, 1960, 1964, and 1968.

Outgoing Presidents tend to be more concerned about an orderly presidential transition than are Presidents-elect. In the future, as the experience of Kennedy and Nixon suggests, incoming Presidents may make arrangements for temporary staff headquarters for the period of two and one half months between election day and their inauguration. Some of the urgent matters that require staff attention as early as possible are preparation of the presidential messages that are expected of a new administration; consultations with leading congressmen and senators looking toward a timetable of legislative action; and the filling of Cabinet and other key posts. Since 1960, each President has charted with the help of task forces the political course of action the President may take in critical areas of public policy. And since the enactment of the Presidential Transition Act of 1964, Congress has made funds available to both the incoming and outgoing president to cover expenses during the transition.

STATESMANSHIP AND POLITICS

This chapter has stressed the political nature of the Presidency. Emphasis on the necessity of manipulation and maneuvering does not in any way question the necessity of the President's having, or being receptive to, creative policy ideas that have great substantive merit. Rather, the point is that many other government officials, officials who have power to check the President, also have firm policy views of whose worth they are sincerely convinced. Faced with these conditions and armed with only a limited authority to command, the President must persuade, negotiate, even bargain and manipulate, if he wants to achieve a positive program.

Knowing what policies to pursue requires the vision of a statesman; putting those policies into actual operation requires the talents of a masterful politician. A successful President needs not only strength of character and a thorough understanding of the long-run needs of the nation but also professional political skills, personal charm, a feel for shifting winds of public opinion, a delicate sense of timing, and that quality which in enemies we call ruthlessness and in friends total dedication. For a President must be able to use, drain, and discard other men to achieve national goals. He must be able to distinguish among what is worth fighting for to the bitter end, what is worth compromising on, and what is worth only capitulation. He must know when to move and when to wait, when to argue and when to agree, when to stand firm and when to compromise, when to reason and when to bargain, when to cajole and when to command. Without doubt, such leaders are rare. The amazing thing is that some have made their way through the labyrinthine paths of American politics to the White House.

SELECTED BIBLIOGRAPHY

Binkley, Wilfred E., *President and Congress*, 3rd ed. (New York: Random House, Inc., 1962). An historical account of presidential-congressional relations.

Blum, John M., *The Republican Roosevelt* (Cambridge, Mass.: Harvard University Press, 1954). A sparkling study of Theodore Roosevelt as President.

Cornwell, Elmer E., Jr., *Presidential Leadership of Public Opinion* (Bloomington, Ind.: Indiana University Press, 1965). The best study of the President as leader of public opinion.

Corwin, Edward S., *The President: Office and Powers*, 4th ed. (New York: New York University Press, 1957). The authorative study of the Presidency from a constitutional and legal perspective.

Donovan, Robert J., *Eisenhower: The Inside Story* (New York: Harper and Row, 1956). An examination of the operation of the Eisenhower Administration during its first few months in office.

Evans, Rowland, Jr., and Robert D. Novak, *Lyndon B. Johnson: The Exercise of Power* (New York: The New American Library, 1966). A critical analysis of Johnson the politician and President by two veteran reporters.

Kallenbach, Joseph, *The American Chief Executive: The Presidency and the Governorship* (New York: Harper and Row, 1966). A camparative study of executive institutions and practices at the national and state levels.

Koenig, Louis W., *The Chief Executive*, rev. ed. (New York: Harcourt, Brace and World, 1968). A comprehensive study of the Presidency, with material on presidential values and styles and comparisons with governors and mayors. Contains extensive bibliography.

Neustadt, Richard E., *Presidential Power: The Politics of Leadership* (New York: John Wiley and Sons, Inc., 1960). A perceptive study that deals not with the Presidency as an institution, not with its legal and constitutional position, nor with the politics of winning nomination and election, but rather with the President's problem of obtaining power for himself while holding office. Told in terms of three case illustrations.

Schlesinger, Arthur M., Jr., *The Age of Roosevelt*, a three-volume history of the years preceding and during F.D.R.'s administrations: Vol. 1: *The Crisis of the Old Order*; Vol. 2: *The Coming of the New Deal*; Vol. 3: *The Politics of Upheaval* (Boston: Houghton Mifflin Company, 1957, 1959, 1960). A distinguished history, colorful and brilliant, illuminating an exciting era of ideas, events, and personalities.

Schlesinger, Arthur M., Jr., *A Thousand Days* (Boston: Houghton Mifflin Company, 1965). A controversial but lively insider's analysis of Kennedy's Presidency.

Sherwood, Robert, *Roosevelt and Hopkins* (New York: Harper and Row, 1948). An extraordinarily rich biographical study of the Roosevelt Administration.

Sorensen, Theodore C., *Kennedy* (New York: Harper and Row, 1965). A well-written and thoroughly detailed account of Kennedy as a senator and President, written by his former Special Counsel.

Wildavsky, Aaron, ed., *The Presidency* (Chicago: Rand McNally, Inc., 1969). A fascinating collection of articles on many aspects of the office.

Williams, Irving, *The Rise of the Vice-Presidency* (Washington, D.C.: Public Affairs Press, 1956). Still the best account of the office, although seriously outdated by important developments in the years since its publication.

Footnotes

[1] Max Farrand, *The Records of the Federal Convention* (New Haven, Conn.: Yale University Press, 1911), I, 65.

[2] Leonard D. White, *The Federalists* (New York: Crowell-Collier and Macmillan, Inc., 1948), p. 14.

[3] Quoted in Theodore H. White, *The Making of the President 1968* (New York: Atheneum Publishers, 1969), p. 147.

[4] Louis M. Koenig, *The Chief Executive* (New York: Harcourt, Brace and World, Inc., 1964), p. 13.

[5] William Howard Taft, *Our Chief Magistrate and His Powers* (New York: Columbia University Press, 1916), p. 139.

[6] *Theodore Roosevelt: An Autobiography* (New York: Crowell-Collier and Macmillan, Inc., 1913), p. 389. Used with the permission of The Macmillan Company.

[7] Richard E. Neustadt, *Presidential Power* (New York: John Wiley and Sons, Inc., 1960), p. 159.

[8] Alan L. Otten, *The Wall Street Journal*, July 6, 1965, p. 16.

[9] Douglass Cater, quoted in Tom Wicker, "Lyndon Johnson Is 10 Feet Tall," *New York Times Magazine*, May 23, 1965, p. 91.

[10] Robert B. Semple, Jr., "Nixon's Presidency Is A Very Private Affair," *The New York Times Magazine*, Nov. 2, 1969, p. 29.

[11] Quoted in Richard E. Neustadt, *Presidential Power: The Politics of Leadership* (New York: John Wiley & Sons, Inc., 1960), pp. 9–10.

[12] Neustadt, p. viii.

[13] *United States v. Curtiss-Wright Export Corp.*, 299 U.S. 304, 318 (1936).

[14] *Missouri v. Holland*, 252 U.S. 416 (1920).

[15] Edward S. Corwin, *The President: Office and Powers*, 4th ed. (New York: New York University Press, 1957), p. 172. (Italics omitted.)

[16] 10 U.S.C. § 332.

[17] 10 U.S.C. § 333.

[18] 10 U.S.C. § 334.

[19] *Panama Refining Co. v. Ryan*, 293 U.S. 388 (1934); see also *Schechter v. United States*, 295 U.S. 495 (1935).

[20] See especially *American Power & Light Co. v. SEC*, 329 U.S. 90 (1946); and *United States v. Sharpnack*, 355 U.S. 286 (1958).

[21] Joseph P. Harris, *The Advice and Consent of the Senate* (Berkeley, Calif.: University of California Press, 1953), p. 397.

[22] Quoted in Rowland Evans, Jr., and Robert D. Novak, *Lyndon B. Johnson: The Exercise of Power* (New York: The New American Library, Inc., 1966), p. 490.

[23] Robert A. Dahl and Charles E. Lindblom, *Politics, Economics, and Welfare* (New York: Harper and Row, 1953), p. 342.

[24] P. 39.

[25] *The American Presidency*, 2d ed. (New York: Harcourt, Brace and World, Inc., 1960), p. 59.

[26] Richard F. Fenno, Jr., "President-Cabinet Relations: A Pattern and a Case Study," *American Political Science Review*, 52 (June 1958), p. 404. (Italics omitted.)

[27] The amendment allows a person who succeeds to the Presidency and serves for not more than two years to run twice for election on his own. If such a person serves an unexpired term of more than two years, he can run only once. Thus a President may serve not more than ten years in the White House.

[28] See *Hollingsworth v. Virginia*, 3 Dallas 378 (1798).

[29] In the first 100 years of the American republic, there were 451 vetoes, only 29 of which were overridden, and over half of these 29 occurred in Andrew Johnson's administration. During the twelve years of his Presidency, Franklin Roosevelt vetoed 631 bills, only 9 of which were overridden. Harry Truman fared less well than his predecessor, since 12 of his 251 vetoes were overridden. During his two terms in office, Dwight Eisenhower used the pocket veto 107 times and his regular veto power on 74 occasions. Only two of the latter were overridden. President Kennedy vetoed only 21 bills; and Johnson was equally sparing, vetoing only 13 public and 17 private bills in his more than five years in office. No serious effort was made to override any of Kennedy's or Johnson's vetoes. Nixon vetoed only one bill during his first year in office and was sustained by Congress. During 1970, Congress overrode his veto of a measure authorizing additional funds for hospital construction and his veto of an appropriation for education.

[30] *Ex parte Merryman*, 17 Fed. Cases 144 (1861).

[31] Benjamin N. Cardozo, *The Nature of the Judicial Process* (New Haven, Conn.: Yale University Press, 1921), p. 168.

Chapter 15 The Presidential Establishment

THE PRESIDENTIAL PERSPECTIVE

This chapter analyzes the President's resources for formulating policies and for managing the executive branch of the federal government. It focuses on the intricate ways in which the President considers and makes policies, including his reliance on official and unofficial advisers both inside and outside the executive branch, and some of the problems in directing the bureaucracy toward the achievement of presidential goals.

Discussions of the Presidency often run the risk of suggesting that the process by which the President makes decisions can be systematized or that certain staffing arrangements and organizational schemes will improve the quality of presidential judgments. Such suggestions are misguided and misleading. How-to-do-it guides to improved executive management—so common in business management literature today—are wholly inappropriate to presidential management because of the breadth and scope of presidential decisions. No corporation executive begins to match the President in terms of multiple responsibilities and the complex issues requiring decisions. No other executive in public life anywhere in the world must resolve so many conflicting issues—with Congress, between departments and expert advisers, with other nations, and with interest groups. Even if the Presidency is stripped of its routine duties and the Office is provided with the best staff assistance, the President's job necessarily remains enormously burdensome. For he cannot delegate to others the duties that make the greatest demands upon human wisdom and energy.

The breadth of the constituency that elected him and the enormous degree to which Americans depend on him for political leadership in formulating policies and getting things done for them give the President, among all public officials, an opportunity to develop the broadest conception of the national interest and the broadest vision in making his decisions. Political executives with lesser responsibilities tend to have progressively narrower and more parochial perspectives that relate directly to the special world in which they live.

The bureau chief, for example, who is responsible directly to a department head or to an assistant secretary, may be the director of a large program employing hundreds or thousands of persons. His budget may reach several millions of dollars annually. He makes decisions and disposes of problems that are complex in analysis, important in their impact on individuals and groups, and delicate in their political consequences. If he is an average bureau chief, he has already served many years in his post, to which he succeeded following a long period of professional work in that bureau. He has become a specialist presiding over public programs in which he is an acknowledged expert. His special world includes not only his bureau but the organized interests and individuals who are affected by his decisions and his bureau's activities, the congressional subcommittees that help to shape the conception of the bureau's mission, and the specialized press that covers his actions and policies. Compared to the pressing reality of this special world, the rest of the federal government tends to appear remote, and the President is a shadowy figure who soon may be succeeded.

A close observer and former member of the bureaucracy[1] has noted:

> It would be unreasonable to expect this official to see his program in the Presidential perspective. The President wants him to be a zealot about his mission, to pursue the goals of his program with skill, enthusiasm, and dedication. To ask him at the same time to be Olympian about his role and his claim on resources—to see in a detached way that he is part of a hive in which many other bees have missions of equal or greater urgency—is to ask him to embrace a combination of incompatible attitudes.

Most bureau chiefs and program managers in the federal government are loyal to the President in the sense that they accept presidential decisions and support them. As we saw in Chapter 14, however, some bureaucrats may have goals of their own which they try to advance by mobilizing support among their clientele groups and congressional subcommittees. Some may be weak or inept in managing their activities and thus unable to follow the President's lead. Some may be so zealous in behalf of their programs that they lose their sense of proportion and fail to relate effectively to their department and to the executive branch. The perspectives and needs of bureau chiefs and the President are to a degree incompatible. What serves one well is likely to constrain the other. Thus, the President cannot escape the necessity of leading the bureaucracy if he wants to achieve his policy goals. No one else approaches the President in the gravity of the decisions he must personally make. According to Sorensen[2]:

> A President knows that his name will be the label for a whole era. Text books yet unwritten and school-children yet unborn will hold him responsible for all that happens. His program, his power, his prestige, his place in history, perhaps his re-election, will all be affected by key decisions. His appointees, however distinguished they may be in their own rights, will rise or fall as he rises or falls. Even his White House aides, who see him constantly, cannot fully perceive his personal stakes and isolation. And no amount of tinkering with the presidential machinery, or establishment of executive offices, can give anyone else *his* perspective.

No other position in American public or private life can in itself be held to qualify a candidate for the post of Chief Executive. Justice Holmes once characterized Franklin D. Roosevelt as a "second-rate intellect but a first-rate temperament." "Perhaps," Neustadt suggests,[3] "this is a necessary combination. The politics of well-established government has rarely been attractive to and rarely has dealt kindly with the men whom intellectuals regard as first-rate intellects." The persistent mystery of American politics is the nature of the temperament that develops expertness in presidential power.

THE PRESIDENTIAL ADVISORY SYSTEM

In the American political system, the President is expected to be the administrator-in-chief of the executive branch and the preeminent policy planner of the nation. He has the responsibility both to develop new ideas and execute policies through the management of government programs. If he is to keep control of the principal activities of the mammoth structure of the executive branch, comprising over six million civilian employees and military personnel, annual purchases of goods and services exceeding $100 billion, twelve departments headed by secretaries of Cabinet rank, over fifty other agencies and commissions, and vast numbers of special units, he needs a great deal of help. And if he is to develop and promote new ideas for public policies and programs, he must be able to draw on advice and policy guidance from both within and outside the government.

In response to these needs the bureaucracy within the Presidency has burgeoned since 1939, when the Executive Office of the President was created. It consists of two groups: the insiders and the outsiders. The insiders include the Cabinet, the personal staff in the White House, and the support staffs in the Executive Office of the President, such as the Office of Management and Budget, formerly known as the Bureau of the Budget. The outsiders include the President's personal friends and political allies, various White House task forces, special study commissions, consultants, and advisory institutions, such as the Urban Institute and The Brookings Institution.

The functioning of presidential policy processes raises central questions. How does the Presidency gather and evaluate information? Where do new ideas come from, and how do they get translated into policy? Who gets access to the White House, and who does not? What strategies of presidential advising tend to work effectively? Do serious problems of democratic philosophy and governing capacity arise when "Chief Executives grow more and more dependent on a nonelected parliament of future planners, chosen not for their representativeness, nor for their ideology, but rather for their professional education and specializations."[4]

THE CABINET

Although the Constitution does not specifically provide for a Cabinet, the Founding Fathers clearly contemplated that the President would look to the heads of departments for advice and counsel. Washington established the tradition of meeting with these officials as a group, thus creating the Cabinet. But it is not a cabinet in the sense in which that term is used in a parliamentary system such as Britain's.

The members of the President's Cabinet do not share with him a constitutional, collective responsibility for policies and decisions on major policy questions. A President is not even bound to consult the Cabinet. For instance, during the Civil War, Lincoln met infrequently with the Cabinet, apparently did not insist that members make a point of being present, and did not always attend himself. Theodore Roosevelt and Woodrow Wilson both regarded their Cabinet members as administrators rather than as a group of policy advisers concerned with the broad strategy of affairs. Wilson did not read his war message to the Cabinet because he did not want to subject its language to review and discussion. Although at first Franklin Roosevelt apparently thought of using his Cabinet more systematically, in the later years the meetings did not amount to much. To Secretary of War Stimson,[5] for example, they "were useful principally as a way of getting into the White House to have a word with the President in private after the meetings were over. . . ."

President Truman tried to make the weekly Cabinet meetings more useful by having the agenda distributed in advance and a record made of the points agreed to after discussion. President Eisenhower extended these innovations by establishing a Cabinet secretariat. Members who wished to have the Cabinet discuss a problem submitted the item to the Cabinet secretary for inclusion in the agenda. Before scheduling it, the secretary or his assistant generally discussed the proposed item with several interested officials in various departments and attempted to screen out minor problems.

President Kennedy reversed the Eisenhower pattern and minimized the importance of Cabinet meetings. President Johnson fell somewhere between the Eisenhower and Kennedy positions; Cabinet meetings under him became more frequent and members were expected to offer the President advice on matters falling outside their respective departmental jurisdictions. President Nixon meets with his Cabinet about once a month or less and seems to prefer smaller Cabinet-level advisory groups on more specific problems. He apparently has enjoyed these various meetings best when they have been informal and free-wheeling, with members sparring over major issues and responding to incessant questioning by the President.

In short, each President makes what use of the Cabinet he wishes. His own working methods determine the procedures of the Cabinet and its contribution as a unifying and creative force in the affairs of the executive branch. The critical fact is, of course, that it is the President, not the Cabinet, who bears the responsibility and must make the crucial decisions.

A President weighs many factors in selecting Cabinet members. He must consider groups and individuals whose support contributed significantly to his election. If his party is badly split, or if there is a national crisis, he may wish to appoint one or two representatives of an opposing faction as Lincoln did when he invited two of his rivals for the 1860 nomination to join his Cabinet. On a broader scale, a President may use Cabinet appointments to try to unify the nation, as Roosevelt did on the eve of World War II when he brought in Republicans to head the Navy and War Departments.

If a President wants to work closely with his Cabinet, personal compatibility is important; and, of course, a chief executive can never afford to ignore ideological compatibility, although other considerations may force him to accept an opponent as a member of his official family. There is no tradition of appointing as head of a department a man who is an expert in the activities for which he will be responsible. Indeed, it is likely to be a matter of chance whether the new appointee will have had any executive experience, although he is quite apt to have some previous exposure to political life either as an elected official or as an adviser.

The leading study[6] of the Cabinet warns both against exaggerating its importance and against dismissing it as an ornamental antique.

> It is weakest in performing the function of interdepartmental coordination and in making direct contributions to decisions through a well-informed, well-organized discussion of policy alternatives. It is most useful as a presidential adviser, in the sense of a political sounding board equipped to provide clues as to likely public or group reactions, and as a forum in which some overall administrative coherence can be secured.

Cabinets may be useful to some degree to a President seeking advice, but the President can never lose sight of the fact that each department has its own interests, its own relations with Congress and powerful interest groups, and its own clientele. Inevitably the secretaries as political leaders of their departments reflect some degree of bureaucratic parochialism in their advice to the President. White House staff advisers, on the other hand, may see problems in a wider context than a Cabinet secretary, but their contact with Congress, interest groups, and actual operations is less. Their views are apt to be less parochial than a secretary's but they may also be less sensitive to the immediate political and administrative setting of the problem under analysis.

WHITE HOUSE PERSONAL STAFF

Of all the components of the presidential advisory system, the public learns more about the activities of the personal assistants to the President than they do about any other advisers or advisory groups. Yet the activities and influence of personal advisers tend to remain subjects of conjecture and gossip.

Small-scale use of aides had been common in the offices of nineteenth-century Presidents. Abraham Lincoln handled White House problems with the help of two or three correspondence clerks. Grover Cleveland answered his own telephone and wrote most of his papers in longhand. Before William McKinley's administration, Presidents had personal or private secretaries to help with correspondence, but these were not recognized as government officials. This arrangement was consistent with the notion that all official matters were referred to appropriate departments for action and that correspondence of the President was personal. President Taft thought it remarkable that the volume of presidential business in his day required the assistance of twenty-five clerks and stenographers. For the first part of this century, one man, Ira Smith, was able to take care of all the mail that came to the White House. Calvin Coolidge used to sit on the corner of Smith's desk while Smith opened the envelopes and passed him his letters. Before Smith retired in 1948, after fifty-one years of service, he had a staff of fifty clerks to help him

Drawing by Tom Little. © 1958 by The New York Times Company. Reprinted
by permission.

with the mail. For twelve years under Franklin Roosevelt, an average of 5000 letters was delivered to the White House each day, and as many as 175,000 letters on a single day.

The recent increase in the number of presidential assistants is equally dramatic and of greater significance. In 1915 Woodrow Wilson was operating the White House with the help of three immediate aides. Herbert Hoover had a personal staff of five, the same number that worked with Theodore Roosevelt in 1907. Under Franklin Roosevelt, the number of administrative assistants varied from six to fourteen. In 1952 the White House staff included fifteen personal assistants to Harry Truman, and it increased to fifty under Eisenhower. The number declined under Kennedy and Johnson, and under Nixon the staff multiplied many times beyond its size in earlier years and included persons borrowed from various departments as well as those employed directly by the White House.

Several senior assistants normally work on problems that concern the President (such as economic stability, national security, patronage and executive recruitment, congressional relations, and speech writing). The press secretary long ago became one of the most influential members of every White House entourage. The appointments secretary is likely to consult the President very frequently. Since he has the task of selecting from the dozens of daily requests for appointments the few whom it is desirable for the President to see.

One of the principal functions of the White House staff is to offset the parochialism of department heads and experts in special fields. These assistants, according to one of the most effective of them, are the only other men in Washington whose responsibilities both enable and require them to look, as the President does, at the government as a whole.[7] Their job is not to replace the Cabinet member or prevent him from seeing the President—although this sometimes happens—but to spot, refine, and define issues for the President. "A good White House staff can give the President that crucial margin of time, analysis, and judgment that makes an unmanageable problem more manageable."[8]

White House assistants also have their limitations. They have less contact and therefore less concern with congressional and other political pressures than do department Secretaries. They tend to be less concerned than department heads with question of organization and management. If the staff man takes on many subordinates to help him in his tasks, he may become another level of clearance between the departments and the President that slows up final determinations.

Franklin Roosevelt must be credited with the first significant development of the personal White House staff and a set of premises for its use.[9] First, Roosevelt limited the personal staff to those who were essential for the conduct of his own work. Routine or second-string activities, including legislative relations, had to be kept out of the White House. Second, Roosevelt tended to give his staff aides specific one-time assignments relating directly to his need to take some action. If they had continuing duties, it was in spheres of recurrent presidential obligations, not in functional subject matters. And third, Roosevelt insisted on keeping his assistants very mobile so that they could provide him with sensitive political intelligence. "FDR intended his Administrative Assistants to be eyes and ears and manpower for *him*, with no fixed contacts, clients, or involvements of their own to interfere when he needed to redeploy them."[10] These premises meant that Roosevelt was his own chief of staff. He could not have lived with a Sherman Adams, as President Eisenhower did, as a staff coordinator and manager.

Unlike President Eisenhower, who preferred fixed assignments for his staff and limited his own involvement to few of them, President Kennedy used a smaller staff organized (like Roosevelt's) on assignments that he expected to lead to action. While Kennedy shared with Roosevelt a taste for competition among assistants in presenting ideas and proposals, he would not tolerate egoism. Kennedy followed Eisenhower in saving his time for the most important business and in keeping and enlarging his personal staff for cultivating congressional support and for science and technology.

The Nixon staff, the largest assembled since 1933, is rather young in age, diverse in experience, and mostly from California. In the first few months, the staff was organized into several power centers concentrating on urban affairs, security policies, congressional operations, environmental protection, and administration. In November 1969, the President revamped his staff organization by concentrating more responsiblities in the Assistant to the President for Domestic Affairs, whose status was much comparable to that of the President's top assistant for national security affairs. He also created the title of Counsellor for assistants who were expected "to anticipate events, to think through the consequences of current trends, to question conventional wisdom, to address fundamentals, and to stimulate long-range innovation."[11]

Despite the very different ways in which Presidents have used their assistants, there has been a tendency toward assigning particular persons continuing responsibility for general programs. To obtain worthwhile advice, Chief Executives, even those who, like Kennedy and Nixon, prefer otherwise, have had to allow most of their advisers to specialize largely in one or at most only several areas. As problems have become more numerous and more complex, staff members have had to spend more time developing expertise.

THE EXECUTIVE OFFICE OF THE PRESIDENT

In addition to his staff of personal advisers within the White House, the President has available a growing body of institutionalized staff support for budgeting, economic policy, national security, and scientific policy. Located within the Executive Office of the President and housed in buildings adjacent to or nearby the White House, these policy staffs constitute a powerful component of the presidential advisory system.

National Security Advisers

Next to grouping the armed services and the military departments under centralized civilian direction, an outstanding feature of the National Security Act of 1947 was the creation of institutional facilities to enable the President to bring about better cooperation and direction in the overlapping areas of foreign and military policy. The 1947 statute established the National Security Council, consisting of the President, the Secretaries of State and Defense, and the Director of Emergency Planning. Its function is to "advise the President with respect to the integration of domestic, foreign, and military policies relating to national security" and to "assess and appraise the objectives, commitments, and risks of the United States in relation to our actual and potential military power, in the interest of national security." The unique task of the NSC is to bring together all significant military and political factors in planning for national security.

Since World War II each President has had to cope with the primary problem of finding effective ways to deal with national security affairs. And each has found that the NSC, which was designed to deal with the Cold War and the possibility of World War III, has been less than an ideal instrument for policy making. Each has used the NSC in his own way, more often than not as supplementary to other White House facilities. Most frequently, "it has been used as the principal arena for debating alternative courses of action and ensuring that all the relevant considerations were thoroughly considered in making a final decision."[15]

A team of experts recruited from the State Department, the Department of Defense, the armed services, and the Central Intelligence Agency (CIA) has provided the staff for the Council's work. In addition, recent Presidents have used a variety of arrangements, including loose, informal working groups, highly structured interagency boards, and special task forces to work on specific issues of national security or on broad developments in the field.

The policy process in national security demonstrates the close relation between each President's personal style and his policy arrangements. The President may want to involve himself in the day-to-day management of national security affairs, or he may prefer to delegate responsibility to department heads acting within guidelines that he sets. He might prefer to rely more on interagency committees and task forces drawn from the key agencies in foreign and security affairs rather than on a dominant, White House staff. Whatever arrangement is preferred, the President needs the help of staff aides for several purposes: to impose some order and coherence on the flow of paper to and from his desk, to keep in touch with all the departments and agencies concerned, and to handle matters that require the utmost security, discretion, and control.

From Truman to Nixon, the trend has been toward a progressive increase in presidential involvement in national security. Each successive President has had more detailed information made available to him; each has dipped deeper into the executive branch agencies in the effort to get better control of issues at earlier stages in their development. And the White House staffs have tended to function as the primary instruments of presidential power.

Despite their enormous complexity, the needs of the President can be readily perceived. First, he must keep fully informed about what is happening that affects national security. Second, he must have means of identifying those issues that potentially concern him. Third, he must try to know and evaluate all aspects of an issue before he makes his decision. Fourth, he must develop workable schemes to coordinate the policies and actions of various department heads. And fifth, the President must establish devices to help assure performance by the bureaucracy in carrying out his decisions and to create understanding—both inside and outside the executive branch—of these decisions and their implications.

President Nixon appeared to set his pattern somewhere between the highly structured central arrangements with maximum delegation of decision-making to Cabinet officers characteristic of Eisenhower and the less formal and more free-wheeling White House-centered schemes of Kennedy and Johnson. Nixon's top assistant for national security affairs seems to be directly involved in both policy planning activities and in the formulation of policies. At the same time, there has been more use of a larger and elaborately organized NSC staff, in accordance with the President's stated intention to use the NSC as the forum for considering major policy questions.

The Domestic Council

In 1970 President Nixon established within the Executive Office of the President a new Cabinet-level forum known as the Domestic Council, chaired by the President. Its membership includes the Vice President, most heads of Cabinet departments, and such other agency heads as the President may designate. It is supported by a staff under an executive director, who serves as one of the President's principal assistants. Like the National Security Council, the staff of the new Domestic Council must work closely with President's personal staff, but it has its own institutional identity. The Council's broad mission is to advise the President on the total range of domestic policy, including goals and objectives, identifying alternative ways of achieving objectives, providing rapid response to presidential requests for policy advice on pressing domestic issues, and maintaining a continuous review of the conduct of significant government programs in the domestic fields. The Council is expected to make substantial use of task forces and other planning or advisory groups, supplemented by its own staff and that of the Office of Management and Budget.

Office of Management and Budget (OMB)

Next to the White House staff the Office of Management and Budget is the most important of the agencies whose primary mission is to help the President control and direct the executive branch. It acquired its present significance in 1939 when, under its original name of Bureau of the Budget, it was transferred from the Treasury Department to the Executive Office of the President. President Nixon transformed the Bureau of the Budget into the Office of Management and Budget in 1970. It is headed by a Director, who is appointed by the President without Senate confirmation. The Office has three main jobs. A primary activity is the formulation and execution of the federal budget, which today is accepted as a major responsibility of the Chief Executive. Before the passage of the Budget and Accounting Act of 1921, department and agencies presented estimates of their financial requirements directly to Congress. There was no general budget for the executive branch until an employee of the House Appropriations Committee assembled the separate budgets submitted by the several departments. Under this system even the most experienced legislators had difficulty in determining the relative needs of competing departments.

The Budget and Accounting Act requires all executive agencies to submit budget estimates to the President and authorizes the Bureau of the Budget (now OMB) on behalf of the President, "to assemble, correlate, revise, reduce, or increase the estimates." This statute gives the President the authority he needs to control expenditures of the executive branch, and it provides a group of specialists to help him use this authority intelligently. By reducing or eliminating funds requested to carry out programs that the President does not support, the Office helps to keep departmental activities within bounds set by the President. Congress, can, of course override these decisions.

Another major task of OMB is to help improve the organization and management of the executive branch, a function it performs in two ways. It provides technical assistance in preparing plans for the reorganization of executive agencies. This phase of its work is especially important when the President is given authority by Congress to carry out extensive structural changes. The Office also assists executive departments and agencies to improve their internal organization and operating procedures. The executive establishment is so vast that it cannot be directed and controlled solely from the executive office of the President. Long-run improvements in organization and operations depend in large part upon the ability of each agency to search out and correct its weaknesses. The staff of OMB is useful in making departments sensitive to opportunities for improvement and in informing all agencies of the best methods of management in use in the government.

A third activity of the Office involves assisting the President in handling legislative matters: by participating in the development of legislative program, by clearing and coordinating departmental advice on proposed legislation, and by making recommendations for presidential action on legislative enactments. In the clearance function, it reviews legislative recommendations submitted by various agencies, examines them for conformity to the President's program, and seeks the views of other agencies with an interest in the legislation. The Office's staff is able to point out conflicts in proposals from different agencies; and in other ways it may prevent competing or ill-advised proposals from being submitted to Congress as administration bills. Congressmen may also find it useful to know that legislative proposals dealing with a single subject but emanating from different departments have been considered side-by-side and that an effort has been made to examine them from a broad perspective.

The Office also keeps the President informed about bills pending in Congress and those that have been passed. With information provided by OMB, the President is able to tell legislative leaders whether a particular bill has his support, whether he is indifferent, or whether it is contrary to his program. The staff surveys interested departments and agencies to find out how they would be affected by a bill that has been passed and on which the President must act. If the consensus is against the bill, the President is informed and probably provided with a draft of a veto message. The President, of course, consults legislative leaders as well as executive officials. If the advice of the legislators conflicts with that of the executive departments, he finds it easier to make up his own mind because of the background of information assembled by the Office of Management and Budget.

In 1970 the Office of Management and Budget was directed to provide leadership within the executive branch for the development of personnel policies and improved practices of executive recruitment.

Presidents rarely get involved in the details of budgetary decision-making, but they do have to make the grand decisions that express their strategic policy judgments. The main responsibility for making the detailed judgments falls on the OMB Director and his staff, with assistance perhaps from the White House staff, all of whom are supposed to reflect the values and priorities of the President. The President cannot avoid major reliance on the budget as an instrument of executive direction and influence. As President Johnson's Budget Director[12] wrote:

> Whereas the budget may have looked from the perspective of the Senate like an intricate collection of compromises among the interests of separate and often conflicting constituencies, it is suddenly seen from the White House as the central focus of efforts to achieve the Presidential vision of national purpose. What appears from lower vantage points to be a catalogue of discrete decisions is viewed from the highest perspective as a series of *choices* among alternatives, many of them perplexing and some of them agonizing.

A principal variable in the work of the Office of Management and Budget is the kind of rapport an agency or department head maintains with the President. He can more readily keep in step with the President on important policy choices if he maintains leverage in dealing with the interest groups concerned with the agency's programs. If there is no organized clientele so concerned, or if it is poorly organized with little political strength, or if the several clientele groups can be played off against each other, the agency head can more readily accommodate himself to the larger perspective of the President. But if the clientele groups are able to push the agency to adopt policies incompatible with the President's program, the Office has the sensitive task of providing countervailing influence. It does so by maintaining special surveillance over agencies where clientele pressure is strong. In these cases, the Office may be in a better political position, safeguarded by its proximity to the President, to make budgetary decisions likely to be unpopular with the agency's clientele. The objective is to guide public spending as much as possible by the President's vision of national purpose rather than the claims of private interests.

The Council of Economic Advisers

The Employment Act of 1946 requires the President to send an economic report to Congress soon after the opening of each regular session. It also created the Council of Economic Advisers to help the President prepare the report, which usually describes the economic state of the nation, discusses trends in employment and production, and appraises federal programs that affect the national economy. The Council recommends actions necessary to maintain the statutory objectives—maximum employment, production, and purchasing power. The Council is composed of three members appointed by the President by and with the advice and consent of the Senate.

The first task of the Council is to analyze, interpret, and forecast economic developments both nationally and internationally. Using the tools of the economist and statistician, the Council sends a steady stream of analyses to the President. In the context of presidential priorities, the advisers then evaluate the contributions of various courses of action to alternative objectives of public policy, pointing up conflicting economic and political hazards. An inescapable aspect of the Council's mission is the education of the President. As a former chairman[13] explains, "The explanatory and analytical models of the economist must be implanted—at least intuitively—in the minds of Presidents, congressmen, and public leaders if economic advice is to be accepted and translated into action." The Council has the task of translating the concepts of economic analysis into forms that are usable as policy guides. This involves the construction of so-called operational concepts such as production gap, full employment surplus, and fiscal drag.

Since the President knows that the Council's advice is not diluted by commitments to operating programs or the interests of particular pressure groups, its members tend to have the advantage of relatively easy access to the White House. But influence on presidential decisions is by no means automatic. As a former chairman[14] has noted:

> Unless the White House took a hand in directing economic traffic through the Council, the policy train often flashed past before we could get out the flag to stop it. One of our major tasks was to establish constructive relationships with the men around the President to help insure that the Council's voice would be heard before final decisions were made, even if it had not been drawn into the early stages of the policy-making process.

In an environment often characterized by bureaucratic aggrandizement the Council has remained compact, flexible, and small. Its professional staff is limited to about fifteen, many of whom are on leave from their university or other regular posts in order to serve full-time for a year or two and perhaps part-time and intermittently thereafter.

Science Advisers

In 1962 the special assistant to the President for science and technology became the director of a new Office of Science and Technology located in the Executive Office of the President. The President's Science Advisory Committee remained attached to the Executive Office as a committee of distinguished outside experts serving part time in advising the President. The combination of full-time science advisers and part-time science advisory groups was paralleled in the defense establishment and in other federal departments concerned with science and technology.

The President's need in this field is not for new ideas for scientific programs in the government; these he can get from the scientific staffs in government offices and from the National Academy of Sciences. Instead, he needs scientific advisers who can help him evaluate proposals from operating agencies, identifying proposals that are based on scientific and professional certainty and those for which equally attractive alternatives are available. These advisers must be able to work with others in the Executive Office to blend scientific advice with advice on the financial, diplomatic, legal, and many other aspects of policy. Above all they must protect him from being presented with advice, ostensibly based on scientific considerations, that will really represent an invasion of his general policy by a special interest.[16]

What the President requires is similar to his needs in other policy areas, advice that is a blend of technology, politics, economics, and law. The expert in science who advises the President must therefore try to collaborate with other specialists and in the process become a generalist who can further the broad public interest concerns of the President.

The development of science policy has engendered feelings of inferiority and anxiety in a Congress already concerned about its power position relative to that of the Presidency and executive branch. In the light of the growing importance of considerations of science and technology in the formulation of policies on environmental pollution, consumer protection, and weapons systems, many congressmen believe that the legislative branch needs its own science advisers and that it should be able to use committee hearings to question the President's science advisers. A consequence of these proposals is that they compromise scientific judgment by forcing advisers to acquire political influence in order to maintain their position.[17]

OUTSIDERS

Personal Friends

In analyzing presidential approaches to staffing, Neustadt[18] writes about President Franklin Roosevelt:

> It never seems to have occurred to FDR that his only sources of such *ad hoc* personal assistance were the aides in his own office. He also used Executive Office aides, personal friends, idea-men or technicians down in the bureaucracy, old Navy hands, old New York hands, experts from private life, Cabinet Officers, "Little Cabinet" officers, diplomats, relatives—especially his wife—toward the end, his daughter—as supplementary eyes and ears and manpower. He often used these "outsiders" to check or duplicate the work of White House staff, or to probe into spheres where White House aides should not be seen, or to look into things he guessed his staff would be against.

Roosevelt's use of outsiders stemmed in part from his dislike "to be tied to any single source of information or advice on anything."[19] All Presidents have felt the need for intimate association with men outside the immediate circle of official aides. This practice goes back at least as far as Andrew Jackson's famous "kitchen cabinet"—a group of personal friends whom he consulted and relied upon more heavily than he did the members of his Cabinet. Abraham Lincoln found such a group invaluable. Woodrow Wilson called upon Colonel House to carry out missions that he considered too vital to entrust to government officials. And during Franklin Roosevelt's administration, especially during the war

Study Panels Flourish in Capital

By JACK ROSENTHAL
Special to The New York Times

WASHINGTON, Dec. 14—In the fall of 1967 John Kenneth Galbraith rebuked President Johnson for his response to the riots that had just crippled Detroit and Newark.

They may have been the worst civil disorder ever, he said to a luncheon meeting of urban affairs experts, yet what had the President done? He had, Professor Galbraith observed acidly, appointed a commission on riots and declared a National Day of Prayer....

The number of Presidential commissions to investigate divisive social issues has increased since then—and so has cynicism about them.

Last week brought the concluding report of still another study group, the National Commission of the Causes and Prevention of Violence, the final major report of a commission appointed in the Johnson Administration....

In the past four years, blue ribbon assemblages have reported at length on crime and law enforcement, Selective Service, rural poverty, civil disorders, housing and urban problems, income maintenance, and now, violence....

When aides to President Nixon took office, they found 169 different advisory commissions, some dating back decades.

Yet they, and many former commissioners and staff members, vigorously defend commissions and reject the cynicism which commissions increasingly have inspired.

They see these major virtues of commissions that they say insure their continuation:

¶ To a considerable degree, commissions do produce national action.

¶ Commissions are vital forces for generating changes in public attitudes that are fundamental to future action.

Commissions often create new bodies of expertise which lay the base for action at the local as well as the national level.

On the first point, action is not always immediate. Representative Alexander Pirnie of upstate New York reached into the big glass bowl to begin the new draft lottery on Dec. 1—nearly three years after the idea of random selection of 19-year-olds had been advanced by the National Advisory Commission on Selective Service.

A major Federal anti-crime program, involving hundreds of millions of dollars in grants for reform of local law enforcement, derives from the work of the President's Commission on Law Enforcement and Administration of Justice.

Operation Breakthrough, the new experimental program for mass-produced housing, resulted from the Commission on Urban Problems headed by former Senator Paul H. Douglas....

There are negative kinds of action as well.

"I think we helped stop excessive killing," says David Ginsburg, a Washington lawyer who was executive director of the National Advisory Commission on Civil Disorders.

Early in the commission's life, he recalls, it stimulated Federal disorder control conferences for hundreds of city officials. "The police became much more sensitive in dealing with disorders," Mr. Ginsburg said, "especially in larger cities. The lessons are only now seeping down to smaller cities."

Of all the recent commissions, the commission on civil disorders won the widest public attention for its efforts in the second area of commission benefit; public education.

"It was maddening to many people," says Representative William M. McCulloch, Republican of Ohio, who served on both the commission on civil disorders and the commission on violence. "But we pointed up something that needed to be pointed up: that we are racist."

The immediate impact of the national crime commission was far less dramatic, but its long-term effects have been widespread, says James Vorenberg, the Harvard law professor who directed its staff.

The most important result was that the commission got across the concept of law enforcement as a system, he said. Too often, it had been regarded as an assortment of independent police, court, and corrections agencies....

Commissions can perform another kind of public education—lending prestige to advanced ideas. One such effort was the President's Commission on Income Maintenance Programs.

This group, appointed by President Johnson, recently submitted its report to President Nixon. It called for a guaranteed annual income of $2,400 for the poor.

It "was not set up because we had any doubts that income maintenance was necessary," said Joseph A. Califano, who was chief domestic affairs aide to President Johnson. "It was because we had to get sophisticated data and try to get blue-chip, prestigious commissioners on the line for something that was highly radical at the time."

A further educational virtue of commissions was identified by former Attorney General Nicholas DeB. Katzenbach, who headed the national crime commission.

"Statements by the Kerner Commission [on civil disorders] like 'white racism' are extremely important," he said. "They help restore the confidence of the black community in the integrity of Government and public institutions."

The same was true of the violence commission's Walker report, he adds. That report sharply criticized police behavior during the Democratic Convention in Chicago. Mr. Katzenbach believes its publication helped reaffirm young people's belief in at least some aspects of Government.

The third function of commissions—developing expertise and research material—probably provokes the most frequent skepticism....

"Perhaps our greatest contribution," says Lloyd N. Cutler, a Washington attorney who directed the violence commission staff, "is to create a literature of violence which simply did not exist. There wasn't even a history of violence before."

© 1969 by The New York Times Company. Reprinted by permission.

years, Harry Hopkins exercised enormous influence as the President's personal and confidential assistant. Although a few of President Truman's intimates were poorly equipped for this service, their indiscretions did not destroy a President's need for personal advisers. No one clearly emerged as President Eisenhower's Colonel House or Harry Hopkins, perhaps because of his development and use of the White House staff. President Kennedy relied heavily on his official White House staff, while President Johnson appeared to count on advice and counsel from congressional leaders and old-time political associates. President Nixon has retained his close friendship with a small group of intimate friends he made while living in New York from 1963 to his election. These friends occupy executive positions in banking, publishing, business, legal practice, and politics and serve as sounding boards for presidential policies and goals.

Task Forces and Commissions

Beginning especially in 1961, the President's need for advice and new ideas has led to tremendous increase in the use of outside specialists, advisers, task forces, study commissions, and White House conferences. Today a President may use thousands of such outsiders in one way or another to advise him on policy. Their activities are submerged in the confidentiality of the Presidency, but when their reports are published, it is somewhat easier to trace the connections between their recommendations and presidential decisions than it is to judge the influence of insiders, whose advice and activities are usually shrouded from public view.

    The first President to use the task force or commission composed of nongovernment persons for policy formulation was Theodore Roosevelt. Hoover used at least 60 commissions, boards, and similar groups; FDR, more than a hundred. Truman used only about 20 major commissions, but they included such important groups as the first Hoover Commission on Organization of the Executive Branch of the Government, the President's Commission on Higher Education, and the President's Committee on Civil Rights. Eisenhower employed a dozen or more on such subjects as reorganization of the executive branch, intergovernmental relations, foreign economic policy, and housing policies. Beginning with Kennedy, their use has multiplied as agents to develop new policy ideas. Kennedy used them particularly to promote provocative proposals; Johnson used them mostly to develop proposals to be incorporated into his legislative program or to take a long-range view of major policy areas.

    Presidential use of such outside groups carries many advantages and disadvantages.[20] The period of time an outside group needs to study a problem and prepare a report generally prevents precipitate action and allows the President and his inside advisers an opportunity to plan their own approach. Perhaps even more important, these outsiders, precisely because they are outsiders, can approach a problem free from an institutionalized commitment to any particular policy or to the interests of any bureau and its clientele. They can take a fresh look; and, if they think it feasible, offer a solution that cuts across established jurisdictional lines of existing agencies. Furthermore, since committee members are usually distinguished citizens, their report can focus congressional and administration attention both directly as well as indirectly by generating reactions from reporters and analysts from the news media.

The principal disadvantage of these advisory committees is inherent in their chief advantage. Because they are outsiders, because they do not have institutional roots in the federal bureaucracy, they will not remain in office to carry through on the long, hard process of translating ideas into viable, operational policy decisions.

Some advisory committees have had great success in convincing both the President and Congress of the wisdom of their proposals. Others have been less skillful or less lucky. Because of this wide disparity in results, it is difficult to generalize about their over-all utility. One leading study[21] concludes that "more and more of the policy initiatives emanate from these White House appointed collectivities." Objections come mainly from the President's competitors for political influence and power. Congressional leaders have some fear that they will be overwhelmed by effective presidential use of this technique. Some professional bureaucrats worry about the White House monopolizing the services of the most noted experts, and, like congressmen, they are concerned lest the President take over all of their policy-making initiative. Professional administrators also worry about the relatively low level of concern advisory groups commonly display toward the operating problems that departments constantly face.

DIRECTING THE BUREAUCRACY

The President as Administrator-in-Chief

Viewed from the White House, the federal bureaucracy appears to be a vast impenetrable jungle. But if it is a jungle, it is one that can be influenced if not controlled. As in all aspects of his mammoth tasks, one of the most useful instruments a President has for exercising leadership is his reputation for knowing what to do and how much can be done and his willingness to put his whole energy into the task. Professional respect may not win over all doubters, but it does greatly increase the likelihood that they will listen attentively.

A President can try to keep his patronage promises to a minimum so he retains as much control as possible over his appointments. While he may not in this way be able to eliminate all problems in dealing with Cabinet officers and agency heads—after all he does not want assistants who have no strong views of their own—a President can reduce his difficulties if he chooses men of ability who think as he does on basic policy issues and who know that they owe their positions to him.

A President may also employ his authority as Chief Executive to assign to various people or agencies in whom he has great trust special missions that may appear to be outside their normal jurisdiction. In addition, he may use this same authority to construct several overlapping networks of responsibility and information. This tactic may make for disorderly organization charts, but it also provides the President with access to different sources of information and at the same time establishes several lines of competition in executing programs. If one fails, the other may succeed, and in any case the existence of competition may spur each on to do a better job. Franklin Roosevelt delighted in this tactic. "His favorite technique," Arthur M. Schlesinger, Jr.,[22] has written, was to keep grants of authority incomplete, jurisdictions uncertain, charters over-lapping. The result of this competitive theory of administration was often confusion and exasperation on the operating level; but no other method could so reliably insure that in a large bureaucracy filled with ambitious men eager for power the decisions, and the power to make them, would remain with the President.

The major organizations within the executive branch are the eleven Cabinet-level departments: State; Defense, Treasury; Justice; Interior; Agriculture; Commerce; Labor; Health, Education and Welfare; Housing and Urban Development; and Transportation. Each department is headed by a secretary who is responsible directly to the President for the satisfactory performance of the activities of his department and is a member of the President's Cabinet. Most civilian employees of the federal government work in these departments. In 1970, the Post Office Department became an independent agency, the U.S. Postal Service.

In addition, there is a highly varied group of more than fifty organizations— agencies, corporations, administrations, commissions, authorities—the heads of which report directly to the President but are not members of his Cabinet. Agency heads are directly responsible for such large organizations as the Veterans Administration, the General Services Administration, the Civil Service Commission, the Panama Canal Company, the Tennessee Valley Authority, the Atomic Energy Commission, the National Aeronautics and Space Administration, and the Selective Service System.

Independent regulatory commissions are part of the executive branch, but they have a special relation to the President. These agencies were established by Congress to regulate such activities as radio, television, and satellite communications, interstate transportation by railroads and trucks, ocean shipping, trade practices, and the interstate distribution of electricity. The statutes under which these commissions operate authorize them to issue rules and regulations having the effect of law as far as private citizens are concerned, and to decide cases arising under the regulations. In addition, their members are usually appointed for rather long and specified terms and are not easily removable by the President.

The impact of presidential staffs on departmental and agency staffs varies greatly. Some agency heads may defer weakly to White House personnel while others stoutly resist. Some learn to develop cooperative responses in the presidential establishment, and some also develop imaginative ways of surmounting the procedures imposed by the executive office of the President. Some devote assiduous attention to cultivating political support in congressional committees and interest group consituencies in order to counter-act presidential influence. Indeed, a persistent theme has been the pervasive development of clusters of power comprising government offices and bureaus, congressional committees, and interest groups. As one commentator[23] has stated, interest groups attempt

to create autonomous and controllable fragments of government, each with a jurisdiction corresponding to the area and scope of the pressure group's interest—autonomous, that is to say, in the sense of independence from the rest of the government, and controllable from the point of view of the pressure group.

Presidential success in combating the drives of individual administrators for maximum autonomy also varies greatly. Some agencies operating in areas relatively unimportant from the point of view of the President's program do not warrant much effort to bring them into line. Others carry on programs that are at the heart of the administration's goals, but even here presidential control may be problematical. A reasonable degree of control can be achieved only by a highly skillful President. Here, as in other aspects of the American political system, powerful centrifugal forces complicate infinitely the art and process of governing. Only political leadership at the most effective level can overcome the splintering of authority, responsibility, and political power that characterizes American politics. Viewed in this perspective a high premium has been placed on the unifying influence of the President.

Organization and Reorganization

The organization of the executive branch is constantly changing. The *United States Government Organization Manual* is published annually, but is often already out of date when it comes off the press. As the federal government takes on new activities, a place must be made for them in the organization structure. For example, in 1958, Congress created the National Aeronautics and Space Administration to conduct space research and develop, test, and operate space vehicles for research purposes. In 1961, Congress established the Arms Control and Disarmament Agency to advise the President on arms controls and disarmament matters, including conduct of research on nuclear detection, reduction of the armed forces, and elimination of the danger of war by accident or miscalculation. The Equal Employment Opportunity Commission was established under the Civil Rights Act of 1964 to investigate complaints of discrimination in employment. The Economic Opportunity Act of 1964 established the Office of Economic Opportunity nominally within the executive office of the President.

In recent years there has been agitation to create several new Cabinet departments dealing with activities that many feel deserve high priority, such as science and technology, transportation, and urban affairs. Citizen groups interested in particular programs like to see them given the prestige of departmental status. And special interest groups prefer that programs that vitally affect them be assigned to agencies subject to their maximum influence.

Nor is adding to the number of government agencies the only way of reflecting changing needs in the organizational structure of government. Desires to reduce governmental costs and to ease the President's responsibility for over-all management of the executive branch are perhaps the best reasons for the continuing reexamination. Beginning in 1932, Congress passed several acts authorizing the President to improve the efficiency of the executive branch by means of reorganization. Presidents have often appointed commissions to study the problem and to recommend improvements. The President's Committee on Administrative Management reported in 1937; another, the Commission on Organization of the Executive Branch of the Government, popularly known as the Hoover Commission, in 1949; and a third, also headed by former President Herbert Hoover, completed its work in 1955. As a result of these and other studies, some improvements have been made, and there is general agreement about other changes that would ease the President's managerial tasks and improve the operations of the executive branch.

Most students of these problems agree that three principal weaknesses should be corrected. First, the President is expected to supervise directly and personally too many people. He is responsible for organizations ranging in importance from the Department of Defense to the Indian Claims Commission. Second, Congress has by statute given many agencies some degree of independence from the President. Third, Congress has often weakened the President's power by specifying the way in which the authority of subordinate executive officials must be exercised.

Increasing the efficiency of the President, however, rarely ranks high on the scale of values for which senior congressmen work. Jealous of their own prerogatives and fearful of executive power that they cannot dominate, these leaders tend to suspect that a President who seeks reorganization of the executive branch is interested in increasing his own power. President Hoover's sweeping reorganization plan was rejected by Congress; charges of dictatorship greeted President Roosevelt's support of the recommendations of his Committee on Administrative Management; and some of President Truman's proposals were turned down for this reason. Moreover, government bureaus and the interest groups that work with them develop vested interests in the existing organization and procedures and oppose reorganization proposals.

In recent years reorganizations have been authorized under the terms of the Reorganization Act of 1949, which grew out of the recommendations of the first Hoover Commission. Under this act the President may submit a reorganization plan to Congress involving a shift of an agency from one department to another or a regrouping of functions within a department or agency. If Congress does not take negative action within sixty days, the plan goes into effect. A simple majority of either the House or the Senate is sufficient to vote a reorganization plan. In the two decades since 1949 over 80 plans were submitted by Presidents, three-fourths of which were accepted by Congress.

EXECUTIVES FOR GOVERNMENT

Political Executives

For decades the system by which the federal government recruits and retains executives to manage federal agencies and offices has remained more or less the same. The system draws on two groups. There are 5000 or more experienced career executives with permanent civil service status who serve as government executives through changes of party control in the President's administration. They are professional administrators providing expert knowledge not only about specific programs but also about the complexities of the political environment. Above this relatively permanent body of career executives are about 500 presidential appointees, or political executives.

The 500 top political executives include the secretaries and assistant secretaries of departments, agency heads and their deputies, heads and members of boards and commissions, and chiefs and directors of major bureaus, divisions, and services. These men and women bear the brunt of translating the aims and philosophy of the administration into operating programs.

The posts occupied by these top political and civilian career executives in federal administration tend to fall into three groups roughly equal in number. About one third serve as agency heads, bureau chiefs, and office and division directors and are responsible for a specific governmental program or operation. Another third are supporting staff specialists, officials who serve as deputies or executive assistants to program heads or who provide managerial services in budgeting, fiscal operations, personnel, management analysis, and general administration. And finally, about a third provide professional services. Typically, they are experts in professional or technical areas—lawyers, economists, physicists, marine biologists.

There are about 200 top federal executive positions as secretaries, undersecretaries, assistant secretaries, and general counsels of the cabinet and military departments; as commissioners of the independent regulatory commissions; and as administrators and deputy administrators of the larger, single-headed agencies.[24] Normally these top political executives serve only one administration. They have come primarily from urban backgrounds and especially from eastern sections of the United States. As a group they are well educated and about 48 years old when they take up their initial political appointments. These executives have mostly been government officials, lawyers, and business men; a few are educators; even fewer are scientists and engineers. While evaluations of performance are hazardous and impressionistic, executives with some previous government service have been more effective than those coming exclusively from the private sector.[25]

On the average these executives stay in their jobs for only two to three years (other than regulatory commissioners, whose median service is longer). Short tenure can be traced to such factors as crushing work load, administrative frustrations, poor congressional relations, difficulties with news media, family problems, fear of loss of promotional prospects and fringe benefits in their interrupted private careers, and salary problems. "The short tenure of many subcabinet officers creates serious obstacles to effective political leadership in federal agencies."[26]

Obstacles to Executive Recruitment

It is not difficult to account for the federal government's disadvantage in obtaining and retaining a fair share of the best executive talent. Opportunities for executives outside government have been plentiful in recent years. Although government salaries at lower and middle levels of employment compare favorably with those in private business, government can never expect to compete with private business in terms of salaries for executives. Its personnel program must of necessity be based on a recognition of this fact of public life. Moreover, the environment of government is so different from that of the business world that there is little or nothing in nongovernmental work that prepares a person for executive work in government. Above all, it is the public nature of the government's business that differentiates it so clearly from nongovernmental enterprise. As the promoter of the public interest, government must be staffed by executives whose perspective is broader than that of a person in private employment. Cost efficiency is just as important to government as it is to a business enterprise, but there is often no way of measuring in monetary terms the value of governmental outputs. It is not enough to say that attacks on poverty, crime, or environmental pollution increase the gross national product or national income level by so many dollars. Equally, and sometimes far more important, are such benefits as improved morale, greater commitment to the political system, and more complete enjoyment of freedom. Computing tangibles is difficult enough; including intangibles in decision-making multiplies work and vulnerability to public criticism from those who would weigh such values on a different scale.

The government official's work is public in another sense of the word. Virtually nothing he does is free from criticism and investigation in Congress, in the press, and over television. Government executives are accountable publicly for what they do or fail to do. Yet Congress has drastically limited the authority of executives by restricting their freedom to organize their offices, hire and fire employees, spend public funds, purchase supplies, and develop new procedures and methods of carrying on their activities. Executives serving temporarily in Washington are usually impressed with—and often oppressed by—the restrictions on their power compared with their former employment.

One overriding consequence of the size of the governmental establishment is that important matters are rarely the concern of a single agency. As a result, a government executive seldom has final authority to handle matters without consulting a host of other officials with different and often competing interests. A related consequence is a continuing need to provide a variety of coordinating devices to mesh the activities and programs of federal agencies. Former Secretary of the Treasury George Humphrey[27] found the interpenetration of government activities to be the most distinctive characteristic of the executive branch:

> Government is vast and diverse, like a hundred businesses all grouped under one name, but the various businesses of government are not integrated nor even directly related in fields of activity; and in government the executive management must operate under a system of divided authority . . . when a government executive decides on a course of action not already established under law, he must first check with other agencies to make certain his proposal does not conflict with or duplicate something being done by somebody else. It is common in government, much too common, for several agencies to be working on different facets of the same activity. The avoidance of overlapping or conflict calls for numerous conferences, for painstaking study of laws and directives, for working out in tedious detail so that what one Cabinet officer does will not bump into what another is doing—or run counter to our interests and activities abroad. . . .
>
> Before coming to Washington, I had not understood why there were so many conferences in government, and so much delay. Now I do. Everything is more complex. . . .

Finally, among the many restraints that tend to deter executive recruitment are a number of statutes known as conflict-of-interest laws. These are discussed in Chapter 16.

Career Executives

Career executives are expected to serve different presidential administrations loyally without regard to party designations. But they cannot help becoming involved in policies and in political matters, for they provide expert political and substantive knowledge and experience that their temporary political chiefs often lack. Although political involvement runs counter to the principle of the neutral professional administrator—a central tenet of the civil service faith—the dual-personnel system often imposes a burden upon the careerist to guide his political superiors through the treacherous jungles and bypaths of Washington politics. The difference between a skillful career executive and an inadequate one is often the former's ability to provide a substantial measure of political skill without becoming excessively involved in partisan politics. As a prominent management consultant[28] concluded:

> . . . large numbers of bureau chiefs cannot avoid making policy or carrying political responsibility. The real trick is to work conscientiously to promote the political policies of the party in power, both parties being presumed to operate in the public interest. Most career executives are better politicians—in the best sense of the word— than are their political supervisors. The present [Eisenhower] administration talked a good deal about a Washington housecleaning in the early months of the first term. While political appointees were changed, and properly, few significant changes were made in the career service. This is not a failure on the part of the administration but rather is evidence that a large number of permanent professionals must be in important posts if our government is to function.

Men who spend a lifetime on a particular job cannot help acquiring the attitude that they know more about the work and what ought to be done than a department head whose tenure ends with the President's. For this reason, department heads may find that their subordinates are not very responsive to new ideas and policies. In unusual cases, subordinate officers of a department may oppose policies that have the support of the department head, the President, and the general public.

Viewed in these terms, the relationships between civil servants and policy officers pose a basic issue. Progressive extension of the career service to important executive positions has created opportunities for competent men and women and thereby has improved the quality of government personnel. At the same time it has become difficult for department heads to inject new ideas and new policies. There is need for some adjustment of the patronage and merit systems that will preserve the values of the career service and maximize the responsiveness of the civil servant to political leadership.

One of the persisting characteristics of the federal career executive is the narrow range of federal programs in which he operates during his career. The doctrine of the federal merit system calls for the establishment of a career service for the entire federal government. In practice, however, a series of "closed" career groups anchored in particular bureaus has been created over the years, and new entrants are normally admitted only at junior levels. The career systems in the operating bureaus have, typically, placed the highest value on technical, specialized training. Consequently, the transferability of administrative skills from one program to another and job mobility across bureau and departmental lines have been minimized. As one expert observer[29] notes:

> . . . our traditional principles have not merely made it difficult to get for government a fair share of the top administrative talent, but they have forced the able men in government careers to concentrate their talents on the interests of particular bureaus or services. And so we have made it almost impossible for the career service to do its main job—which is to look ahead at the great problems that confront the nation, to devise and recommend policies to meet them, and to see that the various departments are effectively coordinated in carrying out the decisions of responsible political authorities.

One of the fundamental governmental needs for the future is administrative talent. Sources of talent within the government may be discovered by broadening the base of education and training and by deemphasizing technical and specialized expertness and parochial assignments within the service. Sources of talent outside the government can be tapped if more effective ways can be found to promote the interchange of talent between government and private employment.

SELECTED BIBLIOGRAPHY

Anderson, Patrick, *The President's Men* (Garden City, N.Y.: Doubleday, 1968). A discussion of the roles and strategies used by White House assistants; highly readable, journalistic introduction to presidential politics.

Bernstein, Marver H., *The Job of the Federal Executive* (Washington, D.C.: The Brookings Institution, 1958). Contains reflections of thoughtful federal executives, both career and political, about their experience in the complex setting of the federal government.

Clark, Keith C. and Laurence J. Legere, *The President and the Management of National Security* (New York: Frederick A. Praeger, 1969). Several contributors present a comprehensive description of how the machinery of national security has worked and what the problems are.

Cronin, Thomas E. and Sanford D. Greenberg, eds., *The Presidential Advisory System* (New York: Harper and Row, 1969). An excellent collection of articles with thoughtful comments by the editors.

Fenno, Richard F., Jr., *The President's Cabinet* (Cambridge, Mass.: Harvard University Press, 1959). The best account of the Cabinet as a political institution, pointing up its weaknesses as a policy making body.

Flash, Edward S., Jr., *Economic Advice and Presidential Leadership* (New York: Columbia University Press, 1965). A thorough analysis of the machinery of economic advice in three presidential administrations.

Jackson, Henry M., *National Security Council: Jackson Subcommittee Papers on Policymaking at the Presidential Level* (New York: Frederick A. Praeger, Inc., 1965). A valuable set of essays that describe and evaluate the National Security Council and discuss the general problems of presidential policy making on foreign and defense questions.

Karl, Barry Dean, *Executive Reorganization and Reform in the New Deal* (Cambridge, Mass.: Harvard University Press, 1963). The genesis and early steps toward administrative management in the federal government, 1900–1939.

Koenig, Louis W., *The Invisible Presidency* (New York: Holt, Rinehart and Winston, Inc., 1960). Interesting portraits of persons who have wielded "behind-the-scenes" power in the White House, including Hamilton, Van Buren, Loeb, House, Corcoran, Hopkins, and Adams.

Mann, Dean E., with Jameson W. Doig, *The Assistant Secretaries* (Washington, D.C.: The Brookings Institution, 1965). An interesting analysis of the problems and processes of appointment of political executives at the Assistant Secretary rank.

Polenberg, Richard, *Reorganizing Roosevelt's Government* (Cambridge, Mass.: Harvard University Press, 1966). An account of the controversy over executive organization in the period 1936–1939, with two chapters on the opposition of the bureaucracy to reorganization.

Price, Don K., *The Scientific Estate* (Cambridge, Mass.: Harvard University Press, 1965). An urbane discussion of key issues of public policy in science and the proper role of science advisers.

Sorensen, Theodore C., *Kennedy* (New York: Harper and Row, 1965). A general account, dealing with President Kennedy's entire political career, but emphasizing the organization and procedures used during his years in the White House.

Stanley, David T., Dean E. Mann, and Jameson W. Doig, *Men Who Govern* (Washington, D.C.: The Brookings Institution, 1967). An analysis of those who have served in recent administrations in political executive positions in the departments, agencies, and regulatory commissions of the federal government.

Sundquist, James, *Politics and Policy: The Eisenhower, Kennedy, and Johnson Years* (Washington, D.C.: The Brookings Institution, 1968). Six case studies of the contributions of key participants in the federal executive and legislative branches to the passage of major domestic policy measures.

Footnotes

[1] Kermit Gordon, "Reflections on Spending," in J. D. Montgomery and A. Smithies, eds., *Public Policy*, Vol. XV (Cambridge, Mass.: Harvard University Press, 1966), pp. 13–14.

[2] Theodore C. Sorensen, *Decision-Making in the White House* (New York: Columbia University Press, 1963), pp. 83–84.

[3] Richard E. Neustadt, *Presidential Power: The Politics of Leadership* (New York: John Wiley and Sons, Inc., 1960), p. 182.

[4] Thomas E. Cronin and Sanford D. Greenberg, *The Presidential Advisory System* (New York: Harper and Row, 1969), p. xix.

[5] Henry L. Stimson and McGeorge Bundy, *On Active Service* (New York: Harper and Row, 1947), p. 561.

[6] Richard F. Fenno, Jr., *The President's Cabinet* (Cambridge, Mass.: Harvard University Press, 1959), p. 155.

[7] Sorensen, p. 70.

[8] Sorensen, p. 71.

[9] See especially Richard E. Neustadt, "Approaches to Staffing the Presidency," *American Political Science Review*, Vol. LVII, Dec., 1963, pp. 855–863.

[10] Neustadt, p. 857.

[11] Office of the White House Press Secretary, Press Release, November 4, 1969.

[12] Kermit Gordon, "Reflections on Spending," in J. D. Montgomery and A. Smithies, eds., *Public Policy*, Vol. XV (Cambridge, Mass.: Harvard University Press, 1966), pp. 12–13.

[13] Walter W. Heller, *New Dimensions of Political Economy* (Cambridge, Mass.: Harvard University Press, 1966), p. 17.

[14] Heller, p. 54. For an examination of the economic advisory machinery in three different administrations, see Edward S. Flash, Jr., *Economic Advice and Presidential Leadership* (New York: Columbia University Press, 1965).

[15] Keith C. Clark and Laurence J. Legere, eds., *The President and the Management of National Security* (New York: Frederick A. Praeger, 1969), p. 5.

[16] Don K. Price, *The Scientific Estate* (Cambridge, Mass.: Harvard University Press, 1965), p. 261–262.

[17] See the discussion in Price, pp. 262–264, 268.

[18] Neustadt, "Approaches to Staffing the Presidency," *American Political Science Review*, Vol. LVII, Dec. 1963, pp. 857-858.

[19] Neustadt, p. 858.

[20] Alan L. Dean, "Advantages and Disadvantages in the Use of *Ad Hoc* Commissions for Policy Formulation," in Thomas E. Cronin and Sanford D. Greenberg, eds., *The Presidential Advisory System* (New York: Harper and Row, 1969).

[21] Cronin and Greenberg, p. xviii.

[22] Arthur M. Schlesinger, Jr., *The Age of Roosevelt*, Vol. 2, "The Coming of the New Deal," (Boston: Houghton Mifflin Company, 1959), p. 528.

[23] Harvey C. Mansfield, "Political Parties, Patronage, and the Federal Government Service," The American Assembly, *The Federal Government Service: Its Character, Prestige, and Problems* (1954), p. 106.

[24] Data in this section are taken from David T. Stanley, Dean E. Mann, and Jameson W. Doig, *Men Who Govern* (Washington, D.C.: The Brookings Institution, 1967).

[25] For corroboration of this view, see Dean E. Mann, with Jameson W. Doig, *The Assistant Secretaries: Problems and Processes of Appointment* (Washington, D.C.: The Brookings Institution, 1965), p. 247.

[26] Stanley, Mann, and Doig, p. 6.

[27] George M. Humphrey, with James C. Derieux, "It Looked Easier on the Outside," *Collier's*, 133 (April 2, 1954), p. 31.

[28] Richard M. Paget, "Strengthening the Federal Career Executive," *Public Administration Review*, 17 (Spring 1957), p. 93.

[29] Don K. Price, "Administrative Leadership," *Daedalus*, Journal of the American Academy of Arts and Sciences, 90 (1961), p. 752.

Chapter 16   The Federal Bureaucracy

THE RISING CURVE OF DEMANDS ON GOVERNMENT

The most striking fact about the federal government in the United States today is the breadth of its activities. They range from eradication of plant pests to international warfare; from control of food and drugs to regulation of railroad rates; from construction of flood-control and power dams to lunar landings; from sale of postage stamps to sale of nuclear energy; from protection of migratory birds to support of windows and orphans; from education of Indian children to stimulation of basic scientific research; from provision of old-age pensions to promotion and maintenance of a healthy economy; from negotiations with prime ministers to diplomatic representation in more than 100 countries.

The program of the federal government is so vast today that it entails expenditures of more than $200 billion each year, the services of about 3 million civilian employees, and the operation of 1800 departments, agencies, bureaus, commissions, corporations, sections, and units. Since 1965 it has cost more to pay interest on the national debt than it did to finance the toal cost of the federal government in 1940. The first Hoover Commission[1] reported in 1949 that "as a result of depression, war, new needs for defense, and our greater responsibilities abroad, the Federal Government has become the largest enterprise on earth." More than two decades later, the evidence supporting this judgment has mounted geometrically.

In the twentieth century and especially after 1930, as American society moved toward further concentration and centralization of private economic and political power, citizens have demanded more and more governmental action to moderate or alleviate their distress, promote their interests, or equalize their opportunities for personal development. The university student today is part of a generation demanding governmental action to combat poverty, eliminate racial discrimination, protect consumers against harmful substances in foods and drugs, reverse the process of urban decay, and reduce environmental pollution. Older people are more concerned with increasing the benefits of social security and improving the quality and availability of medical care at prices they can afford. Other citizens, concerned with violence in American society, are urging governmental action to curb crime, overhaul penal institutions, and improve the administration of law enforcement. And almost all groups call on the national government to devise an effective strategy to eliminate inflation.

These demands—some generated by private citizens, some by public officials, some by interest groups, and some by each of these means—have triggered responses in governmental policies. These responses have tended to be slow rather than rapid, reluctant more often than eager, and piecemeal rather than planned and integrated. In the context of impending catastrophe, obstacles to political action may be overcome more readily; but, as contemporary political experience demonstrates, demands for governmental services normally exceed the government's capacity to plan, organize, finance, and sustain the desired activities. When choices have to be made among competing demands, especially between claims of national security and the alleviation of human misery and poverty, political controversies intensify.

Any policy decision of national significance must have the support of a legislative majority. The President on occasion may set a course of action without the guidance of legislation, but before his action is very far advanced he generally must obtain legislative approval at least in the form of appropriations of funds. This makes interest groups work continuously to convince congressmen of their views of what should or should not be done. All these points of view—of officials in the three branches of government, of economic and professional interests as expressed through political parties and pressure groups, of state and local political leaders, and of the electorate as a whole—interact to influence the response of government.

POLITICS AND ADMINISTRATION

Any governmental activity involves policy decisions about what is to be done and administrative actions to carry out the decisions. These elements may at first seem distinct, but on closer scrutiny they merge. Are policy and administration distinct and separable or are they simply different aspects of the intricate processes of governing? Is it Congress *alone* that formulates policy, and the executive *alone* that administers policy? Is it the Cabinet secretary who decides, and the career civil servant who executes decisions?

Broadly speaking, there are two views. One is that policy-making and administration are different processes, and each should be the responsibility of a distinct group. Thus under a simplistic doctrine of separation of powers the characteristic function of Congress is the formulation of policy; the characteristic function of the executive is the administration of policy. The other view, and the one adopted here, is that policy and administration are so intermingled that those who exercise the powers of government inevitably make *and* execute policy. As we have seen in earlier chapters, in carrying out its role of policy maker. Congress intervenes in a host of ways in administrative matters.

Administrators also share in the law-making function. Most statutes deal with problems in general terms. They declare broad policies and leave it to administrators to formulate more precise rules to carry out those policies. Title VI of the Civil Rights Act of 1964, for instance, announces a sweeping principle: "No person in the United States shall, on the ground of race, color, or national origin, be excluded from participation in, be denied the benefits of, or be subjected to discrimination under any program or activity receiving Federal financial assistance." Converting that principle into a working set of guidelines has been a long, arduous, and continuing process,[2] and each step has been fraught with policy choices. The Johnson administration, somewhat surprised by its ability to persuade Congress to make such a radical pronouncement, at first took a narrow view of its authority. Gradually the Johnson administration moved more boldly to try to end racial segregation in southern states. The Nixon administration, however, was less certain of its course.

In dealing with each school district and deciding whether its plans to adjust the racial composition of its educational programs meet statutory and constitutional standards, federal officials have been making dozens of policy-decisions; and they have been forced to do so by the very terms of the 1964 Act. The Johnson administration's efforts at vigorous enforcement involved as many policy choices as did Nixon's decision to go slow. And the general language of Title VI made either approach legal.

The President is the most important policy maker in the federal government. But even within the executive branch he does not—indeed, cannot—act alone. As we saw in Chapters 14 and 15, he is surrounded by Cabinet officials, friends, personal aides, agency staffs, commissions, task forces, and advisory groups. The information and advice these people channel to him—or keep from him—help shape his perception of problems and his choice among possible solutions. Furthermore, there is a close limit to the number of problems with which he can concern himself and the details of which he can be aware, much less approve. Even department and agency heads must delegate authority to subordinates to cope with the myriad of problems they face every day.

Because of the number and complexity of public needs, popular demands, and unpopular problems, thousands of federal officials have to make decisions that determine whether a veteran gets educational benefits from the GI bill, whether a businessman is entitled to a tax deduction, whether a policeman will be prosecuted for allegedly abusing the civil rights of a member of a racial minority; whether a neighborhood group in a black ghetto can obtain public funds to help organize and express its interests in planning urban renewal or, to revert to an earlier example, whether a southern school district with a "freedom of choice" plan for pupil assignment can qualify for federal aid. Each of these decisions may be relatively unimportant in itself. It may represent only a tiny fraction of the work of the federal government and immediately concern only a few people; but in the aggregate the effect of these decisions is federal policy. Because the administrative process is a policy-making arena, it is also the scene of pressuring by interest groups and lobbying by senators and representatives who want to make sure that their constituent's interests are being protected and fostered.

BUREAUCRACY IN A DEMOCRACY

Politics and Policy Making

In the federal government, public services are typically manned by administrators and employees selected on the basis of specialized competence. They are neither elected nor appointed by elected officials. They are not removable because they differ with their political superiors on policy matters. More and more this appointive public service—the bureaucracy—makes or influences decisions and policies that have great significance. The principle and practice of a career public service based on merit and freed from politics create several interconnected problems. First, insofar as civil servants are freed from political control, they may also be cut loose from democratic control. Second, the more policy administrators make, the more difficult it is for them to avoid political involvement. Since merit in the civil service system refers to technical competence, usually along specialized lines, and not to policy preferences, the most knowledgeable of officials might be the least sympathetic to the policy aims of a particular administration.[3]

Policy preference need not be the same as political partisanship in the sense of party bias. Nor does policy preference necessarily mean personal ambition. As we shall discuss in the next section, a civil servant who accepts his function of assisting political executives can help governments run by whichever party is in office. And, if he accepts certain rules of fair play within the constitutional and legal system, he can both formulate and execute policy without running roughshod over the rights of private citizens.

Still, insofar as one party pursues goals that are more congruent with those of a civil servant, he is apt to be more enthusiastic and probably more effective under that party's rule. Furthermore, there is always the danger that he may try to substitute his own choices for those of his political superiors. Despite the availability of appeal of his decisions within his agency and of judicial review of administrative decisions, a bureaucrat may become arbitrary and oppressive. In short, as long as unanimity is absent and ambition, whether for self, for policy, or for agency, is present, none of these problems can be wholly solved; but their frequency can be reduced and their effects can be softened.

Responsibility

One means of mitigating the effects of bureaucratic independence is to establish lines of responsibility for the purpose of holding a public officer accountable for what he does or fails to do. This objective can be approached by defining clearly the duties of each officer, by providing staff and facilities to enable him to carry out his duties effectively, by establishing ways to evaluate his performance, and by utilizing sanctions to reward distinguished performance and to punish inadequate or unsatisfactory performance.

Every organization tries to create just such a network of accountability, but the size, number, and complexity of operating problems force political executives to rely so heavily on discretion at lower levels as to weaken their capacity to control or influence the organization. Even in the army or the Central Intelligence Agency, or for that matter in nongovernmental organizations such as the Jesuits, networks of formal responsibility are never fully effective: yet they can be of considerable utility in controlling the behavior of civil servants.

More important, however, than regulations imposed and enforced from above are an official's values, personal as well as professional, and his feelings and attitudes about the nature of his work and the character of his relationships with his superiors. These kinds of norms, although they are subjective, may be widely shared; and they may include many of the concepts contained in legal codes of responsibility. But, coming as they do from within a man rather than being imposed from outside, these subjective norms can exert moral pressure that is quite effective in moving an official to follow certain procedures or to defer to certain persons in authority.

The federal government has traditionally placed primary emphasis on the first meaning of responsibility. Over the years, the executive branch has developed rather effective arrangements to enforce legal accountability and to measure performance of assigned duties. But as we noted, the importance of subjective elements of responsibility has been increasing. Consequently, the values, ethical principles, and social orientations of civil servants have become more important in assessing their accountability.

A coherent, articulate, and strong internal sense of responsibility may create difficult problems both for administrators and for the federal government. Moral pressure may undermine as well as reinforce either legal norms of accountability or specific policy directives. And considerations of professional values and standards may point in a different direction from that mandated by a statute. Furthermore, the policy directives a bureaucrat may receive may leave unclear what his agency is supposed to do, or presidential choices may point to a very different course from those made by Congress. Interest group leaders may spin persuasive arguments for an administrator to exercise his legitimate—and perhaps just a bit of illegitimate—discretion to modify a decision. A powerful member of Congress may make it plain that if his wishes in a particular situation are not carried out, the agency's entire program may suffer.

However, the fact remains that a public service without a highly developed internalized sense of responsibility is apt to act like a chaotic collection of private interest groups. Because the Madisonian system fragments and diffuses power, Presidents have to bargain away much of their formal control over their executive departments. Because American leaders and American society have generally neglected to socialize public servants with a professional ethic of special allegiance to the President, the values of individual professional groups in the bureaucracy are tending toward dominance in the federal bureaucracy.

Representation

Representation is a word with many meanings. It can designate an agency relationship in which one person selects another to "act for" him. More broadly it can mean "typical of." In this sense we might say that a senate committee is representative of the party composition of the Senate as a whole. The word can also mean "standing for" or "chosen from." We might, for instance, speak of some members of a presidential committee as representative of industry or labor or of Catholics or Jews, even though there was no election of these "representatives" by the groups from which they were chosen.

Clearly federal bureaucrats are not directly representative of the country as a whole in the sense of being chosen agents. None of them is elected, and few are appointed directly by elected officials. In an indirect sense, however, one can talk of many federal offices as being representative in an agency sense of particular interests and groups. The Department of Agriculture, for example, was established to help farmers, and the principal function of the Department of Commerce has been to further business interests. Other organizations—the Interstate Commerce Commission, for instance—that were initially established to control particular groups, have often become their captives and act more as advocates than as regulators.

Representation in the agency sense, even in the indirect way it operates in the federal bureaucracy, creates great problems. If every federal bureau or commission were to function as an advocate of a particular set of interests, there could be no such thing as federal policy, only an inchoate glob of programs, each making separate demands on the budget and putting forth a myriad of uncoordinated and perhaps mutually contradictory policies. As we have noted so many times, the influence that individual congressmen and interest groups can bring to bear makes mass chaos a constant threat and some confusion a constant reality.

Bureaucratic representation in the sense of "typical of" also has a long tradition in American politics. It was at the core of the Jacksonian spoils system and of the opinion that prevailed until the latter part of the nineteenth century—and still occasionally recurs in odd places, such as Lenin's *State and Revolution*—that government jobs should not go to a professional elite but to ordinary persons lacking specialized skills. The Pendleton Act of 1883, which established a civil service system based on merit, carries through on this concept of representation by requiring a degree of geographical distribution of federal jobs in Washington.

Today the federal bureaucracy is both more and less "typical of" the American people than it was in the past. It is certainly far less representative in terms of education and specialized experience. Civil service positions above the level of clerk are usually staffed by men—and to a lesser extent by women—who are better educated and possess far more technical knowledge than the average citizen. On the other hand, the national bureaucracy is now much more likely to include a cross section of religious, ethnic, and racial groups than it did in earlier years.[4]

Until recently the federal government tended to fill its important civil service positions almost exclusively from among whites, and in the not too distant past predominantly from white Protestants. The political power of white ethnic groups has been reasonably effective in eliminating discrimination against their members, but chicanos, Puerto Ricans, Indians, orientals, and blacks have fared less well. In 1883, when the civil service system was established, the federal government employed only 620 blacks in the District of Columbia. Although that number slowly increased, Woodrow Wilson instituted segregated facilities for black and white federal employees. Actually the first significant moves toward minimizing racial discrimination in federal employment came during World War II, and it was not until the Kennedy administration that the national government made a concerted effort to recruit other than white career officials. By 1967, about 19 percent of the total federal work force were members of racial minorities, but the overwhelming proportion of these people held custodial and other low-level posts. In large part this imbalance is a result of past practices which either kept minority members out or discriminated against them when the time came for promotion or job assignments. To some extent, this situation is a consequence of the fact that minority groups in this country still receive on the average fewer years of education as well as a lower quality education than do whites. An additional contributing factor is that the informal working rules of the federal bureaucracy are grounded in the social mores of the white middle class, with whose nuances many members of minorities groups are not intimately familiar.

Over the long haul, increased representation in the sense of being "typical of" or even "chosen from" can increase the legitimacy of governmental action in the eyes of those segments of the community who see their "representatives" participating in policy making. On the other hand, if minority officials are only token concessions and do not fully share in making important decisions, then such representation is likely to generate only contempt for the system.

Participation in Decision Making

The traditional model of decision making in large-scale organizations, public and private, is that of a pyramid in which decisions are made only by those at the top. This authoritarian design has been under attack for many years for denying opportunities to lower echelon officers and employees to participate in managerial processes and decisions. The arguments in favor of more participation of employees are based more on preference and belief than on empirical research findings. It has been claimed that, in participative management, decisions will be better because more views and knowledge will be contributed; morale will be raised because people are happier with decisions they have helped make; the organization will be more effective and efficient; employees will have greater opportunities for self-fulfillment; employees will be developed more effectively for executive responsibility; and the principles of democracy will be served.

The goal of participation may be reached short of involving employees in making key decisions. It can take such forms as more permissive supervision; use of sensitivity training to encourage employees to be frank with one another and develop mutual understanding; more decentralization of decision making from Washington to field offices; or decision making by groups rather than by single executives.

A curious dilemma can come into play here. As a governmental agency becomes more internally democratic, it may become less democratic in terms of its relations to the larger political system. While policy making by administrators is inevitable, the broader policy decisions are supposed to be made by Congress and the President, not by various layers of civil servants who do not stand for election. Broad participation of civil servants in policy making may, therefore, conflict with the requirements of political democracy.

Citizen Participation and Bureaucratic Responsiveness

The Madisonian system of fragmented power creates special problems of bureaucratic responsiveness since Congress and the President may demand very different kinds of responses from administrators. But one aspect of the general problem of the responsiveness of the public service is shared in all countries—bureaucratic conservatism in the sense of fondness for following established procedures coupled with resistance to ideas and programs that strike out in new directions. In part this trait is a consequence of the number and magnitude of the problems with which public officials must deal. Smooth handling of such a mass of business requires a means of routinizing most work. If every case had to be decided by its own unique procedure, delays in the administrative process would quickly far outrun those in the judicial process.

Despite some miscarriages of justice, routinizing decisions can provide generally effective public services, but only so long as the problems are of the variety with which the procedures were designed to cope. When the problems are new and different, the situation is likely to change radically. In the United States, efforts to diminish poverty ran into just

Urban Renewal Giving the Poor Opportunity to Increase Power

By DAVID K. SHIPLER

More and more slum residents, almost all of them black or Puerto Rican, are exercising a power they have not had for long: the ability to block an urban renewal project in their neighborhoods, or shape its direction, or get a project where there was none before.

There was a time not many years ago when no huge crowds from the city's poverty areas turned up at City Hall to attend Planning Commission hearings, and even if they had the Planning Commission would probably not have listened.

Since the final years of the Wagner administration panels of local residents have attained the power to shape decisions about what kind of housing will go where, who will design and build and own it, and how tenants will be relocated from the tenements to be demolished.

Neighbors Organize

In the 53 urban renewal areas throughout the city, the influence of "the community," as these articulate and outspoken residents are known, flows from their own drive and the initiative of the Federal Government to involve them in the planning process. The city has implemented the Federal mandate.

Black pride and self-assurance have worked in combination with the Federal antipoverty program to produce a sophistication and a battery of neighborhood organizations that have enabled some slum dwellers to find the pressure points of city government.

They can stop projects when they want to, as they have hindered construction of the proposed state office building in Harlem.

At a recent meeting of the Planning Commission the long, wooden benches, like church pews, were crammed with people, and crowds filled the aisles and spilled into the corridor outside.

There was a hush as the people strained to listen to a woman from Harlem who was facing a row of commissioners seated behind a curved dais.

She began in low, angry tones, letting her voice rise finally to a shout. "We need your help." She jabbed a finger toward the dais. "But we'll accept it not on your terms. We'll accept it on our terms!". . .

"If you've planned it yourself, man, you're not going to burn it down," said a young man from Bedford-Stuyvesant. . . .

The city has retained final authority over decisions as it must when it uses Federal money. Washington mandates community participation, but warns against community control.

Stopping short of giving real control has created some suspicion, bitterness and frustration among residents. . . .

The city uses the terms "participation" and "partnership" to describe what officials believe as the proper role of communities. But these are loose words, some community leaders say, and their vagueness has allowed the system of planning to remain highly centralized, despite the community influence. . . .

There has been some movement toward structuring local power. The City Council enacted legislation several months ago requiring the Planning Commission to consult with local planning boards, which are appointed by the borough presidents, before acting on matters affecting their neighborhoods. The commission need not follow the local boards' advice, but it must listen.

Each of the three Model Cities neighborhoods — Central Brooklyn, Harlem-East Harlem and the South Bronx—makes its desires known to the city through an elected board, most of whose members are well-known names in antipoverty organizations, churches and businesses.

The Model Cities program is an attempt to focus government resources on a slum, not only to remake it physically but also to improve municipal services, create jobs and lift people out of poverty. . . .

Since the Model Cities committee decides which organizations are to get certain Federal funds, a conflict of interest question has been raised by the Department of Housing and Urban Development and the Lindsay administration. . . .

. . . In a recent study of antipoverty programs in a dozen cities, Dr. Kenneth B. Clark, a black psychologist who heads the Metropolitan Applied Research Center, concluded, "The poor serve as pawns in a struggle in which their interests are not the primary concern.

"The leaders talk in the name of the poor, and extensive funds are appropriated and spent in their name without direct concern for, or serious attempts at, involvement of the poor."

Such involvement, Dr. Clark said, is "either a sentimental gesture or another cynical exploitation of the poor, which the more sophisticated indigenous will exploit as another 'hustle.' ". . .

City officials contend that residents have never been told they would have the final say. But they believe the great gulf between the poor and the establishment, the deep suspicions about government, are being overcome, slowly.

© 1969 by The New York Times Company. Reprinted by permission.

such a series of large scale difficulties. Urban renewal, for instance, involved not merely physical planning of streets, highways, and buildings, functions bureaucrats could with relative ease, handle directly or indirectly through private agencies; also involved was a myriad of financial and psychological upheavals created by displacement of former slum dwellers. The bureaucracy had little experience in dealing with these kinds of issues; and, on the whole, the poor found officials of both public and private agencies rigid in their procedures, unsympathetic in their approaches, and sometimes openly hostile in their attitudes toward blacks.[5] Early emphasis on the purely physical aspects of planning led to widespread charges that urban renewal really meant only "urban removal," "slum relocation," or, where racial minorities were involved, "urban resegregation." Basically the poor did not know how to communicate effectively either with those who were administering the programs—sometimes did not know how to find out who was responsible— or with elected politicians. When they could express their ideas and opinions, they usually lacked the political power to make them stick.

By the early 1960s there was widespread concern among many federal officials as well as among outside observers and the poor themselves that such programs were tearing up lives and neighborhoods with scant regard for the interests or wishes of the people most immediately affected. Although it is unclear how seriously Congress took this concern,[6] the Economic Opportunity Act of 1964 commanded that community action programs carried out under the statute should be "developed, conducted, and administered with the maximum feasible participation of residents of the areas and members of the groups served." Similar provisions were placed in the Model Cities Act of 1966 and in other legislation passed during this period.

"Maximum feasible participation" has meant, in effect, that federal bureaucrats have had to help create political awareness and power among poor people so that officials could then be responsive to the interests of these people. So far the record of successes and failures has been mixed. Devising a system of representation of the poor in community action programs and model city neighborhood councils has been very difficult. Schemes calling for election of representatives have failed to arouse much interest. Community conventions and designation of community representatives have been tried without much success. Participants in organizing and operating community institutions have had an intensive learning experience. The process of community participation has sometimes disturbed the peace and attacked the organized political power of the community and has therefore led to efforts to eliminate or modify the statutory prescription. Has participation led to new bases of political power for the poor? In a few situations this may be the result, but the long term trend seems to suggest that it will not be an effective antidote to bureaucratic inertia and middle class bias.

SPECIAL OBLIGATIONS OF FEDERAL EMPLOYEES

As part of a larger effort to maintain the integrity of the merit system free from political involvement, to ensure that civil servants will be working for the United States rather than some other country, and to enhance the continuous and efficient operation of public functions, the federal government has imposed a series of special obligations on its employees. Four types of obligations are currently enforced:

1. Loyalty-security programs limit certain kinds of private behavior and associations that might possibly endanger the internal security of the government.

2. The Hatch Act regulates some of the partisan political activities of civil servants.

3. Statutes and administrative orders forbid strikes by public employees and, insofar as they are effective, limit the scope of collective bargaining about salary and conditions of work.

4. Statutes and administrative orders also prohibit certain activities that might cause a conflict of interest between the performance of an employee's official duties and his personal economic gain.

Loyalty-Security Programs

World War II and even more so the Cold War brought into sharp focus questions about the loyalty of government employees. The problem was an old one. To root out "Copperheads," Lincoln's administration had investigated federal employees and sometimes required special oaths of loyalty. But the matter, difficult enough in dealing with modern techniques of espionage, was exacerbated by Senator Joseph McCarthy's charges that, because of alleged treason among presidential advisers and top State Department officials, the United States had surrendered eastern Europe to Soviet control and China to communism. This emotionally laden argument provided a facile explanation to a bewildering set of foreign policy problems and helped start a witch hunt to rid the government of any fool, homosexual, or traitor who dared to assert that Chinese and Russian interests were very different or that the United States might peacefully coexist with both.

Even before Joseph McCarthy launched his crusade, President Truman had begun a comprehensive loyalty program which subjected the bulk of federal employees to investigations to determine their stability, vulnerability to blackmail, and orthodoxy of their political affiliations. Initially the program raised very serious problems of civil liberties; but, as hysteria subsided and judicial decisions and administrative orders brought about procedural reforms, major deprivations of liberty decreased markedly, although they by no means ceased.

Among the more onerous security restrictions has been the loyalty oath; a requirement that prospective employees not only swear to support the Constitution but also avow that they are not Communists, fascists, or subversive persons. Some state oaths have been so all-inclusive in their efforts to purge Communists that a literal reading of their terms would have excluded from government service anyone who fought against Nazi Germany.

Loyalty oaths have been under attack by the courts since 1961. The Supreme Court[7] has come down hard against state loyalty oaths, but it has followed a more complex course in deciding cases involving federal procedures. Actually the Supreme Court has invoked many grounds to outlaw oaths, including the charge that they are bills of attainder (legislative acts that punish without judicial trial), ex-post-facto laws (which impose punishments for acts that were lawful when committed), and the First Amendment (which protects free speech). In 1969 a U.S. district court declared the existing federal oath unconstitutional as an impairment of rights of free speech and association. The Department of Justice did not appeal the ruling, but the Civil Service Commission continued to require the oath for new employees. After several months, however, an official of the American Civil Liberties Union pointed out the oath's illegality; and, somewhat embarrassed, the Commission decided to drop the requirement rather than revise the wording of the oath. New and old employees who are being considered for positions that involve handling classified information, however, are still subject to rigorous security investigations.

Apart from constitutional issues, loyalty oaths have been opposed because of their use as devices to punish religious heretics in Spain and France, Catholics who sympathized with southern rebels after the Civil War, and federal employees under indiscriminate attack by reactionaries in the early 1950s. Many resent oaths because they rest on the assumption that the government can probe the inner workings of the mind. In practical terms, they fail because they do not deter disloyal persons from falsely affirming their loyalty.

Political Activity

The Hatch Political Activities Act of 1939 attempts to enhance the nonpartisan image of the civil service by forbidding most federal employees and state and local employees working in federally aided programs from using their "official authority or influence" to affect the outcome of an election, from taking part in "political management or in political campaigns," and from soliciting campaign contributions from fellow employees. These general prohibitions are supplemented by detailed regulations, allowing employees, for example, to express their political views freely in private but not from public platforms, and permitting them to display campaign stickers on their car bumpers but not on their coat lapels.

In 1967 a bipartisan commission[8] reviewed the operations of the Hatch Act and recommended a general easing of restrictions on the political activities of most federal workers but a tightening of provisions intended to protect employees from coercion. Seeing the crux of its assignment as the reconciling of constitutional freedom with controls against political excesses, it recommended that Congress permit public employees to express their opinions freely in private or in public on any political subject or candidate but prohibit them from engaging in partisan political fund raising, campaign activities while on duty, management of a political campaign even when off-duty, serving as an officer of a political organization at the city level or above, or acting as an official at any polling place. Congress had not acted on these recommendations by the end of 1970.

Unions in Public Employment

A third restraint on federal employees is a statutory—though as the Post Office and the Federal Aviation Administration learned in 1970, not necessarily an effective—denial of the right to strike. The heart of the problem is the potential conflict between the authority of political officials to set public policy and the right of citizens to governmental services, on the one hand, and, on the other, the right of public employees to bargain collectively with political officials over personnel policies and to disrupt or even halt government activity to further their private economic gain. A fundamental principle of the federal merit system has been that appointment and advancement in government employment shall be on the basis of individual merit, not by pressure of organized employees, and not on the basis of seniority. Another basic principle is that pay shall be set according to classification plans that relate pay to the skills and levels of responsibilities involved in certain kinds of work, and not by agreements negotiated in collective bargaining sessions with unions. Working conditions, such as hours of work and leave arrangements, are fixed by Congress or by executive officials under legislative standards, not by general agreements negotiated through collective bargaining as in private industry. A third principle is that grievances are to be handled by appeals to the governmental hierarchy under the supervision of the Civil Service Commission, not through union representation or arbitration.

Despite the hostility of all of these fundamental principles to unionism and collective bargaining, unions representing public employees have grown rapidly in recent years, during a time when they have not been enjoying significant growth in the private sector. In 1970 about one-third of all federal employees were union members. Most of these people were postal workers, though about a quarter held blue collar jobs in other departments and about 15 percent were white collar workers outside the Post Office Department.

In 1962, President Kennedy issued a pair of Executive Orders which laid down the general principles under which the federal government would deal with employee unions. These orders allow decentralized bargaining for unions of federal employees in individual agencies and departments under the general guidance of the Civil Service Commission. A union can win exclusive rights for all employees in an agency or department if a majority of the workers concerned vote for it. Excluded, however, from the scope of negotiable subjects are such matters as the mission of the agency, its budget, organizational structure, personnel assignments, and operating methods. Although the orders specifically stipulate that the government would withdraw union recognition if a strike were called, the Nixon administration did not invoke this provision in 1970 against the postal workers nor against the air controllers.

Despite blatant conflicts between unionism in the public service and principles of a merit system under a democratic government, unions of public employees will probably continue to grow in size and strength. Prohibitions of strikes will gradually erode, and voluntary arbitration will probably increase. It is also likely that unions and governmental agencies will tend to enter into contractual agreements to handle specific problems of employment and rely less on general legislative prescriptions. If these developments occur, there will be a critical need for a mediation or even an arbitration system to prevent crippling strikes that could paralyze the government and the country, and still maintain the power of elected officials.

Regulation of Conflicting Interests

By statute, executive order, and administrative regulation, Congress and the executive branch have established a fourth set of special obligations on federal employees that are designed to prevent and regulate conflicts of interest. The term "conflict of interest" has in this connection a limited meaning. It deals with two interests only: one is the interest of the government employee and the public in the proper administration of the employee's office; and the other is the employee's interest in his private economic affairs. A conflict of interest exists when these two interests clash, or appear to clash. The purpose of regulation is to prevent situations from arising in which the government employee may be tempted to resolve a conflict of interest to his own personal advantage rather than the government's. Regulation attempts to arrange affairs within a government office to prevent an employee from being placed in a position of handling a matter that involves his own personal interest. A simple example is a rule that an agent of the Internal Revenue Service shall not audit or process his own tax return.

The basic statute governing conflicts of interest of federal employees was enacted in 1962.[9] It is supplemented by a series of executive orders, one of which requires separate codes of conduct for each department and agency of the executive branch.[10] The principal section of the statute provides that a person shall not act for the government where his private interests are involved. The method of control is the requirement that an employee disqualify himself from participating in a transaction involving the government in which he has a substantial personal interest. A second injunction prohibits an employee from serving two masters, for example, by assisting others in transactions involving the government. A third prohibition runs against his receiving outside compensation for services performed by him for the government. And a fourth general rule prohibits gifts, favors, and gratuities to a government employee when he has reason to believe that the donor has business relations with the employee's agency or is seeking one or that the action will affect his official performance.

These rules of conduct are aimed at the regular, full-time employee and official. A less strict set of rules governs the behavior on the job of part-time, intermittent, and short-term persons employed by the government.

Supplementary rules promulgated by individual agencies are designed to deal with sensitive areas in agency employment where problems of conflicting interest might arise. Thus the Securities and Exchange Commission prohibits employees from speculating in the stock market; the Housing and Urban Development Department prohibits employees dealing with urban renewal and development matters from participating in any real estate transaction that may be connected with a matter that falls within the jurisdiction of the department; and the Department of Agriculture prohibits employees who have access to confidential data on the commodities markets from engaging in any financial transactions involving these commodities.

PROFESSIONALISM

One of the more important recent trends within the federal bureaucracy has been the growth of a narrowing kind of professionalism. Of necessity, the work of many upper level civil servants has become more specialized. As a result they tend to think of themselves first as engineers or economists and only secondarily as government officials. Professionalism of this kind can have significant psychological impact. It can shift concern away from supposedly critical matters such as furthering presidential policy to raising the prestige of a particular occupational grouping, from recruiting personnel for public service to regulating entrance into a specialized guild, from improving the quality and efficiency of federal programs to refining particular kinds of scientific knowledge. These characteristics of specialization and professionalization are widely shared in all upper echelons of American society and to some extent may be an inevitable byproduct of a technically advanced society. As Daniel Bell[11] has said, the dominant figures of the last century were entrepreneurs, men of broad vision, wide knowledge, and great imagination; in contrast, leadership of the new society rests with the intensively, narrowly trained technician—the engineer, the scientist, the psychologist—working for research laboratories and the universities.

The trend toward professionalism creates complex problems for the public service. Each profession attempts to stake out areas of activity in which members of the profession have exclusive operating rights. It works hard to develop career opportunities and higher salary scales for its members, and tries to toughen standards of education and of entry into the profession. And it tends to work toward a career system of employment with important security provisions for the protection of its members. From a democratic standpoint what is critical is that each profession tends to bring to an organization a special view of the agency's mission and its relation to the rest of the government. Narrow parochialism, no matter how erudite in any substantive field, is not a promising base for formulating policies that must simultaneously cope with a wide range of public problems. The old cliche that "experts should be on tap, not on top" has, if anything, become more appropriate as the problems of an industrial society have become more tightly intertwined. "The danger," Frederick Mosher[12] writes, "is that the development in the public service of the mid-century decades may be subtly, gradually, but profoundly moving the weight toward the partial, the corporate, the professional perspective and away from that of the general interest."

GOVERNMENT BY CONTRACT

Although increased professionalism is a hallmark of modern governmental administration, even a bureaucracy as large and diverse as that of the federal government cannot include a sufficient number of skilled experts in every field to carry on needed public programs. This has been especially true in the promotion of scientific and technological advancement. where the development of governmental responsibility has been rapid and unprecedented. Until World War II the scientific activities of the federal government were not based on a general policy but were developed in connection with specific operations, such as the activities of the Geological Survey and the testing and measurement activities of the National Bureau of Standards. As a result, governmental activities in science emphasized applied research and almost no support of basic research. The experience of World War II drastically altered government-science relations. Universities and industrial laboratories received public funds for the first time, and wholly new nongovernmental bodies working almost entirely on governmental projects were created.

The instrument for extending the government's partnership with the business and the university communities for basic scientific research and development has been the contract. The growth of contracting has indeed been one of the most striking changes in the federal government in recent years. From 60,000 to 80,000 contracts for research and development are processed each at the cost of billions of dollars. And since 1961, about 80 percent of all federal funds for research and development have been spent by non-governmental institutions under contract to the government.

Government by contract has developed without explicit policy guidance from Congress or the Presidency. The causes of this growth are clear. Contracting meets crucial needs of society without building up the personnel and physical resources of the government itself, stimulates private economic activity, avoids rigid civil service salary schedules, competes for scarce talent, and recognizes that many Americans prefer to work for non-governmental agencies.

The decentralized character of governmental activities in this field reflects what may be called the New Federalism. Just as the grant-in-aid system established new patterns of administration and provided a workable compromise between federal centralization and state autonomy in handling problems of national scope, so does the contractual scheme make possible dominant federal financing for scientific research without centralizing operations in Washington. Today the California Institute of Technology can undertake major responsibility for rocket research; the University of California for jet propulsion; the Institute of Defense Analyses for weapons system evaluation; and the Aerospace Corporation for space technology, while industrial giants like Union Carbide, DuPont, Monsanto, General Electric, and others build facilities to produce military hardware and carry out related research programs. Industrial corporations today maintain Air Force bombers and missile ranges under contract, universities administer technical asistance programs around the world, dozens of firms work with the National Aeronautics and Space Administration on manned lunar landings, and private research institutes prepare studies for executive and legislative bodies.[13]

The New Federalism of government contracting produces many benefits, including the obvious ones of flexibility in permitting use of technical experts and their facilities without putting them permanently on the national budget, of subsidizing the spiraling cost of higher education, and of helping maintain a steady flow of scientists into the economy. It is extraordinarily difficult to supervise such a vast, decentralized mass of expenditures, and the work is often so technical and so basic in nature that it is difficult even for experts to be sure of the value of the results. Probably much money is wasted, but it is impossible to prove that losses are outweighed by the important benefits that accrue. A more significant cost than financial uncertainty is the character of the relationships that may be built up between the contracting agencies of the federal government and the private institutions. There are two kinds of dangers here. One is that the contracting agencies, like some regulatory commissions, may be captured by the private institutions, serve as their advocates with Congress and the executive office of the President, and become mere conduits for public money rather than protectors of the public interest. Conversely there is the danger that such relationships may gradually shift the role of the university and the private researcher from that of preserving, creating, and transmitting knowledge to that of acting as the advocate of a particular governmental agency, political party, or public policy.

THE PERFORMANCE OF THE BUREAUCRACY

On the whole, the federal public service is headed by technically skilled, administratively able groups of career executives and specialists. As it inevitably must in a free and affluent society, government continues to suffer some competitive disadvantages with private industry in recruiting and retaining the most competent and imaginative officials. There are, however, enough energetic idealists who see federal service as an attractive opportunity to influence their country and enough men and women who perceive government work as providing more job security than private industry to keep the problem below the critical level.

The fundamental problems of the federal bureaucracy do not turn on personnel matters, but on issues of constitutional structure and professional values and practices. As we have pointed out here and in previous chapters, the fragmentation of power in the Madisonian system as well as the growing complexity of environmental problems allow interest groups and congressmen to push administrators into policy channels different from those charted by the President. Sometimes a department head is the innocent victim of a power struggle between Capitol Hill and the White House. Sometimes, however, he eagerly utilizes the help of friendly interest groups to play Congress off against the President or willingly allies himself with a congressional committee and a cluster of interest groups to ignore if not defy presidential wishes. A more strongly developed internalized sense of responsibility—of loyalty to a broad profession of public service—would do much more to enhance presidential influence over his subordinates than would tighter legal controls, though the latter remain important.

Even an administrator devoted to a military ideal of becoming an obedient subordinate of the President often faces a baffling difficulty. "Policy" frequently means "the decisions which he himself negotiates with other public executives. The broader guidelines that he needs are not available from oracle or priest or political boss, and often not even from the 'higher' levels of an increasingly nonhierarchical hierarchy." [14] Because of the complexity of public problems, because of the diffusion of power, because Presidents have had to bargain with congressmen, because congressmen have commonly been more sensitive to local constituency interests than to national needs, the administrator may find that if anyone is to govern it must be himself. If his perspective is broad, if his authority is vast, if his ability to coordinate with other agencies is great, then all will probably go reasonably well. But, generally speaking, only the President has this perspective and authority, and on important issues he may have had to give up the power to use his authority effectively. The end result may often be incoherent, incomplete, and conflicting mixes of policies and programs, arranged not as a symphony but as a cacophony.

SELECTED BIBLIOGRAPHY

Appleby, Paul, *Big Democracy* (New York: Alfred A. Knopf, 1945). Stimulating lectures on administrative problems of the federal government; just as fresh today as they were when originally published, by a distinguished public executive and academic administrator.

Association of the Bar of the City of New York, *Conflict of Interest and Federal Service* (Cambridge, Mass.: Harvard University Press, 1960). An examination of problems of conflict of interest in the federal executive branch and a detailed program of reform, most of whose recommendations have been enacted into law.

Caiden, Gerald, *Administrative Reform* (Chicago, Ill.: Aldine Publishing Company, 1969). An incisive study of the phenomenon of reform of administration, public and private, and the obstacles in the path of reformers.

Dahl, Robert A., and Charles E. Lindblom, *Politics, Economics, and Welfare* (New York: Harper and Row, 1953). A major study that blends economic and political theory in interpreting the relations between political and economic forces in the formulation and administration of public policy.

Danhof, Clarence, *Government Contracting and Technological Change* (Washington, D.C.: The Brookings Institution, 1968). A detailed study of the origin, development, and problems of government contracting and its impact on technological change in the United States.

Fenno, Richard F., Jr., *The Power of the Purse: Appropriations Politics in Congress* (Boston: Little, Brown, and Company, 1966). The leading study of the activities of congressional committees on appropriations.

Gaus, John M., *Reflections on Public Administration* (University, Ala.: University of Alabama Press, 1947). Valuable insights into the forces influencing the development of administrative institutions in government.

Hyneman, Charles S., *Bureaucracy in a Democracy* (New York: Harper and Bros., 1950). A detailed examination of processes by which the bureaucracy is subject to democratic control, together with thoughtful chapters on the role of department heads as political executives.

Lyons, Gene M., *The Uneasy Partnership* (New York: Russell Sage Foundation, 1969). Problems in the relationships between the social sciences and the federal government and federal policies affecting social science.

Mosher, Frederick C., *Democracy and the Public Service* (New York: Oxford University Press, 1968). Philosophical and ideological trends in the growth of public employment, with emphasis on the growth of professionalism and the role of unions of public employees in the public service.

Mosher, Frederick C., ed., *Governmental Reorganizations* (Indianapolis: Bobbs-Merrill, 1967). A collection of case studies of reorganizations in federal, state, and local governments in the U.S., together with a long essay by the editor focusing on the factor of employee participation in reorganizing attempts.

Redford, Emmette S., *Democracy in the Administrative State* (New York: Oxford University Press, 1969). Further studies in the forces that affect the democratic character of public officials and bureaucratic institutions.

Reagan, Michael D., *The Administration of Public Policy* (Glenview, Ill.: Scott, Foresman and Company, 1969). A description of the linkages between substance and process in the development and administration of public policy.

Rourke, Francis E., *Bureaucracy, Politics, and Public Policy* (Boston: Little, Brown and Company, 1969). A thoughtful treatment of the design and operation of the bureaucracy and its contribution to the formulation of public policy. Contains selected bibliography of relevant books and articles.

Sayre, Wallace S., ed., *The Federal Government Service*, 2nd ed. (Englewood Cliffs, N.J.: Prentice-Hall, 1965). Excellent essays on the politics of the federal personnel system.

Stein, Harold, ed., *Public Administration and Policy Development* (New York: Harcourt, Brace and Company, 1952). A pioneering collection of case studies in administrative action, with a seminal essay on public administration by the editor.

Van Riper, Paul, *History of the United States Civil Service* (New York: Row, Peterson, 1958). The standard history of the federal civil service system.

Wildavsky, Aaron, *The Politics of the Budgetary Process* (Boston, Mass.: Little, Brown and Company, 1964). A thorough study of the role of the Bureau of the Budget and other participants in the formulation of the President's budget.

Footnotes

[1] United States Commission on Organization of the Executive Branch of the Government, *Concluding Report* (Washington, D.C.: Government Printing Office, 1949), pp. 3–4.

[2] See especially Gary Orfield, *The Reconstruction of Southern Education: The Schools and the 1964 Civil Rights Act* (New York: John Wiley and Sons, Inc., 1969).

[3] For an interesting discussion of these general problems, see Frederick C. Mosher, *Democracy and the Public Service* (New York: Oxford University Press, 1968).

[4] For an interesting argument that the federal bureaucracy is actually more representative than Congress, see Norton Long, "Bureaucracy and Constitutionalism," reprinted in his book *The Polity* (Chicago, Ill.: Rand McNally and Company, 1962).

[5] See, for example, James L. Sundquist, "The End of the Experiment," in Sundquist, ed., *On Fighting Poverty: Perspectives from Experience* (New York: Basic Books, Inc., 1969).

[6] Adam Yarmolinsky, who was one of the drafters of the statute, says that the question of political control and resident power did not arise; "The Beginnings of OEO," in Sundquist, ed., *On Fighting Poverty*. John G. Wofford, an early administrator of OEO programs, says, however, that the OEO staff treated the formula of "maximum feasible participation" as "an attempt to deal with the condition of 'powerlessness' that characterized the poor." "The Politics of Local Responsibility," in Sundquist, pp. 79–80.

[7] Some cases are cited in Chap. 19.

[8] Commission on Political Activity of Government Personnel, *Report* (Washington, D.C.: Government Printing Office, December 1967).

[9] U.S.C. §§ 201–218 (1969).

[10] Executive Order No. 11,222, 3 C.F.R. at 591 (1968), issued May 8, 1965.

[11] Daniel Bell, "Note on the Post-Industrial Society," *The Public Interest*, 1 (Winter 1967), p. 27.

[12] Frederick C. Mosher, *Democracy and the Public Service* (New York: Oxford University Press, 1968), 210.

[13] For an analysis, see Clarence H. Danhof, *Government Contracting and Technological Change* (Washington, D.C.: The Brookings Institution, 1968).

[14] Harlan Cleveland, "The American Public Executive: New Functions, New Style, New Purpose," Theory and Practice of Public Administration, *The Annals*, Monograph No. 8 (October 1968), p. 174.

Part VI   The Judiciary

Supreme Court's Focus Is on Policy

By John P. Mackenzie
Washington Post Staff Writer

Accused hijacker Arthur G. Barkley is not the only one who thinks—incorrectly—that the United States Supreme Court is the place where all injustices must be corrected and every man has a right to a hearing.

Barkley, who broadcast his complaints about the high court's "runaround" on a tax matter over the radio of a commandeered airliner before his capture here last week, shares with many other Americans some basic misconceptions about the role of the court. Although few go so far as to demand $100 million in reparations, many people fail to realize that the Supreme Court sits to make judicial policy and often only incidentally to rectify errors.

"Many think the Supreme Court is the place to go whenever you have a pain," one justice has said privately. Other members of the court have complained publicly about the high volume of frivolous appeals and petitions laid on the court's doorstep.

Actually, the justices express more sympathy for persons like Barkley who file reams of paper without a lawyer's aid than they do for some lawyers, who should know better but who insist on wasting their clients' money by seeking relief in the highest court of all. Unlike the highest courts in many lands, the U.S. Supreme Court does not sit to make sure that every lower court decision is decided correctly. And while the court's members quarrel often about applying its rules to specific cases, they agree that the court's job is not even to rectify every outrage that occurs. Even serious miscarriages of justice may be ignored by the court unless they involve concrete violations of the Constitution and laws and a legal issue of widespread importance.

One lawyer whose petition was rejected years ago tells of encountering the late Justice Felix Frankfurter at a social gathering. Frankfurter remarked, a little out of turn, what a shocking thing the lower court had done to the lawyer's client.

When the lawyer, treading cautiously for fear of offending the justice, asked why his petition had been denied, Frankfurter replied, "Oh, my good fellow, that case would never come up again in a million years."

Congress has given the court the unusual power to deny a hearing to any petition from lower courts without stating a reason. As the current term draws to a close, nearly 4000 persons have had pleas rejected, most of them without being told exactly why, while perhaps one in 20 petitions results in a full-dress action with legal briefs, oral argument and a written decision. . . .

Rarely does the high court show collective concern for the plight of one individual unless his case is typical of a major legal problem. Only occasionally does a Clarence Gideon succeed in interesting the judges in his cause with a handwritten petition.

Gideon, convicted of burglary, won review of his case, the appointment of a top Washington lawyer named Abe Fortas and finally a new trial because of the issue he raised: the right to free legal counsel in criminal cases. Members of the court had been waiting for a case like Gideon's to re-examine and overturn a 20-year-old precedent and to rule, as it did in 1963, that every indigent accused of a serious crime is entitled to a lawyer.

For all its celebrated compassion for the underdog, the Supreme Court frequently insists it is not being soft-hearted. Once a man gets his case to the highest legal level he becomes, in the court's view, only a "chance beneficiary" if he wins.

In recent years the power to deny review for no reason has been wielded as vigorously as the equally awesome power to interpret the Constitution. When the famous Miranda confessions decision was handed down in 1966, hundreds of petitioners whose cases were similar to Ernesto Miranda's failed to benefit because the court held its new constitutional rule to apply only to future trials. This was done despite the fact that the losers could have been winners had the court only chosen their cases as the vehicles for deciding the issue at hand. Justice John Marshall Harlan has started to protest this arbitrariness without much success.

What matters to the court is the legal principle involved; the petitioner's main function is to provide the court with a live case or controversy to be used in setting judicial policy and trying to relate judicial decisions to the real world.

This does not mean that the justices, as humans, don't care what happens to the petitioners. It means that often in the nature of their task they can't afford to linger over legal disputes that concern only the parties, however seriously. . . .

© 1970 by The Washington Post. Reprinted by permission.

Chapter 17   The Judicial Process

THE NATURE OF LAW

Law is a magic word in our society. It conjures up mental pictures of demons of enforcement cracking truncheons against skulls as well as images of angels of sweet reason wafting principles of justice down upon men. These elements—coercion, principles, reason, and justice—are vital parts of any general working concept of law.[1] But so is politics. For law sets forth rules that reward some kinds of conduct and punish others. Disputes about law are typically disputes about societal goals, about rights and duties, and about allocations of valuable resources. Decisions about those matters are the products of a political process.

The exact mixture of the first four elements in a legal system are determined by political power, but all four must still be present for law to be operational. To seem to be, as well as actually to be, more than whim, law must be based on broad principles rather than *ad hoc* decisions. So, too, law must seem to be just. Physical force alone does not make law, otherwise a stick-up man would represent legal authority to his victim; but neither does justice alone make law. If it did—or more properly if all men visualized justice in the same way and had the character to follow that vision—then law, indeed all government, would be unnecessary. Obviously, however, in any modern community many views of justice compete, and a substantial portion of mankind often opts for immediate, selfish gain over claims of abstract justice.

For many of the same causes, reason, sweet or otherwise, cannot be equated with law. Logic is a many-edged sword, and one man's syllogism may be another man's fallacy. Moreover, reason, even where men follow it, is instrumental. That is, one can use it to deduce that, given Objective A, Course 1 brings swifter results and costs less than Course 2 or 3. But logic cannot "prove" that Objective A is worthwhile in itself or preferable to Objective B except again in terms of some higher objective. In any event, the strength of reason, like that of justice, is weakest when it runs counter to immediate self-interest. For many people in many situations, "I want" is primary. "I should want, given A, B, and C," is tediously irrelevant.

Because knowing what is just and reasonable does not inevitably lead to doing what is right, there must be some sort of sanction to help persuade men to do good, at least in the sense of respecting the rights of others and of society as a whole. In many small communities, ostracism may be a serious deterrent. In other societies, fear of retribution in the next world may function as an effective threat. These may also be important forces in a complex, modern society, but men have found a need for some form of physical sanctions as well. And here again the Madisonian dilemma we have been discussing in earlier chapters arises: How to give government enough power to control those who would violate the law and yet allow society to control the governors?

One of the attractive features of the concept of law is that the existence of a body of general rules not only makes individuals more secure in their relations with one another by providing a set of norms to govern behavior, but by being announced in advance these principles also limit, at least psychologically, the permissible choices of action by public officials. The notion of a constitution as a body of fundamental law binding on rulers is a concrete example of an effort to make specific the restrictions on officials who have coercive power. The effectiveness of those restrictions depends both on institutional arrangements and on cultural norms, among which, in circular fashion, law generally and the constitution in particular may function.

THE LAWMAKERS

Much of the history of political institutions can be seen as an attempt to find an arrangement that would provide an impartial set of umpires who could judge disputes between individuals but would themselves be controlled. In Western democracies this search has sometimes led to a now familiar division of labor among legislators, administrators, and judges. But, as we have seen, these divisions are hardly clear either in the abstract or in the tangled web of government. In the countries that trace their legal institutions to England, judges have often been lawmakers as much as have legislators. In fact, in England and the United States, judges made far more law than did legislators until well into the second half of the nineteenth century. In the last hundred years, more especially in the last forty, legislators have more and more been trying to formulate the general principles and policies needed to cope with society's problems. But although judges' power has been diminished, it is still important.

Administrators, too, participate in lawmaking. As experts they frequently testify before legislative committees, and many bills debated in Congress have been drafted by executive officials. In addition, like judges, administrators have the task of applying the general terms of statutes to specific situations. Again, like judges, they must sometimes fill in gaps in the law or decide whether—or how—to extend existing principles to new problems. Administrators may also have to confront the problems of constitutionality, for they, too, may be called on to enforce a statute or executive order that, in their judgment, violates the Constitution.

ANGLO-AMERICAN LAW

The Common Law

There are solid historical reasons why these functions of law-making, law-applying, and law-interpreting are so amalgamated in American politics. The roots of American law run deep into the British past, to a time when judges—if one can use the word in anything like its current sense—were royal officials and Parliament was basically a way for the king to raise taxes. These royal officials sat with the king's court at Westminster and also went around the country to settle disputes between citizens. Judges then decided disputes on the basis of what they found to be the "common" custom of the realm, rather than the customs of any particular town, county, or area. Undoubtedly, the judges' social prejudices and regional biases were important elements in deciding what was "common" and what was parochial practice. But rather early in this process, judges began following the rule of *stare decisis*, that is, adhering to previous decisions. In practice this meant that where judges encountered recurrent problems they would apply the same principles; thus the common law took on continuity both across space and time.

Equity

Through the centuries the common law developed as a judge-made, national system of rules covering most of the social and economic problems existing in English society. But that law also began to harden into a rather inflexible set of forms of action that enabled people to obtain relief in court only in standard situations. This rigidity prevented the common law courts from hearing cases that lay outside the fixed pattern. But the English social system was still evolving, and the old ways could not solve all the new problems. As aggrieved persons kept coming to the king for justice, his staff referred these cases to the royal chancellor. Gradually his office, the chancery, also developed into a court, separate from those of the common law, applying a different set of rules that came to be known as equity.

Equity acted as a force for reform in the British legal system. It operated by relatively informal procedures and, initially, chancery judges claimed to apply "natural justice" rather than fixed legal rules. But soon precedents took on much the same vitality there as in the common law. Procedures, too, quickly became fairly well set, although they have remained somewhat less formal than in the law courts. Perhaps the most important difference between equity and the common law lies in the objectives of the proceedings. The common law mainly provides compensatory justice; its chief remedy is money damages. Equity, on the other hand, offers preventive justice. It can order a defendant not to act, to stop acting, or to undo the effects of a former action.

The 1952 steel seizure supplies a good illustration of the operational differences between law and equity. When President Truman ordered the Secretary of Commerce to take over the steel mills to prevent a national strike, the mill managers could, under common law proceedings, have sued the United States, the Secretary, or both, for damages. It would have been difficult, however, to put a price tag on the loss that management would have suffered, and it was at least doubtful whether the United States or the Secretary could have been forced to pay any money at all. Equity offered a different remedy, an injunction (a court order) directing the Secretary to surrender control of the mills to their managers. Naturally, management sought an injunction.[2] In other situations, one might seek an injunction to forbid an official or a private citizen from taking a particular action; for example, a black might ask for an injunction prohibiting a public official from enforcing a literacy test for voting, or a home owner might ask a court to enjoin a builder from constructing an apartment house that would shut off his light.

Although in England courts of law and courts of equity were historically separate institutions, the American Congress in 1789 authorized federal judges to hear both common law and equity cases, a practice generally, although not universally, accepted today in the states. In the middle of the nineteenth century, the British also came around to the single court system.

Toward an Independent Judiciary

Over time, the personnel who staffed both the British common law and equity tribunals began to split off from the rest of the king's court. Although for centuries they retained some of their former status as executive officers and advisers—and despite folklore to the contrary still retain some of this status—these officials developed a new professional identity as judges rather than as administrators. By the early seventeenth century they could claim, as Lord Coke did against James I, a monopoly in interpreting the law. These were matters of slow development, however. It was not until 1701 that the Act of Settlement formally acknowledged that judges were to serve for good behavior during the reign of the king who appointed them, with removal in that time subject to Parliamentary approval. And it was not until 1760 that judicial commissions did not expire on the death of the king.

Despite its slowness, the notion of a judiciary independent of executive and legislature took a firm hold both in British and American culture. Royal abuse of this principle was one of the colonial grievances against George III listed in the Declaration of Independence. Today, even though about two thirds of American states provide for popular election of judges, the American political system still gives them a degree of independence greater than that enjoyed by any other class of officials.

POLITICAL EFFECTS OF JUDICIAL DECISIONS

The substantive content of the rules that judges, especially federal judges, apply can have an important impact on the political system. In deciding cases that appear to concern only two private citizens, a court may be mechanically applying an old rule, modifying that old rule, or creating a new one; that rule, old, new, or modified, if followed by other judges, can affect the rights of many other citizens, either because of lawsuits or because of out-of-court advice given by lawyers. More broadly, the interests involved in a case may be widely shared in society and perhaps even represented by organized interest groups. For instance, a case may revolve around the reciprocal rights and duties of management and labor unions, of manufacturers and their customers, or of corporation executives and stockholders. Here a decision—for instance, one holding a car manufacturer liable to its customers for injuries suffered as a result of inadequate safety features—can have an immediate effect on the lives and property of millions of people.

As we saw in Chapter 7, the right of interest groups to "lobby" in the courts is protected by the First and Fourteenth Amendments.[3] Organized groups can often bring suit themselves, and they can encourage and help others to do so. In addition a group can sometimes join litigation already in progress either directly as a party to the suit, or as an *amicus curiae* (a friend of the court). Facilitating group access to the courts is a technical procedure known as a "class action." Here a single person or a few people sue not only for themselves but for all other members of a clearly defined group sharing a common legal right. For example, a black man might file a class action for an order forbidding voting registrars to discriminate not only against him personally but also against all other qualified black voters.

At another level, a lawsuit, perhaps a criminal prosecution, may raise fundamental issues for the relationships between citizens and their government, for example, how free is free speech? What requirements must a prospective voter meet? A fourth kind of case may present questions about the relations among governmental officials: Who can regulate a particular kind of commercial activity? Only the federal government? Only the states? Or both? If both, under which circumstances does the one have to give way to the other?

Because of the significance of these cases to government officials and interest groups, a judicial decision, even by the Supreme Court, may not end the broader policy conflict surrounding the litigation. The American political process provides avenues to attack judicial decisions just as it does legislative or administrative action. Nevertheless, since it is difficult to uproot judicially endorsed principles, what judges say about general rules is important. If nothing else—and typically there is much else—judicial decisions help shape both the general principles and specific issues around which policy battles are fought.

JUDICIAL DISCRETION

Because of the policy implications of many of their decisions, judges are major political actors whether they choose to be or not. But judges are not automatons; they do not function as dispassionately as computers, searching a memory bank of prefabricated rules and then applying the relevant rule to a factual matrix. Judges frequently exercise choice among competing values and competing policies, and they are forced to do so by the nature of their office.

If the streams of the law—customs, previous judicial decisions, statutes, and constitutional clauses—were crystal clear and all ran in the same direction and if the needs of society were static, judges might be able to exercise only technical skills. None of these conditions obtains, however. Most basically the problems and the needs of American society are constantly changing. Law cannot be static and still provide workable rules for a living society. School segregation may have been a minor issue just after the Civil War when almost all of the newly freed slaves were totally illiterate; but a century or even perhaps a generation later, the problem was vastly different. So, too, employer-employee relations changed as factories came into existence. A hired man on the farm or an apprentice in a small shop might have fared quite well bargaining with his employer on an individual basis, but the creation of huge social institutions where thousands of people worked for a small group of managers posed an entirely different situation. A lone worker simply could not bargain with an Andrew Carnegie or a John D. Rockefeller, unless he could do so collectively through a union. Once unions became legitimate institutions, they in turn raised new social problems with which the law has had to cope.

"The law," Dean Roscoe Pound once observed, "must be stable, yet it cannot stand still." This dilemma of providing a known set of rules while still adapting those principles to cope with changing conditions makes judging an inherently creative process. Further, the sources of the law we mentioned rarely settle the difficult cases. Custom is usually only of marginal help when a new problem arises; indeed custom—the custom of dumping industrial wastes in the nearest stream, for instance, or of providing second-rate schools for second class citizens—may be the cause of the problem. Previous judicial decisions may not cover the situation or, what is more likely, may offer two or more mutually incompatible sets of guidelines. American courts have been functioning for such a long time that it takes an incompetent attorney not to be able to uncover a half dozen precedents to support almost any kind of claim.

Statutory and constitutional clauses may be of more help, but they do not necessarily settle the problem. The Constitution contains a wide variety of vague prohibitions and commands. The Fourth Amendment forbids not all searches and seizures but only those that are "unreasonable." Whether particular electronic methods of surveillance are reasonable or unreasonable is not a question that the men of the eighteenth century faced. The Fifth and Fourteenth Amendments forbid not the taking of "life, liberty, and property," but only their taking "without due process of law," a phrase that defies precise definition. It is also less than clear what the "cruel and unusual punishment" is that the Eighth Amendment outlaws.

Like constitutional clauses, important statutes also tend to be general. In part this is so because vagueness of language is one way of maximizing agreement, in part because there are inherent problems in using words, and in part because congressmen have at times wanted to encourage, or even force, judges to become creative partners in the legislative process. The Sherman Antitrust Act, for example, declares that it is illegal to "monopolize, or attempt to monopolize" trade in interstate commerce. But the statute offers no definition of what is meant by monopoly or monopolization. Senator Sherman[4] candidly sketched the problem for his fellow legislators:

> I admit that it is difficult to define in legal language the precise line between lawful and unlawful combinations. This must be left for the courts to determine in each particular case. All that we, as lawmakers, can do is to declare general principles, and we can be assured that the courts will apply them so as to carry out the meaning of the law. . . .

Even where Congress appears to speak precisely it may not do so consistently. Over a period of time Congress may enact a series of statutes with mutually incompatible provisions. Either because of oversight or inability to reach agreement, congressmen may not specify which provisions take precedence. The antitrust field provides another example. In one series of statutes Congress has apparently instructed federal agencies to attack restraints on trade and to foster free competition. In another series of laws (and in niggardly appropriations to run the enforcement agencies), Congress has seemingly been opposed to too much competition and to too vigorous federal attacks on monopolistic practices.

It is evident that judges frequently have considerable freedom in choosing among policy alternatives. It is also evident that judges, like other human beings, will be influenced in their choices by their own values. Judges will also be influenced by their perceptions of the nature of the problems. To a judge like William O. Douglas, who as a young man was almost killed by a railroad detective, police brutality may seem a more real danger than it does to a judge who was reared in a wealthy, socially prominent family.

Perception and values reinforce each other to the point that judges, like the rest of men, may well see much that they want to see or fear to see in particular controversies. A number of empirical analyses of the voting behavior of justices of the Supreme Court have found a strong relationship between those votes and the values the Justices endorse.[5] When he was still a judge on the Court of Appeals for New York, Benjamin Cardozo[6] summed the matter up in his usual sparsely eloquent style:

> My analysis of the judicial process comes then to this, and little more: logic, and history, and custom, and utility, and the accepted standards of right conduct, are the forces which singly or in combination shape the progress of the law. Which of these forces shall dominate in any case must depend largely upon the comparative importance or value of the social interest that will thereby be promoted or impaired. . . .
> If you ask how [the judge] is to know when one interest outweighs another, I can only answer that he must get his knowledge just as the legislator gets it; from experience and study and reflection; in brief from life itself.

One must be very careful in discussing judicial discretion. It is not the same as judicial license. It is true that judges do not fit the model of completely impartial arbiters; they have prejudices and predilections. Although they may keep most of them under control, they may be carried away by anger as Judge Julius Hoffman was at the trial of the "Chicago 7" in 1970. But the biases we have been talking about are not biases for or against particular persons but for or against certain principles and policies. If the ideal judge is one who is impartial between litigants, then most federal judges come reasonably close to this model. But judges are not intellectual eunuchs; they are not impartial between competing ideas. Before lamenting this fact, one should consider whether a judge who had no respect for the dignity of man or who could look with equanimity on genocide would be a fit official in a civilized society. The troublesome aspects about judicial discretion are how much a judge really can exercise and for what purposes he uses it.

THE FEDERAL COURT SYSTEM

Jurisdiction

One of the chief features of U.S. law is the existence of a dual court structure, one for the federal government and an entirely different set of tribunals run by each state government. Federalism itself does not require this double system. In Australia, Canada, and

India, state courts handle most judicial business with a national supreme court at the top of the hierarchy to further uniformity. The American Constitution permits a similar arrangement, but the First Congress opted in 1789 for a complete set of federal courts to parallel those of the states. Nevertheless, to the despair of litigants and the profit of lawyers, Congress has chosen to give federal courts exclusive jurisdiction in only some of the kinds of controversies—bankruptcy and patents, for instance—listed in Article III of the Constitution as being under national control. The official rationalization is that the workload of federal judges must be kept within manageable limits. Far more important has been the pressure of local officials to enhance their own power and that of state judges.

As a result of overlapping patterns of jurisdiction, a potential litigant often has a choice of courts in which to sue or be sued. Moreover, in matters of criminal law, a defendant may be subjected to prosecution in both state and federal courts, since by the same act—robbing a national bank, for example—he may violate the law of both governments. This, the Supreme Court has ruled, constitutes "double amenability" not double jeopardy; the resulting confusion, the Court[7] has said comfortingly, is a price of federalism. Some Justices have taken a more literal interpretation of the Fifth Amendment, but they have so far been in the minority.

Article III limits the jurisdiction of federal courts to certain kinds of disputes. Those courts can hear only "cases and controversies." These are narrow, technical terms and refer to situations in which opposing litigants have real interests that are in conflict and that conflict either has done or threatens immanent injury to a right that the law protects. The gist of this restriction is that federal cours are not supposed to give advisory opinions[8] or settle mere arguments, however interesting or even important. To these "case" requirements, judges have added so-called "standing to sue" rules. Basically these rules require that a person who invokes federal jurisdiction show that this particular clash of interests involves one of *his* legally protected rights, not a right of the public in general or of other persons,[9] and that the question raised is one that courts can answer and not one whose solution the Constitution leaves to Congress or the President.

Article III's actual listing of the matters under federal jurisdiction is quite simple. Litigation may be heard in courts of the United States either because of the nature of the controversy itself or because of the status of one of the parties to the suit:

A. Nature of the Controversy

If the case involves:

1. a question of the interpretation of the federal Constitution or any federal statute or treaty;

2. a question of admiralty or maritime law.

B. Status of the Parties

Where one of the parties is:

3. the United States government or one of its officers or agencies;

4. an ambassador, consul, or other representative of foreign government;

5. a state government suing:

   a. another state;

   b. a citizen of another state;

   c. a foreign government or its subjects;

6. a citizen of one state suing a citizen of another state;

7. an American citizen suing a foreign government or citizens of a foreign nation;

8. a citizen of one state suing a citizen of his own state where both claim land under grants of different states.

District Courts

Congress has created three tiers of federal courts plus several special courts. At the first or trial level are the district courts. In 1970 there were 90 of these, at least one in every state. At the next level are eleven U.S. courts of appeals to review decisions of the district courts, and at the top is the U.S. Supreme Court, which reviews decisions both of the courts of appeals and of state decisions on federal questions.

The bulk of federal judicial work is done at the trial level. All criminal and most civil cases start here, as do all suits in equity. More than 100,000 cases a year are filed in district courts, but a large share of that number are informally settled by the parties themselves without any action by the court. District judges conduct about 14,000 trials a year and dispose of another 14,000 civil cases by pretrial conferences. Except for relatively infrequent litigation requiring a special panel of three judges, these disputes are presided over by a single judge, although the court itself may have as many as 24 judges attached to it.

District judges are important public officials. In pretrial conferences they generally act as influential mediators and try to get the parties to reach a settlement between themselves. These actions are seldom appealed since the parties themselves agree to them. Even where a formal trial is held, less than a half will be appealed. Thus the district court's decision is not only the first, but more often than not the final judicial ruling in a case. This fact alone gives district judges considerable practical leeway.

Other factors widen that leeway. First, legal rules are no more clear when a district judge has to interpret them than when a Supreme Court Justice does. Indeed, they may be far less so, since, if the case presents a new problem, the Supreme Court has the advantage of having the district judge's solution. In addition, even where the Supreme Court has apparently spoken on a particular problem, the Justices may not have spoken clearly. Besides normal problems of communication, there are special political factors that operate to muddy meaning. Judges, like framers of constitutions and statutes, often have difficulty coming to full agreement. One popular way of compromising differences is to use vague phraseology and leave issues for future resolution. Supreme Court Justices may also take this course when they are simply unsure of what is the best solution, hoping to gain wisdom from the experience accumulated through the efforts of lower court judges to transform general pronouncements into operational rules. The generality of the Supreme Court's directives in the *School Segregation*[10] and early *Reapportionment* cases[11] was in part an attempt to learn by experience.

Whatever the cause, when a district judge is faced with an opaque pronouncement or if he senses that the Justices are about to change an old rule, he must exercise choice, not completely unfettered choice, but still choice. And his selection can shape public policy as well as public law. Even if his decision is appealed, the argument at the next level will be framed by his work.

Fact Finding

A second set of factors, involving determination of the facts of a case, also widen a trial judge's discretion. Unhappily for judges, they are seldom presented with questions about what rule to apply to a neatly outlined problem. Testimony about the facts of a situation is frequently even more conflicting than the rules the opposing parties endorse. Probably most lawsuits center on disputes of fact. Witnesses to the same act recall vividly divergent actions; experts often offer conflicting diagnoses of a defendant's mental health, financial condition, or social practices. Police brutality cases are among the most difficult to decide. The police swear great oaths they never touched the defendant while the defendant vows that he signed a confession only to escape being beaten to death.

Even where witnesses have nothing at stake, there is a real problem in trying to recall events that happened months or even years earlier. An appellate judge is reluctant to disturb a trial judge's or a jury's weighing of conflicting testimony. A witness's demeanor, his nervousness, confidence, dress, or mannerisms may strengthen or weaken his credibility, and an appellate judge never gets to see or hear witnesses. He has to depend on reading the trial record.

Trial courts perform an ancillary emotional function in settling disputes. They provide a forum in which disputants may angrily, although peacefully, attack each other. In the courtroom friendly witnesses are gently examined and hostile witnesses mercilessly cross-examined, and it is here opposing counsel make eloquent pleas to the judge, to the jury, and to the Deity for justice or mercy or revenge. This is an important function. "A day in court" has become a synonym for fair play and a fair chance. Against this background, such tactics of defendants during recent trials of Black Panthers or alleged riot leaders as shouting obscenities at the judge or witnesses threatens not only to disrupt formal processes of adjudication but to destroy the role of the trial as a substitute for brute force.

Trial by Jury

The judge's function narrows when a jury is used. In federal courts a litigant may ask for a jury trial in any common law case where the amount in dispute exceeds $20, just as a defendant in a federal criminal prosecution must be tried by jury unless both he and the prosecution waive the right. The jury takes over the task of fact finding, and the judge is supposed only to make sure that the trial follows regular procedures and to instruct the jury on the rules they should apply to the facts of the case. Yet a clear distinction between facts and law is frequently impossible. In deciding what evidence the jury can hear, the judge participates in fact finding; moreover, he is often allowed to comment to the jury on the weight he believes they should put on certain kinds of evidence. In turn, the jury in its deliberations probably often interprets or creates new legal rules to govern the case.

Although still numerous, jury trials are becoming less common both in the United States and England. In neither country, of course, are juries regularly used in equity cases. There is considerable debate whether the decrease in jury trials bodes good or bad for the legal system. Only two facts are really clear: (1) jury trials typically take much longer and so contribute to the ever growing burdens of administering justice; (2) juries

Chicago 7 Jurors Tell of Compromise

By JOHN KIFNER

Special to The New York Times

CHICAGO, Feb. 19—The verdict in the Chicago conspiracy trial was described today as a hard-fought compromise, with three of the women jurors holding out for acquittal of all seven defendants until a crucial conference in the Palmer House Hotel late Tuesday night.

Six women and two men wanted to convict all of the defendants on both counts of the Federal indictment, according to interviews with the jurors.

Another woman was said to have vacillated between the two groups.

The mediator who negotiated the compromise was the only young person on the jury, Kay Richards, a 23-year-old computer operator.

The jury found all seven defendants not guilty of conspiring to foment rioting at the 1968 Democratic National Convention and acquitted John R. Froines and Lee Weiner of teaching the use of incendiary devices.

David T. Dellinger, Rennie C. Davis, Thomas E. Hayden, Abbie Hoffman and Jerry C. Rubin were found guilty of violating the antiriot provisions of the Civil Rights Act of 1968. The specific counts against each involved speeches made before or during the convention.

Miss Richards told of her role as a mediator in a copyrighted article in this morning's Chicago Sun-Times.

"At first I was a hard-liner for finding all seven of them guilty on both counts," she said. "And then I went soft, I felt as a responsible juror. I had to come up with a solution. So I became the negotiator."

'Better Than Nothing'

Another juror, Mrs. Ruth Petersen, corroborated this account of the negotiations. She said "we'd still be there" if it had not been for Miss Richards's efforts.

The verdict, Mrs. Petersen said, "was better than nothing."

"Half a chicken is better than none at all. Most of us would have found all the defendants guilty on both counts," she said.

"But we didn't want a hung jury," Mrs. Petersen continued. "That would have been a waste of time. We had gone so long and we hated to see all that money gone and time wasted."

The frequently chaotic trial lasted four and a half months, and the jury returned its verdict at the beginning of its fifth day of deliberations.

The jury took three secret ballots when it began deliberations on Saturday, and it quickly became apparent that there were two opposing blocs.

"The point is, we were all anxious to go home," Miss Richards said. "And due to anxiety, one woman in the group of four fluctuated back and forth and would do whatever was decided in order to get home.

"But the way it ended Saturday night, all four were still saying that the seven were innocent of all the charges," she recalled.

The deadlock is said to have continued Sunday. Miss Richards said that on Monday she began to negotiate with the three women for a compromise.

She said that her efforts as mediator also included persuading the majority that there was not enough evidence to convict the seven men on the conspiracy charge and that the case had not been proved against Mr. Weiner and Mr. Froines.

On Monday and Tuesday nights, the jurors asked to be excused after dinner, and the negotiations between the two groups continued from separate rooms in the Palmer House, where the jurors were sequestered during most of the trial.

'Feelings High'

"Feelings were so high, with the two groups against each other, we just didn't feel at ease there in the jury room together," Miss Richards explained.

The compromise was finally reached late Tuesday night, the interviews indicated. The jurors reaffirmed the verdict by a voice vote when they returned to the jury room at 10 A.M. yesterday.

Mrs. Jean Fritz, a housewife who was widely believed to be sympathetic to the defendants, sat in the jury box biting her lip. Her voice was barely audible when the jury was polled on the verdict, and she was crying as she left for home in a marshal's car.

At her neat, white clapboard house in suburban Des Plaines this afternoon, a neighbor who answered the door said that Mrs. Fritz would not speak about the deliberations.

The five men each face a maximum penalty of five years in jail and a $10,000 fine in addition to the sentences they have already been given on contempt of court charges.

© 1970 by The New York Times Company. Reprinted by permission.

are much freer than judges in arriving at a judgment since they do not have to explain or justify their decisions. A reviewing court can never be sure why a jury decided as it did, whether it construed the facts one way and found for the plaintiff or whether it viewed the facts another way and decided that the law was bad and found for the plaintiff anyway. A trial judge or an appellate court can overturn a jury's decision only on a finding that its judgment could not have been based on the evidence presented—a most difficult conclusion to justify, though sometimes easy to suspect.

Even the facts about juries' use of their freedom are not clear—a fittingly ironic commentary on trial court procedures. Some judges and many losing lawyers have asserted that juries decide cases without regard for the legal rules that the judge has expounded to them. More recent and more systematic but still not necessarily conclusive studies of juries indicate that their decisions are usually closer to those of the judges who presided at the trials than most observers had previously thought. The most complete analysis indicates that judges and jurors agree in more than four out of five criminal cases.[12]

Courts of Appeals

Trial judges may make mistakes. More often losing litigants think that trial judges have erred. Even when judges have made no mistakes in a technical sense, different trial judges may have offered different solutions to the same kind of problem. Thus to provide greater certainty, to foster faith in the courts, and also to provide greater uniformity, most judicial systems have established a means for reviewing the judgments of trial courts. In Anglo-American law, to maintain an appeal a litigant normally has to show that the trial court either misconstrued the nature of the conflict, committed procedural errors, applied the wrong legal rules, or drew a palpably illogical conclusion from the evidence.

Generally speaking, an appellate court will not re-try the facts of a case, but the distinction between facts and law is as blurred at the appellate as at the trial level. An appellate judge frequently has to decide for himself whether congressional districts are as equal in population as they can be, or whether a business is mostly in local or interstate commerce. As the Supreme Court said in 1964, its duty to review was "not limited to the elaboration of constitutional principles; we must also in proper cases review the evidence to make certain that those principles have been constitutionally applied."[13]

The federal judicial system has two layers of appellate courts, the courts of appeals and the Supreme Court. Congress has divided the country into ten numbered circuits, each presided over by a Court of Appeals, and an eleventh circuit for the District of Columbia with its own Court of Appeals. In 1970, 97 judges staffed these courts, ranging in size from 3 in the first circuit (encompassing the states of Maine, New Hampshire, Massachusetts, Rhode Island, and the Commonwealth of Puerto Rico), to 15 in the fifth circuit, which included the states of Georgia, Florida, Alabama, Mississippi, Louisiana, Texas, and the territory of the Canal Zone). Circuit judges normally sit in panels of three to hear cases, but in rare and important instances they may all sit together—*en banc*—to hear a controversy.

As its name implies, a Court of Appeals hears only cases initially decided elsewhere; it does not conduct trials. A few kinds of decisions can be taken directly from a district court to the U. S. Supreme Court, but most litigation begun in federal district courts must first go to a Court of Appeals for review. In addition to decisions of district courts, a Court of Appeals may also review orders of certain federal administrative agencies, such as the Interstate Commerce Commission and the Federal Trade Commission.

The United States Supreme Court

The Constitution refers to a Supreme Court but leaves it to Congress to provide for the Court's size and organization and to establish its appellate jurisdiction. From time to time Congress has set the number of Justices at from five to ten, and changes in the Court's size, or attempts to change its size as in 1937, have usually been at least partially the result of partisan efforts to shift the direction of the Court's decisions. There is no inherent magic in the number nine, but since this has been the number of Justices since 1869, it has taken on a sanctity over the years. The Court's appellate jurisdiction has also been a frequent target of congressional attacks but has generally survived these assaults intact. The one significant exception occurred in 1868 when the Radical Republicans, fearing with good reason that the Justices would declare much of military Reconstruction unconstitutional, removed the Court's jurisdiction to hear an appeal in a case pending before it. The Justices dutifully declared they were then without authority to decide the controversy.[14]

The Supreme Court is almost exclusively an appellate tribunal. Article III does provide that the Court shall have original, that is, trial, jurisdiction where a state is a party or where an ambassador, consul, or other representative of a foreign nation is a party. These kinds of cases simply do not arise very often. Ambassadors and other representatives usually have immunity from suit, and it is considered bad policy for a diplomat to sue a citizen of the country to which he is posted. The Justices have interpreted the Eleventh Amendment to exclude suits for money damages by private citizens against their own states[15]; and both Congress and the Court have interpreted Article III as allowing cases falling under the Court's original jurisdiction to begin in other tribunals. As a practical matter, the Supreme Court exercises its original jurisdiction almost solely in suits between states and, less frequently, between a state and the federal government.

The procedure by which cases reach the Supreme Court under its appellate jurisdiction is technically complex both because of the dual stream of litigation coming from state and federal courts and because of the volume of those two streams. Generally speaking, cases reach the Supreme Court in one of three ways: certification, appeal, or certiorari. Judges of a U.S. court of appeals may "certify" to the Supreme Court a question of federal law in a case before them, a question that the judges feel is of such importance or difficulty that it should be resolved immediately by the highest tribunal in the country. This procedure is seldom used.

Appeal is more often resorted to in trying to obtain review. Under existing statutes a losing party may appeal his case to the Supreme Court when: (1) a federal court has declared a state law unconstitutional or has issued an injunction against the enforcement of an act of Congress; (2) the highest court of a state has declared a federal statute, executive order, or treaty unconstitutional; or (3) the highest court of a state has sustained the validity of a state law against a challenge that it violates the U.S. Constitution.

Cases under the third heading are the most numerous, and, while jurisdictional statutes appear to oblige the Supreme Court to hear nearly all of them, the Justices dismiss the overwhelming majority on the grounds that the constitutional challenges are "insubstantial."

The bulk of cases are brought to the Supreme Court by a writ of certiorari (from the Latin, "to be made more certain"). The losing party in a U.S. Court of Appeals or in the highest court of a state, if his claim involves a question of federal law, may petition the Supreme Court to review his case. Granting certiorari, that is, agreeing to hear the case, is strictly a matter of discretion. The Justices vote on whether or not to take each of these cases, four votes, one less than a majority, being necessary to accept the dispute. The Court now receives annually about 3000 such petitions from state supreme courts and from U.S. courts of appeals. The Justices usually consent to hear less than 200 of these.

Special Federal Courts

There are also several federal courts of special jurisdiction. The most important are: the Customs Court, the Court of Customs and Patent Appeals, the Court of Claims, and the Court of Military Appeals. The Customs Court hears appeals from the rulings of customs collectors concerning the appraisal of imported goods and the collection of import duties. The Court of Customs and Patent Appeals reviews the rulings of the Custom Court, hears appeals from some rulings of the Patent Office, and also reviews certain findings of the Tariff Commission about unfair practices in the import trade. The Court of Claims has jurisdiction over most cases involving suits against the United States for damages. The Court of Military Appeals, staffed by civilian judges, reviews court martial proceedings. Decisions of these courts are reviewable by the Supreme Court under much the same procedures as cases from other federal courts, although those of the Court of Military Appeals are usually more difficult to appeal.

JUDICIAL RECRUITMENT

The concept of the judicial office suffers from the same ambiguity inherent in the concept of law. On the one hand, judges have been described as "animate justice." On the other hand, they are government officials who possess considerable political power and, in the United States just as in other democratic nations that have adopted judicial review, they are selected by highly politicized processes. Periodically cries are raised to take judicial appointments "out of politics" and leave the recruitment of judges to bar associations. In practice this suggestion really means taking selection out of one kind of politics, where voters indirectly exercise some measure of control, and putting it into another, the politics of bar associations, where voters have no control.[16]

Historically the British monarch appointed judges and still officially does, although the Prime Minister and his cabinet, especially the Minister of Justice and the Lord Chancellor, make the actual choice. Older American practice tended toward election by state legislatures or nomination by the governor subject to legislative consent. At the end of the Revolutionary War, only Vermont provided for popular election of judges, and in

1832 only Michigan elected all of its judges. But the tides of Jacksonian democracy swept over the courts, and all states admitted to the union since 1846 provide for popular election of all or most judges, as do many of the older states. Federal judgeships, however, have remained appointive offices.

The status of judges in common law countries differs from that in European nations whose legal systems draw on the Roman law tradition. On the continent, judges form a distinct profession separate from the practicing bar. One usually enters the judiciary immediately after graduating from law school, having passed a special set of examinations, and perhaps having undergone additional training for the bench. Promotion and salary increases are regulated much as for other career civil servants. In contrast the Anglo-American tradition draws judges from among practicing lawyers, public officials who went to law school, and less frequently from law professors.[17] These judges seldom have any special training other than having once studied law; indeed, many minor judges may have had no legal education at all. Although differences in training, careers, and outlooks are still striking, some Roman law countries have been broadening their bases of judicial recruitment, especially for "constitutional courts" modeled on the U.S. Supreme Court. An interesting byproduct of this broadening is a tendency for the selection process to become increasingly politicized.

Federal Recruitment

The formal steps in filling vacancies on the federal bench are deceptively simple. The President nominates a candidate and the Senate confirms or rejects him. If confirmed he takes an oath of office and serves during good behavior at a salary that cannot be lowered.

The informal processes are far more complex and much more interesting. A campaign for appointment usually begins long before any particular vacancy occurs. Judgeships, state and federal, are marvelously rich pieces of patronage, "grand political plums," the late Senator Everett Dirksen once called them. It is not so much the money involved for, while federal judges are reasonably well compensated,[18] salaries are lower than what a successful practicing attorney usually earns. The critical factors are the power and prestige a judge commands. Many, perhaps most ambitious lawyers covet these rewards and begin early in their careers to try to achieve them by working hard and faithfully for political party organizations, public officials, or even by running for office themselves.

Before disparaging this ambition one must take a careful look at some of its effects. It may make judges appear less like high priests and more like public officials, but it is at least questionable whether this is bad for a democratic government. A second effect is that this ambition helps keep able, highly trained men in politics. A third effect is to provide a large pool of professionally qualified candidates from which both parties can draw candidates who have practical experience as well as technical knowledge.

The operation of this kind of ambition also provides appointing officials with a basis of prediction about performance. If a judge turns out to be incompetent or is corrupted by power, the country will suffer and the President and his party are likely to be punished at the polls. Thus, it is not imprudent for appointing officials to prefer harder evidence of a man's strength under fire than his own or his friends' assertions of steadfastness.

There is also the matter of a judge's basic political philosophy. A President would be a fool, or a diabolically clever man playing a very subtle double game, willingly to put on the bench a judge who would declare the administration's most cherished policies unconstitutional or interpret statutes to block the administration's goals. It may turn out, of course, that the President misjudges his man or has to choose among lesser evils, but where he has choice he will certainly opt for a judge whose constitutional philosophy is in accord with his own. This is one of the reasons why more than nine out of ten federal judges come from the same political party as the President who nominates them and why Presidents tend to pick men whose views have been tested. As Lincoln[19] said:

> We cannot ask a man what he will do [if appointed], and if we should, and he should answer us, we should despise him for it. Therefore we must take a man whose opinions are known.

Given the wide spectrum of views encompassed by the both political parties, a President is not always limited to his own party for "right thinking" men. A President may, as William Howard Taft, Warren G. Harding, Franklin D. Roosevelt, and Harry S. Truman did, put members of the other party on the bench to enhance an image of non-partisanship while hoping to obtain a judge favorably disposed toward his general politics. President Eisenhower[20] tried this tactic in 1956 when he appointed William J. Brennan· to the Supreme Court. That action may have helped the General gain support among Catholic and Independent votes in the 1956 election, but he was probably displeased by the Justice's liberal opinions. In his angry denunciation of senators who rejected the nomination of G. Harrold Carswell because they said he was a mediocrity with a racist background, President Nixon candidly stated the primary criterion that most Presidents have tried to apply in selecting judges: "First and foremost, they had to be men who shared my legal philosophy. . . ."

A President may also reward an opposition senator or congressman by naming one of his candidates to the bench, although a President or his staff rarely overtly bargains along the straight lines of "You support my bill and I'll nominate your man." But in passing out patronage few Presidents can consistently ignore the needs or wishes of those legislators on whom they depend. And, as will be recalled from earlier chapters, the President often has to rely on legislators from the opposition party to supply the critical votes for his program.

Nomination Process

Once a vacancy occurs in the federal judiciary, a complex and dramatic game begins. Unlike most American contests the objects of this competition is to get off the field and onto the bench. Candidates quickly mass the support they have been building up over the years, and prod bar associations, friendly interest groups, local politicos, and senators and even congressmen. Interest groups who are concerned about using the courts begin to support their own candidates or endorse or oppose those already active. Public officials join in, sometimes to make sure one of their people is selected or to win the post for themselves.

Most recent Presidents have delegated their authority in the nominating process to the Attorney General, who passes this authority down to the Deputy Attorney General. He, in turn, usually works through a small staff. The amount of leeway the President's agents have in their selection depends on the level of the judgeship. Since George Washington's time, senators have played a crucial—at times a dominant—part in naming district judges. If one of the senators from the state in which the vacancy occurs is from the President's party, senatorial courtesy gives him a great advantage. A senator cannot capriciously invoke this tradition to blackball any nominee, but he can come close to doing so. If both senators are from the President's party, his agents may gain leverage by playing one off against the other. But even where the two senators are both in the opposition party, the Deputy Attorney General's staff is well advised to listen to their views, although it is probable—and perfectly acceptable—that the local leaders in the President's party will carry more weight.

At the Court of Appeals level, the President has much more freedom. Every circuit includes at least three states—except, of course, for the District of Columbia circuit but the District has no senators—and while considerations of geographical representation do come into play, a senator cannot assert the kind of proprietary interest he can where the judgeship falls totally within his own state. At the Supreme Court level the President is least restricted, but as the unhappy experiences with the nomination in 1968 of Abe Fortas to be Chief Justice and Homer Thornberry, Clement Haynsworth, and G. Harrold Carswell to be Associate Justices in 1968, 1969, and 1970 show, the President is not completely free.

The Deputy Attorney General's staff has also usually begun some work before the vacancy occurs, and through their contacts the staff members have or quickly build up a list of possible candidates. Senators, congressmen, local leaders, interest group representatives, officials of other executive departments, and perhaps members of other presidential staffs will be in constant touch, suggesting, supporting, or condemning candidates. Incumbent judges may also be drawn into this process; indeed, they may inject themselves into it with gusto. During William Howard Taft's Chief Justiceship (1921–1930), almost any vacancy on the federal bench triggered a series of letters, telephone calls, and visits from the Big Chief to the Department of Justice or even to the White House. In fact, a judge may often have more accurate knowledge than most people of the technical competence of candidates and, from his own political experience, perhaps also of candidates' varying degrees of orthodoxy.

When the Deputy Attorney General's staff members have completed their list— and in the case of district judges that list invariably at minimum overlaps with those of the senators from the state—they ask the Federal Bureau of Investigation to conduct inquiries into the candidates' moral characters and professional reputations. At the same time the staff asks the American Bar Association's Standing Committee on Federal Judiciary to report on candidates' professional qualifications. This report rates candidates on a four-point scale: "Exceptionally well qualified," "Well qualified," "Qualified," "Not qualified."[21]

These investigations may screen out weak candidates but they rarely determine the winner. In the case of district and to a lesser extent circuit judgeships. the remaining names on the list cause continuing negotiation between the staff and the senator or senators. Even for a district judgeship, a senator cannot dictate the choice, unless he has been given that prerogative by the President in exchange for other considerations. A senator may be able to block almost any nominee, but, unless he can win the President's cooperation, he cannot get his own man nominated. On the other hand, without the senator's cooperation it is almost impossible for the President to get his man confirmed. Faced with this kind of stalemate, both sides usually agree to a negotiated peace.

Confirmation

The President announces the nomination by sending the candidate's name to the Senate, where the question is referred to the Committee on the Judiciary. The Committee chairman and his staff have usually long been in touch with the Deputy Attorney General and his staff and have done some preliminary investigations of their own. A member of the Justice Department staff usually sits down with the chairman and goes over the FBI report with him, but no other senator may see it. The ABA committee formally submits its evaluation to the committee. Meanwhile, the committee staff solicits the views of the senators from the nominee's state so the record will be clear, then sets a mutually convenient time for hearings. Because of the work that has preceded nomination, hearings on district or circuit court judgeships are generally dull recitations of virtue more appropriate to funeral eulogies.

In contrast, hearings on Supreme Court nominees are frequently dramatic performances. A few crackpots provide comic relief by explaining how the nominee's eating meat will ruin the morals of the nation, or his refusal to march against the United Nations spells the corruption of American youth. More seriously, some legal experts may offer searing critiques of his judicial philosophy while others present stirring panegyrics, and the debate may expand to such broad topics as the nature of the Union, the relationships between Congress and the courts, and the role of law in society. Committee members and other senators may join in the debate and praise or excoriate the nominee's career or political opinions, questioning him with the zeal of an ambitious district attorney cross-examining a notorious kidnapper. The 1968 hearings on Abe Fortas provide a vivid illustration of what can happen, as Senator J. Strom Thurmond of South Carolina thundered at the nominee: "Mallory—I want that word to ring in your ears—Mallory. . . . Mallory, a man who raped a woman, admitted his guilt, and the Supreme Court turned him loose on a technicality. . . . Can you as a Justice of the Supreme Court condone such a decision as that? I ask you to answer that question."[22] His ears and those of most people within a hundred yards ringing from the senator's shouting, Fortas did refuse to comment and exposed himself to hours of additional berating, reminiscent of the similar way in which Senator Joseph McCarthy had treated Justice William J. Brennan twelve years earlier.

After the hearings have been completed, the committee deliberates and votes on a recommendation to the Senate to confirm or reject the nominee. Both majority and minority members may file a report to accompany their recommendations. The question is then discussed on the Senate floor. Again the matter has usually been long settled for district and circuit judgeships. The suspense over the Haynsworth nomination in 1969 and that of Carswell in 1970 make those instances atypical, but it is not at all unusual for debates over the confirmation of Supreme Court nominees to be both angry and informed.

The nominations of Louis D. Brandeis, Charles Evans Hughes, John J. Parker, and Abe Fortas caused fights comparable to those over Haynsworth and Carswell.

At this stage lobbying is usually at a minimum since by this time the members of the opposition, if there is any, know they are beaten and content themselves with formal speeches. Where, however, the opposition has a chance, lobbying may become intense, with agents of the AFL-CIO, the National Association of Manufacturers, the NAACP, the American Bar Association, Justice Department officials, and members of the President's personal staff crossing each others' trails with promises, blandishments, and fresh evidence about the nominee and grass-roots reactions to him.

Retirement of Federal Judges

Judges on many state courts serve for specified terms, and many other countries have set ages for compulsory retirement from the bench. Article III of the Constitution, however, specifies that federal judges shall serve "during good behavior." Unhappily judges are subject to the same problems of ill health and old age as the rest of men, and may stay on the bench well past the time when they can function effectively. Justice Stephen Field, for example, cast the decisive vote to invalidate the income tax after his mental faculties had failed. He, like Justice Robert Grier before him and Justices Joseph McKenna and Oliver Wendell Holmes after him, was asked by his colleagues to give up his office.

Since impeachment is an inappropriate remedy for bad health, policy makers have sought other solutions. Many people have suggested a constitutional amendment setting a compulsory retirement age—seventy-five is a frequently mentioned figure—but Congress has never proposed such a change. More positively, Congress has enacted generous retirement provisions. A judge who reaches seventy and has had ten years of service may retire at full salary. If he is in ill health, both the age and length of service stipulations may be waived. Nevertheless, most judges do not retire at seventy. "It is extraordinary," Charles Evans Hughes[23] once remarked, "how reluctant aged judges are to retire. . . . They seem to be tenacious of the appearance of adequacy." Ironically, despite having publicly urged judicial retirement at seventy-five, Hughes himself stayed on the Supreme Court until he was seventy-nine.

It may turn out that Congress has unwittingly established a procedure to remove from service district and circuit judges who are no longer able to perform their duties. A federal statute provides that each judicial circuit should have a council composed of judges and members of the bar. The law authorizes this council to "make all necessary orders for the effective and expeditious administration of the business of the courts within its circuit." And in 1965 the judicial council of the tenth circuit ordered that a district judge accused of inefficiency should not hear any additional cases or decide cases already on his docket. The judge thus retained his office and salary but lost his authority.[24]

Federal Judges

The products of this process have generally been honest, competent, and politically knowledgeable public officials. Again, the sanction of punishment at the polls reinforces the moral imperatives the President, his assistants, and the senators bring to bear on such problems. To speak of judgeships as one form of patronage by no means implies that they are auctioned off to the most loyal party workers or parceled out to the opposition like green stamps. As one recent official said, "We feel that we owe certain people jobs but we do not feel that we owe them *specific* jobs."[25] Judgeships are very special kinds of jobs requiring special qualifications.

The uproar over Justice Abe Fortas and Judge Clement Haynsworth in 1969 actually indicates the high standards expected of judges. No one accused either jurist of dishonesty; the charges were rather that each had been insensitive to the nature of judicial office and had created an appearance of impropriety. Fortas had accepted a pension from a foundation established by a shady financier, Louis Wolfson; but when a case involving Wolfson came to the Supreme Court, Fortas disqualified himself from sitting in judgment. Haynsworth continued on the board of directors of a corporation after becoming a federal judge, participated in a decision involving a large customer of that corporation, and bought stock in a firm involved in litigation in his court *after* the case had been decided but *before* the decision had been announced. In both instances, Fortas' liberalism and Haynsworth's conservatism played an important role in galvanizing opposition.

In addition to being competent and honest, the typical federal judge has been a white, male, upper middle-class, highly educated Protestant, who is in middle to later life. Ethnic forces in American life make themselves felt in this part of politics, too, and there are many members of minority groups on the bench, although blacks and women—the latter a majority in American society—are grossly under-represented.

Perhaps more important than the ethnic or socio-economic background of judges is that they are almost all successful lawyers whose commitment to the existing system has been tested in the crucible of practical politics. Most of them are "establishment men" in the broadest sense of that term. Some, like Justice William O. Douglas, may be mavericks who relish tweaking the system, and many other jurists may be equally devoted to political, legal, and social reform, but they come almost exclusively from that group of people clustered just to the right and to the left of the political center. One would be hard put to identify federal judges from the radical right or radical left. This collective biographical fact may help account for what many observers have noted as the inherent conservatism of the bench. Judges may actively work for social change, but it is for change that preserves and perhaps perfects the existing system rather than creates a new system.

SELECTED BIBLIOGRAPHY

Cardozo, Benjamin N., *The Nature of the Judicial Process* (New Haven, Conn.: Yale University Press, 1921). An eloquent and insightful description of the problems of judicial decision making.

Carr, Robert K., *The Supreme Court and Judicial Review* (New York: Holt, Rinehart and Winston, Inc., 1942). A brief commentary on the role of the Court in judicial review of legislation and governmental action.

Danelski, David J., *A Supreme Court Justice is Appointed* (New York: Random House, 1964). A fascinating analysis of the events that led to the appointment of Pierce Butler to the Supreme Court.

Dolbeare, Kenneth M., *Trial Courts in Urban Politics* (New York: John Wiley and Sons, Inc., 1967). A path breaking study of the political roles of state trial courts.

Frank, Jerome, *Law and the Modern Mind* (New York: Brentano's, Inc., 1930). A brilliant and provocative analysis of the role of law in modern society.

Grossman, Joel B., *Lawyers and Judges: The ABA and the Politics of Judicial Selection* (New York: John Wiley and Sons, Inc., 1965). A case study of the efforts of a pressure group to influence federal judicial appointments.

Holmes, Oliver Wendell, *The Common Law* (Boston: Little, Brown and Company, 1881). An analysis of Anglo-American law by one of the most famous Supreme Court Justices.

Hurst, Willard, *The Growth of American Law: The Law Makers* (Boston: Little, Brown and Company, 1950). A penetrating history of the development of law in the United States, emphasizing the role of lawmaking agencies.

Jacob, Herbert, *Debtors in Court: The Consumption of Government Services* (Chicago: Rand McNally and Company, 1969). An investigation of the consequences flowing from efforts of debtors and creditors to use the courts—a broader and more useful book than the title implies.

Kalven, Harry, and Hans Zeisel, *The American Jury* (Boston: Little, Brown and Company, 1966). A fascinating empirical study of the work of juries and how their decisions differ from those of judges.

McWhinney, Edward, *Judicial Review*, 4th ed. (Toronto: University of Toronto Press, 1969). An excellent introduction to judicial review as it operates in seven countries.

Murphy, Walter F., and C. Herman Pritchett, *Courts, Judges, and Politics* (New York: Random House, Inc., 1961). An introduction to the judicial process in the United States.

Peltason, Jack W., *Federal Courts in the Political Process* (New York: Random House, Inc., 1955). A stimulating analysis of judges' involvement in American government.

Plucknett, T. F. T., *A Concise History of the Common Law*, 5th ed. (Boston: Little, Brown and Co., 1956). A scholarly but readable account of the development of English legal rules and institutions.

Watson, Richard A., and Rondal G. Downing, *The Politics of Bench and Bar* (New York: John Wiley and Sons, Inc., 1969). A close examination of the political maneuverings of lawyers and judges to influence judicial selection under a supposedly nonpartisan method of choice.

Footnotes

[1] For general discussions of the nature of law, see; H. L. A. Hart, *The Concept of Law* (Oxford: Oxford University Press, 1961), and Lon L. Fuller, *The Morality of Law* (New Haven, Conn.: Yale University Press, 1964).

[2] *Youngstown Sheet and Tube Co. v. Sawyer*, 343 U.S. 579 (1952).

[3] *NAACP v. Button*, 371 U.S. 415 (1963).

[4] *Congressional Record*, XXI, 2460.

[5] See especially the two books by C. Herman Pritchett, *The Roosevelt Court: A Study in Judicial Politics and Values 1937–1947* (New York: Crowell-Collier and Macmillan, 1948), and *Civil Liberties and the Vinson Court* (Chicago, Ill.: University of Chicago Press, 1954); and Glendon A. Schubert, *The Judicial Mind: Attitudes and Ideologies of Supreme Court Justices 1946–1963* (Evanston, Ill.: Northwestern University Press, 1965).

[6] Benjamin N. Cardozo, *The Nature of the Judicial Process* (New Haven, Conn.: Yale University Press, 1921), pp. 112–113.

[7] See *United States v. Lanza*, 260 U.S. 377 (1922); *Abbate v. United States*, 359 U.S. 187 (1959); and *Bartkus v. Illinois*, 359 U.S. 121 (1959).

[8] Informally and unofficially federal judges occasionally have given advisory opinions. For several examples, see Walter F. Murphy and C. Herman Pritchett, eds., *Courts, Judges, and Politics* (New York: Random House, 1961), Chapter 7. Some state courts are obliged to give advisory opinions when so requested by the governor or the legislature.

[9] The Supreme Court has relaxed this rule in some instances where it would be difficult for the individual whose rights were threatened or denied to bring suit. See, for example, *Pierce v. Society of Sisters*, 268 U.S. 510 (1925); and *Barrows v. Jackson*, 346 U.S. 249 (1953). A class action does not violate the standing rule because the person who brings the suit must show a real, personal interest and that that interest is shared by a definable group of other people as well.

[10] *Brown v. Board of Education*, 349 U.S. 294 (1955).

[11] *Baker v. Carr*, 369 U.S. 186 (1962).

[12] Harry Kalven and Hans Zeisel, *The American Jury* (Boston: Little, Brown and Company, 1966).

[13] *New York Times v. Sullivan*, 376 U.S. 254, 285 (1964).

[14] *Ex parte McCardle*, 7 Wallace 506 (1869).

[15] The Eleventh Amendment, however, does not prevent a citizen from seeking an injunction to prevent a state official from enforcing an allegedly unconstitutional law, nor from suing a state official for damages if his action violates federal law; neither does the Eleventh Amendment bar the federal government from prosecuting a state official for violating federal law. The basic case is *Ex parte Young*, 209 U.S. 123 (1908). These cases begin in the district courts, since the Supreme Court has ruled that they are technically not suits against a state.

[16] See Richard A. Watson and Rondal G. Downing, *The Politics of Bench and Bar: Judicial Selection under the Missouri Nonpartisan Court Plan* (New York: John Wiley and Sons, Inc., 1969).

[17] Migration often runs in the opposite direction in Roman Law countries. There a successful judge may be invited to become a university professor, a professionally more prestigious position than that of most judgeships.

[18] In 1968 Congress raised the salaries of federal judges so that district judges receive $40,000 annually, circuit judges $42,500, and Supreme Court Justices $60,000. The Chief Justice receives $62,500.

[19] Quoted in David M. Silver, *Lincoln's Supreme Court* (Urbana, Ill.: University of Illinois Press, 1956), p. 208.

[20] Since the Senate was not in session, the President gave Brennan a recess appointment that would have expired at the end of the next session of Congress. As soon as Congress reassembled, Eisenhower sent in Brennan's nomination for a regular appointment.

[21] The Nixon Administration did not submit the names of its first three Supreme Court nominees to the ABA committee until after the choice had been made; but, after the unhappy nominations of Judges Haynsworth and Carswell, the Attorney General decided he would consult with the ABA before announcing any future selections.

[22] U.S. Senate, Committee on the Judiciary, *Hearings on the Nomination of Abe Fortas to be Chief Justice of the United States*, Ninetieth Cong., 2d Sess., p. 191 (1968).

[23] Charles Evans Hughes, *The Supreme Court of the United States* (New York: Columbia University Press, 1928), p. 75.

[24] *Chandler v. Judicial Council*, 382 U.S. 1003 (1966), 398 U.S. 74 (1970).

[25] Quoted in Harold W. Chase, "Federal Judges: The Appointing Process," *Minnesota Law Review*, 51 (December 1966), p. 204. This is the most useful study yet made of federal judicial appointments.

Chapter 18   The Supreme Court at Work

DECISION-MAKING PROCEDURES

The United States Supreme Court building provides a fitting home for the magic and majesty that surround law. On the outside, the huge marble palace—modeled on the Parthenon at Athens—reflects the solidity and integrity of established legal rules. Inside, the long, cool corridors radiate the serenity of a temple of justice. From the first Monday in October until late June or early July the Justices meet here to hear and decide the mass of cases that lawyers and litigants feel should go to the highest court in the country. The issues directly involved are always legal, but the ramifications of those issues are frequently political.

The long summer vacation and the Court's practice of sitting for several weeks to hear cases and then recessing for several weeks to read, write, and reflect, combine to make the Justices' pace seem far more leisurely than it really is. The workload is staggering, and as much in self-pity as in jest the Justices have referred to themselves as forming "a chaingang."

Just before 10 A.M. on Mondays through Thursdays when the Court is in session, the Justices meet in the robing room behind the red veloured courtroom, exchange pleasantries, shake hands, and put on their long black robes. Precisely at 10 the curtains part and the Justices march in three dignified groups to take their places behind the great mahogany bench that dominates the small room. As they enter, the crier slams down his gavel and chants:

> The Honorable, the Chief Justice and Associate Justices of the Supreme Court of the United States!
> Oyez, oyez, oyez! All persons having business before the Honorable, the Supreme Court of the United States are admonished to draw near and give their attention, for the Court is now sitting. God save the United States and this Honorable Court.

A few administrative matters such as admission of new attorneys to the Supreme Court bar may consume the first minutes of time; then, if any decisions are ready to be announced, the Justices assigned the task of preparing the Court's opinions summarize the rulings and the reasons for them. The dissenters add short and sometimes caustic comments. With that done, the Chief Justice calls the first case. Probably months before, the Court had agreed to hear the controversy, and the burden of each side's contentions has already been stated and restated in carefully documented written arguments—briefs and reply briefs. Now each side has a chance at oral argument. Usually the Justices allot two hours or less to a case, though in extraordinarily important disputes, such as the *School Segregation* cases, they may allow several days. Counsel—morning clothes used to be required but now business suits predominate—stands at a lectern in front of the Justices in their high-backed leather chairs and begins, "Mr. Chief Justice, may it please the Court . . ." A white light on the lectern flashes when he has five minutes left; when a red light goes on, the lawyer stops, even in mid-sentence. The story is told that Chief Justice Charles Evans Hughes once called time on an attorney in the middle of the word "if."

Oral argument can be a difficult experience for a lawyer. The Justices may be bored by a tedious presentation and stare glumly at the ceiling, whisper and send notes to each other, or dispatch page boys to bring them law books. When he was Solicitor General, William Howard Taft complained that the Justices seemed to choose his time to speak as the best opportunity to catch up on their correspondence; few who were familiar with Taft's oratorical style could question the Justices' taste. Oliver Wendell Holmes used to sketch the outline of an attorney's probable argument and, if counsel appeared to be following a predictable course, catch a short nap.

The Justices prefer a Socratic dialogue to a lecture, and quiet, candid explanation to rhetoric. Questions, sometimes three and four at once, fly at counsel, as the Justices probe for clearer exposition of the facts in this particular dispute and for informed speculation on what the probable consequences of alternative solutions would be. The Justices can be ruthless in their pursuit of the truth—or the lawyer, if he annoys them. When he was Solicitor General before his appointment to the Court, Stanley Reed once fainted during oral argument, and many other attorneys have suffered obvious mental blackouts.

At noon the Justices recess for a half-hour's lunch, then go back into session until 2:30. On Fridays they meet in their conference room to discuss and vote on the cases they have just heard argued, and to decide what other cases to hear. These conferences are secret. Only the Justices may enter the room; any important messages brought to the door are taken by the junior Justice. Each member of the Court brings in with him a locked red leather book in which he records the votes of his colleagues on each of the cases. Some Justices, Frank Murphy and Harold Burton, for example, have taken notes of what was said during conference to guide themselves in writing opinions and perhaps to enlighten history. The Burton and Murphy papers show that conference discussion is usually informed, lively, and often long and heated. As at oral argument, the Justices are concerned about more than technical legal rules; they explore—and debate—with each other, as they did with counsel, the impact of their decisions on public policy. The Chief Justice speaks first, then the other Justices in order of seniority. Each Justice is supposed to be allowed to talk without interruption, but ideas—and sometimes tempers—flash. When the

Chief feels that further discussion would serve no useful purpose, he calls for a vote, and the Justices vote in reverse order of seniority.

If the Chief Justice is with the majority—and some Chief Justices followed John Marshall's tactic of taking advantage of their prerogative of voting last to join the majority—he assigns the job of writing the opinion of the Court either to himself or to one of the other majority Justices. If the Chief Justice is in the minority, the senior Associate Justice on the majority side appoints the opinion writer. That Justice circulates drafts to all of his colleagues, so that those in the majority may make suggestions for changes, and the minority Justices, if there are any, may have an opportunity to answer his arguments. The Justices typically do make suggestions for change—Oliver Wendell Holmes once complained that "the boys generally cut one of the genitals" from his opinions—and an opinion in an important case is likely to go through a half-dozen or more drafts. Each Justice may write his own opinion, dissenting or concurring, though again custom requires that he circulate it to all the Court and provide an opportunity to reply. It happens occasionally that a concurring or dissenting opinion will persuade other Justices to change their minds and end up as the opinion of the Court. A Justice is free to switch his vote up to the minute the decision is announced, and even after that if the loser petitions for a rehearing.

JUDICIAL POWER

In opposing ratification of the Constitution, one delegate to the Virginia convention complained of "the stupendous magnitude" of power conferred on the Supreme Court.[1] One can sense that power even in the quiet of the Supreme Court building, and American constitutional history makes the Virginia gentleman appear guilty of understatement. The scholarly attitude of the Justices notwithstanding, as they read briefs, listen to oral argument, and debate with one another, they are functioning as members of a coordinate branch of government. They have sometimes fully exploited their potential to influence not only immediate public policy, but also the long-range development of the political and social systems. John Marshall's nationalism, Stephen Field's classic economic liberalism, and Earl Warren's civil libertarianism have been dynamic forces shaping American society. Yet the Justices are not all-powerful. They operate from a strong political base and can wield sharp weapons, but they are also subject to many restrictions. Without understanding the sources and instruments of judicial power and the limitations on that power, one cannot begin to grasp the kinds of roles that the Supreme Court—indeed all courts—play in American government.

SOURCES OF JUDICIAL POWER

Legal Sources

Along with all other American judges, the Justices of the Supreme Court are the legitimate heirs of the English jurists who staffed the common law and equity courts, and as such have authority, recognized by custom, statute, and the Constitution, to adjudicate certain kinds of legal disputes. Like their British ancestors, American judges can also interpret acts of the legislature. As we saw in the preceding chapter, the multiplicity of legal rules and the generality of the language of many important statutes force judges to act as policy makers, and, as we also noted, the Constitution reinforces this push. By its own terms the Constitution is law, "the supreme law of the land," and, so the Justices have successfully claimed, is thus as subject to judicial interpretation as other kinds of law.

In practice, constitutional interpretation means judicial review, the authority to declare invalid the actions of other public officials. Yet that power is not mentioned in the Constitution itself. In several early cases the Justices apparently assumed they possessed authority to declare statutes unconstitutional,[2] but the first use of this authority came in 1803 in *Marbury v. Madison*.[3] The specific legal point involved was a narrow, technical one of jurisdiction; but, as so frequently happens, there were important political issues below the surface. Before going out of office the administration of President John Adams had persuaded the lame-duck Federalist Congress to create a number of new judgeships, which Adams filled up with deserving Federalists who might otherwise have been out of power and out of work. Some of these appointments were made so late that John Marshall, who saw no problem in serving as Adams' Secretary of State at the same time he was Chief Justice, did not have time to deliver them before the Jefferson administration took office. Jefferson refused to send out the remaining commissions, and William Marbury, a disappointed justice of the peace in the District of Columbia, went to law to gain his judgeship.

Marbury filed suit in the Supreme Court for an order directing James Madison, the new Secretary of State, to deliver the commission. Marbury claimed that the Judiciary Act of 1789 gave the Court original jurisdiction to issue a mandamus—an order to a public official to do his duty—in such a case. Marshall, who like many conservatives was fearful of the havoc a radical like Jefferson might wreak on the country, was determined to establish once and for all the character of judicial power. The Chief Justice put aside the easy course, which was to hold that the Act of 1789 did not give the Court original jurisdiction in this kind of case—which would have been a fair reading of the statute. Instead he took up the constitutional issue, and found a conflict between Article III's enumeration of the Court's original jurisdiction and that supposedly added by the Act of 1789.

Marshall's opinion was long but his reasoning was direct. First, he took advantage of the opportunity to write a biting 9,000-word indictment of Jefferson's administration, concluding that Marbury indeed had been wronged. The next question, Marshall said, was whether Marbury had sought the correct remedy, and the Chief Justice concluded he had not. The Act of 1789 was in conflict with the Constitution and thus invalid. At this point Marshall then deduced the principle of judicial review by means of a syllogism. Major premise: The Constitution is the supreme law. Minor premise: It is the function of judges to interpret the law, and they take an oath to support the Constitution. Conclusion: Courts must declare invalid any inferior law—for example, an Act of Congress—in conflict with the higher law, that is, the Constitution.

Marshall's logic is not invulnerable; it was attacked at the time by Jefferson and his supporters. It was castigated as an assertion of judicial supremacy and as an effort to retain Federalist control of government. The Constitution, critics noted, was different from ordinary law; it was a political document. As for the judicial oath, every office holder took a similar pledge to support the Constitution. Perhaps the most telling point was made by Senator Breckinridge of Virginia: "Is it not extraordinary," he asked,[4] "that if this high power was intended, it should nowhere appear [in the Constitution]?"

Marshall's decision angered the Jeffersonians, though as much because of his blasting attack on the administration as for his assertion of judicial review. In retaliation they impeached Justice Samuel Chase and came within a few votes of convicting him. Had they succeeded, Marshall would probably have been next; but they failed, and the principle of judicial review—next used by Marshall to declare invalid an executive order issued by President Adams,[5] a decision with which the Jeffersonians found it difficult to quarrel—gradually became part of the American political tradition.

While no one today seriously questions the legitimacy of judicial review itself, just how far a Supreme Court decision obligates coordinate and coequal branches of the federal government is still an unsettled question. The line between judicial review and judicial supremacy is not at all distinct. It is improbable that many people would deny judges' supremacy over the kinds of courtroom procedures covered by Article III of the Constitution. For instance, even some of those who have attacked judicial review have acknowledged that were Congress to provide for a treason conviction on the testimony of one witness rather than two as Article III commands, the Court would be justified in ignoring the statute. There would probably be little opposition to a somewhat broader judicial claim to deny other officials the use of court machinery to enforce laws that the Justices thought unconstitutional.

Some writers, however, have implied a third and much broader claim: A Supreme Court decision binds not only the parties to a case but also the President and Congress in their own policy making outside of the courtroom. Without a doubt the possibility of an adverse Supreme Court decision has had an inhibiting effect on administrative and legislative behavior, but the extent of the legal and moral obligation involved poses a different sort of question. Strong Presidents like Thomas Jefferson, Andrew Jackson, Abraham Lincoln, and Franklin Roosevelt have asserted that in performing their executive duties they must follow their own interpretations of the Constitution. Jackson[6] vetoed the bank bill of 1832 because he thought a national bank unconstitutional even though the Supreme Court had held in *McCulloch v. Maryland* (1819)[7] that Congress could establish such an institution:

> If the opinion of the Supreme Court covered the whole ground of this act, it ought not to control the coordinate authorities of this Government. The Congress, the Executive, and the Court must each for itself be guided by its own opinion of the Constitution. Each public officer who takes an oath to support the Constitution swears that he will support it as he understands it, and not as it is understood by others.

Lincoln put it more generally. He first conceded that a Supreme Court decision was binding on the parties to a case and the principles announced in the opinion should be treated with great respect by other officials. He then went on to say:

> At the same time the candid citizen must confess that if the policy of the government, upon vital questions, affecting the whole people, is to be irrevocably fixed by decisions of the Supreme Court, the instant they are made, in ordinary litigation between parties, in personal actions, the people will have ceased to be their own rulers,

having to that extent, practically resigned their government, into the hands of that eminent tribunal.

Jackson's and Lincoln's arguments, incidentally, would not support *state* officials who claimed authority to nullify a Supreme Court decision, since they are not officers of a coordinate branch of government.

It is also worth noting here that the power of judicial review is not unique to the U.S. Supreme Court. It is shared by every federal court and by all state courts of major jurisdiction, although the Supreme Court can, if asked, usually review decisions of these other courts. Other countries—Argentina, Australia, Canada, the Federal Republic of Germany, Ireland, Italy, Japan, and the Philippines—have also adopted judicial review, modeling their "constitutional courts," as such tribunals are usually called, more or less on the American Supreme Court.

Prestige

In *Federalist #78* Alexander Hamilton ridiculed fears of judicial supremacy by pointing out that federal judges would have "neither purse nor sword." But those judges may have prestige, a firm hold on public esteem, and in democratic politics that can be a vital source of power. Since judges do lack physical force, they ultimately have to depend on the feeling that one *ought* to obey a court decision and that if one of the parties does not, then other public officials *ought* to use their power to compel obedience.

From time to time scholars, newspapermen, lawyers, elected politicians, and judges themselves point to the high or low prestige in which the Supreme Court is currently held. Unfortunately we have little hard data to gauge the relative popularity of the Court in different periods. Without a doubt decisions constantly irritate some groups, ethnic, regional, or ideological, while other decisions please still other groups; but the correlation between noisy praise or condemnation and public opinion is doubtful. It is even hazardous to extrapolate from editorial opinions to those of newspaper readers. What does seem clear, however, is that if one looks at what critics of the Supreme Court have said over the years, the Justices began with no prestige whatever and have since fallen steadily in public esteem. "The Supreme Court," as C. Herman Pritchett[9] observed, "is not what it used to be, and what's more it never was."

Mass polling does offer some promise of clarifying the relationships here, but its use on a scientific basis goes no further back than the 1930s: and even since then there has been relatively little sampling of public attitudes on judicial issues. One systematic study of national public attitudes by Murphy and Tanenhaus[10] reveals a rather low awareness of specific Court decisions. Less than 45 percent of national samples of voting-age adults in 1964 and 1966 could recall any recent Supreme Court action—names of cases, of course, were not asked. When a respondent could recall a decision, it was likely he would disapprove of what the Court had done. Yet more than two out of three of the people who had an opinion, including 40 percent of those who had expressed only critical views of particular decisions, thought that the Court was doing its basic job very well. This difference between criticism of individual decisions and approval of the Court as an institution indicates that the Justices have a reservoir of public support on which

"1969 was a troublesome year ... Do you suppose we could have it stricken from the record?"

GRIN & BEAR IT by Lichty. Courtesy Publishers-Hall Syndicate.

they can draw in emergencies. Additional surveys in the Murphy-Tanenhaus study of practicing attorneys and administrative assistants of senators and congressmen as well as analyses of better educated people in the national samples indicate that this institutional support is deeply and widely shared among those who could be termed political activists and opinion leaders.

Yet three pieces of evidence imply that the Justices' reservoir of public support is not unlimited. First, and perhaps most critical, replies to open-ended questions—that is, questions to which respondents frame their own answers rather than pick among those suggested by the interviewer—showed a wide range of emotions: from respect, admiration, pleasure, and approval on the one hand, to disapproval, anger, and contempt on the other. But there was little evidence of anything like awe or adulation that would remotely imply automatic acceptance of Court decisions.

Second, much of the variation in responses to questions about the Court was closely associated with the general political views of the interviewees. The more people approved of the over-all trend of national public policy from the New Deal to the Great Society, the more they favored specific decisions and supported the Court as an institution.

This close connection between policy views and Court support indicates a complex relationship. In part public approval of political development may be due to Supreme Court decisions; one simply cannot say to what extent this is true. On the other hand, this policy link may mean that certain kinds of decisions can severely drain the Court's reservoir of support and that as general political attitudes changes so must those of the Justices if they are to retain their support. Indirect evidence for this latter interpretation comes from the Gallup polls in the spring of 1937 which show that at one point almost half of those who had opinions favored Roosevelt's plan to pack the Supreme Court.

Third, a large portion of the public either is not aware of the work of the Court or is so slightly aware as to be unable to articulate responses to simple questions. Thus we do not know how deeply, if at all, the support of this silent mass runs, and we must have doubts about the depth of feeling of many of those who answered the questions. We said earlier that more than two out of three persons who answered the question thought the Court was doing its job very well, but only a little more than half of the sample could make any response at all. Moreover, this ignorance or apathy may occur among those most aided by judicial decisions and whose political help would be most needed in time of crisis. One would expect blacks, for instance, to be among the most ardent defenders of the Supreme Court, and so knowledgeable blacks were. But proportionately far fewer blacks than whites demonstrated much knowledge of the Court in particular or politics in general.

The Need for an Umpire

A third source of judicial power is a practical one; a federal system that divides power among state and national units of government, denies some power to each level, and then further fragments power among units of the national government, needs some kind of umpire. The Framers planned this division to cause friction, and in that sense it works very well indeed. But if anything is to get done, there must be ways of overcoming, at least temporarily, that friction. Just as individuals living together need some sort of arbiter to settle disputes, so do government officials who share power. Much of the Supreme Court's business is concerned with drawing boundary lines between the authorities of various government officials.

In a related fashion, other governmental officials may need the Court to help legitimize[11] controversial decisions. In a pluralistic society, any important public policy is likely to hurt the interests of many individuals and groups. Opposition will be based in part on the wisdom of the policy, but especially where there is a vague or general constitutional clause involved, doubts will be raised about the permissibility of the policy under the fundamental law. If it is to survive, every governmental structure must provide some means of quieting these kinds of basic constitutional doubts. In American politics the campaign speech, the ballot box, and the constitutional amendment perform this legitimizing function, but so may a Supreme Court decision. This sharing in legitimization points up the fact that the Justices are far more likely to declare a contested congressional statute constitutional than unconstitutional. From 1789 to 1970 the Supreme Court invalidated national laws in less than 90 instances.

INSTRUMENTS OF JUDICIAL POWER

The most basic instrument of judicial power is jurisdiction, the authority to decide certain kinds of cases and to issue orders to the parties involved. The potential political efficacy of this instrument increases if, as American judges can, courts can issue orders to governmental officials. Reinforcing this authority to grant or deny legitimacy to private or governmental action is the practice of writing opinions. These may be merely turgid explications of technical rules, but in the hands of a master they can become means of influencing not only immediate public opinion but also of shaping long-run political development. The eloquent rhetoric of John Marshall, Louis Brandeis, Oliver Wendell Holmes, Benjamin Cardozo, and Harlan Fiske Stone all took on lives of their own in helping to mold the thinking of later generations.

Just as prestige is an important source of judicial power, so it can also become a weapon of judicial power—and this is precisely the transformation that an opinion writer tries to bring about. Prestige can be strongly reinforced by professional reputation, the respect that other governmental officials have for the skill and determination with which the Justices will use their power. When the Justices can combine a popular feeling that their decisions ought to be obeyed with a belief among public officials that the Justices can create a political backfire to burn those who do not aid compliance, they have forged an instrument to bludgeon the very people who have the physical power to defy them.

The Justices also have certain passive instruments at their command. They can almost completely determine what cases they will accept—which is not to say they can control what cases are brought before them; that is another problem. But without giving any reason beyond the Delphic "want of a substantial federal question," they can refuse to hear any case they wish. Moreover, even when they agree to take a case they may use a variety of technical devices to delay a decision until a time they think more propitious for the objectives they wish to achieve.

LIMITATIONS ON JUDICIAL POWER

Technical Checks

A series of interlocking restrictions operate to restrict judicial power. As a court of law, the Justices must follow certain formal procedures. These are generally somewhat flexible but they are not infinitely malleable. Unlike administrators, judges cannot initiate action. Someone else must bring a case to them and in a form that meets jurisdictional and standing requirements. The Justices can, for instance, sustain the conviction of a brutal sheriff under one of the civil rights laws, but they cannot start such a prosecution themselves. Even where a case has been brought and formal criteria met, the Justices are limited in that they can usually give or deny only what the parties ask for. If a group of dissidents appeals an injunction forbidding a protest march, the Justices cannot put the mayor out of office.

A second restriction limits the binding force of a decision. A court order legally obligates only the parties to a case, those who cooperate with them, and those who succeed to their office or status. A decision that the legislature of Tennessee was gerrymandered would not, of itself, legally compel the government of a neighboring state using exactly the same representational formulas and ratios to redistrict. A separate suit would have to be brought, although, of course, the existence of the first judgment might well move officials of the second state to act on their own. Earlier we mentioned the "class action," a procedure that allows one litigant or a small group of litigants to sue for themselves and all others similarly situated. These kinds of actions widen the scope of a judicial decision, but the resulting order still runs only against specific persons. Again a class action that resulted in an injunction against Mississippi officials would have no binding force in Alabama.

The kinds of orders that a court can issue also limit judicial power. In general, judges can far more easily forbid certain kinds of action than they can command positive action, especially where public officials are involved. The Justices can hold a civil rights statute or a tax law constitutional or unconstitutional, but they cannot compel Congress to pass such a statute. They can,[12] of course, liberally interpret any existing statute to harvest more policy than congressmen realized they had planted.

Public Opinion

If the Court draws much of its power from public esteem, then popular attitudes can also be a check on judicial power—unless, of course, the Court is viewed as being incapable of error and, as we have seen, there is no evidence of such adulation. Like the Lord, the public taketh away as well as giveth, and it may do so with considerably more caprice than the Deity is wont to exercise. The Justices are not apt to try to overturn the system or act as radical reformers, but even in protecting against change they have to restrain themselves from using their power too frequently.

Internal Restrictions

The Justices are also limited by their own concepts of how, as judges, they ought to act. Since they have come to the bench after undergoing a long period of legal training and usually a far longer period of apprenticeship in public service, it is probable that they will have absorbed many of the prevailing norms about judicial action held by the legal profession and by other government officials. These norms may be vague, yet they do in broad terms differentiate behavior perfectly proper to legislators and administrators from that which may be proper to judges. For instance, a legislator who tried to cope with a problem by drafting an entirely new set of rules that swept away all the old rules might be looked on as unwise, but not as acting improperly. A judge in the same circumstances would raise more serious questions. Even though judges sometimes reverse old rulings, the usual way of the common law is to change on a retail rather than a wholesale basis, gradually remolding rules over a period of years, preserving some of the reality and much of the appearance of certainty in the law.

In addition, the Justices cannot help but be aware of at least some of the apparent anomalies of their being appointed officials serving what amounts to life terms in a supposedly democratic government. This realization has undoubtedly moved many Justices to

hesitate to substitute their own judgment for that of popularly elected officials. Many Justices have been able to practice judicial self-restraint with some success, although the claim has been overused.

Institutional Limitations

The Supreme Court rarely makes either the first or the final decision in a case. As we saw in the preceding chapter, its jurisdiction is almost totally appellate. It reviews a lower court decision, reverses or affirms it, writes an opinion explaining the principles behind choices, and then usually remands the case for final dsposition in the court where the litigation began. Thus the Justices, like the President, largely operate through a bureaucracy, but they have even less control over their bureaucracy than does the President over his. The Justices can exercise little if any formal or even informal control over the appointment, retention, or promotion of lower federal judges and probably none whatever in state judicial affairs. The sheer volume of business in the state and federal courts, the frequency with which new issues arise, the vagueness of many legal rules and even of Supreme Court interpretations of those rules mean that Supreme Court Justices are at most leaders of their branch of government, not its masters. The analogy of bureaucracy, judicial or administrative, to international politics, where independent and semi-independent leaders negotiate[13] is well taken. The military model of a disciplined hierarchy saluting and unquestioningly carrying out orders without regard to personal consequences is one which Presidents and Supreme Court Justices may sorely envy but never see.

A second set of institutional checks revolves around the simple fact that the Supreme Court is staffed by nine Justices. The Justices share power with each other as well as with other officials. To hear a case requires a vote of four members and to decide it requires five votes. Since nine is an uneven number one might expect clear cut decisions in all cases where every Justice sat, but in complex litigation there are usually more than two options open. Furthermore, an opinion, to be labelled as that of the Court, must have the assent of at least a majority of the Justices. It is no easy matter to persuade five or more individualistic, strong-willed lawyers to agree on a complicated legal document that is based on certain fundamental and perhaps controversial assumptions of political philosophy and that may have immediate as well as long-run effects on public policy.

A Justice who is determined to write exactly as he himself wishes is apt to find himself writing solo concurring and dissenting opinions. The Justice assigned the task of writing for the Court circulates each draft to all members of the Court, and the majority Justices make suggestions for change. These suggestions may pertain to matters of literary style or they may go to the heart of the substance of a case. Getting agreement, if the case is at all important, typically involves negotiation, compromise, and even bargaining. It can be a complex operation, for a change that one member of the majority demands may be anathema to another. The opinion writer thus sometimes finds himself deliberately writing vaguely so as to alienate as few of his colleagues as possible. The final product, as Justice Holmes once observed, may be a mass of dough but, not since the days of John Marshall has a single Justice been able to dominate the Court. Decisions and opinions are products of what Felix Frankfurter once described as an orchestral rather than a solo performance.[14]

In the business of negotiating, the Justices have incentives and sanctions. The main incentive, of course, is to enshrine as those of the Court the principles that a Justice thinks most fitting to cover this and future situations. The major sanction available to the opinion writer is, if he can somehow still muster five votes, ignoring the wishes of a colleague. His colleague's sanction is the threat to write a separate opinion and to persuade other Justices to join him. Clearly the effectiveness of either sanction depends in part on the closeness of the vote, and in part on the intellectual power of the individual Justices. A 5–4 division puts the opinion writer at a considerable disadvantage, just as a 9–0 judgment gives him great leeway. A threat from a Holmes, a Brandeis, or a Black to circulate a separate opinion means much more than a similar menace from a less skillful writer.

The threat to pull out may be stated bluntly. Harlan Fiske Stone[15] once wrote Felix Frankfurter: "If you wish to write, placing the case on the ground which I think tenable and desirable, I shall cheerfully join you. If not, I will add a few observations for myself." A Justice may also speak more subtly but still clearly. As Stone[16] once wrote Owen Roberts:

> I doubt if we are very far apart in the Cantwell case, but in order that you might get exactly my views, I have written them out and enclosed them herewith.
>
> If you feel that you could agree with me, I think you would find no difficulty in making some changes in your opinion which would make it unnecessary for me to say anything.

Helping to keep the negotiating process within certain bounds is the knowledge among the Justices that they have to work together for many years, and during that time each is likely to have to write a hundred or more opinions of the Court.

Political Restraints

The Supreme Court can say what statutes and executive orders really mean; it can even declare them unconstitutional. These are great powers, but Congress and the President each have a series of weapons they can turn against the Justices. Congress can impeach and remove any judge, increase the number of Justices, confer or withdraw most of the Court's appellate jurisdiction, cut off money for the Court's administrative staff or deny funds to carry out specific decisions, enact new statutes to "correct" judicial interpretations of old law, and propose constitutional amendments to counter the effects of a judicial decision, as the Fourteenth and Sixteenth Amendments did, or even to strike at judicial power itself, as the Eleventh Amendment did. Although it was probably unconstitutional, during Jefferson's administration Congress abolished a whole tier of federal courts and turned the judges out without salaries, and after the Civil War several Radical Republican legislators threatened to abolish the Supreme Court.

The President, as Chief Executive, may forbid administrative officials, ranging from U.S. marshals to the Secretary of Defense, to enforce Supreme Court decisions, and he can pardon anyone convicted of criminal contempt of court for disobeying judicial orders. In choosing nominees for the Supreme Court and lower courts, the President can try to influence future decisions, as can senators in approving or disapproving a

nominee. Utilizing his power of legislative initiative, the President can try to persuade Congress to use any of its powers against the Court; and, as can senators or congressmen, he can draw on his own prestige to attack the Justices.

The wording of the national supremacy clause of Article VI of the Constitution puts state officials on a lower level than federal officers, but state officials can still challenge the Court. Like national officials they may try to undermine the Justices' prestige. And since the feudal structure of both political parties makes senators, representatives, and even federal administrators dependent on local politicos, state officials may be in a strong position to pressure federal officials into opposing Supreme Court decisions.

POWER AND PRUDENCE

This long list of checks raises the question of why the Supreme Court has not been curbed both severely and frequently. In part the answer lies in the fact that these checks are limitations, not barriers. Usually having had prior practical political experience, judges are typically well aware of these restrictions and usually know how to work within them and even how to reduce their strictures. Moreover, Court defenders as well as attackers will be using available channels of political influence, and it is always easier to prevent Congress from acting than to get it to take positive action. A President, too, is likely to be subjected to cross-pressures. While it is less difficult for him to act than it is for Congress, much of the real power he can wield against the Court requires congressional cooperation, or, as in the case of refusing to enforce decisions, can expose him to political dangers both from public opinion and from the fact that recalcitrants are usually state officials whose challenge to the Supreme Court normally becomes in effect a threat to the national supremacy on which much of the President's own power rests.

In part the answer lies in the internal restraints to which all governmental officials are subject. Presidents and members of Congress take their oaths of office as seriously as do judges, and they are usually as devoted to the preservation of the political system as judges are. An independent judiciary exercising judicial review is an integral part of that system. Closely related is the fact that public officials often feel they ought to obey Supreme Court decisions even when they disagree with them. There are, of course, limits on how far officials will go in following a judicial decision—a limit determined in part by the official's view of how far and strongly the opinion of those people who form his particular public will push him or let him go.

In short, Supreme Court Justices and other federal officials are commonly products of the same general political culture and of the same political subculture of professional politicians. They share belief in the "rules of the game" and the existing structures of government. They are also held together by the bond of all being officers of the *federal* government.

Furthermore, because of the frequency with which vacancies occur on the High Bench, about once every twenty-seven months, it is normal for at least a sizable minority if not in fact a majority of the Justices to be quite sympathetic with the general and even the specific goals of an administration. Difficulties may arise, as in the early 1800s or the mid-1930s, when a majority of the Justices are from a different political generation from both the President and a majority of the Congress. Difficulties with state officials whose parochial orientation may put them out of the main stream of national politics are more likely to occur.

Prudential considerations may also deter Congress and the President from using apparently available weapons against the Court, even when it seems that they stand a good chance of winning over a sufficiently large portion of public opinion to escape punishment at the polls. The President and Congress are inevitably rivals for power, and each may need the Court to check the other. Either branch may need the Justices, as John F. Kennedy and Lyndon Johnson did in the civil rights field, to help push the other into taking certain courses of action. Both the President and Congress may need the Court to legitimize certain controversial policy decisions or to take the blame for failures to act. For instance, for President Kennedy and many big-city congressmen, Supreme Court pronouncements about "a wall of separation between church and state" opened a welcome escape from the politically tricky issue of federal aid to parochial schools.

Because of the President's advantages of access to mass media and his more centralized power base, members of Congress may well believe that by crushing judicial power they would put themselves in a far worse position in relation to the Chief Executive. Even where they largely agree with him on substantive policy issues, they may see their status as members of the legislative branch as being protected by a strong judicial check on the White House. They may reasonably fear that were the Supreme Court weakened, the President would dominate the national government. In 1937 many liberal Democrats who had been counted as foes of the Supreme Court drew back from supporting Roosevelt's plan to add six new Justices. The opposition was led by Senator Wheeler, who had run for Vice President in 1924 on the Progressive party ticket on a platform that included curbing the Court and who had later become an ardent New Dealer. These people sensed what one of FDR's advisers put into words:[17] "If the President wins the court fight, everything will fall into his basket."

As a result of all of these factors, there has been intermittent guerrilla warfare between Congress and the Court and between the Court and the President, but not since Jefferson was in the White House have Congress and the President joined to launch a major attack against the Justices, and even that alliance was short-lived. The three branches of government coexist, occasionally in harmony, more often in armed truce, even more frequently in competition, and sometimes in open conflict, but the conflict has typically been for limited objectives. With the two exceptions of Jefferson's first administration and the Radical Republicans in Congress after the Civil War, the gains sought have been within the tripartite institutional structure of the national government.

THE ROLES OF THE SUPREME COURT

In this and the previous chapter, we have been describing not one role but a whole set of roles that Supreme Court Justices and to some extent all federal judges play in the U.S. political system. The Supreme Court is a legal tribunal operating within a flexible but still recognizable set of procedural rules; it is also a dispenser of justice as well as an interpreter of legal rules; at the same time the Court is a coordinate branch of government responsible in an important although limited way for helping to formulate public policy while deciding individual cases.

Like the President, Supreme Court Justices play many roles, all at the same time. First, they are arbitrators of disputes between individual citizens and directly or indirectly between conflicting social interests. Second, where public officials are involved in a case the Supreme Court often has the task of defining the boundaries of authority between various governmental agencies and between government and the individual citizen. Third, in defining the boundaries of public authority the Supreme Court may not only check governmental power, it often helps to legitimize controversial policies and new extensions of political power. Fourth, as appellate court judges, the Justices act as supervisors of the federal judicial system, and even of the fifty state judicial systems insofar as federal law is concerned. Fifth, in deciding cases the Court often modifies existing rules or fashions new rules for new problems. Thus Justices play a legislative role, much to the anger of losing litigants and of those public officials who fear judicial encroachments on their power, disagree with the substantive policy involved, or are vulnerable to pressure from the interests that lost in the judicial process.

Sixth, like bureaucrats Supreme Court Justices may play a representational role. They can be representatives in the sense of "chosen from" rather than "acting for." Customs built-up around Supreme Court appointments require that the Justices come from all sections of the country and that there usually be at least one Catholic and one Jew on the Court. The appointment of Thurgood Marshall probably has begun a tradition of having at least one black Justice. The Court may perform an additional representational function by providing a forum for persons or groups who have too little political power to secure a real voice in other governmental processes. Last, the Justices may also play an ancillary representational role by protecting the integrity of the electoral processes, by trying to safeguard, as in the white primary cases,[18] the rights of racial minorities to vote, or as in the reapportionment decisions,[19] the right of every man to have his vote counted equally with those of his fellow citizens.

Seventh, by the opinions they write, the Justices may help educate the public at large and government officials in particular. It is true that few of these opinions are read by other than a cluster of lawyers, public officials, newsmen, scholars, and students experiencing the joys of political science courses. Yet because these people also write and talk, some general idea of what courts do percolates through much, though certainly not all, of the community. And knowledge that a respected court, especially if it is the Supreme Court, has declared that the Constitution permits or forbids certain kinds of policies may well affect public attitudes. The Supreme Court, Justice Frank Murphy[20] observed, is "the Great Pulpit" in American politics. Here, incidentally, may be the most important legacy of the Supreme Court under Chief Justice Earl Warren: it constantly reminded Americans of the basic concepts like political democracy, social equality, and the presumption of innocence that underlie their system of government.

The Justices may play any or all of these roles well or badly. There are many examples of both wisdom and foolishness in Supreme Court history. The Dred Scott decision,[21] for instance, held in 1857 that Congress had no authority to regulate or prohibit slavery in the territories. What the Justices thought would put an end to the slavery question almost put an end to the Union. The *School Segregation* decisions,[22] on the other hand, supplied a much-needed sermon that a democratic government cannot rest on a caste society.

Two points are fundamental to this discussion. First, the Justices play these roles whether they want to or not. A decision that school segregation was constitutional would have had different but no less important political and educational effects. As Justice Robert H. Jackson[23] once said, "We act in these matters not by authority of our competence but by force of our commissions." Second, as we indicated earlier, even when interpreting the Constitution, a judicial decision is not necessarily final. New statutes, new constitutional amendments, even new judges are practical possibilities. The U.S. political system forces judges to participate in policy making, and requires them to share power not only with each other but also with a large number of other public officials.

SELECTED BIBLIOGRAPHY

Beveridge, Albert J., *The Life of John Marshall* (Boston: Houghton Mifflin Company, 1916, 4 Vols.). The first major biography of a Supreme Court Justice: a classic of its kind.

Bickel, Alexander M., *The Supreme Court and the Idea of Progress* (New York: Harper and Row, 1970). A well-written evaluation of the work of the Warren Court by a former law clerk of Justice Felix Frankfurter.

Carr, Robert K., *The Supreme Court and Judicial Review* (New York: Holt, Rinehart and Winston, Inc., 1942). A brief analysis of the Court's use of judicial review.

Jackson, Robert H., *The Supreme Court in the American System of Government* (Cambridge, Mass.: Harvard University Press, 1955). A Justice's short, trenchant essays on his Court.

Mason, Alpheus T., *Harlan Fiske Stone: Pillar of the Law* (New York: Viking Press, 1956).

———, *William Howard Taft: Chief Justice* (New York: Simon and Schuster, Inc., 1965). Two richly detailed political biographies of Chief Justices of the United States.

McCloskey, Robert G., *The American Supreme Court* (Chicago, Ill.: University of Chicago Press, 1960). A superb historical introduction to the work of the Court.

Murphy, Walter F., *Congress and the Court* (Chicago, Ill.: University of Chicago Press, 1962). A case study of the efforts in the 1950s to curb the Supreme Court.

———, *Elements of Judicial Strategy* (Chicago, Ill.: University of Chicago Press, 1964). An analysis of the political power of the Supreme Court, based on the private papers of several Justices.

——— and Joseph Tanenhaus, *The Study of Public Law* (New York: Random House, 1971). An explanation of why and how political scientists study courts and judges.

Pritchett, C. Herman, *The Roosevelt Court: A Study in Judicial Politics and Values, 1937–1947* (New York: Crowell-Collier and Macmillan, 1948). A path-breaking study of decision making in the Supreme Court.

Schmidhauser, John R., *The Supreme Court* (New York: Holt, Rinehart and Winston, Inc., 1960). A useful analysis of the social backgrounds of Supreme Court Justices.

Twiss, Benjamin R., *Lawyers and the Constitution: How Laissez-Faire Came to the Supreme Court* (Princeton, New Jersey: Princeton University Press, 1942). An important case study of the influence on the Supreme Court by lawyers who argued before it.

Vose, Clement E., *Caucasians Only: The Supreme Court, the NAACP, and the Restrictive Covenant Cases* (Berkeley, Calif.: University of California Press, 1959). An interesting account of how a pressure group utilized judicial power to achieve one of its goals.

Warren, Charles, *The Supreme Court in United States History* (Boston: Little, Brown and Company, 1922), 2 Vols. An old but still excellent history of the Court written from a sympathetic point of view.

Footnotes

[1] Quoted in Alpheus T. Mason, *The Supreme Court: Palladium of Freedom* (Ann Arbor, Mich.: University of Michigan Press, 1962), p. 72.

[2] These early cases are discussed in Charles Warren, *The Supreme Court in United States History* (Boston: Little, Brown and Company, 1922), chapter 1. The more important decisions were: *United States v. Yale Todd*, decided in 1794 but not officially reported until 1852, 13 Howard 52; *Hylton v. United States*, 3 Dallas 171 (1796); and *Calder v. Bull*, 3 Dallas 386 (1798).

[3] 1 Cranch 137 (1803).

[4] *Annals of Congress*, 7th Cong., 1st Sess., p. 179.

[5] *Little v. Barreme*, 2 Cranch 170 (1804).

[6] James D. Richardson, ed., *A Compilation of the Messages and Papers of the Presidents* (Washington, D.C.: Bureau of National Literature and Art, 1908), II, 582.

[7] 4 Wheaton 316 (1819).

[8] Richardson, VI, 9.

[9] U.S. Senate, Subcommittee on Separation of Powers, *Hearings: The Supreme Court*, 90th Cong., 2d Sess., (1968) p. 130.

[10] Walter F. Murphy and Joseph Tanenhaus, "Public Opinion and the United States Supreme Court," in Joel Grossman and Joseph Tanenhaus, eds., *Frontiers of Judicial Research* (New York: John Wiley and Sons, Inc., 1969), p. 273.

[11] Robert A. Dahl, "Decision-Making in a Democracy: The Supreme Court as a National Policy-Maker," *Journal of Public Law*, 6 (Fall 1957), p. 279; and Charles L. Black, Jr., *The People and the Court* (New York: Crowell-Collier and Macmillan, 1960), chapter 3.

[12] See, for example, *Brotherhood of Railroad Trainmen v. Howard*, 343 U.S. 768 (1952), and *Sullivan v. Little Hunting Park*, 396 U.S. 229 (1969).

[13] Robert A. Dahl and Charles E. Lindblom, *Politics, Economics, and Welfare* (New York: Harper and Bros., 1953), p. 342.

[14] For a discussion of the group phase of decision-making on the Supreme Court, see Walter F. Murphy, *Elements of Judicial Strategy* (Chicago, Ill.: University of Chicago Press, 1964), chaps. 3 and 7.

[15] Quoted in Murphy, p. 59.

[16] Quoted in Murphy, p. 59.

[17] The statement was by Thomas Corcoran, quoted in Louis Koenig, *The Invisible Presidency* (New York: Holt, Rinehart and Winston, Inc., 1960), p. 286.

[18] *Smith v. Allwright*, 321 U.S. 649 (1944); *Terry v. Adams*, 345 U.S. 461 (1953).

[19] See Chapter 8 for a listing and discussion of these cases.

[20] Quoted in J. Woodford Howard, *Mr. Justice Murphy: A Political Biography* (Princeton, N.J.: Princeton University Press, 1968), p. 228.

[21] *Dred Scott v. Sandford*, 19 Howard 393 (1857).

[22] *Brown v. Board of Education*, 347 U.S. 483 (1954).

[23] *West Virginia v. Barnette*, 319 U.S. 624, 640 (1943).

Part VII   Civil Liberties

Washington: Repeal the Bill of Rights?

By JAMES RESTON

WASHINGTON, April 18—
You can put it down as a fairly reliable rule that periods of war or fierce domestic controversy tend to threaten or restrict the constitutional liberties of the American people. And with the war in Vietnam and a crime wave at home, we are clearly going through another such time.

The reasons are plain. The uses of physical violence against the people, property and institutions of the United States in defiance of the law have created a climate of fear in the country, and under the dominion of fear, a great many people now seem willing to choose order at the expense of some of their liberties, or at least at the expense of somebody else's liberties.

It is hard to estimate just how far this counterrevolution has gone, but recently C.B.S. News took a nation-wide poll which at least gives us a clue. It concluded that the majority of American adults now seem willing to restrict some of the basic freedoms constitutionally guaranteed by the Bill of Rights.

Specifically, about three-fourths of the 1,136 people interviewed in the telephone poll said extremist groups should not be permitted to organize demonstrations against the Government, even if there appeared to be no clear danger of violence.

Over half of those questioned would not give everyone the right to criticize the Government, if the criticism were thought to be damaging to the national interest, and 55 per cent added that newspapers, radio and television should not be permitted to *report* some stories considered by the *Government* to be harmful to the national interest.

On this ground, no group characterized by the Government as "extremist" could even organize a peaceful assembly against the war. The Government could draft them into war they oppose, but they wouldn't even be able to exercise their First Amendment right to demonstrate against such action.

It would not be hard to demonstrate that any serious criticism of the present Government's war effort in Vietnam gives comfort to the enemy and therefore would be considered by the Government as damaging to the national interest; so should there be no criticism of a war the people have to fight and finance?

The suggested prohibition on reporting things the *Government* thinks damaging to the national interest is even sillier. Most governments think reporting battle-field losses and certainly battle-field atrocities like Mylai are damaging, but even Vice President Agnew hasn't suggested that these reports should be suppressed.

Nor do individual liberties in criminal matters win the support of a majority of those polled by C.B.S. Nearly three out of every five adults (58 per cent) said that if a person is found innocent of a serious crime, but new evidence is uncovered after trial, he should be *tried again*, despite the protection against double jeopardy. And three out of five questioned added that if a person is *suspected* of a serious crime, the police should be allowed to *hold* him in jail until they can get enough evidence to charge him with the crime.

Well, save my old habeas corpus, what goes on here? Are we to fight a war for the liberties of the Vietnamese people and lose our own in the process? Let the Government take us into an obscene war by stealth at the cost of over 40,000 American dead and not be free to criticize its stupidities or even report its blunders?

The Nixon Administration has already mounted an attack on the press and on the Senate for exercising their constitutional freedoms. Chief Justice Burger has just written a lone dissent in the Supreme Court insisting on a far stricter definition of "double jeopardy" than any of the other conservatives on the Court. And Attorney General Mitchell is advocating the right of "preventive detention" of suspected criminals.

This, of course, is not wholly new. After the French Revolution, we had the Alien and Sedition Acts of 1798. During the Civil War, military trials were often substituted for civil trials and habeas corpus was often suspended. The fear of anarchists led to a wave of repressive measures after the First World War, and the fear of Communist subversion turned us over to the tender mercies of Joe McCarthy after the Second World War. But usually the people fought for their liberties, and now they seem to be acquiescing in their erosion.

In face of all the present civil disorder it may be understandable but it is tolerable only if you don't think about it. Maybe we ought to read the Bill of Rights again. After all, it's only 462 words, and we really ought to keep them, at least until the 200th anniversary of the Declaration in 1976.

© 1970 by The New York Times Company. Reprinted by permission.

Chapter 19 Civil Liberties in a Free Society

THE FUNCTIONS OF CIVIL LIBERTIES

Nowhere does the Madisonian dilemma appear so acute as in a discussion of civil liberties. Without strong government to keep the peace and protect people from those who feel little moral restraint in taking what they want or in venting their aggressions, civilized life outside of small, primitively simple societies would be impossible. On the other hand, possession of a near monopoly of physical force can tempt government officials to turn this power to personal benefit. The history of Nazis and Fascists in Germany, Italy, and Spain provides a set of horror stories about the dangers of unchecked "defenders of the people" that are as vivid as the records of Stalinism and Maoism.

In most democratic nations, civil liberties serve two functions. First of all, they are ends in themselves or stepping stones toward such objectives as individual self-development and self-expression. For most people, government is not an end in itself, but rather a means of establishing some of the conditions for the achievement of peace and happiness, and any real degree of happiness requires a large measure of self-determination. The ultimate justification for government is that it provides citizens with an opportunity to live the good life. Without the rights to enjoy privacy, to express oneself in words and symbols, to worship or not worship, to own and dispose of property, the good life, however it is defined, would be impossible for most people.

But many of these same rights are also means to limit government, not merely in the sense of being prohibitions written into a constitution but also in the sense of functioning as live, operating checks. Freedom of speech and press, for instance, do permit self-expression, but they do more. Along with freedom of assembly, they provide a legitimate means of organizing opposition that can protest governmental policies and at the next election challenge and perhaps unseat incumbents. In this sense, freedom of communication and association form the basis of free, democratic government. If opposition is illegal, if alternative policies cannot be formulated, defended, and put to a test in the market of the ballot box, then democracy cannot exist; and it is doubtful if any other kind of free government could survive such restraints. The right to discuss public affairs, Justice Oliver Wendell Holmes[1] once said, "is more than self-expression; it is the essence of self-government." In a similar fashion, other protections, such as advice of counsel or a fair, public trial by jury in a criminal case, function not merely to defend the rights of a particular person but also to protect society as a whole from overzealous or overambitious guardians.

BALANCING

Recognizing the dual functions of civil liberties clarifies rather than resolves the difficulties in achieving freedom and security under limited government. If one is to talk, as so many writers have, of a balance, then he has to face up to certain problems. Balancing individual rights against public authority does not mean placing the interest of the individual on one side of a scale and the interests of society on the other. A free society, as we just pointed out, has an interest in individual liberty as one of the means of keeping the society truly free. If we are to weigh one interest against another, we must label both sets of weights as those of society and somehow calibrate the scale to take this double loading into effect.

The problems of balancing liberty against authority occur in two dimensions, that of the individual against government and that of individual against other individuals. Not only is it necessary to protect freedom from governmental threats but there is also the necessity of keeping individuals from injuring, even inadvertently, others. Protecting society from venal or corrupt officials and from criminals is difficult enough, but many rights, each legitimate in itself, can conflict. For example, one man's freedom to speak and write may conflict with another's right to a trial by an impartial jury. A news editor may believe he has a right, even a duty, to expose crime and corruption in his city, but in so doing, especially if his paper has wide circulation, he may prejudice potential jurors against an accused.

A third problem is that just as society and the needs of its citizens change, so may their relations to one another and to government. Firearms provide a good illustration. On the frontier in the last century, men often fed their families by hunting; there was also constant danger from hostile Indians and white bandits. In that situation, carrying firearms was a fundamental right. In the context of modern American society, however, guns are rarely necessary for food, and private citizens' carrying them for self-protection creates huge dangers.

A fourth problem occurs because of the physical size and diversity of the United States. Complete uniformity of detail in matters of law in all fifty American states would probably be unworkable. In fact, if such uniformity ever did obtain, it would be an indication that the country had outgrown federalism. On the other hand, if national citizenship is to have any real meaning, some rights have to be protected in every part of the country, and protected against state as well as federal violations.

Over the years, Supreme Court Justices have tried to distinguish between rights that are and are not of such fundamental importance to require uniformity. In tracing this dividing line the Justices have admittedly drawn on values that may not be universally shared and have based their decisions on pragmatic judgments about what is workable in society. The problem of finding national protection for rights deemed basic has been difficult because the original Constitution imposed few restrictions on the authority of a state with regard to its own citizens. Section 10 of Article I forbade states to impair the obligation of contracts, or pass bills of attainder or *ex post facto* laws. Section 2 of Article IV declared that citizens of each state shall be entitled to the privileges and immunities of the citizens in the several states, a vague statement that has never had much practical effect.

Chief Justice John Marshall[2] further complicated the situation by ruling that the Bill of Rights limited only the federal government. The question is more difficult than Marshall admitted. The first of the original ten amendments does begin with the words "Congress shall make no law," but this phraseology does not necessarily indicate that the subsequent nine amendments applied only to the national government. Furthermore, what we call the First Amendment was the first amendment ratified, not the first one of the Bill of Rights that Congress proposed, and the language of most of the other amendments is sufficiently broad to apply to both national and state governments. Moreover, there was a specific reason, absent in the case of the other amendments, for restricting the scope of the First Amendment: several states had the equivalent of established religions and proposing a total ban would have lessened the chances of ratification.

Whether right or wrong, Marshall's decision settled the matter until the adoption of the Fourteenth Amendment after the Civil War. Section 1 provided in part:

> No State shall make or enforce any law which shall abridge the privileges or immunities of citizens of the United States; nor shall any State deprive any person of life, liberty, or property without due process of law, nor deny to any person within its jurisdiction the equal protection of the laws.

The command of equal protection forbade discrimination among persons; and the privileges and immunities and the due process clauses laid the basis for an argument that this amendment had "incorporated" the Bill of Rights and thus made those protections effective against the states.

Some Justices have completely rejected the incorporation argument; others have completely accepted it. The result has been a slow process of inclusion and exclusion—in recent years more inclusion than exclusion—of specific rights into the due process rather than the privileges and immunities clause. In 1925, for instance, the Supreme Court held that due process protects freedom of speech against state action.[3] Later the Court included all the First Amendment guarantees,[4] the rights to a fair trial, to privacy, to counsel, to a trial by jury in serious criminal cases, and protections against self-incrimination, double jeopardy, and cruel and unusual punishment.[5] About the only provisions of the Bill of Rights that do not now seem to be applicable against the states are the requirements of indictment by grand jury and of a jury trial in civil cases where the amount in controversy exceeds twenty dollars. One should keep in mind that the peculiarities of American constitutional law make the term "state" cover any official at the state, county, city, town, or other local level.

FORMAT

In this chapter we shall analyze some of the substantive civil liberties such as speech, press, assembly, religion, and citizenship. In the following chapter we take up the problems of criminal justice, and in Chapter 21 we return to the great knot of American politics, race and equal protection of the laws. One of the themes running through this sequence of chapters will be that understanding Supreme Court decisions is a necessary but not a sufficient condition for understanding constitutional rights. As we have already seen, Supreme Court decisions and opinions can act as powerful influences on the policies government officials pursue and, by helping to shape the general political culture, can affect the ways in which members of the general public think and behave. But a Supreme Court ruling seldom immediately settles a policy problem; it is typically only one step in a long, drawn out process. Before a problem is solved—or outlived—Congress, executive officials, state and local officers, and many private citizens usually get involved.

FREEDOM OF COMMUNICATION

Absolutists and Relativists

Discussion, debate, and dissemination of ideas, we have said, form the core of democratic government. Yet the exercise of these rights can raise serious problems. Does the right to criticize a public official stop short of profanity and invective? Can one call a policeman a pig, a fascist, or a "goddamned racketeer" and claim the privilege of the First Amendment? Can one publish malicious falsehoods about neighbors and invoke a similar privilege? Does the right to urge others to join in a cause include a right to plot to rob a bank? Does it include the right to urge a group of hooded and armed Ku Klux Klaners "to bury the niggers," or angry blacks to burn down a ghetto, or young men to refuse to register for the draft? Do the rights of speech and association protect those who organize a conspiracy to overthrow the government by force? Does the right to espouse offbeat ideas include the right to publish and sell pictures of nudes or of human beings engaged in assorted sexual acts?

Faced with these kinds of problems, many people, including some judges, legislators, and police officials have tried to stifle novel, unpopular, offensive, or "dangerous" ideas. At the opposite extreme are those who would leave the communication of ideas, whether by written or spoken means, completely alone. More than three hundred years ago in the midst of a period of bitter revolution, John Milton[6] wrote:

> And though all the windes of doctrin were let loose to play upon the earth, so Truth be in the field, we do injuriously by licensing and prohibiting to misdoubt her strength. Let her and Falsehood grapple; who ever knew Truth put to the wors in a free and open encounter?

Thomas Jefferson[7] echoed Milton in his first inaugural address:

> If there be any among us who wish to dissolve this union, or to change its republican form, let them stand undisturbed as monuments of the safety with which error of opinion may be tolerated where reason is left free to combat it.

More recently Justice Hugo Black* has argued that freedom of expression under the First Amendment is an absolute right. "It is my belief," he has said, "that there *are* 'absolutes' in our Bill of Rights, and that they were put there on purpose by men who knew what words meant, and meant their prohibitions to be 'absolutes.' " And he added, "Our First Amendment was a bold effort . . . to establish a country with no legal restrictions of any kind upon the subjects people could investigate, discuss, and deny."

But if a political censor contradicts the basic notions of free government, unfettered speech and writing can threaten many of the values like peace, privacy, and the right to a reputation that government is supposed to protect. Completely unrestricted speech might even erode, as we saw in the chapter on political campaigning, the electoral process itself. Each of the absolutists just quoted has recognized these dangers and has flavored his absolutism with a pinch of relativism. Milton drew the line at tolerating Catholicism, Jefferson had a "darker side" on civil liberties, and Justice Black's absolutism has run aground on the twin reefs of "symbolic speech" and protection of the right to a fair trial. Black has voted to sustain punishment for wearing black armbands,[9] burning a draft card,[10] and burning an American flag.[11] The distinction which the Justice has drawn in these cases between words and acts is very thin. Not only is the usual purpose of words to cause deeds—"Words are the triggers of action," Judge Learned Hand once wrote—but verbal persuasion is typically interlaced with symbols. "We live by symbols," Oliver Wendell Holmes said, and nowhere is this more true than in politics. The flag, motherhood, the log cabin, the hound's tooth, the full dinner pail, eggheads, paper hats, and slogan buttons are integral parts of American political debates, shorthand representations of politically laden values.

Black has also voted to convict demonstrators for parading, although in an admittedly orderly fashion, outside of a courtroom. Judges and jurors, Black felt, should be insulated from popular influence. "Justice cannot be rightly administered," he explained,[12] "nor are the lives and safety of prisoners secure, when throngs of people clamor against the processes of justice outside the courthouse or jailhouse door."

Black's distinctions may be reasonable, indeed they may be both intelligent and necessary, but in effect they imply that communication of ideas should not always take precedence over other rights and other values. Most other Supreme Court Justices have been less absolutist than Black; although in recent years a majority has usually voted for the same result in particular cases as he has. Most Justices have followed an approach, although many prefer not to admit it, akin to that of balancing of interests. Inevitably a balancing approach, as Black has complained, increases the scope of judicial discretion. There are no rules to tell a judge what weights to put on which interests, or even to decide on which side of the scale particular interests belong. Just as inevitably, the Justices have widely and sharply disagreed with one another on what kinds of speech are constitutionally protected, although the trend during Earl Warren's Chief Justiceship (1953–1969) was certainly toward extending the reach of the First Amendment.

Censorship

On one point, at least, there has historically been wide agreement among judges both here and in other common law countries. Freedom of speech and press protects against prior restraint, that is, against censorship. Under some circumstances, most judges have said, a man may be held responsible for the effects of his words or writings, but he should never have to submit the content of his communication to a censor for advance clearance. Yet, enough cases—frequently decided by divided votes—keep cropping up over the years to indicate that censorship is more prevalent in our society than fiercely libertarian pronouncements by judges would lead one to expect.

In 1931 *Near v. Minnesota*[13] centered around a local district attorney's use of state law that branded as a public nuisance any periodical that regularly published obscene, lewd, or scandalous material. The district attorney had obtained an injunction against future publication of *The Saturday Press,* a weekly newspaper that mixed antisemitism with charges of corruption in Minneapolis politics. "This," a majority of the Supreme Court said about the injunction, "is the essence of censorship," but four of the Justices dissented.

Eight years later, *Hague v. CIO* presented an even more crass kind of censorship, one that has probably occurred more often than it should in local politics. Boss Frank Hague of Jersey City, who once boasted "I am the law," utilized his full power to keep unions out of his private fiefdom. Not only did he deny labor organizers use of public halls in the city and threaten them with arrest if they tried to explain the provisions of federal law to workers, but when organizers did come into town he subjected them to humiliating searches, arrested them for distributing leaflets, and then forced them onto ferries leaving for Manhattan. A federal district judge granted an injunction against Hague, and the Supreme Court affirmed by a 5–2 vote. The majority divided over whether the case should be decided under the privileges and immunities or the due process clause of the Fourteenth Amendment, but the five Justices[14] did agree that, "Wherever the title of streets and parks may rest, they have immemorially been held in trust for the use of the public and, time out of mind, have been used for the purposes of assembly, communicating thoughts between citizens, and discussing public questions."

When Huey Long was running Louisiana much as Hague was running Jersey City—more on the scale of a kingdom than a fiefdom—he instituted a more subtle form of censorship by having the legislature enact a 2 percent tax on the gross receipts of newspapers with a weekly circulation of more than 20,000. Curiously this distinction meant that most of the anti-Long papers had to pay up, while most of those papers who supported Long, the small country weeklies, escaped. The Supreme Court was unanimous in declaring the Kingfish's tax unconstitutional.[15] Incidentally, newspapers are usually subject to the same general statutory regulations as other businesses. For instance, they have to pay regular business taxes, obey labor regulations, and are subject to the antitrust laws.[16] In the Louisiana case, however, the Justices recognized that the law was "a deliberate and calculated device in the guise of a tax to limit the circulation of information to which the public is entitled."

Frequently censorship problems have arisen where cities and towns require licenses for parades and public meetings. The Supreme Court has sustained the validity of such ordinances only where they are essentially nondiscretionary—that is, where the local official can only impose uniform regulations, such as limitations on the times and places for parades and meetings. If the official has discretion to allow a permit to one group and deny it to another, the Court has generally struck down the ordinance.[17]

Moving Pictures, Radio, and Television

A thorny question of coverage arises: What about moving pictures, radio, and television? Usually movies are thought of as art or entertainment, and the Supreme Court[18] in 1915 ruled that they were not covered by the First Amendment. Later, when presented with a case where a film with a social message was censored because it offended racist sentiments, the Justices[19] changed their minds. They added, however, that movies "were not necessarily subject to the precise rules governing other particular methods of expression." In fact the Court subsequently allowed some prior censorship of films, but even more recently[20] has insisted on three sets of procedural safeguards: (1) the burden of proof that a movie is obscene or otherwise objectionable must rest with the censor; (2) the censor must quickly either issue a license or go to court and ask for an order forbidding the showing of the picture; (3) there must be a provision for prompt court review of any action taken by the censor.

The problems of radio and television are complicated by the fact that only a limited number of frequencies and channels are available. Congress has authorized the Federal Communications Commission to allocate these wavelengths under a licensing system and has instructed the Commission to pay attention, in its decisions to grant, renew, or revoke licenses, to the "public interest, convenience, or necessity." Thus there is a potential, at least, for some form of censorship here, although the Supreme Court has sustained the constitutionality of the basic arrangement.

A recent challenge of the FCC's "fairness rule" illustrates the complexity of the problems involved. The fairness rule provides that a radio or television station which in its editorial comments endorses or opposes a candidate for public office or attacks the "honesty, character, integrity or like personal qualities of an identified person or group" must give the other side a chance to reply on the air and at no charge. The Red Lion Broadcasting Company alleged that this rule was a form of censorship both in requiring the station to supply free time and, more subtly, in militating against candid political discussion. The Supreme Court, however, unanimously rejected these arguments.[21] The Justices agreed that the First Amendment was applicable, but it had to be applied in a different way than to ordinary speech or writing. A license did not grant a station a complete monopoly for the political views of its owners. Free communication—the purpose of the First Amendment—required that opponents of a license owner have some opportunity to air their views. Furthermore, the people as a whole retained a right to hear both sides, and that right was paramount. "It is the purpose of the First Amendment to preserve a free marketplace of ideas in which truth will ultimately prevail, rather than to countenance monopolization of that market, whether it be by the Government itself or a private licensee."

Sedition

The most fundamental problem involving freedom of communication and association concerns sedition, that is, a charge of inciting persons to engage in unlawful action against the government. Clearly a democratic society has a right to protect its form of government against coups d'etat and efforts at violent revolution. There has been no serious challenge to the federal government's basic authority to punish sabotage, espionage, or treason. Sedition, however, presents a more delicate issue since it inevitably involves speech or writing. In practice the distinction between a real incitement to violence in the here and now and endorsement of revolution as a moral right is often fuzzy. The distinction causes serious problems for Americans, who because their country was born out of revolution, cannot deny the morality of revolution as a general principle, though they may certainly deny the morality of its application in specific circumstances.

Moreover, no one interested in limited government can afford to forget that public officials may frequently be sorely tempted to regard radical and powerful opponents as revolutionaries. John Marshall certainly viewed Thomas Jefferson as a subversive, and some Federalists called him a seditionist. Indeed, the Adams administration prosecuted many Jeffersonians just for such an offense. One hundred and fifty years later, Senator Joseph McCarthy of Wisconsin managed to brand almost anyone who opposed him as a Communist or Communist sympathizer, just as some members of the New Left tag all opponents as fascists.

The first national sedition statute was the ill-famed companion to the Alien Act of 1798, but after a short and infamous history it lapsed in 1801. During the Civil War, Congress passed a law, still in effect, making it a crime to conspire to overthrow the government by force; and during World War I a new sedition statute, although technically labeled as an espionage act, came into effect. This statute made it a crime to interfere with the draft, obstruct recruiting, encourage disloyalty, incite insubordination in the armed services, hinder sale of U.S. bonds, or "willfully utter, print, write, or publish any disloyal, profane, scurrilous, or abusive language about the form of government of the United States or the Constitution . . . or to bring the form of government . . . or the Constitution . . . into contempt. . . ."

It was in interpreting this act and its amendments that the Supreme Court, speaking through Oliver Wendell Holmes, first formulated the "clear and present danger" test. As initially applied the test served as a justification for affirming the convictions of socialists who had spoken or written in criticism of American participation in World War I.[22] Ironically, it is not clear that Holmes[23] originally meant the test to be a measure of the constitutional power of Congress or to be a rule to determine whether specific words came under the prohibitions of the statute. "The question in every case," he wrote, "is whether the words used are used in such circumstances and are of such a nature as to create a clear and present danger that they will bring about the substantive evils that Congress has a right to prevent."

In any event, excess zeal among state and federal officials in prosecuting both opposition to the war and general political dissent—about 2,000 people were convicted during and shortly after the war—brought Holmes, along with Louis D. Brandeis, onto a different track. Soon the two Justices were using the clear and present danger phrase as a test to determine whether a statute had been constitutionally applied. As Brandeis[24] explained in 1927:

> Fear of serious injury cannot alone justify suppression of free speech and assembly. Men feared witches and burnt women. . . . To justify suppression of free speech there must be reasonable ground to believe that the danger apprehended is imminent. There

must be reasonable ground to believe that the evil to be prevented is a serious one. . . . In order to support a finding of clear and present danger it must be shown either that immediate serious violence was to be expected or advocated, or that past conduct furnished reason to believe that such advocacy was then contemplated.

Holmes and Brandeis, however, were expressing these libertarian views in separate concurring and dissenting opinions, for until the 1930s a majority of the Justices showed little sympathy for First Amendment rights if the speakers were from the political left.

The World War I Act and its amendments were operative only in wartime, and it was not until 1940 that Congress passed a new sedition act that applied in peacetime. This law, popularly known as the Smith Act, defined four different offenses: knowingly advocating violent overthrow of the government; helping organize a society that engages in such advocacy; becoming a member of any such society; and conspiring to commit any of these offenses.

The Smith Act was little used during World War II, but after the Cold War started the Department of Justice began to prosecute groups of Communists for conspiring to advocate violent overthrow of the government and for conspiring to form an organization—the Communist party—to preach and accomplish this result. In 1951 *Dennis v. United States*,[25] a review of a conviction of eleven high-ranking party leaders, marked the first great Supreme Court effort to interpret this statute.

The evidence at the trial had consisted largely of quotations from classics of Marxist literature asserting the inevitability of force to overthrow the established order in capitalist states and the testimony of ex-Communists that they had heard the accused advocate the use of force. The defendants argued that they could not be found guilty unless the government proved that their activity had resulted in a clear and present danger of a substantive evil, namely, the forcible overthrow of the government.

The six Justices in the majority could not agree on the reasoning necessary to uphold the convictions and wrote three separate opinions. In the opinion of Chief Justice Fred Vinson, in which three other Justices concurred, the clear and present danger test was reinterpreted to become a "grave and probable" danger test. In other words, these Justices held that where speech is used to create a particularly grave danger of overthrowing the government, it is sufficient that there should be a probability that the evil result will transpire.

In their dissenting opinions Justices Black and Douglas protested against what they regarded as a drastic dilution of the clear and present danger test. Granting that the "ugliness of Communism" and "its deceit and cunning" were present in the books used by the accused, the dissenters did not feel that the government had proved that the defendants had used speech, or were planning to use speech, in such a way as to create a clear and present danger to the established order.

Following the Supreme Court decision in the *Dennis* case, the federal government proceeded with the prosecution of several score lesser Communist leaders. Virtually all of these defendants were convicted. In 1957, however, in *Yates v. United States*,[26] the Supreme Court set aside convictions of fourteen persons. The majority interpreted the Smith Act as forbidding only advocacy of *action* to achieve the forcible overthrow of government and held that it did not encompass advocacy of the mere abstract *doctrine* of the desirability or inevitability of forcible overthrow. Since the trial judge had failed to charge the jury that the evidence must show that the defendants advocated *action* to overthrow the government, the Court reversed the convictions. It also held that the term "organize," as used in the statute, referred only to the act of founding or establishing an organization and not to the continuing process of carrying on the affairs of an already existing organization. Since it was agreed that the Communist party was finally "organized" no later than 1945, the indictment of the defendants in 1951 was improper under the federal statute of limitations requiring that persons accused of such an offense be prosecuted within three years of the time the alleged offenses were committed. In 1962, Congress amended the Smith Act to include within the word "organize" recruitment of new members and formation of new units of a party, thus reading into the law the meaning rejected by the Supreme Court in the *Yates* case.

In 1961, in *Scales v. United States*,[27] the Court finally passed on the constitutionality of the so-called membership clause of the Smith Act, which makes it a criminal offense to become a member of a society knowing that it advocates overthrow of government by force or violence. In upholding both the validity of the clause and the conviction of Scales under it, the Court ruled that the act reaches only "active," and not merely "nominal" or "passive" members.

In a companion case the Justices reversed a conviction on membership grounds because the evidence had not been sufficient to show that the particular Communist party unit to which the accused belonged had engaged in advocacy of action directed toward forcible overthrow. And the Court[28] reiterated "the premise that Smith Act offenses require rigorous standards of proof." Thus, although the Court has upheld the constitutionality of all phases of the Smith Act brought before it, it has substantially narrowed the coverage of the act and has required the government to carry a heavy burden of proof. These rulings make it extremely difficult to secure convictions under the Smith Act; and they came at a time when federal officials in the executive branch had pretty well concluded that Smith Act prosecutions were a poor way of combatting communism.

In 1950, Congress passed, over President Truman's veto, another major statute aimed at "subversives," the Internal Security Act, popularly known as the McCarran Act. Although portions of the act apply to all "totalitarians," its primary target is Communists. The statute required all "Communist-action" and "Communist-front" organizations, and individual members of the former, to register with the federal government. The Act also created a Subversive Activities Control Board to decide what organizations are required to register. Members of such organizations are subject to varying prohibitions; for example, they may not hold government jobs. The statute also provided for internment of persons whom the government may believe likely to commit espionage or sabotage in time of emergency, and it placed severe immigration and naturalization restrictions upon Communists.

Enforcement of the registration system bogged down in litigation for a decade. Finally in 1961, in a 5–4 ruling, the Supreme Court held that the registration section of the act was constitutional and that the Communist party was required to register under it. The Court postponed, however, a ruling on the validity of the consequences of such registration for party members.[29] Party officials still refused to register, and eventually their case again reached the Supreme Court in 1965. The Court then unanimously ruled that the registration requirements for individual party officers violated the Fifth Amendment's ban against compulsory self-incrimination.[30]

Enforcement of other parts of the McCarran Act has also run into difficulties. The Supreme Court has declared unconstitutional two provisions, one relating to travel by members of the Communist party and the other to a ban on Communists working in defense industries.[31] In addition, no President has yet attempted to apply the preventive detention clauses and some political pressure has been building up for the repeal of this section since it smacks of concentration camps and involves imprisonment without trial. There is, however, an unhappy precedent. During World War II, the federal governmental interned over 100,000 American citizens of Japanese decent and in what must rank as one of the least proud moments of the Court, a majority of the Justices declared such action constitutional.[32]

The Smith and McCarran Acts may have made some small contribution to the demise of communism in the United States, but it is far more probable that the major credit for this decline is due to Stalinist brutality inside and outside the Soviet Union and to the blind dogmatism of the leaders of the American Communist party. On the whole, it is hard to find in these particular statutes—as opposed to laws relating to espionage and sabotage—an intelligent approach to countering subversive activity. They do, however, present serious dangers to free discussion. At a very minimum their enactment shows that members of Congress placed a low value on unobstructed communication and put a low assessment on the capacity of the people to reject Communist propaganda. When public officials denigrate freedom and enshrine orthodoxy they may well shape the general political culture to weaken support for essential civil liberties.

Loyalty-Security Programs

Loyalty-security programs provide another painful illustration of the severe tensions between liberty and authority as well as among various kinds of rights. The issue is not merely that of government's right to protect itself against actual and potential subversives within its own ranks. Also involved is the right of the people to have their government operating in their interests, not those of another nation. But there are also the rights of officials and candidates for public office to exercise their constitutional prerogatives of speaking and thinking freely about political matters.

The problem is how to weed out professional spies and to distinguish among various categories of more or less risky and more or less reliable persons—for even though it may not be true that every man has his price, it is very probably true that almost every man has his breaking point. The difficulties of weighing the typically elusive and intangible evidence available for such judgments impose not only tremendous intellectual problems but also real dangers for civil liberties, especially First Amendment freedoms. To bar a man for preaching the necessity of violent overthrow of the government or for knowingly joining with others who do so may be perfectly reasonable, but such cases just rarely come up. The common situation is that of a man who has espoused unorthodox views or has been a member of groups on the fringes of the political left or right or even, years earlier, of the Communist party. A program that does not distinguish between innocent and knowing membership or between radical hyperbole and seditious words threatens not only to punish individuals for exercising their constitutional rights, but it can also leave the public service staffed largely by timid or unimaginative officials who are welded by fear to the status quo. More generally, by putting a premium on the staid and conventional, such a program, if its contagion affects society as a whole, may choke off all hope of progress.

During the McCarthy period, both state and federal loyalty-security programs were badly abused to expel many people who had dared to endorse novel or unpopular ideas. There is little evidence of hard-line Communists either being discovered or fired, although many may have been kept out of government service. Since that particular form of hysteria has quieted, the federal programs, at least, seem to be operating more fairly. The Supreme Court played an indirect role in this change. Its main contribution was to remind public officials and private citizens of constitutional principles of free expression and association, and at the same time use statutory interpretation to narrow the reach of the federal programs rather than constitutional clauses to invalidate them.[33]

The Justices have been more bold where state programs have been challenged. A central item in both state and federal efforts has been the loyalty oath, a requirement that officials and candidates for public jobs swear not only to support the Constitution but additional affirmations that they are not fascists or Communists and do not seek to overthrow the government by force. These oaths are distasteful and are hardly likely to deter a professional agent or even a security risk, who usually is either vulnerable to some kind of blackmail or is so venal as to be willing to sell out his country. After some initial vacillation, the Supreme Court has come down hard on these oaths as being unconstitutionally vague.[34] And after the Justices had invalidated a whole series of state oaths and a U.S. district court had ruled against the federal requirement,[35] the U.S. Civil Service Commission in 1970 issued a directive dropping the loyalty oath for new federal employees.

Incitement to Riot

On the local level, the dangers of riots and mob action are far more real than any communist-directed efforts at a national coup d'etat. As one would suspect, the Court has reviewed a number of convictions of controversial speakers. Since these local disputes almost always involve state regulations, the Justices have not had open to them the less direct course of statutory interpretation, for by its own rulings the Supreme Court must accept whatever gloss state courts put on their own laws. Squarely faced with constitutional issue, the Justices have, by and large, been more libertarian than in national decisions. In *Brandenburg v. Ohio*,[36] for example, the Justices were unanimous in reversing the conviction of a Ku Klux Klan leader for making a speech before a hooded and armed group, urging them to "bury the niggers" and "send the Jews back to Israel." The Court made the same distinction between advocacy and incitement here that it had made in *Yates v. United States* and held that the state could not punish a speaker unless he was "inciting or producing imminent lawless action and is likely to incite or produce such action."

Political Pressure

The Supreme Court, we saw in Chapter 7, has placed lobbying within the compass of the First Amendment, and this protection holds for all branches of government, including the courts. In the context of American pressure group politics, litigation, the Justices have recognized, is more than "a technique for resolving private differences"; it is "a form of political expression. Groups which find themselves unable to achieve their objectives through the ballot frequently turn to the courts."[37]

Picketing and demonstrations constitute another form of political pressure, a kind of lobbying with the public rather than with government officials, although, of course, protestors are typically acutely aware that officials usually watch their demonstrations closely. While acknowledging that these forms of communication are constitutionally protected, the Supreme Court has also recognized that the physical presence of people carrying placards proclaiming bitterly controversial demands and perhaps jostling or accosting bystanders and opponents, injects a complicating element. And the Court has sustained restraints against picketing that occurred "in a context of violence" or where the demonstrators sought illegal ends.[38]

The Justices have also been more tolerant of demonstrations aimed at other public officials than at fellow judges. *Edwards v. South Carolina*[39] and *Cox v. Louisiana*[40] reveal interesting differences in approach. In *Edwards,* one hundred and eight-seven black students had been arrested for marching around the state capitol grounds carrying placards protesting segregation policies. The police at first merely watched, but when a crowd of several hundred persons gathered and traffic in the area was being slowed, the police told the students to disperse. The students responded by singing patriotic and religious songs while clapping their hands and stomping their feet. The police promptly marched the demonstrators off to jail, and later they were convicted for breach of the peace. The Supreme Court reversed the convictions, pointing out that the students had done no more than exercise their constitutional rights of assembly and petition. The Court stated that the function of these rights was to invite dispute, even perhaps to stir anger and bring about unrest. As long as the students had demonstrated peacefully and had not caused a major traffic obstruction, they could not be punished.

Cox presented parallel facts except that the demonstrators were protesting outside a state courthouse and were convicted under a Louisiana law—modeled on a federal statute—prohibiting picketing "near" a court. Although reversing these convictions on technical grounds, the Justices carefully pointed out that a state could protect courts not only from actual interference but also from any situation that could give rise to a belief that judges and jurors might be unlawfully swayed in their decisions.

While *Cox* did endorse a relatively stringent rule where judges were the target of protest, that decision represents a far more libertarian view than prevailed prior to 1941. The older rule allowed judges to punish as contempt any speech or writing that sharply criticized or in any way implied an effort to influence the judicial process.[41] Since 1941 the Justices have drawn a distinction between words and deeds taking place inside a courtroom and those that occur outside. The Court has allowed judges considerable discretion to punish summarily allegedly contemptuous words or acts that transpire within the court. But for an out of court statement to be punishable, it must "constitute an

"Correctly numbered pages are not a redeeming social value."

Drawing by Savage. © 1969 by The New York Times Company. Reprinted by permission.

imminent, not merely a likely, threat to the administration of justice. The danger must not be remote or even probable; it must immediately imperil."[42] This doctrine does not restrict the power of judges to punish out-of-court disobedience of their decrees as contempt.

Symbolic Speech

The concept of "symbolic speech" adds an interesting and vexing dimension to First Amendment problems. Symbols are an integral part of communication, and, in a sense, although the Justices did not choose to see it that way, demonstrations constitute symbolic speech. Indeed, it would be hard to identify any part of the democratic political process that could not reasonably be so labeled. As we saw earlier, Justice Black's intellectually neat distinction between words and action runs into serious practical difficulties. In its decisions, the Court seems so far to be following a simple pragmatic course. Where the matter has been minor—wearing of black armbands, for instance—the Justices have stressed the communications aspects of the case and the necessity of constitutional protection. Where the issue has been more serious—the burning of draft cards—the Court has emphasized the deed itself rather than communication of ideas and noted that government can punish action.[43]

Obscenity

Sex problems always make interesting law; and writing or speaking frankly about sex directly raises a political issue of the constitutional protection that should be accorded such discussion. Indirectly this kind of communication may help determine how permissive or authoritarian a society will be in its general orientation. Furthermore, the current injunction "to make love, not war" links, whether consciously or not, sexual mores dominant in the older generations with a pentup aggressiveness that expresses itself in institutionalized violence. To the extent that candid discussion of sexual matters is aimed at this or similarly socially relevant relationships, it would seem to come under the rubric of political discussion. It is this kind of content that judges have been searching for when they speak of "redeeming social value" of literature and nonliterature that is otherwise crudely vulgar.

Obscenity cases have given judges great headaches, especially in recent decades when jurists have been more sensitive to the necessity of free transmission of ideas. Judges are also aware of the profits that accrue to merchants who pander to sexual drives, and of the integral part that sexual mores play in shaping much of the rest of social life. Complicating their lives has been the fear that idiosyncratic or outmoded standards of morality might be used to inhibit creativity in the arts as well as political communication. The farce of church officials putting fig leaves on some of Michelangelo's masterpieces still rankles. In all of this pulling and tugging, a majority of the Supreme Court has maintained that the distribution of obscenity itself lies outside of the pale of constitutional protection. But, mere possession of obscene material for personal edification or amusement falls within the ambit of the First Amendment.

The next step, establishing a test to distinguish the obscene from the candid or the merely vulgar, is the critical one, since most definitions tend to be either circular or to depend on highly individualized value judgments. *Roth v. United States* (1957)[44] is a landmark case because the Justices faced up to the problems of definition and tests. The Court emphasized that "sex and obscenity are not synonymous" and defined the latter as "material which deals with sex in a manner appealing to prurient interest." Expressly rejecting a Victorian test that a book might be judged obscene because of isolated passages, the Court established this rule: "whether to the average person, applying contemporary community standards, the dominant theme of the material taken as a whole appeals to prurient interest."

"Prurient" Webster defines as "marked by a restless craving: itching with curiosity"; it is hardly more clear than the word obscenity itself. And in 1966[45] the Justices refined their test to include three elements: "(a) the dominant theme of the material taken as a whole appeals to prurient interest in sex; (b) the material is patently offensive because it affronts contemporary community standards relating to the description or representation of sexual matters; and (c) the material is utterly without redeeming social value."

Unfortunately, in none of their decisions have the Justices been able to agree as to whether "contemporary community standards" are those of the nation as a whole or those of a particular locality. A majority, however, has held that it is legitimate for government officials to consider the way in which an item is advertised as a factor in determining whether its appeal is mainly to prurient interests.[46] Thus the Court affirmed the conviction of the publisher of the magazine *Eros,* who had used advertising methods that were permeated by the "leer of the sensualist" and had, for obvious publicity reasons, tried to get his material mailed from two Pennsylvania towns, Intercourse and Blue Ball. Failing in this he had settled on Middlesex, New Jersey.

Children present special problems where obscenity is possibly involved. In the same year as the *Roth* decision, the Court invalidated a Michigan statute that made it a crime to sell to anyone a book that might be dangerous to the young.[47] "The incidence of this enactment," the Court said, "is to reduce the adult population of Michigan to reading only what is fit for children." And that, the Justices thought, "is to burn the house to roast the pig." On the other hand, the Court later sustained a narrowly worded New York law forbidding sales of girlie magazines to minors.[48]

Roth was an exception in that it involved a federal statute. Most obscenity cases come from state prosecutions. To date, the Court has never found a federal law restricting obscenity unconstitutional, although it has on occasion held that the Postmaster General has exceeded his statutory authority to ban certain material from the mails.[49]

Libel and Slander

Libel and slander refer to words (*printed* in the case of libel, *spoken* in the case of slander) used with malicious intent to defame the character of another person or to expose him to public contempt, hatred, or ridicule. There are obvious tensions between these concepts and that of freedom of the press and speech. For the law, that is, society, to ignore such conduct would leave men's reputations at the mercy of whim and charity, and could gutterize the electoral process. Yet it is difficult to distinguish, especially in the heat of political debate, between fair but biting criticism and character defamation. And historically government officials have used criminal libel laws to punish their opponents and choke off opposition generally.

Faced with this dilemma, a majority of the Supreme Court has opted for a course that takes away from "public figures" as well as public officials a large part of the remedy that private citizens have against defamation. The key decision came in 1964, in *New York Times v. Sullivan.*[50] There the Court reversed a state libel judgment against the *Times* for publishing an advertisement attacking Birmingham, Alabama, officials for mistreating blacks. Conceding that some information in the advertisement was false, a majority of the Justices nevertheless ruled that good faith criticism of government officials was so important to a democracy that the Constitution "prohibits a public official from recovering damages for a defamatory falsehood relating to his official conduct unless he proves that the statement was made with 'actual malice'—that is with knowledge that it was false or with reckless disregard of whether it was false or not." Justices Black, Douglas, and Goldberg would have held that in criticizing a public official a newspaper has absolute immunity from a libel suit.

THE RIGHT TO TRAVEL

The right to disseminate ideas and to join with others who hold similar views implies a right to move freely within the United States and under certain circumstances in and out of the country as well. In addition, the facts of modern economic life often make freedom of movement essential to earning a living. The Supreme Court has long recognized these aspects of travel. Shortly after the Civil War the Court invalidated a Nevada law that tried to stem the state's loss of population by taxing railroads for every passenger carried out of the state.[51] In 1942 the Justices also struck down a California law designed to exclude from entry citizens of other states who might become dependent on local relief.[52] Five Justices based their decision on a finding that California was interfering with interstate commerce. The other four found that the statute robbed citizens of one of the privileges and immunities protected by the Fourteenth Amendment.

In the early 1960s, "freedom riders" underlined the political implications of the right to travel. These riders, both white and black, made trips around the Deep South, usually by bus, to dramatize the discrimination still practiced against blacks in waiting rooms, restaurants, and other facilities connected with interstate commerce. In many instances they encountered not only public hostility but also official resistance in the form of prosecutions for disturbing the peace and inciting violence. Violence, in fact, was frequent, but against the riders. At a cost of many jailings and beatings, the riders ultimately caused the desegregation of a large number of interstate facilities.[53]

Most of the Supreme Court cases concerning foreign travel have involved alleged Communists or travel to Communist countries. The Justices have endorsed two competing principles. On the one hand, they have held that "the right to travel is part of the 'liberty' of which the citizen cannot be deprived without due process of law." On the other hand, they have acknowledged that the federal government's authority to conduct foreign relations, to regulate commerce, and to control immigration can legitimately operate to limit travel rights. In reconciling these principles, the Court has insisted that restrictive regulations be clearly authorized by Congress. As Justice Douglas[54] said for a five-judge majority in 1958 in ruling that Congress had not conferred on the Secretary of State power to deny passports to Communists: "Where activities or enjoyment, natural and often necessary to the wellbeing of an American citizen, such as travel are involved, we will construe narrowly all delegated powers that curtail or dilute them."

The Justices have also stressed that a restrictive statute must be carefully drawn. "Precision," the Court[55] explained in striking down that section of the McCarran Act that made it a felony for a member of Communist-action or Communist-front organization to apply for a passport, "must be the touchstone of legislation so affecting basic freedoms." And, six members of the Court felt, the McCarran Act "sweeps too widely and too indiscriminately across the liberty guaranteed by the Fifth Amendment."

FREEDOM OF RELIGION

Religious freedom is closely connected with freedom of speech, association, and assembly. And one has only to look at the northern counties of Ireland to see how bitterly religion can be linked to politics even in the modern world. The thrust of the American Constitution—not completely successful, as the 1928 and 1960 Presidential campaigns and current controversies over public aid to parochial schools demonstrate—is to take religion completely out of politics. Article VI outlaws religious tests for public officers and the First Amendment forbids Congress—and, by way of the Fourteenth Amendment, the states— to "establish" a religion or to interfere with "the free exercise" of religion. These three prohibitions are closely related and actual cases seldom fall neatly into one category rather than another.

Establishment of Religion

Congress has never tried to "establish" a religion in the literal or even historical sense of that term, and long before the Fourteenth Amendment came into effect all the states had disestablished churches. Establishment, however, is a word much more freighted with meaning. As the Supreme Court explained in 1947,[56] the First Amendment means at least that:

> Neither a state nor the Federal Government can set up a church. Neither can pass laws which aid one religion, aid all religions, or prefer one religion over another. . . . No tax in any amount, large or small, can be levied to support any religious activities or institutions, whatever they may be called, or whatever form they may adopt to teach or practice religion. Neither a state nor the Federal Government can, openly or secretly, participate in the affairs of any religious organization or groups and vice versa.

Despite such a sweeping definition, the Justices have found no barrier to states supplying free bus transportation and free textbooks to parochial school children,[57] holding that these kinds of aid were for "a secular purpose and a primary effect that neither advances nor inhibits religion." Religious education has met with a more mixed reception. In 1948 the Court[58] invalidated a "released time" program for religious instruction. Under this system, unpaid volunteers from local churches gave instructions on school property once a week to children whose parents wanted them to have such training. A majority of the Court thought that use of public property and utilization of compulsory attendance laws to get the children into school in the first place constituted an establishment. Four years later, however, the Court[59] held constitutional a plan similar in almost all respects except that instructions were given off school property.

The widespread practice of prayers and Bible reading in public schools has generated a series of cases. For years the Justices avoided ruling on such rituals, but in 1962 they squarely faced the issue of the constitutionality of a prayer composed by the New York State Board of Regents: "Almighty God, we acknowledge our dependence upon Thee, and we beg Thy blessings upon us, our parents, our teachers, and our country." Any student would be excused from this recitation if his parents requested, but the Court still ruled that the arrangement violated the First Amendment. Government, Justice Black[60] said for the majority, "should stay out of the business of writing or sanctioning official prayers and leave that purely religious function to the people themselves and to those the people choose to look to for religious guidance."

The following year the Justices extended this ruling to strike down a Pennsylvania requirement of daily reading in public schools of verses of the Bible and recitation of the Lord's Prayer. Justice Clark[61] wrote for the Court:

> The place of religion in our society is an exalted one, achieved through a long tradition of reliance on the home, the church and the inviolable citadel of the individual heart and mind. We have come to recognize through bitter experience that it is not within the power of government to invade that citadel, whether its purpose or effect be to aid or oppose, to advance or retard. In the relationship between man and religion, the State is firmly committed to a position of neutrality.

Free Exercise

One of the earliest free exercise cases involved a challenge to an act of Congress outlawing polygamy in the territories. The statute was clearly directed against the Mormons, but in 1879 the Court[62] sustained its validity, distinguishing between the right to believe, which was absolute, and the right to act, which was subject to normal criminal law. Sixty-seven years later the Court held that an anti-prostitution statute could legitimately be applied to Mormons practicing polygamy.[63] A bare majority of the Justices, speaking through Justice Douglas, said that polygamy was "a notorious example of promiscuity" that Congress could punish. The Court recognized the religious motivation behind the practice, but found that immaterial. Had the Mormons advocated merely "serial polygamy," that is, many wives but only one at a time, they would in this century at least have been in the mainstream of American law and culture.

Sunday closing laws have also raised questions both of establishment—sanctioning the Christian day of rest—and of free exercise in that they force Jewish merchants to recognize the Christian sabbath and put them at a competitive disadvantage if they try to observe their own. A majority of the Supreme Court[64] rejected both arguments, but a few years later did hold[65] that a state could not lawfully deny unemployment compensation to a Seventh Day Adventist who refused to accept a job that required him to work on Saturdays.

Small religious sects have frequently suffered from government regulations impinging on their rituals and tabus. The Jehovah's Witnesses have been especially active in bringing offending public officials into court, and their litigation in the 1940s helped develop much of the law of free speech. Interestingly, the Justices preferred to rest their decisions on the somewhat broader grounds of freedom of communication rather than on religious discrimination. The most notable victory of the Witnesses was over compulsory flag salutes. Since the Witnesses take the First Commandment literally—not to worship "graven images"—they refused to allow their children to participate in saluting the flag. In 1940, by an overwhelming 8–1 majority, the Court[66] upheld a requirement of this type, with Justice Harlan Stone the lone dissenter. Three years later the Supreme Court agreed to reconsider the problem. Four of the Justices who had participated in the first decision were now ready to invalidate compulsory flag-salute legislation, and they were joined by two new members of the Court to make up a 6–3 majority that held such legislation an unconstitutional interference with religious freedom.[67]

Test Oaths

In *Torcaso v. Watkins* a unanimous Court invalidated a provision in the Maryland state constitution that required all persons holding office of profit or trust in the state to declare a belief in the existence of God. Torcaso had been denied a commission as a notary public because of a refusal to make such a declaration. The Court[68] said, "This Maryland religious test for public office unconstitutionally invades the appellant's freedom of belief and religion and therefore cannot be enforced against him." The Justices were doing little more here than recognizing that freedom to believe in God is not true freedom unless it includes the right not to believe.

Military Service and Conscientious Objectors

Governmental authority to raise armies by means of compulsory service can endanger the religious freedom of those citizens who are opposed to war on moral grounds. Here two interests may come into direct conflict, that of society in its own self-defense and that of society in attaining one of its goals, freedom of conscience. The problem is made more complex by the difficulty of ascertaining whether a man is truly opposed to war on moral principles or is merely trying to avoid risking his life.

Even in Colonial times the states made some provision for exempting conscientious objectors from service in the militia. And when the federal government first instituted a draft during the Civil War, Congress followed this state practice, though the exemptions were narrow. Again, in World War I, Congress excused from combat service members of any "well-recognized religious sect" whose tenets forbade participation in war.

In 1940, Congress widened the limits to include any person "who, by reason of religious training and belief, is conscientiously opposed to participation in war in any form." Eight years later Congress added that "religious training and belief in this connection means an individual's belief in a relationship to a Supreme Being involving duties superior to those arising from any human relation, but does not include essentially political, sociological, or philosophical views or or a merely personal code."

The Supreme Court has liberally interpreted these provisions. In *United States v. Seegar* [69] the Justices unanimously reversed draft-evasion convictions of three men, two of whom expressed beliefs in a Supreme Being and vaguely related these beliefs to moral objections to war. The third defendant claimed that he was opposed to war on religious grounds but admitted skepticism regarding the existence of a Supreme Being. Rather, he based his opposition to war on a "belief in and devotion to goodness and virtue for their own sakes, and a religious faith in a purely ethical creed." The Justices found that this statement, if sincerely made, entitled him to exemption under the law. In reversing these convictions, the Court tried to formulate two general tests to determine whether individuals who do not belong to sects such as the Quakers should be exempt from military service. The first test is: Does the claimed belief occupy the same place in the life of the objector as an orthodox belief in God holds in the life of one clearly qualified for exemption? The second test is more difficult and factual: Does the objector sincerely believe in the pacifist views he proclaims?

A 1970 case caused the Justices more problems.[70] There the defendant denied that his pacifist views were in any way connected with religion but were solely the result of his reading history and sociology. Speaking through Justice Black, four of the eight participating Justices applied the *Seegar* rules and found that the defendant was entitled to an exemption as a conscientious objector under the draft act. The other four Justices believed that the statute simply could not be stretched to cover beliefs so sharply divorced from religious tenets. But one of the latter four, John Marshall Harlan, thought that insofar as the draft law allowed exemptions on religious grounds it was a violation of the First Amendment. Thus he voted with Black and his colleagues. The result of the case was clear but the future status of the *Seegar* rules became much more doubtful.

THE RIGHT TO FREEDOM

Slavery

So far we have been discussing specific civil rights, but underlying all of these is the right to freedom itself. Closely allied is the right to citizenship which, in a world divided into hundreds of independent nation states, becomes "the right to have rights."[71] Because of the slavery issue, the Framers of the Constitution evaded defining either freedom or citizenship, but the Thirteenth and Fourteenth Amendments repaired these omissions. Unlike most constitutional provisions, the Thirteenth Amendment operates against private persons as well as against government officials:

> Neither slavery nor involuntary servitude, except as a punishment for crime whereof the party shall have been duly convicted, shall exist within the United States, or any place subject to their jurisdiction. Congress shall have power to enforce this article by appropriate legislation.

Most of the controversies that have arisen under this Amendment have centered about real or alleged instances of "involuntary servitude" rather than "slavery." In 1867, Congress passed an Act, making it a federal crime to hold persons in peonage—"a status or condition of compulsory service, based upon the indebtedness of the peon to the master." Thus attempts to force a man to work off a debt are illegal. "The undoubted aim of the Thirteenth Amendment as implemented by the Antipeonage Act," the Supreme Court[72] said, "was not merely to end slavery but to maintain a system of completely free and voluntary labor throughout the United States."

Compulsory military service has, many young people would think, a real element of involuntary servitude, but in 1917 a unanimous Supreme Court[73] gave this proposition short shrift, disposing of it in one long jumbled sentence: "contributing to the defense of the rights and honor of the nation" was a citizen's "supreme and noble duty." While this decision is still ruling law, the Supreme Court[74] in 1968 scalded as "a blatantly lawless" act, a local draft board's revocation of an exemption because the man had turned in his registration card as a protest against the war in Vietnam.

Citizenship

In the infamous Dred Scott case,[75] the Supreme Court held that blacks could not be citizens of the United States. The Fourteenth Amendment overruled this decision and provided very simply that "all persons born or naturalized in the United States, and subject to the jurisdiction thereof, are citizens of the United States and of the State wherein they reside." Despite its straightforwardness, this clause has left many tough questions unresolved. Among the more important have been: Can Congress revoke a person's citizenship as a punishment for crime? Under what circumstances can a man be judged to have given up his citizenship? After some internal disagreement, a majority of the Court has come around to the view that Congress may not revoke a person's citizenship for any reason. An individual may voluntarily renounce it but only by a definite, specific repudiation. The Justices have held[76] that neither desertion from the armed forces in wartime, nor draft evasion, nor voting in a foreign election constitutes a clear repudiation.

SELECTED BIBLIOGRAPHY

Becker, Carl, *Freedom and Responsibility in the American Way of Life* (New York: Alfred A. Knopf, Inc., 1945). A beautifully written analysis of the compatibility of political authority and individual liberty.

Berns, Walter, *Freedom, Virtue and the First Amendment* (Baton Rouge, La.: Louisiana State University Press, 1957). A vigorous attack on the American tradition of freedom of expression.

Brown, Ralph S., Jr., *Loyalty and Security* (New Haven, Conn.: Yale University Press, 1958). A thorough and comprehensive analysis of the loyalty-security problem.

Chafee, Zechariah, *Free Speech in the United States* (Cambridge, Mass.: Harvard University Press, 1941). A classic in civil rights literature, by a noted legal scholar and defender of human liberty.

Clor, Harry M., *Obscenity and Public Morality: Censorship in a Liberal Society* (Chicago, Ill.: University of Chicago Press, 1969). A sophisticated attempt to develop a justification for censorship against obscenity in a free society.

Emerson, Thomas I., *Toward a General Theory of the First Amendment* (New York: Random House, 1963). An effort to construct a formal legal doctrine to guide judges in deciding First Amendment cases.

Fortas, Abe, *Concerning Dissent and Civil Disobedience* (New York: The New American Library, 1968). An argument for dissent within the law, written by Fortas when he was still on the Supreme Court.

Lasswell, Harold D., *National Security and Individual Freedom* (New York: McGraw-Hill Book Company, 1950). An analysis of the dangers of a garrison state, even a supposedly democratic garrison state.

Levy, Leonard W., *Legacy of Suppression: Freedom of Speech and Press in Early American History* (Cambridge, Mass.: Harvard University Press, 1960). A myth-puncturing account of the rather low legal protection accorded freedom of expression in the good old days.

Meiklejohn, Alexander, *Free Speech and Its Relation to Self-Government* (New York: Harper & Brothers, 1948). A provocative and influential thesis that freedom of political expression ought to be an absolute right.

Mill, John Stuart, *On Liberty* (New York: Appleton-Century-Crofts, 1947). Originally published in 1851, a famous attempt to define the proper limits of freedom and authority.

Pritchett, C. Herman, *The American Constitution*, 2d ed. (New York: McGraw-Hill Book Company, 1968), Chaps. 20–28. A lucid presentation of the law of the First Amendment.

Shapiro, Martin, *Freedom of Speech: The Supreme Court and Judicial Review* (Englewood Cliffs, N.J.: Prentice-Hall, Inc., 1966). An introductory analysis of Supreme Court treatment of free speech problems.

Thoreau, Henry D., *On the Duty of Civil Disobedience* (New Haven, Conn.: Yale University Press, 1928). Originally published in 1849; an impassioned disquisition on the moral obligation of the individual to resist unjust governmental authority.

Zinn, Howard, *Disobedience and Democracy: Nine Fallacies on Law and Order* (New York: Random House, 1968). A vigorous effort to rebut Fortas' book as vitiating civil liberties.

Footnotes

[1] *Abrams v. United States*, 250 U.S. 616, 630, dissenting opinion (1919).

[2] *Barron v. Baltimore*, 7 Peters 243 (1833).

[3] *Gitlow v. New York*, 268 U.S. 652 (1925).

[4] See, for example: *Palko v. Connecticut*, 302 U.S. 319 (1937), explaining and justifying choices up to that time; also: *DeJonge v. Oregon*, 299 U.S. 353 (1937), and *Cantwell v. Connecticut*, 310 U.S. 296 (1940).

[5] These cases are discussed in Chapter 20.

[6] John Milton, *Areopagitica*, Hales, ed. (New York: Oxford University Press, 1917), pp. 51–52.

[7] James D. Richardson, ed., *Messages and Papers of the Presidents* (Washington, D.C.: Bureau of National Literature and Art, 1903), I, 321–322.

[8] "Absolutes, Courts, and the Bill of Rights," *New York University Law Review*, 35 (April 1960), p. 865.

[9] *Tinker v. Des Moines*, 393 U.S. 503 (1969).

[10] *United States v. O'Brien*, 391 U.S. 367 (1968).

[11] *Street v. New York*, 394 U.S. 576 (1969).

[12] *Cox v. Louisiana*, 379 U.S. 559, 583 (1965).

[13] 283 U.S. 697 (1931).

[14] 307 U.S. 496, 507 (1939).

[15] *Grosjean v. American Press Co.*, 297 U.S. 233 (1936).

[16] See: *Associated Press v. NLRB*, 301 U.S. 103 (1937); *Associated Press v. United States*, 326 U.S. 1 (1945); *Oklahoma Press Co. v. Walling*, 327 U.S. 186 (1946); *Lorain Journal v. United States*, 342 U.S. 143 (1951).

[17] For instance: *Lovell v. Griffin*, 303 U.S. 444 (1938); *Hague v. CIO*, 307 U.S. 496 (1939); *Cox v. New Hampshire*, 312 U.S. 569 (1941); *Niemotko v. Maryland*, 340 U.S. 268 (1951).

[18] *Mutual Film Corp. v. Ohio*, 236 U.S. 230 (1915).

[19] *Burstyn v. Wilson*, 343 U.S. 495 (1952).

[20] *Freedman v. Maryland*, 380 U.S. 51 (1965).

[21] *Red Lion Broadcasting Co. v. FCC*, 395 U.S. 367 (1969). For an earlier ruling on the basic requirement of a license to broadcast, see *National Broadcasting Co. v. United States*, 319 U.S. 190 (1943).

[22] *Schenck v. United States*, 249 U.S. 47 (1919); *Frohwerk v. United States*, 249 U.S. 204 (1919); and *Debs v. United States*, 249 U.S. 211 (1919).

[23] *Schenck v. United States*, 249 U.S. 47, 53 (1919).

[24] *Whitney v. California*, 274 U.S. 357, 376, concurring opinion (1927).

[25] 341 U.S. 494 (1951).

[26] 354 U.S. 398 (1957).

[27] 367 U.S. 203 (1961).

[28] *Noto v. United States,* 367 U.S. 290 (1961).

[29] *Communist Party v. Subversive Activities Control Board,* 367 U.S. 1 (1961).

[30] *Albertson v. SACB,* 382 U.S. 70 (1965).

[31] *United States v. Robel,* 389 U.S. 258 (1967).

[32] *Korematsu v. United States,* 323 U.S. 214 (1944).

[33] See, for example: *Joint Anti-Fascist Refugee Committee v. McGrath,* 341 U.S. 123 (1951); *Peters v. Hobby,* 349 U.S. 331 (1955); *Cole v. Young,* 351 U.S. 536 (1956); *Vitarelli v. Seaton,* 359 U.S. 535 (1959); and *Cafeteria and Restaurant Workers v. McElroy,* 367 U.S. 886 (1961).

[34] See, for instance: *Baggett v. Bullitt,* 377 U.S. 360 (1964); *Cramp v. Board,* 368 U.S. 278 (1961); and *Elfbrandt v. Russell,* 384 U.S. 11 (1966).

[35] *Stewart v. Washington,* 301 F. Supp. 610 (1969).

[36] 395 U.S. 444 (1969).

[37] *NAACP v. Button,* 371 U.S. 415, 429 (1963).

[38] *Milk Wagon Drivers Union v. Meadowmoor Dairies,* 312 U.S. 287 (1941); and *Giboney v. Empire Storage,* 336 U.S. 490 (1949).

[39] 372 U.S. 229 (1963).

[40] 379 U.S. 536 (1965).

[41] *Toledo Blade v. United States,* 247 U.S. 40 (1918), states the older rule.

[42] *Craig v. Harney,* 331 U.S. 367, 376 (1947); See also: *Nye v. United States,* 313 U.S. 33 (1941); *Bridges v. California,* 312 U.S. 252 (1941); and *Pennekamp v. Florida,* 328 U.S. 331 (1946).

[43] The Court decided the flag burning case, *Street v. New York,* 394 U.S. 576 (1969), on other grounds, but each of the four opinions in the case made it plain that the Justices thought that government could punish a man for publicly burning an American flag.

[44] 354 U.S. 476 (1957).

[45] *Fanny Hill v. Massachusetts,* 383 U.S. 413, 318 (1966).

[46] *Ginzburg v. United States,* 383 U.S. 463 (1966).

[47] *Butler v. Michigan,* 352 U.S. 380 (1957).

[48] *Ginsberg v. New York,* 390 U.S. 629 (1968).

[49] See, for example, *Hannegan v. Esquire,* 327 U.S. 146 (1946). The Court did invalidate on First Amendment grounds a federal law authorizing the Postmaster General to destroy unsolicited mail that he deemed to be Communist propaganda, unless the addressee requested delivery. *Lamont v. Postmaster General,* 381 U.S. 301 (1965).

[50] 376 U.S. 254 (1964). Later decisions following *The New York Times* doctrine are: *Garrison v. Louisiana,* 379 U.S. 64 (1965), and *Rosenblatt v. Baer,* 383 U.S. 75 (1966). In *Curtis Publishing Co. v. Butts* and *Associated Press v. Walker,* 388 U.S. 130 (1967), a majority of the Justices disagreed among themselves about how the *New York Times* rule should be applied, although they did agree on the results in the two disputes.

[51] *Crandall v. Nevada,* 6 Wallace 35 (1868).

[52] *Edwards v. California,* 314 U.S. 160 (1942).

[53] See Law Survey, "Transportation," *Race Relations Law Reporter,* 7 (Spring 1962), p. 311; and *Bailey v. Patterson,* 369 U.S. 31 (1962).

[54] *Kent v. Dulles,* 357 U.S. 116, 129 (1958); see also *Dayton v. Dulles,* 357 U.S. 144 (1958).

[55] *Aptheker v. Rusk,* 378 U.S. 500, 514 (1964); see also *United States v. Lamb,* 385 U.S. 475 (1967).

[56] *Everson v. Ewing Township,* 330 U.S. 1, 15–16 (1947).

[57] *Board of Regents v. Allen,* 392 U.S. 236, 243 (1968).

[58] *McCollum v. Board,* 333 U.S. 203 (1948).

[59] *Zorach v. Clauson,* 343 U.S. 606 (1952).

[60] *Engel v. Vitale,* 370 U.S. 421, 435 (1962).

[61] *Abington School District v. Schempp,* 374 U.S. 203, 226 (1963); see also *Chamberlin v. Dade County,* 377 U.S. 402 (1964).

[62] *Reynolds v. United States,* 98 U.S. 145 (1879); *Davis v. Beason,* 133 U.S. 333 (1890).

[63] *Cleveland v. United States,* 329 U.S. 14 (1946).

[64] *McGowan v. Maryland,* 366 U.S. 420 (1961); *Gallagher v. Crown Kosher Super Market,* 366 U.S. 617 (1961); *Two Guys From Harrison v. McGinley,* 366 U.S. 582 (1961); *Braunfeld v. Brown,* 366 U.S. 599 (1961).

[65] *Sherbert v. Verner*, 374 U.S. 398 (1963).

[66] *Minersville School District v. Gobitis*, 310 U.S. 586 (1940).

[67] *West Virginia v. Barnette*, 319 U.S. 624 (1943).

[68] 367 U.S. 488 (1961).

[69] 380 U.S. 163 (1965).

[70] *Welsh v. United States*, 398 U.S. 333 (1970).

[71] Chief Justice Earl Warren in *Trop v. Dulles*, 356 U.S. 86, 102 (1958).

[72] *Pollock v. Williams*, 322 U.S. 4, 17 (1944).

[73] *Selective Draft Act Cases*, 245 U.S. 366, 390 (1917).

[74] *Oestereich v. Board No. 11*, 393 U.S. 233 (1968).

[75] *Dred Scott v. Sandford*, 19 Howard 393 (1857).

[76] *Trop v. Dulles*, 356 U.S. 86 (1958); *Kennedy v. Mendoza-Martinez*, 372 U.S. 144 (1963); *Rush v. Cort*, 372 U.S. 144 (1963); and *Afroyim v. Rusk*, 387 U.S. 253 (1967).

Chapter 20   Criminal Justice

JUDICIAL DECISIONS AND PUBLIC POLICY

H. L. Mencken once wrote that every night he thanked God for the Bill of Rights and then thanked God that he was too prudent ever to try to use any of them. Mencken was indulging his waspish talent for cynical wit, but his sarcasm had an element of truth. There is often a wide gap between the rights that the Supreme Court finds in the Constitution and the rights a citizen can in fact exercise. Public officials often ignore a Supreme Court decision either because they are not aware of it or because they disagree with it. Deliberate disobedience is less likely to occur where one official or a small group of officials has power to execute the Court's policy or where a decision goes along with prevailing social mores or politically dominant interests. But as the number of officials responsible for enforcement grows and as the new policy diverges from accepted custom or runs counter to what those who wield power want, the difficulties of judicial supervision and the likelihood of an older policy being followed both increase.

Reactions, for instance, to recent Supreme Court rulings on "released time," school prayer, and Bible reading cases range from quick compliance to utter defiance.[1] Similarly, many communities still try to enforce licensing ordinances that in effect permit police to censor and discriminate among those who wish to speak or assemble in public. The example of continuing school segregation seventeen years after *Brown v. Board* is too obvious to need further comment.

Even where government officials comply, private citizens can often impose social and economic sanctions—and occasionally, although usually illegally, physical sanctions as well—on those who voice unorthodox thoughts or offend local customs. A man who is ostracized by his fellow human beings or blacklisted from employment is as effectively punished for exercising his constitutional rights as is a man who serves a short jail term.

THE PROBLEM OF CRIME IN A FREE SOCIETY

Blatant discrepancies between judicial pronouncements and actual practice are frequent in the field of criminal justice. The number of responsible officials is high: there are about 450,000 police officers in the United States and additional thousands of trial judges, prosecutors, and prison and probation officials. Furthermore, crime has become a critical problem as well as an emotionally charged issue, and many recent Supreme Court decisions have declared long-established police customs to be unconstitutional. These rulings have stirred not only anger and resentment, but also official criticism and counteraction.

Indeed, the cliché "law and order" threatens to become a shibboleth to replace the ten-gallon white hat as a means of telling the good guys from the bad. Yet "law" and "order" are very different concepts, and the two are frequently in tension if not opposition, for one of the essential functions of law is to restrain public officials. If order were the sole or even the paramount social value, the only standard of police conduct would be its utility in preventing crime or catching criminals. Yet even then one could not be sure of achieving order, for once freed from outside restraints, a police force might opt for values other than order. Law enforcement officials, it need hardly be said, are subject to the same temptations and failings as the rest of men. In fact, the frustrations and dangers of their work may make them more vulnerable to anger and revenge, as the police "riot" in Chicago during the 1968 Democratic Convention illustrates.

While most Americans apparently agree that life in a police state is too high a price to pay for order, they are willing to allow many restrictions on their freedom for protection against criminals. There is simply no dodging the fact that crime has become a cancer in American society. One can only guess at its incidence since most illegal acts go unreported. The President's Commission on Law Enforcement[2] estimated that in 1965 there were about 2.5 million crimes against property and more than 350 thousand against persons. Since that time, all indications have pointed to a rise both in the total number of crimes and the ratio of criminal acts to population. In 1969, police in the District of Columbia recorded 291 homicides, 326 rapes, and 7071 robberies. (The last category does not include muggings and purse snatchings.) Officials estimated there had been a total of about 13,000 robberies of all kinds in the District that year.

Crimes of violence like rape and robbery do not exhaust the list of illegal activity. The so-called crimes without victims, such as prostitution and gambling, are still prevalent. Use of drugs like heroin, LSD, and the amphetamines infect the young more than the old, but drug abuse—both taking and selling—is widespread. Ghettos are seed beds for these kinds of criminal activities, but the middle and upper classes of suburbia and exurbia have their share of drug problems. And fraud, embezzlement, antitrust violations, false advertising, and income tax evasion are "white collar crimes" typical of the prosperous rather than the poor. A recent survey[3] revealed that more than nine out of ten adults were willing to admit having committed a non-traffic offense for which they could have been jailed.

The dollar cost of crime is high; it ran to about $21 billion in 1965 and has probably increased significantly since then. Moreover, most crimes of robbery and violence occur in big cities; the victims are disproportionately poor and black. The following two tables show how crimes involving violence or the potential of violence threaten the ghetto dweller far more than the even mildly affluent.

In addition, crime's relative injury to a poor man is far more painful than to the well-to-do. A theft of fifty dollars from a business executive causes an inconvenience, or, at most, a brief postponement of a luxury. To an unskilled worker, fifty dollars may represent a week's take-home pay. Its loss can mean a family's being evicted or going almost without food. Where the target of a robbery is a store in a ghetto area, the cost, even the added cost of insurance, is usually passed on to the neighborhood in the form of higher prices. If robberies are frequent the store will probably be closed, throwing additional people out of work and increasing the difficulties of shopping for those who cannot afford an automobile.

The high rate of violent crime has also lowered the quality of life for potential as well as actual victims. It keeps people from enjoying theatres, libraries, parks, and other facilities for leisure, education, and cultural enrichment that urban centers provide as compensation for dirt, pollution, overcrowding, and thousands of other inconveniences. For a man—much less a woman—to go out alone at night on the streets of many neighborhoods in Chicago, New York, or Washington is risky, and only a thief, a policeman, or a fool is apt to walk alone after dark in lonely places like public parks. It comes as a shock to American tourists to see people strolling around European cities like Dublin, Madrid, Paris, or Rome at 2 A.M. In the U.S. these tourists would have locked themselves securely in at nightfall, and, if they were a representative sample of the population, more than a third of them would have guns in their homes to protect against burglars.

A recently returned professional diplomat was struck by the change in American life. He[4] found that people who live in the suburbs of the major cities "are becoming like dwellers in a medieval village, fearful of venturing into the city's perils, cut off from the

VICTIMS OF CRIME BY INCOME
(Rates per 100,000 population)

| Offenses | Income | | | |
	$0–$2,999	$3,000–$5,999	$6,000–$9,999	Above $10,000
Forcible rape	76	49	10	17
Robbery	172	121	48	34
Aggravated assault	229	316	144	252
Burglary	1,319	1,020	867	790
Larceny ($50 and over)	420	619	549	925
Motor vehicle theft	153	206	202	219
Number of respondents	(5,232)	(8,238)	(10,382)	(5,946)

SOURCE: *President's Commission on Law Enforcement and Administration of Justice*, The Challenge of Crime in a Free Society (*Washington, D.C.: Government Printing Office, 1967*), *p. 38.*

VICTIMS OF CRIME BY RACE
(Rates per 100,000 of population)

Offenses	White	Nonwhite
Forcible rape	22	83
Robbery	58	204
Aggravated assault	186	347
Burglary	822	1,306
Larceny ($50 and over)	608	367
Motor vehicle theft	164	286
Number of respondents	(27,484)	(4,902)

SOURCE: *President's Commission on Law Enforcement and Administration of Justice*, The Challenge of Crime in a Free Society (*Washington, D.C.: Government Printing Office, 1967*), p. 39.

stimulation of city life, unwilling to attend cultural events, penned within their own cottages at nightfall for fear of what is abroad in the dark."

Perhaps the most significant cost of crime is that it is eroding the bases of community at a time when a sense of national cohesion is badly needed. Knowledge among whites that blacks commit a very high percentage of crimes like murder or mugging increases fear of housing and school integration and intensifies racial prejudice. For their part, blacks, as the most frequent victims of violent crime, blame the police in particular for their problems and whites in general for not caring about their plight. Cutting across racial lines is an apparently growing distrust of all strangers that may fragment American society in a way that will undermine the social cohesion essential to stable democratic government.

CRIMINAL LAW AND SUBSTANTIVE RIGHTS

Nowhere are the objectives of American criminal law authoritatively spelled out, and those that can be deduced from other constitutional and legal norms as well as from actual practice are not necessarily consistent with each other. Historically, the criminal law was a public substitute for private revenge and without a doubt still retains much of that character. In part the purpose of criminal law has also been to serve as a secular equivalent of Purgatory, a means of cleansing the criminal of his moral guilt, of forcing him "to pay his debt to society" for his sins. Another purpose has been to protect society either by deterring actual or potential lawbreakers or by isolating criminals from the rest of the population. Criminal law may also operate as a means of rehabilitating and reforming the offender.

The incongruities of these aims and the inability of American political leadership to formulate priorities among them contributes mightily to the problems of administering

*"I am against fighting crime piece-meal gentlemen! ... We
need strong legislation that will make ALL crime illegal!"*

GRIN & BEAR IT by Lichty. Courtesy Publishers-Hall Syndicate.

justice. Less confused but by no means clear are the substantive rights that the constitutional system tries to protect from abuse, deliberate or inadvertent, by those charged with
applying criminal sanctions. By substantive rights we mean the essence of what is protected, in contrast to procedural rights, the obligations of public officials to follow certain
specified steps before imposing punishment. The Constitution originally mentioned explicitly no substantive rights, although we can deduce from the various procedural guarantees there and in the Bill of Rights that the basic rights in the field of criminal justice
are those to privacy and dignity, to physical freedom, and to a fair trial if accused of
crime.

The Constitution of 1787 referred directly only to the last two of these. The
Framers safeguarded the right to a fair trial by forbidding either state or national governments to pass bills of attainder, that is, legislative acts that, without a judicial trial, convict a person of crime and impose punishment. Historically, these bills had provided a
convenient way for the British government to jail or execute political offenders and avoid
the risk of acquittal by a sympathetic jury. They were used with some frequency in this

country during the colonial period, but rarely since then. The few cases that have arisen have been marginal.[5] The only clear instance occurred in 1946 when the Court[6] invalidated a provision in a congressional appropriation that no salary could be paid to three named persons because of allegedly subversive activities.

The Constitution also forbids Congress and state legislatures to pass *ex post facto* legislation. In one of its first cases the Supreme Court held that these clauses prohibit only retroactive criminal laws and not all laws that may have a retroactive effect. In other words, an *ex post facto* law is one that: (1) makes criminal an act that when committed was innocent; or (2) increases punishment for a crime after the act was committed; or (3) lowers the degree of proof for a crime, again after the act was committed.

Article III of the Constitution prescribes jury trials for federal offenses and also narrows the definition of treason and limits the punishment that can be imposed:

> Treason against the United States shall consist only in levying war against them, or in adhering to their enemies, giving them aid and comfort. No person shall be convicted of treason unless on the testimony of two witnesses to the same overt act, or on confession in open court.
>
> The Congress shall have power to declare the punishment of treason, but no attainder of treason shall work corruption of blood or forfeiture except during the life of the person attainted.

The Framers protected the basic right to freedom by providing in Article I that: "The privilege of the writ of habeas corpus shall not be suspended, unless when in cases of rebellion or invasion the public safety may require it." Sometimes called "the great writ of liberty," habeas corpus was especially designed to prevent arbitrary arrest or unlawful imprisonment. Where this right is available, any person who is being held by state or federal officers, or the lawyer or friend of the prisoner, may ask the nearest court for a writ, ordering the officers to bring the prisoner into court and show legal cause for holding him. If such cause is not shown or if a charge is not brought, the court will order the prisoner released.

The Constitution does not state whether suspension must be limited to those areas immediately affected by rebellion or invasion, and it does not specify the agency of government that may order the suspension, though the clause occurs in the article describing congressional authority. Early in the Civil War, without congressional authorization, President Lincoln suspended the writ in various parts of the country, both in and outside of combat areas. This action was challenged by Chief Justice Roger B. Taney, who, sitting as a trial judge, as Supreme Court Justices then also had to act, ruled that power to suspend habeas corpus rested exclusively with Congress.[7] Thereafter Congress passed legislation specifically authorizing the President to suspend the writ when he judged such action to be necessary.

Just after the Civil War, the Supreme Court faced the even more difficult question of the constitutionality of a suspension of habeas corpus in an area outside an actual theater of war or rebellion.[8] All nine Justices agreed that the President could not suspend the writ in such areas, and a majority of five believed that Congress could not do so either. There has been no attempt since the Civil War by either Congress or the President to suspend the writ in the United States.

Federal Computers Amass Files on Suspect Citizens

By BEN A. FRANKLIN

Special to The New York Times

WASHINGTON, June 27— The police, security and military intelligence agencies of the Federal Government are quietly compiling a mass of computerized and microfilmed files here on hundreds of thousands of law abiding yet suspect Americans.

With the justification that a revolutionary age of assassination, violent political dissent and civil disorder requires it, the Government is building an array of instantly retrievable information on "persons of interest." . . .

The leader of a Negro protest against welfare regulations in St. Louis, for example, is the subject of a teletyped "spot report" to Washington shared by as many as half a dozen Government intelligence gathering groups.

The name of a college professor who finds himself unwittingly, even innocently, arrested for disorderly conduct in a police roundup at a peace rally in San Francisco goes into the data file.

A student fight in an Alabama high school is recorded—if it is interracial.

Government officials insist that the information is needed and is handled discretely to protect the innocent, the minor offender and the repentant.

Senator Ervin, a conservative, a student of the Constitution, a former judge of the North Carolina Superior Court, and the chairman of the Senate Subcommittee on Constitutional Rights, says that the advent of computer technology in Government file keeping is pushing the country toward "a mass surveillance system unprecedented in American history." . . .

The Government is gathering information on its citizens in the following reservoirs of facts:

¶ A Secret Service computer, one of the newest and most sophisticated in Government. In its memory the names and dossiers of activists, "malcontents," persistent seekers of redress, and those who would "embarrass" the President or other Government leaders are filed with those of potential assassins and persons convicted of "threats against the President."

¶ A data bank compiled by the Justice Department's civil disturbance group. It produces a weekly printout of national tension points on racial, class and political issues and the individuals and groups involved in them. Intelligence on peace rallies, welfare protests and the like provide the "data base" against which the computer measures the mood of the nation and the militancy of its citizens. Judgments are made; subjects are listed as "radical" or "moderate."

¶ A huge file of microfilmed intelligence reports, clippings and other materials on civilian activity maintained by the Army's Counterintelligence Analysis Division in Alexandria, Va. Its purpose is to help prepare deployment estimates for troop commands on alert to respond to civil disturbances in 25 American cities. Army intelligence was ordered earlier this year to destroy a larger data bank and to stop assigning agents to "penetrate" peace groups and civil rights organizations. But complaints persist that both are being continued. Civilian officials of the Army say they "assume" they are not.

¶ Computer files intended to catch criminal suspects—the oldest and most advanced type with the longest success record—maintained by the Federal Bureau of Investigation's National Crime Information Center and recently installed by the Customs Bureau. The crime information center's computer provides 40,000 instant, automatic teletype printouts each day on wanted persons and stolen property to 49 states and Canada and it also "talks" to 24 other computers operated by state and local police departments for themselves and a total of 2,500 police jurisdictions. The center says its information is all "from the public record," based on local and Federal warrants and complaints, but the sum product is available only to the police.

¶ A growing number of data banks on other kinds of human behavior, including, for example, a cumulative computer file on 300,000 children of migrant farm workers kept by the Department of Health, Education and Welfare. The object is to speed the distribution of their scholastic records, including such teacher judgments as "negative attitude," to school districts with large itinerant student enrollments. There is no statutory control over distribution of the data by its local recipients—to prospective employers, for example. . . .

The subcommittee has been advised by the Department of Housing and Urban Development, for example, that its data systems planners have proposed to integrate on computer tape files concerning the following: the identities of 325,000 Federal Housing Administration loan applicants; the agency's own "adverse information file," the Justice Department's organized crime and rackets file, and F.B.I. computer data on "investigations of housing matters." The object, the Department said, is a unified data bank listing persons who may be ineligible to do business with H.U.D.

The I.R.S., with millions of tax returns to process, was one of the earliest agencies to computerize. It has also had a reputation as a bastion of discretion. The privacy of individual tax returns has been widely regarded as inviolate, to be overcome only by order of the President.

But the subcommittee has been told that the I.R.S. has "for many years" been selling to state tax departments—for $75 a reel— copies of magnetic tapes containing encoded personal income tax information. It is used to catch non-filers and evaders of state taxes.

The American Civil Liberties Union office here protested last October that the Constitution protects such acts as an effort merely to "embarrass" a Government official, the persistence of citizens in seeking redress even of "imaginary" grievances, and their participation in "anti-U.S. Government demonstrations." The Secret Service, however, has declined to withdraw or amend its intelligence reporting guidelines.

© 1970 by The New York Times Company. Reprinted by permission.

Immediately after the attack on Pearl Harbor in 1941, however, the governor of Hawaii, then a territory, with the approval of President Roosevelt, placed the islands under martial law, suspending habeas corpus and establishing military tribunals to try civilians. After the war ended the Supreme Court[9] decided that this wholesale suppression of civil government in the islands had been invalid. But a majority of the Justices based their decision on the Organic Act of 1900, under which the governor had acted. The majority, however, strongly intimated that such an extreme form of martial law did violate the Constitution.

The original Constitution made no mention of a right to privacy, but the Fourth Amendment affords some protection in affirming a "right of the people to be secure in their persons, houses, papers and effects against unreasonable searches and seizures. . . ." The First Amendment in setting religious belief outside the scope of government regulation supports privacy and safeguards freedom of association.[10] In protecting a man against self-incrimination, the Fifth Amendment provides additional support. By forbidding quartering of troops in civilian homes in peacetime, the Third Amendment also implicitly recognizes a right to privacy. On the basis of these clauses and the Ninth Amendment, the Supreme Court[11] has ruled, in somewhat mystic language, that privacy is one of the "penumbras" of the Bill of Rights "formed by emanations from those guarantees that give them life and substance."

TWO MODELS OF CRIMINAL JUSTICE

In trying to achieve the diverse purposes of criminal law and in protecting substantive rights, public officials obviously have considerable room for choice. With some oversimplification we can construct two different models of criminal justice.[12] Neither is completely pursued to the exclusion of the other. Like all models these are abstractions from rather than descriptions of reality; but they are useful in providing insights into the quite different attitudes and goals that motivate officials who administer the processes of criminal justice.

First is what may be called the Due Process Model. It operates on the premise that power corrupts and thus tries to counterweight police power with judicial power, imposed largely through tight restrictions on the character and source of evidence admissible in court proceedings. The biases of this model clearly run in favor of the societal interests in individual freedom. While its strictures do not prevent effective law enforcement, they do make the work of police and prosecutors more difficult. The concern of the Due Process Model is with *legal* not *factual* guilt. It assumes that an accused is innocent until proven guilty. More basically, it also assumes that society can more readily tolerate a fairly high degree of lawlessness among private citizens than it can a hyperefficient police force. The skeleton of this model is formed by the procedural guarantees of the Bill of Rights, held together by libertarian Supreme Court decisions.

The Crime Control Model provides a competing concept of the processes of criminal justice. Its biases run in favor of societal interests in law enforcement. Its emphasis is on *factual* rather than *legal* guilt, on standards of police professionalism rather than on judicial supervision as the primary means of channeling official behavior, and on administrative efficiency in apprehending and punishing criminals rather than on procedural niceties. The Crime Control Model also takes cues from the Bill of Rights, but where the Due Process Model construes these guarantees broadly, the Crime Control Model takes a stricter interpretation, giving the benefit of any ambiguous language to police authority rather than to individual liberty.

The two models are different, but they are by no means diametrically opposed. Each accepts the value of limited government and operates within the context of a democratic political tradition. Both reject totalitarian instruments like concentration camps, but they differ sharply on where—and how—to draw the line between permissible and impermissible governmental conduct. Perhaps the fundamental difference is that the Crime Control Model pictures criminal justice as essentially an administrative process in which the policy of apprehending criminals is the central, although not the sole, value; while the Due Process Model sees criminal justice as basically an adversary process in which the accused can challenge before a judge each action of executive officials.

SUPREME COURT PRESCRIPTIONS

While not all Supreme Court Justices would count themselves as friends of the Due Process Model, it is accurate to say that the great expounder of that model—indeed, the primary source of many of its specific principles—has been the Supreme Court since the 1930s and more especially from 1953–1969 under Chief Justice Earl Warren. As one would expect, prosecutors and police officials have been among the most outspoken exponents of the Crime Control Model, though a large number of legislators and quite a few judges have been advocates of this tougher approach. Just as judicial decisions often vary from the Due Process Model, so police practices may sometimes be illegitimate under both models. Not all police have internalized the norms of a dignified, self-respecting profession of law enforcement that the Crime Control Model assumes; and, even where they have, some policemen, like the rest of men, may be unwise, lax, overzealous, or even criminal in their behavior. To understand the processes of criminal law in American government, it is necessary first to analyze the general rules the Supreme Court has laid down to cover the administration of justice, and then to examine actual police behavior to see to what extent and under what conditions it is likely to diverge from either model.

Arrest

To arrest a suspect for an offense, a police officer must have "probable cause" to believe that the man has committed or is about to commit a crime. The difference between mere suspicion and probable cause is hardly precise. Some years ago the Supreme Court[13] defined probable cause as "reasonable ground of suspicion supported by circumstances sufficiently strong in themselves to warrant a cautious man in the belief that the party is guilty of the offense with which he is charged." Generally speaking, a policeman must have some tangible evidence implicating a suspect—perhaps the officer sees a man actually commit a crime or a witness identifies the suspect as the guilty party.

Wherever possible an arresting officer should have a warrant—an order from a magistrate or other judicial official, to whom the officer's evidence of probable cause has been submitted—to take a person into custody. (We use the term *judicial official* or magistrate here because in federal district courts a commissioner appointed by the district judge, rather than the judge himself, normally issues arrest and search warrants, hears charges against an accused, informs him of his constitutional rights, and sets bail. A commissioner cannot, however, preside at a trial or impose punishment. In state systems, a magistrate, usually a minor judge, performs similar functions to those of a commissioner.) Obviously, there are many situations in which a policeman does not have time to go to court, and a warrant is not an absolute requirement for a valid arrest, even under the Due Process Model.

Search

Once an officer has made an arrest he may search the prisoner, but judges in this country have been divided over just how extensive that search can be unless the policeman also has obtained a warrant that follows the Fourth Amendment's requirements specifying the thing sought and the person or area to be examined. Indeed, the Supreme Court has crossed its own trail so often that the Justices have become wary of laying down general principles, claiming that this is the sort of problem "which can only be decided in the concrete factual context of the individual case."[14]

Most recently the Supreme Court has restricted the area to be searched without a warrant to the person of the suspect and the immediate area under his control. The only two purposes of such a search that are legitimate under the Due Process Model are the protection of the safety of the arresting officer and the prevention of the destruction of evidence.[15]

If the police wish to look into a suspect's home or office for evidence connecting him with a crime, they must, under normal circumstances, obtain a search warrant. To secure such a writ, police must go before a judicial officer and show probable cause. As in arrest, there may be circumstances, such as the hot pursuit of a criminal into his home, in which police simply do not have time to go to court to obtain a warrant.[16]

A tricky question of the relationship between search and arrest can arise under the so-called "stop-and-frisk" laws that several states have enacted. These statutes allow a policeman to stop and question a person whom the officer "reasonably suspects" has committed or is about to commit a serious crime. Since an officer may question any citizen, this first part of the stop-and-frisk law raises no new problems. A second provision, however, that the officer, if he "reasonably suspects" that the person is carrying a weapon, may search and arrest him if he is illegally armed, does pose new and grave problems, for the Court has held that an illegal arrest may not be subsequently validated by the fruits of an unlawful search.

The Justices have approached this issue rather gingerly. They have ruled that the standard for determining the validity of such searches is that of "reasonableness" under the Fourth Amendment. Thus each case must be looked at individually. In 1968, a majority of the Justices found it reasonable for an experienced policeman to question and then to search for weapons three men whom he observed repeatedly casing a store. The Court then affirmed their convictions for carrying concealed weapons.[17] Similarly, the

Justices found it reasonable for a police officer to stop and search a man after the officer had heard a noise outside his apartment door and found the prisoner and another man running away. In this case the search revealed that the defendant was carrying burglar tools, and he was convicted for this offense.[18]

On the other hand, the Court[19] reversed a narcotics conviction based on evidence obtained from a search without a warrant. The arresting officer had watched a stranger talk to a number of people whom the officer knew as drug addicts, although he could not overhear any of the conversations and did not see any money or goods change hands. After eight hours of observing, the policeman stopped the suspect and told him, "You know what I want." The suspect reached for his pocket, but the officer grabbed him and found he was carrying heroin. Eight of the Justices believed that the officer had not had probable cause to arrest the suspect, and ruled that "where a policeman has no probable cause to arrest, he can justify a search only because of danger to himself or others, and here he has no reason for such a fear. . . . Before he places a hand on the person of a citizen in search of anything, a policeman must have constitutionally adequate, reasonable grounds for doing so." Had he overheard incriminating remarks in the conversations or seen material exchanged, he might well have been justified in arresting the suspect; and had the arrest been valid, the subsequent search would probably have been also.

The problem, even under the Due Process Model, is one of balancing, first by the policeman and then by the judge, the interests of society in having the law obeyed and the lives and property of citizens protected against society's interests in defending the sanctity of the individual. A search, even a cursory one for weapons, is an intrusion, probably a humiliating intrusion, against privacy and human dignity. The general rule, if there is one, is that "the officer need not be absolutely certain that the individual is armed; the issue is whether a reasonably prudent man in the circumstances would be warranted in the belief that his safety or that of others was in danger."[20]

Yet the second of the three "stop and frisk" cases just discussed involved the arrest of a suspect who was running away from an apartment door. And he was convicted not for carrying a weapon—apparently he was unarmed—but for possession of burglar tools. These instruments may constitute a threat to property but hardly to lives. Thus, while the Court's general statement of principle may be quite reasonable, it is evident that the Justices are still having difficulty applying general rules to specific situations, and they will have even more. In the District of Columbia Crime Control Act of 1970, Congress has allowed police to obtain "no knock" search warrants authorizing them to break into homes without knocking if they can show probable cause that giving a warning would result in danger to the police or other persons, destruction of evidence, or escape of a suspect. This statute also authorizes police to break into a home without knocking if after securing a regular search warrant they learn of circumstances indicating that any of these three conditions would obtain.

Interrogation

The Fifth Amendment provides that no person "shall be compelled in a criminal case to be a witness against himself," and the Due Process Model sets this prohibition in motion as soon as a man is "taken into custody or otherwise deprived of his freedom of action in any significant way."[21] Immediately after arresting a suspect, a policeman is supposed to warn him of his constitutional rights to remain silent and to be represented by counsel at government expense if he cannot afford to pay.

While today American police probably seldom use violence to obtain a confession, it would be a rare man who, under arrest in a police station and surrounded by law officers, did not experience considerable apprehension. From the point of view of solving crimes, this fear is quite functional. The Due Process Model, however, imposes close limits on the amount of psychological coercion to which a suspect may be exposed.[22] To ensure fair treatment, federal law requires U.S. officials to bring a prisoner "without unnecessary delay" before a judicial officer, who examines the charge and the evidence to make sure the suspect is being lawfully detained, and then informs him of the charges against him and of his constitutional rights to silence and to free counsel. The judicial officer also sets the bail that the prisoner must post to be released, if the offense with which he is charged allows bail. In some jurisdictions the magistrate can release the man on his assurance that he will return for trial proceedings.

There is no clear line distinguishing necessary from unnecessary delay. The Supreme Court has said that federal police may wait to bring a prisoner before a magistrate until they have completed routine arrest procedures, checked out his alibi, and talked to the principal witnesses immediately available.[23] What federal officers cannot do is to begin really probing interrogation of the suspect until he has been brought before the magistrate. The obvious purpose is to make certain that the defendant knows his rights— not to promote police efficiency.

Formal state procedures vary but not nearly so much as informal police practices. The Supreme Court has not yet imposed on state officials quite the same requirement of rapid appearance before a magistrate, but the Justices held 5–4 in the famous case of *Miranda v. Arizona*[24] that due process of law obliges all enforcement officers to inform the accused not only of his rights to silence and counsel but also of his right to have free counsel.[25] Furthermore, his lawyer may be present at all times the prisoner is under interrogation. If at any stage the prisoner changes his mind after first waiving his right to counsel, the interrogation is supposed to stop until his attorney can be present. The burden of proof that a defendant has freely and intelligently waived these rights is on the prosecution, if it attempts to introduce at a trial any statement or evidence obtained from questioning the accused.

Formal Charge

In the federal system, a defendant is formally accused of a crime by a grand jury indictment, as required by the Fifth Amendment for all serious offenses. A grand jury is convened by the prosecutor in the jurisdiction. It hears evidence presented by the prosecutor and even occasionally gathers evidence on its own. If a majority of the jurymen feel there is sufficient reason to bring a man to trial, they present a "true bill" and indict, that is, accuse, him.

The grand jury is a cumbersome instrument, and its use is one of the few provisions of the Bill of Rights the Supreme Court has not made obligatory on the states. Although some states still employ this process to initiate judicial proceedings, increasingly they are allowing prosecutors to accuse a defendant formally by filing with a court what is called an "information."

Once a prisoner has been charged, the magistrate may review his earlier decision regarding bail. The Eighth Amendment provides only that "excessive bail shall not be required,"[26] a stipulation that does not prevent complete denial of bail in a capital or very serious case. The judicial officer, if he decides to allow bail, sets a sum of money which the defendant will have to post. The amount is that which in the judicial officer's judgment is sufficient to insure the defendant's appearance at the trial. Since most defendants are not affluent, bail bondsmen do a heavy business. For a fee, usually about 10 percent of the bail, they will post a bond guaranteeing the bail and the defendant's presence at the trial. In most jurisdictions these bondsmen can arrest and return the defendant if he tries to flee.

Bail practice raises several serious problems. First, where bail is denied or set so high that a prisoner cannot raise the money, he may have to stay in prison for weeks and possibly for months. Not only will his earning power be at least temporarily destroyed and his dignity suffer, but his ability to gather evidence and prepare a defense will be curtailed. Ironically, although he may be kept in prison without being found guilty, if he is convicted he may be promptly freed, since suspended sentences are quite common, especially for first offenders.

Second, by making money the basic criterion of whether a man stays in jail, bail practice discriminates against poorer defendants. Congress has done something about this problem. After several pilot studies showed that people released without bail showed up for trial about as often as those who had to put up money, Congress passed the Bail Reform Act of 1966. This statute, affecting only federal criminal procedure, requires that a judicial officer release on their own recognizance those accused of noncapital offenses who are unable to raise bail, unless he has strong reason to believe that the accused will not appear for trial. The statute also authorizes, but does not require, judicial officials to apply the same procedure to persons accused of capital offenses. In addition, Congress provided for swift appellate court review of decisions refusing release of an accused and ordered the Attorney General henceforth to give credit toward any prison sentence for the time a defendant spent in custody awaiting trial.

The problem of bail also involves society's interests in the protection of its members. Criminals released on bail are free to return to their professional work and may even be able to intimidate potential witnesses and jurors. On the other hand, the law's presumption of innocence, not to mention the Fifth and Fourteenth Amendments, seems to bar imprisonment without trial. Traditionally, of course, bail practices have resulted in a measure of deliberate preventive detention. Where judges believe that an accused is dangerous or "socially undesirable," they have often set very high bail (as in recent cases involving Black Panthers) or denied bail altogether. Congress, in the District of Columbia Crime Control Act of 1970, has taken an additional step and has formally authorized preventive detention for up to 60 days for a suspect accused of: (1) threatening a prospective witness or juror; (2) serious crimes, and if the judge believes him dangerous to the community; or (3) a crime of violence and if he has been convicted of such an offense within the previous ten years, committed a crime of violence while on probation, parole, or bail, or is a drug addict. These provisions raise constitutional problems of great importance. Reforming the criminal court system to provide the speedy trial that the Constitution commands would have been a more direct, although a more expensive and complicated, solution.

Trial

State and federal trials for all serious crimes must be by jury,[27] unless the defendant and, in most jurisdictions, the prosecution as well waive that right. Neither the trial nor the grand jury has to be representative of the community at large in the sense of constituting a statistically neat cross-section, but the government may not systematically exclude from the jury panel members of the racial or ethnic group to which the defendant belongs.[28] Somewhat inconsistently, however, the Supreme Court has allowed states to exclude women, even where the defendant is female.[29]

The Sixth Amendment sets procedural minimums for criminal trials: "the accused shall enjoy the right . . . to be informed of the nature and cause of the accusations; to be confronted with witnesses against him; to have compulsory process for obtaining witnesses in his favor, and to have the assistance of counsel for his defense." As at the interrogation stage, the government must provide a lawyer for the accused if he cannot afford to hire one, and the attorney must have ample time to prepare his case.

Under the Fifth Amendment, the defendant cannot be made to take the witness stand, nor can the prosecutor or judge comment to the jury about the defendant's not testifying,[30] although nothing can prevent the jurymen from drawing their own conclusions. "The constitutional foundation underlying the privilege [against self-incrimination]," the Supreme Court[31] has said, "is the respect a government—state or federal—must accord to the dignity and integrity of its citizens."

Beyond these specific constitutional guarantees, appellate courts will look at the trial as a whole to insure that it was fair in substance as well as procedure: to make certain, for example, that the basic statute under which the accused was charged was constitutional, that the trial was not conducted in an atmosphere of fear of violence or mob rule, that the presiding judge was unbiased, that the jury was not unfairly swayed by newspaper or other publicity, that the prosecutor did not introduce perjured testimony, and that a reasonable group of men could have concluded from the evidence actually presented that the accused was guilty.

The Fourth Amendment may come into play again at the trial, as may the Fifth, when the question of admissibility of evidence is involved. Since 1914 the Supreme Court has not allowed federal courts to hear evidence that was illegally obtained,[32] and in 1961 *Mapp v. Ohio*[33] applied a similar exclusionary rule to state trials as well. This policy has a double purpose. First, it is a means—just about the only practical means, though certainly not a completely effective one—of making enforcement officials respect defendants' rights to privacy and to silence. Second, and equally fundamental, this policy protects the integrity of the judicial process. As Chief Justice Earl Warren[34] said in one of his final opinions:

> Courts which sit under our Constitution cannot and will not be made party to lawless invasions of the constitutional rights of citizens by permitting unhindered governmental use of the fruits of such invasions.

It was in part to make sure that any pretrial statement given by an accused to the police was freely made that the Court insisted in *Miranda* on a defendant's right to have his attorney present at the interrogation. Perhaps more often the question of admissibility arises out of evidence obtained through a questionable search. Our earlier discussion in-

"Now, just between you and me and the lamppost . . ."

Drawing by Opie; © 1967 The New Yorker Magazine, Inc.

dicated that the law of search-and-seizure is hardly precise, and electronic surveillance has muddied matters still further.

In its first wiretapping case, *Olmstead v. United States* (1928),[35] the Supreme Court ruled 5–4 that intercepting telephone conversations was not a search and seizure forbidden by the Fourth Amendment. A decade later, however, the Justices found that the Federal Communications Act of 1934 had forbidden unauthorized interception of radio, telegraph, or telephone communications; and, under the exclusionary rule, evidence so obtained was inadmissible in federal courts.[36] Mapp's extension of the exclusionary rule to state proceedings did not automatically make wiretap evidence inadmissible there because the Supreme Court distinguished between evidence obtained in violation of the Constitution—which state courts could not use—and evidence obtained in violation of a statute—which state courts could use.

Gradually, however, a majority of the Court came around to the view that *Olmstead* was wrong and that wiretapping and similar forms of bugging were searches and seizures that came within the scope of the Fourth Amendment.[37] Evidence so obtained by state officers would be admissible in state courts only if the requirements of the Fourth Amendment were met.

This doctrine did nothing to change admissibility of evidence in federal courts since the Court applied a stricter exclusionary rule there. But Congress in the Omnibus Crime Control Act of 1968 amended the Federal Communications Act. Under the newer law, it is illegal under most circumstances for private citizens or government officials to intercept messages. In national security cases, the President may authorize bugging, but otherwise state and federal officials must petition a court of competent jurisdiction for permission and go through much the same procedure and show the same probable cause as in applying for a search warrant. An order can run for a maximum of thirty days, although it can be renewed following an application procedure very similar to the initial request. In emergency situations involving national security or organized crime, the Attorney General may authorize bugging for as long as forty-eight hours, if he uses that time to apply for a court order.

In general the terms of the 1968 statute parallel the standards laid down in several recent Supreme Court decisions, and bar from use in *any* judicial proceeding evidence obtained through illegal eavesdropping. There are, however, still some problems present which may lead the Justices to negate parts of the act. First, an order for thirty days of wiretapping is far more inclusive than the usual search warrant, which allows a search at one time only. Second, the privacy of other people than the person named in the court authorization may be invaded since the suspect may talk with—and about—a large number of people. Third, notice of the authorization will apparently normally be given the suspect only after the surveillance is completed, not as with a search warrant when the order is executed.

Double Jeopardy

If a defendant is acquitted, he can never be retried for that offense again. That is the clear message of the Fifth Amendment: "nor shall any person be subject for the same offense to be twice put in jeopardy of life or limb. . . ."Until recently, however, the Supreme Court had allowed states under limited circumstances to retry a once-acquitted defendant. In 1969, six of the Justices ruled that protection against double jeopardy was so fundamental as to be included in the Fourteenth Amendment.[38]

This protection, however, is still subject to certain exceptions. A particular act might well violate federal and state laws, and the guarantee does not at present protect a person from prosecution by both governments for such an offense. Even where a person has violated only a federal or a state law, the possibility of a double prosecution is not completely ruled out, for a single act may violate two or more criminal statutes. In such circumstances the accused may be tried and convicted for each separate offense. Again, freedom from double jeopardy does not prevent the prosecution from bringing a man to trial a second time when, following a first trial that resulted in a finding of guilt, the accused has persuaded a higher court to set aside the original verdict because of procedural errors.

Punishment

Statutes usually put a floor under and a ceiling over the punishment that a court may impose upon conviction, although the judge typically has wide discretion including that of suspending sentence. The only directly applicable constitutional provision is that of the Eighth Amendment forbidding "cruel and unusual punishments." The Supreme Court has rarely found a sentence to run afoul of this clause. Among those few was a California law making it a crime to be a drug addict; the Justices ruled that it was "cruel and unusual" for a state to make a sickness a crime.[39]

Perhaps most important, the Justices to date have not held the death penalty to be cruel and unusual, although they have ruled that states cannot exclude people from jury panels because they do not believe in capital punishment.[40] The Court[41] has also held that it is unconstitutional to permit only a jury to impose a death penalty, since this provision could deter a defendant from exercising his constitutional right to a jury trial. If the Court does strike down the death penalty, it may eventually do so on the grounds of a denial of equal protection of the laws, since statistical evidence indicates that of those sentenced to death, poor blacks are about the only ones actually executed. White and well-to-do convicts generally have access to quicker and more competent attorneys who take full advantage of all legal technicalities.[42]

Appeal

The Bill of Rights does not specifically mention a right to appeal a conviction, but the federal government and all of the states allow at least one such appeal as a matter of statutory right. State procedures are usually more restrictive than federal, but state prisoners who believe their trials were unfair and who cannot appeal—or who have exhausted their appeals—within the state judicial system may start habeas corpus proceedings in a federal district court. Whatever appeal procedure a state allows, however, cannot discriminate on the basis of ability to pay.[43] A state must, for example, furnish indigent convicts with free legal counsel and free transcripts of the trial record.[44]

ACTUAL POLICE PRACTICES

The Crime Control Model

Procedures under the Crime Control Model (CCM) are nowhere so neatly or completely collected as are the tenets of the Due Process Model in Supreme Court decisions; but basically the Crime Control Model would differ from the rulings we have just described by: (1) giving greater weight to a policeman's trained judgment in weighing probable cause for arrest and placing less emphasis on the need for a warrant to arrest or search; (2) interpreting the reasonableness of searches more broadly to expand police authority beyond the limits set by the Supreme Court; (3) allowing police ample time to interrogate a suspect thoroughly before taking him before a magistrate; and (4) setting back the time when the right to counsel becomes operative until after the suspect has been brought before a magistrate. At the trial, the CCM would permit at least the prosecutor to comment on a defendant's failure to take the stand and would allow illegally obtained evidence to be introduced but would permit prosecution of the officer or officers who engaged in the illegal activity. At the appellate stage, the Crime Control Model would restrict the number of appeals available to a defendant and would eliminate many of the technical grounds which courts now allow prisoners to use to challenge their convictions. The CCM would not, however, condone violence against a defendant or threats of violence nor questioning over such a long period as to coerce a suspect; neither would it authorize arrests or searches on an official's whim or fancy—though it would on the basis of a "reasonable suspicion."

It is easy to understand why a law enforcement officer would prefer the wider freedom that the Crime Control Model would give him. It is also easy to understand—although not to justify—why a policeman would sometimes violate the standards of both the Due Process and Crime Control Models. To him crime is not merely a mass of unpleasant statistics or dollar costs. He works every day amidst the human suffering it causes and sees the blood, gore, wasted lives, and crippled minds of adults and, worse, of youngsters who will never have a chance at a decent living. If he takes his job seriously, he is likely to come to despise lawbreakers and to be sincerely motivated to protect society from their activities; and he is likely to be frequently angered by the requirements and assumptions of the Due Process Model. For instance, when he makes an arrest he does not presume the accused is innocent. If the officer were not convinced of the suspect's guilt, he would not in most instances make the arrest at all. He has conducted an investigation, examined the evidence, and drawn what to him are logical conclusions.

His motivation to curb crime is functional for his ambition, since his promotion within the police hierarchy depends in great part on his success in solving cases and in making arrests that lead to convictions. As a trained expert, he may also take professional pride in his work, and criticism by newspaper editors, elected politicians, or superiors on the force that he or his colleagues are behaving inefficiently can be stinging. In short, the law enforcement officer has to please many people other than judges, and even all judges are not proponents of the Due Process Model or of recent Supreme Court decisions. A wide variety of public officials and people in quasi-public positions may serve as reference groups from whom the policeman takes cues about proper behavior, and they sometimes permit and even occasionally directly order him not to follow the Due Process Model.

For instance, the Crime Control Act of 1968 repudiated several Supreme Court decisions, including *Miranda v. Arizona.*[45] In this act, Congress established voluntariness as the primary standard for admissibility in federal courts of statements made by defendants to the police. Judges, the statute says, may consider the nature of the warnings about constitutional rights that police gave, but neither delay in bringing a prisoner before a magistrate nor failure to advise him of his rights of itself renders a confession involuntary. Whether this statute is constitutional is another matter. It does explicitly contradict *Miranda,* but that case was decided by a 5–4 vote, and two of the majority left the Court shortly after the decision. The point here is that Congress in this statute and President Nixon in explicit criticism of the Supreme Court as being soft on criminals, have given federal officials very different instructions than has the Supreme Court; and the U.S. Department of Justice as well as several state governments have challenged the *Miranda* doctrine in the judicial process. Under circumstances such as these, a policeman can find heavy reinforcement for his dislike of the Due Process Model.

Investigatory Procedures

Police often follow the general principles of the Due Process Model. This is especially likely when they are working on a "big case," a serious felony like premeditated murder or large scale narcotics peddling that will probably involve a lengthy trial in which a judge will scrutinize not only the nature of the evidence but the way in which it was obtained; but as we shall see in a few pages, the normal course of the criminal process is "justice without trial."[46] Police are also apt to follow this model in dealing either with affluent citizens or with the more successful professional criminals since both types of people are likely to know their legal rights, to have their own lawyers, and perhaps also to have quick access either to political influence or to the news media. In many cases where the police think the matter is minor and the offender basically a decent citizen, they may go beyond the bounds of this model and give him more generous treatment than that required by even the most libertarian Supreme Court ruling.

In the usual case, however, the law enforcement officer will probably be somewhat tougher and follow the Crime Control Model. Indeed, as we noted earlier, he may even violate the professional standards which that model presumes. When, for instance, a detective spots a woman whom he knows to have a record of convictions for prostitution strolling along the street late at night, he usually concludes she is out for business rather than pleasure. So, too, he may be familiar with the habits of small-time thieves, pickpockets, runners for numbers rackets, and operators of floating crap games. He will also frequently see drug addicts who he knows are selling narcotics or stealing in order to keep themselves supplied. In fact, since heroin addiction is both debilitating and expensive, junkies account for a large proportion of all crime, perhaps as much as half in some urban areas. With their minds shot, they can do little to get the money necessary to feed their habit other than steal, practice prostitution, or sell dope themselves.

As a practical matter, the police can pick up most of these people and search them for incriminating evidence without satisfying either the strict standards of probable cause of the Due Process Model or the more permissive criteria of the Crime Control Model. Both the suspect and the officer may know the law forbids such action, but both also know that if the petty criminal or even the innocent poor man or woman complicates the policeman's work by insisting on his rights, the policeman can make his life miserable. For the same reasons, after being taken into custody the accused is not apt to insist on his right to silence—although he may lie outrageously—or to counsel, at least at the interrogation stage.

Studies of the impact of the *Miranda* decision on the behavior of suspects have showed that a large percentage of prisoners who are advised of their rights—and not all by any means are informed—quickly waive them.[47] In part they do so because they wish to appear cooperative, in part because they really do not understand what is being told them—criminals are typically well below average in intelligence—and in part because they do not trust lawyers to take their side against the police. *Miranda,* of course, makes little difference to the successful professional criminal since he knows precisely what his rights are and is not likely to say anything to the police unless he gets something, such as a promise of leniency or immunity, in return.

A standard police technique is to allow a petty crook to go free, letting him know that he can be leaned on at leisure, and then to use both gratitude and fear to persuade him to act as an informer. In payment for occasional tips, a policeman may give him a few dollars—often out of the officer's own pocket—and not go out of his way to check into how he earns his living otherwise. The efficiency of a police force in arresting big-time criminals is a function of its intelligence system, which in turn is based largely on underworld informants. Police agents can infiltrate a gang only at grave risk and great difficulty, and can do so only once before blowing their cover. But the society of criminals has its own communications nets, and tapping into several of these can provide steady payoffs, well worth the cost of letting a few small fish go free.

The Trial Substitute

Even where a more serious offense is involved, the police may, through deliberate choice, ignorance, or over-zealousness, go beyond the bounds of the Due Process or Crime Control restrictions. They may have arrested the suspect on a flimsy suspicion, have searched his property more extensively than the Fourth Amendment permits, failed to provide proper warnings or questioned him longer than the law allows before charging him before a magistrate, or even threatened physical violence. But none of these flaws is necessarily fatal to a conviction, for one of the most important facts about American criminal justice is that most cases never go to trial. An overwhelming majority and, in some jurisdictions, perhaps as many as nine out of ten non-traffic convictions are obtained through guilty pleas.

Thus far more often than not, the culmination of the legal process is not a trial where a judge can examine police procedures, but a bargaining process that takes place over the charge lodged against the defendant. The prisoner may tacitly begin his bargaining by cooperating with the police and by not insisting on his rights. Even if the police do not let him go free, they may be willing to book him on a less serious offense. It is with the prosecutor, however, that the main bargaining occurs. In some jurisdictions the judge may participate in the negotiations; in others both the prosecuting and defense attorneys must stipulate that no bargaining occurs, although everyone, including the judge to whom the stipulations are made, knows that it has.

In essence, the defendant offers to plead guilty if the prosecutor will ask the judge for leniency or will reduce the charge—for example, from assault with a deadly weapon to simple assault, or from selling drugs to illegal possession of narcotics. If there have been police irregularities at the arrest or investigation stages, the defense attorney can use this fact in his negotiations, stressing that part of the prosecution's evidence would be thrown out of court.

Both sides are pushed toward this kind of bargaining. The defendant often has been convicted at least once before and knows that the evidence against him, even that part which may be admissible, is weighty, possibly damning; while his own protestations of innocence—which may be all that he can offer in his defense—are not likely to be convincing. Even if he is innocent and can put up a good defense, if he is poor and cannot raise bail, he may have to stay in jail longer awaiting trial than he would if convicted and sentenced. In December 1969, for instance, over 600 prisoners in New York City jails had been awaiting trial for more than six months. Moreover, it is a statistical fact that judges tend to impose stiffer punishment on persons convicted after a full trial than they do for the same offense if the accused pleads guilty.[48] And, of course, the defendant can usually plead guilty to a lesser crime than he would be tried for.

For his part, the prosecutor usually has a small, overworked staff facing a huge backlog of cases. There is always a big trial demanding attention. If he can get rid of less important business without riling the police or making a mockery of the law, a busy prosecutor is generally all too happy to do so and to conserve his time for the really tough ones. To maximize his bargaining position, the prosecutor often charges the defendant with a more serious crime than the one on which he thinks he can get a conviction if the case actually goes to trial.

The judge usually knows what is going on, even where plea bargaining is illegal. He also realizes that he presides over a court designed to serve a small, uncomplicated rural society, a court that could not possibly function in a modern industrial environment if it had to accord the full and fair trial of the Due Process Model to even a small percentage of defendants. His docket is stacked with cases. A typical judge on an urban court that handles lesser criminal cases may have to dispose of more than a thousand nontraffic

Gamblers' Links to Police Lead to Virtual 'Licensing'

By DAVID BURNHAM

New York gamblers maintain an intimate and financially rewarding relationship with many policemen that at times perverts law enforcement into a system of "licensing" the city's vast gambling industry, according to some police sources.

This association between gamblers and many of the policemen assigned to the department's specialized anti-gambling units was described by police officials, policemen and former policemen in a six-month survey undertaken by The New York Times on the problems of police corruption.

A special committee set up by Mayor Lindsay to investigate corruption after he learned that The Times was planning to publish its survey said yesterday that it would hold its first meeting tomorrow morning. Citizens were urged to report any specific information they had on wrongdoing.

The names of the policemen who discussed corruption with The Times during the survey are being withheld to protect them from possible reprisals.

While many policemen are not corrupt, interviews with a number of policemen, during which they referred to notes and other records, suggested that large numbers of plainclothes men—the policemen assigned to controlling gambling—become tainted and in effect regulate the industry.

"Each plainclothes unit has a regular monthly meeting to decide which gamblers to take on and which gamblers to drop—because they've become too hot," one plainclothes man explained.

"At this monthly meeting, they also talk about how much each gambler should be charged," he continued. "The decision is based on how much he takes in."

The plainclothes man said that numbers operators sometimes tried to shortchange the police by lying about the number of "collectors" employed to pick up bets. "When they do this," a plainclothes man said, "they fine the gambler the amount he held back on them.

"At the same time," he continued, "if a plainclothes man arrests a gambler who is "on the pad" by mistake, he also will be fined—maybe a hundred bucks or so."

The plainclothes man also said that arrests sometimes were made by appointment. "Me and this other guy spotted this collector and we grabbed him and he said he was a cousin—paying the cops.

"The guy I was working with said he was sorry, but they had a complaint and had to make a collar. The gambler told him he understood, but 'please don't hold me up now, it's my busiest time.' "

So the collector and the cop made an appointment—he agreed to be in front of the precinct house at the end of the business day, the policeman said. "And sure enough, three hours later, he was standing there with a smile on his face and his made-up evidence—a few phony policy slips —in his hand.

On another occasion, several plainclothes men arrested a collector who was operating in a hallway.

"He said he was a cousin," the policeman said," and asked us to let him go. I said no soap, we had to have a collar. He said he understood and would be glad to provide a flunkie to take the arrest."

Because the policeman telling the story wanted to make the arrest—and not be considered an enemy by his colleagues—he said he developed a little story.

"I told him I was sorry," the policeman recalled, "but that I thought internal security might be watching and I didn't want to get in trouble by bringing in a substitute."

A number of New York policemen agree that the basic payment to corrupt plainclothes men from gamblers was $800 to $1,000 a month—tax free—with lieutenants sometimes getting double.

But they agree that some plainclothes men make a great deal more.

"You really are limited only by your own initiative," one plainclothes man said. "Like you can go out and make your own scores. I heard one guy openly boasting that he made $60,000 in the past two years."

Although the Times survey showed there were many sources of police graft, virtually all knowledgeable experts agreed that the highly organized and superbly efficient gambling industry contributed the most.

There are two major kinds of illegal gambling in New York. One is the "policy game," or "numbers racket"—a six-day-a-week lottery. The other is bookmaking, where individual citizens can place bets on events such as football games and horse races.

Estimates of the annual take of the gamblers vary. But two New York Treasury Department agents a few years ago set the yearly gross of the five major policy games in New York City alone at $1.5-billion.

Some law enforcement experts say in general only that those gamblers who pay bribes are allowed to operate.

As a result, the primary function of corrupt policemen in big cities "is not the enforcement of law, but the regulation of illegal activities," William F. Whyte wrote in his book about law enforcement, "Street Corner Society."

© 1970 by The New York Times Company. Reprinted by permission.

cases every month, and perhaps as many traffic offenses. His colleagues on courts of higher jurisdiction are not quite so busy, but they, too, usually are far behind in their dockets.

In 1969, the Supreme Court[49] ruled that trial judges had to investigate guilty pleas to make sure that they were "intelligent and voluntary." If judges physically can find time to carry out this mandate, its principal effect on plea bargaining is likely to be to bring it out in the open. That would be no small gain, since it would inject a much more potent element of judicial supervision into what is supposed to be a legal proceeding.

CRIME, SOCIAL REFORM, AND REHABILITATION

Crime control is tightly linked to broader reform. No program to keep the streets safe can be successful over the long run unless drug addiction is dramatically lessened and the economic and social conditions which encourage crime are drastically improved. The frustrations of overcrowded urban life and of ubiquitous forms of discrimination, the unhappiness of broken homes, and the humiliation and deprivations of living off welfare in a land of plenty may not cause crime, but they do make crime appear a more attractive alternative, a dangerous though possibly effective means of escape from the nightmare of the ghetto.

These basic facts have been hammered home time and again, but they have received only the beginnings of ameliorative action from governmental officials. Not quite so fundamental but still important in controlling crime is the penal system itself. Confusion over the purposes of criminal law is depressingly reflected in what happens when a judicial sentence is carried out. Prisons at best are custodial institutions that do little to rehabilitate offenders. At worst prisons are schools—with rather strict rules about compulsory attendance—in which amateur offenders are trained to become proficient professionals.

Probation services are not markedly more efficient in helping to rehabilitate exconvicts. Officers are usually too heavily overworked to do much more than keep records on those whom they are supposed to be guiding. The President's Commission on Law Enforcement found that in 1965, 97 percent of probation officials were supervising more cases than they could carefully administer, and there has been little improvement since then. "What we must weigh in the balance," Chief Justice Warren Burger noted in a speech in 1970, "is the rationality of a system which is all contest and conflict and virtually no treatment of what is at the heart of the problem—a disorganized and inadequate human being who cannot cope with life." Given the large number of Americans—about 2 million a year—who are put on probation, or enter juvenile training schools, reformatories, jails, or penitentiaries, this absence of help not only reveals a lack of humane concern but also offers a bleak outlook for a more law-abiding society.

SELECTED BIBLIOGRAPHY

Banton, Michael, *The Policeman in the Community* (New York: Basic Books, Inc., 1964). A basic study of the relationship between the police and the public.

Blumberg, Abraham S., *Criminal Justice* (Chicago, Ill.: Quadrangle Books, 1967). A searing analysis of plea bargaining and its implications for due process of law.

Campbell, James S., J. R. Sahid, and D. P. Stang, *Law and Order Reconsidered: A Staff Report to the National Commission on the Causes and Prevention of Violence* (Washington, D.C.: Government Printing Office, 1969). A very useful study that helps update and reevaluate the earlier work of the President's Commission on Law Enforcement and Administration of Justice, cited below.

Chevigny, Paul, *Police Power: Police Abuses in New York City* (New York: Pantheon Books, 1969). A sharply critical account of the behavior of a relatively good police force; argues that abuses are the results of social pressures on the police.

Free, Daniel J., and Patricia M. Wald, *Bail in the United States* (New York: The Vera Foundation, 1964). A good general discussion of the problems of bail reform; the bibliography is extremely useful.

Packer, Herbert L., *The Limits of the Criminal Sanction* (Stanford, Calif.: Stanford University Press, 1968). An exciting inquiry into the relations between society and criminal law, and a challenge to the social utility of much of that law.

President's Commission on Law Enforcement and Administration of Justice, *The Challenge of Crime in a Free Society* (Washington, D.C.: Government Printing Office, 1967). A monumental study surveying the entire field of criminal justice and making more than 200 specific recommendations for reform.

Skolnick, Jerome H., *Justice Without Trial: Law Enforcement in Democratic Society* (New York: John Wiley and Sons, Inc., 1966). A skillfully done work combining the rich detail of an original case study with broad generalizations from existing knowledge.

Sykes, Gresham M., *The Society of Captives: A Study of a Maximum Security Prison* (Princeton, N.J.: Princeton University Press, 1958). A short but fascinating account of life in a state prison.

Westin, Alan F., *Privacy and Freedom* (New York: Atheneum Publishers, 1967). A thorough study of the right to privacy and of threats to its enjoyment.

Whittemore, L. H., *Cop: A Closeup of Violence and Tragedy* (New York: Holt, Rinehart & Winston, Inc., 1969). Three vignettes of the working lives of policemen; provides a series of informative insights into the human problems of law enforcement.

Footnotes

[1] Gordon Patric, "The Impact of a Court Decision: Aftermath of the McCollum Case," *Journal of Public Law*, 6 (Fall 1957), p. 455; Frank J. Sorauf, "*Zorach v. Clauson:* The Impact of a Supreme Court Decision," *American Political Science Review*, 53 (September 1959), p. 777; Robert H. Birkby, "The Impact of the Bible Reading Decision," *Midwest Journal of Political Science*, 10 (August 1966), p. 304; and William K. Muir, Jr., *Prayer in the Public Schools: Law and Attitude Change* (Chicago, Ill.: University of Chicago Press, 1967). See also Harrell R. Rodgers, Jr., *Community Conflict, Public Opinion and the Law: The Amish Dispute in Iowa* (Columbus, Ohio: Charles E. Merrill Publishing Company, 1969).

[2] President's Commission on Law Enforcement and Administration of Justice, *The Challenge of Crime in a Free Society* (Washington, D.C.: Government Printing Office, 1968), p. 18.

[3] President's Commission on Law Enforcement, p. 43.

[4] Jack Perry, "It's Order from within that U.S. Needs," *Washington Post and Times Herald* (February 5, 1970), p. C5.

[5] See *Cummings v. Missouri*, 4 Wallace 277 (1867); *Ex parte Garland*, 4 Wallace 333 (1867).

[6] *United States v. Lovett*, 328 U.S. 303 (1946).

[7] *Ex parte Merryman*, Fed. Cases No. 9,487 (1861).

[8] *Ex parte Milligan*, 4 Wallace 2 (1866).

[9] *Duncan v. Kahanamoku*, 327 U.S. 304 (1946).

[10] *NAACP v. Alabama*, 357 U.S. 449 (1958).

[11] *Griswold v. Connecticut*, 381 U.S. 479, 484 (1965); see also *Katz v. United States*, 389 U.S. 347 (1967).

[12] This distinction is based largely on Herbert L. Packer, *The Limits of the Criminal Sanction* (Stanford, Calif.: Stanford University Press, 1968), Chapter 8.

[13] *Stacey v. Emory*, 97 U.S. 642, 645 (1877).

[14] *Sibron v. New York*, 392 U.S. 59 (1968).

[15] *Chimel v. California*, 395 U.S. 752 (1969).

[16] *Warden v. Hayden*, 387 U.S. 294 (1967).

[17] *Terry v. Ohio*, 392 U.S. 1 (1968).

[18] *Peters v. New York*, 392 U.S. 40 (1968).

[19] *Sibron v. New York*, 392 U.S. 40, 64 (1968).

[20] *Terry v. Ohio*, 392 U.S. 1, 27 (1968).

[21] *Miranda v. Arizona*, 384 U.S. 436, 444 (1966).

[22] *Leyra v. Denno*, 347 U.S. 556 (1954).

[23] *Mallory v. United States*, 354 U.S. 449 (1957).

[24] 384 U.S. 436 (1966).

[25] *Gideon v. Wainwright*, 372 U.S. 335 (1963), laid down the doctrine that states, as well as the federal government, would have to provide indigent defendants with free legal counsel, where they were accused of serious crimes. Before then, the Court had required states to provide free attorneys but only under special circumstances. *Powell v. Alabama*, 287 U.S. 45 (1932); *Betts v. Brady*, 316 U.S. 455 (1942). *Gideon*, however applied only to trials, not to police interrogations.

[26] As of the fall of 1970, the Supreme Court had not held that states were bound by this provision, but that states are so bound is a logical deduction from many decisions.

[27] *Duncan v. Louisiana*, 391 U.S. 1945 (1968) applied this rule to the states.

[28] *Norris v. Alabama*, 294 U.S. 587 (1935); *Hernandez v. Texas*, 347 U.S. 475 (1954).

[29] *Hoyt v. Florida*, 368 U.S. 57 (1961).

[30] *Griffin v. California*, 380 U.S. 609 (1965).

[31] *Miranda v. Arizona*, 384 U.S. 436, 460 (1966); the decision making the self-incrimination clause binding on the states was *Malloy v. Hogan*, 378 U.S. 1 (1964).

[32] *Weeks v. United States*, 232 U.S. 383 (1914).

[33] 367 U.S. 643 (1961).

[34] *Terry v. Ohio*, 392 U.S. 1, 13 (1968).

[35] 277 U.S. 438 (1928).

[36] *Nardone v. United States*, 302 U.S. 379 (1937).

[37] *Berger v. New York*, 388 U.S. 41 (1967); *Katz v. United States*, 389 U.S. 347 (1967).

[38] *Benton v. Maryland*, 395 U.S. 784 (1969).

[39] *Robinson v. California*, 370 U.S. 660 (1962); compare *Powell v. Texas*, 392 U.S. 514 (1968), sustaining the constitutionality of a state law against public intoxication and incidentally holding that the factual record was inadequate to extend the definition of drug addiction as a sickness to alcoholism.

[40] *Witherspoon v. Illinois*, 391 U.S. 510 (1968).

[41] *United States v. Jackson*, 390 U.S. 570 (1968).

[42] Marvin E. Wolfgang, Arlene Kelly, and Hans C. Nolde, "Comparisons of the Executed and the Commuted among Admissions to Death Row," *Journal of Criminal Law, Criminology, and Police Science*, 53 (September 1962), p. 301. A brief study by the Southern Regional Council, "Race Makes the Difference," October, 1969, shows that in seven southern states blacks are likely to receive heavier punishment for most crimes than are whites.

[43] *Douglas v. California*, 372 U.S. 353 (1963); compare *Johnson v. Avery*, 393 U.S. 483 (1969).

[44] *Griffin v. Illinois*, 351 U.S. 12 (1956); *Draper v. Washington*, 372 U.S. 487 (1963).

[45] Other provisions of the act run directly counter to *Mallory v. United States*, 354 U.S. 449 (1957); and *United States v. Wade*, 388 U.S. 318 (1967).

[46] This section depends heavily on Jerome H. Skolnick, *Justice Without Trial: Law Enforcement in Democratic Society* (New York: John Wiley and Sons, Inc., 1966). Depending on the circumstances, however, police are apt to use extra- or illegal wiretapping more frequently in big cases, rather to obtain leads than use as evidence in court. Police have to be careful about such techniques because the Supreme Court has, under the so-called "fruits of the poisoned tree" doctrine, ruled that evidence obtained indirectly through illegal means is just as tainted as evidence directly obtained

through illegal means. *Nardone v. United States*, 308 U.S. 338 (1939). This is a follow-up case to that cited in note 36. The problem for the defense, of course, is to find out how the police got their information. In any event, scandals involving the Internal Revenue Service, publication in 1969 of extensive tapes of conversations among alleged Mafia leaders in New Jersey, and revelations that federal officials tapped telephones of Martin Luther King and Elijah Muhammad contradict assurances by the Director of the Federal Bureau of Investigation and various U.S. Attorneys General that the FBI rarely resorts to wiretapping. What data we have indicates that state use of electronic surveillance is even more widespread, although it may well be less efficient in catching criminals.

[47] Many of these studies are discussed in U.S. Senate, Committee on the Judiciary, *Hearings: Controlling Crime through More Effective Law Enforcement*, 90th Cong., 1st Sess. (1967). See also, Note, "Interrogations in New Haven: The Impact of *Miranda*," *Yale Law Journal*, 76 (July 1967), p. 1519; and Richard H. Seeburger and R. Stanton Wettick, Jr., "Miranda in Pittsburgh—A Statistical Study," *University of Pittsburgh Law Review*, 29 (October 1967), p. 1.

[48] Note, "The Influence of the Defendant's Plea on Judicial Determination of Sentence," *Yale Law Journal*, 66 (December 1956), p. 204.

[49] *Boykin v. Alabama*, 395 U.S. 238 (1969).

Chapter 21 Equality and the New Black Politics

THE AMERICAN DREAM

"I have a dream," Martin Luther King[1] said in 1963. As he described it, it was an old dream, one that blacks in the United States had been experiencing for at least a hundred years. It was a dream of having a fair share of the respectability, the material welfare, and the values of white middle-class society. Even more, it was a dream of being an integrated part of that society and as such was fundamentally an American dream. It meant enjoying that equality of human dignity which the Declaration of Independence had proclaimed to be a self-evident truth, that equality before the law which the Fourteenth Amendment had enshrined as a fundamental constitutional principle, and that material prosperity that had driven generations of Americans. The black man was closer to seeing that dream come true when Reverend King spoke than when Lincoln had signed the Emancipation Proclamation, but equality in a racially integrated society was still a distant goal.

Indeed, to many whites King's dream of people of all races living together as sisters and brothers was a nightmarish hell of a "mongrel society." To many blacks, the dream of integration had become a dangerous fantasy rather than a guiding hope. A century of second-class citizenship, of living in sharecropper shacks or rat-infested urban ghettos had left a trail of bitter disillusionment. As Stokely Carmichael and Charles Hamilton[2] said: "we reject the goal of assimilation into middle-class America, because the values of that class are in themselves anti-humanist and because that class as a social force perpetuates racism."

The great problem of American domestic politics remains that of converting the black dream of equality into reality, either within or alongside white middle-class society, and doing so promptly. The alternatives are chaos and civil war or brutal repression. This was a problem the Founding Fathers tried to ignore, but it would not follow the example of the old soldier and quietly fade away. In fact, by adopting the Madisonian system of fragmented power and doing nothing about slavery, the Framers compounded the difficulties of succeeding generations. Since slavery was a going institution that became more rather than less profitable after 1800, it took positive governmental action to end it, just as removing the discriminatory vestiges of slavery has required positive governmental action. And, the Madisonian system makes positive governmental action on a national scale hard to come by.

With government officials unable and/or unwilling to solve the basic problems, all sides have resorted to violence. Before 1861 there were at least 250 abortive slave revolts, including Nat Turner's rebellion in 1831 and John Brown's raid in 1859. It took a civil war to end slavery, but even that bloody conflict has not exorcised violence from racial relations. The Ku Klux Klan and less-organized white mobs lynched more than three thousand blacks from 1882 to 1959, and the North experienced savage race riots, as in Springfield in 1908, East St. Louis in 1917, Chicago in 1919, and Detroit in 1943. Freedom riders and civil rights workers in the South have frequently been beaten and some murdered, while white police actively or passively cooperated. In the 1960s race riots in northern ghettos became such a common summer happening as not to merit headlines outside of the affected city.

THE FIGHT FOR EQUALITY

Separate and Unequal

For a short time after the Civil War, the carpetbag governments of southern states, backed by the bayonets of the Union Army, directed, protected, fostered, and exploited the newly freed slaves' drive for equality. The Compromise of 1877, however, left the White House to northern Republicans and the black man to southern Democrats. Lynchings were frequent and segregation common, though not as common as one might think. It was not until the 1890s that southern states enacted most of their segregation legislation and began effectively to bar blacks from voting.[3] The Supreme Court quickly put the seal of constitutional legitimacy on these efforts. The landmark case was *Plessy v. Ferguson,* decided in 1896. It sustained the constitutionality of a Louisiana statute requiring railroads to segregate passengers. For seven members of the Court, Justice Brown[4] said that if a segregation statute implied black inferiority, "it is not because of anything found in the act, but solely because the colored race chooses to put that construction on it." Dissenting alone, John Marshall Harlan[5] said "our Constitution is color-blind, and neither knows nor tolerates classes among citizens." He branded segregation "a badge of slavery," and snarled a prediction that "the judgment this day rendered will, in time, prove to be quite as pernicious as the decision made by this tribunal in the *Dred Scott* case."

"Separate but equal" was now ruling constitutional law, while "separate and unequal" immediately became ruling practice. Twenty years after *Plessy* there was not a single high school for blacks in rural areas of the Deep South, and both southern and northern states spent proportionately much less for black education than for white. In 1930, for example, southern states were spending on an average of four times as much for each white child enrolled in a public school as for each Negro child enrolled; by 1952 this gap had narrowed to less than two to one, but less inequality did not make for greater equality. During oral argument in the *School Segregation* cases the Attorney General of Virginia[6] confessed to the Supreme Court:

> Sad to relate, I am ashamed to say, that during many of these years of the past we have been grossly neglectful of our responsibilities in bringing equal facilities for the Negro race in Virginia.

As the following table shows, the Attorney General need not have limited his statement to Virginia.

EXPENDITURES PER PUPIL IN AVERAGE DAILY ATTENDANCE IN SOUTHERN STATES AND THE DISTRICT OF COLUMBIA

	White Schools	Negro Schools
1939–1940	$41.99	$16.29
1949–1950	115.68	72.70
1951–1952	131.93	89.82

SOURCE: *Carol J. Hobson*, Statistics of Public Elementary and Secondary Education of Negroes in the Southern States 1951–52 (*Washington, D.C.: Government Printing Office, 1955*), *p. 17*.

The NAACP

The modern struggle for black equality began shortly after the turn of this century with the Niagara Movement and then the founding of the National Association for the Advancement of Colored People in 1909. Initially led as much by liberal whites as by blacks, the NAACP pursued a gradualist, legally oriented strategy. It would attempt, its first president[7] said, "to smooth the path of the Negro race upward, and create a public opinion which will frown against discrimination. . . . We want to make race prejudice if we can as unfashionable as it is now fashionable. We want to arouse the better feelings of the white people." And to arouse these "better feelings," the Association began publishing its own magazine, *The Crisis*, lobbying in Congress, and, most important, re-educating judges by bringing cases before them. Given the lack of black voting power to influence elected officials and, on the other hand, the flagrant violations of black rights, this strategy had a certain practical attractiveness. From 1915 on, the NAACP was active in almost every piece of civil rights litigation that reached the U.S. Supreme Court. The Association benefited not only from the free services of several distinguished white lawyers but also from those of a group of young blacks who were educated at Howard Law School.

In 1938 the NAACP turned its Court operations over to a separate unit, the Legal Defense and Education Fund, and placed it under the direction of an energetic and ambitious young lawyer named Thurgood Marshall. What had been a series of scattered battles now became a coherent campaign, as Marshall's staff launched a coordinated series of attacks against racial restrictions on voting and against discriminatory practices in transportation, housing, education, and criminal justice. Operating much like a pressure group in the legislative process, the Fund urged blacks to use the courts to secure their rights, then picked the most promising cases to support.

One southern senator complained that Marshall seemed to have "an almost occult power" over Supreme Court Justices; what he did have was a bench sensitive to the issue of discrimination and a hardworking staff that could prepare not only astute legal arguments but dig up the factual data that proved the existence of real discrimination. While some NAACP lawyers would be doing these kinds of work, other staff members would be encouraging liberal professors to write books and articles that would support the general constitutional philosophy of the Association. In addition some lawyers would coordinate the NAACP's legal strategy with other liberal groups, such as the American Jewish Congress, the AFL–CIO, and the American Civil Liberties Union, so that they could join together to present a multifaceted argument to illuminate the judicial mind. As a final fillip, Marshall or a member of his staff would practice oral argument before a panel of Howard Law School professors, each one of whom would play the role of a particular Supreme Court Justice.[8]

The NAACP's list of victories is impressive. In case after case the Supreme Court reversed convictions of Negroes secured from juries from which black citizens had been systematically excluded.[9] The white primary and its substitutes came crashing down.[10] In the field of transportation, the Justices first ordered that railroads live up to the second half of the "separate but equal" rule,[11] then found such state laws to be an unconstitutional burden on interstate commerce.[12] Under the stimulus of Marshall and his staff, the Court held that racially restrictive real estate convenants—contracts in which the buyer of a piece of property promised never to sell it to a black and, in some cases, to a Catholic or a Jew—were legally unenforceable.[13]

It was in the field of education that the most famous battles were fought. The NAACP's strategy meshed with that of the Justices and was in the gradualist tradition of the common law: to move slowly, to proceed step by step in undermining the legal bases of segregation rather than trying to sweep them away in one sudden assault. The NAACP began its campaign at the graduate level, showing that sometimes separate facilities simply did not exist or if they did were physically unequal.[14] By 1950, it was clear that Jim Crow was doomed. In that year, in *Sweatt v. Painter*,[15] the Justices looked not merely at physical facilities to determine equality but also at intangibles, such as academic reputation, status of alumni, and the kinds of personal contacts that could be made in the two institutions. No segregated school could meet those criteria, no matter how much money southern states were willing to pour into a black educational system.

The crowning achievement of the NAACP came in 1954 in the school segregation decisions, *Brown v. Board of Education*.[16] Speaking for a unanimous Court, Chief Justice Earl Warren referred to the harmful effects that compulsory, state-ordained segregation inflicted on the minds of black school children, who were, in effect, quarantined from the rest of society. The Chief Justice's conclusion was direct and simple: "Separate educational facilities are inherently unequal." The Court then postponed until the following term argument and a ruling on how its decision would be implemented. In 1955, the Justices opted to send the cases back to lower court judges with instructions to require that the states end discriminatory practices "with all deliberate speed," a formula that became a highly permissive one.[17]

Within a few years the Justices had tidied up and found segregation in public recreational facilities[18] and in local[19] as well as interstate transportation to be as unconstitutional as in schools. The first great crisis came in Little Rock, Arkansas, in 1957, when white rioters and the National Guard under orders from Governor Orval Faubus kept black children from entering a previously segregated school. Reluctantly, President Eisenhower sent federal troops to execute a desegregation order. Afterwards, the Justices sternly rebuked state officials who had claimed authority to nullify a federal court decision:[20]

> In short, the constitutional rights of children not to be discriminated against in school admission . . . can neither be nullified openly and directly by state legislators or state executive or judicial officers, nor nullified indirectly by them through evasive schemes. . . . Article 6 of the Constitution makes the Constitution the 'supreme Law of the Land.' . . . The federal judiciary is supreme in the exposition of the law of the Constitution. . . . No state legislator or executive or judicial officer can war against the Constitution without violating his undertaking to support it.

Implementation

These were bold words, but they went unheeded. The fight to implement the 1954 ruling was anything but a mopping up operation. Border state officials made some earnest but many more token efforts to desegregate. The Deep South said never and enacted reams of new legislation in what for almost nine years was a successful attempt to secure school segregation behind a morass of legal technicalities. Counterattacking to keep Marshall's legal staff off balance, southern states passed new acts, initiated sweeping legislative investigations, or began litigation to outlaw the NAACP.

If nothing else—and there was little else to show in the first few years—the Supreme Court had jarred the national conscience, and public opinion polls showed a marked and steady increase in national opinion favoring integration and even some changes in Deep-Southern opinion as well. With the moral force of the segregation rulings behind them and lukewarm support from the Eisenhower administration, the NAACP and its liberal white allies were able to get the Civil Rights Act of 1957 through Congress. As we saw in Chapter 8, this statute largely protected only voting rights, and even there turned out to be ineffective. The law's real value was symbolic. As the first civil rights statute passed since Reconstruction, it represented an acknowledgment, albeit a not overly enthusiastic one, by Congress and the President of federal responsibility for protecting the rights of black citizens. The Civil Rights Act of 1960 was an improvement, but only a slight one. Like the 1957 law, it was limited in scope and established cumbersome legal procedures rather than effective administrative remedies.

Six years after the *School Segregation* decisions, hardly a black child in the Deep South, except in North Carolina, was attending an integrated grammar or high school, and there were few more blacks in "white" southern colleges. Indeed, in 1956 when Autherine Lucy, a qualified black girl, had tried to enter the University of Alabama, white rioters came close to murdering her; and, to placate the mob, University officials expelled her. Even along the border states there was a series of similiar, although less dramatic, outbursts of mob violence against public school desegregation, and being spat on and greeted with signs "Nigger go home!" was common fare for black children who dared to rely on legal processes to secure constitutionally guaranteed equality.

Progress in other fields was only slightly less glacial. Despite the two new federal voting rights laws, few blacks in the South were able to register to vote. White officials used a string of tricks and subterfuges to keep blacks from the polls. Most better restaurants and hotels simply would not accept black patrons, and even lunch counters either had separate seats for blacks or required them to eat their food off the premises. Despite an Interstate Commerce Commission order, some railroads continued to run separate cars for blacks and to maintain separate waiting rooms and restaurants. In local transportation, of course, blacks were still required to sit in the back of the bus.

Economic conditions were almost as depressing. To some extent, blacks benefited from general American prosperity; between 1947 and 1960, for example, the real income of the average black family doubled. The gap between black and white income, however, had narrowed only slightly. In fact, the gap was still so great that in 1960, the average black family had barely exceeded the average white family income of 1947, and the average black family had to live on 55 percent of the income of the average white family. With craft unions adamantly refusing to let Negroes join, with most employers at best reluctant to hire blacks, especially black males, for anything but menial jobs, and with segregated and usually inferior educational facilities open to their children, the future held no rousing promise for most southern blacks.

Progress in the North was also frustratingly disappointing, and by 1960 two out of every five black citizens were living outside the South; by 1970 nearly half of all American blacks were living in northern cities. In these states there were no enforced statutes requiring segregation. On the contrary, there were many protective civil rights acts on the books,[21] most of them ineffectual. Actual practice, however, was effectively discriminatory and equally as humiliating as in the Deep South, sometimes even more so since discrimination in the North would often come in surprising forms. The crowded, crime-ridden, garbage infested urban ghetto was hardly the promised land. And the northern black was caught in the same vicious circle as his southern brother: poor education drastically reduced his chances of obtaining a good job even when he had a chance at one; low pay (or welfare) forced him to live in a dirty slum, to rear his children in a morally debilitating atmosphere, and to send them to an inferior school where they would be poorly equipped to compete in the white world outside the ghetto. Northern blacks had the vote; but, contrary to much democratic folklore, voting is not a universal antidote for social ills, and certainly for blacks in the year 1960 there had been few tangible payoffs.

Montgomery

A sweeping change in the nature of black politics began in 1955, when Mrs. Rosa Parks refused to give up her seat on a Montgomery, Alabama, city bus to a white man. Her refusal galvanized blacks in the community to protest against segregation; and they invited a young minister named Martin Luther King, Jr., to lead them. Under King's direction, the blacks of Montgomery mounted a long and eventually successful boycott of the city bus lines. They won not only a Supreme Court decision that segregation in local transportation was unconstitutional,[22] but also begrudging compliance from city officials.

King handled this crisis in a way quite different from the traditional approach of the NAACP. A lawsuit was a part of his strategy, but it was not the central part. His group, the Southern Christian Leadership Conference, which despite its regional title soon became a national organization, stressed direct action, such as demonstrations, protests, and boycotts rather than litigation and lobbying. Influenced by Ghandi's writing and the effective way in which he had ousted the British from India, King's movement was built around a philosophy of nonviolence. His immediate goal was to sear the conscience of the nation and "awaken a sense of moral shame" among those who opposed equality.

King's commitment to nonviolence was a deeply ingrained product of his religious training, but his advocacy of direct action was flexible and tactical, and his ideas developed as he and other blacks accumulated experience in its use. Protest, of course, is not a novel vehicle in American politics. As we saw in Chapter 7, its immediate purpose is less to persuade those against whom the protest is directed than to dramatize grievances and by so doing arouse outside groups to whose pressure the apparent target is sensitive.[23] The dramatic and direct aspects of protest gave it an appeal to a people seething with idealism, resentment, and frustration. In 1960, a group of young black college students in Greensboro, North Carolina, began the first of a series of sit-ins at lunch counters that refused integrated service to black customers. Soon sit-ins, freedom rides, marches, and other forms of mass demonstrations became the standard tactics of black politics. Soon, too, the ghetto riot would become a common means of expressing black rage.

The Civil Rights Acts of 1964, 1965, and 1968

King's eloquence, the moral appeal of nonviolence, the idealism of his followers, and the young black and white students who joined similar groups dedicated to sweeping but nonviolent change, made him popular among white liberals as well as among blacks. Helping his campaign were not only civil libertarians, but a number of people who were completely hostile to everything he stood for. In 1963, in full view of network television, Eugene "Bull" Connor, Chief of the Birmingham police, turned dogs and fire hoses on black demonstrators. A few months later when Governor George Wallace used state police in a vain effort to prevent school desegregation, another wave of violence broke out. The most shocking incident was the dynamiting of a black church that killed four young girls attending Sunday school. There had been twenty other church bombings in Birmingham since the school segregation cases, but Governor Wallace's public defiance of the law ensured that these murders would get wide notice.

Some experts claim that "Bull" Connor and his dogs performed the most effective work for passage of the 1964 Civil Rights Act, but George Wallace and the church bombers helped arouse what President Kennedy described as a national sense of shame and anger. This new statute was the most comprehensive civil rights law ever enacted in the United States. The Act:

1. Allows the Attorney General to initiate in the name of the United States school desegregation suits, if asked to do so by a local resident, establishes machinery

for positive federal assistance to communities trying to desegregate, and requires the U.S. Office of Education to make comprehensive surveys of school integration at all levels.

2. Permits the Attorney General to bring suit to end discrimination because of race, color, religion or national origin in places of public accommodation, such as hotels, motels, restaurants, theaters, or sports arenas, that are operated by an agency of the state or federal government, or that serve patrons in interstate commerce, or that sell goods that move in interstate commerce. There are many specific exceptions to the statute's coverage, including private clubs, bars, neighborhood theaters, and small boarding houses.

3. Permits the Attorney General to bring suit to desegregate publicly owned facilities, such as parks and recreation areas.

4. Forbids unions or management in industries or unions with twenty-five or more workers to discriminate in hiring, promoting, or classifying employees.

5. Provides certain protections for voters described in Chapter 8.

6. Perhaps most important, prohibits discrimination in any federally assisted program and allows U.S. officials to enforce this prohibition by cutting off federal aid from any program that does discriminate.

Passage of the Voting Rights Act of 1965 (described in Chapter 8) was also speeded by continued recalcitrance of southern officials in allowing blacks to vote. Most tragically, civil rights foes assisted passage of the Fair Housing Act of 1968. This bill, which forbids discrimination in the sale or rental of about 80 percent of all housing, had been meandering through two years of congressional debate. In April, 1968, when Martin Luther King was murdered, it had been passed in somewhat different forms by both houses, and anger at the assassination helped legislators settle their differences. Within a week the bill was signed into law.[24]

THE NEW LEADERSHIP

The Eclipse of the NAACP

Ironically, these new statutes came at a time when many black leaders were growing less and less interested both in integration in general and civil rights legislation in particular. These had been the historical goals of the NAACP, but that organization had lost its leadership preeminence by the early 1960s. The very success of the NAACP's legal campaign helped to undermine its influence.[25] In sweeping away so completely the constitutional bases of discrimination, it had achieved one of its primary aims. It had also created a surge of expectations that were to be dashed.

Victory and disillusionment with its results set the stage for a new kind of approach and a new kind of leadership. As Bayard Rustin,[26] an older black moderate, said, blacks had become "concerned not merely with removing the barriers to full *opportunity,* but with achieving the fact of equality." Lawsuits had created opportunity, another kind of strategy was needed to attain equality. Moreover, actually attaining equality meant a broadening of focus, even a diverting of focus away from the South and its official barriers against equal opportunity to the North, where equality had been only glimpsed not gained.

In a sense, Martin Luther King represented a transition phase in black leadership. His dream of an integrated society and his philosophy of nonviolence linked him to the older traditions of the NAACP and its white liberal allies. His tactics of mass action and his radical rhetoric set the tone for newer black politics. "We want our Freedom Here; we want it Now, not tomorrow; we want it All, not just part of it," he would say. But his willingness to ally his organizations with white liberals and to sit down and compromise with white racists was part of the older Fabianism of the NAACP.

The New Groups

The NAACP had never had a monopoly of leadership among blacks, and during the 1950s a number of organizations had been gaining influence. By the early 1960s several of these had built up broad popular bases for themselves. Some adopted and adapted King's tactics of mass action, but most of them rejected King's dream. Black separatism became a real force in Negro politics, although as we shall shortly see, separatism still has the endorsement of only a minority of black citizens. The most outspoken separatists are the Black Muslims,[27] the followers of Elijah Muhammad. They are completely alienated from white society. Totally without faith in court decisions or legislation, they advocate segregation but of a black supremacist kind, and teach the eventual emergence of a black nation in the United States. The Muslims have trained a quasi-army, "the fruit of Islam," to police and protect their meetings, offices, and temples. Officially their leaders deny advocating violence against "the white devils," but avow they will resist force with force. Muslims have tried to educate their followers to achieve economic independence from whites and have integrated their social and political teachings with a theology borrowed in part from Mohammedanism but also in part the creation of Elijah Muhammad.

More politically active have been groups like the Congress of Racial Equality (CORE) and the Student National Coordinating Committee (SNCC). Both were initially biracial, but in 1966 they began squeezing out their white members, although they still accept and even solicit money from whites. SNCC and CORE have drawn most of their members from young adults, frequently college students, and have recently suffered heavy competition from a proliferation of black organizations on campuses.

In some respects more like the Muslims, in others more like SNCC or CORE, the Black Panthers have grown from a small group of militants organized in Oakland, California in 1966 by Bobby Seale and Huey Newton to a nationwide paramilitary force.[28] Members wear uniform jackets modeled on those of World War II German army officers and, in a sardonic commentary on the permissive gun laws that so many conservatives support, frequently and legally appear in public carrying sidearms and carbines. On one occasion a group of them staged an armed protest in the California state capitol.

Headed by a relatively young group of leaders, the Panthers have appealed mainly to ghetto blacks in their late teens and early twenties, many of whom, like their Minister of Information, Eldridge Cleaver, have long police records. Yet some of them—Cleaver, for instance—have displayed considerable literary talent, and they have been the most systematically ideological of any of the militant organizations, endorsing the principles of

Panthers Indoctrinate The Young

By CHARLAYNE HUNTER

Early one morning last week, as women in housecoats sat perched in windows trying to escape the heat, and men casually gathered on stoops along a decaying street in the Brownsville section of Brooklyn, the sound of voices came floating out of a church, shattering the quiet, idle scene.

"Power to the people," a young man shouted.

A chorus of young voices replied, "Power to the people."

"What is the main thing we want to get rid of?" shouted the young man.

"Pigs," answered a chorus of voices.

"And how we gonna do it?" the young man asked.

"Kill him," said one small voice.

The young man remained silent.

"Leave him like he is," said another.

The young man continued to remain silent.

"Put the right thinking in him," said another small voice.

"Right on," replied the young man.

"Right on," replied the chorus of young voices.

On the second floor of the Good Shepherd Mission at the corner of Hopkinson and Sutter Avenues, two young men stood at the front of a small room, while seventeen boys and girls, ranging in age from four to fourteen years old, sat at wooden armchair desks.

The two young men, Henry McIntyre and Roscoe Lee, both teen-agers, are Black Panthers and the children made up the first class here of students in a new Panther program — the Liberation School.

Within the last six months, the Panthers have been concentrating on programs for slum children. The first of these was a breakfast program that Panthers say feeds 10,000 youngsters in cities throughout the country.

At the beginning of the summer, however, a directive went out to all chapters from Panther headquarters in Oakland, Calif., stating that during the summer the breakfast program would be replaced by the Liberation Schools except where both programs could be run without difficulty.

The Brownsville chapter kept both programs and feeds more youngsters—50 to 60—than it teaches. All of the students receive breakfast and lunch.

Panthers are basically Marxist-Leninist and see as their enemy the capitalist system and its exponents—known in Panther circles as "Pigs."

"We take them on field trips to point out the contradictions," a Panther guide, Henry Mitchell, explained to a visitor.

"They see streets that are not clean and they see fire trucks speeding up the streets where they play but no fires. When there is a fire, the Pig Department is seldom around in time to save the property or the lives of the people.

"We take them out on Prospect Avenue—to a block of delapidated houses—to check out the genocide. We show them exposed lead pipes where they can get lead poisoning and TB."

The children are shown the "contradictions" and are taught about the "pigs." One portion of the three-hour class was devoted to a discussion of the "pigs."

Teacher: "What is a pig?"

Student: "A pig is a low-down person who can be any color who beats us up and tells lies."

Teacher: "How many types of pigs are there?"

Student: "Four kinds."

Teacher: "Name them."

Student: "The avaricious business man pig ["who may be a landlord or a store owner," the teacher interjected], the police pig, the president pig and the National Guard pig."

The teacher then says that there is a fifth type of pig—the faceless pig. "You see him but you don't know him," he said. "He's the one who comes into the street and tells people to be cool. He gets paid for snooping around." There was mention of a "demagogic politician pig," but no discussion.

The curriculum could be described as free-wheeling, provided the teachers remain within the scope of the 10-point Panther program. The daughter of a female Panther captain Brenda Hyson, a pretty 6-year-old named Semele, was asked by her teacher to name one point of the program. Her eyes brightened and faultlessly she replied:

"We want freedom and the power to determine our own destinies."

Of the seventeen youngsters in the class, 15 are girls. When asked about the significance of that, the Panther guide replied.

"That's a good thing. We've got to eliminate male chauvinism. We've oppressed our women more than any of the pigs and we've got to make the point now that they are our other half rather than our inferior half."

Other points that Panthers connected with the Liberation School make include teaching family unity and obedience to party leaders. The children are taught chants like "Free Huey" (Huey P. Newton, a Panther founder and Minister of Defense now in jail on a manslaughter conviction) and "Free All Political Prisoners," as well as the one about the fugitive Panther Minister of Information, Eldridge Cleaver.

"Where's Eldridge?" the teacher shouts.

"He's free, eating watermelon and the pigs can't touch him," came the reply, loudly and in unison.

The two teachers in the class dropped out of high school and do not plan to return. They say they "gave up on the pig's school," and now attend the people's school"—sessions in political awareness—held at the Panther office a block away.

When asked if they would encourage their young summer pupils to give up regular school the Panther guide said, "They'll be sent to school because there are laws. But there'll be a vast difference in their ability to learn."

© 1969 by The New York Times Company. Reprinted by permission.

Marxism-Leninism and more especially of Maoism. Indeed, in their early days, all party members were supposed to carry a copy of the sayings of Chairman Mao. Their Ten Point Program is phrased in revolutionary rhetoric, but many of the specific demands are essentially similar to those that white and black reformers have long been urging. The Panthers' tactics, however, are radically different from those of liberal groups. "Arm yourself" is their advice to blacks; arm, organize, and force whites to respect the rights of blacks. In their first few years, the Panthers spoke of the gun as the exclusive instrument of black freedom; and, although official pronouncements have become somewhat less strident, there remains a heavy emphasis on violence. "We are special," David Hilliard,[29] the Panthers' chief of staff says. "We advocate the very direct overthrow of the Government by force and violence. By picking up guns and moving against it because we recognize it as being oppressive and in recognizing that we know that the only solution is armed struggle."

Many whites and blacks discount these revolutionary pronouncements as mostly rhetoric; but a number of urban police departments have been deeply worried by the large caches of arms Panthers have been building up and their avowed purpose of sniping at policemen. As a result of mutual fear, there has been a series of bloody clashes between police and party members. In each instance, both sides have accused the other of premeditated murder or attempted murder.

Perhaps because of their Marxist ideology or because they saw themselves as too heavily outnumbered in a predominantly white country, the Panthers rather quickly moderated their initial black nationalsim. "An undying love for black people," Eldridge Cleaver[30] has warned, "that denies the humanity of other people is doomed." To accept black racism is to accept the evils of white racism, he argues. In the same vein, other Panther leaders have shifted the blame for black problems from whites generally and placed it on a capitalistic economic system. And, after purging some of their more nationalistic leaders, the Panthers have freely allied with white radicals and Puerto Rican ghetto groups under their slogan "Power to the People."

Political Style

It is difficult to compile a detailed catalogue of the political objectives and tactics of each of these groups. Except for CORE and the Muslims, they are all of recent origin, their leadership has frequently changed, and they differ drastically among themselves in objectives and tactics. One can, however, contrast in very general terms the new political style of the militants with the older style of the NAACP.

First, the new militants consider themselves as part of a "liberation" movement, whereas the NAACP and even Martin Luther King saw themselves as part of a civil rights movement. Liberation here has international overtones. Many of the younger black leaders perceive the black citizen's struggle as one facet of a larger struggle of colored races all over the world to escape from white colonialism. In this sense the Panthers' Marxist ideology represents an exaggeration of a more widespread view. Liberation also has a broad connotation. It means much more than achieving specific constitutional rights like equality before the law. It also means freedom from white political, economic, and social domination, all summed up by the ambiguous phrase "Black Power."

Whatever else it means, "Black Power" includes political power—black voters and black officials working for black interests. There is sufficiently widespread agreement on this aspect of the new politics that the NAACP, CORE, and King's SCLC could all work together in the voter registration drives that SNCC began. Some years ago, Negro leaders denied the existence of a bloc black vote, although it was often a reality, albeit rarely a potent one. Newer leaders are frankly, publicly striving to create a bloc vote to put blacks into office and to keep white racists out.

"Black capitalism" is much more controversial.[31] Despite official blessings from the Nixon administration, it appears to have generated little faith among Negroes that private enterprise, white or black, will put black advancement ahead of the profit motive. But all the newer black leaders stress economic liberation and urge blacks to build up and patronize their own business establishments. They also put job opportunities at or near the top of their priorities; and here equal opportunity, many leaders explain, is not good enough now. Because of past discrimination, they argue, blacks need and deserve preferential treatment to have even a hope of catching up.

Most vital in the eyes of many current black leaders is freedom from white cultural hegemony, a reorientation toward a fresh set of values congruent with the life history, styles, and aspirations of black people. In place of Martin Luther King's dream, some of the new leaders opt for a totally segregated society, absolute black separatism in the style of the Muslims. Others urge what has been called "militant pluralism,"[32] the creation or perhaps re-creation of a distinct black culture, an appreciation of the unique worth of black history and the actual and potential black contribution to civilization—in short, a pride in a black heritage similar to that which Irish-, Polish-, Jewish-, and Italian-Americans take in their origins. "My fight," John O. Killens[33] has written, "is not to be a white man in a black skin, but to inject some black blood, some black intelligence into the pallid main stream of American life, culturally, socially, psychologically, philosophically."

Like Martin Luther King, most of the new leaders do not reject favorable court decisions or legislation, and again like King, they emphasize mass action. But most of them emphatically reject King's philosophy of nonviolence. Robert F. Williams,[34] ousted as president of a local NAACP chapter for advocating countering force with force, has said that "the power of non-violence and love is a farce." As would be expected, the Panthers are most outspoken on this issue. As Cleaver[35] put it in 1969: "We must get it clear in our minds that we will shoot anyone who uses a gun, or causes others to use guns, to defend the system of oppression, racism, and exploitation. . . . We must face the fact that we are at war in America." At other times, it should be added, Cleaver and his followers play down appeals to violence. On announcing a possible return to the United States in early 1970 to face criminal charges, he said that he was coming out of exile to fight "not with fire, not with guns—but with solid political and scientific knowhow."

Most of the militant leaders do not advocate violence, but neither do they shrink from it. Like the Muslims, they preach the right of self-defense as an essential part of human dignity. "White people," Carmichael and Hamilton[36] state, "must be made to understand that they must stop messing with black people, or the blacks *will* fight back." The ghetto riots constitute sharp warnings that black retaliation is not an empty threat.

Socially the NAACP spoke for the black middle and upper classes; its leaders were usually middle-aged and older men, often white. The new political leaders are black, and they tend to be much younger, although some who began their careers in the 1950s are discovering that aging is a universal failing of the living. These new leaders claim, at least, to speak for the poorer masses of their race, for the proletariat of the ghetto. The NAACP and Martin Luther King's SCLC were liberal reformers. They wanted change and they wanted it fast, but they were willing to work within the system to get that change and to pay the system's price of incremental advancement. They saw the race problem largely the way Gunnar Myrdal, the noted Swedish sociologist, had portrayed it in his seminal study, *An American Dilemma*:[37] as a painful clash between white norms and white practice. The reformers thought that this clash would ultimately be resolved in favor of the norms, the "better opinion" to which the NAACP directed its efforts, the moral conscience at which Martin Luther King's philosophy of nonviolence was aimed.

The newer leaders tend to reject Myrdal's thesis and accept that of Charles Silverman:[38]

> The tragedy of race relations in the United States is that there is no American Dilemma. White Americans are not torn and tortured by the conflict between their devotion to the American creed and their actual behavior. They are upset by the current state of race relations, to be sure. But what troubles them is not that justice is being denied but that their peace is being shattered and their business interrupted.

Some of the newer leaders are also reformers; some, like the Panthers, are revolutionaries; but even the reformers are radicals. They speak with Martin Luther King's rhetoric of Freedom Now, but they are generally far less willing to negotiate and compromise than he was. Robert F. Williams was not much to the left of the bulk of the new leaders when he said,[39] "FREEDOM NOW!—or let it burn, let it burn." Working within the existing system has much weaker appeal; the new leaders are fed up with delays and distrust promises. Black Power, Carmichael and Hamilton have explained, "is a call to reject the racist institutions and values of this [white] society."[40] They add[41] that the "political and economic institutions of this society must be completely revised if the political and economic status of black people is to be improved." As a self-proclaimed revolutionary, Eldridge Cleaver[42] could put it more bluntly:

> As long as I am alive and this system which creates all this suffering, all this pain, is also alive, I will know that I have not done enough, I will not have given my all to destroy it. And it has to be destroyed in its lair. . . .

The closest approaches to blueprints for the new society are the separate nation scheme of the Muslims and the revolutionary socialism that the Panthers describe as the prerequisite to Communism. But most black leaders find the separate-nation concept unrealistic and Marxist ideology unpalatable. The older black characterization of a black Communist as "an Uncle Tom with a union card"[43] is reflected in Stokely Carmichael's quip that while he might not know a great deal about Marx, he did know that he did not want blacks following any Honkie. There are a few vague shapes of the new institutions in the margins of militant speeches and writings. Among these are neighborhood control, that is, black control in black neighborhoods, of schools, police, and other public services.

In their plans for reshaping society, many of the new militants see whites as playing a minor role—at least in a positive sense. They are hostile to or at most wary of the older kinds of alliances with white liberal groups. Indeed, the white liberal has become the whipping boy for the new leaders. It is he, not the racist, who is charged with betraying the black. The racist is described as an enemy, but an open enemy; the liberal is a hypocrite who stabs the black in the back. Unlike the Panthers and the NAACP, many of the newer groups are willing to establish coalitions only for limited purposes, and, when they do, they insist, as do the Panthers, on either running the alliance or being full and equal partners.

THE BLACK COMMUNITY

Who Speaks for Whom?

The writings of notables, whether black or white, do not always correlate strongly or even positively with the views of the masses for whom they claim to speak. Data taken from a survey of more than 5,000 people in 15 cities, conducted in 1968 for the National Advisory Commission on Civil Disorders, indicate that the new black leaders as yet represent the opinions of only a minority, although a politically active minority, of urban blacks. Analysis of surveys of blacks, black social scientists have warned,[44] has to proceed warily because many black citizens are sufficiently suspicious of the white establishment as to "put on" the interviewer, even if he, too, is black. But the overt responses of blacks to the Commission display sufficient internal consistency that we feel justified in cautiously using them as indicators of black sentiment.

These data[45] show that if the NAACP has lost its leadership of the most

---

BLACK OPINION OF BLACK LEADERS (1968)

Q: "Now I want to read you a list of people active in civil rights. For each one, please tell me whether you approve or disapprove of what the person stands for, or don't know enough about him to say."

	Approve	Partly Approve and Partly Disapprove	Disapprove	Don't Know
NAACP	75%	11%	3%	11%
Roy Wilkins	50	12	3	35
Martin Luther King	72	19	5	4
H. Rap Brown	14	13	45	28
Stokely Carmichael	14	21	35	30

SOURCE: *Angus Campbell and Howard Schuman, "Racial Attitudes in Fifteen American Cities," in* Supplemental Studies for the National Advisory Commission on Civil Disorders (*Washington, D.C.: Government Printing Office, 1968*), p. 21.

politically active black citizens, it retains a hold on the affections of a large majority of black people. It is hard to judge the depth of that affection, to be sure; and qualifying the Association's popularity is the fact that more than one out of every three blacks did not know enough about Roy Wilkins, the NAACP's executive secretary, to offer an opinion about him, a somewhat larger group than was unacquainted with two militants, H. Rap Brown and Stokely Carmichael.

Pluralism versus Separatism

A vital set of questions for the future of American politics is how wide and how deep the desire for racial separatism runs both among blacks and whites. The opening chapter spoke of the many cultures in American society and offered evidence to support the proposition that in gross terms one can say that having two societies, one black, one white, is not an impending danger but a long standing reality. That reality, however, need not represent a permanent condition. Three broad kinds of change are possible: First, there could be an acceleration of currently divisive forces that would separate blacks and whites into two hostile, watertight communities. Second, Martin Luther King's dream of an integrated society could become a reality. Third, the pluralism that has supposedly characterized much of American life could encompass a black cultural identity, just as it has included a respected cultural identity for other ethnic groups. If the third alternative comes about, integration, but of a kind that stops well short of cultural assimilation, would still be possible.

BLACK OPINION ON RACIAL SEGREGATION

Statement	Percentage of Negroes Agreeing
Believe stores in "a Negro neighborhood should be owned and run by Negroes"	18
Believe school with mostly Negro children should have Negro principal	14
Prefer to live in all Negro or mostly Negro neighborhood	13
Believe school with mostly Negro children should have mostly Negro teachers	10
Agree that "Negroes should have nothing to do with whites if they can help it"	9
Believe that whites should be discouraged from taking part in civil rights organizations	8
Prefer own child to go to all or mostly Negro school	6
Believe close friendship between Negroes and whites is impossible	6
Agree that "there should be a separate black nation here"	6
Prefer child to have only Negro friends, not white friends too	5

Source: Angus Campbell and Howard Schuman, "Racial Attitudes in Fifteen American Cities," in Supplemental Studies for the National Advisory Commission on Civil Disorders (Washington, D.C.: Government Printing Office, 1968), p. 16.

There is some evidence indicating that however unlikely King's dream is to materialize in the near future, the third alternative of peaceful pluralism has a solid base of support within the black community, and passive support among whites. The results of the survey conducted for the National Advisory Commission on Civil Disorders make it clear that only a small minority of blacks prefer racial separatism. The following table shows that barely 6 percent want their children to go to a black school or believe there should be a separate black nation or that whites and blacks cannot have close friendships.

Running through these and other survey data is also strong support for black cultural identity and economic independence. Almost all blacks believe that they should take more pride in their history and that there should be more businesses operated by blacks. A substantial majority agree that blacks should buy, where possible, from stores run by blacks. A minority, but a large one, endorses the idea of having black children learn an African language. What emerges is a portrait showing "a substantial number of Negroes want *both* integration and black identity."[45]

Perceptions of Discrimination and Progress

As would be expected, blacks perceive a great deal of discrimination in housing and employment, and they are generally cynical about the current policies of large corporations to seek out blacks—77 percent of the blacks interviewed said they thought all of this was for show, not for real. But a heavy majority of blacks claimed to believe that, despite discrimination, they can get ahead in America. Education had a strongly positive effect on the optimism of black men about social advancement, but curiously did not seem to affect women's outlooks. Most encouraging, perhaps, is that a majority of blacks sense a marked lessening of racial discrimination in recent years. Sixty-two percent said there had been a lot of progress over the past ten or fifteen years.

There were many objective indicators to substantiate these subjective judgments. Various programs combatting poverty have pumped millions of dollars—not always wisely—into a series of projects to aid urban blacks. Although housing segregation has, if anything, increased school segregation in the North, in the South, despite the Nixon administration's wavering, the threat of withholding federal funds has dramatically increased the number of black children attending racially mixed schools. In the fall of 1970, about one half of black children in southern states were attending integrated schools. More important for the long haul, in the country as a whole, the proportion of blacks with a high school education rose from 36 percent in 1960 to 60 percent in 1969.

Black financial resources also increased. The average income of the black family went from $3,233 in 1960 to $5,359 by the end of 1968. The story in housing facilities, although still mostly segregated housing, was similar. In 1960, 44 percent of blacks were still living in unsafe or inadequate shelters or in buildings without basic plumbing facilities. By 1968 this figure had been cut almost in half, to 24 percent.

White Attitudes

Where race is concerned, it can also be misleading to accept responses from whites at face value. Surveys consistently show a decided majority supporting the idea of desegregation, but deeper probing, even of nonsouthern respondents, typically reveals real unease when it comes to sending their own children to schools with a large number of blacks or to having more than a few blacks living in the immediate neighborhood. Many if not most whites are worried by the high crime rate among black citizens and fear violence against themselves and their children, or at very least a loosening of middle-class standards of morality. That the behavior of blacks is little different from that of whites of similar social, economic, and educational backgrounds apparently causes discomfort but not a change of attitude.

Without a doubt, a strong current of distaste for blacks runs through white American society. The survey conducted for the National Advisory Committee on Civil Disorders asked both whites and blacks how many white people they thought disliked blacks. Caucasians perceived even more widespread racial hostility than did blacks. Almost half again as many blacks as whites said that they thought only a few white people disliked blacks.

Whites, however, claimed awareness of far less discrimination against blacks than did the blacks. While Caucasians apparently concede that blacks are worse off than they themselves are, a majority see the cause in the blacks themselves rather than in social conditions brought about by discrimination. But only 6 percent of all whites believed that the black man's problems were rooted in his nature. Interestingly, a greater proportion of whites perceive racial discrimination in housing than in employment; but only a minority (40 percent) of whites favor fair housing laws while two out of three support fair employment legislation. Moreover, although 44 percent of Caucasians admitted they would mind having a black living next door, 86 percent claimed they would not mind at all having a qualified black supervisor at work.

There is also considerable white sentiment favoring governmental action "to bring the poorer schools up to the standard of the better schools," a code that probably translates "improve black schools." In any event, 78 percent of whites said they would approve such governmental action, and 59 percent said they believed government should improve housing conditions in "rundown and overcrowded" areas—again probably interpreted as a euphemism for black ghettos.

SURVEY OF OPINIONS ABOUT RACIAL HOSTILITY (1968)

	Whites	Negroes
Only a few whites dislike Negroes	25%	38%
Many whites dislike Negroes	60	45
Almost all whites dislike Negroes	10	12
Don't know	5	5
	100%	100%

SOURCE: *Angus Campbell and Howard Schuman, "Racial Attitudes in Fifteen American Cities," in* Supplemental Studies for the National Advisory Commission on Civil Disorders *(Washington, D.C.: Government Printing Office, 1968), pp. 25, 31.*

These data offer little joy to integrationists, but, if the two immediate and tangible goals of black leadership are improving the quality of black education rather than integration per se and obtaining full and fair employment, then there are some grounds for encouragement. In addition, while none of these questions was aimed directly at learning white attitudes toward black pluralism, the resulting patterns of opinions indicates at least passive support for black cultural identity.

Counterbalancing white perceptions of racial dislike were responses to a query about the kinds of friends white adults would like to see their children have. Two out of three said they would like to see their children have black friends or did not care about race in such matters. Again, these responses may be more liberal than actual emotions. But even if they and the answers to questions about approving integration in general represent more what whites believe is right than what they actually feel, they still offer some hope in indicating that moral pressure is at work. Increased black self-respect might increase white respect as well, and that seems badly needed. Furthermore, cultural pluralism and limited integration might be a welcome compromise to many fearful whites.

FUTURE PROSPECTS

Blacks are more ready to accept a pluralistic, integrated society than are whites, and most blacks perceive considerable progress in achieving equality. But the questions remain whether these gains can be consolidated and continued rapidly enough to keep the overwhelming majority of blacks willing to work within the existing system by peaceful means. Since blacks have historically been the "last hired and the first fired," their economic advances have been less secure than those of whites.

While the newer liberation groups may have been more radical than a majority of the black community in 1968, they did then and still speak for a politically active minority whose influence far exceeds its numerical strength. Continued inequality can only increase that influence, and there remains operative much relative deprivation in psychic as well as material terms. Discrimination is still widely, though usually illegally, practiced in both North and South. In more tangible terms, black gains have by no means bridged the gap between them and whites. Despite its increase, in 1969 the average income of the black family was only 60 percent of that of Caucasians. Only 6 percent of whites lived that year in substandard housing, as compared to almost a quarter of all blacks. Not only had a much larger proportion of whites finished high school, but on the whole they had had better education than blacks with the same number of years of schooling. Over the long run "open admission" or preferential admission policies of colleges may help construct a better balance, but that pay-off will be immediate only in symbolic terms.

A majority of blacks' seeing progress is not the same as their making an irrevocable commitment to the existing political system. The militants' rejection of "progress" for "freedom" will undoubtedly become more popular. Data from the Commission on Civil Disorders[46] survey show that younger blacks are not only much more outspoken than their elders about the need to achieve both material advancement and cultural autonomy, but also more separatist in their views and much more willing to condone violence or even to assert a willingness to use force to attain their goals. A study of attitudes in the

BLACK OPINION ON MEANS TO GAIN RIGHTS (1968)

"As you see it, what's the best way for Negroes to try to gain their rights—use laws and persuasion, use nonviolent protests, or be ready to use violence?"

Means	Percent
Laws and persuasion	39
Nonviolent protests	38
Be ready to use violence	15
Don't know	8
Total	100

SOURCE: *Angus Campbell and Howard Schuman, "Racial Attitudes in Fifteen American Cities," in* Supplemental Studies for the National Advisory Commission on Civil Disorders (*Washington, D.C.: Government Printing Office, 1968*), *p. 52.*

Watts area of Los Angeles after the riots of 1965 produced similar results.[47] Younger blacks were more politicized but less committed to either political party and more disaffected with the American political system than were older black citizens. Some of this hostility is currently being reflected in the increasing frequency of racial clashes in integrated high schools around the country.

Violence has only minority approval within the black community as a whole, but it has markedly greater support than separatism. Almost one of every six urban blacks said that he or she believed that readiness to use violence was the most effective way of furthering the cause of black citizens. This is a small minority in percentage terms, but it constitutes about a half million black people between the ages of 16 and 69 living in the fifteen cities surveyed. And that, by any standards, is a volatile basis for a guerrilla force.

Only the Muslims, the Panthers, and, on the other side, a few white leaders like George Wallace have neat formulas to ease much less resolve racial tensions. One thing is clear, however: those tensions will not be substantially lessened until blacks—and other ethnic minorities like Puerto Ricans, Mexican-Americans, and Indians—have both achieved equality of opportunity and attained a return from that opportunity that does not significantly differ from that received by whites.

SELECTED BIBLIOGRAPHY

Broderick, Francis L., and August Meier, eds., *Negro Protest Thought in the Twentieth Century* (Indianapolis, Ind.: Bobbs-Merrill Company, Inc. 1965). An excellent collection of essays that helps put current problems in sharp perspective.

Brown, Claude, *Manchild in the Promised Land* (New York: The New American Library, Inc., 1965). A shocking but fascinating autobiographical account of life in the Harlem ghetto.

Carmichael, Stokely, and Charles V. Hamilton, *Black Power: The Politics of Liberation in America* (New York: Random House, Inc., 1967). An angry analysis of the politics of American race relations by a black radical leader and a black social scientist.

Cleaver, Eldridge, *Soul on Ice* (New York: McGraw-Hill Book Company, 1968). Autobiographical essays by the talented Minister of Information of the Black Panthers.

Dollard, John, *Caste and Class in a Southern Town*, 3rd ed. (Garden City, N.Y.: Doubleday and Company, Inc., 1957). An old but important study of overt and hidden patterns of race relations.

Essien-Udom, E.U., *Black Nationalism* (Chicago, Ill.: University of Chicago Press, 1962). A first rate analysis of the Black Muslims.

Grier, William H., and Price M. Cobbs, *Black Rage* (New York: Basic Books, Inc., 1968). Interesting reinforcement by two black psychiatrists of the conclusions of social scientists about the effects of discrimination on the human mind and soul.

Frazier, E. Franklin, *Black Bourgeoisie* (New York: The Free Press of Glencoe, 1957). A jaundiced view of the black middle class, the group from which the older black leadership was drawn and to which it was oriented.

Hayden, Tom, *Rebellion in Newark: Official Violence and Ghetto Response* (New York: Random House, Inc., 1967). A white radical's graphic account of the Newark riots of 1967.

King, Martin Luther, *Stride Toward Freedom: The Montgomery Story* (New York: Harper and Brothers, 1958).

———, *Why We Can't Wait* (New York: The New American Library, Inc., 1963). Two introductions to King's philosophy of nonviolence and his tactics of mass action.

Lockard, Duane, *Toward Equality: A Study of State and Local Anti-Discrimination Laws* (New York: Crowell-Collier and Macmillan Co., 1967). An analysis of the difficulties in enacting and enforcing civil rights legislation.

Myrdal, Gunner, *An American Dilemma* (New York: Harper and Row, 1944). This book has become a classic in the study of race relations and has had a great impact on American political and social thought. It is also available in a second edition but that of 1944 is the one that has had great influence.

National Advisory Commission on Civil Disorders, *Report* (Washington, D.C.: Government Printing Office, 1968). The justly famous Kerner Commission study of the causes of race riots.

Orfield, Gary, *The Reconstruction of Southern Education* (New York: John Wiley & Sons, Inc., 1969). A useful analysis of the impact of the Civil Rights Act of 1964.

Seale, Bobby, *Seize the Time: The Story of the Black Panther Party and Huey P. Newton* (New York: Random House, Inc., 1970). A fascinating account of the Panthers' activities and problems by one of the organization's co-founders.

Skolnick, Jerome H., *The Politics of Protest* (New York: Simon and Schuster, Inc., 1969). Originally a task force report to the National Commission on the Causes and Prevention of Violence; a broad survey of protest movements with an excellent chapter on the new black politics.

Vose, Clement E., *Caucasians Only: The Supreme Court, the NAACP, and the Restrictive Covenant Cases* (Berkeley, Calif.: University of California Press, 1959). A scholarly study of the NAACP as a pressure group.

Woodward, C. Vann, *The Strange Career of Jim Crow*, 2d rev. ed. (New York: Oxford University Press, 1966). A revealing history of the origins of segregation statutes.

X., Malcolm (Malcolm Little), *The Autobiography of Malcolm X* (New York: Grove Press, Inc., 1964). The autobiography of a charismatic black leader.

Footnotes

[1] Martin Luther King, Jr., "I Have a Dream: Address to the March on Washington," reprinted in Francis L. Broderick and August Meier, eds., *Negro Protest Thought in the Twentieth Century* (Indianapolis, Ind.: The Bobbs-Merrill Company, Inc., 1965), p. 400.

[2] Stokely Carmichael and Charles V. Hamilton, *Black Power: The Politics of Liberation in America* (New York: Random House, Inc., 1967), p. 41.

[3] The best general account is C. Vann Woodward, *The Strange Career of Jim Crow*, 2d ed. (New York: Oxford University Press, 1966).

[4] 163 U.S. 537, 551 (1896).

[5] At p. 559.

[6] *Oral Argument in the School Segregation Cases*, U.S. Supreme Court, October Term 1952 (Washington, D.C.: Ward and Paul Co., n.d.), p. 187.

[7] Quoted in Clement E. Vose, *Caucasians Only: The Supreme Court, the NAACP, and the Restrictive Covenant Cases* (Berkeley: University of California Press, 1959), p. 32. This is a very valuable case study of the NAACP's legal strategy and tactics.

[8] See Vose, *Caucasians Only*.

[9] *Smith v. Texas*, 311 U.S. 128 (1940); *Hill v. Texas*, 316 U.S. 400 (1942); *Cassell v. Texas*, 339 U.S. 282 (1950); *Avery v. Georgia*, 345 U.S. 559 (1952); and *Whitus v. Georgia*, 385 U.S. 445 (1967).

[10] *Smith v. Allwright*, 321 U.S. 649 (1944); *Terry v. Adams*, 345 U.S. 461 (1953).

[11] *Mitchell v. United States*, 313 U.S. 80 (1941).

[12] *Morgan v. Virginia*, 328 U.S. 373 (1946), involved buses but the same rule became applicable to railroads: *Henderson v. United States*, 339 U.S. 816 (1950).

[13] *Shelley v. Kraemer*, 334 U.S. 1 (1948); *Barrows v. Jackson*, 346 U.S. 249 (1953).

[14] *Missouri ex rel. Gaines v. Canada*, 305 U.S. 337 (1938); see also *Sipuel v. Board of Regents*, 332 U.S. 631 (1948).

[15] 339 U.S. 629 (1950).

[16] 347 U.S. 483 (1954).

[17] 349 U.S. 294 (1955).

[18] *Dawson v. Baltimore*, 350 U.S. 877 (1955); *Holmes v. Atlanta*, 350 U.S. 879 (1955).

[19] *Gayle v. Browder*, 352 U.S. 903 (1956).

[20] *Cooper v. Aaron*, 358 U.S. 1, 17 (1958).

[21] For a summary of these statutes, see Duane Lockard, *Toward Equal Opportunity* (New York: Crowell-Collier and Macmillan, 1968).

[22] *Gayle v. Browder*, 352 U.S. 903 (1956).

[23] See Michael Lipsky, "Protest as a Political Resource," *American Political Science Review*, 62 (December 1968), p. 1144.

[24] In *Jones v. Mayer*, 392 U.S. 409 (1968), decided two months after the 1968 housing act went into effect, the Supreme Court sustained the constitutionality of an all but forgotten civil rights act of 1866 that forbade racial discriminaion in buying or selling real estate.

[25] Francis L. Broderick and August Meier, eds., *Negro Protest Thought in the Twentieth Century*, p. xxxi.

[26] Bayard Rustin, "From Protest to Politics," reprinted in Broderick and Meier, p. 411.

[27] See E.U. Essien-Udom, *Black Nationalism* (Chicago, Ill.: University of Chicago Press, 1962), for the best account of the Muslim movement.

[28] For an excellent description of the Panther party by a former member, see Earl Anthony, *Picking Up the Gun* (New York: Dial Press, 1970); one of the co-founders of the party has written a somewhat different account: Bobby Seale, *Seize the Time: The Story of the Black Panther Party and Huey P. Newton* (New York: Random House, Inc., 1970).

[29] *The New York Times*, December 14, 1969.

[30] Eldridge Cleaver, "Three Notes from Exile," *Ramparts*, 8 (September 1969), p. 32.

[31] See Theodore L. Cross, *Black Capitalism: Strategy for Business in the Ghetto* (New York: Atheneum Publishers, 1969); and William F. Haddad and G. Douglas Pugh, eds., *Black Economic Development* (Englewood Cliffs, N.J.: Prentice-Hall, Inc., 1969).

[32] Jerome H. Skolnick, *The Politics of Protest: A Task Force Report Submitted to the National Commission on the Causes and Prevention of Violence* (New York: Simon and Schuster, 1969), p. 162.

[33] John O. Killens, "Explanation of the 'Black Psyche,'" reprinted in Broderick and Meier, p. 350.

[34] Robert F. Williams, "USA: The Potential of a Minority Revolution," reprinted in Broderick and Meier, p. 326.

[35] Cleaver, "Three Notes from Exile," p. 35.

[36] Carmichael and Hamilton, p. 53.

[37] Gunnar Myrdal, *An American Dilemma* (New York: Harper and Row, 1944).

[38] Charles Silverman, *Crisis in Black and White* (New York: Random House, Inc., 1964), pp. 9–10.

[39] Robert F. Williams, in Broderick and Meier, p. 333.

[40] Carmichael and Hamilton, p. 44.

[41] P. 66.

[42] Cleaver, "Three Notes from Exile," p. 29.

[43] Wilson Record, *The Negro and the Communist Party* (Chapel Hill, N.C.: University of North Carolina Press, 1951), p. 310.

[44] William W. Ellis, *White Ethics and Black Power: The Emergence of the West Side Organization* (Chicago, Ill.: Aldine Publishing Company, 1969), p. 20.

[45] These data are taken from Angus Campbell and Howard Schuman, "Racial Attitudes in Fifteen American Cities," in *Supplemental Studies for the National Advisory Commission on Civil Disorders* (Washington, D.C.: Government Printing Office, 1968).

[46] Campbell and Schuman, "Racial Attitudes in Fifteen American Cities," p. 6.

[47] David O. Sears, "Black Attitudes toward the Political System in the Aftermath of the Watts Insurrection," *Midwest Journal of Political Science*, 13 (November 1969), p. 515.

Part VIII Public Policies

Diplomatic Dissent

Restive 'Young Turks' Lead Reform Movement At State Department

By Stephen Grover

Staff Reporter of The Wall Street Journal

WASHINGTON—Secretary of State William P. Rogers confesses to a worrisome problem.

"The thing I've noticed, and I'm trying to do something about it," he says, "is that I don't feel I have an action group at my command as they do at other departments. Sometimes I have a feeling things aren't going to get done."

That disclosure won't electrify veteran observers of State. It is the perpetually beleaguered department that John F. Kennedy, in a moment of pique, called "a bowl of jelly." Now Mr. Rogers and President Nixon find themselves confronted—as their predecessors were—by an irksome paradox in the business of making and executing foreign policy.... A young and reform-minded Foreign Service Officer, puts the problem this way: "We have first-rate people and a second-rate system."

... Small wonder, say the critics, that recent Presidents have come to work around the State Department, rather than through it, and that the making of foreign policy has all but moved to the White House. . . ."

Mr. Kennedy tended to bypass Dean Rusk, then Secretary of State. Lyndon Johnson maintained a closer relationship with Mr. Rusk than Mr. Kennedy did, but he relied heavily on his foreign affairs adviser, Walt W. Rostow. Now there is much evidence that Mr. Nixon leans more heavily on Henry Kissinger, his foreign affairs adviser, than he does on Secretary Rogers. . . .

Perhaps more significant, however, is a show of militancy by a group of young FSOs called "Young Turks" for their aggressive leadership of the American Foreign Service Association, an FSO group. At their urging, for instance, the department agreed last month to the creation of an ombudsman as a grievance mechanism. . . .

Some of State's difficulties seem to be as inescapable as the weather. Mr. Rusk calls it a "department of frustration," since it "deals with that part of the world that doesn't automatically respond to our command."

Mr. Rusk raises another point: The State Department often doesn't get credit for its triumphs. "The State Department is in the same position as the CIA," says Rep. Wayne Hays of Ohio, a ranking member of the House Foreign Affairs Committee. "Its mistakes show; a lot of its successes don't. If State succeeds in getting a foreign government to adopt a certain policy, it can't very well announce that fact in public."

But even observers with a bias in State's favor sharply indict many of its ways. Perhaps most vexing, as President Kennedy discovered, is that the State Department often takes a long time to act. ... On one afternoon in 1961, the colony of British Guiana (now the nation of Guyana) seemed to be threatened by a Communist takeover. Mr. Bundy ordered a policy position paper on the situation; State replied that the paper would take a week or two to prepare.

As columnist Stewart Alsop recounted the story, a Foreign Service Officer explained that the paper would "have to be drafted, and then move up through the various levels of the office of Inter-American Affairs. Then there would be clearances and concurrences—European Affairs, International Organization Affairs, Intelligence and Research, Political Affairs. Then when it got up near the Secretary's level, there would be inter-agency clearances—the Pentagon, the Central Intelligence Agency, maybe Treasury or Commerce. And finally the paper would have to be cleared by the National Security Council.

"A policy in an afternoon? Good God!"

On the question of State's reputed slowness to move, Secretary Rogers cautions that many problems indeed do require extensive and thoughtful analysis. "Months may elapse before a decision can be made," he says....

... in installations abroad and in Washington, State has difficulty imposing its will on the other agencies that have foreign dealings. And it has an internal problem: State Department people in Washington are covered by two personnel systems, the Foreign Service and the Civil Service.

The major difference is that Foreign Service people must agree to work abroad during much of their careers, while Civil Service people may remain at home....

Congressman Hays says he never has understood "how a Secretary of State can run a hydra-headed thing" that has employes covered by two systems. Three years ago he introduced a bill that would have merged the two groups of employes within State. The bill was killed in a Senate committee.

Mr. Hays traces the defeat to persistent lobbying by the American Foreign Service Association, the FSO organization. . . .

The problem is that the AFSA has a new orientation. It now is controlled by the "Young Turks" who advocate merging the services.

The new AFSA, in fact, advocates a single Foreign Service combining State Department personnel with those of related agencies such as AID, which has 17,000 employes, USIA, with 11,200 employes, the Peace Corps and the Arms Control and Disarmament Agency....

In addition to creating the ombudsman, State's leadership already has listened to another suggestion of the Young Turks. It agreed last summer to the creation of a new staff, the Office of Planning and Coordination, in the Secretary's office, to aid him in long-range planning, suggesting alternative policies and coordinating foreign relations activities. . . .

© 1969 by The Wall Street Journal. Reprinted by permission.

Chapter 22 Foreign and Military Policies

U.S. STRATEGY IN INTERNATIONAL AFFAIRS

For two and a half decades the central element in American foreign policy has been a belief that the Soviet Union and Communist China mortally threaten the security of the United States. American leaders have accordingly followed three basic and closely interrelated policies: containment, deterrence, and economic assistance to actual and potential allies as well as to uncommitted nations.

Containment

Late in the summer of 1945, the United States, Great Britain, and the Soviet Union concluded a bloody war against Germany, Japan, and their allies. Within two years, however, the United States and Britain found themselves in a cold war with their erstwhile partner. After the Germans surrendered, Soviet troops, contrary to agreements with the United States, continued to occupy northern Iran, and in 1945–1946, Russia began pressing Turkey for territorial concessions. At the end of the war Russian troops occupied most of eastern Europe, and the guerrilla leaders who had taken control of Albania and Yugoslavia were Communists. After some generally unsuccessful efforts to use free elections to legitimate their power, the Russians had by 1947 added Poland, Hungary, Rumania, Bulgaria, and Czechoslovakia to their satellite empire. Meanwhile, Communist guerrillas were pushing Greece into anarchy.

Confronted with these moves, the United States initially vacillated. But when Britain decided it could no longer defend the Mediterranean, President Truman reacted with a forthrightness that characterized his years in the White House. He protested to the Russians against their failure to leave Iran, implying that the United States was prepared to use force to free that country of foreign troops. Truman also sent American economic and military assistance to Turkey and Greece, enabling the Turks to withstand Soviet demands and the Greeks to crush the Communist guerrillas. In a speech before Congress in March 1947, the President made it clear that the United States was following a general policy, not making a series of unconnected decisions. Proclaiming what came to be called the Truman Doctrine, he declared:

> At the present moment in world history nearly every nation must choose between alternative ways of life. The choice is too often not a free one. . . . I believe that it must be the policy of the United States to support free peoples who are resisting attempted subjugation by armed minorities or outside pressures.

After mid-1947 the Truman Doctrine became the central tenet of containment, the policy of resisting Communist efforts to take over other nations. Despite criticisms that it was too timid or too aggressive, too rigid, or too grandiose, containment remained a basic element in American foreign policy for more than twenty years.

As another component of this policy the United States has entered into a series of regional military alliances providing for collective defense. In Europe it is a member of the North Atlantic Treaty Organization (NATO); in the Western Hemisphere, of the Organization of American States (OAS); in the Pacific, of the South East Asia Treaty Organization (SEATO) and the Australia-New Zealand-United States Treaty arrangement (ANZUS). In addition, the United States has bilateral alliances with a number of nations, including Korea, Japan, and the Philippines.

The first real and also successful test of the containment doctrine came in 1948, when the United States fought the Russian blockade of Berlin by airlifting food, coal, medicine, and other supplies that kept the citizens of West Berlin existing for almost a year until the Russians lifted their blockade. The policy was severely tested a second time in 1950, when North Korean armies, trained and equipped by the Russians, crossed the thirty-eighth parallel and invaded South Korea. Again Truman responded swiftly by ordering American air and naval units to support the South Koreans, and shortly thereafter, he committed American ground troops to the war.

The war in Vietnam presented a third crucial test, one that many critics believe shows that containment policy has become badly outmoded. The success of the North Vietnamese and Viet Cong in eroding the authority of various South Vietnamese governments first brought about an increasingly sharp American military response. Then, as tactical military victories proved inadequate to shore up the government in Saigon, it brought a slowing down and subsequently a halt in bombing of the North, a long desultory series of peace talks in Paris, and gradual withdrawal of American troops.

If the purpose of intervention in Vietnam was to contain communism, that policy was certainly unsuccessful. The exact extent to which disengagement from that unhappy country spells the end of containment as a vital part of American policy in Asia remains to be seen. The reaction of vocal elements in Congress and the electorate against the war suggests that, unless there is aggression of the most flagrant sort, it may be practically impossible in the near future for the United States to fight another small war to stop the spread of communism.

Some defenders of containment urge its continuance and claim that Vietnam represents a misuse of the policy rather than a fundamental flaw in the concept itself. The object of containment, they contend, should have been China, not communism in the abstract, for experience in Europe shows that communism can take on forms that are not inimical to American interests. Given the nationalism of Vietnamese leaders, a strong, united country, even one controlled by Ho Chi Minh's disciples, would be a more realistic barrier against the spread of Chinese influence than a fractionalized set of puny dukedoms. To the moral argument that many South Vietnamese refuse to live under an authoritarian Communist regime and that most of those who favor any sort of free government would probably not survive the kind of blood bath the Communists used in Hanoi in the 1950s and in Hue in 1968 to purge potential opponents, these realistic defenders of containment reply in a way curiously like that of many doves. First, they note, South Vietnamese governments have not been noted for respecting life and liberty. Second, continuing the war would kill more, though probably different, people than the Communists would if they took over in the South. Most important, the realists assert, American interests in checking China and eliminating the effects of poverty at home take precedence over the interests of the South Vietnamese.

Economic Assistance

Economic aid has been an integral part of containment. American money and material were important factors in enabling Greece and Turkey to resist Communist pressures. Later the United States adopted the Marshall Plan, an attempt to rebuild the economies of western European nations. Foreign aid has also been an expensive and important aspect of American efforts to build up the capabilities of developing countries to resist both external aggression and internal subversion.

Assistance from the United States restored prosperity to western Europe to the extent that by 1970 West Germany had become one of the richest nations in the world, and France, who after World War II was economically destitute, militarily impotent, and politically disunited, felt strong enough in 1966 to withdraw most of its support from NATO and ask that American forces go home. In Southeast Asia, Latin America, the Middle East, and Africa, foreign aid began from a base of poverty and ignorance, in an atmosphere more medieval than modern. Except in Japan the results have been less encouraging than in Europe, although in many instances there has been some progress. There has, however, been a growing disillusionment among Americans about using their tax dollars as a means of universalizing the great society, especially when recipients, like the normal human beings they are, demonstrate little or no gratitude.

Deterrence

Following traditional practice, the United States quickly demobilized most of its armed forces after World War II and relied on its monopoly of nuclear weapons for national defense. This monopoly, however, was short-lived. By 1949, the Russians had atomic bombs and soon developed aircraft capable of dropping those bombs on the continental United States. In a few more years, perhaps earlier than the U.S., the Soviets developed operational hydrogen bombs. In response to these renewed threats to national survival, the United States developed the concept of deterrence. Although it can take a number of forms, including aggression or preventive war, in practice deterrence has meant maintenance of a military capacity to launch a devastating retaliation against any nation that attempts an attack against the United States or its major allies.

This objective requires, among other things, a strategic force prepared to survive an assault and able to retaliate effectively. The problem is immense mainly because an aggressor has enormous advantages. Even without total surprise, the first thermonuclear blow against military bases, political centers, and large cities could be decisive. Consequently, the strength of a deterrent force cannot be measured in numbers of bombers and missiles. It is also necessary to consider vehicles that can be readied on short notice; the numbers than can survive the initial attack and still be operational; and the proportion that could get through enemy defenses to hit assigned targets.

The problem is delicate. The deterring force must be sufficiently large to hold out the likelihood of devastation for any nation that launches an attack; and foreign policy decisions must reflect determination so that the threat of retaliation will be credible. Yet the deterring force must not be so awesome, nor its power so suddenly escalating, nor foreign policy decisions so belligerent than an opponent will be panicked into making a surprise attack out of fear that tomorrow he will be overwhelmed.

Since neither the United States nor Western Europe has been attacked, defendants of the doctrine argue that deterrence has been a success. Yet if this is the case, it is a success that has brought its own share of great problems. The money needed to create and maintain the weapons systems is money that cannot be used to end hunger, disease, and poverty. More important, deterrence, as practiced by the Russians and Chinese no less than by Americans, carries the potential to destroy the world. Not only is there a constant possibility of deliberate use of the massive weapons involved or of an accident that could provoke retaliation, but advancing technology is also making it more difficult to construct any sort of international arms agreement that could be effectively policed. Development of MIRV warheads—Multiple Independently Targeted Re-entry Vehicles, military jargon for big missiles that can fire a number of smaller projectiles—means that a single submarine with its standard equipment of 16 Poseidon missiles can launch the equivalent of 160 nuclear-tipped rockets, enough destructive power to wipe out any country. Faced with the impossibility of constantly keeping track of every submarine and every mobile missile base of every country, American, Chinese, and Russian leaders might well conclude that they simply cannot afford to expose themselves by taking any real steps toward disarmament.

Postponing such steps poses threats beyond deliberate or accidental use of nuclear devices by one of the major powers. As technological knowledge has deepened, it has also spread. If left alone for another decade, it is probable that a number of smaller countries, will develop atomic weapons and at least short-range delivery systems. Chances of both accidental and calculated use and counter-use multiply each time another nation joins the nuclear club. Again, however, checking the spread of atomic weapons would require the active and honest cooperation of China, Russia, and the United States, and that kind of cooperation does not seem likely in the near future.

CHANGES IN THE INTERNATIONAL SETTING

End of the Myth of Global Communism

From the late 1940s through the 1950s, popular and often official discussions of foreign policy interpreted communism as a monolithic specter haunting the world. All Communists were pictured as equally dangerous. Loyalty to the cause of revolution and to the destruction of capitalism was held to transcend every national and ethnic difference. Some early evidence contradicted this simplistic view, and soon other events were to prove that it no longer provided, if it ever had, a true perspective.

In 1948, Russia broke its alliance with Yugoslavia because of Tito's unorthodox politics, and in 1953, riots broke out in East Germany. In 1956, the Hungarians revolted against their Communist government and were beaten down only after a brutal, full-scale intervention by Russian troops. These were significant indications of unrest and discontent, yet still on a scale that the Soviets could control. But in a few more years the monolithic unity of the Communist bloc had splintered into a myth. Even after a ruthless Russian invasion of Czechoslovakia in 1968 that put down efforts to liberalize that country's regime, Rumanian and other East European leaders continued on many points to oppose, though not to defy, Soviet hegemony. On the other hand, all of the former eastern European satellites except Albania and Yugoslavia have remained closely tied to Russia, if not by ideological bonds then by the presence of the Red Army.

Russia itself has felt warming winds of change. After Stalin's death in 1953, new groups came to power in the Kremlin. First there were several coalitions; then Nikita Khrushchev commanded the government, though never with Stalin's iron hand. Khrushchev stayed in power for almost seven years before his ouster in 1964, when another coalition took over. What each of these regimes had in common was a desire to liberalize Soviet society, not in the sense of transforming it into a Western-style democracy but of replacing terror with more efficient forms of social control and of meeting popular demands for increased production of consumer goods. The Russian people had twice built up their industry, the first time after the 1917 Revolution, the second after the devastation of World War II; and it was not unnatural that they wanted some immediate share of the material goods they had twice sweated and bled for.

Economic progress in the Soviet Union has widened the most significant division in the Communist camp. Since the possibility of prosperity has increased almost as fast as that of atomic destruction, Russian revolutionary ardor has waned, while the Chinese have grown more strident in their calls for militant action against the West.

The Russians, to be sure, have not been averse to continuing their imperialism by deposing liberal Hungarian and Czech governments, threatening West Berlin, supporting Castro's Cuban revolution, strengthening their penetration of the Arab world, and, far more seriously, in 1961 by placing intermediate-range missiles in Cuba. But the confrontation with the United States, in which President Kennedy coldly and firmly offered Khrushchev a choice between withdrawal and war, was sobering. Soviet leaders realize that if any of them survived a hydrogen war, they would inherit a radioactive desert. On the other hand, Chinese leaders, with little experience with atomic weapons and a surfeit of several hundred million people, apparently find the prospect of nuclear war less terrifying or less real.

From differences in emphasis on fine points of Marxist doctrine, the Sino-Soviet dispute shifted to name-calling and open hostility. Whether the real cause was ideological or the refusal of Soviet leaders to share atomic weapons with their allies, the split took on major proportions in 1966. The Russians angrily withdrew military and economic aid from the Chinese and began competing with them for leadership of Communist parties around the world. The Chinese readily joined in this competition, branding the Russians as lackeys of American imperialism. In a few more years, clashes between Soviet and Maoist troops along the Siberian border were becoming frequent, and by 1969 some Russian leaders were more or less openly debating the pros and cons of a nuclear first strike against China.

The Erosion of Bipolarity

In the 1960s, the bipolarity of the post World War II period began to disintegrate. In addition to the emergence of Communist China as a major world power along with the United States and the Soviet Union, the trend has been toward a more pluralistic world. It is not bi- or tri-polarity that has come to an end. Rather it is the unchallenged dominance of the super powers over their blocs that has been weakened.

Paralleling the fissures in the Iron Curtain have been breaks in the American alliance. Great Britain has remained a staunch ally, but a progressively weaker one in military terms. For all practical purposes France decided in 1966 to go it alone. While De Gaulle's abdication is bringing France closer toward the United States and Great Britain, how much closer remains to be seen. Through the mid-1960s, West Germany and Japan more or less dutifully played the music in the American band as Washington arranged the score. More recently, with a rain of prosperity drowning out guilt feelings about World War II, both nations have been acting more on their own, friendly to and in a military sense dependent on the United States, but now soloists if not composers and arrangers.

American experience in Vietnam has also generated greater disposition to acknowledge the limits of national power in a complex, pluralistic world. One of the evidences of this process has been the decline of oversimplified cold war ideologies. Other signs are the struggles of nationalist forces in score of countries, new and old, to break free from traditional political systems, the marked drift of western European interests away from the United States, and the shaky condition of many western and Communist alliance systems. Securing the cooperation of its old allies has become much more sensitive and problematical for the United States, and disillusionment with the results of foreign aid leads to further cutbacks in these appropriations.

The International Position of the United States

In the absence of a clear and unambiguous external danger, Americans are less united in their understanding of what threatens American interests abroad. Public opinion has been deeply affected by the protracted war in Vietnam, and a significant portion of the population has turned toward isolationism. If the United States decides not to fight additional limited wars with its own conventional forces, it has essentially three choices open to counter future moves by Russia or China to bolster allies who are threatened by indigenous Communist movements: to support with advice and logistics the local government being threatened; to return to the policy that John Foster Dulles, Eisenhower's Secretary of State, popularized as "massive retaliation"; or to revert even further back to isolation. The first of these alternatives has always been the most attractive, but in Korea, Vietnam, and Laos military and economic aid were not sufficient. Alone they probably never can be unless the local government has strong support from its own people or can be quickly persuaded to execute the reforms needed to build that support.

Massive retaliation is a threat to respond with atomic weapons to almost any hostile advance. As a bluff this kind of policy may have a limited degree of success. If the bluff is fully believed by another nuclear power, however, it may provoke a preemptive first strike. If the bluff is called, it will provoke either a hydrogen holocaust or an embarrassing retreat. A drift toward isolation is more probable than any policy as perilous as massive retaliation, although diplomatic history since 1914 indicates that this planet has become far too small for isolation to be more than a dangerous dream.

INSTRUMENTS OF FOREIGN POLICY

In its international relations, the ultimate purpose of a country is to persuade other countries, by peaceful means if possible, to allow it to attain its national objectives. The basic instruments of persuasion are military force, propaganda, economic power, and diplomacy.

Military Force

Military force may take the shape of a lone saboteur to agents who stir up internal discord and plot revolution to guerrillas who fight a hit and run war to huge conventional armies and navies to MIRV missiles, chemical and hydrogen warheads and even to bacteriological weapons. For comprehensive purposes of national security, however, the development of effective military forces requires a mammoth national effort that involves the educational system of the country, its technological capabilities, manufacturing facilities, and labor force as well as the activities of millions of civilians and men and women in uniform.

Four aspects of military power today raise immensely difficult problems. First, security requires a growing industrial base to enable the country to maintain a long-term state of readiness to produce the constantly changing weapons required for defense, and an expanding pool of scientific talent to meet the challenge of basic research and changing technology. Second, translation of scientific development into operational weapons is difficult and time consuming. The time spread from drawing-board design to full-scale manufacture of working weapons has become longer. Third, national capacity to survive may depend on the speed with which active military forces can be alerted and supplemented by reserves. Military planners can no longer count on an extended period of mobilization prior to the outbreak of hostilities. War comes too quickly—and perhaps too finally—for that. The fourth aspect of contemporary military strategy is the necessity for a versatile military establishment. The force than can deliver a crushing blow or deter a massive attack on the United States is not necessarily the most effective kind in limited warfare.

Faced with these problems, military planners must establish priorities of development among ground, sea, and air—and soon possibly space—forces. They must decide how much of limited defense funds should be spent for scientific research, basic and practical, satellite systems, improved missiles and anti-missiles, atomic-powered ships or planes, radar networks, and fallout shelters. The problems of choice are difficult. First of all, the costs of mistakes are awesome. If insufficient funds and lack of imagination go into weapons development and basic research, the country may suddenly find that other nations have available a totally new weapons system that makes American weapons obsolete. If the weapons of limited wars in contrast to those of massive wars are ignored or underrated, the nation's ability to aid its allies may be shattered.

From 1919 to 1940, the equipment of American ground forces scarcely changed. Today, however, the hallmark of weapons systems is their astonishing rate of obsolescence. Almost before a weapon goes into production, it tends to become obsolete. Since the Korean war, weapons technology has become infinitely more complex. Missiles and rockets can be produced today for any desired range. Earth satellites and lunar probes give way to space platforms and human exploring of outer space. New weapons are likely to be more massive in their capacity for destruction, more difficult to protect against, and far more costly. In the 1960s, a nuclear submarine cost more than 10 times as much as a World War II submarine, and its operating costs are more than three times those of a conventional submarine. It has been estimated roughly that each new weapons system costs more than double the one it replaces.

Military power is often regarded by relatively poor countries as a matter of prestige, even in the absence of threats to national security. Underdeveloped countries are buying weapons from pistols to the most advanced fighter-bombers and radar systems, and their military budgets are rising faster than their gross national products. Since 1965, the expenditures by developing countries for arms has been increasing sharply, and the supply of arms has become big business in the United States, the Soviet Union, France, Britain, Italy, West Germany, Switzerland and other countries. Major governments may use arms deliveries as political as well as economic instruments.

Propaganda

Propaganda is a second major instrument of foreign policy. While communications between governments must involve messages betwen public officials, propaganda is typically aimed at a wider public audience. Because of recent experience with "big lie" techniques of Nazi and Communist agencies, there is a tendency to think of propaganda as intrinsically a tool of deceit and deception. Propaganda may, however, be designed to tell the truth—sometimes a powerful weapon. Propaganda is an old and commonly used instrument of foreign policy that the United States has employed since the Revolutionary War. Its fundamental purposes in international relations are akin to those of public relations in the business world—to build up a desirable public image of a country and its aims to help persuade others of the rightness or expediency of allowing that nation to attain its objectives. This image need not be a benevolent one. Machiavelli long ago claimed that in politics it was better to be feared than loved,[1] and propaganda is often used to instill dread. Nor need propaganda be restricted to such media as radio, television, or newspapers. Mere detonation by the Russians in 1961 of hydrogen bombs equivalent to more than 50 million tons of TNT was convincing evidence to many neutralists and even to pro-Western government officials of the might of the Soviet Union.

The first highly organized, centrally administered efforts of the United States to utilize propaganda as an effective instrument of foreign policy occurred during World War I, when the United States established the Committee of Public Information to produce speeches, editorials, pictures, movies, and pamphlets demonstrating the depravity of the Germans and the wonderful virtues of Americans and their gallant allies. In World War II the United States ran an Office of War Information, and the armed forces devoted great attention to psychological warfare. After the war, Congress established the U.S. Information Agency, whose primary function is to build up the American image abroad. The USIA represents an effort to put propaganda on a permanent and professional basis. Although the complaint has been made that the agency tends to communicate with persons already friendly to the U.S., USIA officials assert that they spend a large portion of their annual budget trying to save the fallen and to convert unbelievers by selecting specific means most likely to reach specific audiences. The agency has staff in almost every American embassy and operates the Voice of America radio network and libraries around the world.

Economic Power

Economic power constitutes a third instrument that has both a positive and a negative edge. Economic power may be used negatively as a set of sanctions against a nation, such as a boycott of goods, a discriminatory tariff, an embargo, or a refusal to give credit. Its most extreme form is a blockade, use of military force to cut off another nation's foreign trade.

Positively, economic aid may take the form of a program such as the Marshall Plan, designed to help allies or potential friends to build themselves up so that ultimately they can defend themselves. It may be given as money, credit to buy goods, goods themselves, or expert advisers or even workers to carry out projects. As an alternative or an addition to direct aid, one nation might offer economic inducements to a second nation so that it might in turn help out a third. While aid may create a favorable climate of opinion, both official and general, it is doubtful that economic assistance can buy national friendship. For most national leaders gratitude is a luxury, and they calculate cooperation with other countries in terms of current or anticipated benefits, rather than of past favors. Sophisticated leaders of the wealthier nations realize this, of course, and seek to support regimes whose interests are compatible with their own.

Since 1961, administration of American nonmilitary aid has been consolidated under the Agency for International Development (AID), which comes directly under the authority of the Secretary of State. AID annually disperses about $2 billion in outright grants or loans; it spends some for research into economic opportunities, some to guarantee private investments in developing countries. The agency also oversees U.S. contributions to international organizations and is responsible for administering several special operations, including the Alliance for Progress, designed to assist Latin America, and the Food for Peace program, under which American surplus farm products are sold or donated to needy countries.

Diplomacy

Military force, economic power, and propaganda give a nation the potential to achieve its aims; diplomacy can transform this potential into reality. Diplomacy is a magic word, conjuring up romantic visions of sophisticated parties and delightfully dark images of international intrigue, with liberal quantities of beautiful women and fine wine. The reality, however, is less glamorous. In its simplest form diplomacy is no more than an instrument of conveying official communications between governments.

In its broader meaning diplomacy is not itself an instrument of persuasion but a force that energizes and gives direction to foreign policy by skillful use of the other instruments. It may involve decisions of when to promise economic assistance or threaten military action; it may involve bargaining to trade one advantage for another; it may involve frank statements that a certain course of action means war. In all phases of its operation diplomacy requires couching promises, demands, and threats in language calculated to achieve an objective while preserving the self-respect of other parties to the negotiations.

In international politics prestige and reputation are at least as important as in domestic affairs. Like a President who wishes to lead congressmen, a government that would persuade other governments must exhibit not only wisdom and prudence but also determination and, to an even greater degree than in internal politics, power. Folklore frequently places great hope on the efficacy of diplomacy. It may be the brain of policy instruments without whose coordination the most abundant economic, military, and propaganda resources are worth very little, but it needs a healthy body to command. Occasionally a shrewd diplomat, like the Frenchman Talleyrand at the Congress of Vienna in 1815, may capitalize on jealousy and suspicion to divide his opponents and so accomplish near miracles. Far more often, however, the effectiveness of diplomacy is limited by the potential of the other instruments as well as by national determination to use any or all of them.

ACCOUNTABILITY FOR FOREIGN POLICY

Influence of Domestic Policies

The formation of foreign policy is affected by numerous physical factors, such as a nation's geographical location, climate, and natural resources; and by such diverse human elements as the state of economic development, the status of scientific knowledge, the size and education of the population, and the personalities of particular public officials. Moreover, in any practical sense it is impossible to isolate foreign policy from domestic policy. One cannot, for instance, speak intelligently about problems of international trade without knowing about conditions of the national economy; about military power without knowing about allocations of resources for scientific research and development; or about foreign aid without knowing about the urgency and cost of domestic social welfare programs.

Because of its great wealth, the United States has been able to afford a large military establishment and to provide economic and military assistance to dozens of other countries. It has been both policeman and provider for much of the world. But because poverty sits only half-hidden in the shadowy alleys of American abundance, the allocation of so many resources to defense has meant that many domestic problems have been given scant attention and money. For instance, continuing research and partial deployment of the Safeguard Anti-Ballistic Missile system—a system whose defenders concede would not be effective against anything more than an accidental Russian firing or a primitive Chinese attack—cost more than $759 million in 1970 alone. A slightly smaller amount of money would provide annually an adequate diet for 500,000 hungry families—about 2 million people—in the United States, and more than twice that number in most other countries.

Dissatisfaction with the war in Vietnam has fed demands that the United States devote less of its wealth to policing the world and more to fulfilling the promises of abundance to its own people. Yet, whatever the merits and demerits of specific programs like the ABM, as long as China and the Soviet Union maintain and augment their military capabilities and display a willingness to use that power to dominate other nations, the United States can hardly afford to disarm unilaterally or, given the years of lead time required to develop new weapons systems, to fall behind in technology. Like their two principal competitors, the American people are caught in the tragic trap of an arms race.

The need to cope with the unequal distribution of wealth will become a more significant factor shaping American foreign policy, just as that wealth and its accompanying scientific knowledge have in the past been important factors. Foreign policy-making in the United States has also been heavily influenced by a number of institutional forces, such as presidential leadership, sharing of powers, decentralized political parties, and bureaucratic organizations.

Checks on Presidential Power

The speed with which many policy decisions must be made, the secret nature of the information on which they are based, the highly technical character of much of that information, and the need to weave together dozens of policy threads—all these make inevitable a high degree of concentration of power in the White House. No one but the President can speak for the nation in the midst of an international crisis. However necessary to survival, this concentration poses in a different context the basic problem that James Madison set before the Constitutional Convention: How to have a government that is strong but still controllable. Certainly many of the institutional checks written into the Constitution are either inoperative or function too slowly to be immediately effective when quick decisions about war, peace, and the many states in between must be formulated.

The judicial process is even less suited than the legislative process to make foreign policy choices, and while judges have sometimes spoken brave words about limitations on executive power[2] in foreign affairs, they have usually done so *after* a crisis. During the actual period of emergency, they have sometimes been unable to act because it takes too long to bring a case before them, or because they have preferred to avoid a constitutional decision,[3] have refused to second guess military decisions,[4] or have disclaimed expertise in international politics.[5] Immediate public opinion is hardly a meaningful restriction since it would be silly to expect any more than a tiny fraction of the electorate to be able on short notice to acquire the information needed to judge a situation intelligently.

There are, of course, some important checks on presidential power in foreign and military affairs. Probably most crucial are the restrictions that the President, his staff, and advisers internalize: their moral consciences and their ambitions to be remembered as wise, just, devoted, patriotic, and determined men.

Furthermore, as in domestic affairs, the President has to operate through other officials and, as we have seen, bureaucracy can impose severe limitations on his ability to do either good or evil. The Department of State is only one of more than forty agencies concerned with making and implementing foreign policy. The National Security Council is responsible for long-range planning. The work of the Department of Defense and the three armed services departments intimately involves foreign policy, both in deploying American forces abroad and in advising officials of other governments. The Central Intelligence Agency is by definition as well as inclination wrapped up in foreign affairs. Less well known are the roles played by many Cabinet-level departments such as Treasury, Agriculture, Labor, and Commerce, and many smaller agencies as well, such as the Atomic Energy Commission, the Export-Import Bank, the Civil Aeronautics Board, and the Tariff and Maritime Commissions.

Congressional power in foreign and military affairs is, more often than not, weak. In resources, intelligence reports, and ability to act, it is normally no match for the Presidency. Nonetheless Congress can intervene, sometimes crucially, by using its powers of investigation, confirmation, treaty ratification, and legislative consideration of foreign policy measures. For example, any treaty the President agrees to will have to be approved by a two-thirds vote of the Senate. Even if the President chooses to avoid this restriction by signing an executive agreement,[6] he is apt sooner or later to need, just as he would need for a treaty, legislation from Congress to carry the agreement into effect, even if that legislation is only an appropriation. Moreover, many of the personnel through whom the President has to work—Cabinet members, ambassadors, the Joint Chiefs of Staff, the Director of the CIA, and a number of other agency heads—have had to be confirmed by the Senate. So too most of the instruments available to him—military force, economic assistance, and intelligence-gathering potential—have all been shaped and will continue to be shaped by congressional action.

Questions about the ability of Congress to control the foreign commitments of the executive branch turn largely on the possibility that Congress could reclaim the war powers that it has largely forfeited through disuse. While the Constitution gives to Congress alone the power to declare war, American Presidents have intervened militarily—and without congressional permission—when they believed that the national interest would be served by armed intervention. The Tonkin Gulf resolution, of August 10, 1964, on which President Johnson relied for legislative authorization to take the United States into war in Vietnam, was nothing more than "a casual nod from Congress."[7] That resolution has been condemned by critics as a deliberate inflation by the President of a trivial naval incident into a major crisis in order to induce Congress to give to him a free hand in the Vietnam war. It also seemed to imply recognition of the doctrine that the President has "inherent power" to commit the country to war without congressional action. Behind the constitutional question of the overlapping powers of the President to repel attacks on the United States and the those of Congress to declare war lie the practical difficulties in evaluating in advance the full implications of a crisis in international affairs that leads to military commitments or diplomatic initiatives backed by a show of force. In these situations Congress tends to support the President, usually with sweeping, patriotic declarations. Only in hindsight and with fuller knowledge of the actual consequences of presidential discretion does Congress challenge the President's commitment of military power. After-the-fact criticism of presidential leadership tends to reflect dissatisfaction and disillusion with American intervention, but is not an exercise of better congressional control over foreign commitments of the President.

While quick judgments on foreign and military affairs by the electorate are likely to be woefully inadequate, the check of the ballot box is a real if sometimes distant one. Hubert Humphrey in 1968 paid for what many people regarded as President Johnson's sins in 1966 and 1967. Here Congress can play an important role since the House and Senate each provide forums for discussion of long-run policies. Hearings can highlight possible alternatives, and testimony of expert witnesses can bring out the probable risks and rewards attendant to each course. Similarly, floor debate can help clarify both problems and solutions. While few citizens read verbatim records of congressional proceedings, much of the information elicited on Capitol Hill gets absorbed into the news media and percolates down to the general public in a diluted but still potable form.

The existence of these checks may provide some psychological comfort, but in any crisis situation the degree of effectiveness of all but the limitations imposed by conscience, ambition, and bureaucratic resistance can easily be overestimated. For any of the other restraints to function, the country must survive the emergency and do so with its governmental structure largely intact. Given the destructive power available in the world, these may be tenuous assumptions. Unhappily, there can also be little doubt that, under the guise of defending the national interest, an evil or demented President could, with the innocent or guilty cooperation of very few leaders, destroy the nation or wreck constitutional government. So far the United States has maintained the Madisonian balance, but probably not primarily because of the institutional checks that Madison constructed.

Growing centralization of power in the office of the Secretary of Defense since 1950 has resulted in clashes between the executive and legislative branches. In 1962, a Senate subcommittee investigating censorship of speeches of military officers refused to accept a plea of executive responsibility for withholding the names of censors. The subcommittee feared that such a policy would further erode the ability of Congress to get the facts on controversial matters and to exercise its constitutional right to raise and maintain armies. Secretary of Defense McNamara argued that executive responsibility for editorial censorship or any other administrative act meant that top executives were accountable for actions of their subordinates. But the subcommittee accepted only the argument of executive privilege—the right of a President and, on his order, his official family, to withhold from Congress information pertaining to the operations of the executive branch, a practice initiated by President Washington and followed by succeeding Presidents.

Congressmen often view such changes in Defense Department organization and procedures with alarm because they seem to reduce legislative supervision of the armed services. Veterans organizations normally give Congress strong support, and the military services have had long experience in developing alliances with congressional committees to dilute, delay, or prohibit concentration of authority, whether in a Secretary of Defense or in a single super Chief of Staff. In addition, some legislators consider centralization of Defense Department activities an issue involving the separation of powers. Since Congress has constitutional authority to raise and support armies and naval forces, it cannot carry out its duties and maintain civilian supremacy in military matters, some people assert, unless it preserves strong authority over the military. On the other hand, the President, as commander in chief, needs to have effective control over the military. If generals or admirals can execute an end run around the President and his Secretary of Defense and appeal to Congress or to public opinion, presidential control is substantially weakened. This clash—between the rights of the President and those of Congress—is built into the system of shared and separated powers. Short of a constitutional amendment, neither side can find a legal solution; it is inevitably a political problem involving negotiation and compromise and probably only temporary agreements.

THE POLICY-MAKING BUREAUCRACY

The Secretary of State

Responsibility for day-to-day operations and coordination of foreign policy falls on the Secretary of State. He may from time to time negotiate directly with foreign officials, but most of his work involves four major functions. First, he must keep the President informed on all important developments in international politics and offer cogent advice on the best course of action. Second, he must try to run the Department of State, a management task that has baffling dimensions. Third, he is responsible for coordinating the work of American ambassadors and special agents in their negotiations with foreign governments as well as the operations of more than forty other federal agencies involved in international relations.

A fourth function pertains to public relations. To create a receptive mood for requests for appropriations and implementing legislation, he must periodically persuade congressmen of the wisdom of administration policies. To keep the President and his party in power, he also must help persuade American public opinion that the government is making sound and intelligent decisions. At the same time, the Secretary must maintain the prestige of the United States by persuading foreign officials of the good faith and firm resolve of the United States.

Before Woodrow Wilson went to the Paris Peace Conference in 1919, no American President had gone abroad to negotiate with a foreign government, and even at home foreign relations had been conducted almost exclusively by the Secretary of State or his subordinates. From Franklin D. Roosevelt to the present, however, each President has engaged in personal diplomacy. Summit conferences and meetings with individual chiefs of state have been taking place at frequent intervals. Presidents Wilson, Roosevelt, Kennedy, Johnson, and Nixon at times concentrated their energies on foreign policy, insisted on making most of the crucial and many of the trivial decisions themselves; Harry Truman, however, depended heavily on the advice of Secretaries of State George C. Marshall and Dean Acheson; and Dwight Eisenhower gave John Foster Dulles wide latitude in forming American policy.

Although a President today has to be far more involved in foreign policy problems than his predecessor a few generations ago, the office of Secretary of State remains a potentially powerful post. Dean Acheson[8] has called the relationship between a President and his Secretary of State "an intensely personal one." The Secretary's real power depends in large part on the degree of confidence that the President has in his judgment, on the President's willingness to delegate authority, on the Secretary's readiness to accept full responsibility, and on how compatible the temperaments of the two men are. James Byrnes grated on Harry Truman and had to resign; John Foster Dulles complemented Eisenhower's personality and made full use of the President's confidence.

The Department of State

Compared to other Cabinet departments, the Department of State is not large. Its budget of $400 to $450 million is the smallest of the twelve departments. Still it employs about 25,000 persons, including about 11,500 foreign nationals working overseas and mans about 260 diplomatic missions, including 115 embassies. Much of the information and advice on which the President and the Secretary of State act are provided by the Department's staff. Few of these people individually have a significant influence on policymaking; yet their combined impact is often decisive. Through their activities much intelligence is generated and transmitted, a good share of international negotiations is carried on, and the basis is laid for most foreign policy decisions.

Abroad the functions of the Department are divided between consular offices, whose primary objective is to safeguard the interests of American citizens, and diplomatic missions, that represent and protect American political interests. Consular officers typically perform such mundane but necessary tasks as assisting American businessmen to find new markets, helping tourists who get into trouble with local police, issuing new passports to Americans who have lost theirs, obtaining visas for foreigners who wish to visit the United States, and administering American law, so far as it is applicable, to citizens abroad. In addition, consular officers are expected to keep their antennae tuned for hints of political developments that may concern the United States. Diplomatic officers run the embassies and represent the United States to the government of the country in which they are stationed. As official representatives of a sovereign nation they have the privilege of immunity from most local laws. In return they have the burden of participating in many ceremonial observances. Diplomats present the views of the United States to foreign officials and in turn relay to Washington the views of the other government. Even more than their consular colleagues, diplomats are expected to collect political information relevant to the national interest. And as anyone can gather from frequent expulsions of

"Your foreign policy suggestions show vision, intelligence and gumption, Sneedby! . . . Frankly, you're making us all pretty nervous!"

GRIN & BEAR IT by Lichty. Courtesy Publishers-Hall Syndicate.

diplomats (they cannot be arrested for espionage because of their immunity), the line between spying and obtaining information is at times a fine one. Indeed, one can expect that several of the embassy staff will be professional spies or counterspies who use their diplomatic immunity and mobility in a foreign country to establish espionage networks.

At the first working level of the Department in Washington are the country directors, relatively senior career officers who supervise departmental activities involving a single country or group of countries in the same geographic region. They in turn are directed by five assistant secretaries of state, each one heading a regional bureau for Africa, Europe, the Western Hemisphere, East Asia and the Pacific, and the Near East and South Asia. Another assistant secretary supervises relations with the United Nations and other international organizations. The assistant secretaries also preside over regional inter-departmental groups responsible for coordinating the overseas operations of all federal agencies. In addition the top management of the Department includes two undersecretaries, two deputy undersecretaries, and seven assistant secretaries. The latter are in charge of such matters as congressional relations, economic affairs, and intelligence and research.

William P. Rogers[9] commented late in 1969, after he had served several months as Secretary of State, "I don't feel I have an action group at my command as they do at other departments. Sometimes I have a feeling things aren't going to get done." When he was Ambassador to India, John K. Galbraith wrote: "The State Department, to a remarkable degree, is the sum of less than its parts." Because it is mired in paper work, critics complain that it takes forever to make a decision or produce a recommendation. It operates mostly by committees and, critics charge, individual officers often fear to jeopardize their careers by speaking up.

Some of the Department's operating problems may be endemic. Secretary Rusk called it a "department of frustration" since it "deals with that part of the world that doesn't automatically respond to our command." The Department moreover often does not get credit for its successes because it cannot announce that a foreign government has agreed to adopt a certain policy that had been pressed on it by the United States. Former ambassador William Atwood has observed that "State has no constituents, nobody who wants to increase its annual appropriations, no aircraft companies or farm lobbies or veterans' organizations to fight its battles on Capitol Hill." The complaint that there are too many employees both in Washington and overseas has been acknowledged at least to the extent that that staff reductions were imposed beginning in 1968. The flow of paper, however, remains mammoth. Each day the Department's communications center receives or sends out over 200,000 words, or more than the combined files for a day of the Associated Press and United Press International, the two big U.S. wire services. And many messages are copied 100 times or more for distribution around the globe.

Like President Kennedy in 1961, President Nixon hoped to strengthen the Department of State by assigning to the Secretary authority over all interdepartmental operations of the U.S. government overseas. In a sweeping order on February 7, 1969, the President[10] made the Secretary responsible for the direction, coordination, and supervision of all overseas activities except those of the military forces. In addition, to stress the close relation between foreign and military policy, the President directed the Department to play a "central and dynamic role" in national security affairs, acting through various policy advisory groups of the National Security Council.

The Foreign Service

The Foreign Service, the professional guild of the State Department, has remained relatively small. Today it includes about 3,500 Foreign Service Officers (FSO) plus several hundred reserve officers—persons with certain kinds of technical expertness who have foreign service status for a limited period. Almost every officer today has a college degree and more than half have done graduate work at a university.[11]

Basically there are three ways of entering the Foreign Service; by competitive examination for American citizens between the ages of 21 and 31, lateral entry above the normal entry rank, and transfer from another department. Examinations are usually given every year, although none was offered in 1968 or 1969 because of a shortage of openings. The examination is designed to test a candidate's capacity to reason, to express himself in English, and to utilize his general knowledge. Those who pass take an oral examination given by senior officers who probe further the general knowledge of the candidates and judge whether they are likely to become good officers. There are also security checks and personal interviews. Special efforts are made to recruit and train young officers from minority groups. Standards of appointment are high, and only about one out of five or six candidates passes the written examination, and of these only one out of two or three survives the oral testing. About 100 are appointed annually, although cutbacks in the late 1960s reduced the intake sharply. Those accepted are usually appointed at the junior level and typically undergo a period of additional training at the Foreign Service Institute in Washington before they are assigned overseas.

Ambassadors

An ambassador is the President's personal representative to a foreign government. Legally he is the senior American officer in a foreign country and has authority over all U.S. government officials serving there except for operational military forces under an area commander. An ambassador's real, as contrasted with his legal, authority may be somewhat different from his formal instructions. He must be able to control his own mission and at the same time win or retain support in the Department of State and Congress for his policy objectives. His problems with members of his mission are analogous to those of the President in dealing with the federal bureaucracy or to those of the Secretary of State in coordinating overlapping governmental activities. A large embassy may have officials from more than three dozen federal agencies. The ambassador has usually had no voice in selecting and perhaps little say in promoting these officials or in choosing the objectives toward which they are working. When the overseas staff members includes CIA agents, military officers, psychologists working for USIA, tax specialists from the Internal Revenue Service, and agricultural experts, ambassadorial control is at best difficult. Ambassadors often have additional trouble dealing with Washington. From Belgrade, George Kennan,[12] for example, complained that the State Department's flow of information to him was insufficient to enable him to place his own negotiations in perspective. On any matter outside the jurisdiction of the Department to resolve, the ambassador, according to Kennan, was likely to get passed over or lost in a bureaucratic maze. He was most frustrated in his relations with Congress because he found that his assessments of Yugoslav developments went largely ignored on Capitol Hill.

    The role of the ambassador in diplomatic negotiations has declined in recent years because crucial negotiations are often carried out directly between the State Department and the foreign ministry of the other country or, less frequently, between the President and the head of a foreign government. For less important matters, the Department may use cables or jet trips by special envoys to give ambassadors detailed instructions that restrict their discretion. The Department may even dispatch a special representative to handle negotiations.

    The appointment of ambassadors is guided by various criteria. Sometimes a President uses the position as patronage to pay off past political debts or to gain future advantage. On the whole, patronage has been declining, at least to the extent that few mediocre men are appointed. Today about 60 to 70 percent or more of all ambassadors are career Foreign Service Officers, and most of the others have had considerable experience in public life and have often been distinguished public servants.

The Defense Establishment

The National Security Act of 1947,[13] as amended and altered by later statutes and presidential reorganization plans, provides the basic organizational structure for managing the program of national security. It created a Department of Defense to supervise and coordinate all military activities. The three military departments—Army, Navy, and Air Force—were included as subdepartments. The Defense Department (DOD) was designed to establish integrated policies and procedures for the three military departments, even though each is organized under its own Secretary. Only the Secretary of Defense is a member of the Cabinet. DOD also has under it the Joint Chiefs of Staff, unified and special military commands, and a group of Defense Staff Officers assigned to research and development, systematic analysis of defense operations and weapons systems, civil defense, and logistics planning. In addition the defense establishment includes highly specialized, top secret intelligence and security forces, an intricate worldwide network of defense communications, and several general and specialized supply services for the military departments and various defense agencies.

According to former Secretary Robert S. McNamara,[14] the Defense Department is the "greatest single management complex" in the United States and probably the world." The Secretary is the President's principal assistant on defense matters, has charge of the awesome military power of the United States under the direction of the Commander-in-chief, and supervises a global enterprise of thousands of installations, 1.3 million civilian employees, and over 3 million men and women in uniform. His burdens are beyond exaggeration. As the first Secretary of Defense to achieve substantial success in defense administration, McNamara[15] writes:

> ... the direction of the Department of Defense demands not only a strong, responsible civilian control, but a Secretary's role that consists of active, imaginative and decisive leadership of the establishment at large, and not the passive practice of simply refereeing the disputes of traditional and partisan factions.

> ... the dynamics of efficient management in so complex an institution as the Department of Defense necessarily require the use of managerial tools and increasing efforts to determine whether the "cost" of each major program and each new project is justified by the "benefit" of strength it adds to our security.

> ... the Department's primary role of combat readiness is fully consistent with innovative programs designed to utilize at minimal cost its potential for significantly contributing to the solution of the nation's social problems.

In the Defense Reorganization Act of 1958, Congress authorized a direct line of command from the Secretary of Defense to operational commands in the field, and clarified the general authority of the Secretary to supervise the service departments. Congress, however, preserved its surveillance of the services in three ways: It retained the right of individual service chiefs and secretaries to bring complaints to Congress "on their own initiative"; it provided for a legislative veto over decisions of the Secretary to transfer, merge, or abolish traditional service functions; and it specifically protected the National Guard, the Marine Corps, and naval aviation against alteration by the President.

The Joint Chiefs of Staff are the top military planners in the Defense Department. Their major task is the formulation of strategic war plans. Its members are the chief of naval operations, the chiefs of staff of the Army and of the Air Force, and, where matters involve the Marine Corps, the commandant of the Marine Corps. In addition, the President designates a fifth officer to serve as chairman. Since 1958, the chairman has had power to vote in sessions of the Joint Chiefs and authority to select the director of the Joint Staff to supervise an enlarged roster of military officers. The Joint Staff was enlarged in order to permit the Joint Chiefs to deal with operational problems as well as strategic planning. Congress, however, specifically prohibited a single chief of staff system and an over-all armed forces general staff. Interservice rivalries and clashes of personality have often hampered the effectiveness of the Joint Chiefs. Such clashes make more difficult the task of reconciling and compromising divergent strategic views of the various services. It is hard for the members to avoid being advocates of a service point of view. Each is dedicated to his own service and its concepts of proper strategy and tactics, indeed is responsible for its status and morale. When money is scarce each battles vigorously to protect his own branch; and more than one member of the Joint Chiefs has resigned in anger and taken his fight with his colleagues or with the administration to the public. Because the Joint Chiefs of Staff have been unable to eliminate interservice rivalries, the Secretary increasingly has acted as referee and arbitrator.

As discussed in Chapter 15, the uses of the National Security Council vary with each President. Initially it was intended to function as a five-man super Cabinet to provide advice to the President on the integration of domestic, foreign, and military policies relating to national security. The statutory members are the President, the Vice President, the Secretary of State, the Secretary of Defense, and the Director of the Office of Emergency Planning. Presidents have often invited others to sit in when he thought it appropriate. One of President Nixon's first moves as chief executive was to "restore the National Security Council to the role set by it in the National Security Act of 1947." Accordingly the President indicated that the Council would be the principal forum for the consideration of policy issues he must decide, meet regularly and often, and be supported by a series of committees and groups to prepare forward planning and to facilitate the handling of immediate operational problems. The President then assigned to these NSC bodies a comprehensive series of studies covering the principal national security issues confronting the country. The President further prescribed the approach for examination of the key issues: to "assure that all pertinent facts are established, and all options presented —complete with pros, cons, and costs—so that decisions can be made with a clear understanding of their ramifications." The purpose of this procedure, the White House[16] added, "is to bring the full range of choices to the President and his principal advisers—not to bury them."

The Central Intelligence Agency, an extremely important part of the national security organization, functions under the National Security Council, planning, developing, and coordinating all foreign intelligence activity. Its work centers on discovering how strong a possible enemy is and what he is up to. In recent years the CIA has employed about 20,000 American citizens plus thousands of foreign-born personnel. The most vital function the CIA performs is the production of "national estimates." These should be reasoned appraisals of such matters as a country's potential for war, its strategic capabilities, and its vulnerability to attack or pressure. The value of national estimates depends upon the soundness of the data and judgment that go into them. Intelligence information is gathered from such open sources as technical journals and other published documents, but it is also gathered by secret agents and by the intelligence services of the Army, the Navy, the Air Force, the CIA, and by similar agencies of friendly governments.

In order to protect the CIA's cloak and dagger operations from publicity that would undermine its effectiveness, Congress exempted it from normal legislative surveillance and from supervision by the General Accounting Office. But many politicians regard the CIA as an inviting target of investigation. Its files would reveal tales of mystery, intrigue, espionage, and critical decisions affecting national security. The CIA's bungling of the Cuban refugees' effort at the Bay of Pigs in 1961 to overthrow the Castro regime and its manipulation of student organizations, revealed in 1967, make it particularly vulnerable to criticism, but so far the CIA's friends on Capitol Hill have protected it against attempts to subject its operations to closer scrutiny.

THE MILITARY-INDUSTRIAL COMPLEX

For the first time since Senator Gerald Nye's famed investigation of the "merchants of death" in the 1930s, the nation entered into a great debate in 1969 about the power and influence of the military. Simply stated, the issue is whether we have created a system that threatens America and all that it stands for, whether a military-industrial complex, consisting of the Pentagon and its network of defense suppliers, research facilities, and private services dependent on military or defense-related customers, key leaders in Congress, and lobbyists for military spending, is beyond democratic control and is driving inexorably toward further military involvements. Has the military-industrial complex become a powerful force for the perpetuation of global military involvements?

The term itself was used first by President Eisenhower in his famous farewell address of January 17, 1961, when he cautioned his fellow Americans to beware the twin dangers to freedom arising from the military-industrial complex and the scientific technological elite:

> ... this conjunction of an immense military establishment and a large arms industry is new in the American experience. The total influence—economic, political, even spiritual—is felt in every city, every state house, every office of the Federal Government. We recognize the imperative need for this development. Yet we must not fail to comprehend its grave implications. Our soil, resources, and livelihood are all involved; so is the very structure of our society.

> In the council of government, we must guard against the acquisition of unwarranted influence, whether sought or unsought, by the military-industrial complex. The potential for the disastrous rise of misplaced power exists and will persist.

Military research and development has been one of the major growth areas of the American economy. Since 1950, military spending and defense-related employment have doubled. Although a few analysts and critics claim otherwise,[17] most observers believe that the M-I complex has not developed through a deliberate conspiracy of industry, military, labor, and other groups. Rather, in the words of Senator Eugene McCarthy,[18] one of its principal critics, "the influence of the military in American life today is something that has happened to us almost without critical judgment and without real evaluation of the process." And as a large part of the American economy has been devoted to defense activities, the M-I complex has "acquired a constituency including factory workers, clerks, secretaries, even grocers and barbers. Local politicians and community leaders may not find it easy to plead for the extension of activities that no longer serve a military purpose. Many, nevertheless, manage to overcome such scruples.[19]

The Economic Impact of Defense

Some of the key dimensions of the military-industrial complex can be suggested by its size, its pervasive impact on the economy, its methods of doing business, its real or alleged inefficiencies, obstacles to its accountability, and its distortion of national priorities.

Size alone raises real fear about the capacity of elected government officials to maintain basic control of foreign and military policy and of the political and economic system of the country. Defense has become the largest employer; one out of every nine or ten jobs today is in defense. Together with their families, defense workers may total as much as one-fifth of the American population. Universities receive a major share of their income

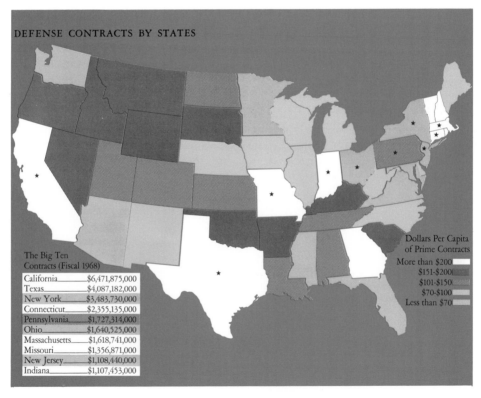

DEFENSE CONTRACTS BY STATES

The Big Ten
Contracts (Fiscal 1968)

California	$6,471,875,000
Texas	$4,087,182,000
New York	$3,483,730,000
Connecticut	$2,355,135,000
Pennsylvania	$1,727,314,000
Ohio	$1,640,525,000
Massachusetts	$1,618,741,000
Missouri	$1,356,871,000
New Jersey	$1,108,440,000
Indiana	$1,107,453,000

Dollars Per Capita
of Prime Contracts

More than $200
$151-$200
$101-$150
$70-$100
Less than $70

SOURCE: U.S. Department of Defense, 1968.

from defense contracts and grants. Money flows into every state from defense-related activity, and at least 80 percent of all congressional districts are directly affected. Some towns are completely dependent on defense activity, and in some states, individual defense contractors occupy critical positions of economic influence: Lockheed in Georgia, Boeing in Kansas and Washington, Bath Iron Works in Maine, McDonnell-Douglas Aircraft in Missouri, and Martin-Marietta in Colorado.

Since the early 1950s defense activity has given the American economy a new and different look. Defense spending amounts to about 10 percent of the gross national product, compared to 4–5 percent in the years immediately after World War II. While money is pumped into every state of the union, over half of all defense spending goes to ten states, led by California, Texas, and New York. In Connecticut, it accounts for about 20 percent of all personal income, in Alaska 30 percent. Because the livelihoods of so many hinge on continued defense spending, which in turn depends on the development of new military gear, critics charge that a new "weapons culture" has developed, and that the prospect of unemployment for defense contractors spurs weapons development. Defense industries, it is charged, must constantly come up with new projects to keep them busy. And once a weapons system is developed, the pressures to produce it are immense. "Military men want the most advanced weapons available; corporations seek the business because of their need to grow; and politicians, particularly those in areas economically dependent on defense industries, push new projects because of the employment they mean for their constituents."[20] A leading critic concludes: "The military-industrial complex isn't a conspiracy. It's a confluence of thinking."[21]

The high rate of defense spending has continued for two decades and has become a substantial and normal factor in the economy. Defense business is only a small part of the total business of many companies, while in others major production efforts demand greater concentration of defense activity. Shifts in the mix of defense spending are major factors in economic growth and stagnation. In the late 1950s and early 1960s, defense spending concentrated on missiles and other items required for a strategic retaliatory force. With increasing U.S. involvement in Vietnam there has been a shift from aerospace, electronic, and missile industries to more conventional weapon production, such as planes, helicopters, tanks, and uniforms.

Industrial involvement in defense can be measured in two ways. The first is each industry's share of total defense outlays. The second is the reliance of each industry on defense income. A few industries—such as aircraft, missiles, communications equipment, shipbuilding, and ordnance—rate high in both ways. In the late 1960s about 68 percent of defense-generated employment was in manufacturing and about 26 percent was in services such as transportation, warehousing, and wholesale and retail trade. Small firms are most likely to receive contracts in textiles and clothing, construction, small weapons, and other more conventional items.[22]

Defense spending directly affects regional economic growth in the United States and is distributed unevenly in the country. Shipbuilding is concentrated in coastal areas; aircraft and missile production are usually found where the climate allows year-round testing and launching; large manufacturing firms are found in densely populated areas with the largest labor forces; only large military installations are located in outlying areas such as Hawaii and Alaska. Subcontracting tends to be concentrated geographically, with

New York and California accounting for at least a third of the value of contract awards. While the defense sector has stimulated economic growth in some areas, it has retarded growth in others.

The Department of Defense and military contractors employ over one-half of all industrial scientists and engineers in the U.S., a reflection of the heavy emphasis in defense employment on technical skill and brain power. Nondefense industries have found it difficult to meet the salary competition for technical work, especially for research and development. The draft has increased labor turnover, and defense employment is predominantly white because poorly educated blacks have lacked the required skills. Training and skill count more heavily in civilian defense work than in other types of employment.

In still other ways defense spending has directly affected economic life. High levels of defense spending have contributed to the inflationary push of recent years and also to the deficit in the balance of payments.

The primary method of doing defense business has been the contract, the great majority of which are entered into not on the basis of competitive bidding but on the basis of administrative determination within the Department of Defense following negotiations with manufacturers. As John Kenneth Galbraith[23] asserts:

> In fiscal 1968 only about one-tenth of all defense contracts were subject to competitive bidding. A shade under 60% went by negotiation to contractors which were the only source of supply. Here there was no chance whatever that another firm could horn in on the business. There was, indeed, no market between the firm and the Government. One public bureaucracy simply sat down and worked things out with another public bureaucracy.

In 1969, for the first time in many years, widespread critism of Pentagon efficiency became commonplace in Congress. Huge cost overruns on the Lockheed C5A Galaxy, a new Air Force freighter large enough to hold 14 jet fighters or 50 automobiles, generated acrimonious debate about the inefficiency of DOD methods of doing defense business. Critics charged DOD with carelessness, fiscal management, lack of candor in explaining soaring costs, and maintaining cozy relationships with contractors. Such charges fed public disenchantment with high military budgets and created a credibility gap between the public and DOD executives, civilian and military.

Major criticism was directed at "low balling," deliberate under-estimating of the probable costs of developing a new weapons systems in full expectation of securing additional contract awards to finance the total project at its eventual—and much greater—cost. Two complicating aspects of these charges should be noted. The first is that the political context of congressional treatment of authorizations and appropriations for defense has encouraged low estimates of costs. The second is that the estimating task is infinitely complex, mainly because of the long lead time required to move a new weapon from drawing board to combat operation. A new missile or a new warplane today takes about eight years from initial design to first flight. McNamara's[24] special contribution to the processes of defense spending was to "bring a more orderly and efficient process to Pentagon procurement—a process that reduced cost overruns to an average of 'only' 100 percent, vs. the 200 percent average that had been common in the 1950s."

Who is in Control?

In any analysis of the problem of accountability, the makeup of the armed services and appropriations committees in the House and Senate is crucial. These committees are composed of men who have large defense establishments in their districts which they probably helped to obtain. The committee chairmen are usually southerners whose patriotism has never been questioned by the American Legion or the FBI. The Charleston, S.C. district of Mendel Rivers, chairman of the House Armed Services Committee, illustrates the point dramatically. His district includes

> an Air Force base
> an Army depot
> Naval shipyard
> a Marine air station
> a Naval station
> The Parris Island boot camp
> two Naval hospitals
> a Naval supply center
> a Naval weapons station
> a fleet ballistic missile submarine training center
> a Polaris missile facility
> an AVCO Corp. plant
> a Lockheed plant
> a G.E. plant under construction
> an 800 acre plot purchased by Sikorsky Aircraft Division of United Aircraft

The annual military payroll among Rivers' constituents alone is $2 billion. The main entrance to the Air Force base is known as "Rivers Gate." A housing project on the Navy base is Men-Riv Park. His campaign platform is "Rivers delivers."

It is probable that Rivers and Senator Richard Russell, former chairman of the Senate Armed Services Committee, and other key legislators in military affairs need not ask for such facilities in their districts or states. The military are anxious to please them and often take the initiative in arranging for installations in their districts. In any case, all installations cannot be accounted for by political preferential treatment.

Accountability is further complicated by the transfer of more than 2,000 retired military officers of colonel or higher rank to employment by defense firms. Lockheed alone employs 200 or more retired senior officers. The charge that the relationship between military buyers and sellers is "incestuous" is difficult to prove, but it seems very unlikely that defense firms expect no advantage to flow to them as a result of the appointment of former officers to company posts.

Prospects of democratic accountability of government decision-makers is also complicated by the extensive use by the Pentagon of public relations to present its point of view at home and around the world. In addition to a staff of more than 6,000 public relations men, the Pentagon had in 1970 more than 300 legislative liaison officers promoting its interests on Capitol Hill at an annual cost of $4.1 million. This force is augmented substantially by the lobbyists for individual defense firms.

Perhaps the strongest case against the military-industrial complex is its role in distorting national priorities. So long as $80 billion is devoted annually to defense activities, political obstacles to spending to alleviate the distress of poverty, urban decay, and poisoning of the environment may be insurmountable. Critics see in this situation the creation of a warfare state whose economy is geared to defense activities, an "economy of death" that takes precedence in its claims on national resources over "the quality of life."

Because of the real or apparent uncontrollability of the defense juggernaut and opposition to continuing American involvement in the Vietnam war, Americans began in 1969 to challenge the military machine and to demand better answers to the question of the proper place of the defense establishment in government and society. As W. Averell Harriman, veteran diplomat and public executive[25] said:

> It is interesting that it took eight years for the Congress and the public to understand what President Dwight Eisenhower was talking about when he warned about the military-industrial complex. It is only recently that we have begun to question the new weapons programs, the wisdom of immediate deployment of the ABM, and testing of the MIRV. Until now, the pressure from Congress has been to appropriate more money than the Administration requested for new weapons programs. Pressure comes now in the opposite direction. The turn around is due largely to the unpopularity of the war and the urgency of domestic needs. We are beginning to recognize the dangers of a militaristic attitude on the part of our country. Our security will not come from the number of our weapons. It will come from the strength of our moral force at home and abroad, from our economic and social strength, and from the unity of our people.

SELECTED BIBLIOGRAPHY

Acheson, Dean, *Present at the Creation: My Years in the State Department* (New York: W. W. Norton and Company, 1969). A fascinating autobiographical account of one man's involvement in diplomacy and government, by a former Secretary of State.

Barnet, Richard J., *The Economy of Death* (New York: Atheneum, 1969). The thesis that the economy of life in the U.S. has been starved to feed the economy of death.

Bemis, Samuel F., *A Diplomatic History of the United States*, 5th ed. (New York: Holt, Rinehart and Winston, Inc., 1965). The latest edition of the standard diplomatic history of the United States.

Clark, Keith C., and Laurence J. Legere, eds., *The President and the Management of National Security* (New York: Frederick A. Praeger, 1969). Authoritative studies of various aspects of the administration of national security affairs.

Galbraith, John Kenneth, *Ambassador's Journal* (Boston: Houghton Mifflin Company, 1969). A lively account of the author's tour of duty as Ambassador to India.

Javits, Jacob K., Charles J. Hitch, and Arthur F. Burns, *The Defense Sector of the American Economy* (New York: New York University Press, 1968). Brief, insightful presentations of basic issues.

Kennan, George F., *American Diplomacy: 1900–1950* (Chicago, University of Chicago Press, 1951). Historical treatment of American foreign policy, by a former leading participant in its formulation.

Kissinger, Henry A., *American Foreign Policy, Three Essays* (New York: W. W. Norton and Company, 1969). Three essays on the conduct of foreign policy, central issues of policy, and the Vietnam negotiations.

Kolko, Gabriel, *The Roots of American Foreign Policy, an Analysis of Power and Purpose* (Boston: Beacon Press, 1969). An account by an economic determinist who believes that the class structure of American society determines American foreign policy.

McNamara, Robert S., *The Essence of Security, Reflections in Office* (New York: Harper and Row, 1968). Speeches while serving as Secretary of Defense, edited for publication in book form.

Morgenthau, Hans J., *A New Foreign Policy for the United States* (New York: Frederick A. Praeger, for the Council on Foreign Relations, 1969). A trenchant critique of the "new globalism" of American foreign policy, together with a prescription of prudence for the future.

Osgood, Robert E., Robert W. Tucker, and others, *America and the World: From the Truman Doctrine to Vietnam* (Baltimore, Md.: The Johns Hopkins University Press, 1970). Analyses of America's basic international position from conventional, revisionist, and imperialist perceptions.

Pusey, Merlo, *The Way We Go To War* (Boston: Houghton Mifflin Company, 1969). An excellent historical treatment of the growing power of Presidents to engage in war without prior congressional authorization.

Roberts, Chalmers M., *The Nuclear Years: Action and Reaction in the Arms Race, 1945–1970* (New York: Frederick A. Praeger, 1970). A thorough study of the history of the arms race and efforts to control it.

Footnotes

[1] Niccolo Machiavelli, *The Prince* (New York: Random House, Inc., 1940), Modern Library ed., Chap. 17.

[2] *Ex parte Milligan,* 4 Wallace 2 (1866); *Duncan v. Kahanamoku,* 327 U.S. 304 (1946).

[3] *Hirabayashi v. United States,* 320 U.S. 81 (1943); *Ex parte Endo,* 323 U.S. 283 (1944).

[4] *Korematsu v. United States,* 323 U.S. 214 (1944).

[5] *United States v. Curtiss-Wright Corp.,* 299 U.S. 304 (1936), *United States v. Chemical Foundation,* 272 U.S. 1 (1926). In *Ex parte Merryman,* 17 Federal Cases 144 (1861), Chief Justice Roger B. Taney upbraided Lincoln for imprisoning civilians without trial, but Taney was sitting as a circuit judge and while he spoke as Chief Justice of the United States he did not speak for the U.S. Supreme Court. For a general discussion of the effectiveness of judicial checks on the President's control of foreign relations, see Glendon A. Schubert, Jr., *The Presidency in the Courts* (Minneapolis, Minn.: University of Minnesota Press, 1957), chapters 4–8.

[6] Executive agreements have much the same force within the United States as treaties—*United States v. Belmont,* 301 U.S. 324 (1937), and *United States v. Pink,* 315 U.S. 203 (1942)—but there is serious question whether under international law they bind succeeding Presidents.

[7] See the analysis of Merlo J. Pusey, *The Way We Go To War* (Boston: Houghton Mifflin Company, 1969).

[8] "The President and the Secretary of State," in Don K. Price, ed., *The Secretary of State* (Englewood Cliffs, N.J.: Prentice-Hall, Inc., 1960), p. 37. See also Dean Acheson, *Present at the Creation, My Years in the State Department* (New York: W. W. Norton and Company, 1969).

[9] Quoted by Stephen Grover, "Diplomatic Dissent," *Wall Street Journal,* Nov. 12, 1969, p. 1. Other quotations in this and the following paragraph are taken from this article.

[10] The documents are collected in U.S. Senate, Committee on Government Operations, Subcommittee on National Security and International Operations, "The National Security Council, New Role and Structure," Committee Print, Feb. 7, 1969 (Washington: Government Printing Office, 1969).

11 John E. Harr, *The Anatomy of the Foreign Service* (New York: Carnegie Endowment for International Peace, 1965), presents a detailed analysis of the composition of the foreign se vice.

12 See Kennan's testimony in U.S. Senate, Subcommittee on National Security Staffing and Operations, *The Administration of National Security*, 88th Congress, pp. 358–360 (1965). For more recent accounts, see John K. Galbraith, *Ambassador's Journal* (Boston: Houghton Mifflin, Company, 1969), Charles E. Bohlen, *The Transformation of American Foreign Policy* (New York: W. W. Norton and Company, 1969), and Ellis A. Briggs, *Anatomy of Diplomacy* (New York: David McKay Co., 1968).

13 61 Stat. 495.

14 Robert S. McNamara, *The Essence of Security* (New York: Harper and Row, 1968), p. 87.

15 McNamara, pp. x–xi.

16 White House Announcement of the Structure, Role, and Staff of the National Security Council, Feb. 7, 1969. It is reprinted in U.S. Senate, Committee on Government Operations, "The National Security Council," Committee Print, 1969.

18 Quoted in Alfred L. Malabre, Jr., "The War Business," *The Wall Street Journal*, May 28, 1969, p. 1.

19 Arthur F. Burns, "The Defense Sector: An Evaluation of its Economic and Social Impact," in Jacob K. Javits, Charles J. Hitch, and Arthur F. Burns, *The Defense Sector and the American Economy* (New York: New York University Press, 1968), p. 84.

17 For example, Gabriel Kolbo, in *The Roots of American Foreign Policy* (Boston: Beacon Press, 1969) argues that the class structure of American society, dominated by the business community, determines American foreign and military policy. He sees the generals doing the bidding of the ruling business class. Richard J. Barnet, in *The Economy of Death* (New York: Atheneum, 1969), presents a sophisticated analysis explaining why the United States has made war preparations the central activity of its government. A leading factor is the role of the national security managers—the politicians, businessmen and bureaucrats—who run national security affairs. "The principal militarists in America," he says, "wear three-button suits," and they "have been far readier than the military to commit American forces to actual combat."

20 Jerry Bishop, "The War Business," *The Wall Street Journal*, June 6, 1969, p. 1.

21 Ralph Lapp, author of *The Weapons Culture* (New York: W. W. Norton and Company, 1968); quoted in Bishop.

22 For a very useful analysis, see Charles J. Hitch, "The Defense Sector: Its Impact on American Business," in Javits, Hitch, and Burns, *The Defense Sector and the American Economy*.

23 John Kenneth Galbraith, "The Big Defense Firms Are Really Public Firms and Should Be Nationalized," *The New York Times Magazine*, Nov. 16, 1969, p. 167.

24 The Military–Industrial Complex," *Newsweek*, June 9, 1969, p. 79.

25 W. Averell Harriman, "Our Security Lies Beyond Weapons," *Look*, August 26, 1969, p. 37.

Chapter 23 Economic Policies

PUBLIC POLICIES AND THE ECONOMY

Since the days of the Founding Fathers, government has been deeply involved in promoting and regulating the economy. Under the leadership of Alexander Hamilton, George Washington's administration took steps to promote trade, to protect struggling American industry from foreign competition, and to establish a stable currency and banking system. Before the Civil War the states chartered corporations in order to promote industries whose operations were considered to be in the public interest. To stimulate "internal improvements" state legislatures sometimes authorized the purchase of stock of private corporations by their state governments.

As a result of these and similar policies, the United States has historically maintained a dynamic economic system with changing mixtures of public and private enterprise and changing forms and degrees of governmental interference and noninterference. Sooner or later we have called upon government to protect the private economy from destroying itself by its indulgence in greed or avarice and to help the economy in other ways when it appears to be unable to take care of itself. Thus as government grew along with business and labor, its activities became more significant for the economy.

The Changing Mix of Public and Private Enterprise

The American economic system today is a combination of private and public enterprise, of monopoly and competition. Most of the nation's business is private in character; it is financed by private capital rather than by public funds; and it is controlled by private persons rather than by government officials. But the balance between privately and publicly controlled enterprise is not firmly fixed. Private economic interests in the fields of business, agriculture, and labor have frequently changed their minds concerning government intervention in private enterprise. Severe economic depressions, natural disasters such as floods, earthquakes, and fires, and, above all, wars have also created irresistible pressures upon government to promote and regulate economic activity in the public interest. The American economy remains essentially private in character, but it depends substantially upon government activity and control to safeguard and promote the public interest and to maintain private enterprise.

The mixture of governmental and private economic activity is influenced by the development of public policies in five major ways.

1. As purchaser of goods and services the federal government accounts directly for one-tenth of all economic activity in the country.

2. As entrepreneur the federal government operates a vast postal system, maintains a monopoly on most nuclear energy developments, runs electric generating plants, railroads, and steamship lines, manufactures clothing, and operates many retail and service enterprises for military personnel. It has used its funds to establish new nonprofit institutions to perform tasks once handled by government staffs or business firms.

3. As regulators of business enterprise federal agencies directly influence or control business decisions on prices, services, advertising of products, and corporate financial structure.

4. Throughout American history the federal government has used public funds to promote and subsidize various business and economic activities. Ship operators and airlines, publishers and direct mail advertisers who use second and third class mail, mineral producers who supply materials for the defense stockpiles, farmers, grazers, and many other groups are the recipients of federal subsidies or financial aid. By lending money and guaranteeing loans to urban developers, college students, farmers, underdeveloped nations, small businesses and others, the federal government promotes economic life. In other ways—dredging harbors, financing airport construction, making grants to states for highway construction, and maintaining protective tariffs—federal programs stimulate, protect, and promote economic activities.

5. By encouraging foreign trade and investment by American business through loans, guarantees, and tax concessions the federal government has increasingly affected the international activities of American firms.

The Public Economy

One of the most significant trends today is that more people carry more public responsibility than before. No longer can the public official be distinguished from the private executive merely by determining whether he works for a "public" agency. Today in almost all large organizations, governmental and nongovernmental, the line between what is public and what is private has become blurred. Perhaps the major factor accounting for this change is the growth in size and influence of large-scale private organizations —industrial corporations, banks, universities, private foundations. The decisions and actions of these "private" agencies deeply affect the public interest and in turn are heavily affected by the public interest. Decisions in contemporary society about involvement in the affairs of other nations, flights to the moon, urban ghettos, labor-management relations or atomic testing are made by governmental executives as well as public officials.

Both sides have helped batter down old barriers between public and private actions and decisions. Private enterprise often seeks governmental involvement in its affairs, many times to bail business out when things go wrong through poor managerial judgment, and sometimes to put the stamp of public approval on private behavior. And government agencies contract with private organizations to carry out more and more public functions.

In the economic arena the American system of private enterprise may be just as enterprising as it was a generation ago. But what has gradually come into being is a *public economy* in which the relations between public and private actions and interests are becoming more subtle and more dynamic. As a result, traditional analyses and descriptions have become unusable as realistic explanations of the American economy today. In determining economic policy, such concepts as laissez faire have yielded to the imperatives of national security at home and of economic and political developments in emerging countries.

To illustrate the development of the public economy, this chapter deals with several areas of national economic policy, including government spending and taxing, the regulation of business activity, and economic growth and stability.

GOVERNMENT SPENDING

Some Significant Data

The financial activities of government strategically influence economic development throughout the United States. The multiplication of functions at all levels of government since the outbreak of World War I has profoundly complicated this process. Total expenditures of all governments in the United States rose from approximately $2.5 billion in 1913 to more than $13 billion in 1932 and to over $100 billion in the peak war year of 1945. They fell off during the period 1945–1950 but climbed again in the 1950s to about $100 billion or more, approached $200 billion by 1964, and by 1970 the total exceeded $300 billion. All of these figures are in current dollars and therefore exaggerate the increases.

In the 1930s and the early 1940s, state and local governments spent $7 to $9 billion annually for all of their programs and activities. After 1945 these expenditures rose sharply, exceeding $50 billion by 1960, and $100 billion by 1968 excluding federal grants-in-aid.

Spending by the federal government similarly increased over the years. As a percentage of total government expenditures it rose from 29 percent in 1913, to 37 percent in 1932, to a peak of 75 to 95 percent during World War II, dropping to about 65 percent in 1968. By 1970, federal expenditures fell just short of $200 billion. Another indication of the increasing significance of government spending is the relation between public expenditures and total national spending which was about 9 percent of the national income in 1900 and rose by 1970 to 30 percent.

In recent years government—federal, state, and local combined—has collected in taxes and other revenues the equivalent of one-fourth of the nation's total output. Very

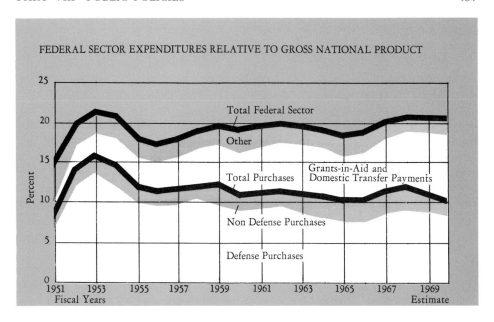

FEDERAL SECTOR EXPENDITURES RELATIVE TO GROSS NATIONAL PRODUCT

SOURCE: *U.S. Bureau of the Budget*, Special Analysis: Budget of the United States, 1971 (*Washington: Government Printing Office, 1970*).

roughly, 40 percent of tax revenues goes toward national government spending for military and security purposes; about 20 percent finances so-called transfer payments (money collected by government from one group of citizens as taxes and paid out to others, as welfare payments and payments under the several social insurance programs and as interest on the public debt); and 40 percent goes for the purchase of goods and services, including

GOVERNMENTAL REVENUES AND EXPENDITURES, 1967–1968

| | Revenue (in billions of dollars) | | | |
	Federal	State	Local	Total
From own sources	165.2	52.5	47.9	265.6
From intergovernmental transfers	—	15.9	22.3	
	Expenditures (in billions of dollars)			
For own programs	166.4	44.3	71.9	282.6
For intergovernmental transfers	18.1	22.0	0.4	

SOURCE: *U.S. Bureau of the Budget.*

the payrolls of government employees. Whereas total government expenditures for goods and services absorbed only 8 percent of the country's total output in 1929, government today buys 20 percent or more of all goods and services produced by the economy.

Despite these enormous increases in government spending in recent years, the proportion of gross national product (GNP) represented by federal government expenditures ranged from 18 to 20 percent in the 1960s. (GNP expresses the market value of all goods produced and services rendered.) By making contracts with private businesses for the purchase of equipment and supplies, by financing the construction of buildings and housing, by making benefit payments to veterans and other groups, and by paying salaries and wages to their employees, governments directly affect the incomes and economic activity of millions of Americans.

With public budgets absorbing nearly a third of the total national income and concentrating on critical national concerns, budgetary decisions of governments have become strategic in their influence on economic life and on society generally. Perhaps the three major types of budgetary decisions are:

1.   What is the proper balance between government spending and private sector spending?

2.   How should the resources of the public sector be divided among public programs? What are the priorities and how can resources be allocated in order to achieve them?

3.   How does government spending and taxing affect the general level of economic activity and the course of economic growth and stabilization?

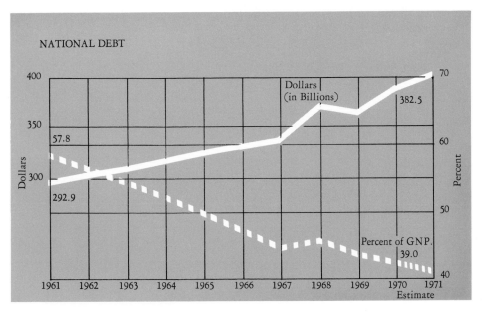

SOURCE: *U.S. Bureau of the Budget.*

Why Government Spending Has Increased

Several factors account for the vast expansion of government functions and costs, but the unifying factor is the growth of public demands for more public services.

1.   As we have seen, the cost of national defense has risen dramatically. Periods of war and preparation for war have required phenomenally large outlays, not only for military personnel and equipment but also for research. War-induced costs, including interest on the public debt and pensions, medical care, and education for veterans, help to account for much of the increase in government spending at the national level.

2.   Conventional government functions of maintaining roads and highways and providing public education have expanded greatly to meet modern needs and larger populations. Heavier expenditures for highways and education explain in considerable measure the increase of the cost of government at state and local levels.

3.   The growth of cities and the concentration of population in urban areas have created needs for more police and fire protection, food inspection, promotion of health and sanitation, protection against pollution of the environment, high-speed transportation, traffic control, and recreation—all products of urbanization.

4.   Efforts to prevent recessions and depressions have resulted in the initiation and continuation of government programs. For example, an emergency program to reduce unemployment tends to become an accepted governmental responsibility in good times as well as bad.

5.   Attempts to increase the share of the poor in economic growth has meant welfare payments as well as expenditures for general education and vocational training of

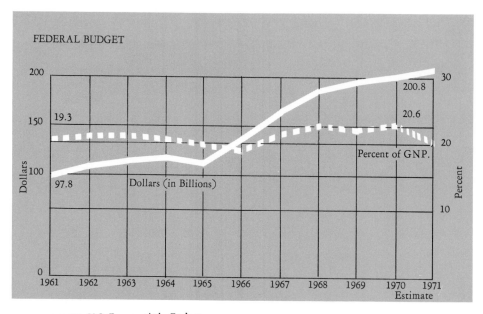

SOURCE: *U.S. Bureau of the Budget*

FEDERAL EXPENDITURES AND RECEIPTS BY FUNCTION, 1969–1971
(In millions of dollars)

	Expenditures[a]		
	1969	1970	1971
Function	Actual	Estimate	Estimate
National defense	81,240	79,432	73,583
International affairs and finance	3,785	4,113	3,589
Space research and technology	4,247	3,886	3,400
Agriculture and rural development	6,221	6,343	5,364
Natural resources	2,129	2,485	2,503
Commerce and transportation	7,873	9,436	8,785
Community development and housing	1,961	3,046	3,781
Education and manpower	6,825	7,538	8,129
Health	11,696	13,265	14,957
Income security	37,399	43,832	50,384
Veterans benefits and services	7,640	8,681	8,475
Interest	15,791	17,821	17,799
General government	2,866	3,620	4,084
Allowances:			
Revenue sharing	—	—	275
Civilian and military pay increases	—	175	1,400
Contingencies	—	300	900
Undistributed intragovernmental transactions:			
Employer share, employee retirement	−2,018	−2,307	−2,366
Interest received by trust funds	−3,099	−3,781	−4,273
Total	184,556	197,885	200,771

	Receipts		
	1969	1970	1971
Source	Actual	Estimate	Estimate
Individual income taxes	87,249	92,200	91,000
Corporation income taxes	36,678	37,000	35,000
Social insurance taxes and contributions (trust funds)	39,918	44,805	49,108
Excise taxes[b]	15,222	15,940	17,520
Estate and gift taxes	3,491	3,500	3,600
Customs duties	2,319	2,260	2,260
Miscellaneous receipts[b]	2,916	3,681	3,614
Total budget receipts	187,792	199,386	202,103

[a] *Includes costs of adjustments in postal field service pay accompanying postal reform.*
[b] *Includes both federal funds and trust funds.*
SOURCE: *U.S. Bureau of the Budget.*

adults. Similarly the contemporary revolution in civil rights and race relations has generated public programs of manpower development, community action, housing, and education.

6.   Increases in the numbers of aged persons and children in the population have stimulated further demands for programs to improve social security and to combat poverty.

Two aspects of governmental spending deserve special attention: intergovernmental transfers and the budgetary implications of an end of the Vietnam war.

Intergovernmental Finance

Between 1955 and 1970 federal grants to state and local governments increased from $3 billion to about $25 billion. Moreover, federal grants have become relatively more important to state and local governments as a source of revenue. In 1955 federal aid accounted for about 10 percent of all general funds available to state and local governments. By 1969, this figure had risen to 18 percent. Today over 150 bureaus and offices in a score of federal departments and agencies administer more than 1000 separate programs distributing federal grants to state and local governments. A continuation of the average annual rate of increase of 11 percent in the amount of grants would yield a level of grants of about $35 billion in 1975.

In addition, local governments in 1968 received about $20 billion from the states, with the largest state aid going to education. Taking federal and state aid together,

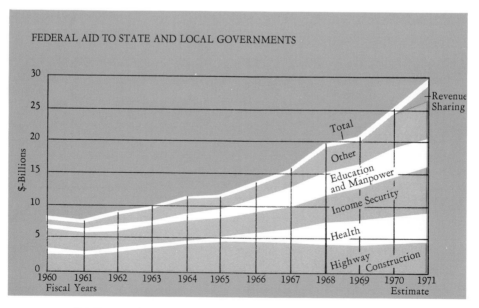

SOURCE: *U.S. Bureau of the Budget.*

there is a pronounced anticentral city and antimetropolitan bias in existing programs of intergovernmental transfers. In 1969, for example, direct state and federal aid supported 27 percent of all public expenditures within central cities, compared to 29 percent of those in suburban areas and 37 percent of all local expenditures in the remainder of the nation. Looked at in terms of local tax effort, direct federal and state aid amount to only 44 percent of central city taxes. The comparable figures for suburbia are 53 percent, and for the rest of the nation, 74 percent.

The anticentral city bias of federal and state aid is particularly strong in education. Suburban school districts in 1962 received $37.66 per capita in educational assistance compared to only $20.73 per capita in the central city. On a per student basis, the gap is wider. For example, in 1966–1967, in New York State the average difference between aid to the central cities of the state's six metropolitan areas and the school districts in the rest of the counties was $100 per pupil.

Apart from transfers of funds among governments, the intergovernmental system of finance is featured by a concentration of federal expenditures in certain regions of the country. In the fiscal years 1965–1967, more than one fourth of all allocated federal expenditures was spent in three states: California, with 14.5 percent; New York, with 7.6 percent; and Texas, with 6.1 percent. In each of 10 states federal expenditures were less than one-half of one percent of the U.S. total: Vermont, Wyoming, Nevada, Delaware, New Hampshire, Idaho, South Dakota, Montana, North Dakota, and Maine.[1] The state with the smallest population, Alaska, had the highest federal expenditure per capita— nearly three times the state with the largest population, California. The next highest states in federal per capita expenditure were the District of Columbia, Hawaii, and, Maryland.

Civilian versus Military Spending

The critical nature of urban problems and the mounting opposition to the war in Vietnam have highlighted the conflict between civilian and military spending. According to Charles Schultze,[2] a former Director of the Budget, four factors will determine the amount of money available for civilian programs during 1969–1974. Two factors add to the "fiscal dividend" once expected cessation of U.S. military combat in Vietnam comes. They are, first, an increase in federal revenues yielded by a growing economy; and the budgetary savings that could be realized from a ceasefire and troop withdrawal. Two factors reduce the fiscal dividend: the increase in civilian expenditures which accompanies growing population; and the probable increase in non-Vietnam military expenditures implicit in currently approved military programs and commitments. A closer look at each of these four factors is in order.

1. *The revenue yield from economic growth*   Assuming a conservative annual inflation rate of about 2 percent and continuing healthy economic growth, federal revenues should grow about $15 to $18 billion a year, or $85 billion at the end of five years. Assuming further the elimination of some taxes, the net growth over five years in federal revenues might scale down to about $70 billion.

2. *Vietnam ceasefire and troop withdrawal*   Estimates of the annual costs in 1970

of U.S. military operations in Vietnam are $26 billion. Assuming that some of these costs would continue, for example, training exercises for B-52 squadrons, savings might net about $20 billion a year, but the full amount would be realized only gradually. Within 18 months to two years, however, these savings of $20 billion, when added to the net additions from economic growth of $70 billion, would reach $90 billion yearly by 1974.

3. *Built-in growth of civilian expenditures*   A larger population leads almost automatically to higher public expenditures for Medicare, for the operation of public parks, for social security, for tax administration, and other normal activities of government. Schultze estimates these costs at $35 billion by 1974. Subtracting this amount from the $90 billion of savings leaves a fiscal dividend of about $55 billion.

4. *Probable growth in non-Vietnam military budget*   Even if major changes in defense policies are not made, military spending for non-Vietnam purposes is likely to increase. First, military and civilian pay will be raised at a conservative cost of about $1.5 billion annually. Second, weapons systems already approved will have to be paid for, for example, Minuteman III and Poseidon missiles, with MIRV's; the Safeguard ABM system; new F-15 air-to-air combat fighter; and a new continental air defense system. Third, costs for these weapons systems will escalate. Fourth, some weapons systems that are now under development are likely to be approved for future deployment. And fifth, the strategic arms race is likely to continue and create a demand for new weapons systems. Schultze concludes that a conservative estimate of these additional non-Vietnam military costs is $20 billion yearly, which further reduces the available fiscal dividend post-Vietnam to about $35 billion a year. It is clear that the country is faced with a series of basic decisions over the next several years on military programs and weapons systems. Moreover, the outcome of these decisions will largely determine the resources that can be made available to meet urgent domestic needs.

TAX POLICIES

Fiscal Objectives

The U.S. government, one of the world's biggest enterprises, must raise over $200 billion annually to pay for programs and activities. Taxes levied to finance expenditures have an immediate as well as a long-range impact on the entire national economy and the distribution of income among individuals. Fortunately, need for additional revenues has been accompanied by increases in economic activity.

Traditionally the primary objective of taxation has been to raise revenue. Most new tax measures are formulated in order to finance new or expanding governmental activities, but taxes may have other purposes. Perhaps the oldest example of a nonfinancial tax is the protective tariff, which is designed to "protect" domestic industry against competition from foreign goods by placing on them a tax sufficiently high to discourage their importation. Other nonfinancial taxes are special levies on chain stores, oleomargarine, narcotics, gambling devices, and products of child labor.

Taxation also may be designed to redistribute income among individuals, influence consumer buying habits and investment practices, or curb inflation. Heavy taxation of a particular commodity may have the effect of discouraging consumers from buying it. Reliance on heavy taxation rather than on borrowing to finance government emergency activities may pre-empt private funds that otherwise might have been invested in business enterprises or deposited in banks. Heavy taxes levied on personal and corporate income in periods of rising prices may reduce the purchasing power of individuals and corporations and may help keep prices of commodities from rising. Changes in the tax rate may also serve as an incentive to an employer to undertake certain desirable business practices. For example, many states will reduce the tax levied on an employer in the state unemployment insurance system if he maintains stable employment in his plant.

Constitutional Limitations on the Power to Tax

Under Article I of the Constitution Congress has power to lay and collect taxes and pay debts, provided three conditions are met:

1.   All duties and excise taxes are levied uniformly throughout the United States.
2.   Direct taxes, except those on income, are apportioned among the states according to population.
3.   No tax is levied on articles exported from any state.

Under these constitutional provisions only one federal tax is expressly forbidden, a tax on exports. The requirement that all duties and excises be uniform means that all persons in similar situations with respect to income, property, or type of business must be taxed alike regardless of their geographical location. In order to permit a uniform federal income tax the Sixteenth Amendment was adopted in 1913. It gives Congress power "to lay and collect taxes on incomes, from whatever source derived, without apportionment among the several states, and without regard to any census or enumeration."

Under the Constitution if Congress has power to regulate an activity such as interstate commerce, it may do so by means of a regulatory tax. Broadening scope of the commerce clause of the Constitution has meant that there are very few limitations on the power of the national government to tax for non-revenue purposes.

A second implied limitation on the taxing power is sometimes applied by the Supreme Court. In *McCulloch v. Maryland*[3] the Supreme Court under Chief Justice John Marshall declared that a state may not tax an instrumentality of the federal government. In this case the Court invalidated a Maryland tax falling on a branch of the United States Bank located in Maryland. Shortly after the Civil War the Supreme Court held that Congress could not tax an instrumentality of state government, and the term "instrumentality" was interpreted to include the salary of a state judge.[4] In 1895, the immunity of state instrumentalities from federal taxation was extended to cover the income from state and municipal bonds.[5]

From 1920 to 1937, the principle of intergovernmental tax exemption was carried even further. As late as 1937, the Court reaffirmed the doctrine that a state could not tax the salary of a federal employee.[6] Since 1937, however, intergovernmental tax immunities have been whittled down considerably, and earlier cases establishing immunity have been overruled.

Under the doctrine of federal supremacy the legal issues involving *state taxation of federal instrumentalities* are fairly well settled. Congress may permit states to tax a federal instrumentality; conversely, it may forbid such taxation. The area of controversy is now limited primarily to instances in which Congress has not expressed itself with respect to immunity from state and local taxation. Gradual changes in constitutional interpretation in the tax field illustrate both the flexibility and uncertainty of the language of the Constitution and the wide measure of discretionary authority possessed by the Supreme Court.

The constitutional status of state instrumentalities is still somewhat confused. A liberal reading of the Sixteenth Amendment would seem to settle the basic issue, since that amendment expressly grants Congress authority to tax income "from whatever source derived." Judges, however, have preferred to see the problem as more complex. Perhaps the most important rule used by the Supreme Court to resolve the issue is that a state's immunity from federal taxation does not extend to instances in which the state enters an ordinary private business, for example, the operation of retail liquor stores.[7] The determination of what is an ordinary private business has been troublesome. A waterworks was declared a regular government function, whereas a college football contest and the bottling and sale of mineral waters were held to be private businesses subject to federal taxation.[8]

Types of Taxes

Each level of government emphasizes particular types of taxation: the federal government relies mainly on income taxes, the states on sales taxes, and local governments on property taxes. For example, in 1970, $129 billion in federal tax revenues were derived from taxes on personal and corporate incomes. Federal taxes on the *income* of individuals and corporations have become increasingly important since the adoption of the Sixteenth Amendment in 1913. Because income taxes are based on ability to pay, they are considered equitable, although loopholes in the tax law may enable a wealthy person to avoid or minimize his tax liability. They are rather easily administered when tax payments are withheld from wages and salaries. Moreover, they are a reasonably reliable source of income even though income tax revenues rise in periods of prosperity and decline during depression.

There are several federal *excise taxes* on specific commodities such as gasoline, cigarettes, and automobiles. Taxes have also been imposed from time to time on the use of telephones and telegraph, safe deposit boxes, and transfers of stocks and bonds.

There are no federal *property taxes,* and in this century state property taxation has been almost abandoned. On the other hand, property taxes remain the chief revenue source for units of local government. They are often considered unfair, because property ownership does not necessarily represent ability to pay taxes, and inadequate, because they provide an unsteady source of revenue. Their main defect, however, has been difficulty of administration.

Death taxes are levied on the transfer of property. They are known as estate and inheritance taxes. The former is imposed on the estate of a deceased before its transfer to his heirs and is payable by the estate. An inheritance tax is levied on the shares received and is payable by individual heirs. Such taxes are justified by the social objective of reducing inequalities of income and wealth among the people generally. The national government and nearly all states administer some form of death tax.

Since the enactment of social security legislation in 1935, *employment taxes* have become important. Both employers and employees who are covered by old-age insurance pay a federal tax on employees' wages. Similarly, a federal employment tax is levied on employers to finance unemployment insurance. Social security taxes are levied principally upon workers' income and fall most heavily on the low-paid workers. On the other hand, employment taxes on employees are rather directly related to benefits received and help to prevent the dependence of the aged and unemployed.

Dividing and Sharing Tax Revenues

One of the most difficult fiscal problems involves allocating tax sources among levels of government. Rapid increases in costs of public services have forced all governments to search for new and more productive methods of raising money. As a result, duplication and waste have flourished. For example, income and sales taxes are levied by all levels of government; but because of political pressures from their constituents, state officials have generally refused to use income taxes to meet more than a small portion of their needs. In the past, restrictions in state constitutions and statutes typically forbade or restricted municipalities from imposing sales and income taxes, and where these sources have been available, their use puts local businesses at a disadvantage in competing with firms in nearby communities.

Many state governors have urged the national government to give up certain excise taxes, such as those on gasoline and liquor, for the exclusive use of the states, both as a way of helping finance state activities and of halting an alleged centralization of power in Washington. Revenue-sharing plans, which we discussed in Chapter 4, represent an effort to meet at least the first of the governors' objectives by providing for an automatic distribution of a portion of federal revenues to the states with few or no restrictions on their use.

Reactions to these schemes have been mixed. Some economists and public officials believe that state legislatures that are dominated by rural and suburban interests would find ways to discriminate against central cities. Some experts object strenuously to bloc grants to states that share no responsibility for raising the funds. Some prefer that the federal government reduce taxes and give the states the opportunity to raise their taxes. Still others believe that revenue sharing has been oversold; they believe that the states could make more efficient efforts to raise the revenues they require directly without depending on handouts from the federal government. And lastly, some critics believe that the distribution formula, which depends heavily on relative revenue effort, would aid wealthy suburbs at the expense of central cities.

On balance, revenue sharing appears to be justified on three grounds. First, the states do not have equal capacity to pay for local services. Second, the federal government already uses the best tax sources and therefore leaves a substantial gap between state-local needs and fiscal capacity. And third, states are limited in their initiatives taken on their own behalf because state competition means that no state can push rates much higher than those of neighboring states. The main problem is how to treat large cities fairly, given the tendency of states to discriminate against their large cities.

Taxes and the Distribution of Income

During the Great Depression of the 1930s and World War II, the gap in pre-tax income between persons of high and low income was significantly reduced. From 1929 to 1944, the share of personal income received by the top five percent of the nation's consuming units (including families and unrelated individuals) declined from 30 percent to 20.7 percent, and the share of the top 20 percent dropped from 54.4 percent to 45.8 percent. By 1952, the share figures of these two groups had scarcely changed, and by 1967, only a small downward change occurred.

In 1967, the top five percent of families (excluding individuals not living with a family) was down to 15 percent of pre-tax income, and the top 20 percent was down to 41 percent. Similarly the shares of those at the bottom of the income ladder changed very little since World War II. However, those in the top 15 percent of the taxpayers (with incomes in 1967 over $12,000) had improved their share of personal income at the expense of the lower 85 percent. The relative loss by the lower 85 percent may have been offset by transfer payments not included in the income figures. These payments are for social security, unemployment compensation, and welfare.[9]

TAXES AND TRANSFERS AS PERCENT OF INCOME, 1965

Income Classes	Taxes			Transfer Payments	Taxes Less Transfers
	Federal	State and Local	Total		
Under $2,000	19	25	44	126	−83[a]
$ 2,000– 4,000	16	11	27	11	16
4,000– 6,000	17	10	27	5	21
6,000– 8,000	17	9	26	3	23
8,000–10,000	18	9	27	2	25
10,000–15,000	19	9	27	2	25
15,000 and over	32	7	38	1	37
Total	22	9	31	14	24

SOURCE: Economic Report of the President, *1969. Income excludes transfer payments, but includes realized capital gains in full and undistributed corporate profits.*
[a] *The minus sign indicates that the families and individuals in this class received more from federal, state, and local governments than they, as a group, paid to these governments in taxes.*

One of the objectives of taxation is to redistribute income more equitably. What has been the effect of the tax system on the distribution of income? What are the trends? Recent estimates bearing on the questions were prepared by the Council of Economic Advisers for the year 1965.[10]

Four conclusions can be drawn from recent studies.

1. Since the mid-1930s the federal tax system has been roughly proportional in the lower- and middle-income classes, and clearly progressive for the highest classes, though not necessarily for the top 1 percent.

2. State and local taxes are aggressive throughout the income scale.

3. The combined federal, state, and local tax burden is heaviest in the very bottom and top brackets, and lowest in the middle brackets.

4. The tax burden of the poor is extremely heavy in proportion to income, although the burden is substantially offset by transfer payments, which made up 56 percent of the total income of those earning less than $2,000 in 1965.

The tax reform legislation of 1969, however, removed many of the poor from federal income tax rolls. A urgent problem is to free the poor from the burden of the payroll tax for social security and Medicare. It can be readily accomplished by providing that no one below a stated income level (poverty line) shall be subject to these taxes. If this change were made, the poor would be relieved of paying an estimated $1.5 billion annually in payroll taxes.

GOVERNMENT REGULATION OF BUSINESS

Historical Development

Most regulatory or promotional activities of government have originated at the state or local level. An exception may be seen in the case of a totally new form of enterprise, such as the production and use of atomic energy, which emerges so suddenly and upon such a broad scale that national control is immediately necessary. But in times past, when economic enterprise was conducted almost exclusively on a local scale, it was only natural that pressure for government to promote or to regulate enterprise was felt first at the local level. So long as businesses remained relatively small and produced goods and services for local markets, cities and states were able to devise and administer regulatory policies with a considerable degree of success. But as business enterprise expanded beyond the political boundaries of single communities, local government controls became less effective and the pressure for regulation soon spread to the states.

Before the Civil War, such government regulation or promotion of the economy as existed was primarily local or state. Thereafter, until the close of the nineteenth century, state governments assumed increasing responsibility for the satisfactory handling of economic problems. Then as transportation facilities improved, business enterprise burst through state boundaries, and goods were soon being sold and consumed thousands of miles away from the places where they had been produced. Many businesses hitherto local or statewide in scope now expanded and entered regional or national markets. The corporate form of business enterprise was perfected and eased the transition from locally owned and managed establishments to great national concerns owned by hundreds of thousands of security holders and operated by professional managers. State governments inevitably found the regulation of these new forms of business enterprise increasingly difficult and, frequently, constitutionally impossible. Agrarian groups who suffered at the hands of railroads or workers and consumers who were exploited by manufacturers were soon pressing Congress to establish national controls.

Government policies concerning economic enterprise in the United States have not developed according to a carefully conceived plan or systematic philosophy. Instead, they have evolved through trial and reflect the traditional experimental approach that has prevailed in the common law and in almost all phases of American social development. The immediate motivation of governmental control has usually been a desire to protect the free enterprise system against forces or conditions threatening to destroy it from within. For example, antitrust regulation is supposed to defend small enterprises against monopoly. Moreover, the pressure for such a policy has come largely from businessmen themselves. In the relations between business and the government, solutions of particular problems have usually been designed to mitigate "felt abuses" and "specific evils."

Although executive, legislative, and judicial officials have all participated—and still do—in formulating and administering public economic controls, the role played by legislators and judges has declined and that of administrative officials has become more important. Before 1860, most government control of the economy in the United States was the work of city councils and state legislatures, with very little assistance from executive agencies. But as the economy became increasingly industrialized after the Civil War, legislatures soon found themselves unable to cope with the burden of regulation. Led by Massachusetts in 1869, the states began to establish commissions to administer regulatory statutes. Congress established the first federal regulatory agency, the Interstate Commerce Commission, in 1887. This step marked a new era in government regulation of business— an era characterized by greater federal direction of economic affairs and by increasing use of administrative bodies as the agencies of control.

The Courts and Government Regulation of the Economy

Judges have always played an important part in government control of the economy. Even before legislatures or administrative agencies, they were actively engaged in regulating and promoting economic enterprise in England and America. An important function of the common law court in England was to settle litigation growing out of business conflicts between private persons, particularly those having to do with contractual obligations; American judges willingly—indeed eagerly—assumed their function.

As early as 1824, in the case of *Gibbons v. Ogden,* the U.S. Supreme Court profoundly affected the course of government control of the economy. The Court invalidated a monopoly in the operation of steamboats in New York-New Jersey waters that the New York legislature had granted and upheld the license that a competing firm had obtained from the federal government. The court ruled that the federal commerce power conferred primary authority on Congress to control commerce, including navigation, between two or more states, and it sustained a federal statute providing for the free issuances of licenses to coastal vessels. In an important sense, this ruling marked the beginning of federal anti-trust policy.

Starting in the last third of the nineteenth century, conservative lawyers were able to persuade judges—and when the lawyers became judges to hold—that the Constitution forbade most governmental restraints on business activities. In economic affairs, the Supreme Court noted, freedom was the rule, restraint the exception. Infused with the sociology of Social Darwinism, the economics of laissez faire, and the politics of judicial supremacy, American judges invalidated state and federal regulations on a wholesale basis. Between 1890 and 1937 the U.S. Supreme Court alone struck down 228 state statutes. "Purely as a matter of arithmetic," Felix Frankfurter[11] observed as he looked at an earlier set of figures, "this is an impressive mortality rate."

Judges had an arsenal of weapons at their disposal. Initially they used the commerce clause of Article I of the Constitution to restrain states from economic regulation, the rationale being that states were invading federal jurisdiction. By the 1890s, however, judges had found that the due process clause of the Fourteenth Amendment was a more flexible instrument. Statutes that abridged "freedom of contract"—a right that was no less rigid or absolute for not being in the Constitution—by setting minimum wages or that regulated rates or prices took away property "without due process of law." Courts also levelled the due process clause of the Fifth Amendment against the federal government and, more importantly, the Tenth Amendment. Federal efforts to regulate such matters as child labor, collective bargaining, and wages and hours of work, judges said in a neat twisting of earlier decisions restricting state police power by the terms of the commerce clause, invaded state jurisdiction.

Thus judges created a vast no-man's land in which both state and federal regulations were unconstitutional. As Justice Harlan Stone[12] wrote to his sister in 1936:

> Our latest exploit was a holding by a divided vote that there was no power in a state to regulate minimum wages for women. Since the Court last week said this could not be done by the national government, as the matter was local, and now it is said that it cannot be done by local governments even though it is local, we seem to have tied Uncle Sam up in a hard knot.

The knot did not stay tied. The great clash between Franklin D. Roosevelt and the conservative majority on the Court resulted in a reversal of judicial policy so fundamental that Edward S. Corwin[13] termed it a "constitutional revolution." Two of the older justices saw the light after the 1936 landslide for Roosevelt, and younger judges who came to the Court after 1937 were all avid opponents of laissez faire and Social Darwinism, although by no means did they remain foes of judicial power once they got on the bench. Speaking for the Court in 1963, Justice Black[14] summed up the constitutional law of economic regulation that had developed since the New Deal: "Whether the legislature takes for its textbook Adam Smith, Herbert Spencer, Lord Keynes, or some other is no concern of ours."

GOVERNMENT POLICY AND ECONOMIC GROWTH

Growth Trends

Measured in terms of growth, the performance of the American economy has been very impressive. From 1870 to 1930, the national output of goods and services increased about 3 percent a year. During the 1930s, there was little growth in production, but after the outbreak of World War II the growth trend accelerated to 9 percent a year from 1939 to 1945. Since then the annual growth trend has been about 4 percent a year.

Another way of describing economic growth trends is to note that during the seventy-five years before World War II the United States doubled its national output about once every twenty-four years. At present rates of production national output doubles itself once every eighteen years. Equally important, increases in productivity have been accompanied by a dramatic rise in social services that help to raise the standard of living.

It is estimated that living standards have doubled every thirty-five years since 1875. As the population has increased, millions of families have shifted from the lowest income to the middle-level income brackets. In the two decades from 1947 to 1967, the median income of American families (based on the value of the dollar in 1967) rose by 76 percent, and the proportion of families with total incomes of $10,000 or more grew from 22 to 34 percent during the same period. The poverty level was reduced from 22 percent of the population in 1959 to 13 percent in 1968. Yet in 1970 about 12 percent or 25 million persons were still living in poverty, with an equal number on the fringes. The face of American prosperity is scarred by misery and distress.

The heart of the poverty problem is that a majority of poor people live outside the main stream of economic development and their status is not likely to be improved through continued economic growth alone. Most of them are the very old, the very young, the very sick, and the very least educated. They are typically, Harrington[15] has said, the people whom industrial civilization has rejected. For most of them, poverty is not a condition that ebbs and flows with good and bad times, but a relatively permanent state. Only specially tailored programs can make a significant portion of them economically self-sufficient. Welfare payments have been a common means of helping these people; but, while necessary to keep them alive, welfare payments alone do little or nothing to get at the basic causes of poverty. In fact, as we shall see in the next chapter, regulations surrounding such programs often operate to perpetuate poverty. Proposals for a negative income tax—direct government payments to families based on the amount by which their incomes fall short of a minimum subsistence level—display more imagination. If coupled with programs to educate the young and to retrain adults physically able to work, these recommendations offer some hope of eliminating at least some of the bases of poverty.

Governmental Promotion of Economic Growth

In the economic sphere the basic goal of American government has been to preserve the private enterprise system and create conditions that generally stimulate a climate of confidence in which it may thrive. We have already discussed how government directly influences economic growth by purchasing goods and services and by taxing the income of individuals and firms to pay for these costs and services. Government also influences the economic climate in a host of indirect ways. The tax system, for example, may encourage or dampen incentives to produce efficiently. Monetary and fiscal powers may worsen or prevent serious hardships caused by sharp fluctuations in the economy. If wisely used, these instruments may help promote economic growth by curtailing inflation and deflation. Regulation of domestic and foreign trade, bankruptcy rules, patent laws, regulation of labor-management relations, and enforcement of rules of business practice—all these affect private conduct in economic life; so do government activities, in stockpiling scarce strategic commodities, disposing of agricultural surpluses, managing procurement of materials for defense and other purposes, and competing with private businesses.

One of the primary ways in which government stimulates economic development is to remove rigidities that impede growth. For example, from time to time since 1890, the nation has been committed fitfully to combating monopolies and collusive practices that undermine the force of competition in economic enterprise. The intent is to strengthen competition to keep alive a more vigorous economic system.

American governments at all levels have traditionally devoted a share of public funds to activities and services designed to promote economic activity. Public expenditures in support of growth have become an essential part of the economy. In the future Americans are likely to spend even larger sums of money to support an expanded school system, to redevelop urban areas on a vast scale, and to raise living and cultural standards in metropolitan areas. More and better highways will increase the tempo of economic growth. In order to meet domestic requirements funds will probably have to be devoted to constructing additional health and hospital facilities, developing recreational areas, and stimulating applied and basic research.

The growth potential of the national economy depends heavily on the supply of natural resources. Consumption of many raw materials in recent years has been enormous. In 1900, for instance, American production of all raw materials exceeded consumption by 15 percent. By 1950, consumption exceeded production by 9 percent, and some estimates indicate that by 1975 this figure will reach 20 percent. The problem here is to stimulate innovation and inventive thinking leading to scientific and technological breakthroughs. Probably the greatest single force toward economic growth in the future will continue to be scientific advance. Already the world may be on the verge of a major revolution in available energy. In addition to the nuclear resources, advances in polymer chemistry, solid-state physics, and electronics foreshadow greater human control over the forces of nature. New knowledge about human cells and about the processes of reproduction and growth in plants promises to extend life and to increase agricultural production.

Government can speed the translation of scientific advance into economic growth by investing in human and physical resources. Public outlays for research and development tend to encourage complementary private investment. Outlays for manpower training improve labor skills and productivity. Private investment in plant and equipment, a key determinant of industrial capacity, can be stimulated by easy monetary policies and selective tax reductions, such as the investment credit and depreciation reform of 1962 and the reductions in corporate tax rates in 1964 and 1965. When the economy is not operating at full capacity, economic policy that stimulates private investment can contribute to renewed prosperity; when there is full employment, increases in capital investment can be achieved only if current consumption is restrained by such measures as higher personal income taxes.

Many tools are available to the government in pursuing the goals of rapid economic growth and full employment, but some are more easily used. Changes in monetary policy can be made quickly by executive authority, but changes in tax rates require congressional approval. The speed of congressional action has varied. Congress acted rapidly in 1969 to reform income taxes and in 1954 and 1965 to reduce excise taxes, but took thirteen months to enact the comprehensive Revenue Act of 1964.

Whatever the choice of instruments, there are three prerequisites of successful economic policy. The first is firm and timely knowledge of the direction and pace of economic trends. While the federal statistics program has made rapid strides in recent years, important gaps remain, such as data on capital stock and capacity, employee fringe benefits, and job vacancies. The second prerequisite is professional understanding of the workings of the economy as a basis for accurate diagnosis of problems and prediction of future trends and evaluation of alternative policy measures. The third is public understanding and acceptance of policy objectives.

In the light of the growing reliance of postwar Presidents on economic advice and the rising influence of economic policy on the nation's economic development, the period since 1960 has been called the age of the economist. A President who hopes to achieve great societies at home and abroad has a vested interest in economic growth. As one of the most influential economic advisers of recent Presidents noted:[16]

> ... policies that enable an economy to grow and prosper give substance to Presidential pledges to "get the country moving again" or to move toward a great and good society. That society takes root far more readily in the garden of growth rather than in the desert of stagnation. When the cost of fulfilling a people's aspirations can be met out of a growing horn of plenty—instead of robbing Peter to pay Paul—ideological road blocks melt away, and consensus replaces conflict.

GOVERNMENT POLICY AND ECONOMIC STABILITY

Like all industrial economies, that of the United States is vulnerable to cyclical fluctuations. Since the economy cannot stabilize itself at relatively high levels of production and employment, governmental powers must be used to prevent or overcome economic recessions or depressions and to hold back inflationary pressures that threaten stability.

The Employment Act of 1946 affirms the responsibility of the national government to utilize the full resources at its command to maintain employment opportunities and to promote maximum production and purchasing power. The position taken by President Eisenhower in 1956 reflects the accepted role of government today:[17]

> Experience ... over many years has gradually led the American people to broaden their concept of government. Today we believe as strongly in economic progress through free and competitive enterprise as our fathers did, and we resent as they did any unnecessary intrusion of government into private affairs. But we have also come to believe that progress need not proceed as irregularly as in the past, and that the

Federal Government has the capacity to moderate economic fluctuations without becoming a dominant factor in our economy.

The Employment Act was a product of the depression and World War II. It placed major responsibility on the President for a continuing review and appraisal of economic developments, for diagnosing economic problems, and for prescribing remedies. While much of the drive behind the enactment of this legislation stemmed from the prolonged depression of the 1930s, the key problem arising after World War II was containing the pressures of excess demand that generate inflationary booms rather than overcoming or avoiding depressions.

Combating Recessions

Government expenditures may be planned for periods of economic depression to offset deficiencies in private spending. These expenditures substitute public funds for private spending in order to maintain national income at a desired level. They may take the form of relief payments to the unemployed, construction of public buildings, dams, and highways, or purchases of the output of an industry to keep factories and mines at work or to keep prices from falling further. A balanced budget, that is, a budget in which current expenditures are met out of current revenues, is impossible if a policy of compensatory spending during a depression is followed. Compensatory spending, therefore, is linked to deficit financing.

In practice, one of the greatest difficulties in such a program is to locate the points at which public funds should be injected into the economy. The general objective is to spend in such a way as to put money into the hands of people who will use it to buy the things they need for immediate use; as the economists say, to increase the supply of money to those who have the highest marginal propensity to spend. This shoring up of private spending for consumer goods is then expected to lead to expanded production to meet increased demands. As purchasing power, consumption, and employment reach higher levels, the government must determine when and how much public spending may be tapered off. As the goal of full employment is approached, taxation must be increased or spending reduced to obtain surplus revenues to retire some of the debt created by the compensatory spending policy.

Compensatory spending may adversely affect the confidence of the business community, and this, in turn, may seriously affect the outcome of the spending program. For example, deficit spending may create doubts in the minds of some businessmen about the ability of the government to meet its financial obligations and to carry its increased debt burden. Or fears that government may continue to compete with private business on a permanent basis may offset some effects of public spending.

Of all the antirecession measures available to government, tax reduction may be one of the most effective. When unemployment increases and production exceeds demand, lowering taxes will leave more money in the hands of consumers for spending and will stimulate business to expand. Some economists have recommended a permanent tax policy that regularly lowers taxes during a recession and restores them to higher levels as soon as the recession is over. Economists now seem to know enough about the economy to predict the effect of changes in tax rates and tax structures on the level of economic activity. Congress, however, is usually reluctant to alter taxes at any time, and it may be unable to do so with sufficient speed in periods of unemployment.

A declining economy can also be stimulated by easing the terms on which credit is available to borrowers. Although an "easy money" policy in which credit is freely available on advantageous terms cannot in itself cure a depression, it can spur economic activity. The policies of the Federal Reserve System are crucial in the control of credit facilities. The ability of banks to make loans and investments depends on the amount of their reserves, or deposits in the Federal Reserve banks. The Board of Governors of the Federal Reserve System can affect the reserve position of the banking system in three ways. It can encourage credit expansion or tighten the money supply by changing the minimum ratio of reserves to deposits that each member bank in the system must hold. In its open-market operations, it can reduce the reserve balances of member banks by selling U.S. Government securities and increase those balances by buying securities. It can influence the amount of money member banks may borrow from a Reserve Bank by changing the interest charge, which is known as the discount rate.

Since World War II recessions have focused attention on unemployment insurance programs as counter-cyclical instruments. These programs are intended to provide cash benefits to regularly employed workers during limited periods of involuntary unemployment. Over 50 million workers are now covered, including about 80 percent of those in nonagricultural employment. Nearly all states provide benefits for a maximum of 26 weeks. In 1967, about one-third of all beneficiaries in three states in the South and one-quarter in 25 other states had exhausted their benefits while still unemployed. Permanent improvement in the system would strengthen efforts to offset economic downturns and stimulate economic recovery.

Containing Inflationary Pressures

As we noted earlier, the Employment Act of 1946 emphasized the objectives of fully utilizing resources to attain high employment. At the time of its enactment few considered the danger of inflation to be nearly as great as the danger of relapse into depression. Since then concern has sometimes been expressed that the antidepression and high-employment themes in the act might bias the American economy toward inflation.

One of the most difficult economics problems is caused by the conflicts among the multiple goals of federal economic policy—full employment continuous economic growth, and only a mild inflation. When, as has happened, inflation is accompanied by unemployment, the characteristic problem of the American economy in recent years, the most direct means of curbing unemployment—increasing government spending, lowering taxes and lowering credit—are likely to increase inflation. Conversely the most direct means of curbing inflation are likely to throw more people out of work.

The Kennedy and Johnson administrations tried to encourage responsible action by large firms and large unions in exercising influence over the production, distribution, and pricing of goods by creating guideposts for noninflationary price and wage behavior. This so-called jawbone technique of regulation by calculated exhortation consisted of setting advisory limits on increases in prices and wages by corporations and unions, and enlisting public support to maintain cost-price stability. The general guidepost for wages provided that the annual rate of increase of combined wages and fringe benefits per man-hour worked should equal the national trend rate of increase in output per man-hour. The general guidepost for prices provided that they should remain stable in those industries in which the increase of productivity keeps pace with the national trend, rise in those industries in which the increase of productivity is smaller than the national trend, and fall in those industries in which the increase in productivity exceeds the national trend. Following their effective application in several cases since 1962, the guideposts suffered a severe setback when the government failed to secure a noninflationary settlement of the 1966 airlines strike. In 1967 they were abandoned. The Nixon Administration chose to rely on credit restrictions and a tight money supply in its effort to slow down the inflationary spiral in 1969 and 1970.

SELECTED BIBLIOGRAPHY

Anton, Thomas J., *The Politics of State Expenditure in Illinois* (Urbana, Ill.: University of Illinois Press, 1966). The experiences of one state in appropriating and spending funds for state programs.

Bernstein, Marver H., *Regulating Business by Independent Commission* (Princeton, N.J.: Princeton University Press, 1955). A history and analysis of the role of the independent regulatory commission at the federal level.

Burkhead, Jesse, *Public School Finance* (Syracuse, N.Y.: Syracuse University Press, 1965). A thorough review of the financing of public schools.

Cary, William L., *Politics and the Regulatory Agencies* (New York: McGraw-Hill Book Company, 1967). The former chairman of the SEC reflects on his experience as a regulator of business enterprise.

Caves, Richard, *Air Transport and its Regulators* (Cambridge, Mass.: Harvard University Press, 1962). Although written from an economic perspective, this case study contains useful insights into the political and administrative problems of this phase of transportation policy

Friedman, Milton, and Walter W. Heller, *Monetary and Fiscal Policy* (New York: W. W. Norton and Company, 1969). Dialogue between apostles of widely differing views on economic policies to stabilize the economy.

Manley, John F., *The House Committee on Ways and Means* (Boston: Little, Brown, and Company, 1970). An insider's analysis of the critical role of the committee of Congress that writes tax legislation.

Maxwell, James A., *Financing State and Local Government* (Washington, D.C.: The Brookings Institution, 1965). A comprehensive review and analysis of the various taxes and other fund raising means used by state and local governments.

Netzer, Dick, *Economics of the Property Tax* (Washington, D.C.: The Brookings Institution, 1966). The economic effects of the property tax, its incidence and distribution and relation to the cost of housing, land use, and the future of urban and suburban development.

Okun, Arthur, *The Political Economy of Prosperity* (Washington, D.C.: The Brookings Institution, 1970). Essays by a former chairman of the Council of Economic Advisers on problems of stabilization policy.

Peacock, Alan T. and Jack Wiseman, *The Growth of Public Expenditure in the United Kingdom* (Princeton, N.J.: Princeton University Press, 1961). A leading study of the British experience in governmental spending and financing.

Schultze, Charles L., *The Politics and Economics of Public Spending* (Washington, D.C.: The Brookings Institution, 1968). An insightful discussion by a former Director of the Budget.

Sharkansky, Ira, *The Politics of Taxing and Spending* (Indianapolis, Ind.: Bobbs-Merrill Company, Inc., 1969). A study of the underlying political nature of decisions on taxing and spending in federal, state, and local governments.

Weidenbaum, Murray, *The Modern Public Sector* (New York: Basic Books, 1969). An examination of the blurry line between private enterprise and the governmental sector of the economy, with emphasis on recent changes and trends.

Wilcox, Clair, *Public Policies Toward Business,* rev. ed. (Homewood, Ill.: Richard D. Irwin, Inc., 1970). A comprehensive treatment of public policies in a wide range of regulatory fields and national economic affairs.

Footnotes

[1] Data are from U.S. Congress, House of Representatives, Committee on Government Operations, Intergovernmental Relations Subcommittee, "Federal Revenue and Expenditure Estimates for States and Regions, Fiscal Years 1965–67 (Washington, D.C.: Government Printing Office, 1968), Ninetieth Congress, 2d Session, p. 3.

[2] Charles L. Schultze, testimony in U.S. Congress, Joint Economic Committee, Hearings before the Subcommittee on Economy in Government, "The Military Budget and National Economic Priorities," Ninety-first Congress, 1st Session, November 1969, pp. 57–70.

[3] Wheaton 316 (1819).

[4] *Collector v. Day,* 11 Wallace 113 (1870).

[5] *Pollock v. Farmers' Loan and Trust Co.,* 157 U.S. 429 and 158 U.S. 601 (1895). See also *Brushaber v. Union Pacific Railroad Co.,* 240 U.S. 1 (1916); *Evans v. Gore,* 253 U.S. 245 (1920).

[6] *New York* ex rel. *Rogers v. Graves,* 299 U.S. 401 (1937).

[7] *South Carolina v. United States,* 199 U.S. 437 (1905).

[8] The taxation of the sale of mineral waters is considered in *New York and Saratoga Springs Commission v. United States,* 326 U.S. 572 (1946).

[9] See Joseph A. Pechman, "The Rich, the Poor, and the Taxes They Pay," *The Public Interest,* No. 17 (Fall 1969), pp. 21–43, especially 25.

[10] Council of Economic Advisers, *Economic Report of the President,* 1969.

[11] Felix Frankfurter, "The United States Supreme Court Molding the Constitution," *Current History* (May 1930), p. 239.

[12] Quoted in Alpheus T. Mason, *Harlan Fiske Stone: Pillar of the Law* (New York: The Viking Press, 1956), p. 426.

[13] Edward S. Corwin, *Constitutional Revolution, Ltd.* (Claremont, Calif.: The Claremont Col'eges, 1941).

[14] *Ferguson v. Skrupa,* 372 U.S. 726, 732 (1963).

[15] Michael Harrington, *The Other America: Poverty in the United States* (New York: Crowell-Collier and Macmillan, Inc., 1962).

[16] Walter W. Heller, *New Dimensions of Political Economy* (Cambridge, Mass.: Harvard University Press, 1966), pp. 11–12.

[17] *Economic Report of the President,* transmitted to the Congress January 24, 1956 (Washington, D.C.: Government Printing Office, 1956), p. 10.

Chapter 24   Welfare Policies

POVERTY AMID PLENTY

The welfare system of the United States was designed in the 1930s to deal with the lack or loss of employment in a depression economy, rather than the current problem of the persistence of poverty in a high-employment economy. The fundamental fact in the consideration of antipoverty policies in the United States today is that the prosperity that has generally prevailed since the end of World War II has produced the highest level of affluence for the largest number of Americans in history, but it has failed to eliminate poverty and extreme deprivation. While the number of Americans living in poverty has declined, especially in the 1960s, a hard core of poor people remains. They are "largely those unequipped by reason of some disability—age, sickness, or other physical incapacity, lack of education or training, discrimination because of race, or some other circumstance over which they have no control—to find gainful employment either in the private or public sectors of the economy, even though jobs are available."[1]

How Many Poor Americans?

During the depression of the 1930s, one-third of the nation, or about 40 million people lived in poverty. Despite rising employment and a national commitment to maximum employment, the proportion of the population estimated to be poor fell only to about 22 percent by 1959, and the absolute number of people below the poverty line remained about the same as it was a quarter of a century earlier. It has only been in the 1960s that the poor have declined rapidly both proportionally and in absolute numbers. Between 1959 and 1968, about 14 million persons moved out of poverty as officially defined, and the number of the poor was reduced to about 25 million or 13 percent of the population. Nevertheless, a presidential commission reported in 1969 that it found "severe poverty and its effects throughout the Nation, and among all ethnic groups." Millions of persons, the commission stated, "do not have a sufficient share of America's affluence to live decently. They eke out a bare existence under deplorable conditions."[2]

Economic growth and expanding job opportunities rather than antipoverty programs have been mainly responsible for reducing the number of poor. From 1959 to 1969, the gross national product jumped from $484 billion to $932 billion, while the unemployment rate dropped from 5.5 percent to 3.5 percent. As a result, 13 million new jobs were created, raising total employment in the country from 65 to 78 million persons, an increase of 20 percent. To illustrate the profound effect of this economic boom, in 1968 alone, some 2.4 million persons moved out of poverty, including 1.6 million whites and 800,000 nonwhites, mainly blacks.[3]

White persons have clearly benefited more from economic prosperity than other racial groups. From 1959 to 1968, 11 million whites, a reduction of 39 percent, moved out of poverty, compared to 3 million blacks, a reduction of 27 percent. In 1968 a black citizen had a one-in-three chance of living in poverty, while a white person had approximately

PERSONS BELOW THE POVERTY LEVEL[a]
(1959–1968)

	Number Below Poverty Level (Millions of persons)			Percent Below Poverty Level		
	Total	White	Nonwhite	Total	White	Nonwhite
1959	39.5	28.5	11.0	22	18	56
1960	39.9	28.3	11.5	22	18	56
1961	39.6	27.9	11.7	22	17	56
1962	38.6	26.7	12.0	21	16	56
1963	36.4	25.2	11.2	19	15	51
1964	36.1	25.0	11.1	19	15	50
1965	33.2	22.5	10.7	17	13	47
1966	30.4	20.8	9.7	16	12	42
1966[b]	28.5	19.3	9.2	15	11	40
1967[b c]	27.8	19.0	8.8	14	11	37
1968[b]	25.4	17.4	8.0	13	10	33

[a] *The poverty concept used in this table is based on the revised definition, adopted in 1969, of $3,553 for a family of four in 1968.*
[b] *Based on revised methodology which reflects improvements in statistical procedures used in processing the income data.*
[c] *Because of a coding error, data for 1967 are not strictly comparable with those shown for 1966 and 1968. It is estimated that this error may have overstated the number of poor families in 1967 by about 175,000 and the number of poor persons by approximately 450,000.*
SOURCE: *U.S. Bureau of the Census, Current Population Report, Series P–20, No. 180 (August 18, 1969).*

a one-in-ten-chance. In absolute numbers, however, there are twice as many whites who are poor as black persons who are poor.

In 1968, about half of the poor lived in metropolitan areas and mainly in central cities. Of the poor in central cities, 43 percent were black, but in suburban communities less than 10 percent of the poor were black. In the decade since 1959, the number of poor persons on farms decreased from 8 to 2.3 million, and the proportion of poor persons in the total farm population declined from about 50 percent to 23 percent, a result achieved primarily by migration of the rural population to the cities. Based on the official definition of poverty (see the next section), at the end of 1968, about half of all poor families lived in the South; and over one-third of the poor lived in families in which the family head worked throughout the year. More than 3 million adults worked full-time the year round at jobs that did not pay a wage above the poverty standard; and 10 percent of all families, or 5.1 million out of 50.5 families, had incomes under $3,000 a year.

The Definition of Poverty

According to the analysis of the Social Security Administration, the poverty threshold for a nonfarm family of four was an income of $2,973 in 1959, $3,410 in 1967, $3,553 in 1968, and more than $3,700 in 1970, taking price increases into account. According to this formula, poverty is defined in terms of annual average money income, after allowing for the size of the family, sex of the head of the family, number of children, farm or nonfarm residence, and changes in the cost-of-living index. Under the formula, a certain minimum human diet is priced every year, and any household that has to spend more than a third of its income to buy this minimum diet is defined as poor.

The poverty threshold under this definition is enough only for bare existence. It is not adequate as a benchmark for policies to combat poverty. One level above this threshold is the "near-poverty" standard, which was about $4,700 for an urban family of four in 1969. Next is the "lower living standard," averaging about $6,400 in 1969. In contrast median family income in 1968 was $8,937 for white families and $5,360 for black families.

Significant Trends in the Poor Population

The incidence of poverty declined the least during the 1960s for the elderly, poor children, poor households headed by women, and individuals not living in family units. Poverty is more prevalent among persons aged 65 and over than among any other age group. In 1968, the elderly poor numbered 4.6 million and constituted about a fourth of all aged persons. The proportion of poor in the over-65 group is double among the blacks over that of whites. As a group the aged poor are not likely to escape from poverty through their own efforts. Half of them live alone, and two-thirds of them are female. In the total population of the poor, the proportion of the aged poor increased from 15 percent in 1959 to 18 percent in 1968.

The largest group among the poor are children under eighteen. About 10.7 million children, or 15 percent of all children under eighteen are classified as poor. Sixty percent of these live in families headed by a female. The proportion of poor children remained unchanged during the 1960s, but those in families headed by a disabled male or by a female who did not work increased from 7 to 11 percent of all poor persons. Poor children are most numerous in black families, especially those headed by females, and this number has been increasing.

The greatest incidence of poverty is found among poor households with dependent children that are headed by women. Among whites, 36 percent of such households were poor in 1968, compared to 62 percent of such black households. Altogether, 7 million persons lived in these households in 1968, including 4.4 million children under eighteen. Between 1959 and 1968, while the total number of poor persons declined, the number of black poor people in families headed by women increased about 700,000 or 24 percent.

Poverty is three times as high among individuals not living in family units as it is among persons living in families. In 1968, 4.7 million individuals were counted as poor in this group. About one-third of individuals not living in families were poor, compared to a poverty rate of 11 percent for persons living with their families. Of these poor individuals not living in families, 72 percent were women, of whom two-thirds were aged.

CLASSIFICATION OF POOR IN RELATION TO ABILITY TO WORK, 1959 AND 1968

	1968 Number (millions)	Percent	1959 Number (millions)	Percent
All Poor Persons	25.4	100	39.5	100
1. Elderly persons (65 years and over)	4.6	18	5.8	15
2. Persons in household headed by disabled male under 65	1.4	6	1.5[a]	4
3. Persons in households headed by female under 65 who did not work	4.0	16	4.0[a]	10
Subtotal (1 + 2 + 3)	10.0	39	11.3	29
Adults	7.2	28	8.6	22
Children under 18	2.8	11	2.7	7
4. All others	15.4	61	28.2	71
Adults	7.5	29	13.7	34
Children under 18	7.9	31	14.5	37
Persons in household headed by Male	15.0	59	29.1	74
Female	10.4	41	10.4	26

[a] *Estimate based on unrevised data.*
SOURCE: *U.S. Bureau of the Census,* Current Population Reports, *Series P-20, No. 198 (August 19, 1969).*

CHANGE IN THE NUMBER OF POOR PERSONS BETWEEN 1959 AND 1968,
BY RACE, AGE, SEX OF FAMILY HEADS, AND FAMILY STATUS
(Millions of persons)

	Total			Households Headed by Male			Households Headed by Female		
	All Races	White	Nonwhite	All Races	White	Nonwhite	All Races	White	Nonwhite
All Persons	−14.1	−11.1	− 3.0	−14.1	−10.4	−3.7	0	−.7	+.7
Persons in families	−13.9	−10.9	− 3.0	−13.8	−10.2	−3.6	0	−.7	+.7
Heads	− 3.3	− 2.6	− .7	− 3.1	− 2.4	− .8	−.2	−.2	+.1
Children under 18	− 6.5	− 5.0	− 1.5	− 6.7	− 4.7	−2.1	+.3	−.3	+.6
Other members	− 4.1	− 3.3	− .8	− 4.0	− 3.2	− .8	−.1	−.1	0
Unrelated individuals	− .2	− .2	− .04	− .2	− .2	− .1	0	0	0
Persons 65 years & over	− 1.1	− 1.0	− .1					0	0
Persons 18–64 years	− 6.5	− 5.1	− 1.4					0	0

Percent Change in the Number of Poor Persons

	Total			Households Headed by Male			Households Headed by Female		
	All Races	White	Nonwhite	All Races	White	Nonwhite	All Races	White	Nonwhite
All Persons	−35.7	−38.9	−27.4	−48	−49	−48	0	−10	+21
Persons in families	−40.1	−44.6	−29.4	−50	−51	−49	0	−16	+24
Heads	−39.3	−41.5	−33.0	−49	−48	−52	− 8	−17	+ 7
Children under 18	−37.6	−44.0	−25.0	−52	−52	−50	+ 6	−14	+35
Other members	−45.7	−48.2	−37.7	−49	−51	−51	−13	−21	0
Unrelated individuals	− 4.7	− 4.8	− 4.7	−15	−14	−19	0	− 1	+ 6
Persons 65 years & over	−19.0	−20.0	−12.5						
Persons 18–64 years	−39.0	−42.0	−32.0						

sources: *U.S. Bureau of the Census*, Current Population Reports, *Series P–23, No. 28; Series P–20, No. 189; and unpublished data.*

High Court Upsets City Welfare Rule

By FRED P. GRAHAM

Special to The New York Times

WASHINGTON, March 23— The Supreme Court ruled 5 to 3 today that welfare recipients have a constitutional right to formal hearings, with trial-like constitutional safe-guards, before officials may cut off their benefits.

The ruling marked the first time that the Court had said that welfare officials must satisfy the Constitution's requirement of "due process of law" in terminating payments to welfare clients. Procedures now in use in New York City and California were declared unconstitutional under the ruling.

As a result of the decision, welfare benefits cannot be canceled until the recipient has been given notice of the reasons he is considered eligible and an opportunity to appear with a lawyer before "an impartial decision-maker" to testify and cross-examine adverse witnesses.

Welfare clients are entitled under the ruling to be represented by lawyers, but the state does not have to furnish counsel. After the hearing, the decision-maker must submit a written ruling, giving reasons for cutting off benefits if that has been done.

Administrative Jam Feared

Welfare officials, joined by the Justice Department as a friend of the court, had warned that such a ruling in behalf of the nine million persons reported receiving public assistance could swamp welfare systems with demands for hearings while ineligible people remained on relief.

But the Court, in an opinion by Justice William J. Brennan, Jr., held that humanitarian considerations outweigh such administrative and fiscal concerns.

He conceded that persons such as a discharged Government employe, a blacklisted Government contractor, and "virtually anyone else whose government largesse is ended" are not entitled to prior hearings. But a welfare recipient who has been mistakenly cut off the rolls has lost "the very means by which to live while he waits" for a hearing, Justice Brennan said.

Public assistance is "not mere charity," he said, but a means to "promote the general welfare, and secure the blessings of liberty" as stated in the preamble to the Constitution. He concluded that the Constitution requires that payments be given without interruption to those who are eligible for them.

Justice Brennan was joined by Justices William O. Douglas, John M. Harlan, Thurgood Marshall and Byron R. White.

Chief Justice Warren E. Burger and Justices Hugo L. Black and Potter Stewart dissented.

Chief Justice Burger's dissent contained his most detailed statement of a philosophy of judicial self-restraint since President Nixon appointed him as a means of bringing "balance" to the liberal court. He objected to the constitutional ruling when the Department of Health, Education and Welfare has announced plans to impose rules, effective next July, that would be similar to those announced today.

"We ought to hold the heavy hand of constitutional adjudication and allow evolutionary processes at various administrative levels to experiment, given their flexibility to make adjustments in procedures without long delays," he said.

Black Scores Court

"The Court's action today seems another manifestation of the now familiar constitutionalizing syndrome: Once some presumed flaw is observed, the Court then eagerly accepts the invitation to find a constitutionally 'rooted' remedy," he added.

Justice Black delivered a long, extemporaneous dissent, in which he termed welfare a "gratuity" that is "nice for those who do not work but receive payments from the Government—that is to say, those who do work."

He charged that the Supreme Court was legislating by using the vague due process clause of the 14th Amendment to impose its own view of what the law should be.

The 84-year-old Justice added that "those who will take time to study the Constitution for themselves" would find "language that anyone could understand—even the Supreme Court" to the effect that the due process clause applies only to a denial of a person's property, and not his claim on the Government.

Today's ruling grew out of two decisions by three-judge federal District courts, in which the New York welfare procedure was declared unconstitutional and a similar California rule was upheld.

New York welfare officials outside New York City have been granting hearings before termination of benefits in recent months, but hardpressed city officials adopted a system whereby clients were given notice and an opportunity to reply in writing —but no hearing—before their payments were cut off. A full hearing was granted after the termination.

Today's decision will apparently affect the rights of welfare clients in all states, although its impact would be lessened if Congress enacted President Nixon's proposed welfare reform proposal. The President's plan would make all persons below a certain income level eligible for benefits, with the Federal Government having the responsibility to determine eligibility.

Presumably, the Federal Government would still have to grant hearings before it could cut off a family's benefits because its income was too high or because a potential breadwinner had refused to take a job or training.

© 1970 by The New York Times Company. Reprinted by permission.

Shortcomings of the Welfare System

In 1970, about 10 million out of 25 million poor persons received cash payments from some public assistance program. As these figures suggest, programs providing insurance benefits and public assistance payments were then grossly inadequate. Under the social security system, social insurance payments for the aged are too low to enable the poor to reach a needed minimum of income without additional public assistance payments or direct relief. In the public assistance programs administered by the states, standards for public assistance have been kept at miserably low levels, and payments to the needy have not been adjusted to changes in the cost of living. In only a few states do payments to aid dependent children exceed the poverty threshold.

One of the central problems of the welfare system is that half of the poor do not receive social security benefits, public assistance payments, or any other public transfer payment, such as veteran pensions. Some of the poor, for example, shun public assistance because of the stigma attached to it.

In its operations, the welfare system has led to several unfortunate consequences. An unemployed father who has exhausted his eligibility for unemployment compensation can help his family better by deserting in order to make it eligible for direct relief. Mothers are encouraged by the system to make fathers leave the home, and a pregnant girl has no material incentive to marry the father of her child. The system has also discouraged people from moving to places where living costs might be lower or job opportunities better. It encourages concentration of the poor in racial or ethnic enclaves in the inner city at a time when economic growth is greater in suburban communities. And it encourages lying and cheating—about a man in the house, number of dependent children, marital status—and strengthens the cynicism of the poor toward the institutions of government and the legitimacy of public authority.

How Social Institutions Reinforce Poverty

A recent study[4] of poverty has noted that poverty, for many people, is more than just a lack of income.

> It also involves a deprived and defeatist state of mind, a persistent lack of capability for improving one's own situation, and an inferior or dependent position in society. Moreover, major social institutions repeatedly reinforce these maladies—even when those institutions are specifically intended to alleviate poverty.

Unless institutions can be reformed, the study concludes, efforts to eliminate poverty by giving aid directly to the poor are bound to fail.

How do the institutions of society reinforce poverty? Several principal ways can be suggested. Social institutions provide assistance to the poor in ways that increase or emphasize their dependency, rather than stimulating feelings of adequacy or efforts at self-improvement. They tend to exploit the ignorance of poor people by imposing on them higher costs than other people pay for similar goods and services. They omit poor people from social insurance schemes that lighten the burden of certain social maladies.

In addition, social institutions tend to create unnecessary obstacles which prevent poor people from taking advantage of opportunities to improve their incomes, living conditions, and general capabilities. By imposing middle-class standards and behavior patterns upon lower-class groups, they weaken the abilities of poor people to improve themselves.

Several examples of the effect of social institutions on poverty can be cited. Retail prices for food and other staples paid by residents of big-city, low-income neighborhoods are often higher than those paid by residents of higher-income areas, mainly because poor people tend to shop in small local stores instead of larger chain stores. Poor people often pay interest rates averaging 50 percent higher for merchandise purchased on credit. Most lenders will not provide mortgages to poor people for purchasing or improving houses in their areas, even if the borrower has good credit. The lowest quality schools with the least qualified teachers are usually concentrated in poor neighborhoods, especially in big cities. Urban highways avoid middle- and upper-income areas, but are often deliberately routed through low-income areas, particularly black neighborhoods. New jobs are created mainly in suburban areas at some distance from central-city low-income neighborhoods. And police practices in low-income areas increase the probability that young men, especially blacks, will develop official police records for acts that would not create such records in higher-income areas. Such institutional perversities tend to undermine the ability of the poor to escape from poverty.

OPTIONS IN COPING WITH POVERTY

At the risk of oversimplification, it is useful to outline briefly the principal alternatives of public policy that are available to combat poverty. The first deals with *aggregate demand*. Its objective is to improve the performance of the total economy so that opportunities will spill over or trickle down to the poor. This approach, which proved to be the most successful one for the period from World War II to the 1960s, became increasingly ineffective by 1970. A second option lies in *improving job capacities* by giving special attention to individuals and groups that are unable to enter the labor market. Some of the possibilities here include the creation of special, protected jobs for the unemployed and the training of people to enter the regular labor in the near future.

Because of the heavy incidence of poverty in certain regions of the country, like the Appalachian area, a third alternative of *area development* emerged in the 1960s. Following this approach, a region would be given special help when it demonstrated that it could not keep up with general performance of the national economy. A fourth approach emphasizes the *redistribution of income*. Minimally, this goal might be achieved by increasing the level of benefits and assistance payments under the old-age insurance scheme and various public assistance programs. A more ambitious effort would be to establish an income maintenance program, like the negative income tax, or by guaranteeing an annual income at a satisfactory level to all people.

An approach that has been adopted widely in the United States is to provide more *goods and services for the poor*. Income-in-kind might provide better schools, more health care, more financial assistance to obtain better housing, and distributions of food. A supplementary option would be to try to help poor people by giving them grants and loans to launch them on a business enterprise. The program of minority entrepreneurship, or black capitalism, of the Department of Commerce illustrates this option. A very different approach is to attempt to *overcome the powerlessness of the poor* by helping them to develop an economic and power base, for example, by giving the poor control over public programs and funds that are funnelled into slum and ghetto neighborhoods.

In the past, the United States has not opted for any coherent program or coordinated set of policies to combat poverty. Rather it has retained old policies and programs developed during the Great Depression and has added on various other policies without any central or unifying theme. In the wide-ranging public debates of recent years over strategies for fighting poverty, two of the options noted have been emphasized: the redistribution of income and the provision of more goods and services for the poor. The sections that follow discuss these policy options and their promise for coping with poverty.

SOCIAL INSURANCE AND VETERANS PROGRAMS

Old-Age, Survivors', and Disability Insurance (OASDI)

In 1929, about three-fourths of all relief funds for the aid of the poor were supplied by state and local governments and the remainder was provided by churches and private welfare organizations. All of these programs were geared to the needs of a predominantly rural population with a high level of economic opportunity. The depression of the 1930s shattered the nation's vision of unlimited economic opportunity, and the destitution and mass misery of those days were beyond the capacity of state and local governments to alleviate. Only the national government was in a position to provide adequate relief programs. Thus in 1935 Congress enacted the Social Security Act, marking the transition from private charity and public poor laws to contributory social insurance and wide governmental assistance to needy persons.

The Social Security Act established a national, wage-related, contributory system of old-age benefits for certain employees and self-employed persons. The Old-Age, Survivors', and Disability Insurance scheme (OASDI) makes payments to eligible workers who are 65 years or older, or to those aged 62 at a reduced rate, to the wives or widows of retired workers if they are over 62, and to their dependent children under 18 (or 22, if they are in school or college). In 1969, nearly $27 billion in benefits were paid out, and 25 million persons, or one out of every eight Americans, received monthly benefit checks, one-fourth of whom were under 60 years of age.

Old-age and disability benefits are financed by federal payroll taxes paid by workers, employers, and self-employed persons on wages and salaries up to a specified maximum ($7,800 in 1970). The principle of requiring contributions of employees is based on the belief that a contributory system establishes a self-respecting method of providing for old-age. Automatic increases in payroll taxes are scheduled by statute. Monthly benefits under OASDI have more than tripled since payments began in 1940 and will probably continue to rise as legislators and political leaders respond to or anticipate demands for liberalizing benefits. Today over 75 percent of all persons over 65 are receiving monthly old-age insurance benefits or will be eligible for them when they retire, and 95 percent of widowed mothers and their children have some survivors' protection.

Over-all, the social insurance system works satisfactorily for those who earned adequate incomes steadily during their lifetime and have some savings to supplement their old-age benefits. For the poor, however, who have been unable to build up adequate annuities in their OASDI accounts, the benefits for which they are eligible are insufficient to pull them above the poverty line. They require cash support to make up deficiencies in their income-earning capacities.

Programs for Veterans

Today nearly half of all Americans are either veterans or veterans' dependents or survivors and are potentially eligible to receive benefits ranging from school books to medical costs and from housing loans to burial flags. Benefits are frequently in the form of cash payments for disabilities or for pensions for survivors. Some veterans are eligible also for complete medical care in the hospitals of the Veterans Administration. In 1970, veterans' benefits and services cost $8.7 billion, only about a third of which goes to poor people. Unlike the social insurance program that links benefits to earnings, veterans' compensation is linked to injury and disability.

CASH ALLOWANCES FOR THE NEEDY

In 1968, about 10 million poor people were receiving some form of cash allowance under five programs of public assistance. The increase in the number of welfare recipients has been marked. Nationally it has increased about 43 percent from 1966 to 1969, and in that same period in New York City it has doubled. Between 1960 and 1969, the amount of cash allowances under public assistance programs has also doubled, from $3.3 to $6.5 billion. In 1969, the federal government contributed more than half of the total, and the state and local governments provided the remainder. Analysis[5] of the assistance rolls indicates that the vast majority of those on relief are "either too young, too old, too sick, or too disabled to be self-supporting."

Five Programs of Public Assistance

Four of the five major types of programs providing cash allowances for the needy were established by the Social Security Act. In these four programs, which cover nearly 90 percent of all people on welfare, the federal government serves as a partner with the states in their financing and administration. The fifth program, for which state and local governments are solely responsible, is general assistance and involves no federal financing. The five programs include the following:

> 1. *Old-age assistance,* to be distinguished from old-age insurance under OASDI, provided cash payments for about 2 million persons in 1969, or a fifth of all welfare recipients. Those receiving assistance are mainly women. The decline in the number of recipients of old-age assistance is explained by the improved availability of old-age benefits under the social insurance program.

2. *Aid to the blind* was paid to about 80,000 recipients in 1969, compared to slightly more than 100,000 in 1960.

3. *Aid to the permanently and totally disabled* went in 1969 to 770,000, more than doubled the 1960 number.

4. *Aid to families with dependent children* (AFDC) accounts for over half of all welfare recipients today. It is the largest, most expensive, and most rapidly growing of all the welfare programs. It increased from about 3 million recipients in 1960 to 6.7 million in 1969. Costs have more than tripled in this period, rising to $3.4 billion in 1969, and are expected to double again by 1975.

5. *General assistance,* or direct relief, is provided by state and local governments without federal aid. Most recipients in this category have been unable to qualify for other federally-supported programs. General assistance programs are more limited than federally aided programs. Some states give only emergency or short-term aid, and several others restrict aid to defined special situations.

Both cities and states have used many devices to reduce their relief rolls. Some have required a minimum period of residence, although in 1969 the U.S. Supreme Court held that a state residency requirement resulted in a denial of equal protection of the Social Security Act.[6] Still other states and cities have attempted to bar narcotics addicts, unwed mothers, and pregnant women. In the late 1960s, however, state courts began to upset these infringements on rights to assistance. In 1968, the U.S. Supreme Court struck down a rule that a state would not make payments in a case of dependent children if there was a man in the house.[7]

Fifty Different Welfare Programs

Under the Social Security Act, the federal government provides grants to the states under various matching arrangements for assistance programs for the elderly, the blind, the disabled, and dependent children. Each state decides whether to accept all or part of the available federal grant; it can assume the burden of matching federal grants entirely; it can share with local governments the financial burdens. Within federal standards, the states are free to set their own policies and rules of eligibility. Federal requirements include the following:

A person must be in need in order to receive assistance.
The state must consider all of a person's income in determining need.
The state must submit to the federal government a plan for administering assistance programs.
The program must be operated on a statewide basis.
The program must be administered by a single state agency.
Opportunity must be provided for a fair hearing for any person whose application for aid is denied.

In setting their own rules and determining levels of payment, states have acted without regard for their impact on other states or on the national welfare. Consequently, variations in levels of payment have been great. More than a score of states have not accepted all available federal funds. In the program to aid dependent children, only half of the

RECIPIENTS AND AMOUNTS OF MONEY PAYMENTS UNDER PUBLIC ASSISTANCE BY PROGRAM, 1950–1969[a]

Year	Total	Old Age	Families with Dependent Children	Disabled	Blind	General Assistance
			Number of Recipients[b] (thousands)			
1950	6,052	2,786	2,233	69	98	866
1955	5,816	2,538	2,192	241	102	743
1960	7,098	2,305	3,073	369	107	1,244
1965	7,802	2,087	4,396	557	85	677
1966	8,073	2,073	4,666	588	84	663
1967	8,893	2,073	5,309	646	83	782
1968	9,725	2,028	6,086	703	81	827
1969	10,426	2,044	6,725	770	80	807
			Payments[c] (millions)			
1950	$2,354	$1,454	$ 547	$ 8	$ 53	$ 293
1955	2,517	1,488	612	135	68	214
1960	3,262	1,626	994	236	86	320
1965	3,993	1,594	1,644	417	77	261
1966	4,304	1,630	1,850	487	85	252
1967	4,931	1,698	2,250	574	87	323
1968	5,660	1,673	2,824	656	88	420
1969	6,462	1,724	3,425	760	91	462
			Percent of Total Payments by Program			
1950	100.0	61.8	23.2	0.3	2.3	12.4
1955	100.0	59.1	24.3	5.4	2.7	8.5
1960	100.0	49.9	30.5	7.2	2.6	9.8
1965	100.0	39.9	41.2	10.5	1.9	6.5
1966	100.0	37.9	43.0	11.3	2.0	5.8
1967	100.0	34.4	45.6	11.6	1.8	6.6
1968	100.0	29.6	49.9	11.6	1.5	7.4
1969	100.0	26.7	53.0	11.8	1.4	7.1

[a] *Calendar years.*

[b] *For 1950 through 1968, as of December 31; 1969 data are for August 31, 1969.*

[c] *Excludes administrative costs. The payments for 1969 are estimates based on 8-months' average.*

SOURCE: *U.S. Department of Health, Education, and Welfare.*

states make payments that meet their own cost standards for the basic needs of a family of four. In 1970, 28 states denied assistance to any family with a male head of household, thus encouraging deception and the breakup of families. Payments to dependent children in the ADFC program ranged from a low of $10.20 per month per child in Mississippi to $66.40 in New Jersey. Under old-age assistance, payments varied from $39.40 per month in Mississippi to $116.25 per month in New Hampshire. Comparable variations existed from state to state in programs for the blind and the disabled.

Even though payments for public assistance are inadequate, states and cities have been under severe financial strain. In many large cities, welfare costs have doubled or tripled within a few years. By 1970 there was general agreement among the leaders of the two major political parties that the federal-state system of public assistance was a colossal failure and required major overhauling.

The Family Assistance Program

Discussions of reform proposals in 1969 and 1970 have highlighted three general ways of changing the system of public welfare They include modest tinkering with the present system, a children's allowance system, and a cash income supplement. Each of these is noted briefly. The first option is to change the present welfare system first to raise public assistance payments in the lowest states, second to help the working poor, especially low-wage men with large families, and third to take some of the financial burden off state and local governments. It is possible to raise payment levels by placing a floor under state programs. For example, states might be required to pay each dependent child at least $30 a month, and the federal government could bear all of the cost of the payments up to the minimum. This step would also work toward giving the national government full control of the four federally aided programs of public assistance. This sort of tinkering would have only minimal effects unless the federal government also extended larger grants to states for supplementary assistance to the working poor.

The second option would scrap the present welfare program in favor of a system of children's allowances or family assistance allowances. Such an allowance would go to all families, not just the poor. It would be based on the number of children or family size. There would be no income test, and payments would be subject to income tax so that middle and upper income people would have part or most of their payments taxed away. Children's allowances of this sort are in effect in more than 60 countries of the world today, including most western European countries. They have the advantage of maintaining incentives to work and encouraging families to stay together. Allowances are easy to administer and involve no stigma or indignity. The principal limitation of this option is its cost. In order to make allowances sufficient to meet the needs of the poor, the program would be very costly.

A third possibility is to abolish the system of public assistance in favor of a new program to provide a cash income supplement to all low-income families. Administered by the federal government through the tax system, it would provide some minimum level of income that varies according to family size and permit families to keep a significant portion of their earnings above this minimum in order to provide a strong incentive to work. The major argument about this strategy centers on the amount of the minimum payment.

If it were placed near the 1970 poverty level of $3700 for a family of four and strong inducements to work were provided above this level, it would cost more than $20 billion. If the level were placed much lower, some families now receiving public assistance would be worse off.

The family assistance plan presented by President Nixon to Congress in 1969 and modified in 1970 combines some elements of tinkering with more radical change. For the four federally aided public assistance programs, the plan placed a floor under payment levels with higher federal contributions. The more radical part is the family assistance scheme, a compromise between a children's allowance and a general income supplement. It provided for an income allowance of $1,600 to a family of four that has no other earnings. It encourages such a family to work by allowing it to keep the first $720 of earnings above this minimum without any reduction in its basic payment and to keep half of all earnings above $2,320. Thus a family of four would get some help from the government if it earns less than $3,920 during the year. The minimum payment of $1,600 would apply in all states and thus reduce the wide disparity in assistance payments.

The most important feature of the plan is that it would apply to all families with children and therefore provide cash assistance to the working poor for the first time. It is estimated that it would extend aid to at least 6 million families previously outside the public assistance scheme. The minimum payments would in effect eliminate federally aided public assistance in ten states whose payment levels are above the federal minimum level.

The Nixon plan of family allowances had three limitations. Couples without children and single persons were left out of the plan entirely. The minimum payment was set too low to alleviate the poverty of many families and individuals. And while it gave considerable relief to poorer states, it did not help the industrial states of the North and West whose welfare payments already exceed the new federal minimum. Whatever its limitations, the plan was a major attempt to revise and reorient federal welfare policies. It seems destined to chart the course of welfare policy for the decade or two ahead and for the 1970s and 1980s play the sort of role played by the Social Security Act from 1935 to 1970.

GOODS AND SERVICES FOR THE POOR

Federal programs to help the poor either provide cash allowances or goods and services to supplement their meager income. The previous sections reviewed various income supplement policies and programs. The following sections outline briefly the major federal programs that provide income-in-kind for poor and low-income families.

Two general arguments have often been cited in support of such programs. The first reason is that government must compensate for the inadequate market supply of essential goods and services available to the poor at a low enough cost, especially housing and medical care. Even if poor people were given enough income to purchase such goods and services, it is alleged, the increased demand of the poor might bid up the prices of these services and the poor would be no better off than they were before. The second general argument is the belief that many poor people are not able to spend money income wisely because they lack essential training, knowledge, and experience to have the judgment to know what is good for them. Therefore, it is argued, they should receive goods and serv-

"How about a financial grant from the private sector for a culturally deprived under-achiever?"

© 1969 by Better Homes and Gardens. Reprinted by permission.

ices in-kind rather than the equivalent cash income to insure that they consume what they need. In federal programs for public housing, food stamps, and social services for recipients of public assistance, public officials and employees restrict the choices open to the poor and impose public standards on them.

Food for the Hungry

For many years prior to 1965, food programs for the hungry had been run primarily as dumping grounds for surplus farm goods or as devices to raise farm income. Backed, however, by welfare, labor, religious, and philanthropic organizations, liberal congressmen succeeded in making hunger a key political issue in the late 1960s. One consequence was the beginning of a movement to win acceptance of the idea that hunger had to be dealt with directly, regardless of agricultural surplus problems.

By 1970, five basic food programs were in operation. First, the School Lunch Program, founded in 1936, provides matching cash grants to the states for nonprofit school lunches. Food is often donated by the Agriculture Department from government surplus stores, and a 1962 amendment authorized subsidized meals for needy children. Subsequent legislation has provided additional federal funds for breakfasts for needy children.

Second, since 1954, Congress has authorized special milk programs to help clear surplus milk from the market. The government purchases milk and donates it to schools. In 1968, a committee of inquiry reported that only 18 million out of 50 million public elementary and secondary school children participated in the milk program. Fewer than 2 million were able to get free or reduced-price milk at lunch, even though there were 6 million school-age children from families whose parents earned less than $2,000 a year or were receiving aid to families with dependent children. Many states made no contribution to the costs of the program, and the children had to pay the difference between the federal grant and the charge made by the school cafeteria.

Third, the food stamp program, begun in 1961 on an experimental basis, was made permanent in 1964. Poor people who live in counties and cities that decide to participate in the program may buy food stamps. These stamps are then redeemable at participating grocery stores for food that costs more than the purchase price of the stamps. The difference is paid by the federal government.

The fourth program covers direct distribution of food to counties and cities not participating in the food stamp program. Under the Agricultural Act of 1949, local officials obtain surplus food from federal stockpiles and then donate it to the poor. In 1969, about 22 different foods were included in these distribution programs. Costs have run slightly higher than those for the food stamp program. The fifth program, the so-called Section 32 program, under a 1935 statute, authorizes the Secretary of Agriculture to use 30 percent of U.S. Customs receipts each year for various purposes, including increasing domestic consumption. Part of this annual fund of hundreds of millions is used to buy perishable fruits and vegetables where surpluses are threatened and give them to institutions and to school lunch and direct distribution programs.

In 1968, the Senate appointed a Select Committee on Nutrition and Human Needs, chaired by Senator George McGovern, South Dakota. On the basis of field studies and extensive hearings, the committee reached a number of conclusions in its interim report of 1969. It found that "clinically validated malnutrition exists in serious proportions in the United States and is a particularly acute problem among infants, pre-school, and school children from low-income families." Malnutrition, it declared, is perhaps the primary factor in the retarded intellectual development of poor children. It stressed especially the devastating emotional and psychological effects of hunger on families that cannot meet their food needs. Poverty-level families, were trapped in a vicious cycle of malnutrition and ill health. Even more dramatically, the Committee found that "despite rising incomes over the past decade, malnutrition has increased among Americans at all income levels."

Finally, the Committee concluded that federal food assistance programs had had only a minimal remedial effect.[8]

They have neither served a significant proportion of those in need of assistance, nor been administered to provide sufficient food or food stamps to enable the few who do participate to provide themselves and their families with an adequate diet. They have been neither funded nor administered to alleviate the problem of poverty-related hunger.

Health and Medical Care

The correlation between poverty and ill health has been well documented. In 1969, a leading government study[9] reported that poor families have more disabling heart disease, nervous disorders, mental illness, orthopedic ailments, and visual defects than the population at large. They obtain much less prenatal care, dental care, and immunization against children's diseases. Poor health among children and teenagers reduces their educability and consequently reduces their opportunities for productive employment.

Federal health programs are aimed mainly at groups outside the labor force—the aged and recipients of public assistance. One of the most important welfare statutes of recent years is the Medicare law, passed in 1965, establishing a medical care program for the aged under the social security system. To those over 65, Medicare provides benefits that are related not to the income of the aged but to the cost of health services. The basic plan provides hospital insurance benefits, including 90 days of hospital care, outpatient services, 100 days of home nursing care, and 100 health care visits annually. This part of the program is financed by adding to the payroll taxes paid by employers and employees and self-employed persons under OASDI. A supplementary plan pays 80 percent of the cost of a variety of medical services, including doctor bills, after a $50 deduction. It is financed by a small monthly fee paid by each participant, matched by a federal tax contribution. In 1968, about one-third of the benefits under the basic plan went to the poor, and a high proportion went to the near-poor.

A different program, called Medical Assistance, or more popularly, Medicaid, is run by the states and financed partly by federal grants-in-aid. Its purpose is to finance medical care for recipients of public assistance. It was initiated in 1965 by Title XIX of the Social Security Act. Any state may qualify for federal grants in support of Medicaid by meeting federal standards. Under a qualified state program those eligible for Medicaid include: all those receiving payments under the four federal-state public assistance programs (the indigent aged, dependent children, the blind, and the totally and permanently disabled); crippled, aged, or otherwise handicapped persons who have just enough money to live on—and therefore do not qualify for the standard public assistance programs—but who cannot afford medical care; all children under twenty-one who do not qualify for public assistance as dependent children but whose families do not earn enough to pay for medical expenses. The effect of these provisions is to make federal funds available to participating states for all medically needy persons under twenty-one and over sixty-five as well as adults between those ages who are blind or disabled or members of families with dependent children. Moreover, those over sixty-five who exhaust their medical benefits under medicare can be assured of aid under Title XIX.

By 1970, 44 states had adopted Title XIX programs covering about 10 million people. The high costs of the program led some states to reduce eligibility for medical assistance. It is not known what percentage of the medically needy are covered by, or make use of, the Medicaid programs, or what percent of the total medical costs incurred by persons covered under Title XIX are borne by the program. The quality of service rendered under the program is also unknown; no controls are imposed on physicians and studies of the delivery of services have not been made.

In addition to Medicare and programs to assist some of the non-elderly poor, the federal government finances medical services for various groups. The largest of these is the group of veterans of the armed services. An interesting new development is the work of the Office of Economic Opportunity in creating Neighborhood Health Centers. This effort is the first by a federal agency to bring permanent health-care facilities to deprived areas.

The evidence of the results of the first years of Medicare is mixed and not yet conclusive. Only a beginning has been made in making adequate medical care available to the elderly. Because of the way in which the relevant regulations operate, Medicare pays only 40 percent of the medical bills of the aged. Medicaid apparently has supplied only marginal assistance.

HOUSING

In 1968, a presidential committee reported that 7.8 million American families—about one out of eight—cannot afford to pay the market price for acceptable housing. The committee estimated that during the 1970s 7.5 million families will remain unable to afford acceptable housing.[10] Continuing increases in population have maintained a steady pressure on the available supply of housing and have produced increases in the price of housing. It seems very unlikely, therefore, that the federal family assistance program can supply sufficient income to the needy to enable them to afford decent housing.

The major federal housing program has been Public Housing, which began in 1937. Today, more than 700,000 units of public housing provide homes for about 2.5 million people. Responsibility for developing and administering federally-subsidized housing projects lies with local housing authorities. In 1968 the median income of all families residing in public housing was about $2,800, and the median monthly rent was about $54. One-third of these units were occupied by elderly persons. About half of all public housing units are occupied by black tenants. In many cities, public housing projects have become all black-tenanted.

Under the Leased Housing program, which was established in 1965, a local housing authority may enter into a contract with a private owner to provide housing for a family, negotiate a rent, and guarantee its payment. A low-income family that qualifies for this program pays a share of the rent to the housing authority, which is responsible to the landlord for the entire rent. Unlike the public housing program, the leased housing program operates in the existing housing market and therefore it helps to promote economic integration. Rental units in this scheme are not part of large low-income housing projects and can be made available more quickly than public housing can be constructed.

The Rent Supplement program, also enacted in 1965, is expected to encourage private profit and nonprofit groups to build low-rent housing. The program authorizes the federal government to contract with local housing sponsors (mainly nonprofit, limited dividend, or cooperative housing organizations) to make supplementary rent payments to owners of certain dwellings that make housing available to low-income families and individuals. To be eligible for a rent supplement, a tenant's income cannot exceed certain maximum levels. In addition, he must be either elderly, physically handicapped, displaced by government action, come from substandard housing, or have been an occupant of a dwelling damaged or destroyed by natural disaster. Rent supplements cover the difference between 25 percent of the tenant's income—the amount he is considered able to pay for rent—and his rent in standard housing. As the tenant's income rises, his rent supplement is reduced. Unlike Public Housing, no family is required to leave a rent-supplemented project because of rising income. It is estimated that about 135,000 persons lived in 45,000 units at the end of 1970.

In the Public Housing and Rent Supplement programs, less than two-thirds of the beneficiaries have annual incomes under $3,000. Subsidies to private organizations apparently have not been sufficient to reduce housing costs and rents to a level that enable many of the poor to benefit.

In 1966, Congress established a model cities program to rebuild entire urban areas by pumping in federal funds. The legislation authorized federal grants to urban areas to finance a coordinated attack on physical blight and decay and social deterioration. Participating cities would be eligible to receive federal grants equal to as much as 80 percent of the amount they were required to provide as their share of the total cost. Special funds were authorized for antipoverty and other social programs in order to overcome the traditional emphasis of urban renewal projects on physical development.

In 1968, Congress added to the battery of new housing legislation a measure directed mainly to home ownership and rental assistance for the needy, but it also included a host of provisions on mass transit in urban areas, interstate land sales, flood insurance, and other urban developmental problems. The home ownership plan provides a federal subsidy to purchase a home amounting to the difference between 20 percent of the family's monthly income and the required monthly mortgage payments.

The imaginative and innovative legislation on housing and urban development of the 1960s has produced disappointing results to date. Far fewer housing units for low- and middle-income families were built than Congress planned. Most of the housing built under these programs has not been available to the neediest families but rather to the richest eligible families. Moreover, optimistic plans for renovation of sound but rundown houses and apartment buildings for low-income families have lagged badly.

Many factors have contributed to the failure of housing policies for the poor. The credit squeeze, rising mortgage interest rates, difficulties in acquiring land for subsidized housing, and rigidities in governmental administration at all levels have been major obstacles. Congress has been unwilling to provide substantial funds to carry out authorized programs. Because of these problems the Office of Economic Opportunity has tried to stimulate housing development by nonprofit groups by funding development corporations specializing in nonprofit construction. Even here little success has been achieved. The legislation of the 1960s has tended to serve moderate and some low-income families rather than poor families.

The future of income-in-kind programs is not clear. Many students of problems of poverty seem to despair of the prospects of developing effective administration of programs to provide better housing, education, health care, and food for the poor. They find in one or another plan to increase cash allowances or family income greater possibilities for alleviating poverty. Perhaps one of the major factors leading to such preference is the democratic appeal of the notion that the non-poor should *not* decide what the poor need. Another is the belief that the capacity of poor persons to exercise adequate judgment about their needs and how to meet them may be greater than the administrative and political capacity of governmental institutions and their bureaucracies to administer income-in-kind programs effectively and compassionately.

JOBS AND SCHOOLS FOR THE POOR

Training for Jobs

As noted earlier, the maintenance of a sound and stable economy at levels of prosperity has not been sufficient to solve the problems of poverty. Great national effort is needed to create jobs for poor people that open to them opportunities for advancement instead of confining them to jobs with low pay, demeaning work, and little prospect for self-improvement. Congress took a major step in the development of federal manpower programs in enacting the Area Redevelopment Act of 1961, focusing on the training of the unemployed in economically stagnant areas. The Manpower Development and Training Act of 1962 (MDTA) provided training for experienced workers with family responsibilities who had lost their jobs because of technological changes. Amendments in 1963 and 1965 channeled federal efforts at job training more directly into areas of greatest need in the economy. Job training for poor youths and adults was authorized under the Economic Opportunity Act of 1964. In 1966, amendments to the legislation of 1962 authorized programs to train and educate workers 45 years and older to meet serious labor shortages and to upgrade workers to enable them to move into trades where labor shortages existed.

In the main, federal manpower programs now concentrate on training younger men with little or no work experience, especially the hard-core unemployed. Both institutional and on-the-job training are provided. Institutional training, which enrolls more than half of the trainees, is in vocational schools. From 1963 to 1968, over one million persons were enrolled in programs financed under the 1962 act. Of these, 600,000 completed their courses, and the Labor Department estimates that 75 percent of these have been employed.

In response to demands for special employment training for youth, the Economic Opportunity Act of 1964 created three training programs: the Job Corps, the Neighborhood Youth Corps, and Vista. Young men and women from 16 to 21 can enroll in the Job Corps for two years and work in conservation camps and urban job-training centers, where they receive general education, vocational training, and work experience. Most of the urban job centers are run by private industrial firms. Criticisms of the program have been directed mainly to the high cost per enrollee and the relations between the tough youngsters in the program and their nearby communities.

The Neighborhood Youth Corps has developed programs of part-time employment for students in low-income families. Vista (Volunteers in Service to America) is a domestic version of the Peace Corps. It enrolls trained persons in community service projects in various parts of the country. The federal government covers the living and travel expenses of enrollees and pays them a small salary for their work in helping Indians, the poor, the mentally ill and retarded, and migratory workers.

By 1970, federal, state, and local governments had done little to meet the special and widespread problems of working women who head households, even though the increase in the number of poor persons in such households, especially black, accounts for the major increase in the welfare rolls. The most promising way to help such women and their families is to establish a national program of day-care centers in order to free welfare mothers to take training or jobs voluntarily. At the same time, the federal government would be able to use these centers to operate an educational program for disadvantaged preschool children.

Education

A central difficulty in coping with problems of poverty has been the failure of public schools to serve those at the bottom of the economic and social ladder. Slum children are usually years behind middle-class children in the skills that lead to success in school. The gap widens as poor children move through high school, increasing from 2.4 years in the sixth grade to 3.5 years in the twelfth. In a labor market where most new jobs require literacy and some mathematical skill, this gap becomes a serious handicap to a great many black and other poor children.

In the 1960s, recognition of the close relation between educational opportunity and economic achievement led to greater federal involvement in public education. In the gradual growth of federal aid to education, a landmark statute is the Elementary and Secondary Education Act of 1965. Like many major developments in public policy, this measure was more than twenty years in the making. Two factors contributed to its enactment. First, evidence of inequality in educational opportunity and achievement had been mounting. For example, examinations of draftees during World War II had disclosed spectacular differences in educational achievement in different states. And second, sustained prosperity had made many citizens and political leaders more sensitive to disclosures of persistent poverty in the society.

The 1965 statute was present essentially as an antipoverty measure whose prime purpose was to help needy children get a more adequate education. The act authorized a program to aid pupils from low-income families by making grants to school districts. It also authorized grants to school districts for the purchase of textbooks and library materials. For example, in 1970, $1.2 billion in federal aid was granted to school districts educating 8–9 million children of poor families. Reports from educators and black organizations, however, charged that federal funds often failed to reach eligible children and were used instead to purchase equipment or construct buildings that failed to provide compensatory instructional programs for deprived youngsters. Funds earmarked for disadvantaged children were often misused, wasted, or diverted from the poor, especially in the South.[11]

Innovative programs for educating poor children have been developed with some success by the Office of Economic Opportunity. About half a million prekindergarten children each summer have been enrolled in Head Start programs designed to raise their levels of educational achievement. More recently, Head Start has developed the Parent and Child Center Program, which tries to provide a variety of services to the poor child from early infancy. By 1969, 31 of these centers were operating. Out of Head Start came Follow Through, a program which continues services to poor children through the primary grades. Upward Bound is a special program providing supplementary funds to prepare high school students for college. From 1965 to 1968, from 65 to 80 percent of these students did enter college, and about three out of four of them have remained in college to com-

FEDERAL EXPENDITURES TO AID THE POOR, FISCAL YEAR 1970
(Billions of dollars)

Social Security	$10.0
Welfare	
Public assistance	3.9
Nutrition	
Food Stamps	0.6
Child nutrition	0.5
Health	
Medicare	2.4
Medicaid	2.1
OEO programs	0.1
Employment	
Manpower development	1.0
Unemployment insurance	0.6
Employment services	0.2
Work incentives	0.1
Education and Youth	
Disadvantaged children	1.1
Educational opportunity	0.1
Other	0.5
OEO programs	0.5
Housing	
Public housing and rent supplements	0.3
Model cities and other	0.2
Other	
Veterans Administration	3.0
other HEW programs	1.3
other agencies	0.5
other OEO programs	0.5
Indian affairs	0.1
Rural poverty	0.1
Total	$29.7

SOURCES: *U.S. Bureau of the Budget and Office of Economic Opportunity.*

plete their studies. Finally, Talent Search seeks out disadvantaged high school youths with potential for educational achievement and encourages and assists them to gain entrance to college. In addition, OEO administers the National Teacher Corps, which recruits future teachers of economically disadvantaged children and develops new patterns of teacher training. While the available funds have been slim, the program appears to produce interesting ideas and experiments.

CAN WE ELIMINATE POVERTY?

In 1970, it is estimated that the federal government spent about $30 billion in various programs to aid the poor. Despite the range of federal programs designed to help the poor and the funds invested in them, they operate with only marginal impact on hardcore poverty. As the discussions in this chapter have suggested, federal antipoverty policies have suffered from two principal defects. First, the welfare structure which the country inherited from the emergency of the 1930s has been entirely inadequate to cope with problems of poverty in a high-employment economy. And second, individual policies and programs have proved to be inadequate, and they have not formed a coherent set of strategies for dealing in a coordinated way with the massive problems of poverty. Despite the growing federal expenditures for welfare and related purposes, the programs discussed in this chapter are mostly underfinanced. While some of them are imaginative, many others are outmoded and even trivial in relation to the problems they were designed to alleviate or eliminate.

Students of poverty problems and political leaders have turned increasingly to the formulation of various types of income maintenance programs to provide cash income supplements to low-income families. Thus the way has been opened to refashion the backward-looking welfare scheme that has emerged since 1935 into an income supplement program, supported by adequate programs of training and education and improved programs providing essential goods and services for the poor.

SELECTED BIBLIOGRAPHY

"American Minority Groups and Contemporary Education," *Journal of Negro Education,* Vol. 38, Summer 1969. A symposium on problems of public education for blacks and other minorities.

Banfield, Edward C., *The Unheavenly City* (Boston: Little, Brown and Co., 1970). Provocative and sophisticated attack on liberal views of the urban crisis and a statement of the case for solving urban problems through natural and historical processes of growth and demographic change.

Birch, Gerbert G., and Gussow, Joan D., *Disadvantaged Children* (New York: Harcourt Brace Jovanavich, Inc. and Grunne and Stratton, Inc., 1970). Discussion of the danger confronting children born at and into poverty.

Downs, Anthony, *Who Are the Urban Poor?* (Committee for Economic Development, CED Supplementary Paper Number 26, October 1968). A short monograph that summarizes factual findings about urban poverty and lucidly discusses policy alternatives.

Ferman, Louis A., ed., "Evaluating the War on Poverty," *The Annals,* Vol. 385, September 1969. A symposium that includes some of the leading authors on problems of poverty.

Harrington, Michael, *The Other America: Poverty in the United States* (New York: Crowell-Collier and Macmillan, Inc., 1962). The book that helped to spur a concerted attack on problems of poverty.

Kahn, Alfred J., *Studies in Social Policy and Planning* (New York: Russell Sage Foundation, 1969). Authoritative analysis of policies and strategies to combat poverty.

Kosa, John, A. Antonovsky, and I. K. Zola, eds., *Poverty and Health* (Cambridge, Mass.: Harvard University Press, 1970). Several specialists explore the social aspects of health and illness, especially the differences between the quality of medical care received by the poor and the nonpoor.

Kotz, Nick, *Let Them Eat Promises: The Politics of Hunger in America* (Englewood Cliffs, N.J.: Prentice-Hall, 1969). A skillful reporter's portrait of the phenomenon of hunger in America and why a partial attack on it has failed.

Levitan, Sar, *The Great Society's Poor Law* (Baltimore, Md.: The Johns Hopkins University Press, 1969). An evaluation of the programs of OEO to combat poverty.

Levitan, Sar and Garth L. Mangum, *Federal Training and Work Programs in the Sixties* (Ann Arbor, Michigan: The Institute of Labor and Industrial Relations, The University of Michigan, 1969). A full discussion of manpower programs of the Labor Department and OEO.

Marris, Peter and Martin Rein, *Dilemmas of Social Reform: Poverty and Community Action in the United States* (New York: Atherton Press, 1967). Excellent analysis of the community action movement as an antipoverty strategy.

Riessman, Frank, *Strategies Against Poverty* (New York: Random House, 1969). A short book that discusses three major antipoverty strategies: Saul Alinsky's local conflict model, the welfare rights strategy, and the new careers design.

Schussheim, Morton J., *Toward a New Housing Policy: The Legacy of the Sixties* (Committee for Economic Development, Supplementary Paper Number 29, 1969). Brief, readable review of national housing policy and its results.

Somers, Anne R., *Hospital Regulation: The Dilemma of Public Policy* (Princeton, N.J.: Industrial Relations Section, Princeton University, 1969). A pioneering study of the relations between hospitals and government.

Steiner, Gilbert Y., *Social Insecurity: The Politics of Welfare* (Chicago, Ill.: Rand McNally, 1966). Intensive analysis of the political forces operating in the field of welfare policies.

Sundquist, James L., ed., *On Fighting Poverty: Perspectives from Experience* (New York: Basic Books, 1969). History and analysis of the origin and development of the Economic Opportunity Act and the OEO.

Tobin, James, Joseph A. Pechman, and Peter M. Mieszkowski, "Is a Negative Income Tax Practical?" *The Yale Law Journal,* Vol. 77, November 1967. A leading article on the negative income tax as the best way to provide income security.

United States, President's Commission on Income Maintenance Programs, Report, *Poverty Amid Plenty* (Washington: Government Printing Office, November 1969). First rate report on poverty in the United States, what the federal government was doing about it in 1969, and the Commission's recommendations for an income maintenance program.

Footnotes

[1] Committee for Economic Development, *Improving the Public Welfare System* (New York: April 1970), pp. 9–10.

[2] President's Commission on Income Maintenance Programs, "Poverty Amid Plenty" (Washington, D.C.: Government Printing Office, November 1969), p. 2.

[3] Hereafter, the term "blacks" is used instead of the conventional statistical term "nonwhites" because blacks account for the overwhelming majority of nonwhite persons in the statistics of poverty.

[4] Anthony Downs, *Who Are the Urban Poor?* (Committee for Economic Development, Supplementary Paper No. 26, October, 1968). p. 38.

[5] Report from the Steering Committee of the Arden House Conference on Public Welfare (New York, 1968), p. 21.

[6] *Shapiro* v. *Thompson,* 394 U.S. 618 (1969).

[7] *King* v. *Smith,* 392 U.S. 309 (1968).

[8] These quotations are found in U.S. Senate, Select Committee on Nutrition and Human Needs, Interim Report, "The Food Gap: Poverty and Malnutrition in the United States" (Washington, D.C.: Government Printing Office, 1969), pp. 5–7.

[9] The President's Commission on Income Maintenance Programs, *Poverty Amid Plenty,* p. 133.

[10] President's Committee on Urban Housing, "A Decent Home" (Washington, D.C.: Government Printing Office, 1968).

[11] See especially "Schools Accused of Misusing Funds Granted for the Poor," *New York Times,* Nov. 9, 1969, p. 1. This article summarizes a report of the NAACP Legal Defense and Education Fund and the Southern Center for Studies in Public Policy.

Part IX State and Local Politics

STATES SHORE UP GOVERNORS' ROLE

Reform of Bureaucracies Is Also Being Undertaken to Benefit the Taxpayers

By JOSEPH B. TREASTER

Movements are underway in statehouses across the land to streamline archaic bureaucracies and put more power in the hands of Governors.

The motivating argument is that taxpayers will get more for their money. Generally, this argument is overriding fears that a concentration of power may lead to abuses.

In many cases, it was these fears that over the last 50 years led to a proliferation of state agencies and the dilution of the Governor's authority.

In an apparent effort to reverse the trend, Wisconsin, Colorado and Florida have completely reorganized their executive branches within the last few months, and more than 15 other states have instituted some changes of this type. . . .

Certain similarities have emerged in the approaches taken by states in their reorganizations, including the following:

¶Consolidation of several related offices into a handful of "superagencies" whose heads report directly to the Governor.

¶Authorization of a Governor to appoint the directors of the superagencies.

¶Authorization of a Governor to initiate and install reorganization plans subject to legislative veto.

¶Extension of a Governor's term of office to four years with a provision for re-election.

¶Limiting the state officials to be selected by popular election to the Governor and a Lieutenant Governor, with the others being appointed by the Governor.

Some of the changes have required constitutional amendments and state officials maintain that millions of dollars are being saved in the process. But so far, little public excitement has been generated. . . .

In Wisconsin, an aide to Gov. Warren P. Knowles said that compressing 90 Wisconsin offices into 28 and further subdividing them into three cabinets that meet once or twice a month, with the Governor presiding, lacked "sex appeal to the general public at election time, but the Governor thinks it was a major accomplishment."

Similar revamping in Colorado cut the number of agencies and departments from 143 to 17. And in Florida, 200 bureaus, boards, agencies and commissions were reduced to 22 with the Governor directly responsible for nine of them.

According to a plan approved by the Massachusetts Legislature, the Governor will superimpose nine appointed Secretaries on the 170 existing state agencies and offices. Initially, operations will remain unchanged, but over a two-year period the Secretaries are supposed to mold their units "into the most efficient and responsive structure possible.". . .

Across the nation, consolidations have most often been in the fields of health and welfare, transportation, natural resources and law enforcement.

In Florida, the Department of Health and Rehabilitative Services brought together such related functions as health, youth services, mental health, mental retardation, vocational rehabilitation, adult corrections and family services or welfare.

One-Stop Service

"Our aim," said State Representative Richard A. Pettigrew of Miami, "was to provide one stop service for the indigent and I think we are achieving it."

The Department of Transportation in Oregon encompasses the previously independent Highway Commission, the Department of Motor Vehicles and the Board of Aeronautics in the newly created divisions for ports and mass transit.

Edward Westerdahl, the Oregon Governor's administrative assistant, recalled how once a freeway and a major bridge had been planned for a place in Portland where another agency was intending to make a $60-million airport expansion.

"Tens of thousands of dollars spent on plans which nullified each other would never have been spent under a unified system," he said.

Minnesota collected under the umbrella of the Department of Public Safety the State Highway Department, the State Bureau of Criminal Apprehension, the Police Training Board, the Fire Marshal, the Civil Defense Agency, automobile registration and driver's license divisions.

When Utah created the Natural Resources Division, including fish and game, parks and recreation, forestry and fire control and four other departments and boards, it was able to eliminate some jobs, use joint offices and centralize accounting, purchasing and printing. . . .

© 1970 by The New York Times Company. Reprinted by permission.

Chapter 25 State and Local Governments

PERSPECTIVES ON THE SYSTEM

The contemporary American state and local government system comprises about ninety thousand units of government providing vitally needed services to a population of more than 200 million persons. These governments employ over 9 million people and spend in excess of $100 billion annually. The activities of state and local governments have a direct, substantial, and often intimate impact on the individual. As a parent, a citizen is concerned with the way in which the state and the community foster the health, welfare, and education of his children; he is affected by marriage and divorce laws, by control of contagious disease, by statutes regulating ownership and operation of automobiles, by rates of publicly or privately owned utilities. As a home owner or apartment dweller, he is affected by zoning and planning activities of his municipal government, by housing or slum clearance programs, by fire and police protection, by collection of garbage, by recreational opportunities. If he lives in a large city, he may ride to and from work on a transportation system owned and operated by the local government. If he lives in the country, absence of a public water supply or sewage disposal system may make him drill an artesian well or keep a septic tank functioning properly. Thus wherever he lives a citizen finds himself, as a taxpayer, concerned about the cost and the efficiency of the state and local governments.

A mixture of old and new is everywhere evident in the world of state and local government—in dusty rural roads and in expensive super highways; in dilapidated one-room schoolhouses and in consolidated schools designed by avant-garde architects and equipped for the teaching of drama, home economics, and automobile repair, as well as the "three R's"; in compulsory vaccination programs and elaborate medical centers; in old-fashioned constables and justices of the peace and in well-trained state police and experienced judges presiding over juvenile, traffic, probate, and other special courts.

Strong institutions of state and local government have been regarded in the United

States as essential ingredients of a dynamic democratic society and a stabilizing force that helps to prevent development of a monolithic political structure. Such terms as "states rights," "home rule," "local autonomy," "decentralization," and "community control" are charged with emotion and are common elements in political rhetoric. Many, however, question these values in the face of the pressures generated by the forces of urban growth and change which have created a widening gulf between city and suburb, sizable disparities among suburbs, and demands for more and better services that cannot be financed by state or local governments.

The typical governor, viewing the problems of government from his statehouse office, finds it easy to conclude that the national government is an overbearing paternalistic monster enmeshed in red tape and bureaucracy which has preempted the best tax sources available. As he turns his view toward cities demanding home rule, however, he rationalizes that municipalities are prone to abuse the discretionary powers they already possess and that the state represents the optimum focus for governmental authority and responsibility. A mayor, on the other hand, caught in the vise of mandatory service costs and limited revenues, may see state officials as penny pinchers, agents of a rural political machine or of a rural-suburban alliance and thus unwilling to solve the complex problems of the older cities. As a result, he may look yearningly toward the federal government in hopes of tapping its great fiscal resources to help meet such urban needs as slum clearance, mass transit facilities, and jobs for the poor.

Traditionally, state and local units of government have been valued as laboratories in which social, economic, political, and administrative projects or devices may be tested before being widely applied. The laboratory analogy has limitations. A device successfully applied in one jurisdiction may yield unfortunate results elsewhere. Another limitation is inherent in the competition between states. Policymakers in a given state may hesitate to embark upon costly social experiments that will raise taxes because they fear that business will move away to a lower-tax state. Federal leadership, for example, was necessary for the development of an adequate social security system. Furthermore, some experiments are beyond the fiscal resources of most state governments, or involve problems too far-flung to be resolved by individual states or even adjoining, cooperating states.

Another benefit of the decentralization of American government is the wide variety of opportunities for public service offered by state and local governments. Almost half a million Americans fill state and local elective posts on school boards, city councils, and township committees, and in state legislatures, while thousands more serve on planning boards, parking authorities, and advisory bodies of all sorts.

Toward a Balanced View

There are four ideas that may help provide a foundation for a more balanced and realistic approach to the study of state and local politics. First, some measure of local self-government is a practical imperative in a country with the territorial expanse of the United States. Although allocations of power and responsibility among the various units of the federal system have been in constant flux, it is difficult to conceive of any feasible arrangement under which the national government could assume direction of all the tasks now discharged independently by states, counties, municipalities, or their agencies. Federal activities have expanded substantially in the face of the increasing integration of the nation in economic and social terms and of the threat of economic instability and international conflict. But the states and their local offspring have not thereby been stripped of their importance. If federal responsibilities have increased, so have those of state and local governments, in part because, as Chapter 5 pointed out, most new federal domestic programs work through the states or their subdivisions. Indeed, state and local governments are playing more important roles today than ever before.

Second, the negative aspects of decentralization cannot be overlooked. The fact that state and local political institutions are indispensable components of the American constitutional system makes it essential to identify and alleviate their most serious shortcomings. Notwithstanding notable advances in some jurisdictions, government at the grass roots abounds in anachronisms, inequities, ineffectiveness, and corruption.

Third, the battle to maintain states' rights is dear to the hearts of many people and cannot be waved aside as a mere game of semantics. But the main parties to the controversy are seldom interested in fine points of political philosophy. Rather, they are practical men who, like their fathers and grandfathers, believe that their objectives will be served best if the center of power is in the states rather than the federal government—or vice versa when the political climate along the Potomac is compatible. Controversies over states' rights have been only phases of deeper power struggles within society.

Fourth, the urban revolution of the second half of the twentieth century is profoundly transforming the familiar state-local pattern of government in ways not yet clearly discernible. A vast body of literature has rapidly accumulated on the maladies of the city, the fragmentation of political power in the metropolis, prescriptions for reversing or checking present trends in urban development, and the deepening involvement of the federal government in the problems of the metropolis.

THE CHANGING SETTING OF LOCAL GOVERNMENT

Change has been a dominant characteristic of the American pattern of local government. Distinctive cultural patterns influenced the political development of communities and sections of the country. Within a single city or state are frequently vast racial and religious differences along with variations in education, income, wealth, and occupational status. Sections of the nation and great metropolitan areas developed such patterns during and after the great waves of immigration. The Irish early became a dominant element in the politics of Boston and New York: Germans, in Wisconsin; Scandinavians in Minnesota.

As the members of one minority group win acceptance, they may in turn resist the efforts of other minority groups to better their status and political influence. In many cities, the onetime dominant Irish-Americans have reluctantly had to yield substantial political power to the Italian-Americans, who in turn have resisted the demands of blacks for a piece of the action, who themselves have not wanted to share their political rewards with the newcomers from Puerto Rico. On the whole, discrimination does not seem to make its victims more altruistic once they are in power.

Economic and geographic factors have a powerful influence on state and local governments. Natural resources, proximity of markets, transportation, adequacy of rainfall,

Nearly 1,500 Negroes Hold Elective Public Office

By JOHN HERBERS

Special to The New York Times

WASHINGTON, March 30—A nationwide survey by two private organizations shows that almost 1,500 Negroes are holding elective public office in the United States.

This is a large increase in recent years. In municipal, county and state elections held last year, probably 100 blacks were added to the list.

The survey was conducted by the Metropolitan Applied Research Center, Inc., of New York and Washington and the Voter Education Project of the Southern Regional Council in Atlanta.

Despite the increase, black elected officials still make up only three-tenths of 1 per cent of more than 500,000 elected officials across the country. Negroes comprise about 11 per cent of the population.

According to the survey, which resulted in the first complete national list of black elected officials, there are 48 mayors, 575 other city officials, 362 school board members, 168 state legislators, 114 judges and magistrates, and 99 other black law enforcement officials.

There is one Negro United States Senator, Edward W. Brooke, Republican of Massachusetts, and there are nine Negro members of the House of Representatives. One Negro holds statewide elective office, State Treasurer Gerald A. Lamb of Connecticut, according to the list.

These, along with a few in other, minor categories, add up to 1,469. The survey was completed on Feb. 1 and the sponsors said it was likely a handful of black officials had been overlooked in the survey.

Of the total, 38 per cent live in the 11 Southern States. Many of these live in small towns and rural areas. The remaining 62 per cent live mostly in cities.

About half of all blacks in the United States still live in the South.

Missouri has the largest black delegation in the state legislature—two Senators and 13 Representatives. Ohio, with 13 black legislators, is the only state in which the percentage of Negroes in the legislature is greater than the percentage of blacks in the state.

Georgia has the largest number of black legislators in the South—two Senators and 12 Representatives. Three states with more than two million blacks—Alabama, Arkansas and South Carolina—have no blacks in their legislatures.

The only major cities in which Negroes make up a majority of the city council are Detroit and Gary, Ind. Only in Pittsburgh is the percentage of blacks on the city council significantly above the percentage of blacks in the population. Blacks make up 21 per cent of the population while black officials hold 33 per cent of the Pittsburgh council seats.

Jacksonville, Fla., which is 47 per cent black, is the only Southern city in which Negroes are represented on the council in approximate proportion to their number in the population. There, four of nine councilmen are black.

Women comprise 8.5 per cent of all black elected officials. There are 13 black women state legislators. Most of the others are school board members.

Eight states—Idaho, Maine, Montana, North Dakota, Oregon, South Dakota, Utah and Vermont—have no black elected officials.

There is no way to compare accurately the number of black elected officials now with those in prior years, because no one counted them before.

"Certainly there are many more now than there used to be," said Mrs. Eleanor Farrar, director of the Washington office of the research center. "We keep finding blacks who have been in public office for years without being listed anywhere or even counted."

The increase has been most noticeable in the South, where as late as 1965 the total number of black elected officials were estimated at only 75. Most of the 565 now listed were elected after passage of the Voting Rights Act of 1965, which paved the way for the mass registration of Negro voters in the South.

© 1970 by The New York Times Company. Reprinted by permission.

fertility of the soil, diversification of the local economy, strength of organized labor—all help condition the way in which economic life is organized and economic benefits are distributed. Cities may vary markedly as centers of finance or industry or residential communities. Differences in family income are reflected in differences in the ability of the states to finance services and activities. Major industries bring their influence to bear on state and local politics in some subtle and some not so subtle ways.

State and local politics also are influenced by the changing urban-rural pattern. By 1980, nine out of ten Americans will live in metropolitan areas. More and more land will become urbanized. The evidence points to more interlocal agreements, authorities, and special districts, greater dependence of older cities on the federal government, less social homogeneity in suburbia, and probably little success in developing comprehensive strategies for regional development to guide the investments that cities, suburbs, states, and the federal government will continue to make.

This is a period of crisis for state and local government. The symptoms of weakness, disorganization, and ineffectiveness are all too evident. In rural areas many local governments are too small and weak to operate effectively and democratically; their legislative bodies are generally not representative; their affairs are usually handled casually by amateur, part-time personnel on a highly personal or private basis. Yet the "myth of the beneficence of little government" persists "in the face of the demonstrated incapacity of the bulk of the minor units to discharge with satisfaction the services required of government today."[1]

In urban areas the capacity to govern effectively is greater, but government often is overwhelmed by the complexity, costs, and conflicts inherent in urban problems. Traffic on major arteries becomes more congested despite new expressways; public transportation facilities deteriorate or disappear. The density of air traffic rises, creating a new hazard to life and property in addition to air pollution and the disruption of work, leisure, and sleep. Many cities are threatened with water shortages because of population increases, industrial expansion, and wasteful consumption. Despite unprecedented expenditures for education, many public schools especially in the inner city are seriously deficient. Although ambitious programs of urban renewal and industrial revitalization are constantly developed, the spread of blight and economic decline rarely is arrested in the older cities. Meanwhile, urban crime, especially among juveniles, is rising, and group and racial conflict sharpens and turns to violence.

STATES IN THE FEDERAL SYSTEM

In the distribution of powers, as we have seen, the Constitution confers certain express and implied powers upon the national government, permits the sharing of some of these with the states, and reserves all powers not granted to the national government, nor forbidden to the states, to the state governments and to the people.[2] Among the states' constitutional powers are those of chartering cities and creating counties. This distribution of functions is never static and is increasingly shared by the three governmental levels. Generally, however, the states exercise great authority in regulation of political parties and elections; administration of justice and educational and public health services; control of corporations, public utilities, and financial institutions; and regulation of motor vehicles. In a number of substantive areas, including agriculture, conservation and development of natural resources, public welfare, regulation and promotion of labor, and transportation, both levels of government exercise significant powers.

In the American federal system the states serve as units of the federal government, as independent entities, and as intermediaries between the national and local governments. As political units of the federal government, the states are the instruments through which national elections are conducted and the character of the American party system is determined. This emphasis upon the state as the basic unit of national politics has produced significant and sometimes curious results. Choosing the President on the basis of state electoral votes has given the larger states more influence in presidential politics than one would expect from their population alone. Until recently, the power of the states over the electoral process—which rurally dominated legislatures often gerrymandered to serve their own interests—impaired the representative character of the House of Representatives. And state and local control of the party machinery has resulted in decentralized parties.

As administrative units of the federal government, the states sometimes take over more or less complete responsibility for certain functions, such as operating agricultural experiment stations at land-grant colleges and universities or maintaining the National Guard. They also carry out many federal grant-in-aid programs, as pointed out in Chapter 4.

In their role as separate entities the states have a spotty record. The caliber of state legislative bodies is not conspicuously high. In some states the courts have been notable weak, both in terms of competence and integrity. Recent scandals involving senior judges in Illinois and Oklahoma point to a dangerous degree of corruption. In some states as in Massachusetts and New York, judges enjoy exceptionally strong reputations. The governorship has often attracted men of outstanding ability, particularly in states with diversified cultures and economies. But state governors typically lack power and efforts to improve administration have usually been spasmodic or have come only as a belated answer to widespread ineffectiveness or corruption.

Despite increases in the functions of state government, the position of the states as independent entities has been steadily weakened in the twentieth century. Technological and economic change has ignored state boundaries. Inadequate responses on the part of the states, the expansion of interstate commerce, and the crises of depression and war have brought into play the superior resources of the federal government.

In recent years, the national government often has been more concerned with local units of government, such as cities and school districts, than with state governments. For example, federal grants-in-aid for pollution abatement, urban transit, and model city programs are designed to finance activities that have traditionally been the responsibility of local units of government. In some programs, the states serve as an intermediary between the national and local governments, receiving and distributing the federal moneys or seeing to it that federally prescribed conditions are observed locally. But this intermediate role often is superfluous, with the result that both federal agencies and local governments usually prefer to bypass the states, much to the consternation of state officials who want to control the flow of federal funds to their subdivisions.

The Legal Status of Local Government

In a legal sense the state-local relationship is a far cry from the federal-state relationship. In the latter it is possible to talk of reserved power and of other constitutional limitations on national action. In state-local relations, however, the state legislature has supremacy unless there are provisions to the contrary in the state constitution. This fact, coupled with the misuse and abuse of such power, stimulated action almost a century ago by the localities to redress the balance in favor of a substantial degree of local autonomy. Since many abuses of state power resulted from the enactment by state legislatures of special charters and special laws affecting individual municipalities, one of the first efforts at reform was directed toward amending state constitutions to require that state laws relating to municipalities be uniform in character. But it proved impossible to force all local units into such a Procrustean bed of uniform legislative control. After all, special legislation is not inherently evil or harmful; ideally, it should permit the adaptation of local government to peculiar problems and to special environment conditions. Thus rigidities of uniform legislation soon led state legislatures to undertake to classify cities and other local units and to legislate for them by "class" rather than individually or on a uniform basis. In time legislative classification of cities became a thinly disguised means of returning to the old system of special legislation for individual municipalities; for example, only one city might be placed in a given class and so-called uniform legislation then enacted for that class. These difficulties all combined to bring about the "home rule" movement to combat the extreme doctrine of state supremacy.

STATE CONSTITUTIONS

A starting point for studying the forms of state and local government is necessarily the state constitutions. Like the Constitution of the United States, their function is to determine the form of government, provide for governmental machinery, specify the political procedures to be followed in the performance of governmental tasks, and safeguard certain rights of the people. Good form does not ensure good government, but sound organization may facilitate the actions of officials trying to serve the public interest. Failure to set forth a rational ordering of authority and responsibility may confuse honest officials, cloak the incompetent, and aid the corrupt.

State constitutions vary considerably in length, subject matter, and phraseology. Generally, they contain separate major sections dealing with basic civil rights; suffrage; legislative, executive, and judicial branches; local government; finance; public education; highways; military powers; amending procedures; and a variety of miscellaneous provisions on public utilities, banks, and corporations. Nothing in the federal Constitution requires the states to separate institutions of powers. But every state constitution has always provided for more or less independent legislative, executive, and judicial branches.

Most state constitutions suffer from the afflictions of old age, including a fondness for a patchwork of amendments rather than periodic governmental overhauls through basic constitutional revision. There is also a tendency to be garrulous at the expense of relevance.

The average state constitution is over eighty years old and is a long, detailed document containing a great deal of material better left to statutory or administrative treatment. Generally the longer the constitution, the more often it requires amendment.

Procedures for amending state constitutions vary widely. In some states it is almost as easy to adopt an amendment as to enact a new statute; in others the process is so difficult as to render amendments virtually impossible. Amendments are usually proposed by a state constitutional convention, by the state legislature, or by initiative through a petition signed by a designated percentage of the electorate. In most states proposed amendments are then subject to final approval in a referendum election, although the vote required for adoption ranges from a simple majority of those voting on the issue to a two-thirds majority of those taking part in the election.

Provisions for calling constitutional conventions also vary considerably. In most states a proposal to call a constitutional convention must be approved by the electorate in a referendum. Even mandatory provisions for periodic constitutional conventions are not always complied with. And it is frequently possible for vested interests to protect their status by framing the call for a convention in such a way as to bar the convention from altering specific sections of the constitution.

Constitutional revision recently has been the subject of official action in approximately half the states. The attack on constitutional deficiencies is part of a broader movement to modernize state governments as a means to more efficient, if not less expensive operation. These efforts feature replacing part-time political appointees with full-time professional administrators to head boards and commissions; lengthening the terms of governors and legislators; consolidating departments and agencies in a smaller number of large departments; providing greater flexibility in raising and spending state revenues; and equipping legislatures for more effective lawmaking.

The basic form of state government is patterned closely after that of the national government. It provides for an elective chief executive, known in all states as the *governor,* a bicameral legislature (in all but one state), and an independent judiciary. Within this basic framework, however, there are many variations. In some states only the governor and a lieutenant governor are elected; all department heads and other administrative officers are appointed, usually by the governor. In other states a "long-ballot" form of government prevails; department heads are elected and in large measure are beyond the governor's control. There are also variations in the terms of executive and legislative officers, eligibility for reelection, division of authority between governor and legislature, use of the veto power, and appointment of nonelective officers.

CHANGING ROLE OF THE GOVERNOR

The governor is the official chief of state and the most prominent officer of state government. From Colonial times on, however, the formal authority of govenors has constantly fluctuated. Because of the antagonism of Americans toward executive power in the original thirteen states, the governor was popularly elected only in Massachusetts and New York, while in the other eleven states he was elected by the legislature. Although lip service to separation of powers required an executive department, great care was taken to prevent the governor from having substantial independent power. The Jacksonian revolution stressed the right of the people to exercise close control over the officers of government and therefore favored popular election not only of the governor but also of several other state executive officers. This resulted in the development of a "plural executive" form of government that deprived the governor of control over such state executive officers as the secretary of state, the treasurer or comptroller, the attorney general, and the superintendent of education. In nearly every state the governor was further limited by the establishment of semi-independent commissions and authorities whose directors were elected by the legislature or were appointed for terms that overlapped his.

Although progress in strengthening executive power has been made in several states, in others the governor is still merely one of several elective officials, some of whom may be his political rivals. An elected auditor may be handling both the executive pre-audit function and the legislative postaudit. An independent commission may be whipping up the support of interest groups for a program that will wreck the governor's plan for a balanced budget. Problems may have developed in a department over which the governor has no control but for which the voters will hold him responsible.

To be strong the governor must have an adequate staff of administrative aides and assistants. He needs a financial assistant to supervise the preparation of his budget and carry on budgetary research. Similarly, he needs an assistant to coordinate long-range planning activities of the operating agencies, a personal legal counsel (if the attorney general is not part of his team and subject to his control), an assistant to prepare reports, speeches, and messages to the legislature, and an assistant to handle personnel problems.

To support his broad legislative program the governor can use department heads and executive staff members to prepare specific bills that will be introduced by friendly legislators. Executive lobbyists can exert pressure on individual legislators. A governor can use his patronage and other powers to persuade legislators to get behind his program. The veto power also is an effective weapon. In the vast majority of states the governor has an item veto, which enables him to eliminate or reduce items in appropriations bills.

The part-time, amateur character of the typical state legislature has given the governor both an opportunity and an incentive to become a stronger legislative leader. As the focal point of the administrative branch of the government, the governor is in a good position to outline the only comprehensive program that can be presented to the legislature. The executive budget has become the basis of the state fiscal program, with the legislature cutting or adding small amounts to demonstrate its not very real independence. If the governor uses the various available devices to attract public attention, the legislature is compelled to give his proposals careful consideration. Special messages with headline-winning requests, carefully prepared press releases, and radio and television appearances have all added to the governor's arsenal of persuasive weapons.

But even the strongest governors find that their powers are unequal to the demands placed on their office in a rapidly urbanizing and changing society. Because of his role and his visibility, the governor is responsible for everything—he is expected to revive his state's lagging economy, increase state aid for local schools, build more roads, and clean up his state's polluted waters; he is blamed for prison scandals, teachers' strikes, riots in the cities, and failure to secure defense contracts. In every state, he is caught in the crossfire between the public's demands for more services and its unwillingness to pay for them through increased taxes. When the governor recommends that the legislature raise taxes, as almost always he must, he risks his political future. The political mortality rate for governors during the past two decades was twice that of members of Congress. A particularly bleak election year for governors was 1962, when 13 of the 27 governors who ran for re-election were beaten; and only six of the winners were able to increase their pluralities.

STATE LEGISLATURES

With the exception of Nebraska, each state has a bicameral legislature consisting of an upper and a lower house, usually called the senate and the house of representatives, respectively. New Hampshire has the largest legislative body, Delaware, the smallest of the bicameral legislatures. Terms of office are generally two or four years. Salaries are usually low and legislators try to supplement their incomes through outside activities. Legislatures of nineteen states meet annually, and thirty-one hold biennial regular sessions. Only seventeen states have regular sessions unrestricted in length.

State legislatures are organized like Congress. The presiding officer of the lower house is a speaker; that of the senate, the lieutenant governor, except in a dozen states lacking a lieutenant governor, where the presiding officer is selected by the majority party. Committee systems vary and may include standing committees in each house, special committees, joint committees, and investigative committees that may operate between sessions. Since 1946, there has been a strong trend toward reduction in the over-all number of committees. Committee chairmen are frequently powerful, and at times autocratic, figures. Where party control is strong, the caucus device is frequently utilized, sometimes in such a way that the minority plays a futile role in the legislative process. Low pay, high turnover, and short sessions have strengthened oligarchic rule by the speaker, party leaders, and key committee chairmen in most legislatures.

State legislatures are characterized by chronic weakness and popular distrust. Members often lack prestige and ability. As a recent study concluded:[3]

> State legislatures have failed to meet the challenge of change because they have been handicapped by restricted powers, inadequate tools and facilities, inefficient organization and procedures, unattractive features that produce excessive turnover in legislative service and lack of public understanding and confidence and because legislatures themselves have been unduly timid in using the powers already in their possession to strengthen their role.

The experts who agreed on this finding made several proposals for improvement. They called for minimizing constitutional limitations on legislatures and abandoning the popular initiative as inconsistent with representative government. More affirmatively, they recommended constitutionally requiring periodic reapportionment, adoption of a unicameral legislature in some states, reduction in size of several legislatures, annual plenary sessions without limitation of time or subject, increased compensation and benefits and reimbursement of expenses, and adoption of tax incentives to encourage popular financial support of candidates. Other recommendations included better professional and secretarial staff for legislators, better central services for bill drafting, law revision, library and reference service, research facilities, adequate office space and assistance, a strong system of standing committees, codes of ethics for legislators, and electronic voting.[4]

Legislative Apportionment

Until recently under-representation of urban citizens in state legislatures was a primary fact of political life. The urban-rural imbalance in state legislatures became steadily more acute as farm population declined and suburbs swallowed up the countryside around central cities.

As of 1960, nearly half of the states had not reapportioned their legislatures since the 1950 census. The Vermont House of Representatives had not been changed by apportionment since the state constitution was adopted in 1793. Alabama had not reapportioned its legislative seats since 1901. Numerous other state legislatures had failed, over many decades, to carry out legislative apportionment as required by state law or constitutional provisions.

The shift to legislative apportionment based on population began immediately after the Supreme Court's 1962 landmark decision in *Baker v. Carr* and accelerated rapidly following the 1964 decisions in *Wesberry v. Sanders* and *Reynolds v. Sims*. In the next few years, more equitable apportionment was won in most states only after furious political battles, including a concerted effort to propose a constitutional amendment to permit the states to apportion one legislative chamber on a basis other than population. This proposal, the so-called Dirksen Amendment, failed to get the required two-thirds majority in the U.S. Senate in 1965 and again in 1966. Both before and after these defeats, rural elements and conservative interests in state after state struggled hard to retain their privileged position in the legislature. But where legislatures failed to act, judges directly intervened either to speed action or to formulate reapportionment plans themselves.

Suburbanites have been the major beneficiaries of reapportionment, since suburbia was the most under-represented area prior to 1960 and is where almost all of the nation's population growth takes place. Except for some of the older urban centers which are losing population, cities also have benefitted from redistricting, especially in the South and the Southwest. The effects of redistricting on the political parties is more difficult to measure. In national terms, neither the Republican nor the Democratic party has been affected in a major way; there is considerable variation, however, in the party advantage derived from reapportionment from state to state.

STATE AND LOCAL JUDICIAL ORGANIZATION

In spite of differences of structure and jurisdiction, most state judicial systems follow roughly the same pattern. At the lowest level are courts presided over by justices of the peace and magistrates. These courts usually handle only relatively minor breaches of the peace, traffic cases, and disputes between private parties involving small amounts of money. In criminal cases sentences are limited to small fines up to $200 and short stays in the local jail. Some magistrates have power to order that persons accused of serious crimes be held in custody pending the presentment of their cases to a grand jury.

At the second level are county and municipal courts. For the most part these are courts of original jurisdiction which hear civil and criminal cases of somewhat greater importance than those that come before magistrates and justices of the peace. In about half the states county courts have appellate jurisdiction over judgments rendered by magistrates and justices of the peace. In large cities municipal courts often have specialized divisions such as traffic courts, juvenile courts, and night courts.

At the third level are basic courts of original jurisdiction, in which serious civil and criminal cases are tried. These bear such names as district court and superior court. Finally, at the fourth level are courts of appeals, in which the judgments of lower courts in the state-local judicial system receive a final review. A few states have both intermediate and high courts of appeals, and a few split the task of review between a high court of criminal appeals and a supreme court which reviews civil cases. In most states, however, a single supreme court performs much the same appellate function in the state judicial system as does the Supreme Court in the federal system.

State judicial systems have long been criticized for their decentralization, political domination, and nonuniformity. The rural justice of the peace and the municipal magistrate have been frequently described as incompetent, venal, and unable to dispense justice. Judges at higher levels have also been criticized, as we noted earlier, both on grounds of integrity and capability, although usually less sharply than local magistrates. The Conference of (State) Chief Justices reported several years ago that decentralization in state judicial systems had led to serious jurisdictional problems and duplication. The conference recommended that greater administrative power be vested in the chief justice of the state supreme court. The group also found that (1) research assistants are increasingly needed by trial and appellate judges; (2) lack of adequate statistics and docket information is a major problem in more than half the states and, as a result, there is a trend to establish agencies to coordinate such data; (3) salaries of judges have increased substantially but generally remain too low to attract men of unusual talent to the state bench; (4) during recent decades there has been an increasing tendency by state legislatures to give the courts their own rule-making responsibility; and (5) rules are being revised to achieve more simplicity in line with the simplified rules of federal civil procedure. The chief justices also took cognizance of a growing concern about the proper selection of judges and expanded consultation among trial and appellate judges to consider methods of hearing cases and drafting and filing opinions—with a higher degree of efficiency and more effective justice resulting in a number of instances from these consultations.

Some progress in judicial reorganization has been made in recent years. In some states, such as Alaska, Hawaii, New Jersey, and Wisconsin, the state judiciary has been substantially integrated into a coherent system working under a chief justice and an administrative office. Several other states have also established adminstrative offices to provide state chief justices and supreme courts with more efficient assistance. Judicial salaries have been increased; improved provisions have been adopted. Interstate associations of trial judges, chief justices, and court administrative officers have worked toward continuing improvement in state judicial machinery and procedures, but too often the state judiciaries remain as Roscoe Pound[5] described them in 1906, "A Congress of independent, uncoordinated *baronies* fraught with delay and threatened by corruption."

UNITS OF LOCAL GOVERNMENT

A governmental agency is a unit of government if it is "an organized entity having governmental attributes and sufficient discretion in the management of its own affairs to distinguish it as separate from the administrative structure of any other governmental unit."[6] From 1942 to 1967, the number of governmental units in the United States declined by more than 70,000. The most striking change involved school districts, whose extensive reorganization produced a steady decline to under 22,000, less than one-fifth the 1942 total. On the other hand, the number of special districts increased sharply, primarily in response to suburbanization.

Organized county governments are found in all but three states: Alaska, Connecticut, and Rhode Island. In Louisiana they are "parishes" rather than counties. County governments vary in political significance. In New England their function is generally limited; in the middle Atlantic and midwestern states they assume greater importance and share power with other units of local government. In the South and West the county is the basic local agency of the state and is sometimes virtually the only unit of local government in rural areas. Since 1942, almost no change has occurred in the number of counties across the nation. A new county was created in Los Alamos, New Mexico, and a handful of others changed their status or were consolidated with other local units. While the average number of counties per state is sixty-one, the southern and midwestern states generally have more.

The county was designed to be the local administrative unit of state government and still serves as a judicial unit; as a law-enforcement unit through the services of the sheriff and the county prosecutor; as the records office for licenses, deeds, and mortgages; and as an educational unit, including a county superintendent of education as the representative of the state with some supervisory and advisory functions over local schools. More and more, however, counties have become a major provider of local government services, particularly in metropolitan areas. Among the responsibilities assumed by counties in recent years are water supply, waste collection and disposal, libraries, parks, operation of hospitals and airports, planning, and, in some instances, urban renewal.

An important obstacle to the development of counties as effective instruments of modern local government has been their lack of executive leadership and centralized administration. Most counties are governed by boards of three to five or more commissioners, which have both legislative and administrative powers. County boards usually are elected, except in the South. There is a close similarity between this form of county government and the commission form of municipal government. In a few states, urban counties have been reorganized to provide an elected chief executive, as in New York, or an appointed county manager, as in California. In most counties, however, executive power is weakened by the common practice of electing separate administrative officers, such as coroner, treasurer, clerk, assessors, sheriff, auditor, recorder, superintendent of schools, highway superintendent, and welfare administrator.

Some critics think the county has outlived its usefulness, viewing it as anachronistic and the epitome of inefficiency. In their opinion its existence can be justified, if at all, only in extensive and sparsely populated areas where local government is needed but where the size and distance between settlements make the municipal corporation an impracticable device. More recently, however, the view is increasingly expressed that the urban county can contribute much to a solution of the problems of local government. Most of those who adopt this attitude readily acknowledge that county government must first be overhauled if it is to serve the public need efficiently and responsibly. Disturbed by the excessive number of independent governmental units in urban areas, they look upon the county as an instrument that can be utilized to increase coordination of effort, especially in such fields as urban planning and development.

"Municipalities" is a general term covering *incorporated* urban places, including cities, boroughs, villages, and towns. There are about 18,000 and their number is increasing with the spread of urbanization. Concentration of population increases the need for a special brand of local government or administration to provide paved streets, water, and other utilities, traffic regulation, rapid-transit systems, health and other inspectional activities, regulation of apartment dwellings, police and fire protection, slum clearance, and so on. Generally, municipalities are smaller in area and wealthier on a per capita basis than nonurban units of local government.

Another unit called the township is found in twenty-two states, principally in the northwestern and northcentral states. This class also includes local units known as "towns" in the six New England states, and some "plantations" in Maine and "locations" in New Hampshire. Of the 17,000 units in this category, few have as many as 10,000 inhabitants.

In contrast with the basic units of local government that are multipurpose in nature, many districts have been created for special purposes. The largest category of such districts is the independent school district. In twenty-nine states responsibility for public education is vested in such districts. In Rhode Island, Maryland, Virginia, and North Carolina there are no independent school districts, and educational facilities are provided by county, city, or town governments. In the remaining states a mixed system prevails. Because of more liberal reorganization laws facilitating consolidation, annexation, and abolition of school districts, the number of these units has dropped dramatically in recent years. School disrticts vary widely in the type of educational system they provide. One-sixth of all districts do not operate any schools. The 1000 largest districts account for more than half of all the public school enrollment in the nation.

In addition to the school districts, there are over 14,000 other special or *ad hoc* districts, generally established to administer a single function of government. Some have no taxing power but instead collect charges or tolls, or levy special assessments. Sixteen percent of these special districts are concerned with soil conservation, 18 percent with fire protection, 15 percent with drainage, 7 percent with housing, and 8 percent with cemeteries. About two thirds of the special districts fall into these classes. Other types include those dealing with highways, irrigation, water supply, sewage disposal, mosquito abatement, weed eradication, libraries, port administration, flood control, parks and recreation, and other functions. There is no consistent pattern from state to state. Nine states, each with at least 500 special district governments, account for six out of ten such local units.

A significant addition to the category is the "authority," a special body created in many states to construct and operate toll roads and bridges, public buildings, and port and airport facilities. The typical authority is a self-supporting public corporate body administered by commissioners with a wide range of autonomous power. The Port of New York Authority, for instance, is administered by a board of twelve, six members appointed by the governor of New York and six by the governor of New Jersey. Most authorities are financed by bond issues that are not subject to constitutional debt limits.

FORMS OF MUNICIPAL GOVERNMENT

Three Basic Plans of Municipal Government

Out of the necessity of adjusting to social and economic change has come a variety of plans for modernizing and improving local government. Local political units have been more inclined to experiment than have state governments. Municipalities have tried weak executives and strong executives; they have experimented with blending executive and legislative responsibilities collectively and individually in the members of a small governing body; they have appointed professional executives operating under policies laid down by a body of elected laymen. And they have tried such devices as proportional representation and nonpartisan elections.

This experimentation has produced three major forms of municipal government:

1. *The mayor-council plan*—an elected mayor and an elected council; including strong-mayor cities, in which the mayor has important duties as chief administrator, and weak-mayor cities, in which the council has more direct control of administration.

2. *The commission plan*—a titular mayor, designated by an elected commission from among its members, who serve collectively as a legislative body and individually as administrators of the several departments.

3. *The council-manager plan*—a titular mayor, designated by an elected council from among its members, the employment by the council of an experienced public administrator as a manager to have full charge of municipal operations, all administrative officers being appointed by the manager.

About half of all municipalities, and almost all of the larger ones, have a mayor-council form of government. The mayor is almost universally elected by the people to serve a term of from one to six years, with a two-year term most frequent. With few exceptions, the council is a unicameral body ranging in size from two to fifty. The size of the council tends to decrease with the size of the city.

Council members are selected in partisan elections in some 56 percent of the cities; in nonpartisan elections in the others. In more than one-third of the cities the councilmen are elected at large; in an equally large group a ward system is used to provide representation of different areas and/or groups in the community. One-fourth of the cities use a combined system of at-large and ward elections. As in the case of mayors, length of term of office tends to be either two or four years.

Distribution of power between mayor and council varies considerably from one city to another. In weak mayor systems the mayor's authority is severely limited; there may be other elected executives and various boards and commissions beyond his control; his appointive power may be virtually nil. In one-third of the cities he has no veto power at all—either over the budget or over ordinances passed by the council. At the extreme he may have little more than a ceremonial function, handing out symbolic keys to the city or proclaiming the annual "Clean-up Week."

In the strong-mayor forms—which also vary considerably—greater authority and responsibility are typically placed in the hands of the elected executive. The mayor is likely to have substantial power to appoint and remove department heads, authority to prepare and present an executive budget, and a veto power than can be overridden only by an extraordinary majority of the council. The strong mayor shares the legislative function with the council and at the same time has to a considerable degree control of the executive branch.

There has been a general trend in the direction of strengthening the mayor, especially in the larger cities. But as is the case with the governor, the authority of even the strongest mayor is inadequate to the problems he must face in the typical big city. With the increasing difficulties of the cities and the intensification of racial confrontation and violence in the 1960s, the number of big-city mayors who retired, either voluntarily or involuntarily, rose dramatically.

For some years after the turn of the century civic reformers believed they had discovered a foolproof form of city government in the commission plan, which, they alleged, boldly violated the traditional doctrine of separation of powers by placing both legislative and executive powers in a small group of men. Under this plan each elected commissioner heads an executive department, and the group acts as a legislative council. Today about one out of five cities from 50,000 to 500,000 population follows the commission plan.

Critics charge that the commission form encourages personal political machines, dissipates executive leadership, and undermines responsible administration. In one large city the commissioner of public works, who had antagonized the majority element, was stripped of his duties and was left in control of a single garbage truck. Disillusion with this form has been reflected in the growth of the strong-mayor and council-manager plans.

The council-manager plan assumes some separation of politics and administration. The council is the policy body, and the appointive manager serves as chief administrator subject to the control of the council. Council-manager cities usually have relatively small councils, the members of which are elected more often on a nonpartisan than a partisan basis. The councilmen and the mayor usually receive lower salaries than is the case under the mayor-council and commission forms. In the manager-plan city the mayor normally serves as the ceremonial chief of the city, presides at council meetings, and participates fully in policy discussions of the council. The council appoints the manager, approves the budget, enacts ordinances, and generally supervises the administration of city activities.

Concomitant with the growth of the manager plan has been the development of a profession of city management. Special training courses have been established at many universities and colleges; many cities pay substantial salaries to their professionally trained chief executive; and managers typically move from smaller to larger communities as they gain experience and a professional reputation in their field.

Policy and politics are persistent problems for most city managers. Typically, he finds it difficult to remain as neutral with respect to policy formation as the spirit of the original plan suggested he should be. Charged as he is with providing efficient services to the citizens of a city and the possessor of most of the information needed to make policy choices, he is necessarily drawn into policy discussions concerning the substantive prob-

lems of municipal government. Yet his nonpartisan, professional status is likely to handicap him as a participant in the rough-and-tumble of municipal politics, especially in a
city with a strong partisan tradition or a substantial level of conflict on local issues. And
if he tries to acquire personal political strength he is likely to find himself under fire from
at least some members of the city council. If he pushes too hard in their direction he may
well lose his job. Thus a successful manager must walk a narrow tightrope in attempting
to provide civic leadership without becoming embroiled in the controversies of the community. He is most likely to do this in a municipality where the level of conflict is relatively low. As a result, the manager plan has proved to be most successful in homogeneous
cities, particularly middle-class suburbs. On the other hand, the plan has made little headway in the larger heterogeneous municipal jurisdictions.

THE CHALLENGE OF URBANIZATION

Despite the massive growth in public demand for improved services and more positive
programs to overcome urban decay, it is unlikely that Americans will be willing to pay the
price for a thoroughgoing reorganization and reform of the structure of state and local
government. Yet by inaction they are paying and will continue to pay a high price for
maintaining the existing decentralized pattern:[7]

> When each jurisdiction goes on its own separate way, urban sprawl continues, with its
> companions of spreading blight, cheap commercial developments along major high-
> ways, inadequate parks, congested schools, mediocre administration, smog, traffic jams,
> recurrent crises in mass transportation, and the hundred and one irritations of undi-
> rected growth. . . . In place of a coordinated attack on the less attractive by-products
> of urbanization, each jurisdiction tries to avoid the conditions it regards as unpalatable,
> to protect its own, and to let its neighbors fend for themselves.

Still the grass roots attachment to local autonomy remains strong even in the face
of mounting evidence of needs for wider regional or metropolitan structures of government embracing a range of existing local forms. In fact, in many of the larger muncipal
jurisdictions, demands from reformers and central business district leaders for metropolitan government have been drowned out in recent years by cries from the neighborhoods,
particularly those in the black ghettos, for community control over education and other
services, for decentralization of large and often insensitive urban bureaucracies, and for
other measures to make local government more responsive to the local groups it serves.
Responsiveness is generally a good thing in a democracy, but responsiveness by fragmented
governmental units to disparate demands practically destroys the possibility of concerted
governmental action, the only real hope of solving rather than painting over the basic
problems.

SELECTED BIBLIOGRAPHY

The American Assembly, Alexander Heard, ed., *State Legislatures in American Politics*
      (Englewood Cliffs, N.J.: Prentice-Hall, 1966). Stimulating and informative essays
      by six distinguished political scientists.

Book of the States (Chicago: Council of State Governments, published biennially). The best source of current information about the organization and activities of state governments.

Fesler, James W., ed., *The 50 States and Their Local Governments* (New York: Alfred A. Knopf, 1967). A comprehensive review of state and local governments and their problems.

Jacob, Herbert, and Kenneth Vines, eds., *Politics in the American States* (Boston, Mass.: Little, Brown and Company, 1965). A recent general discussion of the political systems of each of the states.

Kallenbach, Joseph E., *The American Chief Executive: The Presidency and the Governorship* (New York: Harper and Row, 1966). A comparative study of the chief executive office in national and state politics, which provides the best recent analysis of the political problems of state governors.

Municipal Year Book (Chicago: International City Managers' Association, published annually). A valuable source of current information about local government.

Stone, H. A., Don K. Price, and Kathryn Stone, *City Manager Government in the United States* (Chicago: Public Administration Service, 1940). The standard study of the city-manager movement.

Footnotes

[1] Roscoe C. Martin, *Grass Roots* (University, Ala.: University of Alabama Press, 1957), p. 83.

[2] See Chapter 4 for further discussion of the constitutional status of the states in the federal system.

[3] Final Report of the Twenty-ninth American Assembly, State Legislatures in American Politics, 1966, p. 5.

[4] Final Report, p. 5.

[5] Roscoe Pound, "The Causes of Popular Dissatisfaction with the Administration of Justice," 1906 address before the American Bar Association; reprinted in Walter F. Murphy and C. Herman Pritchett, eds. *Courts, Judges, and Politics* (New York: Random House, 1961), pp. 41–46.

[6] U.S. Bureau of the Census, *Governments in the United States in 1952* (Washington, D.C.: Government Printing Office, May 1953), p. 6.

[7] Robert C. Wood, *Metropolis Against Itself* (New York: Committee for Economic Development, 1959), p. 42.

Chapter 26 State and Local Governments in Action

STATE AND LOCAL POLITICS IN NATIONAL ELECTIONS

A foreign visitor to the United States at the time of a presidential election could hardly fail to find the election results in many states baffling. For example, in 1964, he might well have been confused by the results in California, giving the Democractic candidate for the Presidency 59 percent of the popular vote and at the same time electing a Republican to the U.S. Senate. In that year Delaware similarly voted 61 percent for Johnson while re-electing a Republican Senator. The balloting in these states suggests that one kind of factor was controlling in the presidential election while very different factors were crucial in senatorial and gubernatorial elections, even though all of the elections were held on the same day and came at the close of a general campaign.

These apparent political anomalies underscore the commanding and often domi-nant role of state and local forces in American politics. This fact is basic to an understand-ing of political life in the United States. It provides the clue to otherwise incomprehen-sible political events, and it suggests why political leaders often choose such different routes in pursuing their interests and promoting their political ambitions. Moreover, these forces are highly volatile, and successful politicians, at least in states and communities in which politics run a free and dynamic course, are those who can sense the changing moods of the voters. Even in a presidential election local forces can work at cross purposes to national political sentiments. Of course, national politics is more than the sum of state and local politics. The outcome of most national elections is the result of a close interplay be-tween national, state, and local political factors.

In the United States elections, even for federal office, are conducted by state and local officials. Normally, state laws provide for administration of elections by local authori-ties under a minimum of state supervision. Local officials must handle several tasks: ballots have to be prepared; polling places designated; officials to conduct the voting selected and supervised; ballots, booths, voting machines, and other supplies distributed to the polling places; voters identified as they appear to vote; and the ballots counted at the completion of voting. Parties and officials compete eagerly for control of election machinery, both for the privilege of dispensing election day jobs to the party faithful, and to prevent others than party regulars from inquiring too closely into the details of election administration.

PARTY SYSTEMS

Both major parties are organized at national, state, and local levels. Their greatest strength is usually found at the local level, where the grass roots unit of political organization is the precinct or election district containing from 300 to 1000 voters. Precinct leaders and party committeemen and committeewomen are often chosen in the same primaries in which candidates for office are nominated. Thus participation in the primaries can shape the entire party organization, from the precinct leader at the bottom up through ward, county, and state committees to the national committee.

In contrast to the continuity of leadership, the financial strength, and the generally superior organization found in many cities and counties, state party organizations are usually weak and the national parties still weaker. State parties occasionally develop temporary strength when a dominant leader arises who is able to count on the support of one or more strong local organizations. Sometimes a county leader may extend his sway over the party organizations in neighboring counties and bid for state power. Strong local bosses may also dominate opposition parties, maintaining them in permanent minority status through financial and patronage aid, and thereby preserving the fiction of a biparty system. Frequently the election of a congressman or a U.S. senator is only of peripheral interest to local bosses. Occupied first with maintaining their local empires, they are likely to place the next highest priority on controlling the statehouse. County organizations are generally much more interested in the election of a governor whom they think they can influence and from whom important favors can be obtained than they are in a senator who will be sitting in faraway Washington.

Relations between state organizations and local party units differ widely. Sometimes the state organization may be little more than a creature of the most formidable of the local parties. In other states the strongest urban unit may struggle bitterly against a state party leadership that is allied with the smaller and weaker rural party organizations. The intensity of the conflict between state and local party units depends to an extent upon whether the state party is in or out of power. A forceful governor endowed with ample patronage may be able to control dissidents in his party. It is usually more difficult to maintain cohesion in the party when it is out of power. There are times when local organizations are concerned above all with enhancing their own interests. They may even turn against a powerful state organization if they feel that they have been treated badly by the state committee in the distribution of patronage.

The significance of the party system can scarcely be overestimated, for parties provide the political framework within which the federal governmental system operates. They set the style of operation for those who wield political power. Because the national role of the parties tends to be limited to the activities of nominating and electing a President and organizing the houses of Congress for action or inaction, as the case may be, the parties push strongly in the direction of decentralizing and diffusing political power. Evidence can be found in the tendency to devolve upon state and local governments much of the responsibility for administering new or enlarged federal domestic programs, such as airport and highway construction and unemployment compensation. Such national legislation inevitably takes strategic account of state and local views.

Lack of discipline and unity within the national parties gives American politics one of its most distinctive characteristics: an openness that allows individuals and organizations broad opportunties to influence national as well as state and local policy. The party system functions so as to diffuse, rather than concentrate, political power. As one observer notes.[1]

> The American parties, unlike any other, are highly responsive when directives move from the bottom to the top, highly unresponsive from top to bottom. Congressmen and senators can rarely ignore concerted demands from their home constituencies; but no party leader can expect the same kind of response from those below, whether he be a President asking for congressional support or a congressman seeking aid from local or state leaders.

On the other hand, the nature of the party system and the constitutional arrangements of the federal system often prevent the states from taking effective action on the most critical issues of modern metropolitan and suburban life. To the extent than urban problems outpace the political capacity of state and local governments to deal affirmatively with them, centralization of power in the national government may be stimulated. Thus the decentralization of power in the American federal system, to which the state-local party system is a key contributor, may generate its own antidote in the form of irresistible demands for national governmental action.

Variations in State Party Systems

On the basis of their voting history most states can be classified as solidly Democratic or Republican or as leaning toward one party or the other. But in many states traditional patterns are changing as the forces of urbanization and industrialization create more competition between the parties.

In the South where one-party control of state government has been most pervasive, the Republicans have been steadily gaining strength in recent years. The first southern state to elect a Republican governor in the twentieth century was Florida, where the influx of population from north of the Mason-Dixon line has hastened the erosion of traditional voting patterns. In other southern states, such as North Carolina, Texas, and Virginia, Republicans now compete seriously with the Democrats in gubernatorial elections and in a growing number of state legislative districts. In 1969, Virginia's Republicans captured the governorship of the Old Dominion for the first time in a century. Even in Deep South states such as Georgia and South Carolina, where the Democrats have been all-powerful for a century and where the Republican party was maintained chiefly to avail itself of federal largesse during periods of GOP reign in Washington, Republicans have mounted strong gubernatorial candidates; although they still do not contest many seats in the state legislature.

By the same token, Democrats have posed a growing threat to the dominant Republicans in states such as South Dakota, Vermont, and New Hampshire where the Republican nomination has been tantamount to election under all but extraordinary circumstances. Unlike the one-party systems which prevailed in the South until recently, however, the Democratic party in most of the normally Republican states has been a viable force that occasionally has won major contests, usually on the coat-tails of a presidential landslide. In spite of the odds against it, the party puts up candidates in most elections, almost always participating in campaigns for top state and local offices. In recent years Democratic governors have been elected in such solidly Republican states as Maine, Iowa, and Kansas. In these states the existence of an opposition party, primed to exploit the foibles and irregularities of the majority in the not always quixotic hope of winning control, provides the voter with a continuing choice but also sharpens the majority party's sense of responsibility and its awareness of and responsiveness to a changing social and economic environment.

The most competitive party systems are found in states in the advanced stages or urbanization and industrialization, for example, Massachusetts, Connecticut, New Jersey, and Illinois. Political battles in these states resemble national campaigns and the struggle for power is intense and persistent. Seldom can either party take victory for granted, and the changing of the guard at the state capitol, at least in the governor's office, is a fairly regular event. The two-party system emerges in its most active form in these states. Each party is a composite of many groups and factions and sometimes the infighting may be more furious than clashes between the two parties. The rub is that even here the composition of either or both houses of the state legislature often fails to reflect the voting for state-wide offices. When the governor and the legislative majority represent different parties, political stalemate may result.

Bossism and Corruption

"Boss" and "bossism" are familiar terms in the vocabulary of American politics. The boss has usually been defined as the head of a political organization held together by the spoils of politics and capable of deciding whom the party shall nominate for office and of influencing strongly the outcome of elections. Charges of "boss rule" crop up in almost every political campaign, but frequently they are no more than the stock in trade of the opposition candidate. On the other hand, the view that bosses belong exclusively to a bygone and cruder era in American politics is naïve.

On occasion, local party leaders may serve as links between government and the underworld. To operate illicit enterprises in narcotics, prostitution, and gambling, as well as to penetrate legitimate activities such as garbage hauling, construction work, or labor unions, criminals must arrange with police, prosecutors, judges, and other officials for the privilege of doing business. Indeed, the modus operandi of the "Dons" of the Cosa Nostra families often closely resembles that of the old political boss: constantly doing favors for both the weak and the powerful, building up a reservoir of debts that can later be called in. One of the more tangible favors to politicians may be sizable campaign contributions.

The classic political machine had a hierarchic organization firmly dominated by the boss. Patronage was important in building a corps of party faithful and maintaining discipline. Usually party officials held public office in order to reduce the expenses of party organization and to keep the reins of power in the "right" hands. In recent years there have been substantial variations from this classic pattern. The hierarchic form has been diluted, authoritarianism has been reduced, and patronage has probably become less important an ingredient in party organization. The number and importance of public jobs to support party workers has declined as civil service systems have taken root and a full-employment economy has become a relatively permanent phenomenon. Social services that used to be provided by the machine for partisan purposes are now more commonly supplied by professional welfare workers. While doorbell ringers have not lost their function, they increasingly share the task of political communication with the mass media, especially television. And antimachine groups have used the primary system from time to time to upset boss control.

Many students of American parties believe that a striking change in political party organization has been the splintering of the power formerly vested in a single boss and the substitution instead of groups of profession politicians operating in more limited areas. Often the single, omnipotent boss about whom little was known has been replaced by a number of leaders who tend to be more exposed to public examination.

Yet the boss, in the older sense of the term, lives on, mainly perhaps because the citizen needs, or believes he needs, a political broker who will listen sympathetically to his problems and has enough organizational strength to intervene on his behalf with a particular agency of government. A father, for example, who has denounced politicians and bossism all his life may turn to a state or local political leader when his son meets obstacles in seeking admission to the medical school of the state university. A contractor who wants a bigger share of public-works contracts presents his grievances not to the purchasing agent of a municipality but to its political taskmaster. These citizens represent sources of power as much as did the impoverished and disoriented immigrants of the gaslight era. The individual who can aid them soon becomes a repository of good will—the substance of which bosses are made.

If Americans widely believe that politicians are engaged in a dirty business, it is partly because many private citizens persist in utilizing party organizations for personal gain, ranging from fixing a traffic ticket to legitimizing by ordinance and statute otherwise illegal business practices worth thousands or even millions of dollars. In boss-ridden cities the party boss and his aides are accessible to citizens who want some governmental act of commission or omission for which they are willing to make some suitable payment. In other areas a party functionary may merely be an intermediary who "introduces" a citizen to appropriate government officials and tries to obtain for him a sympathetic hearing. Often particular party leaders are known for their close relationship with governmental officials, one with the police department, another with the prosecutor's office, another with the tax assessor, and so on.

Even when an activity is legal, such as the operation of a race track under license granted by the state or a city, relations between operators and government or party officials may be intimate and questionable. The stockholders in such enterprises often include a large number of party leaders, perhaps to ensure adequate police assistance in the handling of traffic and large crowds in attendance. For decades the liquor business has put large sums of money into politics in order to maintain valuable operating privileges.

EXPANDING SCOPE OF STATE AND LOCAL ACTIVITIES

State and local activities have expanded as America has been industrialized and urbanized, as citizens have demanded new services, as technological change has alternately created and solved problems, as the basic role of government has shifted from the negative one of maintaining law and order to the positive one summed up in the phrase "welfare state." Private charity has been supplemented by public welfare responsibility; the function of health has increasingly taken on a public character. Free public education has become more deeply imbedded in the American tradition and has expanded greatly at all levels, but in particular at the college and university stage. Increasingly, economic enterprises have requested or received some type of governmental intervention. Interest groups have developed for the purpose of expanding or delimiting governmental activity in this or that area.

Public Education

A convincing case can be made for the claim that providing educational opportunities is the most important service that government renders in the United States. National defense and highway construction may each cost more money in any given year than do the public schools, but neither is so basic to the maintenance of a free society or to the promotion of the individual citizen's happiness and chances of material success in a technological society. Furthermore, without adequate defense against foreign enemies a nation's very existence would be endangered, but national defense can do no more than preserve the status quo; it does not in and of itself create wealth, contribute to progress, or make life more worthwhile. Similarly, though highways are essential to a mobile people in an industrial society, ability to move around is merely a means to an end. But unless the masses of the people can be trained to understand and conserve the social values of a democracy, as well as to develop and put to good use individual talents and aspirations, the very basis of a free society is in danger.

The dimensions of public education are huge. Over 4.8 million people, or more than half of all state and local employees, are engaged in the operation of public schools. Total annual state and local expenditures for education reached $36.4 billion in 1968. In addition to elementary and secondary schools, most states and a number of cities maintain expensive systems of technical schools, colleges, and universities. As would be expected, the states vary considerably in their patterns of educational organization and in the financial effort involved. For example, although the South is far below the other regions of the United States in terms of per capita income, it ranks highest in the proportion of its income spent for public education. A striking change in recent years has been the increasing financial assistance supplied by the states to the local units that operate grade and high schools and to colleges and universities.

Because of the central importance of education, the magnitude of public effort in this field, and the tremendous variations in educational quality among and within states, public education generates a great deal of conflict at the state and local level. Controversies periodically erupt in most state capitals over the amount of state school aid available for the localities, the formulas under which assistance will be distributed within the state, and the allocation of funds to state colleges and universities. Incessant pressures for more tax dollars for education also produce conflict at the local level, which is reflected in strug-gles over school budgets, the rejection of bond issues, and spirited campaigns between "spenders" and "economizers" for positions on local school boards. In addition, two of the most explosive factors in politics—religion and race—underlie much of the conflict over public educational policies at the state and local level. Rapidly rising costs have led parochial school leaders and their clients to press their claims for broad-scale public sup-port of private education; and these efforts have borne fruit in a growing number of states despite the opposition of those who favor a strict separation of church and state. Problems rooted in race permeate the politics of education—unequal educational opportunity and facilities, desegregation, busing, decentralization, and community control, and open admis-sions to public colleges and universities.

Welfare and Public Health

Another tremendous shift has taken place in expanding public responsibility for what was once considered almost exclusively a private or "charity" activity. The county poor-house, which long symbolized government's responsibility in the welfare field, has to a large extent been replaced by social insurance, which combines collective responsibility with individual dignity. Large areas of social security, such as unemployment compensa-tion and public assistance, are joint federal-state responsibilities. Many other welfare activities, however, are local responsibilities—although financial aid and supervision may come from the state and federal governments.

Despite the advances made in reducing insecurity by state and local governments with federal assistance, the decentralized welfare system has many flaws. Even in federally aided programs, there are wide variations in the levels of support provided in different states. In 1968, the average monthly payment to a family receiving Aid to Families with Dependent Children in the United States was $167.80, but in Mississippi families re-ceived only $34.50 while the average AFDC grant in New York was $248.65. Moreover, the unequal distribution of people requiring public assistance has placed heavy burdens on those jurisdictions with large concentrations of poor residents, particularly the older and larger cities. Since a considerable share of the welfare burden is borne by the local taxpayer, the administration of public assistance at the local level frequently has as its primary goal the reduction of the welfare rolls rather than the needs of the poor. As a result of these shortcomings, as well as of the rapid growth of dependency in the 1960s, pressures have intensified for state and particularly federal assumption of the full costs of welfare and the adoption of alternative systems such as the negative income tax or guaranteed annual income which promise to reduce or eliminate local determinations of need. Another product of these forces has been the growing militancy of welfare recipients who demand reforms that will make the system more responsive to their needs and interests.

The states spend a great deal of money every year in maintaining hospitals and asylums and in subsidizing local public-health units. In 1968, state and local expenditures for health and hospitals exceeded $6.8 billion. Despite rising state and local budgets and a rapid growth in federal assistance, escalating costs and mounting public needs have outrun the capacity of most state and local governments to provide adequate facilities and care.

City hospitals and state institutions frequently are overcrowded, understaffed, and lacking in modern equipment and techniques. Another weak link in the health chain is the lack of full-time public-health personnel in many rural counties and small municipalities. In too many areas the health officer is a part-time, poorly paid physician who naturally devotes most of his efforts to private practice. Public health involves many routine activities, such as the inspection of meat, milk, and water and of restaurants and food markets and periodic examination of school children. But the principal function at state and local levels has been the provision of hospital care and services.

Providing Transportation Facilities

Roads are by far the most important state and local responsibility in the field of transportation. The major burden for constructing and maintaining the highways which are used by almost 100 million motor vehicles falls on state governments, which spent $14.7 billion on roads in 1967. About 30 percent of the states' highway funds come from the federal government. Most of this federal aid is earmarked for the construction of the 42,500-mile National System of Interstate and Defense Highways, two-thirds of which was completed in the thirteen years following congressional authorization of the program in 1956.

Highways have always been an important source of political benefits or spoils. Many a governor has been elected or re-elected on the platform of providing good rural roads or through political efforts of jobholders in the highway department. Highway spending often is a major source of patronage since it provides a means of favoring certain contractors or politically loyal localities. Because road-building is an extremely "political" function of most state governments, highway programs frequently generate a good deal of controversy. Conflict also arises because of the key role highways play in determining the economic fortunes of the communities they touch or bypass, as well as from their capacity to alter radically the physical setting of an urban neighborhood or modify significantly the property tax base of a local government. As a result of these latter factors in particular, highway-locating decisions in metropolitan areas have become one of the most hotly contested issues in state and local politics, pitting highway engineers against city planners and conservationists, neighborhood against neighborhood, and municipality against municipality.

Most other transportation responsibilities fall to local governments and local public authorities which operate bus and mass transit systems, airports, parking facilities, and public docks. During the late 1960s, a few states transformed their highway agencies into departments of transportation. But except for the states of the heavily urbanized northeast, most continued to confine their efforts to the construction and maintenance of roads.

Law Enforcement

Organized police systems exist in three-fourths of the states and in virtually all municipalities. Supplementing these groups are county sheriffs and rural constables. At the federal level the FBI cooperates with state and local police. Need for police protection varies generally with population and other factors. Highly urbanized communities have the greatest need, as measured by crime statistics and the size of police forces. They also have the most severe problems—in recruiting able personnel, in combatting corruption, and, most important, in narrowing the gulf between the police and blacks—an important source of tension and violence in the older neighborhoods of every American city.

Generally, state police organizations have won respect as disciplined outfits, well trained and well equipped. They do not usually operate within city limits but supplement local law-enforcement activities in rural areas. In some places they perform all police functions, while in a dozen states they are limited to enforcing traffic laws and to preventing crime on the state highways. Although traditionally the police function has been decentralized (even though a municipal policeman is supposed to enforce state law as well as municipal ordinances), the recent trend has brought increased federal activity and increased state supervision of local police.

Regulation of Business and Labor

State and local governments have many programs and policies that affect the business sector of the economy. State governments regulate the activities of banks, securities dealers, insurance companies, especially in states where the insurance business is concentrated, and public utilities. State regulation also extends to the licensing of lawyers, doctors, dentists, barbers, undertakers, and a host of other professionals. Regulation here frequently reflects the guild spirit, with governmental power a handmaiden of professional groups.

Regulatory activities of local governments generally are more limited than those of the state. Municipalities tend to confine themselves to such activities as setting taxi and transit fares, enforcing building standards, and in some cases control rents. The narrower scope of the local regulatory function principally reflects the character of the American economy. Most corporations whose functions affect the public interest, and thus should be under public control, engage in business on a state or interstate basis, thus from a practical standpoint they can be supervised only by state or federal agencies. As an interesting sidelight, the concept of public regulation of privately owned enterprise is favored in state governments over proposals for public ownership. At the local level, however, public ownership of utilities has long been widely accepted, as any list of municipally owned enterprises shows.

Labor is naturally interested in state policies affecting such matters as minimum wages, workmen's compensation, unemployment compensation, cash sickness benefits, mediation of labor disputes, and strikes in public utilities. The 1950s witnessed a strong movement to enact "right to work" statutes aimed at outlawing the union shop and weakening the bargaining power of unions. On the other hand, some states have developed costly programs of social welfare and labor benefits.

Influencing the Pattern of Development

The basic character and physical structure of urban and rural communities depend in large part upon the activities of state and local governments. The physical appearance of city, suburb, and town is affected by zoning ordinances, building codes, and other regulations concerned with the use of property and construction activities; slum clearance programs;

aids to public and private housing; the planning, construction, and maintenance of high-ways, bridges, and airports; the construction of schools, hospitals, and other public build-ings; and the development of parks, playgrounds, and other recreational areas. Policies governing the cutting of timber, the conservation of other natural resources, and the sup-ply of water for industrial consumers also have obvious effects.

Until recently these and other vital aspects of the physical environment, such as fire fighting and fire prevention, have been controlled almost solely by chance, or by the short-run perspectives of a particular unit of state or local government. Most areas of the United States have been greatly changed by the hand of man, operating for the most part without government restriction and without any planned pattern. The rate of population growth and the devastating impact of uncontrolled technology and development on the environment necessitate more effective planning and public control than has been provided by state and local governments in the past, or seem likely to provide in the immediate future.

STATE AND LOCAL FINANCE

Revenues and Costs

Since 1927, when state and local government spending was about $8 billion, the costs of state and local government have gone up more than twelvefold. And in recent years these governments have increased their revenues about 10 percent annually. This steady growth in revenues and expenditures has been a response to public demands for more and more governmental action. These demands in turn partly reflect the need to provide costly ser-vices for ever-larger urban and suburban populations. They have been generated also by technological and scientific advances; by more enlightened attitudes toward problems of housing, slum clearance, and urban renewal; by rising prices; and by remarkable advances in medical science and hospital services that have prolonged life and lowered death rates. Although almost all state and local governments have faced critical financial problems since 1950, state-local revenues have shown a strong capacity to grow with the economy. Substantial increases in state-local spending have been accompanied by sharp rises in per-sonal income, increases in the total output of goods and services, and general prosperity since 1942.

In the 1920s, when governmental expenditures were relatively modest, local gov-ernments accounted for about 80 percent of state-local expenditures, and they raised most of the required revenue themselves, chiefly through the property tax. When property values collapsed during the depression of the 1930s demands for welfare and other bene-fits forced first the states and then the federal government to take a more active role. The increase in state-local revenues between 1927 and 1938 was provided entirely by the states, which experimented with new sources of revenue, including sales and income taxes and federal aid. It was largely during the period of the depression that the present tax systems of state and local governments took shape.

During World War II revenues were plentiful, but needed expenditures were commonly deferred because of the shortage of materials and manpower. After the war state and local governments were staggered by great new revenue and spending requirements. In the intervening years, almost every governmental unit has been forced to increase taxes and spending levels to construct schools, hospitals, and highways, meet higher prices and salaries for traditional functions, and undertake new programs stimulated by population growth, rising income levels, and higher aspirations of community residents. Education, as we have seen, takes the largest share of state and local money. The next largest goes for highways, followed by public welfare.

In fiscal year 1968, total state expenses were about $66 billion—up 100 percent from 1961. California ranks first, accounting for about 13 percent of all state expenditures. The nation's cities account for about two-fifths of total expenditures by local government, and their costs have been mounting nearly 10 percent annually. Revenues and expenditures of municipalities are somewhat smaller than those of school districts but substantially larger than those of counties, special districts, and townships.

Limitations on State and Local Taxing Power

Within constitutional limitations states are free to distribute tax burdens as they see fit. The federal Constitution contains certain specific prohibitions, such as denying power to levy import, export, and tonnage taxes. Nor can states, without congressional consent, tax instrumentalities of the national government. Interstate commerce is peculiarly within the province of national authority; states are forbidden to levy taxes that discriminate against or unduly burden it. States, however, are permitted to tax enterprises and individuals engaged in interstate commerce in accordance with principles and doctrines developed and applied by the Supreme Court. For example, a state may tax corporations and persons engaged in commerce, applying the tax against real estate or a proportion of movable property used within that state, or in terms of a share of gross or net income that was earned within that state.

In a real sense, however, political or practical limitations weigh more heavily than do constitutional limitations. Tax laws tend to reflect the balance of power among groups in the state or community. A state may be free to enter a tax field, but if the federal government is already active in that area the state officials are apt to recognize the practical obstacles involved. Individuals or corporations, who are taxed too heavily may vote offending legislators out of office, or these people may threaten to move to other states, as we noted in Chapter 23, since states and communities compete with one another, tax policy must be considered in terms of attracting or driving away industry. In an election year the party in power rarely imposes a new tax or raises the rates of old ones. If a sales tax is being given serious consideration, interest groups will attempt to shape the legislation to their advantage.

The Major Sources of State and Local Revenue

The *property tax* remains the principal local revenue source, but most state governments have abandoned it, turning to new means of supporting themselves, such as sales and income taxes and federal grants-in-aid. The property tax now yields more than $26.8 billion to local governments, accounting for 66 percent of all revenue from local sources. The rest comes mostly from local sales taxes. The property tax violates many generally accepted criteria of fairness. It bears little relationship to the ability of the owner to pay; assessed valuations may be thrown out of line as a result of shifts in the business cycle; assessors may be incompetent or dishonest and are often prone to assess rural property at lower levels than comparable urban property. Slow and uneven progress is being made toward scientific, nonpartisan assessment practices. There is increasing pressure to substitute appointive for elective assessors, to enlarge the primary area of assessment, provide a system of genuine statewide equalization of assessments, and in general to strengthen a systematic approach to the problem. In many areas, however, these goals are still remote.

All but two states—Alaska and Delaware—have a *general sales tax,* and for most states it constitutes the basic revenue source. The states as a whole receive over half of their total tax revenue from general and selective sales taxes, the rest being derived mainly from income taxes and fees for motor vehicle and operators' licenses. Many of these taxes were initiated during the depression when state and local governments were hard pressed to find revenues for relief and other purposes. The sales tax is defended on the ground that it produces a large and stable income to finance essential operations. It is criticized on the grounds that it falls most heavily on citizens least able to pay and that it may produce an undesirable deflationary effect during periods of economic decline. In addition, the sales tax is easily evaded if nearby states or cities do not make use of it. When food, medicine, nonluxury clothing, housing, and other basic essentials are exempted, the sales tax burden appears to be socially sound and equitable since it is then paid in rough proportion to easily disposable personal income. A general sales tax with such exemptions has the further appeal of being easy to administer and politically more acceptable than a personal income tax.

Four out of five states use the *income tax* as a source of revenue. Wisconsin was the first in 1911. In times of inflation the rates produce increased revenues, thereby helping to sop up inflationary dollars; in a depression period the revenues from the same rates fall off sharply. For this reason many experts prefer the greater stability of the sales tax.

State and local governments have a variety of other revenue sources, including death and gift taxes, various licenses, general corporation licenses, and severance taxes. Municipalities are increasingly using the nonproperty type of tax and a variety of fees, licenses, and permits as revenue sources to supplement the traditional property tax. Special assessments are a traditional revenue source and are used to help finance improvements such as sewers or streets that particularly benefit a certain group of property owners. Parking meters have become a familiar part of the street scene in many municipalities. In some communities fees are charged for garbage disposal or for other services. Frequently, municipally operated enterprises bring a profit to the city's treasury.

Hard-pressed municipalities have often turned to state legislatures for financial assistance. In some cases, instead of grants-in-aid, legislators have changed taxing or borrowing limitations or have given the cities new taxing powers. Some cities have entered the sales tax field; others have adopted income taxes that apply to payrolls and business profits. Such taxes enable a city to place part of the tax burden on those who use the city as a place of business or employment but who return each evening to the suburbs. Admissions taxes on theatrical productions and sports events may also hit the suburbanite who wants to use the central city.

The Intergovernmental Economy

Federal aid has become a critical factor in financing certain essential government functions. For the past two decades such grants have been extended to state and local governments and even some private organizations to broaden opportunities for elementary, secondary, and higher education; to develop economically depressed areas of the country; to finance health services and medical care; to stimulate efforts to revitalize urban centers; and to launch a concerted attack on poverty. In 1968, federal-aid payments constituted about 16 percent of total state and local revenues.

PERSONNEL FOR STATE AND LOCAL GOVERNMENTS

More than 9.4 million people are employed directly by state and local governments in the United States, more than half of them in education. Three to five hundred thousand employees have been added annually. Included in the broad category of government personnel are governors, mayors, managers, and other top management officials, as well as thousands of schoolteachers, highway engineers, firemen, policemen, doctors, janitors, garbage collectors, and so on. The vast majority are appointed to their positions, sometimes on the basis of merit, sometimes on the basis of political favoritism (which does not necessarily exclude qualified people), sometimes because no one else is available. In the top management group are found elective as well as appointive officials, some motivated by strong political ambitions, some dedicated to serving the public interest in a reasonably selfless manner.

In terms of their administrative responsibilities, top managers in state and local government are not well paid, especially when contrasted with private enterprise. Few states pay their governors $30,000 or more. In private enterprise an analogous executive would command from three to even ten times as much. Municipal official salaries frequently run substantially higher than those of key state officials. The top salaries for mayors and city managers often exceed gubernatorial salaries. Salaries of officials vary depending on professional qualifications. A public works director is frequently an engineer; a superintendent of schools has a doctorate in education. Particularly since the advent of social security, welfare administrators have been selected on the basis of professional qualifications.

The merit system has made less headway in state and local governments than in the federal government. In 1967, only thirty states had merit systems with general coverage; the others have had to establish systems to cover state personnel involved in federal grant-in-aid programs, particularly under the federal Social Security Act.

The municipal record—particularly in the larger cities—is somewhat better. Virtually all cities of over 100,000 population have civil service systems. Of cities of from 10,000 to 100,000 population, only 60 percent have such systems and only one-fourth have reasonably complete civil service coverage of all their employees. Schoolteachers have a merit system of their own; although selected generally by local school boards, they must meet minimum certification requirements established by the states.

Civil service systems, of course, may merely camouflage the operations of patronage systems. A personnel agency may wink at exceptions to the law; or it may be inadequately financed and staffed; or laws may be passed granting blanket exemptions to certain types of jobs. Veterans' preference laws may greatly weaken the system, or in times of a tight labor market the scarcity of personnel may result in low standards.

One-fourth of all state-local employees are employed by the states, one-fourth by municipalities; school districts hire almost one-third and counties one-eighth. The remaining 5 percent is employed by townships and special districts other than school districts. Changes in employment by occupation reflect the current demand for new or improved governmental services. Sharp increases have occurred in recent years in highway workers, police, public health and hospital employees, teachers, and public welfare workers.

The manpower needs of state and local governments in the years immediately ahead are destined to become even more critical. Present estimates indicate that total government employment will reach 13 million by 1975, and nearly all the increase will be in state and local programs and services. There already exists a shortage of well-trained, highly qualified personnel in state and local governments. Many jurisdictions now have difficulty attracting and holding professional, managerial, and technical personnel. Salaries continue to be a serious source of dissatisfaction for municipal executives. Patronage persists in many governments, and effective personnel management is an exception. In response to the man-power crisis in state and local government President Johnson in 1966 and 1967 called for a program of federal assistance to state and local governments to develop more effective career services for their employees and to improve the quality of government.

Public services, as administered by state and local governments, vary widely in quality. Some clearly match the level of federal services, but others leave much to be desired. A number of severe problems demand analysis and solution: how to overcome overspecialization of career services, especially in the middle and upper ranks; how to gain recognition and high prestige for able public servants; how to recruit and develop talent for key posts—executive, managerial, professional, and technical. While these problems are also present in federal practice, they are even more critical for state and local units, which have customarily been far less energetic in attacking them.

The urgency of improving the competence and capacity for leadership in state and local public service is hard to exaggerate. As a leading student has concluded:[2]

> One of the most important national goals for the American democracy is the building of a talented, expert and innovative public service in the national, state, and local governments. It is these public servants who must be relied upon to bring to the political process not only high technical expertise and a sense of continuity but also more than a minor share of the inventiveness, the long-range perspectives, and the conscious explication of those public interests which would not otherwise be emphasized in the public debate which precedes and follows the making of policy decisions. The responsibility for the continuous improvement of the public service rests most clearly and properly upon the elected chief executives, but it is also a task in which every leading institution in our government and society—legislatures, political parties, interest groups, communication media, and educational systems—has its own distinctive opportunity and high obligation to contribute.

SELECTED READINGS

Banfield, Edward C. and James Q. Wilson, *City Politics* (Cambridge, Mass.: Harvard University Press, 1963). The best general account of the governmental process in the American city.

Key, V. O., Jr., *American State Politics* (New York: Alfred A. Knopf, Inc., 1956). An outstanding analysis of state politics emphasizing the role of the political parties.

Lockard, Duane, *New England State Politics* (Princeton, N.J.: Princeton University Press, 1959). An informative study of the political process in six states.

Masters, Nicholas A., Robert H. Salisbury, and Thomas H. Eliot, *State Politics and the Public Schools* (New York: Alfred A. Knopf, Inc., 1964). A survey of the dynamics and mechanics of educational policy-making in three states, Michigan, Illinois, and Missouri.

Sayre, Wallace S., and Herbert Kaufman, *Governing New York City* (New York: Russell Sage Foundation, 1960). An extensive study of the political system governing the nation's largest city and the dynamics of its political process.

Wilson, James Q., ed., *City Politics and Public Policy* (New York: John Wiley and Sons, 1968). Eleven essays which explore the linkages between the political process and policy outputs.

Footnotes

[1] Morton Grodzins, "The Federal System," in *Goals for Americans,* Report of the President's Commission on National Goals (Englewood Cliffs, N.J.: Prentice-Hall, Inc., 1960), p. 275.

[2] Wallace S. Sayre, "The Public Service," in *Goals for Americans,* Report of the President's Commission on National Goals, p. 296. Copyright 1960 by Prentice-Hall, Inc. Reprinted by permission of the publishers.

Epilogue

We have tried to understand the American system of government by placing it in its historical, cultural, and institutional setting and then by describing how its formal and informal processes operate—the choice of leaders, the practical and ideal restrictions on their power, and the character of citizens' rights. We have also described how the system produces and carries out policy decisions, summarized the content of many of those policies, and indicated some of the ways in which they shape American life.

Without a doubt politics in the United States is a fascinating as well as impressive process. That essentially the same legal structure has survived for more than 180 years is a monument to the wisdom of the Framers of the Constitution and the skill of succeeding generations of politicians. That it has survived *and* produced a great measure of individual freedom and a general level of prosperity unequaled in the world is even more significant. Yet, to us of the 1970s there are dismaying items on the debit side of the ledger. The United States is facing grave crises in both foreign and domestic affairs, and, of course, each generation's crises seem to people of that time far more serious than those of earlier periods.

The current international situation raises many of the same issues as has the debate that has gone on intermittently since 1898 over America's role as a world power. One could almost say that the issues are similar to those George Washington discussed with his advisers over the proper course to follow after the outbreak of the French Revolution or those that Thomas Jefferson considered before sending the Navy and Marines to retaliate against the Barbary Pirates. There is one all important difference, however: the present problems occur against a backdrop of nuclear and biological weapons that can obliterate life on this planet.

By the time this book is read, the Vietnamization of the war in Southeast Asia may have become a reality, or the war itself may be completely over. But it is not likely that questions about Laos, Cambodia, Thailand, Malaya, Korea, Formosa, or the locus of the next "war of liberation" will have been settled, any more than will questions about American policy in the Near East, Subsaharan Africa, or Latin America or toward the former satellites of Eastern Europe. Nor is it likely to be at all clear how the United States can help developing nations to maintain their independence, attain some degree of internal freedom, and achieve a measure of prosperity. If imperialism has become repugnant to most Americans, isolationism can only be a fatuous dream in a shrunken world. We can ask Cain's ancient question about being our brothers' keepers, but the answer will be unchanged.

The problem in foreign affairs is to find wisdom. In domestic politics, it is to find both wisdom and power to carry out that wisdom. For the first time since the Civil War, the legitimacy of the entire political system is being openly questioned by a number of minorities. Not only are there the usual ragings about revolution from the lunatic fringes of the right and the left, but the young, the black, the poor, and a solid core of serious intellectuals are increasingly dubious not simply about particular policy decisions or specific instances of corruption but, more fundamentally, about the piecemeal way in which the American political system deals with its problems. More than a hundred years after Emancipation, racial injustice is still eroding ideals of human dignity as well as the constitutional command of equality; urban blight is spreading; private industries continue to scar the landscape, pollute the water, and foul the air at fantastic rates. The welfare system can be most charitably described as inadequate, if indeed it is a system at all. In the midst of abundance millions of children go hungry every day and thousands are literally starving to death. Black ghettos are crowded with well-fed rats and ill-nourished people, people as rejected as the rural poor of Appalachia or the Indian poor on the reservations. And they are giving signs that their patience is not as boundless as their poverty.

Crime threatens to turn central cities into jungles, and an epidemic of narcotics addiction menaces an entire generation. The system of criminal justice limps, and functions at all only because it has to operate in but a small percentage of cases. Rehabilitation of convicted criminals is warmly endorsed in speeches but ignored in budgets. Only a handful of dedicated officials show deep concern.

It is incredible that the richest nation on earth, one that can wage massive wars, rebuild the economy of Western Europe, design and deploy intercontinental ballistic missiles, and put men on the moon and rockets on Mars, would not have the physical resources to cope with poverty, crime, and racial injustice at home. The cause must lie elsewhere, perhaps in what Duane Lockard[1] has called "perverted priorities," putting secondary things first. Or it may lie in what Theodore J. Lowi[2] terms "interest group liberalism," a belief that government not only *does* work through a bargaining process among powerful interest groups but that that is the way government *ought* to function.

In either case, the Madisonian system of fragmented power must bear much of the blame. As we have seen, the legal structure of federalism itself poses no real obstacle to the exercise of national power; the difficulties lie in an informal feudalism that permeates the whole atmosphere of American government. The parties, the Congress, the President's bureaucracy, and even to some extent the national courts are infused with a kind of fractionalism that shatters and obscures authority and responsibility. To be adopted, a national policy must usually be cut and sewn into a bizarre, almost psychedelic pattern so that almost every important congressman's special constituency interest gets a piece of the action.

To be carried out a policy must be further skewed to fit the ideas and ambitions of state and federal bureaucrats and the interests they represent. Rationality in terms of programmatic efforts to attack a serious problem rarely plays a central role in this bargaining process.

As long as the demands on government were small, as long as those making the demands could be satisfied with immediate symbolic gains and incremental material gains, the Madisonian system performed well. It still performs well for groups who have become politically entrenched, who want only to tinker with the status quo. But it is hard on newcomers. And there is now a large group, the blacks, who are relatively new actors in politics and have not been and do not seem likely soon to be absorbed into the mainstream of American life. They are being joined in their discontent by other racial minorities and by masses of poor whites. More than a decade ago, a distinguished political scientist[3] warned that the system was so preoccupied with cleavages among those who were participating in politics that it had "become insensitive to the interests of the largest minority in the world." Members of that minority are now demanding real not merely symbolic gains; they are demanding them quickly rather than slowly; and they are demanding them on a national rather than on a piecemeal scale.

The values protected by a regime of fragmented power are numerous. Such a regime safeguards the rights of many minorities by providing them with a number of vantage points from which they can oppose and even block hostile governmental action. It promotes stability and peaceful change by encouraging negotiation, bargaining, and compromise. It produces public policy by a process approaching consensus, albeit consensus among a restricted clientele.

The system not only checks ambition against ambition, it also checks intelligence against intelligence and virtue against virtue. Built in is the assumption that no single man or small group of men is all wise or all virtuous or is likely to have a near monopoly of what wisdom and goodness humans are apt to possess. The system thus forces competition among ideas as well as among men, and so allows voters a choice. It also provides an institutional base for opponents of immediately popular notions.

These are not trivial accomplishments. Limited government and even popular government must inevitably rest on the legitimacy of opposition to those currently in power and in favor. Indeed, it must be kept in mind that in the current crisis the Madisonian system is providing a public, institutional forum for many minority groups pressing for reform. Public opinion surveys indicate that only a minority of American adults, and a smaller minority of white adults, now see the problems of urban unrest as critical, or favor federal action to desegregate schools, or enforce fair employment practices, or provide a minimum standard of living for all citizens. Majoritarian parliamentary systems in Australia, England, and India have done no more—in fact it could be argued, far less—for racial minorities than has the American system over the past two decades. But in England and Australia race has never become anywhere near as serious or as large a problem as in the United States; religious beliefs of the untouchables themselves have given the Indians some lead time in coping with caste discrimination.

The crux of the dilemma facing the United States is how to preserve the great and obvious benefits its system bestows while lowering the costs of operating that system to the point where government, especially the federal government, can cope effectively and democratically with the unholy trinity of crime, poverty, and racial injustice. By "effectively" we intend no utopian vision of government officials wiping out social problems like a platoon of janitors cleaning blackboards; we mean only that government formulate and administer programs that will bring remedies substantial enough to provide real help in the present and realistic hope for the future. By "democratically" we mean securing the approval of a majority of the people in the country, not for the details of any plan but for the general ends and means of a coherent program.

To win approval for what must be done requires leadership that is skilled at both persuasion and manipulation. In the past, the United States has sometimes found that kind of leadership, usually in war, but occasionally in peace. Most recently Lyndon B. Johnson was able to build on the legacy of John F. Kennedy to begin a war against poverty and a campaign for civil rights that went beyond tokenism. His tragedy was in dissipating his financial resources and his political capital in Vietnam just when his management of Congress was creating and exploiting opportunities for far-reaching social reform.

If the American political system is to survive without repression, it will be because of positive political leadership that faces up to the problems and convinces both private citizens and public officials that these problems are serious and interrelated; that they must be attacked, attacked immediately, and attacked together by coordinated and probably expensive programs. As we have said so many times in this book, if there is to be positive leadership in American politics, it can only come from the President. Even then the Madisonian system may stalemate. But without presidential leadership there is no hope that the system can move with any speed or controlled direction.

American government has truly become presidential government. The great challenge to the President is to bring together not just a majority of worried whites sufficiently numerous to keep his party in control of the White House another four years, but to bring the whole people together. In confronting problems of both foreign and domestic policy, his task is to unite, not to divide black against white, not to placate those who prefer the status quo—for the problems cannot be wished away—but to motivate them to act like prudent conservatives and opt for change while the option is still theirs. His task is not to cool but to warm, not to calm but to excite, not to stagnate but to lead.

Footnotes

[1] Duane Lockard, *The Perverted Priorities of American Politics* (New York: Crowell-Collier, Macmillan, Inc., 1970).

[2] Theodore J. Lowi, *The End of Liberalism: Ideology, Policy, and the Crisis of Public Authority* (New York: W. W. Norton and Company, Inc., 1969).

[3] Elmer E. Schattschneider, *The Semisovereign People: A Realist's View of Democracy in America* (New York: Holt, Rinehart and Winston, Inc., 1960), p. 108.

For Further Research

The student should be aware of certain general sources of information about political subjects. *The International Encyclopedia of the Social Sciences* (New York: The Macmillan Company and the Free Press, 1968) contains seventeen volumes of essays by leading authorities on almost all major topics in the field of political science. There are also a number of learned journals to which the student may profitably turn in a search for articles on subjects of interest to him. The *American Political Science Review* (1527 New Hampshire Ave., N.W., Washington, D.C.) is published by the American Political Science Association, which is the national association of the political science profession. Several regional political science associations also publish journals: Academy of Political Science (sponsored by Columbia University)—*Political Science Quarterly* (Fayerweather Hall, Columbia University, New York City); The American Academy of Political and Social Science (sponsored by the University of Pennsylvania)—*The Annals* (University of Pennsylvania, Philadelphia); Southern Political Science Association—*Journal of Politics* (University of Florida, Gainesville); Midwest Conference of Political Scientists—*Midwest Journal of Political Science* (Wayne State University Press, Detroit); Western Political Science Association and Pacific Northwest Political Science Association—*Western Political Science Quarterly* (Institute of Government, University of Utah, Salt Lake City). Other journals useful to the student of politics are *The Public Interest, Public Policy, Trans-action, Public Opinion Quarterly* and *Commentary.*

Many government publications provide an excellent record of the operations of Congress. The work of the congressional committees is recorded in documents known as *Hearings,* which contain the verbatim testimony given by witnesses at the public hearings of each committee, and as *Reports,* which give the complete formal reports of each committee to the House or the Senate.

The official record of the work of the two houses themselves is found in the *House* and *Senate Journals,* which the Constitution directs shall be kept. These publications provide only the bare record as to the putting of formal motions, the vote on bills, and similar matters. They are far less widely known or used than is the *Congressional Record,* which provides a nearly verbatim reporting of everything that is said or done on the floor of each house. The *Record* dates back only to 1873. The record of congressional debate for the years before 1873 is to be found in three privately printed publications: the *Annals of Congress,* for the period 1789–1824; the *Register of Debates,* for the period 1824–1837; and the *Congressional Globe,* covering the period 1833–1873. The present-day *Record* is published in two editions: a daily issue, which appears within twenty-four hours of a meeting of Congress, and a permanent edition, consisting of a dozen or more bound volumes appearing at the close of a year's session.

The statutes enacted by Congress are available in three forms. Immediately following its enactment, a statute is published in the *Slip Law* format, a pamphlet providing the text of the single law. The *Slip Law* citation of a statute is given in this form: Public Law 637–83d Congress; Chapter 886–2d Session. The *United States Statutes at Large* are bound volumes containing in chronological order the text of all laws passed by each Congress. The *Statutes at Large* citation of a law is given in this form: 60 *Stat.* 812 (the sixtieth volume of the *Statutes at Large* at page 812). Third, the laws of the United States are found in various codified collections. A "code" represents an attempt to do two things: (1) to weed out statutes that have been repealed or superseded and to present only the law that is actually in effect at the time the code is published; and (2) to arrange the laws topically, rather than chronologically, so that all statutory provisions dealing wih a single subject, such as immigration, agriculture, or internal revenue, may be found in one place. The federal government revises and republishes the *United States Code* at frequent but irregular intervals, but the government does put out annual supplements to keep the *Code* up to date. The latest full revision was in 1964. Two private publishers also put out a 100-odd volume set entitled the *United States Code Annotated.* These books, also kept current by annual supplements, contain summaries of legislative history and judicial interpretations as well as the actual statutes. The *Code* citation of a provision of law is given as follows: 18 U.S.C. 241 (the 18th title of the *United States Code* section 51).

A private organization, Congressional Quarterly, Inc. (1735 K Street, N.W., Washington, D.C.), issues a weekly publication known as the *Congressional Quarterly Weekly Report.* The *Quarterly* is designed primarily for use by newspapers and contains a remarkably detailed and accurate summary of congressional activities. Roll-call votes on important issues are reproduced, substantive analyses of pending bills are provided, and the work of interest groups is examined. At the end of the year this material is presented systematically in a single volume called *The Congressional Quarterly Almanac.* Congressional Quarterly, Inc. has also published two large volumes summarizing much of national politics since World War II, *Congress and the Nation, 1945–1964* (1965) and *Congress and the Nation, 1965–1968* (1969).

Biographical information about the current members of Congress can be found in the *Congressional Directory* (Washington, D.C.: Government Printing Office), published in several editions each year. *The Biographical Directory of the American Congress* (Washington, D.C.: Government Printing Office, 1950) contains a brief biography of every person who served in the Congress (and its predecessor bodies) between 1774 and 1949.

The Statistical Abstract of the United States, published annually by the Government Printing Office, is a treasure house of important and trivial information about American political, social, and economic life. A useful supplement to these annual reports is *Historical Statistics of the United States: Colonial Times to 1957* (Washington, D.C.: Government Printing Office, 1960). *The United States Government Organization Manual,* the official organization handbook of the federal government, is revised annually; it describes the agencies of the legislative, judicial, and executive branches.

Publication of court decisions has always been an important characteristic of the

American and British Judicial systems. All of the opinions of the Supreme Court—majority, concurring and dissenting—are published each year in a series of volumes known as the *United States Reports*. Until shortly after the Civil War the volumes bore the name of the Court reporter and were privately published. Thus the citation of the *Dred Scott* case is 19 Howard 393 (the 19th volume edited by Howard, beginning at page 393). Since 1875, the volumes have been cited simply as *United States;* the *School Segregation Cases* are found in 347 U.S. 483 (the 347th volume of the *United States Reports* beginning at page 483). In addition to the *United States Reports,* which is an official publication of the federal government, two editions of Supreme Court decisions are published by private concerns. One of these is known as the *Supreme Court Reporter* (the citation of the *School Segregation Cases* is 74 S. Ct. 686), and the other as the *Lawyers' Edition,* now in its second series (the citation of the *School Segregation Cases* is 98 L.ed. 873). These private publications carry additional aids that make them somewhat more useful to students than the official edition.

Many of the most important rulings of the lower federal courts are published by the West Publishing Company of St Paul. There are five separate series. The rulings of the lower federal courts from "the earliest times" to 1880 are contained in thirty volumes known as the *Federal Cases.* The cases are numbered (1 to 18,313) and arranged alphabetically rather than chronologically, since lower-court decisions were not published contemporaneously until 1880. From 1880 to 1924 lower-court cases were reported year by year in chronological fashion in 300 volumes known as the *Federal Reporter.* In 1924, the *Federal Reporter* (2d series) was started. In 1932, this series was limited to the decisions of the courts of appeals, and beginning in that year the miscellaneous rulings of the district courts were reported in a series known as the *Federal Supplement.* Federal decisons relating to rules of procedure are now published in the *Federal Rules Decisions.* The work of lower federal courts is so vast that the West Company publishes only a fraction of the total number of decisons.

The Supreme Court's interpretations of the Constitution are summarized in a number of casebooks—for example, Alpheus T. Mason and William M. Beaney, eds., *American Constitutional Law,* 4th ed. (Englewood Cliffs, N.J.: Prentice-Hall, Inc., 1968)—and textbooks—for example, C. Herman Pritchett, *The American Constitution,* 2d ed. (New York: McGraw-Hill Book Company, 1968). The massive work, *The Constitution of the United States of America: Analysis and Interpretation,* is an encyclopedic reference. The latest (1964) edition, edited by Norman J. Small, leans heavily on an earlier version edited by Edward S. Corwin. The volume is published by the Government Printing Office.

The Constitution of the United States of America

(LITERAL PRINT)

[PREAMBLE]
We the People of the United States, in Order to form a more perfect Union, establish Justice, insure domestic Tranquility, provide for the common defence, promote the general Welfare, and secure the Blessings of Liberty to ourselves and our Posterity, do ordain and establish this Constitution for the United States of America.

ARTICLE I

Section 1

[LEGISLATIVE POWERS]
    All legislative Powers herein granted shall be vested in a Congress of the United States, which shall consist of a Senate and House of Representatives.

Section 2

[HOUSE OF REPRESENTATIVES, HOW CONSTITUTED, POWER OF IMPEACHMENT]
    The House of Representatives shall be composed of Members chosen every second Year by the People of the several States, and the Electors in each State shall have the Qualifications requisite for Electors of the most numerous Branch of the State Legislature.

    No Person shall be a Representative who shall not have attained to the Age of twenty-five Years, and been seven Years a Citizen of the United States, and who shall not, when elected, be an inhabitant of that State in which he shall be chosen.

    Representatives and *direct Taxes*[1] shall be apportioned among the several States which may be included within this Union, according to their respective Numbers, *which shall be determined by adding to the whole Number of free Persons, including those bound to Service for a Term of Years,* and excluding Indians not taxed, *three fifths of all other Persons.*[2] The actual Enumeration shall be made within three Years after the first Meeting of the Congress of the United States, and within every subsequent Term of ten Years, in such Manner as they shall by Law direct. The Number of Representatives shall not exceed one for every thirty Thousand, but each State shall have at Least one Representative; *and until such enumeration shall be made, the State of New Hampshire shall be entitled to chuse three, Massachusetts eight, Rhode-Island and Providence Plantations one, Connecticut five, New-York six, New Jersey four, Pennsylvania eight, Delaware one, Maryland six. Virginia ten, North Carolina five, South Carolina five, and Georgia three.*[3]

When vacancies happen in the Representation from any State, the Executive Authority thereof shall issue Writs of Election to fill such Vacancies.

The House of Representatives shall chuse their Speaker and other Officers; and shall have the sole Power of Impeachment.

Section 3

[THE SENATE, HOW CONSTITUTED, IMPEACHMENT TRIALS]

The Senate of the United States shall be composed of two Senators from each State, *chosen by the Legislature thereof,*[4] for six Years; and each Senator shall have one Vote.

Immediately after they shall be assembled in Consequence of the first Election, they shall be divided as equally as may be into three Classes. The Seats of the Senators of the first Class shall be vacated at the Expiration of the second Year, of the second Class at the Expiration of the fourth Year, and of the third Class at the Expiration of the sixth Year, so that one third may be chosen every second Year: *and if vacancies happen by Resignation, or otherwise, during the Recess of the Legislature of any State, the Executive thereof may make temporary Appointments until the next Meeting of the Legislature, which shall then fill such Vacancies.*[5]

No person shall be a Senator who shall not have attained to the Age of thirty Years, and been nine Years a Citizen of the United States, and who shall not, when elected, be an Inhabitant of that State for which he shall be chosen.

The Vice President of the United States shall be President of the Senate, but shall have no Vote, unless they be equally divided.

The Senate shall chuse their other Officers, and also a President pro tempore, in the Absence of the Vice President, or when he shall exercise the Office of President of the United States.

The Senate shall have the sole Power to try all Impeachments. When sitting for that Purpose, they shall be on Oath or Affirmation. When the President of the United States is tried, the Chief Justice shall preside: And no Person shall be convicted without the Concurrence of two thirds of the Members present.

Judgment in Cases of Impeachment shall not extend further than to removal from Office, and disqualification to hold and enjoy any Office of honor, Trust or Profit under the United States: but the Party convicted shall nevertheless be liable and subject to Indictment, Trial, Judgment and Punishment, according to Law.

Section 4

[ELECTION OF SENATORS AND REPRESENTATIVES]

The Times, Places and Manner of holding Elections for Senators and Representatives, shall be prescribed in each State by the Legislature thereof; but the Congress may at any time by Law make or alter such Regulations, except as to the Places of chusing Senators.

The Congress shall assemble at least once in every Year, and such Meeting shall be on the first Monday in December, unless they shall by Law appoint a different Day.[6]

Section 5

[QUORUM, JOURNALS, MEETINGS, ADJOURNMENTS]

Each House shall be the Judge of the Elections, Returns and Qualifications of its own Members, and a Majority of each shall constitute a Quorum to do Business; but a smaller Number may adjourn from day to day, and may be authorized to compel the Attendance of absent Members, in such Manner, and under the Penalties as each House may provide.

Each House may determine the Rules of its Proceedings, punish its Members for disorderly Behavior, and, with the Concurrence of two thirds, expel a Member.

Each House shall keep a Journal of its Proceedings, and from time to time publish the same, excepting such Parts as may in their Judgment require Secrecy; and the Yeas and Nays of the Members of either House on any question shall, at the Desire of one fifth of the present, be entered on the Journal.

Neither House, during the Session of Congress, shall, without the Consent of the other, adjourn for more than three days, nor to any other Place than that in which the two Houses shall be sitting.

Section 6

[COMPENSATION, PRIVILEGES, DISABILITIES]

The Senators and Representatives shall receive a Compensation for their Services, to be ascertained by Law, and paid out of the Treasury of the United States. They shall in all Cases, except Treason, Felony and Breach of the Peace, be privileged from Arrest during their Attendance at the Session of their respective Houses, and in going to and returning from the same; and for any Speech or Debate in either House, they shall not be questioned in any other Place.

No Senator or Representative shall, during the time for which he was elected, be appointed to any civil Office under the authority of the United States, which shall have been created, or the Emoluments whereof shall have been encreased during such time; and no Person holding any Office under the United States, shall be a Member of either House during his Continuance in Office.

Section 7

[PROCEDURE IN PASSING BILLS AND RESOLUTIONS]

All Bills for raising Revenue shall originate in the House of Representatives; but the Senate may propose or concur with Amendments as on other Bills.

Every Bill which shall have passed the House of Representatives and the Senate, shall, before it become a Law, be presented to the President of the United States; if he approve he shall sign it, but if not he shall return it, with his Objections to that House in which it shall have originated, who shall enter the Objections at large on their Journal, and proceed to reconsider it. If after such Reconsideration two thirds of that House shall agree to pass the Bill, it shall be sent, together with the Objections, to the other House, by which it shall likewise be reconsidered, and if approved by two thirds of that House, it shall become a Law. But in all such Cases the Votes of both Houses shall be determined by Yeas and Nays, and the Names of the Persons voting for and against the Bill shall be entered on the Journal of each House respectively. If any Bill shall not be returned by the President within ten Days (Sundays excepted) after it shall have been presented to him, the Same shall be a Law, in like Manner as if he had signed it, unless the Congress by their Adjournment prevent its Return, in which Case it shall not be a Law.

Every Order, Resolution, or Vote to which the Concurrence of the Senate and House of Representatives may be necessary (except on a question of Adjournment) shall be presented to the President of the United States; and before the Same shall take Effect, shall be approved by him, or being disapproved by him, shall be repassed by two thirds of the Senate and House of Representatives, according to the Rules and Limitations prescribed in the Case of a Bill.

Section 8

[POWERS OF CONGRESS]

The Congress shall have Power

To lay and collect Taxes, Duties, Imposts and Excises, to pay the Debts and provide for the common Defence and general Welfare of the United States; but all Duties, Imposts and excises shall be uniform throughout the United States;

To borrow Money on the Credit of the United States;

To regulate Commerce with foreign Nations, and among the several States, and with the Indian Tribes;

To establish an uniform Rule of Naturalization, and uniform Laws on the subject of Bankruptcies throughout the United States;

To coin Money, regulate the Value thereof, and of foreign Coin, and fix the Standard of Weights and Measures;

To provide for the Punishment of counterfeiting the Securities and current Coin of the United States;

To establish Post Offices and post Roads;

To promote the Progress of Science and useful Arts, by securing for limited Times to Authors and Inventors the exclusive Right to their respective Writings and Discoveries:

To constitute Tribunals inferior to the supreme Court;

To define and Punish Piracies and Felonies committed on the high Seas, and Offences against the Law of Nations;

To declare War, grant Letters of Marque and Reprisal, and make Rules concerning Captures on Land and Water;

To raise and support Armies, but no Appropriation of Money to that Use shall be for a longer Term than two Years;

To provide and maintain a Navy;

To make Rules for the Government and Regulation of the land and naval forces;

To provide for calling for the Militia to execute the Laws of the Union, suppress Insurrections and repel Invasions;

To provide for organizing, arming, and disciplining, the Militia, and for governing such Part of them as may be employed in the Service of the United States, reserving to the States respectively, the Appointment of the Officers, and the Authority of training the Militia according to the discipline prescribed by Congress;

To exercise exclusive Legislation in all Cases whatsoever, over such District (not exceeding ten Miles square) as may, by Cession of particular States, and the Acceptance of Congress, become the Seat of the Government of the United States, and to exercise like Authority over all Places purchased by the Consent of the Legislature of the State in which the Same shall be, for the Erection of Forts, Magazines, Arsenals, dock-Yards, and other needful Buildings;—And

To make all Laws which shall be necessary and proper for carrying into Execution the foregoing Powers, and all other Powers vested by this Constitution in the Government of the United States, or in any Department or Officer thereof.

Section 9

The Migration of Importation of such Persons as any of the States now existing shall think proper to admit, shall not be prohibited by the Congress prior to the Year one thousand eight hundred and eight, but a Tax or Duty may be imposed on such Importation, not exceeding ten dollars for each Person.[7]

The privilege of the Writ of Habeas Corpus shall not be suspended, unless when in Cases of Rebellion or Invasion the public Safety may require it.

No Bill of Attainder or ex post facto Law shall be passed.

No Capitation, or other direct, Tax shall be laid, unless in Proportion to the Census or Enumeration herein before directed to be taken.[8]

No Tax or Duty shall be laid on Articles exported from any State.

No Preference shall be given by any Regulation of Commerce or Revenue to the Ports of one State over those of another; nor shall vessels bound to, or from, one State, be obliged to enter, clear, or pay Duties in another.

No Money shall be drawn from the Treasury, but in Consequence of Appropriations made by Law; and a regular Statement and Account of the Receipts and Expenditures of all public Money shall be published from time to time.

No Title of Nobility shall be granted by the United States: And no Person holding any Office of Profit or Trust under them, shall, without the Consent of the Congress, accept of any present, Emolument, Office, or Title, of any kind whatever, from any King, Prince, or foreign State.

Section 10

[RESTRICTIONS UPON POWERS OF STATES]

No State shall enter into any Treaty, Alliance, or Confederation; grant Letters of Marque and Reprisal; coin Money; emit Bills of Credit; make any Thing but gold and silver Coin a Tender in Payment of Debts; pass any Bill of Attainder, ex post facto Law, or Law impairing the Obligation of Contracts, or grant any Title of Nobility.

No State shall, without the Consent of the Congress, lay any Imposts or Duties on Imports or Exports, except what may be absolutely necessary for executing its inspection Laws: and the net Produce of all Duties and Imposts, laid by any State on Imports or Exports, shall be for the Use of the Treasury of the United States; and all such Laws shall be subject to the Revision and Control of the Congress.

No State shall, without the Consent of Congress, lay any Duty of Tonnage, keep

Troops, or Ships of War in time of Peace, enter into any Agreement or Compact with another State, or with a foreign Power, or engage in War, unless actually invaded, or in such imminent Danger as will not admit of Delay.

ARTICLE II

Section 1

[EXECUTIVE POWER, ELECTION, QUALIFICATIONS OF THE PRESIDENT]

The executive Power shall be vested in a President of the United States of America. *He shall hold his Office during the Term of four years and, together with the Vice President, chosen for the same Term, be elected, as follows:*[9]

Each State shall appoint, in such Manner as the Legislature thereof may direct, a Number of Electors, equal to the whole Number of Senators and Representatives to which the State may be entitled in the Congress: but no Senator or Representative, or Person holding an Office of Trust or Profit under the United States, shall be appointed an Elector.

The electors shall meet in their respective States, and vote by ballot for two Persons, of whom one at least shall not be an Inhabitant of the same State with themselves. And they shall make a List of all the Persons voted for, and of the Number of Votes for each; which List they shall sign and certify, and transmit sealed to the Seat of the Government of the United States, directed to the President of the Senate. The President of the Senate shall, in the Presence of the Senate and House of Representatives, open all the Certificates, and the Votes shall then be counted. The Person having the greatest Number of Votes shall be the President, if such Number be a Majority of the whole Number of Electors appointed; and if there be more than one who have such Majority and have an equal Number of Votes, then the House of Representatives shall immediately chuse by Ballot one of them for President; and if no person have a Majority, then from the five highest on the List the said House shall in like Manner chuse the President. But in chusing the President, the Votes shall be taken by States, the Representation from each State having one Vote; A quorum for this Purpose shall consist of a Member or Members from two-thirds of the States, and a Majority of all the States shall be necessary to a Choice. In every Case, after the Choice of the President, the person having the greatest Number of Votes of the Electors shall be the Vice President. But if there should remain two or more who have equal vote, the Senate shall chuse from them by Ballot the Vice President.[10]

The Congress may determine the Time of chusing the Electors, and the Day on which they shall give their Votes; which Day shall be the same throughout the United States.

No Person except a natural born Citizen, or a Citizen of the United States, at the time of the Adoption of this Constitution, shall be eligible to the Office of President; neither shall any Person be eligible to that Office who shall not have attained to the Age of thirty-five Years, and been fourteen Years a Resident within the United States.

In Case of the Removal of the President from Office, or his Death, Resignation, or Inability to discharge the Powers and Duties of the said Office, the same shall devolve on the Vice President, and the Congress may by Law provide for the Case of Removal, Death, Resignation, or Inability, both of the President and Vice President, declaring what Officer shall then act as President, and such Officer shall act acccordingly, until the Disability be removed, or a President shall be elected.

The President shall, at stated Times, receive for his Services, a Compensation, which shall neither be encreased nor diminished during the Period of which he shall have been elected, and he shall not receive within that Period any other Emolument from the United States, or any of them.

Before he enter on the Execution of his Office, he shall take the following oath or Affirmation:—"I do solemnly swear (or affirm) that I will faithfully execute the Office of President of the United States, and will to the best of my Ability, preserve, protect and defend the Constitution of the United States."

Section 2

[POWERS OF THE PRESIDENT]

The President shall be Commander in Chief of the Army and Navy of the United States, and of the Militia of the several States, when called into the actual Service of the United States; he may require the Opinion, in writing, of the principal Officer in each of the executive Departments, upon any Subject relating to the Duties of their respective Offices, and he shall have Power to grant Reprieves and Pardons for Offences against the United States, except in Cases of Impeachment.

He shall have Power, by and with the Advice and Consent of the Senate to make Treaties, provided two thirds of the Senators present concur; and he shall nominate, and by and with the Advice and Consent of the Senate, shall appoint Ambassadors, other public Ministers and Consuls, Judges of the Supreme Court, and all other Officers of the United States, whose Appointments are not herein otherwise provided for, and which shall be established by Law: but the Congress may by Law vest the Appointment of such inferior Officers, as they think proper, in the President alone, in the Courts of Law, or in the Heads of Departments.

The President shall have Power to fill up all Vacancies that may happen during the Recess of the Senate, by granting Commissions which shall expire at the End of their next Session.

Section 3

[POWERS AND DUTIES OF THE PRESIDENT]

He shall from time to time give to the Congress Information of the State of the Union, and recommend to their Consideration such Measures as he shall judge necessary and expedient; he may, on extraordinary Occasions, convene both Houses, or either of them, and in Case of Disagreement between them, with Respect to the Time of Adjournment, he may adjourn them to such Time as he shall think proper; he shall receive Ambassadors and other public Ministers; he shall take Care that the Laws be faithfully executed, and shall Commission all the Officers of the United States.

Section 4

[IMPEACHMENT]

The President, Vice President and all civil Officers of the United States shall be removed from Office on Impeachment for, and Conviction of, Treason, Bribery, or other high Crimes and Misdemeanors.

ARTICLE III

Section 1

[JUDICIAL POWER, TENURE OF OFFICE]

The judicial Power of the United States, shall be vested in one supreme Court, and in such inferior Courts as the Congress may from time to time ordain and establish. The Judges, both of the supreme and inferior Courts, shall hold their Offices during good Behavior, and shall, at stated Times, receive for their Services, a Compensation, which shall not be diminished during their Continuance in Office.

Section 2

[JURISDICTION]

The judicial Power shall extend to all Cases, in Law and Equity, arising under this Constitution, the Laws of the United States, and Treaties made, or which shall be made, under their Authority;—to all Cases affecting Ambassadors, other public Ministers and Consuls;—to all Cases of admiralty and maritime Jurisdiction;—to Controversies to which the United States shall be a party;—to Controversies between two or more States;—*between a State and Citizens of another State;*—between Citizens of different States,—between Citizens of the same State claiming Lands under Grants of different States, *and between a State,* or the Citizens thereof, *and foreign States, Citizens or Subjects.*[11]

In all Cases affecting Ambassadors, other public Ministers and Consuls, and those in which a State shall be Party, the supreme Court shall have original Jurisdiction. In all the other Cases before mentioned, the supreme Court shall have appellate Jurisdiction, both as to Law and Fact, with such Exceptions, and under such Regulations as Congress shall make.

The Trial of all Crimes, except in Cases of Impeachment, shall be by Jury; and such Trial shall be held in the State where the said Crimes shall have been committed; but when not committed within any State, the Trial shall be at such Place or Places as the Congress may by Law have directed.

Section 3

[TREASON, PROOF AND PUNISHMENT]

Treason against the United States, shall consist only in levying War against them, or in adhering to their Enemies, giving them Aid and Comfort. No Person shall be convicted of Treason unless on the Testimony of two Witnesses to the same overt Act, or on Confession in open Court.

The Congress shall have Power to declare the Punishment of Treason, but no Attainder of Treason shall work Corruption of Blood, or Forfeiture except during the Life of the Person attained.

ARTICLE IV

Section 1

[FAITH AND CREDIT AMONG STATES]

Full Faith and Credit shall be given in each State to the public Acts, Records, and judicial Proceedings of every other State. And the Congress may by general Laws prescribe the Manner in which such Acts, Records and Proceedings shall be proved, and the Effect thereof.

Section 2

[PRIVILEGES AND IMMUNITIES, FUGITIVES]

The Citizens of each State shall be entitled to all Privileges and Immunities of Citizens in the several States.

A person charged in any State with Treason, Felony or other Crime, who shall flee from Justice, and be found in another State, shall on Demand of the executive Authority of the State from which he fled, be delivered up to be removed to the State having Jurisdiction of the Crime.

No person held to Service or Labour in one State, under the Laws thereof, escaping into another, shall, in Consequence of any Law or Regulation therein, be discharged from such Service or Labour, but shall be delivered up on Claim of the Party to whom such Service or Labour may be due.[12]

Section 3

[ADMISSION OF NEW STATES]

New States may be admitted by the Congress into this Union; but no new State shall be formed or erected within the Jurisdiction of any other State; nor any State be formed by the Junction of two or more States, or Parts of States, without the Consent of the Legislatures of the States concerned as well of the Congress.

The Congress shall have Power to dispose of and make all needful Rules and Regulations respecting the Territory or other Property belonging to the United States; and nothing in this Constitution shall be so construed as to Prejudice any Claims of the United States, or of any particular State.

Section 4

[GUARANTEE OF REPUBLICAN GOVERNMENT]

The United States shall guarantee to every State in this Union a Republican Form of Government, and shall protect each of them against Invasion; and on Application of the Legislature, or of the Executive (when the Legislature cannot be convened) against domestic Violence.

ARTICLE V

[AMENDMENT OF THE CONSTITUTION]

The Congress, whenever two thirds of both Houses shall deem it necessary, shall propose Amendments to this Constitution, or, on the Application of the Legislatures of two thirds of the several States, shall call a Convention for proposing Amendments, which, in either Case, shall be valid to all Intents and Purposes, as Part of this Constitution, when ratified by the Legislatures of three fourths of the several States, or by Conventions in three fourths thereof, as the one or the other Mode of Ratification may be proposed by the Congress; *Provided that no Amendment which may be made prior to the Year One thousand eight hundred and eight shall in any Manner affect the first and fourth Clauses in the Ninth Section of the first Article;*[13] and that no State, without its Consent, shall be deprived of its equal Suffrage in the Senate.

ARTICLE VI

[DEBTS, SUPREMACY, OATH]

All Debts contracted and Engagements entered into, before the Adoption of this Constitution, shall be as valid against the United States under this Constitution, as under the Confederation.

This Constitution, and the Laws of the United States which shall be made in Pursuance thereof; and all Treaties made, or which shall be made, under the Authority of the United States, shall be the supreme Law of the Land; and the Judges in every State shall be bound thereby, any Thing in the Constitution or Laws of any State to the Contrary notwithstanding.

The Senators and Representatives before mentioned, and the Members of the several State Legislatures, and all executive and judicial Officers, both of the United States and of the several States, shall be bound by Oath or Affirmation, to support this Constitution; but no religious Test shall be required as a Qualification to any Office or public Trust under the United States.

ARTICLE VII

[RATIFICATION & ESTABLISHMENT]

The Ratification of the Conventions of nine States, shall be sufficient for the Establishment of this Constitution between the States so ratifying the Same.[14]

Footnotes

[1] Modified by Sixteenth Amendment.
[2] Modified by Fourteenth Amendment.
[3] Temporary provision.
[4] Modified by Seventeenth Amendment.
[5] *Ibid.*
[6] Modified by Twentieth Amendment.
[7] Temporary provision.
[8] Modified by Sixteenth Amendment.
[9] Number of terms limited to two by Twenty-second Amendment.
[10] Modified by Twelfth and Twentieth Amendments.
[11] Modified by Eleventh Amendment.
[12] Repealed by the Thirteenth Amendment.
[13] Temporary provision.
[14] The Constitution was submitted on September 17, 1787, by the Constitutional Conventions, was ratified by the conventions of several states at various dates up to May 29, 1790, and became effective on March 4, 1789.

done in Convention by the Unanimous Consent of the States present the Seventeenth Day of September in the Year of our Lord one thousand seven hundred and Eighty seven and of the Independence of the United States of America the Twelth. *In Witness* whereof We have hereunto subscribed our Names,

G:⁰ WASHINGTON—
*Presidt, and Deputy
from Virginia*

New Hampshire	JOHN LANGDON NICHOLAS GILMAN
Massachusets	NATHANIEL GORHAM RUFUS KING
Connecticut	WM SAML JOHNSON ROGER SHERMAN
New York	ALEXANDER HAMILTON
New Jersey	WIL: LIVINGSTON DAVID BREARLEY WM PATERSON JONA: DAYTON
Pennsylvania	B FRANKLIN THOMAS MIFFLIN ROBT MORRIS GEO. CLYMER THOS. FITZSIMONS JARED INGERSOLL JAMES WILSON GOUV MORRIS
Delaware	GEO READ GUNNING BEDFOR JUN JOHN DICKINSON RICHARD BASSETT JACO: BROOM
Maryland	JAMES MCHENRY DAN OF ST THOS. JENIFER DANL CARROLL
Virginia	JOHN BLAIR — JAMES MADISON JR.
North Carolina	WM BLOUNT RICHD DOBBS SPAIGHT HU WILLIAMSON
South Carolina	J. RUTLEDGE CHARLES COTESWORTH PINCKNEY CHARLES PINCKNEY PIERCE BUTLER
Georgia	WILLIAM FEW ABR BALDWIN

Amendments to the Constitution

The first ten amendments were proposed by Congress on September 25, 1789;
ratified and adoption certified on December 15, 1791.

AMENDMENT I

[FREEDOM OF RELIGION, OF SPEECH, AND OF THE PRESS]
Congress shall make no law respecting an establishment of religion, or prohibiting
the free exercise thereof; or abridging the freedom of speech, or of the press; or the right
of the people peaceably to assemble, and to petition the Government for a redress of
grievances.

AMENDMENT II

[RIGHT TO KEEP AND BEAR ARMS]
A well regulated Militia, being necessary to the security of a free State, the right
of the people to keep and bear Arms, shall not be infringed.

AMENDMENT III

[QUARTERING OF SOLDIERS]
No Soldier shall, in time of peace be quartered in any house, without the consent
of the Owner, nor in time of war, but in a manner to be prescribed by law.

AMENDMENT IV

[SECURITY FROM UNWARRANTABLE SEARCH AND SEIZURE]
The right of the people to be secure in their persons, houses, papers, and effects, against unreasonable searches and seizures, shall not be violated, and no Warrants shall issue, but upon probable cause, supported by Oath or affirmation, and particularly describing the place to be searched, and the persons or things to be seized.

AMENDMENT V

[RIGHTS OF ACCUSED PERSONS IN CRIMINAL PROCEEDINGS]
No person shall be held to answer for a capital, or otherwise infamous crime, unless on a presentment or indictment of a Grand Jury, except in cases arising in the land or naval forces, or in the Militia, when in actual service in time of War or in public danger; nor shall any person be subject for the same offence to be twice put in jeopardy of life or limb; nor shall be compelled in any Criminal Case to be a witness against himself, nor be deprived of life, liberty, or property, without due process of law; nor shall private property be taken for public use, without just compensation.

AMENDMENT VI

[RIGHT TO SPEEDY TRIAL, WITNESSES, ETC.]
In all criminal prosecutions, the accused shall enjoy the right to a speedy and public trial, by an impartial jury of the State and district wherein the crime shall have been committed, which district shall have been previously ascertained by law, and to be informed of the nature and cause of the accusation; to be confronted with the witnesses against him; to have compulsory process for obtaining Witnesses in his favor, and to have the Assistance of Counsel for his defence.

AMENDMENT VII

[TRIAL BY JURY IN CIVIL CASES]
In suits at common law, where the value in controversy shall exceed twenty dollars, the right of trial by jury shall be preserved, and no fact tried by a jury shall be otherwise re-examined in any Court of the United States, than according to the rules of the common law.

AMENDMENT VIII

[BAILS, FINES, PUNISHMENTS]
Excessive bail shall not be required, nor excessive fines imposed, nor cruel and unusual punishments inflicted.

AMENDMENT IX

[RESERVATION OF RIGHTS OF PEOPLE]
The enumeration in the Constitution, of certain rights, shall not be construed to deny or disparage others retained by the people.

AMENDMENT X

[POWERS RESERVED TO STATES OR PEOPLE]
The powers not delegated to the United States by the Constitution, nor prohibited by it to the States, are reserved to the States respectively, or to the people.

AMENDMENT XI

[Proposed by Congress on March 4, 1794; declared ratified on January 8, 1798.]
[RESTRICTION OF JUDICIAL POWER]
The Judicial power of the United States shall not be construed to extend to any suit in law or equity, commenced or prosecuted against one of the United States by Citizens of another State, or by Citizens or Subjects of any Foreign State.

AMENDMENT XII

[Proposed by Congress on December 9, 1803; declared ratified on September 25, 1804.]
[ELECTION OF PRESIDENT AND VICE-PRESIDENT]
The Electors shall meet in their respective states, and vote by ballot for President and Vice-President, one of whom, at least, shall not be an inhabitant of the same state with themselves; they shall name in their ballots the person voted for as President, and in distinct ballots the person voted for as Vice-President, and they shall make distinct lists of all persons voted for as President, and of all persons voted for as Vice-President, and of the number of votes for each, which lists they shall sign and certify, and transmit sealed to the seat of the government of the United States, directed to the President of the Senate;—The President of the Senate shall, in presence of the Senate and House of Representatives, open all the certificates and the votes shall then be counted;—The person having the greatest number of votes for President, shall be the President, if such number be a majority of the whole number of Electors appointed; and if no person have such majority, then from the persons having the highest numbers not exceeding three on the list of those voted for as President, the House of Representatives shall choose immediately, by ballot, the President. But in choosing the President, the votes shall be taken by states, the representation from each state having one vote; a quorum for this purpose shall consist of a member or members from two-thirds of the states, and a majority of all states shall be necessary to a choice. And if the House of Representatives shall not choose a President whenever the right of choice shall devolve upon them, before the fourth day of March next following, then the Vice-President, shall act as President, as in the case of the death or other constitutional disability of the President. The person having the great-

est number of votes as Vice-President, shall be the Vice-President, if such a number be a majority of the whole numbers of Electors appointed, and if no person have a majority, then from the two highest numbers on the list, the Senate shall choose the Vice-President; a quorum for the purpose shall consist of two-thirds of the whole number of Senators, and a majority of the whole number shall be necessary to a choice. But no person constitutionally ineligible to the office of President shall be eligible to that of Vice-President of the United States.

AMENDMENT XIII

[Proposed by Congress on January 31, 1865; declared ratified on December 18, 1865.]

Section 1

[ABOLITION OF SLAVERY]
Neither slavery nor involuntary servitude, except as a punishment for crime whereof the party shall have been duly convicted, shall exist within the United States, or any place subject to their jurisdiction.

Section 2

[POWER TO ENFORCE THIS ARTICLE]
Congress shall have power to enforce this article by appropriate legislation.

AMENDMENT XIV

[Proposed by Congress on June 13, 1866; declared ratified on July 28, 1868.]

Section 1

[CITIZENSHIP RIGHTS NOT TO BE ABRIDGED BY STATES]
All persons born or naturalized in the United States, and subject to the jurisdiction thereof, are citizens of the United States and of the State wherein they reside. No State shall make or enforce any law which shall abridge the privileges or immunities of citizens of the United States; nor shall any State deprive any person of life, liberty, or property, without due process of law; nor deny to any person within its jurisdiction the equal protection of the laws.

Section 2

[APPORTIONMENT OF REPRESENTATIVES IN CONGRESS]
Representatives shall be apportioned among the several States according to their respective numbers, counting the whole number of persons in each State, excluding Indians not taxed. But when the right to vote at any election for the choice of electors

for President and Vice-President of the United States, Representatives in Congress, the Executive and Judicial officers of a State, or the members of the Legislature thereof, is denied to any of the male inhabitants of such State, being twenty-one years of age, and citizens of the United States, or in any way abridged, except for participation in rebellion, or other crime, the basis of representation therein shall be reduced in the proportion which the number of such male citizens shall bear to the whole number of male citizens twenty-one years of age in such State.

Section 3

[PERSONS DISQUALIFIED FROM HOLDING OFFICE]
No person shall be a Senator or Representative in Congress, or elector of President and Vice-President, or hold any office, civil or military, under the United States, or under any State, who, having previously taken an oath, as a member of Congress, or as an officer of the United States, or as a member of any State legislature, or as an executive or judicial officer of any State, to support the Constitution of the United States, shall have engaged in insurrection or rebellion against the same, or given aid or comfort to the enemies thereof. But Congress may by a vote of two-thirds of each House, remove such disability.

Section 4

[WHAT PUBLIC DEBTS ARE VALID]
The validity of the public debt of the United States, authorized by law, including debts incurred for payment of pensions and bounties for services in suppressing insurrection or rebellion, shall not be questioned. But neither the United States nor any State shall assume or pay any debt or obligation incurred in aid of insurrection or rebellion against the United States, or any claim for the loss of emancipation of any slave; but all such debts, obligations and claims shall be held illegal and void.

Section 5

[POWER TO ENFORCE THIS ARTICLE]
The Congress shall have power to enforce, by appropriate legislation, the provisions of this article.

AMENDMENT XV

[*Proposed by Congress on February 26, 1869; declared ratified on March 30, 1870.*]

Section 1

[NEGRO SUFFRAGE]
The right of citizens of the United States to vote shall not be denied or abridged

by the United States or by any State on account of race, color, or previous condition of servitude.

Section 2

[POWER TO ENFORCE THIS ARTICLE]
The Congress shall have power to enforce this article by appropriate legislation.

AMENDMENT XVI

[Proposed by Congress on July 12, 1909; declared ratified on February 25, 1913.]
[AUTHORIZING INCOME TAXES]
The Congress shall have power to lay and collect taxes on incomes, from whatever source derived, without apportionment among the several States, and without regard to any census or enumeration.

AMENDMENT XVII

[Proposed by Congress on May 13, 1912; declared ratified on May 31, 1913.]
[POPULAR ELECTION OF SENATORS]
The Senate of the United States shall be composed of two Senators from each State, elected by the people thereof, for six years; and each Senator shall have one vote. The electors in each State shall have the qualifications requisite for electors of the most numerous branch of the State Legislature.

When vacancies happen in the representation of any State in the Senate, the executive authority of such State shall issue writs of election to fill such vacancies: Provided, That the Legislature of any State may empower the executive thereof to make temporary appointment until the people fill the vacancies by election as the Legislature may direct.

This amendment shall not be so construed as to affect the election or term of any Senator chosen before it becomes valid as part of the Constitution.

AMENDMENT XVIII

[Proposed by Congress December 18, 1917; declared ratified on January 29, 1919.]

Section 1

[NATIONAL LIQUOR PROHIBITION]
After one year from the ratification of this article the manufacture, sale, or transportation of intoxicating liquors within, the importation thereof into, or the exportation thereof from the United States and all territory subject to the jurisdiction thereof for beverage purposes is hereby prohibited.

Section 2

[POWER TO ENFORCE THIS ARTICLE]
The Congress and the several states shall have concurrent power to enforce this article by appropriate legislation.

Section 3

[RATIFICATION WITHIN SEVEN YEARS]
This article shall be inoperative unless it shall have been ratified as an amendment to the Constitution by the legislatures of the several states, as provided in the Constitution, within seven years from the date of the submission hereof to the states by the Congress.

AMENDMENT XIX

[Proposed by Congress on June 4. 1919; declared ratified on August 26, 1920.]
[WOMAN SUFFRAGE]
The right of the citizens of the United States to vote shall not be denied or abridged by the United States or by any state on account of sex.

Congress shall have power, by appropriate legislation, to enforce the provision of this article.

AMENDMENT XX

[Proposed by Congress on March 2, 1932; declared ratified on February 6, 1933.]

Section 1

[TERMS OF OFFICE]
The terms of the President and Vice-President shall end at noon on the 20th day of January, and the terms of the Senators and Representatives at noon on the 3rd day of January, of the years in which such terms would have ended if this article had not been ratified; and the terms of their successors shall then begin.

Section 2

[TIME OF CONVENING CONGRESS]
The Congress shall assemble at least once in every year, and such meeting shall begin at noon on the 3rd day of January, unless they shall by law appoint a different day.

Section 3

[DEATH OF PRESIDENT-ELECT]
If, at the time fixed for the beginning of the term of the President, the President

elect shall have died, the Vice-President elect shall become President. If a President shall not have been chosen before the time fixed for the beginning of his term, or if the President elect shall have failed to qualify, then the Vice-President elect shall act as President until a President shall have qualified; and the Congress may by law provide for the case wherein neither a President elect nor a Vice-President elect shall have qualified, declaring who shall then act as President, or the manner in which one who is to act shall be selected, and such person shall act accordingly until a President or Vice-President shall have qualified.

Section 4

[ELECTION OF THE PRESIDENT]
The Congress may by law provide for the case of the death of any of the persons from whom the House of Representatives may choose a President whenever the right of choice shall have devolved upon them, and for the case of the death of any of the persons from whom the Senate may choose a Vice-President whenever the right of choice shall have devolved upon them.

Section 5

Sections 1 and 2 shall take effect on the 15th day of October following ratification of this article.

Section 6

This article shall be inoperative unless it shall have been ratified as an amendment to the Constitution by the legislatures of three-fourths of the several States within seven years from the date of its submission.

AMENDMENT XXI

[Proposed by Congress on February 20, 1933; declared ratified on December 5, 1933.]

Section 1

[NATIONAL LIQUOR PROHIBITION REPEALED]
The eighteenth article of amendment to the Constitution of the United States is hereby repealed.

Section 2

[TRANSPORTATION OF LIQUOR INTO "DRY" STATES]
The transportation or importation into any State, Territory, or Possession of the United States for delivery or use therein of intoxicating liquors, in violation of the laws thereof, is hereby prohibited.

Section 3

This article shall be inoperative unless it shall have been ratified as an amendment to the Constitution by conventions in the several States, as provided in the Constitution, within seven years from the date of the submission hereof to the States by the Congress.

AMENDMENT XXII

[Proposed by Congress on March 21, 1947; declared ratified on February 26, 1951.]

Section 1

[TENURE OF PRESIDENT LIMITED]
No person shall be elected to the office of President more than twice, and no person who has held the office of President, or acted as President, for more than two years of a term to which some other person was elected President shall be elected to the Office of the President more than once. But this Article shall not apply to any person holding the office of President when this Article was proposed by the Congress, and shall not prevent any person who may be holding the office of President, or acting as President, during the term within which this Article becomes operative from holding the office of President or acting as President during the remainder of such term.

Section 2

This Article shall be inoperative unless it shall have been ratified as an amendment to the Constitution by the legislatures of three-fourths of the several states within seven years from the date of its submission to the States by the Congress.

AMENDMENT XXIII

[Proposed by Congress on June 21, 1960; declared ratified on March 29, 1961.]

Section 1

[ELECTORAL COLLEGE VOTES FOR THE DISTRICT OF COLUMBIA]
The District constituting the seat of Government of the United States shall appoint in such manner as the Congress may direct:

A number of electors of President and Vice President equal to the whole number of Senators and Representatives in Congress to which the District would be entitled if it were a State, but in no event more than the least populous State; they shall be in addition to those appointed by the States, but they shall be considered, for the purposes of the election of President and Vice President, to be electors appointed by a State; and they shall meet in the District and perform such duties as provided by the twelfth article of amendment.

Section 2

The Congress shall have power to enforce this article by appropriate legislation.

AMENDMENT XXIV

[Proposed by Congress on August 27, 1963; declared ratified on January 23, 1964.]

Section 1

[ANTI-POLL TAX]
The right of citizens of the United States to vote in any primary or other election for President or Vice President, for electors for President or Vice President, or for Senator or Representative of Congress, shall not be denied or abridged by the United States or any State by reasons of failure to pay any poll tax or other tax.

Section 2

The Congress shall have power to enforce this article by appropriate legislation.

AMENDMENT XXV

[Proposed by Congress on July 7, 1965; declared ratified on February 10, 1967.]

Section 1

[VICE PRESIDENT TO BECOME PRESIDENT]
In case of the removal of the President from office or his death or resignation, the Vice President shall become President.

Section 2

[CHOICE OF A NEW VICE PRESIDENT]
Whenever there is a vacancy in the office of the Vice President, the President shall nominate a Vice President who shall take the office upon confirmation by a majority vote of both houses of Congress.

Section 3

[PRESIDENT MAY DECLARE OWN DISABILITY]
Whenever the President transmits to the President pro tempore of the Senate and the Speaker of the House of Representatives his written declaration that he is unable to discharge the powers and duties of his office, and until he transmits to them a written

declaration to the contrary, such powers and duties shall be discharged by the Vice President as Acting President.

Section 4

[ALTERNATIVE PROCEDURES TO DECLARE AND TO END PRESIDENTIAL DISABILITY]

Whenever the Vice President and a majority of either the principal officers of the executive departments, or of such other body as Congress may by law provide, transmit to the President pro tempore of the Senate and the Speaker of the House of Representatives their written declaration that the President is unable to discharge the powers and duties of his office, the Vice President shall immediately assume the powers and duties of the office as Acting President.

Thereafter, when the President transmits to the President pro tempore of the Senate and the Speaker of the House of Representatives his written declaration that no inability exists, he shall resume the powers and duties of his office unless the Vice President and a majority of either the principal officer of the executive department, or of such other body as Congress may by law provide, transmit within four days to the President pro tempore of the Senate and the Speaker of the House of Representatives their written declaration that the President is unable to discharge the powers and duties of his office. Thereupon Congress shall decide the issue, assembling within 48 hours for that purpose if not in session. If the Congress, within 21 days after receipt of the latter written declaration, or, if Congress is not in session, within 21 days after Congress is required to assemble, determines by two-thirds vote of both houses that the President is unable to discharge the powers and duties of his office, the Vice President shall continue to discharge the same as Acting President; otherwise, the President shall resume the powers and duties of his office.

Index